Nāgārjuna's Treatise on the Ten Grounds

To refrain from doing any manner of evil,
to respectfully perform all varieties of good,
and to purify one's own mind—
This is the teaching of all buddhas.

The Ekottara Āgama Sūtra
(T02 n.125 p.551a 13–14)

A Note on the Proper Care of Dharma Materials

Traditional Buddhist cultures treat books on Dharma as sacred. Hence it is considered disrespectful to place them in a low position, to read them when lying down, or to place them where they might be damaged by food or drink.

Nāgārjuna's Treatise On the Ten Bodhisattva Grounds

The Daśabhūmika Vibhāṣā

As Translated into Chinese
By Tripiṭaka Master Kumārajīva
(*c* 410 CE)

Annotated English Translation by Bhikshu Dharmamitra

Kalavinka Press
Seattle, Washington
www.kalavinkapress.org

Kalavinka Press
8603 39th Ave SW
Seattle, WA 98136 USA
(www.kalavinkapress.org)

Kalavinka Press is associated with the Kalavinka Dharma Association, a non-profit organized exclusively for religious educational purposes as allowed within the meaning of section 501(c)3 of the Internal RevenueCode. Kalavinka Dharma Association was founded in 1990 and gained formal approval in 2004 by the United States Internal Revenue Service as a 501(c)3 non-profit organization to which all donations are tax deductible.

Donations to KDA are accepted by mail and on the Kalavinka website where numerous free Dharma translations and excerpts from Kalavinka publications are available in digital format.

Edition: SZPPS-EO-1019-1.0
Kalavinka Buddhist Classics Book 13b

ISBN: 978-1-935413-16-5 / Library of Congress Control #2019032385

Library of Congress Cataloging-in-Publication Data

Names: Dharmamitra, Bhikshu, 1948- translator. | Kumārajīva, -412? translator.
Title: Nāgārjuna's treatise on the ten Bodhisattva grounds : the Daśabhūmika vibhāṣā / as translated into Chinese by Tripiṭaka Master Kumārajīva (c 410 ce) ; annotated English translation by Bhikshu Dharmamitra.
Other titles: Daśabhūmivibhāṣāśāstra. English
Description: Szpps-eo-1019-1.0 | Seattle, Washington : Kalavinka Press, 2019. | Series: Kalavinka Buddhist classics; book 13b | Includes bibliographical references. | Summary: ""Nāgārjuna's Treatise on the Ten Bodhisattva Grounds" is Bhikshu Dharmamitra's extensively annotated original translation of Ārya Nāgārjuna's "Daśabhūmika Vibhasa" rendered from Tripiṭaka Master Kumārajīva's circa 410 ce Sanskrit-to-Chinese translation. It consists of 35 chapters that explain in great detail the cultivation of the ten highest levels of bodhisattva practice leading to buddhahood, focusing almost exclusively on the first two of the ten bodhisattva grounds. This is a work which has never been translated into English before"-- Provided by publisher.
Identifiers: LCCN 2019032385 | ISBN 9781935413165 (paperback)
Subjects: LCSH: Tripiṭaka. Sūtrapiṭaka. Avataṃsakasūtra. Daśabhūmikasūtra--Criticism, interpretation, etc. | Bodhisattva stages (Mahayana Buddhism) | Nāgārjuna, active 2nd century. Daśabhūmivibhāṣāśāstra.
Classification: LCC BQ1632.E5 D343 2019 | DDC 294.3/823--dc23
LC record available at https://lccn.loc.gov/2019032385

Kalavinka Press books are printed on acid-free paper.
Cover and interior designed by Bhikshu Dharmamitra.
Printed in the United States of America

Dedication

Dedicated to the memory of the selfless and marvelous life of the Venerable Dhyāna Master Hsuan Hua, the Guiyang Ch'an Patriarch and the very personification of the bodhisattva's six perfections.

Dhyāna Master Hsuan Hua

宣化禪師

1918–1995

Acknowledgments

The accuracy and readability of this translation have been greatly improved by many corrections, preview comments, and editorial suggestions generously contributed by Bhikkhu Bodhi, Bhikshu Jianhu, Feng Ling, Nicholas Weeks, and Jon Babcock.

Expenses incurred in bringing forth this publication were underwritten by generous donations from Craig and Karen Neyman, Madalena Lew, Shuyu Yang, Jiajing Li, Kam Chung Wong, Loritta Chan, David Fox, Nicholas Weeks, Yuen-Lin Tan, and the BDK English Tripiṭaka Project. Sponsorship of Adobe Indesign book layout was provided by Anagarika Mahendra.

Were it not for the ongoing material support provided by my late guru's Dharma Realm Buddhist Association and the serene translation studio provided by Seattle's Bodhi Dhamma Center, creation of this translation would have been much more difficult.

Additionally, it would have been impossible for me to produce this translation without the Dharma teachings and personal inspiration provided to me by my late guru, the awesomely wise and compassionate Dhyāna Master Hsuan Hua, the Guiyang Ch'an Patriarch, Dharma teacher, and exegete.

Finally, I owe an immense debt of gratitude to the members of the liver care and transplant teams at Seattle's University of Washington Medical Center who cured me of liver cancer in 2010 and then gave me a liver transplant several months later. In particular, if it weren't for over a decade of wonderfully attentive and compassionate care by Dr. Renuka Bhattacharya, now medical director of UW's liver transplant program, the kindness and skill in three major surgeries by my transplant surgeon, Dr. Jorge Reyes, and the marvelous generosity of an anonymous liver donor, I would have died years ago and thus never could have completed the scriptural translations I have produced in the last eight years.

Outlining in This Work

The thirty-five chapter titles in this work are from the Taisho Chinese text. All other outline headings originate with the translator. Buddhist canonical texts are often so structurally dense that they are best navigated with the aid of at least a simple outline structure such as I have supplied here.

List of Abbreviations

AN	Aṅguttara Nikāya
BB	Buddhabhadra (T278)
BCSD	Hirakawa's *Buddhist Chinese-Sanskrit Dictionary*
BDK	Bukkyo Dendo Kyokai English Tripiṭaka
BHSD	Edgerton's *Buddhist Hybrid Sanskrit Dictionary*
BR	Bodhiruci (T1522)
CBETA	Chinese Buddhist Electronic Text Association's edition of the Taisho edition of the Chinese Buddhist canon.
CDB	*The Connected Discourses of the Buddha*
DN	*Dīgha Nikāya*
DR	Dharmarakṣa (T278)
DSBC	Digital Sanskrit Buddhist Canon's digitized edition of *Daśabhūmikasūtram,* edited by P. L. Vaidya.
EA	*Ekottara Āgama*
KB	Kumārajīva and Buddhayaśas (T286)
KJ	Kumārajīva
MDPL	*Materials for a Dictionary of the Prajñāpāramitā Literature*
MLDB	*The Middle Length Discourses of the Buddha*
MN	*Majjhima nikāya*
Mppu	*Mahāprajñāpāramitā upadeśa*
MW	Monier Williams' *A Sanskrit-English Dictionary*
N	Nāgārjuna
NDB	*Numerical Discourses of the Buddha*
PTS	Pali Text Society
SA	Śikṣānanda (T279)
SD	Śīladharma (T287)
SN	Saṃyutta Nikāya
SYMG	The Song, Yuan, Ming, Gong editions of the Chinese Buddhist canon.
SZPPS	*Shizhu piposha lun*
T	Taisho Chinese Buddhist Canon via CBETA (Version 2004. ed. Taibei)
VB	Venerable Bhikkhu Bodhi

General Table of Contents

Dedication	5
Acknowledgments	7
Outlining in This Work	7
List of Abbreviations	8
General Table of Contents	9
Directory to Chapter Subsections	11
Translator's Introduction	31
Introduction Endnotes	39
Nāgārjuna's Treatise on the Ten Grounds	41
Ch. 1 - The Introduction	43
Ch. 2 - Entering the First Ground	61
Ch. 3 - The Characteristics of the Ground	81
Ch. 4 - Purification of the Ground	97
Ch. 5 - The Explanation of the Vows	107
Ch. 6 - On Producing the Bodhi Resolve	139
Ch. 7 - On Training the Mind	147
Ch. 8 - On the Avaivartika	159
Ch. 9 - On the Easy Practice	175
Ch. 10 - Getting Rid of Karma	195
Ch. 11 - Distinctions with Regard to Merit	207
Ch. 12 - Distinctions with Regard to Giving	219
Ch. 13 - Distinctions with Regard to the Giving of Dharma	241
Ch. 14 - The Characteristics of the Refuges	249
Ch. 15 - The Five Moral Precepts	259
Ch. 16 - On Realizing the Faults of the Householder's Life	269
Ch. 17 - On Entering the Temple	283
Ch. 18 - The Jointly Shared Practices	307
Ch. 19 - The Fourfold Dharmas	319
Ch. 20 - Mindfulness of the Buddhas	337
Ch. 21 - Forty Dharmas Exclusive to Buddhas (Part 1)	357
Ch. 22 - Forty Dharmas Exclusive to Buddhas (Part 2)	369

Ch. 23 - Forty Dharmas Exclusive to Buddhas (Part 3) 397
Ch. 24 - Verses Offered in Praise 427
Ch. 25 - Teachings to Aid Mindfulness-of-the-Buddha Samādhi 437
Ch. 26 - The Analogy Chapter 455
Ch. 27 - A Summarizing Discussion of the Bodhisattva Practices 471
Ch. 28 - Distinctions in the 2nd Ground's Courses of Karmic Action 485
Ch. 29 - Distinctions Pertaining to Śrāvakas and Pratyekabuddhas 521
Ch. 30 - Distinctions Pertaining to the Great Vehicle 535
Ch. 31 - Guarding the Moral Precepts 567
Ch. 32 - An Explanation of the Dhūta Austerities 591
Ch. 33 - Aids to Gaining the Fruits of Śīla 619
Ch. 34 - In Praise of the Moral Precepts 639
Ch. 35 - The Karmic Rewards of the Moral Precepts 647
Translation Endnotes 655
Bibliography 727
Glossary 729
About the Translator 741
Kalavinka Buddhist Classics' Fall, 2019 Title List 743

Directory to Chapter Subsections

I. Chapter One: The Introduction 43
A. Verses Declaring the Three Refuges and the Treatise's Intent 43
1. Q: Why Explain the Ten Grounds? 43
2. A: The Plight of Beings and the Availability of Saviors 43
3. Q: Can Non-Bodhisattvas Also Transcend Saṃsāra? 44
4. A: Yes, But the Great Vehicle Requires the Ten Grounds 44
5. Q: How Long for Two Vehicles to Achieve Transcendence? 44
6. A: Two Vehicles are Rapid; Bodhisattvas Require Many Lives 44
7. Q: Is There Any Difference in the Quality of Liberation? 45
8. A: Nirvāṇa Does Not Differ; Levels of Awakening Are Very Different 45
9. Q: If Nirvāṇa Is Identical, Why Not Quickly Depart? 45
10. A: This is a Weak and Inferior Statement Devoid of Compassion 45
a. Without Bodhisattvas, How Could The Two Vehicles Exist? 45
b. This Would Put an End to the Three Vehicles and the Three Jewels 46
1) The Four Types of People 46
2) The Immense Superiority of One Who Perfects the Ten Grounds 47
11. Q: I Am Convinced, So Please Continue To Explain the Verses 47
B. Nāgārjuna Continues Explaining His Introductory Verses: 47
1. Q: Is Generating the Resolve Sufficient To Become a Bodhisattva? 48
2. A: Of Course Not, But Perhaps Yes. 48
3. Q: Why only praise the Bodhisattva's Solid Resolve? 49
4. A: It Is Essential For Success and Those Without It Would Turn Back 49
a. Why, Absent Solid Resolve, One Abandons the Bodhisattva Path 49
1) Fear of Continued Existence in Saṃsāra 49
2) Fear of the Hells 49
3) Fear of Rebirth in the Animal Realm 51
4) Fear of Rebirth in the Hungry Ghost Realm 52
5) Fear of Rebirth in the Human Realm 52
6) Fear of Rebirth in the Deva or Asura Realms 53
b. The Contrasting Response of One with Solid Resolve 53
1) The Bodhisattva's Vow 53
2) The Bodhisattvas Compassion, Vigor, and Success 53
3) Eight Bodhisattva Dharmas 53
C. Nāgārjuna Continues to Explain His Introductory Verses 54
1. Q: This Is Just as in Scripture. Why Be Redundant? For Fame, etc.? 54
2. A: This Treatise Is Not Composed for Self-Serving Reasons 54
3. Q: If Not, Then Why? 54
4. A: Out of Kindness and Compassion and for No Other Reason 54
5. Q: Why Just Repeat What Scripture Already Explains? 55
6. A: Some Beings Require or Delight in More Thorough Explanations 55
7. Q: How Are Others' Unique Predilections Any of Your Business? 56

8. A: Because I Have Resolved Not To Abandon Anyone 56
9. Q: What Are the Qualities of Such a Good Person? 56
10. A: Immediate Dharma Understanding; Also, 10 Qualities, as Below: 56
11. A Vibhāṣā Helps Those Who Find Sutras Hard to Fathom 57
12. Such Explanation of Dharma Is an Offering to the Buddha 57
13. By Explaining Dharma One Lights the Dharma Lamp 58
14. This Leads To Accumulating the Four Bases of Meritorious Qualities 58
a. Truth 58
b. Relinquishment 58
c. Quiescence 58
d. Wisdom 59
15. Nāgārjuna's Final Statement of Intent 59

II. Chapter Two: Entering the First Ground 61
A. Q: What Are the Ten Grounds? 61
B. A: The Ten Grounds Taught by All Buddhas Are As Follows: 61
C. Q: How Does One Enter and Cultivate the First Ground? 63
D. A: Five Stanzas on First Ground Cultivation 63
1. The Meaning of "Roots of Goodness" 63
a. Abhidharma Categories of "Roots of Goodness" 63
b. The Meaning of "Roots of Goodness" That is Relevant Here 64
2. The Meaning of "Practicing the Practices" 64
a. Seven Dharmas Essential to "Thorough Practice" 64
b. The Importance of Dhyāna to Implementing the Practices 65
3. The Meaning of "Accumulating the Provisions" 65
a. "Provisions" Includes the Topics Referenced Earlier 65
b. "Provisions" Also Includes the Practice of 22 Good Dharmas 65
4. The Meaning of "Thoroughly Making Offerings to all Buddhas" 66
5. The Meaning of "Protected by the Good Spiritual Friend" 67
6. The Meaning of "Complete Development of Resolute Intentions" 67
a. Q: Compared to Scripture, Isn't This a Deficient Explanation? 67
b. Q: No. Each Ground Involves Specific Resolute Intentions 69
7. The Meaning of "Compassionate Mindfulness of Beings" 70
8. The Meaning of "Resolute Faith in the Unsurpassable Dharma" 70
9. The Meaning of "Bringing Forth the Vow" 70
a. Q: Why Do You Say, "After I Have Achieved Liberation"? 70
b. A: If One is Not Already Liberated, One Cannot Liberate Others 70
c. Q: For What Sort of Benefit and with What Sort of Resolve? 71
d. A: To Gain the Ten Powers and Enter the Stage of Certainty 71
1) Q: What Are the Ten Powers? 71
2) A: They Are as Follows 71
3) To Gain The Powers, One Makes the Vow and Becomes Irreversible 72
a) Q: Does Everyone Then Reach the Stage of Certainty? 72
b) A: Some Do; Some Do Not 72
4) Q: If Some Do Not, Why Claim Certainty Relies on Resolve? 72
5) A: Because This Is True of Some Bodhisattvas 73

a) Q: What is the Nature of This Initial Resolve? 73
b) A: The Initial Resolve Is Characterized by These 41 Aspects 73
(1) Q: Doesn't "Permanence" of Resolve Contradict Dharma? 75
(2) A: You Misunderstand the Concept 75
10. The Meaning of "Birth In the Family of the Tathāgatas" 75
a. The Meaning of "Tathāgata" 75
b. The Meaning of "the Family of the Tathāgatas" 77
c. The Meaning of "Having No Transgressions or Faults," etc. 78
d. Q: Why Is the First Ground Said To Be "Joyful"? 79
e. A: Because of the Immense Significance of the First Ground 79
III. Chapter Three: The Characteristics of the Ground 81
A. Q: What Are the Characteristics of the First Ground Bodhisattva? 81
B. A: He Immediately Acquires Seven Qualities (Verse) 81
1. Q: Why Only Say, "For the Most Part" He Has These Seven Traits? 83
2. A: Because He Still Hasn't Done Away with the Contaminants 83
3. Q: Is His Joyfulness Acquired by Him or Is It a Feature of This Ground? 83
4. A: It Is Due to Mindfulness of Buddhas & the Stage of Certainty 83
a. Q: What Is Unique about the First Ground Bodhisattva's Joyfulness? 84
b. A: He Realizes He Will Definitely Become a Buddha 84
c. From Which Types of Fear Has This Bodhisattva Been Freed? 86
d. Fear of Not Surviving, Death, the Wretched Destinies, etc. (Verse) 86
1) Fear of Not Surviving 86
a) Why Does This Bodhisattva Not Fear Failing to Survive? 86
b) Due to Great Merit, Endurance, Wisdom, and Easy Satisfaction 86
2) Fear of Death 88
3) Fear of the Wretched Destinies 91
4) Fear of Great Assemblies 92
5) Fear of Ill Repute and Fear of Being Disparaged 93
6) Fear of Imprisonment, shackles, manacles, or Beatings 93
e. Realizing Nonexistence of Self As the Basis of Fearlessness 93
1) Q: Why Does This Bodhisattva Have No Conception of a Self? 94
2) A: He Delights in Emptiness and Sees the Body as Not Self (Verse) 94
IV. Chapter Four: Purification of the Ground 97
A. Q: How Should the 1st Ground Bodhisattva Cultivate Its Purification? 97
B. A: One Cultivates 27 Dharmas (Verse) 97
1. "The Power of Faith Becomes Ever More Superior" 98
a. Q: Of the Two Types of Superiority, of Which Do You Speak? 98
b. A: Both "More" and "Better Quality" 98
2. "One Practices Deeply the Mind of Great Compassion" 98
3. "The Mind of Kindness" 98
4. "Tirelessly Cultivating the Mind of Goodness" 98
5. "One Finds Joyous Delight in Sublime Dharmas" 99
6. "Always Drawing Near to the Spiritual Guide" 99
7. "A Sense of Shame" and "a Dread of Blame" 99
8. "Reverence" 99

9. "Gentle and Harmonious" 99
10. "Delighting in Contemplating Dharmas" 99
11. "Staying Free of Attachment" 99
12. "Single-Mindedness" 99
13. "Striving to Acquire Abundant Learning" 100
14. "Refraining from Coveting Offerings of Benefits and Support" 100
15. "Staying Far from Cheating, Flattery, and Deception" 100
a. The Five Types of Wrong livelihood 100
1) Feigning Uniqueness 100
2) Taking Advantage of a Close Relationship 101
3) Inducement through Instigation 101
4) Manipulation through Praising and Blaming" 101
5) Seeking to Gain Benefits Based on One's Benefits 102
16. "One Does Not Defile the Family of the Buddhas" 102
17. "Not Damaging Moral Precepts" and "Not Cheating the Buddhas" 103
a. Might a Bodhisattva at the Stage of Certainty Break Precepts? 103
b. This Is Possible If He Has Not yet Cut off the Afflictions 103
18. "Deeply Delighting in All-Knowledge" and "Remaining Unmoving" 104
19. "Always Cultivating Ever More Superior Dharmas" 104
20. "Delighting in World-Transcending Dharmas," "Not Worldly Ones" 104
21. "Cultivating What Is Difficult to Cultivate" 105
22. Q: How Does One "Securely Abide" and Not Retreat? 106
23. A: By Always Practicing and Completely Developing These Dharmas 106
24. The Meaning of "Bodhisattva" and "Superior Dharmas" 106

V. Chapter Five: Explanation of the Vows 107
A. The First Bodhisattva Vow 107
B. The Second Bodhisattva Vow 107
C. The Third Bodhisattva Vow 108
D. The Fourth Bodhisattva Vow 109
E. The Fifth Bodhisattva Vow 109
F. The Sixth Bodhisattva Vow 110
G. The Seventh Bodhisattva Vow 114
1. An Exhaustive List of the Characteristics of Evil and Impurity 114
2. A Description of the Characteristics of Pure Lands 120
H. The Eighth Bodhisattva Vow 131
I. The Ninth Bodhisattva Vow 132
J. The Tenth Bodhisattva Vow 132
K. The Infinitely Vast Scope and Duration of the Ten Bodhisattva Vows 133

VI. Chapter Six: On Producing the Bodhi Resolve 139
A. The Seven Bases for Producing the Bodhi Resolve 139
1. The Influence of a Buddha 140
2. The Motivation to Protect the Dharma 140
3. Compassion for the Suffering of Beings 141
4. The Instructive Influence of a Bodhisattva 142
5. The Aspiration to Emulate the Conduct of Bodhisattvas 142

6. Inspiration Provoked by an Act of Giving 143
7. Inspiration Arising from Observing a Buddha's Physical Marks 143
B. The Relative Probability of Success in these Seven Bases 144

VII. Chapter Seven: On Training the Mind 147
A. A: Practicing Dharmas Resulting in Failure Entails Loss 147
1. Q: Which Dharmas Result in Loss 147
2. A: There Are Four Such Dharmas (Verse) 147
3. Q: Are There Only These Four or Are There More? 150
4. A: There Are Numerous Additional Cases (A Series of Verses) 150
a. Q: What Is Meant by "the Works of Māras"? 151
b. A: There Are Numerous Examples, As Follows: (List) 152
B. Q: Which Dharmas Cause One to Make the Vows Again in Each Life? 156
C. A: They Are as Follows: (Verse) 156

VIII. Chapter Eight: On the Avaivartika 159
A. Q: What Are the Distinguishing Characteristics of an Avaivartika? 159
B. A: There are Five Defining Dharmas, as Follows: (Verse) 159
1. Maintaining a Mind of Equal Regard toward Beings 159
2. Not Envying Benefits and Support Obtained by Others 160
3. Not Speaking of a Dharma Master's Transgressions 160
4. Resolute Faith in the Profound and Sublime Dharma 160
5. Not Craving to Be the Object of Others' Reverence 160
6. One Does Not Retreat from Complete Enlightenment 160
C. Two Types of Reversible Bodhisattvas, Ruined Versus Progressing 161
1. Q: What Are the Signs of a "Ruined" Reversible Bodhisattva? 161
2. A: Seven Characteristics, as Follows: (Verse) 161
a. Absence of Determination and Ability 161
b. Delighting in Inferior Dharmas 162
c. Being Deeply Attached to Fame and Offerings 162
d. Having a Mind That Is Not Upright and Straight 162
e. Feeling a Miserly Cherishing toward Others' Households 163
f. Not Having a Resolute Belief in the Dharma of Emptiness 163
g. Only Esteeming All Manner of Verbal Discourse 163
h. These Are the Marks of One Fallen into Ruination 163
3. Q: What Are the Traits of the Reversible Bodhisattva Who Succeeds? 163
4. A: He Has Five Qualities, as Follows: (Verse) 164
a. Not Apprehending the Existence of any "Self" 164
b. Not Apprehending the Existence of Any "Being" 165
c. Not Engaging in Discriminations While Speaking on Dharma 166
d. Not Apprehending the Existence of Bodhi 167
e. Not Seeing a Buddha by His Signs 168
D. Q: What Are the Characteristic Signs of an Avaivartika? 169
E. A: The Avaivartika Has Numerous Characteristics, as Follows: 170

IX. Chapter Nine: On the Easy Practice 175
A. Q: How Difficult! Is There an Easier Path to the Avaivartika Ground? 175
B. A: How Weak & Inferior! But, If You Want That, I Will Explain 176

1. The Practice of Calling on Ten Buddhas, One in Each Direction 176
2. Q: Can One Instead Call on Other Buddhas and Bodhisattvas? 183
3. A: Yes, There is Amitābha as Well as Other Such Buddhas 183
a. Amitābha's Original Vows and a Praise Verse 185
4. Also, the Seven Buddhas of the Past as Well as Maitreya 188
5. Also, by Calling on Ten Other Buddhas 190
6. Also, by Calling on All Buddhas of the Three Times 191
7. Also, by Calling on the Great Bodhisattvas 192

X. Chapter 10: Getting Rid of Bad Karma 195
A. Q: Is Buddha Mindfulness All One Must Do to Become Irreversible? 195
B. A: One Should Also Repent, Entreat, Rejoice & Dedicate Merit 195
1. How Does One Perform These Endeavors? 195
2. "Repentance" Is Performed as Follows: 195
3. Q: How Does One Go about "Entreating"? 198
4. A: "Entreating" Is Performed as Follows: 198
5. Q: What is meant by "Rejoicing"? 200
6. A: "Rejoicing" Is Performed as Follows: 200
7. Q: What Is Meant by "Dedication"? 201
8. A: Dedication Is Performed as Follows: 202
9. Q: Which Ways of Performing These Accords with the Buddhas? 204
10. A: Whichever Ways Accord with This Passage from Scripture 204

XI. Chapter 11: Distinctions with Regard to Merit 207
A. Q: How Should One Repent, Entreat, Rejoice, and Dedicate Merit? 207
B. A: With Reverence and Pressed Palms, Three Times Each Day & Night 207
C. Q: What Karmic Result Ensues from Doing This? 207
D. A: If One Did This but Once, the Merit Would Be Incalculably Great 207
E. Q: Why Have You Not Discussed the Merit Arising from Repentance? 212
F. A: The Merit Arising from Repentance Is the Greatest 212
G. Q: How Can You Say That Repentance Gets Rid of Karmic Offenses? 213
H. A: Although Not Eliminated Entirely, They Are Greatly Reduced 214

XII. Chapter 12: Distinctions with Regard to Giving 219
A. With More Merit & Mental Pliancy, the Bodhisattva Develops Faith 219
B. The Bodhisattva's Sympathy for Beings Leads to Compassion for Them 219
C. The Bodhisattva Is Then Motivated to Rescue Beings from Suffering 219
D. Due to Kindness & Compassion, He Devotes Himself to Giving 220
1. The Bodhisattva Is Willing to Give Everything to Beings 220
2. Q: Is His Giving Done for Merit or Due to Kindness and Compassion? 222
3. A: He Knows, Has Faith, May Have the Heavenly Eye & So Gives All 222
a. Q: As You Said He Knows Them, Please Explain These Karmic Results 222
b. A: Akṣayamati Bodhisattva's Explanation Is As Follows: 222
c. The Karmic Results of Other Sorts of Giving 224
d. He Avoids Wrong Giving and Gives In Accordance with Emptiness 225
1) Q: Will You Please Discuss These Two Types of Giving? 225
2) Akṣayamati Bodhisattva Explains Them as Follows: 225
a) The Types of Impure Giving 225

b) Giving Conjoined with Emptiness, Signlessness, or Wishlessness 228
c) Impure Giving Versus Pure Giving 229
(1) The Bases for Presence or Absence of Purification 230
(2) Q: Of These Four, Which Should Be Practiced? 231
(3) A: Practice Two That Are Pure and Avoid Selfish Motives 231
(4) Q: How Can One Possessed of Desires Practice Pure Giving? 232
(5) A: Do Not Accumulate Things That Engender Miserliness 232
(a) Q: How Can One Accomplish This with One's Own Body? 232
(b) A: Consider One's Body to Be Like a Medicine Tree 232
E. The Bodhisattva's Dedication of the Merit Arising from His Giving 233
1. Q: How Many Types of Right and Wrong Dedication are There? 233
2. There Are 4 Pure Objectives of Dedication and 3 Not Practiced 234
a. The Three Types of Dedication One Does Not Practice 234
b. The Four Types of Dedication Done for the Sake of Pure Objectives 234
1) Q: Which Dharmas Diminish Its Benefit and Which Increase It? 234
a) A: There Are Four Causes of Diminishment, as Follows: 235
b) For Increase, Stop These Four and Adopt Three Types of Thought 235
F. One Gives for the Sake of Causing 3 Dharmas and Seeking 2 Dharmas 236
1. Q: You Said One Doesn't Seek Rewards. Isn't This Contradictory? 239
2. A: No, Because This Wealth Is Gained & Used Only to Benefit Beings 239
G. One Also Gives to Cut Off Two Dharmas and Gain Two Dharmas 239
H. One Also Gives to Increase Three Types of Wisdom 240
I. Others Say That Giving Is Practiced to Increase Two Dharmas 240
J. In Summary, the Bodhisattva Should Practice Four Kinds of Giving 240

XIII. Chapter 13: Distinctions with Regard to the Giving of Dharma 241
A. Dharma Giving Is Supreme and the Wise Should Practice It 241
B. Q: Why Do You Say Only the Wise Should Practice Dharma Giving? 241
C. A: Erroneous Interpretations Do Not Benefit Anyone 241
1. Q: What Do You Mean by "Erroneous Interpretations"? 241
2. A: Wrong Ideas of Spurious Origin (Four Cases from Scripture) 241
D. Q: How Does One Know That Dharma Giving Is Supreme? 243
E. A: The Sutras Say So 243
F. A Sutra Explains Propriety in Speaking Dharma as Follows: 243
1. Four Qualities of a Qualified Dharma Speaker 244
2. Four Correct Behaviors When Ascending the High Seat to Teach 244
3. Four More Correct Behaviors for When One Sits on the High Seat 244
4. Another Four Correct Behaviors When Sitting on the High Seat 245
5. Eighteen More Qualifications For One Who Sits on the High Seat 245
6. Four More Dharmas To Be Observed When Sitting on the High Seat 246
G. A Scriptural Citation Regarding the Buddha's Teaching of Dharma 246
H. Conclusion: In Dharma Giving, One Should Practice Accordingly 247

XIV. Chapter 14: The Characteristics of the [Three] Refuges 249
A. Distinctions Regarding Material Giving versus Dharma Giving 249
1. Laity Excel at Material Giving & Monastics Excel at Dharma Giving 249
2. Monastics Are Better Trained to Practice Dharma Giving 249

3. The Hazards to Monastics of Devotion to Material Giving 250
B. Taking Refuge in the Three Jewels 251
1. Q: What Is Meant by Taking Refuge in the Buddha? 251
2. A: The Primary Aspects of Taking Refuge in the Buddha 251
3. Q: What Is Meant by Taking Refuge in the Dharma? 252
4. A: The Primary Aspects of Taking Refuge in the Dharma 252
5. Q: What Is Meant by Taking Refuge in the Sangha? 252
6. A: The Primary Aspects of Taking Refuge in the Sangha 253
7. The Meaning of Mindfulness of the Buddha, Dharma, and Sangha 255
a. The Meaning of Mindfulness of the Buddha 255
1) Q: What Is Meant by "Mindfulness of the True Buddha"? 255
2) A: "Mindfulness of the True Buddha" as Set Forth in a Sutra 255
b. The Meaning of "Mindfulness of the Dharma" 257
c. The Meaning of Mindfulness of the Sangha 258
C. A Concluding Statement on the Three Refuges 258

XV. Chapter 15: The Five Moral Precepts 259
A. The Lay Bodhisattva Cultivates Goodness and Avoids Bad Actions 259
B. One Relinquishes Self Benefit, Benefits Others & Repays Kindness 259
C. Q: Relinquishing Self-Benefit to Benefit Others Is Wrong 260
D. A: No. This Is Good Even in Worldly Terms & Also Benefits Oneself 260
E. One Should Steadfastly Observe the Five Moral Precepts 262
1. Q: Does This Bodhisattva Only Observe These Precepts? 264
2. A: Uphold The 5 Precepts & Also Practice the Other Good Actions 264
a. He Should Explain Dharma for Beings & Proceed to Teach Them 264
b. One Should Provide Beings with Whatever They Are Deficient In 265
c. The Bodhisattva Teaches All Sorts of Evil Beings 265
d. When Evil Beings Disturb Him, He Must Not Think In These Ways: 265
e. He Should Redouble His Resolve & Act Like a Great Physician 266
f. Failing in This, He Would Be Worthy of the Buddhas' Censure 266

XVI. Chapter 16: On Realizing the Faults of the Householder's Life 269
A. The Bodhisattva Should Know the Faults of the Householder's Life 269
B. Q: What Are the Faults of the Householder's Life? 269
C. A: They Are Well Described in This Passage from a Sutra 269
D. Also Practice Giving, Uphold Precepts, and Contemplate Almsmen 271
1. Five Threefold Contemplations Whenever Seeing an Almsman 272
2. It Is Due to Almsmen That One Is Able to Perfect the Six pāramitās 273
3. One Knows the Benefits of Giving and the Faults of Miserliness 274
a. Q: What Are the Merits of Giving and Faults of Keeping the Gift? 274
b. A: Using True Wisdom, the Bodhisattva Understands as Follows: 274
4. Contemplate Relatives and Possessions as Like Mere Illusions 275
5. One Should Reflect on Them All as the Results of Karma 276
6. Use the Following Threefold Contemplations of One's Spouse 277
7. Use Wisdom to Reduce Bias Toward One's Own Children 279
8. Take up This Threefold Contemplation of One's Children 280
9. Use The Following Thoughts to Develop Equal Regard for All 280

XVII. Chapter 17: On Entering the Temple 283
- A. One Should Be Able to Relinquish Whatever One Is Attached to 283
- B. Q: If One Is Attached to Something, What if Someone Asks for It? 283
- C. A: Exhort Oneself to Abandon Miserliness and Relinquish It 283
- D. If One Is Still Unable to Relinquish It, One May Politely Decline 284
- E. If a Divided Sangha Stops Functioning, One Should Try to Mediate 284
- F. On Abstinence Days, the Lay Bodhisattva Takes the Eight Precepts 285
  - 1. Q: How Should One Practice This Abstinence Dharma? 285
  - 2. A: Solemnly Vow to Uphold the Eight Precepts as Follows: 285
  - 3. Q: Should One Treat Bad Monks with Disdain and Anger? 287
  - 4. A: Do Not Adopt a Disdainful or Angry Attitude toward Them 287
  - 5. Q: If Hatred Is Wrong, What Attitude Is Most Appropriate? 288
  - 6. A: Feel Pity for Him and Condemn His Afflictions Instead 288
- G. On Entering a Temple, One Should Be Respectful and Make Offerings 294
- H. One Should Reflect on the Merit of Becoming a Monastic 294
- I. Ninety-Nine Reflections on the Advantages of Monastic Life 295
- J. One Should Develop a Deep Yearning to Become a Monastic 300
- K. Three Aspirational Thought When Bowing at a Stupa or Temple 301
- L. On Meeting Any Monk, Serve, Follow Instructions, and Assist 301
- M. Avoid Causing Afflictions in Those Not Receiving One's Gifts 303
- N. Giving as an Opportunity to Encourage Highest Bodhi Resolve 304
- O. Do Whatever Is Necessary to Preserve and Protect the Dharma 304
- P. When Giving, Have No Regrets or Selfish Motives & Dedicate Merit 305

XVIII. Chapter 18: The Jointly Shared Practices 307
- A. A: The Jointly Shared Practices Are as Follows: (List) 307
  - 1. Patience, Dharma Giving, Dharmas Patience, and Contemplation: 307
    - a. Patience 308
    - b. Dharma Giving 308
    - c. Dharmas Patience 308
    - d. Contemplation 309
    - e. Not Distorting the Dharma 309
  - 2. Esteem for Dharma, Nonobstruction, Offerings & Resolute Faith 309
    - a. Esteem for the Dharma 309
    - b. Offerings in Support of the Dharma 310
    - c. Resolute Faith 310
  - 3. Emptiness, Non-Greed, Congruent Actions & Words, Lamp Light 310
    - a. Cultivation of Emptiness 310
    - b. Not Being Covetous or Envious 311
    - c. Acting in Accordance with One's Own Words 311
    - d. Giving Lamp Light 311
  - 4. Music, Means of Transport, Right Vows, the Means of Attraction 311
    - a. Giving Musical Performances 311
    - b. Giving Means of Transport 312
    - c. Right Vows 312
    - d. Thought Imbued with the Means of Attraction 312

5. Benefiting and Comforting Beings and Equal Regard for All Beings 312
a. Q: How Can One Differentiate a Buddha from Other People? 313
b. A: A Buddha Possesses the Thirty-Two marks 313
1) Q: How Can One Understand Such Matters? 313
2) A: Each of the Thirty-Two marks Has Three Distinctions 313
a) Q: What Is Meant by Each Mark Having Three Distinctions? 313
b) A: This Refers to Each Mark's Substance, Fruition, and Karma 313
XIX. Chapter 19: The Fourfold Dharmas 319
A. One Should Cultivate the Causes for Gaining the 32 Marks 319
1. Fourfold Dharmas Causing Either Loss or Gain of Wisdom 319
a. Four Dharmas Causing Loss of Wisdom 319
b. Four Dharmas Causing Attainment of Wisdom 319
2. Fourfold Dharmas Causing Decrease or Increase of Good Roots 320
a. Four Dharmas That Decrease One's Roots of Goodness 320
b. Four Dharmas That Increase One's Roots of Goodness 320
3. Fourfold Dharmas That Increase or Stop Flattery and Deviousness 321
a. Four Dharmas Involving Flattery and Deviousness 321
b. Four Dharmas Characteristic of a Straightforward Mind 321
4. Fourfold Dharmas of Ruined Bodhisattvas & Those Well-Trained 322
a. Four Dharmas Practiced by a Bodhisattva Fallen into Ruin 322
b. Four Dharmas Practiced by the Well-Trained Bodhisattva 323
5. Fourfold Bodhisattva Mistakes versus Good Paths of Conduct 323
a. Four Kinds of Bodhisattva Mistakes 323
b. Four Paths of Good Bodhisattva Conduct 324
6. Four Dharmas Indicative of an Imitation Bodhisattva 324
a. Q: How Can One Abandon Imitation Bodhisattva Dharmas? 324
b. A: Cultivate Four Qualities of the Initial Bodhisattva Practices 324
1) The Four Qualities of the Initial Bodhisattva Practices 325
2) To Develop The Qualities, Draw Near to a Good Spiritual Guide 325
a) Fourfold Good and Bad Spiritual Friends 325
i) The Four Kinds of Good Spiritual Friends 325
ii) The Four Kinds of Bad Spiritual Friends 326
3) Four Questions on the Good Effects of Good Spiritual Friends 326
a) Answer #1: The Meaning of the Four Vast Treasuries 327
b) Answer #2: The Meaning of Going Beyond the Works of Māra 327
c) Answer #3: The Meaning of Producing Measureless Merit 327
d) Answer #4: The Meaning of Accumulating All Good Dharmas 327
7. Eight Twofold Dharmas the Bodhisattva Must Completely Abandon 328
a. The Two Hollow Attachments 328
b. The Two Types of Bondage 328
c. The Two Hindrance Dharmas 328
d. The Two Defiling Dharmas 329
e. The Two Ulcerous Sores 329
f. The Two Abyss-Like Dharmas 329
g. The Two Dharmas Leading to Being Burned 329

h. The Two Types of Illnesses 329
1) Q: Which Dharmas Lead to Bodhi & Which Earn Āryas' Praise? 329
2) A: The Four Truths' Practices and Four Additional Dharmas 329
a) The Four Dharmas Characteristic of Cultivating the Truths 330
b) The Four Dharmas Praised by the Three Classes of Āryas 330
8. The Bodhisattva's Relinquishing Mind & Freedom from Weariness 331
a. The Bodhisattva Doesn't Weary of Providing Two Kinds of Benefit 331
b. Q: Why Are Bodhisattvas Taught to Understand Worldly Dharmas? 332
c. A: Knowledge of the World Enables Dharma Teaching Expedients 332
9. One Must Have a Sense of Shame, Dread of Blame, and Respect 333
10. The Bodhisattva Must Never Retreat from Completing His Works 333
a. Q: How Can the Bodhisattva Succeed in Completing His Works? 334
b. A: He Has Patience, Makes Offerings, and Follows Teachings 334
11. Right Practice of Ten Dharmas Enabling 1st Ground Purification 334
a. Faith 334
b. Compassion 335
c. Kindness 335
d. Relinquishing 335
e. Tirelessly Patient Endurance 335
f. The Ability to Understand the Meaning of Teachings 335
g. Serving as Guide for Beings' Minds 336
h. A Sense of Shame and Dread of Blame 336
i. Making Offerings to the Buddha 336
j. Abiding in the Buddha's Teachings 336
XX. Chapter 20: Mindfulness of the Buddhas 337
A. On Finishing 1st Ground Practices, the Bodhisattva Sees Buddhas 337
1. Q: Is There Any Other Way to Be Able to See the Buddhas? 337
2. A: On Entering the Pratyutpanna Samādhi, One Sees the Buddhas 337
3. Q: How Can One Acquire This Samadhi? 337
4. A: Envision the Buddhas with the 32 Marks and 80 Characteristics 338
a. Recollection of the Buddhas' Qualities and Accomplishments 338
b. Recollection of the 32 Marks of the Buddhas 338
c. Recollection of Other Qualities of the Buddhas 340
d. Recollection of More Special Qualities & Abilities of Buddhas 342
e. Contemplative Recollection of the 80 Secondary Characteristics 344
f. Envisioning the Buddhas in an Assembly, Teaching, on the Lion Seat 348
1) Envisioning the Buddhas as They Sit on the Lion's Seat 348
2) Envisioning the Audience as the Buddhas Teach Dharma 348
3) Envisioning the Manner in Which They Teach Dharma 349
4) Envisioning the Effects of the Buddhas' Teaching of Dharma 350
5) Instruction on This Type of Contemplative Mindfulness 351
6) The Importance of Praising the Major Marks and Secondary Signs 351
a) Verses in Praise of the Buddhas' 32 Marks 351
b) Verses in Praise of the Buddhas Secondary Characteristics 353
c) Summation on Importance of Such Recollective Contemplation 355

XXI. Chapter 21: Forty Dharmas Exclusive to Buddhas (Part 1) 357
A. Introduction to the Forty Dharmas Exclusive to Buddhas 357
B. 1) Sovereign Mastery of the Ability to Fly 358
C. 2) [The Ability to Manifest] Countless Transformations 360
D. 3) Boundless Psychic Powers of the Sort Possessed by Āryas 361
E. 4) Sovereign Mastery of the Ability to Hear Sounds 363
F. 5) Immeasurable Power of Knowledge to Know Others' Thoughts 364
G. 6) Sovereign Mastery in [Training and Subduing] the Mind 364
H. 7) Constant Abiding in Stable Wisdom 365
I. 8) Never Forgetting 366
J. 9) Possession of the Powers of the Vajra Samādhi 366

XXII. Chapter 22: Forty Dharmas Exclusive to Buddhas (Part 2) 369
A. Q: Your Claim That Omniscience Exists Is False for these Reasons 369
B. A: Wrong. As I Shall Now Explain, The Buddha Truly Is Omniscient 377

XXIII. Chapter 23: Forty Dharmas Exclusive to Buddhas (Part 3) 397
A. 10) Thorough Knowing of Matters That Are Unfixed 397
B. 11) Thorough Knowing of Formless Absorption Phenomena 400
C. 12) The Knowledge of All Matters Related to Eternal Cessation 403
D. 13) Thorough Knowing of Non-Form Dharmas Unrelated to Mind 404
E. 14) The Great Powers Pāramitā 405
F. 15) The Four Unimpeded Knowledges Pāramitā 405
G. 16) The Pāramitā of Perfectly Complete Replies and Predictions 406
H. 17) Invulnerability to Harm by Anyone 409
I. 18) Their Words Are Never Spoken without a Purpose 410
J. 19) Their Speech Is Free of Error 412
K. 20) Complete Use of the Three Turnings in Speaking Dharma 413
L. 21) They Are the Great Generals among All Āryas 413
M. 22–25) They Are Able to Remain Unguarded in Four Ways 414
N. 26–29) They Possess the Four Types of Fearlessnesses 415
O. 30–39) They Possess the Ten Powers 417
1. The First Power 417
2. The Second Power 418
3. The Third Power 419
4. The Fourth Power 420
5. The Fifth Power 420
6. The Sixth Power 421
7. The Seventh Power 421
8. The Eighth Power 421
9. The Ninth Power 422
10. The Tenth Power 422
P. 40) They Have Achieved Unimpeded Liberation 422
Q. Summary Discussion of the Dharmas Exclusive to the Buddha 423

XXIV. Chapter 24: Verses Offered in Praise 427
A. The Importance of Praises to Mindfulness-of-the-Buddha Practice 427
B. The Praise Verses 427

1. Verses in Praise of the Forty Dharmas Exclusive to the Buddhas 427
2. Verses Praising the Four Bases of Meritorious Qualities 430
a. Verses Praising the Truth Basis of Meritorious Qualities 431
b. Verses Praising the Relinquishment Basis of Meritorious Qualities 431
c. Verses Praising the Quiescence Basis of Meritorious Qualities 433
d. Verses Praising the Wisdom Basis of Meritorious Qualities 434
3. Concluding Praise Verses 436

XXV. **Chapter 25: Teachings Aiding Mindfulness-of-the Buddha Samādhi** 437
A. Initial Instructions on the Mindfulness-of-the Buddha Samādhi 437
B. Four Dharmas Capable of Bringing Forth This Samādhi 439
C. Four More Dharmas Capable of Bringing Forth This Samādhi 440
D. Four More Dharmas Capable of Bringing Forth This Samādhi 440
E. Four More Dharmas Capable of Bringing Forth This Samādhi 440
F. Four More Dharmas Capable of Bringing Forth This Samādhi 441
G. Four More Dharmas Capable of Bringing Forth This Samādhi 441
H. Five More Dharmas Capable of Bringing Forth This Samādhi 441
I. Five More Dharmas Capable of Bringing Forth This Samādhi 442
J. The Guidelines for Lay and Monastic Cultivation of This Samādhi 442
1. Twenty Guidelines for Lay Cultivators of This Samādhi 443
2. Sixty Guidelines for Monastic Cultivators of This Samādhi 443
3. Fifty Dharmas Supporting Cultivation of This Samādhi 446
K. The Benefits of Cultivating This Pratyutpanna Samādhi 448
L. This Samādhi's Various Stations and Levels of Cultivation 451
M. Various Qualitative Variations in How This Samādhi Manifests 451
N. Various Abhidharmic Classifications of This Samādhi 452
O. The Practitioner's Offerings, Roots of Goodness, and Teaching 452
P. The Practitioner's Use of the Four Means of Attraction 453
Q. The Practitioner's Dedication of Roots of Goodness 453

XXVI. **Chapter 26: The Analogy Chapter** 455
A. The Bodhisattva Should Study, Cultivate, and Reach the Grounds 455
B. Seven Practices Characteristic of the First Ground Bodhisattva 455
C. Eight Accomplishments Associated with Entering the First Ground 456
D. The Essential Aspects of the Bodhisattva's First Ground Cultivation 457
E. Additional Factors That the Bodhisattva Must Learn 458
F. The Benefit of Knowing These Dharmas and Their Skillful Means 461
G. An Analogy for a Bodhisattva's Knowledge of the 10 Grounds Path 461

XXVII. **Chapter 27: A Summarizing Discussion of Bodhisattva Practices** 471
A. A Brief Presentation Intended to Finish the First Ground Discussion 471
B. Q: Before Finishing, Please Summarize the Bodhisattva Path 472
C. A: A Series of Statements Summarizing the Bodhisattva Practices 472
1. Practice All Bodhisattva Dharmas & Abandon All Transgressions 472
2. Be Single-Minded and Non-Neglectful in Practicing Good Dharmas 473
3. Two Dharmas That Subsume the Path to Buddhahood 473
4. Three Dharmas That Subsume the Path to Buddhahood 473
5. Four Dharmas That Subsume the Path to Buddhahood 474

6. Five Dharmas That Subsume the Path to Buddhahood 474
7. Six Dharmas That Subsume the Path to Buddhahood 474
8. Seven Dharmas That Subsume the Path to Buddhahood 475
9. Eight Dharmas That Subsume the Path to Buddhahood 475
10. Nine Dharmas That Subsume the Path to Buddhahood 476
11. Ten Dharmas That Subsume the Path to Buddhahood 476
12. Faults to Be Urgently Abandoned on the Path to Buddhahood 477
a. One Fault That Must Be Urgently Abandoned on the Buddha Path 477
b. Two Faults That Must Be Urgently Abandoned on the Buddha Path 477
c. Three Faults to Be Urgently Abandoned on the Buddha Path 478
d. Four Faults to Be Urgently Abandoned on the Buddha Path 478
e. Five Faults to Be Urgently Abandoned on the Buddha Path 479
f. Six Faults to Be Urgently Abandoned on the Buddha Path 479
g. Seven Faults to Be Urgently Abandoned on the Buddha Path 480
h. Eight Dharmas to Be Urgently Abandoned on the Buddha Path 480
i. Nine Dharmas to Be Urgently Abandoned on the Buddha Path 481
j. Ten Dharmas to Be Urgently Abandoned on the Buddha Path 481
13. The 32 Dharmas of Genuine Bodhisattvas 482
14. Seven Additional Dharmas of Genuine Bodhisattvas 484

XXVIII. Ch. 28: Distinctions in the 2nd Ground's Karmic Actions 485
A. The Ten Resolute Intentions Necessary for Entering the 2nd Ground 485
1. The Straight Mind and the Pliant Mind 486
2. The Capable Mind 486
3. The Restrained Mind 486
4. The Quiescent Mind 486
5. The Truly Sublime Mind 486
6. The Unmixed Mind 486
7. The Unattached Mind 487
a. Q: Doesn't an Unattached Mind Contradict the Bodhisattva Vow? 487
b. A: No, One Must Accord with the Mind of Equanimity 488
c. Q: Why Must the Bodhisattva Again Develop the Straight Mind, etc.? 489
d. A: Now, on the 2nd Ground, These Minds Become Solidly Established 489
e. Q: What Is the Result of Deep Delight and Solid Establishment? 489
f. A: These Types of Mind Will Forever After Be Effortlessly Invoked 489
g. Q: What Are the Fruits of Acquiring These Ten Types of Mind? 490
h. A: He Will Attain the Second Ground and a Threefold Stainlessness 490
B. The 2nd Ground Bodhisattva's Ten Courses of Good Karmic Action 490
1. Q: How Many Are Physical, How Many Verbal & How Many Mental? 490
2. A: Physical and Mental Are Threefold and Verbal Are Fourfold 491
C. Definitions of Each of the Ten Courses of Good & Bad Karmic Action 491
1. Killing 491
2. Stealing 491
3. Sexual Misconduct 492
4. False Speech 492
5. Divisive Speech 493

6. Harsh Speech 493
7. Scattered or Inappropriate Speech 493
8. Covetousness 493
9. Ill Will 494
10. Wrong Views 494
11. Right View 494
D. Abhidharma Categories Analyzing the 10 Courses of Karmic Action 495
1. Twenty Factors Used in Abhidharmic Analysis of Actions 495
2. The Twelvefold Discussion of Origins and Such 505
3. The Seven Types of Bad Actions, Their Origins, and Four Distinctions 508
4. More Subsidiary Distinctions Related to the Good and Bad Actions 510
5. Distinguishing "Karmic Deeds" versus "Courses of Karmic Action" 511
6. Four Distinctions: "Karmic Deeds" and "Courses of Karmic Action" 512
7. Three Kinds of Purity Used to Move Beyond the First Ground 513
8. The 10 Courses of Good and Bad Karma As Arbiters of One's Destiny 514
9. Resolving to Abide in the 10 Good Actions & Teach This to Others 515
10. One Should Learn the Rebirth Results of the 10 Good & Bad Actions 516

XXIX. Chapter 29: Distinctions Pertaining to the Two Vehicles 521
1. Q: Which Beings Can Use the 10 Courses to Fulfill the Śrāvaka Path? 521
a. Stanza #1 Commentary 522
b. Stanza #2 Commentary 524
c. Stanza #3 Commentary 524
d. Stanza #4 Commentary 525
e. Stanza #5–6 Commentary 526
f. Stanza #7 Commentary 526
2. Q: Who Can Use the Ten Courses to Become a Pratyekabuddha? 527
a. Stanza#1 Commentary 528
b. Stanza#2 Commentary 528
c. Stanza #3 Commentary 529
d. Stanza #4 Commentary 530
e. Stanza #5 Commentary 531
f. Stanza #6–7 Commentary 532

XXX. Chapter 30: [Distinctions Pertaining to] the Great Vehicle 535
A. Q: Which Beings Can Use the Ten Courses to Become Buddhas? 535
B. A: The Ten Courses Enable Buddhahood for Beings of This Sort (Verse) 535
C. An Extensive Line-by-Line Explanation of the Verse's Deep Meaning 536
1. "Superiority of the Bodhisattva's Cultivation of the Ten Courses" 536
a. Five Ways in Which the Bodhisattva's Practice is Superior 537
1) Superiority of Vows 538
2) Superiority of Solid Resolve 538
3) Superiority of Resolute Intentions 539
4) Superiority of Thoroughgoing Purity 539
5) Superiority in the Use of Skillful Means 540
2. The Bodhisattva's "Measureless Cultivation" 540
a. Immeasurability of Time 540

b. Immeasurability of Roots of Goodness 540
c. Immeasurability of Objective Conditions 541
d. Immeasurability of Ultimate Ends 541
e. Immeasurability of Dedication of Merit 542
3. The Bodhisattva's "Extraordinary Cultivation" 542
a. His Extraordinary Capacity to Endure 542
b. His Extraordinary Vigor 542
c. His Solidity of Resolve 543
d. His Extraordinary Wisdom 543
e. His Extraordinary Karmic Fruits 543
4. The Bodhisattva's Vows 544
a. The "Solidity" of His Vows 544
b. The "Goodness" of His Vows 544
5. The Bodhisattva's "Great Compassion" 545
6. The "Unimpeded" Nature of the Bodhisattva's Compassion 545
7. The Bodhisattva's "Thorough Practice of Skillful Means" 546
a. His Knowledge of "the Correct Place and Time" 546
b. His Knowledge of "What Delights the Minds of Others" 547
c. His Knowledge of "What Causes Others to Turn & Enter the Path" 547
d. His Knowledge of "What Constitutes the Correct Sequence" 547
e. His Knowledge of "How to Lead and Guide Beings" 550
8. The Bodhisattva's "Patient Endurance of Pain and Anguish" 551
9. The Bodhisattva's "Never Abandoning Any Being" 552
10. The Bodhisattva's "Deep Delight in the Buddhas' Wisdom" 553
11. "Delight in Those Who Practice the Buddhas' Powers & Masteries" 554
12. The Buddhas' "Practice of the Powers" 554
13. The Buddhas' "Practice of the Sovereign Masteries" 555
14. The Bodhisattva's "Ability to Refute All Wrong Views" 556
15. The Bodhisattva's "Preservation and Protection of Right Dharma" 556
16. The Bodhisattva's "Valor" 558
17. The Bodhisattva's "Ability to Endure" 559
18. The Bodhisattva's "Vigor" 560
19. The Bodhisattva's "Solid Resolve in Teaching Beings" 561
20. The Bodhisattva's "Not Coveting His Own Happiness" 561
21. The Bodhisattva's "Not Coveting a Measurelessly Long Life" 562
22. The Bodhisattva's "Supremacy in All Endeavors" 563
23. The Bodhisattva's "Freedom from Fault in All the Works They Do" 564
24. The Bodhisattva's "Complete Purity" & "Success in Supreme Bases" 564
25. How the Ten Courses Enable the Attainment of Buddhahood 565

XXXI. Chapter 31: Guarding the Moral Precepts 567
A. General and Specific Results of the Ten Courses of Karmic Action 567
1. The Ten Courses of Good Karmic Action 567
a. General Karmic Results of the Ten Courses of Good Karmic Action 567
b. Specific Karmic Results of the Ten Courses of Good Karmic Action 567
2. The Ten Courses of Bad Karmic Action 568

a. General Karmic Results of the Ten Courses of Bad Karmic Action 568
b. Specific Karmic Results of the Ten Courses of Bad Karmic Action 568
B. The Bodhisattva's Implementation of Moral Virtue on the Path 569
1. Cherishing the Dharma and Increasing Kindness and Compassion 569
2. The Motivation to Teach Beings and Cause Them to Enter the Path 570
3. The Genesis of a Bodhisattva's Wish to Rescue Beings from Suffering 570
4. The Vow to Cause 2 Vehicles Practitioners to Enter the Mahāyāna 572
5. The Power of the Precepts and Deep Entry into the Second Ground 574
6. Reaching the 2nd Ground, the Bodhisattva May See a 1000 Buddhas 575
7. One Makes Offerings to the Buddhas & Receives the 10 Courses Again 576
8. Having Received Them Again, One Forever Upholds the Precepts 576
9. One Abandons Miserliness, Practices Giving, & Delights in Precepts 576
C. Śīla Pāramitā's Aspects, Arising, Powers, Purification & Distinctions 577
1. The Sixty-Five Aspects of the Perfection of Moral Virtue 577
2. The Arising of the Moral Precepts 580
3. The Powers of the Moral Precepts 582
4. The Purification of the Moral Precepts 582
5. Distinctions in the Moral Precepts 583
D. The Essential Constituents of Śīla (Moral Virtue) 584
1. Q: Does Moral Virtue Consist Only of Good Actions of Body & Speech? 584
2. A: No, There Are Other Factors Integral to Moral Virtue 584
3. The Supreme Cultivation of Moral Virtue 585
a. Q: Please Explain the Bases of Supreme Cultivation of Moral Virtue 585
b. A: No "I," No "Mine," No Elaboration, and Inapprehensibility 585
c. Scriptural Descriptions of Supreme Cultivation of Moral Virtue 585
d. The Inexhaustibility of the Bodhisattvas' Moral Virtue 587
4. A Clarification Regarding Aspects versus Essence of Moral Virtue 588

XXXII. Chapter 32: An Explanation of the Dhūta Austerities 591
A. Having Seen 10 Benefits, Wear Correct Robes and Go on Alms Round 591
1. The Ten Benefits of the Appropriate Robes 591
2. The Ten Benefits of Obtaining One's Food from the Alms Round 592
B. Dwelling in a Forest Hermitage 592
1. To Derive the Benefits of Dhūta Practice, Do Not Accept Invitations 592
2. Having Observed Ten Benefits, Remain in Solitude with 3 Exceptions 593
3. The Ten Benefits of Dwelling in Solitude in Forest Hermitage 593
4. When Leaving, One Should Maintain the Perception of Emptiness 593
5. Ten Reasons a Forest Dweller Might Come to a Temple or Stupa 594
6. The Forest Dweller's Vigorous Cultivation of Right Dharma 594
7. Scriptural Citation on the Correct Purposes of a Forest Dweller 595
8. The Appropriate Dharmas of a Forest Dweller 597
9. The Means for Extinguishing Fear 597
10. Four Cases in Which a Forest Dweller May Gather with Others 601
11. The Aspects Defining Hermitage Dwelling Approved by the Buddhas 602
12. Hermitage Dwelling as a Means to Fulfill the Six Perfections 604
13. The Buddha's Four Prerequisite Dharmas for Hermitage Dwelling 604

14. Other Bodhisattvas for Whom Hermitage Dwelling Is Beneficial 605
15. Four Fourfold Dharmas for the Forest Dweller 605
16. The Bad Results of Forest Dwelling without Wisdom and Vigor 606
C. Additional Discussions of the Dhūta Austerities 607
1. A Listing and Brief Discussion of The Other Ten Dhūta Austerities 608
2. The Benefits of the Other Ten Dhūta Austerities 609
a. The Ten Benefits of Wearing Cast-Off Robes 609
b. The Ten Benefits of Taking One's Single Meal in a Single Sitting 609
c. The Ten Benefits of Always Sitting and Never Lying Down 610
d. The Ten Benefits of Not Accepting Food at the Wrong Time 610
e. The Ten Benefits of Possessing Only One Three-Part Set of Robes 610
f. The Ten Benefits of Accepting Robes Woven from Animal Hair 611
g. The Ten Benefits of Laying out One's Sitting Mat Wherever One Is 611
h. The Ten Benefits of Dwelling beneath a Tree 611
i. The Ten Benefits of Dwelling in a Charnel Field 612
j. The Ten Benefits of Dwelling out in the Open 612
3. Additional Discussion of Matters Related to Hermitage Dwelling 613
a. Five Types of Monks Who Dwell in a Forest Hermitage 613
b. Additional Discussion of When One May Leave a Hermitage 613
1) Proper Motivation When Leaving the Forest Hermitage 614
2) Generating the Motivation to Benefit Both Self and Others 614
c. On the Importance of Revering One's Spiritual Teacher 615
1) On the Difficulty of Repaying the Kindness of One's Teacher 615
2) On Maintaining the Proper Attitude toward One's Teacher 616
3) On Taking Direction from One's Teacher 616
4) On Not Seeking Praise or Benefit in Relating to a Teacher 616
5) On Making the Teacher's Good Qualities Well Known 616
6) On the Need to Become a Good Lineage-Preserving Disciple 616

XXXIII. Chapter 33: Aids to Gaining the Fruits of Śīla 619
A. On the Purification of Śīla, Moral Virtue 619
1. Four Dharmas Enabling Purification of Moral Virtue 619
2. Four More Dharmas Enabling Purification of Moral Virtue 620
3. Four More Dharmas Enabling Purification of Moral Virtue 620
4. Four More Dharmas Enabling Purification of Moral Virtue 621
5. Four More Dharmas Enabling Purification of Moral Virtue 625
6. Four More Dharmas Enabling Purification of Moral Virtue 628
7. Four Kinds of Monks Who Break the Moral Precepts 631
8. Four Kinds of Monks of Which One Should Become the Fourth 631
a. He Who Is a Monk Only in Form and Appearance 632
b. He Who Merely Feigns Extraordinary Deportment 632
c. He Who Is a Monk Only for Fame and Self-Benefit 633
d. The Monk Who Genuinely Carries on Right Practice 633
9. Wrong Motivations for Upholding the Practice of Moral Virtue 634
10. Right Motivations for Upholding the Practice of Moral Virtue 635
11. The Benefits of Perfecting the Practice of Moral Virtue 636

XXXIV. CHAPTER 34: IN PRAISE OF THE MORAL PRECEPTS 639

XXXV. CHAPTER 35: THE KARMIC REWARDS OF THE MORAL PRECEPTS 647

A. THE SECOND GROUND BODHISATTVA AS A WHEEL-TURNINING KING 647

B. THE WHEEL-TURNING KING'S TREASURES 647

1. HIS GOLD WHEEL TREASURE 647
2. HIS ELEPHANT TREASURE 648
3. HIS HORSE TREASURE 648
4. HIS PRIME MINISTER OF MILITARY AFFAIRS TREASURE 648
5. HIS TREASURY MINISTER TREASURE 648
6. HIS JEWEL TREASURE 649
7. HIS JADE MAIDEN TREASURE 649

C. FOUR QUALITIES OF THE WHEEL TURNING KING 651

D. A DESCRIPTION OF A WHEEL-TURNING KING'S DOMAIN, RULE & QUALITIES 651

Translator's Introduction

As the latest in my series of translations of bodhisattva path texts important in the history of Classic Indian and Chinese Mahayana Buddhism, I present here my English translation of Tripiṭaka Master Kumārajīva's rendering from Sanskrit of Nāgārjuna's *Treatise on the Ten Grounds* (*Daśabhūmika-vibhāṣā*).[1] This is a text devoted to explaining in great detail the aspects of practice involved in ascending through the ten "grounds," "planes," or "levels" of bodhisattva path cultivation that are described in the *Ten Grounds Sutra* (*Daśabhūmika-sūtra*) and in the nearly identical "Ten Grounds" chapter of the *Flower Adornment Sutra* (*Avataṃsaka-sūtra*). (In order to encourage and facilitate deeper study of this topic, I have translated both of these closely related texts which are available under separate cover from Kalavinka Press.)

Although Dharmarakṣa was the first one to translate this text into Chinese, his 265 CE translation of this treatise has been lost.[2] The edition of Nāgārjuna's *Treatise on the Ten Grounds* that I have translated here is the only one that exists in any language, namely the 17-fascicle *Shizu piposha lun* (十住毘婆沙論) or *Daśabhūmika-vibhāṣā* that is preserved in the Taisho edition of the Buddhist canon (T no. 1521). It was translated from Sanskrit into English by Tripiṭaka Master Kumārajīva as dictated to him from memory by Tripiṭaka Master Buddhayaśas sometime between the latter's arrival in Chang'an in 408 and his return to Kashmir four years later.

Although, having studied it closely, I find this 35-chapter treatise to be beautifully and awesomely complete in itself as a close description of the principles and practices necessary for entering and mastering the first two of the ten bodhisattva grounds, it is probable that this text as translated by Kumārajīva was originally part of a much larger work. Fortunately, the edition that we have is, in and of itself, a wonderfully thorough training manual for moving from the life of a common unenlightened person to that of an irreversible bodhisattva well along on the path to buddhahood.

A Brief Description of the Treatise Contents

As noted above, this text consists of 35 chapters[3] in 17 fascicles that describe in great detail the principles and practices involved in entering the bodhisattva path and in perfecting in correct sequence the practices of the first and second grounds, "The Ground of Joyfulness" and "The Ground of Stainlessness."

Chapter 1, "The Introduction," discusses the author's motivations and aims in composing this treatise. Chapters 2 through 27 explain the first ground's practices. Chapters 28 through 35 explain the second ground's practices.

Chapter 2, "Entering the First Ground," through Chapter 17, "On Entering the Temple," focus on the practice methods of the lay bodhisattva. Chapter 18, "The Jointly Shared Practices," through Chapter 27, "Summarizing the Practice [of the First Ground]," focus more on the bodhisattva practices that are common to both the lay bodhisattva and the monastic bodhisattva. Chapter 28, "Distinctions in Courses of Karmic Action on the Second Ground," through Chapter 35, "The Karmic Rewards of the Moral Precepts," focus somewhat more strongly on the practices of the monastic bodhisattva or very advanced lay practitioner.

A Condensed Description of Each Chapter's Contents[4]

To give the reader a quick idea of the general content of each of the chapters, I present immediately below only the briefest of general descriptions. For a much more detailed outline of the contents of each chapter, I refer the reader to my 18-page "Directory to Chapter Subsections" which follows immediately after the "General Table of Contents.

1) The Introduction: This chapter consists of a general discussion of the whole treatise, a description of Nāgārjuna's motives in writing the treatise, and a close explanation of the "refuge" verse that opens the treatise.

2) Entering the First Ground: This chapter lists the names and meanings each of the ten grounds, explains how one enters the first ground, and discusses why this ground is called "The Ground of Joyfulness."

3) The Characteristics of the Ground: This chapter describes the character of the first-ground bodhisattva, focusing in particular on this bodhisattva's distinctive features. It also explains why his mind is for the most part joyful and explains the nature of his fearlessness.

4) Purification of the Ground: This chapter describes 27 dharmas involved in purifying the first ground.

5) The Explanation of the Vows: This chapter describes the bodhisattva's ten great vows in great detail.

6) On Producing the Bodhi Resolve: This chapter describes and explains the seven causes and conditions involved in generating the resolve to achieve the utmost, right, and perfect enlightenment.

7) On Training the Mind: This chapter describes the many different sorts of causes and conditions that might cause the bodhisattva to lose his resolve to reach the enlightenment of a buddha.

8) On the Avaivartika: This chapter describes the characteristics of the bodhisattva who has fallen into ruination and the characteristics of the bodhisattva who has become irreversible on the path to buddhahood.

9) On the Easy Practice: This chapter describes using the path of "the easy practice," mindfulness of the buddhas, to succeed in reaching the ground of the *avaivartika* or "irreversible" bodhisattva.

10) Getting Rid of Karma: This chapter describes the methods for purifying past bad karma, specifically referencing repentance, entreating, rejoicing in others' merit, and dedication of merit.

11) Distinctions with Regard to Merit: This chapter discusses the merit and karmic rewards of repentance, entreating, rejoicing, and transference of merit and also explains how repentance results in less severe retribution from grave karmic offenses.

12) Distinctions with Regard to Giving: This chapter discusses the karmic rewards of giving and also explains what constitutes pure giving and impure giving.

13) Distinctions with Regard to the Giving of Dharma: This chapter explains the superiority of Dharma giving over material giving and discusses the qualifications of someone who teaches the Dharma.

14) The Characteristics of the Refuges: This chapter discusses how one takes refuge in the Buddha, the Dharma, and the Sangha as well as how one practices mindfulness of the Buddha, mindfulness of the Dharma, and mindfulness of the Sangha.

15) The Five Moral Precepts: This chapter explains the practices beneficial to self and beneficial to others while also explaining the dharma of the five lay precepts.

16) On Realizing the Faults of the Householder's Life: This chapter details for the lay bodhisattva the faults of the household life, thereby encouraging the layperson to consider the advantages of becoming a monastic. It also describes the practice of the six perfections.

17) On Entering the Temple: This chapter describes the practices adopted by the layperson on entering the grounds of stupas and temples, explains how to take and maintain the eight abstinence precepts, and compares the lay practice with monastic practice.

18) The Jointly Shared Practices: This chapter describes the practices common to both lay and monastic bodhisattvas while also describing a buddha's 32 major marks and the karmic causes that bring them about.

19) The Fourfold Dharmas: This chapter explains how wisdom is the origin of the 32 marks while also setting forth many fourfold lists that explain how wisdom is acquired, how wisdom is lost, how one's roots of goodness are devoured, how one's roots of goodness increase, and so forth.

20) Mindfulness of the Buddhas: This chapter describes the method for acquiring the *pratyutpanna* samādhi wherein one is allowed to see the Buddhas. It explains that one should cultivate mindfulness and contemplation of the Buddhas' form bodies in reliance upon their 32 major marks and 80 subsidiary characteristics.

21) Forty Dharmas Exclusive to Buddhas (Part 1): This chapter lists 40 dharmas exclusive to buddhas and discusses the first nine of those 40 dharmas that serve as the basis for practicing mindfulness of all buddhas' Dharma body.

22) Forty Dharmas Exclusive to Buddhas (Part 2) – Challenges to the Reality of Omniscience: This entire chapter is devoted to refuting the various challenges to the claim that buddhas are omniscient.

23) Forty Dharmas Exclusive to Buddhas (Part 3): This chapter begins by explaining the tenth of the exclusive dharmas, that of "thorough knowing of matters that are unfixed," continues by explaining the rest of the 40 exclusive dharmas, and then ends by introducing an additional 44 exclusive dharmas.

24) Verses Offered in Praise: This chapter explains that one is to use the 40 dharmas exclusive to the Buddhas in one's practice of mindfulness of the Buddha and then presents praise verses to be used as a means for successfully entering the mindfulness-of-the-Buddha samādhi.

25) Teachings to Aid the Mindfulness-of-the-Buddha Samādhi: This chapter sets forth the method for acquiring the *pratyutpanna* samādhi while also describing the karmic rewards derived from this samādhi.

26) The Analogy Chapter: This chapter sets forth the analogy of the great guide leading fellow travelers across treacherous terrain to a great city while also describing in greater detail the knowledge essential to deeply understanding and practicing the bodhisattva path.

27) A Summarizing Discussion of the Bodhisattva Practices: This chapter presents a general explanation of all the dharmas practiced by the bodhisattva along with a discussion of the differences between the practitioner who is a bodhisattva in name only and the practitioner who truly is a genuine bodhisattva.

28) Distinctions in the Second Ground's Courses of Karmic Action: This chapter begins by introducing ten types of resolute intentions that should be adopted by the first-ground bodhisattva wishing to reach the second ground. It continues then with detailed explanations of each of the ten courses of good karmic action and the ten courses of bad karmic action.

29) Distinctions Pertaining to Śrāvakas and Pratyekabuddhas: This chapter begins by asserting that the ten courses of good karmic action enable the practitioner to access the ground of a *śrāvaka*-disciple, the ground of a *pratyekabuddha,* and the ground of a buddha. It then describes which sorts of beings may reach the grounds of *śrāvaka*-disciples and *pratyekabuddhas* by relying upon the practice of the ten courses of good karmic action.

30) Distinctions Pertaining to the Great Vehicle: This chapter describes which sorts of beings may reach the ground of a buddha through cultivation of the ten courses of good karmic action. It also asserts that a bodhisattva's cultivation of the ten courses of good karmic action is superior to such cultivation as undertaken by adherents of the *śrāvaka*-disciple and pratyekabuddha vehicles.

31) Guarding the Moral Precepts: This chapter describes the general and specific karmic rewards resulting from cultivating the ten courses of good karmic action. It then presents sixty-five aspects of the perfection of moral virtue in accordance with *The Jeweled Summit Sutra.*

32) An Explanation of the Dhūta Austerities: This chapter describes the correct practice of the twelve *dhūta* austerities, their benefits, and the conditions under which they may be set aside.

33) Aids to Gaining the Fruits of Śīla: This chapter describes the dharmas that enable purification of one's practice of moral virtue. It also describes four types of monks of which the first three are worthy of censure and the fourth is to be emulated.

34) In Praise of the Moral Precepts: This chapter begins by asserting that, "The bodhisattva who purifies his observance of the moral precepts in this manner is able to gather together all sorts of meritorious qualities and derive all manner of benefits." It then proceeds to quote Akṣayamati Bodhisattva's extensive praise of the moral precepts.

35) The Karmic Rewards of the Moral Precepts: This chapter describes the second-ground bodhisattva's manifestation as a wheel-turning king who instructs beings in the practice of the ten course of good karmic action.

On the Completeness and Ultimacy of This Treatise

Although this treatise primarily focuses its discussions on how to understand the principles, how to develop the qualities, and how to master the skills required to reach the first two of the bodhisattva grounds, its utility is not limited to accomplishing that already very amazing, beautiful, and daunting feat. In fact, the discussions in this text are so wide-ranging and deep that they apply to the entire path to buddhahood. Indeed, if one were to deeply study this text together with the Ten Grounds Sutra,[5] one would then already possess a very complete map of how to proceed all the way to the perfect enlightenment of a buddha.

So many other additional aspects of knowledge, wisdom, powers, skills, and qualities are mastered on these first two grounds that I think it would be fair to say that most of us would need to cultivate the bodhisattva path for many hundreds of lifetimes before we could move beyond the teachings presented in this wonderful treatise by Nāgārjuna.

As noted in Chapter 29, this treatise does indeed provide all of the teachings a practitioner would need to reach all the way to buddhahood: "These ten courses of good karmic action enable the practitioner to reach the grounds of the *śrāvaka* disciples, also enable him to reach the ground of the *pratyekabuddhas*, and also enable him to reach the ground of the Buddhas."

In the very next chapter, Chapter 30, Nāgārjuna answers the question, "Which sorts of beings can the ten courses of good karmic action also cause to reach the ground of buddhahood?", doing so by setting forth the following verse distinguishing these bodhisattvas from practitioners attracted to the individual-liberation paths idealizing arhats and *pratyekabuddhas*:

> The way they practice the ten courses of good karmic action
> is superior to that of the two other classes of practitioners,
> for they engage in measureless extraordinary cultivation
> superior to that of anyone else in the world.
>
> They bring forth vows that are both solid and good,
> perfect the great compassion that cannot be impeded,
> adeptly take on the practice of skillful means,
> and patiently endure every sort of pain and anguish.
>
> They do not abandon any being,
> deeply cherish the wisdom of the Buddhas,
> and delight in those who completely and thoroughly practice
> the Buddhas' powers and sovereign masteries.
>
> They are able to refute all ideas involving wrong views
> and accept and protect the Buddhas' right Dharma.
> They are valiant, able to endure, and vigorous,
> and are possessed of solid resolve in teaching beings.
>
> They do not covet or become attached to their own happiness
> or to living a measurelessly long life.
> They are supreme in all their endeavors
> and free of fault in all the works they do.
>
> They possess every kind of purity
> and come forth through the practice of all the supreme bases.[6]
> The courses of good karmic action enable these persons
> to reach the ground of the Bhagavats who possess the ten powers.

A close perusal of the above verses should bolster the practitioner's confidence in the completeness and ultimacy of the teachings presented in this treatise.

In Summation

I first happened on this text many years ago when searching the Buddhist canon for the most important bodhisattva path texts to translate into English. I immediately fell in love with it and started translating it back in 2004, but had to take a break from it for a few years due to health reasons and also because I was preoccupied with fourteen other bodhisattva path manuscripts I published as the first ten Kalavinka Press volumes in 2009.

I finally finished a first draft translation of this treatise in late spring of 2011 which I did not finish revising until early 2018, this because I was deeply involved in creating a translation of the Ten Grounds Sutra (now available) and the *Avataṃsaka Sutra* (which, though long since completed, is still being revised and edited).

I have always felt that Nāgārjuna's *Treatise on the Ten Grounds* is one of the most important and most inspiring bodhisattva path texts in the Buddhist canon and one that simply *must* be translated into English as soon as possible. Hence it gives me great pleasure to finally be able to bring forth this translation for the perusal of English-speaking Dharma students and practitioners devoted to the deep study of the bodhisattva path.

Although, aided by the critical comments of a group of Dharma friends and colleagues, I have given this translation my best effort and the greatest care to ensure accuracy, I am aware that there may still be room for refinements here and there. To that end, I invite constructive comments by email via the Kalavinka.org website. That said, I remain very confident that this book will suffice to advance the western reader's understanding of right practice of the bodhisattva path as taught by Ārya Nāgārjuna.

Bhikshu Dharmamitra
Seattle
April 23, 2019

Introduction Endnotes

1. Although it is common to see the Sanskrit title of this work reconstructed in English academic articles as "*Daśabhūmika-vibhāṣā-śāstra,*" this based on its Chinese title as *Shizhu piposha lun* (十住毘婆沙論), "Ten Grounds Vibhāṣā Treatise," Hirakawa reconstructs this title as simply "*Daśabhūmika-vibhāṣā,*" probably because he recognized that the *lun* (論) or "treatise" in the Chinese title was only ever intended by Kumārajīva and other translators to notify the Chinese reader that a *vibhāṣā* is a kind of treatise. That is to say, he most likely did *not* intend it as a translation of the Sanskrit word *śāstra*.
2. In an article on Nāgārjuna, Joseph Walser writes: "Of two things we can be fairly certain. First, according to two sixth-century catalogues of Buddhist texts translated into Chinese, Dharmarakṣa translated a work called the *Treatise Commentary on the Sūtra of Ten Stages* (the *Daśabhūmika-vibhāṣa-śāstra*) in 265 CE that he ascribes to Nāgārjuna." (Powers, p. 498)
3. Although the Taisho edition of this text restarts the chapter numbering after Chapter 27 by designating Chapter 28 as "Chapter One," I instead fol-low the chapter numbering of the SYMG editions, all of which number this treatise as consisting of a series of 35 continuously numbered chapters. The apparent rationale for the Taisho edition's restarting the numbering at Chapter 28 is to call the reader's attention to the fact that the first 27 chapters are at least nominally devoted to explaining the first ground whereas the final 8 chapters constitute a new section consisting of N's explanation of the second ground. In any case, the reader should be aware that headings of these sorts for the most part originate with the Chinese translation team, not with the Indian text.
4. This condensed description of each chapter borrows from and expands upon a very similar Chinese language narration found as part of "A Simplified Introduction to the Daśabhūmika Vibhāṣā" (十住毘婆沙論簡介) by the Chinese Buddhist monk Hou Guan of the Fuyan Buddhist Studies Institute (福嚴佛學院, 釋厚觀, 09/18/2001). As of this writing (July, 2018), the document can be found at this URL:
   http://www.fuyan.org.tw/main_edu/1521-00c.doc
5. My complete translation of the Ten Grounds Sutra is available from Kalavinka Press.
6. These "four bases of meritorious qualities" are truth, relinquishing, quiescence, and wisdom.

Nāgārjuna's Treatise On the Ten Bodhisattva Grounds

The Daśabhūmika Vibhāṣā

(T26.1521.20a02–122b13)

Composed by Ārya Nāgārjuna

Translated into Chinese in the Later Qin Era by
Tripiṭaka Master Kumārajīva from the State of Kuchā

Annotated Chinese-to-English Translation by Bhikshu Dharmamitra

Chapter 1
The Introduction

I. Chapter One: The Introduction

A. Verses Declaring the Three Refuges and the Treatise's Intent

I bow down in reverence to all buddhas,
to their unsurpassable great path,
to those in the bodhisattva sangha
who, equipped with solid resolve, abide on the ten grounds,

to the *śrāvaka* disciples, to the *pratyekabuddhas*,
and to those free of a self and anything belonging to a self.
I shall now explain the meaning of the ten grounds,
doing so in accordance with the utterances of the Buddha.

1. Q: Why Explain the Ten Grounds?

Question: You are now about to explain the meaning of the bodhisattva's ten grounds. What are the reasons for this explanation?

2. A: The Plight of Beings and the Availability of Saviors

Response: The dangers and difficulties of the six rebirth destinies of the hells, animals, hungry ghosts, humans, devas, and *asuras* are terrifying and induce great fearfulness. In the churning whirlpool currents of the great sea of *saṃsāra,* the beings therein swirl about, going forth and coming back in accordance with their karma. This is what forms that sea's towering waves. Their tears, milk, flowing sweat, pus, and blood form its masses of noxious spume.

Their leprous sores, emaciation, regurgitated blood, and urinary disorders, their ascendant-energy febrile diseases, their carbuncles and flowing abscesses, their vomiting and bloating—all of these different sorts of diseases are that sea's *rākṣasas.*

Their worries, anguish, and bitter afflictions form its waters. Their being beset with troubles, weeping and wailing in grief—these are the sounds made by the churning of its waves. All of their feelings of bitterness and affliction—these are its "boiling and burning mountain."[1] Death is that cliff bank on the shore beyond which no one can climb.

The winds of their karma associated with the contaminants and connected to the fetters and afflictions pound and blow at them unpredictably. They are cheated and deceived by the four inverted views.[2] Their delusions and ignorance create a great black darkness.

Throughout the course of beginningless time, these common people, under the sway of their affections, have always moved along in the midst of this. So it is that they come and go in this fashion in the great sea of *saṃsāra* without ever reaching the far shore.

But there may be those who, having reached it, are also able to rescue and bring across an incalculable number of beings. It is due to these causes and conditions that we now set forth an explanation of the ten grounds of the bodhisattva.

3. Q: Can Non-Bodhisattvas Also Transcend Saṃsāra?

Question: Is it the case that, if a person is unable to cultivate the ten grounds of the bodhisattva, he will not succeed in crossing beyond the great sea of *saṃsāra*?

4. A: Yes, But the Great Vehicle Requires the Ten Grounds

Response: Someone cultivating the vehicles of the *śrāvaka* disciples or the *pratyekabuddhas* can cross beyond the great sea of *saṃsāra*. If, however, someone aspires to use the unsurpassable Great Vehicle to cross beyond the great sea of *saṃsāra*, this person certainly must perfect the cultivation of the ten grounds.

5. Q: How Long for Two Vehicles to Achieve Transcendence?

Question: In the case of those cultivating the vehicle of the *śrāvaka* disciples or the *pratyekabuddhas*, how long must they pursue their practice before they succeed in crossing beyond the great sea of *saṃsāra*?

6. A: Two Vehicles are Rapid; Bodhisattvas Require Many Lives

Response: In the case of those who cultivate the vehicle of the *śrāvaka* disciples, some may succeed in crossing beyond it in as little as a single lifetime. Some will require two lifetimes and yet others may require an even greater number of lifetimes. This is a matter dependent upon the relative sharpness or dullness of one's faculties. It is also a matter dependent upon the causes and conditions of one's cultivation in earlier lifetimes.

In the case of those cultivating the vehicle of the *pratyekabuddhas*, some will require seven lifetimes to succeed in crossing beyond whereas others will require eight lifetimes.

In the case of those who cultivate the Great Vehicle, some may require a number of great kalpas as numerous as the sands of a single Ganges River, and some may require a number of great kalpas as numerous as the sands in two, three, or four Ganges Rivers, and so forth until we come to those requiring kalpas as numerous as the sands contained in ten, one hundred, one thousand, ten thousand, or a *koṭi* of Ganges Rivers. They may require an even longer period of time than that.

Only after that may they completely fulfill the cultivation of the bodhisattva's ten grounds and then realize buddhahood. This too is a matter dependent on the relative sharpness or dullness of one's faculties. This too depends on the causes and conditions of one's previous-life cultivation.

7. Q: Is There Any Difference in the Quality of Liberation?

Question: The *śrāvaka* disciples, the *pratyekabuddhas*, and the buddhas all succeed in reaching the far shore [of liberation from *saṃsāra*]. Are there or are there not any differences in the liberation they each achieve?

8. A: Nirvāṇa Does Not Differ; Levels of Awakening Are Very Different

Response: This matter requires differentiation: As regards the achievement of liberation from the afflictions, there are no differences. It is on the basis of this achievement that one enters the nirvāṇa without residue. In this respect as well, there are no differences. This is because [nirvāṇa] has no distinguishing characteristics.

It is only with respect to the matters of a buddha's degree of liberation from the obstacles to extremely deep *dhyāna* absorption and his degree of liberation from the obstacles to [the knowledge of] all dharmas that there exist distinguishing factors relative to the *śrāvaka* disciples and the *pratyekabuddhas*. The degree of difference in these is so extensive that no amount of description could ever come to the end of it. No accurate comparison can be made even by resort to analogy.

9. Q: If Nirvāṇa Is Identical, Why Not Quickly Depart?

Question: That which all Three Vehicles take as the goal of training is the nirvāṇa without residue. If there are no distinctions in the nirvāṇa without residue, what use could there be for us in going and coming in *saṃsāra* for great kalpas as numerous as the Ganges' sands, fulfilling the ten grounds' practices? That would not be nearly as good as using the vehicles of the *śrāvaka* disciples and the *pratyekabuddhas* to put a swift end to all suffering.

10. A: This is a Weak and Inferior Statement Devoid of Compassion

Response: This sort of statement is weak and inferior. It is not the beneficial discourse of someone possessed of the great compassion.

a. Without Bodhisattvas, How Could The Two Vehicles Exist?

Suppose all bodhisattvas emulated your small-mindedness so devoid of kindly or compassionate intent and thereby became unable to energetically and assiduously cultivate the ten grounds. In such a case, how could any *śrāvaka* disciple or *pratyekabuddha* aspirant ever attain liberation?

b. This Would Put an End to the Three Vehicles and the Three Jewels

What's more, in such a case, there could not even be any differentiation into the Three Vehicles. How is this the case? All *śrāvaka* disciples and *pratyekabuddhas* come forth in direct reliance upon a buddha. If no buddhas existed, then, on what basis could they come forth? If there was no cultivation of the ten grounds, how could there be any buddhas? If there were no buddhas, there would also be no Dharma and no Sangha. Therefore your statement advocates complete severance of the lineage of the Three Jewels. These are not the wise words of a great man, and they are not such as could survive critical examination. Why [do I say this]?

1) The Four Types of People

There are four types of people in the world. The first benefits himself, the second benefits others, the third benefits both, and the fourth benefits no one. Among these, those who benefit both are able to cultivate kindness and compassion and benefit others. These are renowned as superior people.[3] As has been stated:

People of the world are so deserving of pity:
They always turn away from what otherwise benefits them,
and, even as they single-mindedly seek wealth and happiness,
they fall on down into the net of false views.

Always haunted by the fear of death,
they flow along, turning about in the six rebirth destinies.
It is those greatly compassionate bodhisattvas
who, by their ability to rescue them, are rare.[4]

Beings, when confronted by the arrival of death,
have no one able to rescue or protect them
from their immersion in deep darkness
wherein they are entangled in the net of afflictions.

If there are those able to bring forth and implement
the greatly compassionate resolve,
because they shoulder the burden of beings' welfare,
they undertake a heavy responsibility to act on their behalf.

In a case where someone brings forth the resolute determination
to undergo alone all manner of suffering through their diligence
only to then take the fruits of peace and security gained
and share them as a gift to be bestowed on everyone—

These are the most supreme sorts of persons
that are praised by all buddhas.
They are also those who, rare indeed,
are great treasuries of meritorious qualities.

There is a saying commonly heard in the world:
"May this family never produce a bad son,"
one only able to benefit himself
while remaining unable to bestow benefit on others.

If, however, they produce a son who is good,
one well able to bring benefit to others—
This one is for them like the moon when full,
for he casts shining brightness upon his entire family.

There are people possessing all manner of merit
who avail themselves of all different sorts of causes and conditions
to then bestow on others benefit that is as vast as a great ocean
and that is also as expansive as the great earth itself.

There is nothing whatever that they seek from the world.
Rather they abide in it only out of kindness and pity.
The birth of such persons is precious indeed
and the lives that they lead are the most superior of all.

2) The Immense Superiority of One Who Perfects the Ten Grounds

So it is that, although there are no distinctions as regards the liberation from afflictions achieved by *śrāvaka* disciples, by *pratyekabuddhas*, and by buddhas, there are nonetheless still huge distinctions associated with the buddhas' perfect fulfillment of the bodhisattva's ten grounds, with the liberation of countless beings, and with the bestowal of benefit on so many as they abide so long in *saṃsāra*.

11. Q: I Am Convinced, So Please Continue To Explain the Verses

Question: The Buddha does indeed possess the great compassion. For the sake of his disciples, you have set forth all manner of praises. This kindness and pity for beings is truly as you have described. You have used different sorts of reasons and considerations to make clear the distinctions, to invoke awakening, and to lead beings forth. When those aspiring to practice kindness and compassion hear this, their minds are purified. I have become deeply pleased by this. Please do explain those earlier verses set forth in preparing to explain the ten grounds' meaning.

B. Nāgārjuna Continues Explaining His Introductory Verses:

Response:

[I bow down in reverence to all buddhas,
to their unsurpassable great path,
to those in the bodhisattva sangha
who, equipped with solid resolve, abide on the ten grounds, …][5]

"Reverence" refers here to the reverently respectful mind. "Bow down" refers to bending down the body and touching someone's feet. "All buddhas" refers to the buddhas of the ten directions and the three periods of time.

"Their unsurpassably great path" refers to the knowing, seeing, and penetrating comprehension in accordance with reality of all dharmas without exception. It is because there are none superior to it that it is said to be "unsurpassable." It is because it is cultivated by great men that it is said to be "the great path."

As for "the bodhisattva sangha," it is by virtue of generating the resolve to practice the unsurpassable path that one is described as a "bodhisattva."

1. Q: Is Generating the Resolve Sufficient To Become a Bodhisattva?

Question: Does one only need to bring forth this resolve to then become a bodhisattva?

2. A: Of Course Not, But Perhaps Yes.

Response: How could it be that, by merely generating this resolve, one thereby becomes a bodhisattva? If a person brings forth this resolve, he definitely must be able to accomplish the cultivation of the unsurpassable path. Only then might one qualify as a bodhisattva.

Then again, it may in fact be that the mere production of the resolve also qualifies one as a bodhisattva. How might that be? Apart from that initial generation of this resolve, there could be no realization of the unsurpassable path. This accords with the statement in the large edition of the *Sutra*[6] that declares that one who has but newly brought forth this resolve thereby qualifies as a bodhisattva.

This is comparable to the case of a bhikshu who, even though he has not yet realized the path, is nonetheless referred to as "a man of the path." This "nominal" bodhisattva then engages in a gradual cultivation whereby he transforms this into a genuinely realized dharma. Later on, in the explanation of the "Ground of Joyfulness," we shall set forth a comprehensive explanation of the characteristics of a bodhisattva who truly qualifies as such.

Now, as for "Sangha," all bodhisattvas of the past, future, and present from the stage of the initial generation of the resolve on through to the path of the vajra unimpeded liberation[7] all qualify as members of the "Sangha."

"Solid resolve" refers to having a resolve comparable to Sumeru, the king of mountains. As such, it cannot be hindered and cannot be destroyed. It is also comparable to the great earth which cannot be moved at all.

"Abiding on the ten grounds" refers to "the Ground of Joyfulness" and the other grounds. These will be extensively discussed later on.

3. Q: Why only praise the Bodhisattva's Solid Resolve?

Question: If bodhisattvas possess additional especially superior meritorious qualities, why do you only praise "the solid resolve"?

4. A: It Is Essential For Success and Those Without It Would Turn Back

Response: It is due to the meritorious qualities of a solid resolve that the bodhisattva is able to accomplish his great works and refrain from falling down into the Two Vehicles' paths.

a. Why, Absent Solid Resolve, One Abandons the Bodhisattva Path

1) Fear of Continued Existence in Saṃsāra

As for one who possesses only a weak resolve, he becomes terrified of *saṃsāra* and then thinks to himself, "Why should I dwell for so long in the midst of *saṃsāra*, enduring all sorts of bitter affliction? That would not be nearly so good as to quickly avail myself of the vehicles of the *śrāvaka* disciples and the *pratyekabuddha*s whereby I might swiftly bring about the cessation of suffering."

2) Fear of the Hells

So, too, when one who possesses only a weak resolve sees or merely hears of:

The Living Hells (*saṃjīva naraka*);[8]
The Black Line Hells (*kālasūtra naraka*);
The Unification Hells (*saṃghāta naraka*);
The Screaming Hells (*raurava naraka*);
The Great Screaming Hells (*mahāraurava naraka*);
The Burning Hells (*tāpana naraka*);
The Great Burning Hells (*pratāpana naraka*);
Or the Great Non-intermittent Hells (*āvici naraka*)—[9]

Or the subsidiary hells, including:

The Flaming Embers Hells (*kukūla naraka*);
The Boiling Excrement Hells (*kuṇapa naraka*);
The Burning Forest Hells (*ādīptavana naraka*);
The Sword Tree Hells (*asipattravana naraka*);
The Road of Knives Hells (*kṣuramārga naraka*);
The Copper Pillar Hells (*tāmrastambha naraka*);
The Piercing Thorns Hells (*ayaḥśalmalīvana*);
Or the Brine River Hells (*khārodakā nādi naraka*)—

Or the instruments of punishment therein, such as the hatchets, battle-axes, daggers, lances, spears, halberds, bows and arrows, iron scrapers, hammers, cudgels, javelins, spikes, short swords, iron nets,[10] iron pestles, or iron wheels—

Or the use of such instruments of punishment to subject one's body to hacking, chopping, slicing, piercing, beating, striking, flaying, splitting open, tying up, shackling, roasting, boiling, interrogating with beatings, grinding up, pounding to a pulp—

Or the foxes, dogs, tigers, wolves, lions, and fearsome beasts struggling forth, gnashing at, pouncing on, and gulping down [the flesh of] one's body—

Or having one's flesh pecked at and devoured by the iron-beaked crows, owls, hawks, and vultures—

Or being hotly pursued by fearsome ghosts that force one to climb up sword trees and scramble up and run down flaming mountains, having one's neck run over by flaming iron carriages, being pursued and beaten with hot iron staves, being nailed down with a thousand nails, being cut apart and scraped out with knives, being plunged into darkness in a place with furiously dancing flames and stench, being placed onto a hot iron sheet that scorches the body as one is subjected to the slicing off of one's flesh, having one's skin completely peeled off and then used to tie up one's hands and feet, being thrown into a cauldron of water leaping in a raging boil, having one's body stewed as one is beaten with iron bats until one's head is broken and one's eyes pop out, being run through with an iron spit and plunged into flames where one's entire body is burned by flames as one's blood flows out and spills onto the ground—

Or being immersed in a flowing river of excrement or being driven along, running down a road of horrors where one is sliced and pierced by its knives, swords, and iron thorns, having daggers spontaneously rain down as if in a storm of flying blades that slice away the limbs of one's body, having a horrible flooding river of bitter salt, painful stench and filth swallow up one's body, having one's flesh entirely rot away and its flesh fall off, leaving only a skeleton that the hell minions drag along, kicking it, stamping it, beating it, and striking at it—

There are countless such intensely painful torments wherein one's life span is extremely long even as one seeks to die and yet remains unable to do so.

If one possessed of only a weak resolve were to see or merely hear of such experiences as these, how could he not be so stricken with terror that he would seek to be saved by the vehicles of the *śrāvaka* disciples and the *pratyekabuddhas*?

Also, one may fall into the Hells of Cold and Ice:

The Arbuda Hells;
The Nirarbuda Hells;
The Aṭaṭa Hells;
The Hahava Hells;
The Huhuva Hells;
The Blue Lotus Blossom Hells;
The White Lotus Blossom Hells;
The Hells of Varicolored Lotuses;
The Red Lotus Blossom Hells;
Or the Vermillion Lotus Blossom Hells.

One resides in these places of deep darkness and immense terror. One is born therein as retribution for slandering worthies and *āryas*.

These hells may take the form of a building, of a mountain peak, or of a river port hillside where one is blown by a harsh and horribly cold wind that makes a fierce, frightening, and mournful sound that blasts at the bodies [of the hell-dwellers] as if rolling through [fields of] dry grass. The flesh of the body then falls away like leaves dropping in the winter. The cold peels open one's wounds and both pus and blood come flowing forth. The filth and stench of the body are difficult to bear. The cold wind cuts one open as one experiences excruciating pain and bitter anguish. There is only one's lamentation, grief, weeping, and wailing. There are no other thoughts. Though one screams and wails, one is stranded alone without anyone to rely on. These punishments are all experienced because one has slandered worthies and *āryas*.

When one who possesses only a weak resolve sees or merely hears of these matters, how could he not become stricken with fear, seeking then to avail himself of the vehicles of the *śrāvaka* disciples and the *pratyekabuddhas*?

3) Fear of Rebirth in the Animal Realm

Also, among the animals, there are those such as boars, dogs, jackals, cats, foxes, gibbons, rats, monkeys, apes, tigers, wolves, lions, rhinoceroses, leopards, bears, elephants, horses, oxen, sheep, centipedes, venomous snakes, vipers, scorpions, tortoises, fish, turtles, dragons, snails, clams, crows, magpies, owls, hawks, and pigeons. All manner of birds and beasts such as these assail and kill each other.

Moreover, the snares, nets, predation, butchery, and slicing that are found there are not of a single sort. If born there, one is restrained with a halter, one has reins threaded through one's nose and strapped around one's head, one bears burdens, one is subjected to beating with cudgels and staves, and one is afflicted with hooks that pierce one's skin and flesh, causing it to split open and hurt unendurably. One is also immersed in smoke, burned by fire, and caused to endure agonizing pain of a myriad sorts. On dying, one's skin is peeled away, and one's flesh is devoured. One encounters therein countless such sorts of excruciating pain.

When one who possesses only a weak resolve hears of or sees these matters, how could he not become stricken with fear, seeking then to avail himself of the vehicles of the *śrāvaka* disciples and the *pratyekabuddhas*?

4) Fear of Rebirth in the Hungry Ghost Realm

Also, among the needle-throated hungry ghosts, there are those such as the fiery-mouthed hungry ghosts, the blazing-goiter hungry ghosts, the vomit-eating hungry ghosts, the rinsings-eating hungry ghosts, the pus-eating hungry ghosts, the excrement-eating hungry ghosts, the *bhūta* ghosts,[11] the *kumbhāṇḍa* ghosts, the *yakṣa* ghosts, the *rākṣasa* ghosts, the *piśaca* ghosts, the *pūtana* ghosts, the *kaṭa-pūtana* ghosts, and all other such ghosts. They have disheveled beards and hair, long nails, and large noses. Their bodies contain a multitude of insects, and are characterized by dreadful stench and filth. They are pierced by numerous sorts of torments and are constantly afflicted by the misery of miserliness, jealousy, hunger and thirst.

They are unable to acquire any food. Even when they do succeed in finding it, they are unable to even swallow it. They always seek after impurities such as pus, blood, excrement, urine, snot, spittle, and rinsings. Those that are strong attempt to steal these things by force, yet, even then, still cannot eat them. They are naked, have no clothes, and hence experience doubly intense cold and heat. A vicious wind blows on their bodies, spins them around, and afflicts them with bitter pain. Mosquitoes, horseflies, and poisonous insects bite them and feast upon their bodies. Their bellies are filled only with sensations of constantly burning hunger that roasts them like blazing flames.

When one who possesses only a weak resolve sees or merely hears of these matters, how could he not become stricken with fear, seeking then to avail himself of the vehicles of the *śrāvaka* disciples and the *pratyekabuddhas*?

5) Fear of Rebirth in the Human Realm

Moreover, among humans, there are the sufferings of separation from those one loves, encounters with those one detests, the sufferings of aging, sickness, and death, and the sufferings of the poverty-stricken in pursuit of whatever they seek, as well as the countlessly many other such sufferings.

6) Fear of Rebirth in the Deva or Asura Realms

In addition, there are also the sufferings encountered by the devas and the *asuras* when they must fall back again [from their bliss-filled celestial existences].

When one who possesses only a weak resolve observes these sufferings, how then could he not become stricken with fear, seeking then to avail himself of the vehicles of the *śrāvaka* disciples and the *pratyekabuddhas*?

b. The Contrasting Response of One with Solid Resolve

1) The Bodhisattva's Vow

When a person with a solid resolve observes all the sufferings and afflictions endured by those in the hells, among animals, and among the hungry ghosts, devas, humans, and *asuras*, he brings forth the mind of great compassion and has no fear. He makes this vow, saying, "All of these beings have deeply entered into such a deteriorated and afflicted state. They have no one to rescue or protect them and have no place of refuge. If I myself am to realize nirvāṇa, I must also bring about the liberation of beings such as these."

2) The Bodhisattvas Compassion, Vigor, and Success

Relying on the mind of great compassion, he is assiduous in his practice of vigor and, before long, achieves what he has vowed to do. It is for this reason that I state that, among all the meritorious qualities of a bodhisattva, solid resolve is foremost.

3) Eight Bodhisattva Dharmas

Additionally, the bodhisattva possesses eight dharmas through which he is able to accumulate all meritorious qualities:

The first is the great compassion;
The second is the solid resolve;
The third is wisdom;
The fourth is skillful means;
The fifth is non-negligence;
The sixth is diligently applied vigor;
The seventh is constantly focused mindfulness;
And the eighth is the good spiritual guide.

Knowing this, one who has only initially generated the resolve therefore swiftly takes up these eight dharmas, doing so with the same urgency as felt by someone whose turban has caught fire. Having done so, he should then cultivate all the other types of meritorious qualities.

C. Nāgārjuna Continues to Explain His Introductory Verses

[I also bow down] to the *śrāvaka* disciples, to the *pratyekabuddhas*,
and to those free of a self and anything belonging to a self.
I shall now explain the meaning of the ten grounds,
doing so in accordance with the utterances of the Buddha.][12]

Additionally, it is in reliance on these same eight dharmas that there come to be the four pairs and eight classes of practitioners within the *śrāvaka*-disciple sangha, namely the practitioners on the verge of stream entry, those who have already become stream enterers, and so forth.[13]

As for "the *pratyekabuddhas*, and those free of a self and anything belonging to a self," even when there are neither buddhas nor the Dharma of a buddha currently extant in the world, there are still some who achieve enlightenment that are referred to as "*pratyekabuddhas*."[14] Because all worthies and *āryas* have transcended the covetous attachment to a self and anything belonging to a self, they are referred to as "those free of a self and anything belonging to a self."

As for "I shall now explain the meaning of the ten grounds in accordance with the utterances of the Buddha," the ten grounds are set forth in proper sequence in the scriptures. Now, we shall accord with that sequence in providing a complete explanation of them.

1. Q: This Is Just as in Scripture. Why Be Redundant? For Fame, etc.?

Question: Your explanations are no different from those contained in the scriptures. Since the meaning of the scriptures is already complete, what need do we have of your additional explanation? Is this not presented simply to display your own abilities and seek fame and benefit?

2. A: This Treatise Is Not Composed for Self-Serving Reasons

Response:

It is not for the sake of making a personal display
of literary adornments,
nor is it due to coveting profit or support
that I now compose this treatise.

3. Q: If Not, Then Why?

Question: If it is not for such reasons as these, why do you compose this treatise?

4. A: Out of Kindness and Compassion and for No Other Reason

Response:

It is because I wish, through kindness and compassion,
to liberally benefit beings.
It is not due to any other cause or condition
that I now compose this treatise.

One observes that beings endure suffering in the six destinies of rebirth while having no one to rescue or protect them. It is from a wish to bring about the liberation of such beings that one summons the power of wisdom to compose a treatise such as this. It is not for the sake of displaying one's own wisdom power, nor is it due to coveting either fame or profit. Nor is there any sort of intention involving jealousy, arrogance, or the seeking of offerings.

5. Q: Why Just Repeat What Scripture Already Explains?

Question: This matter of kindly pity in benefiting beings has already been discussed in the scriptures. What need is there to explain it yet again, thus needlessly subjecting yourself to wearisome hardship?

6. A: Some Beings Require or Delight in More Thorough Explanations

Response:

> There are those who, on merely encountering a scripture of Buddha,
> reach a penetrating knowledge of the supreme meaning.
> There are others who, only on receiving a well-presented explanation,
> then gain a comprehension of its genuine meaning.

There are those persons possessed of sharp faculties and deep wisdom who, on hearing the profound scriptures spoken by the Buddha, are immediately able to reach a penetrating comprehension of the supreme meaning. The so-called "profound scriptures" refers to those describing the ten bodhisattva grounds. "The supreme meaning" is just the meaning of the ten grounds as understood in accordance with reality.

There are those treatise-authoring masters possessed of kind and compassionate minds who, in accordance with the utterances of the Buddha, compose treatises in explanation of them that are graced by well-adorned phrases and sentences. There are those persons who, because of these, are then able to gain a penetrating comprehension of the meaning of the ten grounds. This is as described here:

> There are people who are fond of literary finery
> in which there are adornments of passages and sentences.
> There are those who are fond of verses in praise,
> and there are those who are fond of the various sorts of sentences.
>
> There are those who are fond of analogies
> and others who understand through causes and conditions.
> In each case, their preferences differ.
> Hence I adapt explanations to each and thus do not forsake them.

The "passages and sentences" above refer to those in which there is adornment of the meaning contained in the sentences but in which there are no poetic verse lines.

"Verses" refers to descriptive paraphrasing of the import of the sentence passage's meaning in which the lines are based on a fourfold, fivefold, or sevenfold word count, or on some other similar schema. The verse construction is basically of two types. In the case of the first, it is a verse-form comprised of four-line stanzas referred to as a *gāthā*. In the case of the second, it is a verse-form comprised of six-line stanzas referred to as a *geya*.

"The various sorts of sentences" refers to the phraseology used in making direct statements. As for "analogies," because people may not understand an especially profound concept, one uses comparative statements to cause them to comprehend. In some cases analogies are factually based, and in other cases they are artificially contrived. As for "causes and conditions," these involve tracing causal origins.

So it is that one adapts to individual preferences "and thereby does not forsake them."

7. Q: How Are Others' Unique Predilections Any of Your Business?

Question: Beings do delight in different things, but what business is that of yours?

8. A: Because I Have Resolved Not To Abandon Anyone

Response: Because I have brought forth the resolve determined to pursue the unsurpassable path, I avoid forsaking anyone at all. Thus I endeavor to benefit them by using whatever powers I may possess. In some cases, this is done by giving material things and in other cases, it is done with Dharma. This is as described here:

If there be a person possessed of great wisdom
who is able to hear a scripture like this,
one need not explain it for him yet again,
for he will then fathom the meaning of the ten grounds.

This is to say that, if there be a person possessed of merit and sharp faculties, then, simply by hearing the *Ten Grounds Sutra,* he will immediately comprehend its meaning and thus he will have no need of additional explanations. It is not for persons of this sort that I compose this treatise.

9. Q: What Are the Qualities of Such a Good Person?

Question: What is it that defines such a good person?

10. A: Immediate Dharma Understanding; Also, 10 Qualities, as Below:

Response: It is one who, on merely hearing the words of the Buddha, is immediately able to spontaneously comprehend them. He is like a grown man able to drink down even intensely bitter medicine when, for little children, one must mix it together with honey.

As for the "good person," generally speaking, there are ten dharmas that qualify one as such. What are the ten? They are:

First, faith;
Second, vigor;
Third, mindfulness;
Fourth, concentration;
Fifth, good physical actions;
Sixth, good verbal actions;
Seventh, good mental actions;
Eighth, an absence of greed;
Ninth, an absence of hatred;
And tenth, an absence of delusion.

11. A Vibhāṣā Helps Those Who Find Sutras Hard to Fathom

As I was explaining:

When people take the text of the scriptures
to be difficult to study and recite,
if one but creates a *vibhāṣā*[15] for them,
this will provide great benefit to people such as these.

If a person with dull faculties is inclined toward indolence and arrogance, because he finds the text of the scriptures to be difficult, he may be unable to study and recite them. By "difficult," we refer to the texts being lengthy, difficult to recite, difficult to expound upon, and difficult to master.

Where there are those who are fond of such things as adorned phrases, refinement achieved through a variety of expressions, analogies, and verses—it is in order to benefit just such persons as these that I compose this treatise. Thus your earlier statement that the scriptures of the Buddha alone are sufficient to provide benefit to beings—this along with your questioning the need for additional explanations—such statements as those are incorrect. As I have stated:

12. Such Explanation of Dharma Is an Offering to the Buddha

The reflections made in composing this treatise
have involved the deep-seated generation of a mind of goodness.
Through illuminating these dharmas,
one makes an incomparably fine offering to the Buddha.

Because, when composing this treatise, the reflections and analyses have been accompanied by abundant mindfulness of the Three Jewels and the bodhisattva sangha while also bearing in mind giving, moral virtue, patience, vigor, *dhyāna* concentration, and wisdom, this deep-seated generation of a mind of goodness then becomes a form of self-benefit.

Because I have expounded and elucidated this right Dharma, this also qualifies as an incomparably fine offering to the Buddhas. This is what constitutes the benefiting of others. As has been stated:

13. By Explaining Dharma One Lights the Dharma Lamp

In explaining the Dharma, one lights the lamp of Dharma
and erects thereby the banner of the Dharma.
This banner serves for worthies and *āryas*
as the emblematic seal of the sublime Dharma.

14. This Leads To Accumulating the Four Bases of Meritorious Qualities

As I now compose this treatise,
truth and relinquishment as well as quiescence and wisdom,
these four bases of meritorious qualities,
are thereby naturally cultivated and accumulated.[16]

Now, in composing this treatise, these four kinds of meritorious qualities are naturally cultivated and accumulated. It is for this reason that the mind remains free of weariness in carrying out this endeavor.

a. Truth

As for "truth," everything that is true and genuine qualifies as "truth." Among all of those things that are genuine, the words of the Buddha are what is truly genuine. This is because they are not subject to change and ruination. As I present an explanation of this Dharma of the Buddha, this constitutes the accumulation of the "truth" basis.

b. Relinquishment

"Relinquishment," refers to giving. Giving is of two sorts, namely the giving of Dharma and the giving of material wealth. Among the two kinds of giving, it is the giving of Dharma that is supreme. This is illustrated by the statement of the Buddha to the bhikshus wherein he said, "First, one should engage in the giving of Dharma. Second, one should engage in the giving of material wealth. Of the two kinds of giving, it is the giving of Dharma that is supreme." So it is that, when I engage in the giving of Dharma, this constitutes the accumulation of the "relinquishment" basis.

c. Quiescence

When I explain the meaning of the ten grounds,[17] there is no accumulation of evil karma by body, mouth, or mind. Additionally, there is no arising of thoughts characterized by covetousness, anger, delusion, or any of the other fetters. Because these sorts of karmic offenses are blocked off, this constitutes the accumulation of the "quiescence" basis.[18]

d. Wisdom

When one explains the Dharma for others, then one gains great wisdom as the karmic result. This act of explaining the Dharma constitutes the accumulation of the "wisdom" basis.

It is in this manner that, in composing such a treatise as this, one accumulates the bases for these four meritorious qualities. Additionally, as I have stated:

15. Nāgārjuna's Final Statement of Intent

As I explain this treatise on the ten grounds,
one's mind becomes purified.
Due to a profound zeal to develop this sort of mind,
one remains intensely diligent and free of weariness.

If anyone hears, accepts, and upholds this
so that his mind becomes possessed of purity,
I, too, find deep delight in this,
and thus single-mindedly proceed with composing this treatise.

The meaning of these two stanzas has already been made clear. Hence it is unnecessary to discuss it again. It is solely for the sake of purifying one's own mind as well as the minds of others that this explanation of the meaning of the ten grounds is undertaken. When this pure mind reaches the point that it should reach, one gains a great karmic reward. This accords with the Buddha's words to Kālodāyin when he said, "Do not feel animosity toward Ānanda. In fact, if Ānanda had not received my prediction that he would attain arhatship after my nirvāṇa, because of this pure mind karma of his, he would have instead been bound for seven successive rebirths as the king of the Paranirmita Vaśavartin Heaven."[19] This is as extensively described in the scriptures.

The End of Chapter One

Chapter 2
Entering the First Ground

II. Chapter Two: Entering the First Ground

A. Q: What Are the Ten Grounds?

Question: These words you have spoken have awakened my mind and I have been extremely pleased by them. If you were to now explain the ten grounds, there would certainly be many who would benefit. What are the ten grounds?

B. A: The Ten Grounds Taught by All Buddhas Are As Follows:

Response:

The dharma of the ten grounds contained herein
has been, is now, and shall continue to be explained
by the buddhas of the past, the future, and the present
for the sake of all buddhas' sons,

The first ground is known as the Ground of Joyfulness.
The second is known as the Ground of Stainlessness.
The third is known as the Ground of Shining Light.
The fourth is known as the Ground of Blazing Brilliance.

The fifth is known as the Difficult-to-Conquer Ground.
The sixth is known as the Ground of Direct Presence.
The seventh is known as the Far-Reaching Ground.
The eighth is known as the Ground of Immovability.

The ninth is known as the Ground of Excellent Intelligence.
The tenth is known as the Ground of the Dharma Cloud.
In analyzing the aspects of the ten grounds,
we shall next present extensive explanations.[20]

"Herein" refers to the sphere of the meaning set forth in the Great Vehicle. "Ten" is simply a term of enumeration. "Grounds" refers to the various stations on which a bodhisattva resides in accordance with his roots of goodness.

"Buddhas" refers to all *tathāgatas* of the ten directions and three periods of time. "Explaining" refers to instruction and explication. As for "buddhas' sons," the true sons of all buddhas are the bodhisattvas. It is for this reason that the bodhisattvas are referred to as "buddhas' sons."

It is because all buddhas of the past, the future and the present explain these ten grounds that the text says, "has been, is now, and shall continue to be explained."

As the bodhisattva on the first ground begins to gain the flavor of good dharmas, his mind abounds in joyfulness. It is for this reason that it is referred to as "the Ground of Joyfulness" (*pramudita*).

On the second ground, as one cultivates the path of the ten good karmic deeds, one leaves behind all stains. It is for this reason that it is referred to as "the Ground of Stainlessness" (*vimala*).

On the third ground, as one engages in vastly comprehensive learning and speaks Dharma for beings, one becomes able to provide radiant illumination. It is for this reason that it is referred to as "the Ground of Shining Light" (*prabhākara*).

On the fourth ground, one's giving, moral virtue, and extensive learning so increase that one's awe-inspiring qualities blaze forth abundantly. It is for this reason that it is referred to as "the Ground of Blazing Brilliance" (*arciṣmati*).

On the fifth ground, the power of one's meritorious qualities becomes so completely full that none of the *māras* are able to bring about one's ruin. It is for this reason that it is referred to as "the Difficult-to-Conquer Ground" (*sudurjaya*).

On the sixth ground, the issue of obstruction by *māras* has come to an end and all path dharmas of the bodhisattva have manifest directly before him. It is for this reason that it is referred to as "the Ground of Direct Presence" (*abhimukha*).

On the seventh ground, one has gone far beyond the three realms and has gained close proximity to the station in which one becomes a Dharma king. It is for this reason that it is referred to as "the Far-Reaching Ground" (*dūraṃgama*).

On the eighth ground, one's vows cannot be moved even by devas, by Māra, by Brahmā, by any *śramaṇa*, or by any brahman. It is for this reason that it is referred to as "the Ground of Immovability" (*acala*).

On the ninth ground, one's wisdom becomes ever more radiant, supple, and superior. It is for this reason that it is referred to as "the Ground of Excellent Intelligence" (*sādhumati*).

On the tenth ground, the bodhisattva becomes able to simultaneously rain down the Dharma rain in countless worlds throughout the ten directions just as when, after the kalpa-ending blaze, there then falls a great universally drenching rain. It is for this reason that it is referred to as "the Dharma Cloud Ground" (*dharmamegha*).

C. Q: How Does One Enter and Cultivate the First Ground?

Question: Now that we have heard the names of the ten grounds, how does one enter the first ground, gain the characteristic features of that ground, and carry forth cultivation of that ground?

D. A: Five Stanzas on First Ground Cultivation

Response:[21]

Having densely planted one's roots of goodness,
having thoroughly practiced the practices,
having well accumulated all the provisions,
having thoroughly made offerings to all buddhas,

having become protected by the good spiritual friend,
having completely developed the resolute intentions,
having become compassionately mindful of beings,
and having resolute faith in the unsurpassable Dharma—

Once one has become completely equipped with these eight dharmas,
at one's own behest, one should bring forth the vow, saying,
"After I have achieved my own liberation,
I shall return and liberate other beings."

For the sake of gaining the ten powers,
one enters the congregation of those at the stage of certainty.[22]
Then one is born into the family of the Tathāgatas
that is free of any transgressions or faults.

One immediately turns away from the worldly path
and enters the supreme path that goes beyond the world.
It is because of this that one gains the first ground.
This ground is referred to as "the Ground of Joyfulness."

1. The Meaning of "Roots of Goodness"

"Plants one's roots of goodness densely" refers to cultivating and accumulating all forms of meritorious qualities, doing so in a manner that accords with Dharma. This is what is meant by "dense planting of roots of goodness."

"Roots of goodness" refers to not being influenced by greed, not being influenced by hatred, and not being influenced by delusion. It is because all good dharmas are born from these three factors that one is then able to speak of "roots of goodness." So too, all forms of bad dharmas are born from greed, hatred, and delusion. It is because of this that these three are known as "roots of evil."

a. Abhidharma Categories of "Roots of Goodness"

In the Abhidharma, these are distinguished in various ways whereby they are categorized as connected with the desire realm, as connected with the form realm, as connected with the formless realm, or as having no specific connection, the result being that, taken together, there are twelve such categories. Additionally, they are categorized as being "associated with the mind," or as "not associated with the mind," thus yielding a total of twenty-four categories. Of these [twelve roots of goodness], the roots of goodness free of the contaminants are cultivated and attained in the acquisition of *anuttarasamyaksaṃbodhi*, whereas the other nine [roots of goodness] are cultivated and accumulated on the bodhisattva grounds.

Additionally, when one has not yet brought forth the resolve, one engages in cultivating and accumulating them over a long period of time. In some cases, three of these categories may be present in a single thought. In some cases, six of these categories may be present in a single thought. In some cases, nine of these categories may be present in a single thought. And in some cases, twelve of these categories may be present in a single thought.

In some cases, one collects only those associated with the mind while not collecting those unassociated with the mind. In some cases, one collects those unassociated with the mind while not accumulating those associated with the mind. In some cases, one collects those associated with the mind as well as those unassociated with the mind. In some cases, one accumulates neither those associated with the mind nor those unassociated with the mind. All such analytic distinctions regarding roots of goodness are such as one will find extensively discussed in the Abhidharma.

b. The Meaning of "Roots of Goodness" That is Relevant Here

The roots of goodness that are relevant here are those that are planted as one strives to realize the unsurpassable path for the sake of beings. All good dharmas that one cultivates may be referred to as "roots of goodness." It is because they are able to produce the wisdom of all-knowledge that they are referred to as "roots of goodness."

2. The Meaning of "Practicing the Practices"

In "practicing the practices," "thorough practice" refers to that which is characterized by purity. "The practices" refers to the upholding of the moral precepts. One remains pure in upholding the moral precepts while practicing in accordance with the correct sequence. It is when this upholding of the moral precepts is combined with seven dharmas that it qualifies as "thorough practice."

a. Seven Dharmas Essential to "Thorough Practice"

Which factors constitute these seven? They are as follows:

First, a sense of shame;
Second, a dread of blame;
Third, extensive learning;
Fourth, vigor;
Fifth, mindfulness;
Sixth, wisdom;
And seventh, pure livelihood characterized by pure physical and verbal actions.

As one implements these seven dharmas, one remains perfect in upholding all of the moral precepts. It is this that qualifies as "thorough practice of the practices."

b. The Importance of Dhyāna to Implementing the Practices

Additionally, it is explained in the scriptures that the *dhyānas* constitute the stations in which one implements the practices. Hence it is the realization of the *dhyānas* that constitutes the thorough practice of the practices. In this treatise, we do not assert that it is definitely required that one use the *dhyānas* in the generation of the resolve. Why is this? When the Buddha was abiding in the world, countless beings brought forth the resolve but did not necessarily possess the *dhyānas* when they did so. Moreover, the practice of the laity's householders also qualifies as thorough practice."[23]

3. The Meaning of "Accumulating the Provisions"

As for "having well accumulated all the provisions," this refers to the [other] factors mentioned in the above verse, namely:

a. "Provisions" Includes the Topics Referenced Earlier

Densely planting roots of goodness;
Thoroughly practicing the practices;
Making many offerings to the Buddhas;
Being protected by the good spiritual friend;
Completely developing the resolute intentions;[24]
Being compassionately mindful of beings;
And having resolute faith in the supreme Dharma.

These are what constitute the "provisions."

b. "Provisions" Also Includes the Practice of 22 Good Dharmas

Also, the fundamental practice of the good dharmas—these must certainly have been cultivated. These also constitute "provisions." Specifically, these include:

Giving;
Patience;

A straightforward character;
A mind that refrains from flattery;
Dwelling harmoniously with others;
Happiness free of resentment;
Being, by nature, utterly committed [to the practice];
Not concealing one's faults;
Not cherishing one-sided attachments;
Not being perversely cruel;
Not being contentious;
Not being presumptuous;
Not being negligent;
Doing away with arrogance;
Remaining free of affectation;
Not praising oneself;
Being able to endure things as they are;
Possessing a decisive mind;
Being able to courageously accept whatever comes;
Not abandoning or changing teachers;
Finding satisfaction with but few desires;
And being fond of solitude.

Once one's practice accords with all such dharmas, one can then gradually perfect the especially supreme meritorious qualities. It is because these dharmas have not yet become solidly established that they are referred to as "fundamental" practices.[25] If one departs from these dharmas, one cannot advance to realization of the superior and sublime qualities. It is because of this that the combination of these fundamental practices and the above eight dharmas constitute the first ground's "provisions."

4. The Meaning of "Thoroughly Making Offerings to all Buddhas"

Now, as for "thoroughly making offerings to all buddhas," this is just like the practice of those bodhisattvas who, in life after life, always make many offerings to all buddhas, doing so in accordance with the Dharma.

Offerings are of two types. The first involves listening well to the Great Vehicle's right Dharma, no matter whether that presentation is extensive or abridged. The second involves such matters as making offerings of the four requisites while providing respectful and reverential service. It is the complete implementation of these two dharmas in making offerings to the Buddhas that qualifies as "thoroughly making offerings to all buddhas."

5. The Meaning of "Protected by the Good Spiritual Friend"

As for "good spiritual friend," although the bodhisattva has four different types of good spiritual friends, the type that is being referred to here is the one who is able to teach him to enter into the Great Vehicle and to perfect the *pāramitās* while also being able to cause him to dwell on the ten grounds. This refers then specifically to those buddhas, bodhisattvas, and even *śrāvaka* disciples who are able to instruct, benefit, and inspire him with joy in the Great Vehicle Dharma while also preventing him from retreating from it.

"Protecting" refers to [the good spiritual friend's] ability to always maintain kindness and sympathy as he instructs and influences one to increase his roots of goodness. It is precisely this that is meant by "protection."

6. The Meaning of "Complete Development of Resolute Intentions"

"Complete development of resolute intentions" refers to being deeply delighted in the Buddha Vehicle, the unsurpassable Great Vehicle, the vehicle of all-knowledge. This is what is meant by "completely developing the resolute intentions."

a. Q: Compared to Scripture, Isn't This a Deficient Explanation?

Question: In the "Unity Chapter,"[26] Akṣayamati Bodhisattva tells Śāriputra:

> Every instance of a bodhisattva's production of an intention is a "resolute intention." In proceeding from one ground to another ground, it is known as "the advancing mind." In the increasing of meritorious qualities, it is known as "the excelling mind." In the realization of unsurpassable endeavors, it is known as "the mind of utmost supremacy." In its assimilation of superior dharmas, it is known as "the superior mind."
>
> In its direct manifestation of the acquisition of dharmas of the buddhas, it is known as "the mind of direct manifestation." In its accumulation of beneficial dharmas, it is known as "the mind that engages with conditions." In its penetrating understanding of all dharmas, it is known as "the mind that achieves liberation." In its tireless fulfillment of vows, it is known as "the resolute mind." In its fulfillment of vows, it is known as "the joyful mind."
>
> In its independent achievement of endeavors, it is known as "the unaccompanied mind." In its abandonment of any signs of corruption, it is known as "the well-trained mind." In its freedom from all forms of evil, it is known as "the mind of goodness." In its separating far from evil people, it is known as "the unmixed mind."
>
> In its making a gift even of one's head, it is known as "the mind that relinquishes what is difficult to relinquish." In its rescuing of

persons who have broken precepts, it is known as "the mind that supports those who find difficulty in the precepts." In its enduring of evil inflicted by inferior beings, it is known as "the mind that is patient with what is difficult." In its ability to forgo the realization of nirvāṇa, it is known as "the mind that remains vigorous even when difficult." In its refraining from coveting [states encountered in] *dhyāna,* it is known as "the mind that cultivates *dhyāna* concentration even when it is difficult."

In its insatiable development of the roots of goodness that aid acquisition of the path, it is known as "the mind that maintains wisdom even when it is difficult." In its ability to bring all endeavors to completion, it is known as "the mind that completes all practices." In its skillfulness in carrying on wisdom-based reflection, it is known as "the mind that abandons pride, extreme pride, and pride in oneself."

In its not cherishing any sort of reward, it is known as "the mind that serves as a field of merit for all beings." In its contemplation of the profound dharmas of the Buddhas, it is known as "the fearless mind." In its refraining from obstructionism, it is known as "the mind that increases meritorious qualities." In its constant production of vigor, it is known as "the inexhaustible mind." In its ability to shoulder even heavy burdens, it is known as "the undiscouraged mind."

Moreover, as for the meaning of "the resolute intentions," this refers to [the mind of] one who remains equally mindful of beings and brings forth an all-encompassing kindness for all of them. He makes offerings to those who are worthy and good, is compassionately mindful of evil people, and esteems and reveres teachers and elders.

He rescues those who have no one to rescue them. He serves as a refuge for those who have no refuge. He serves as an island for those who have no island. He serves as the ultimate resort for those who have no last resort. He is able to serve as a companion for those who have no companions.

Even in the midst of those who are devious, he practices the straight mind. Even when among those people who have become corrupted, he practices genuine and correct thought. Even when among those who engage in flattery, his mind is free of flattery.

Among those who are ungrateful, he practices gratitude. Among those who are unaware of how to act, he practices the correct way of acting. Among those who are unbeneficial, he is able to act in a beneficial manner.

Among those beings inclined toward deviance, he practices right action. Among arrogant people, he remains free of arrogant behavior. Among those who do not accord with instructions, he does not become resentful or angry. Even among beings who have committed offenses, he always strives to protect them. Even amidst all of the transgressions committed by beings, he refrains from focusing on their faults.

He makes offerings to those who serve as fields of merit, accords with their instructions, and finds no difficulty in accepting their transformative teaching. When dwelling in a forest hermitage,[27] he is single-mindedly vigorous. He does not seek benefits or offerings and does not indulge any stinting attachment to his own body or life.

Moreover, because his mind is inwardly pure, he is free of deceptiveness. Because he practices good verbal karma, he does not praise himself. Because he is readily satisfied, he does not act in an intimidating fashion. Because his mind is free of defilement, he behaves gently and harmoniously. Because he accumulates roots of goodness, he is able to enter the realm of *saṃsāra*. Because he acts for the sake of all beings, he patiently endures all forms of suffering.

The bodhisattva possesses an inexhaustible number of such characteristics associated with resolute intentions.[28]

Now, however, you only present a simple explanation of the characteristics of resolute intentions. How is this not a deficient explanation?

b. Q: No. Each Ground Involves Specific Resolute Intentions

Response: No, this is not a deficient presentation. Akṣayamati provides in a single place a comprehensive description of all of the characteristics of the resolute intentions. However, here, we are concerned with their distribution as they occur on the various grounds.

This *Ten Grounds Sutra* provides specific explanations of the characteristics of the resolute intentions as they occur on each succeeding ground. Thus the bodhisattva in every case gains realizations of aspects of the resolute intentions in accordance with the particular ground upon which he abides. The meaning of the resolute intentions is defined according to each particular ground.

Now, on the first ground, we describe two types of resolute intention: The first is the one involved in bringing forth great vows. The second is the one involved in dwelling at the stage of certainty.

Therefore one should realize that it is by according with their respective locations on each of the ten grounds that one presents a thorough explanation of [these various aspects of what constitutes] "the resolute intentions." Thus the circumstantial basis of your challenge, "How is this not a deficient presentation?" is incorrect.

7. The Meaning of "Compassionate Mindfulness of Beings"

Now, as for "having become compassionately mindful of beings," it is on the basis of having completely developed compassion that one is referred to as "compassionate." What then is meant by "compassion"? This refers to a feeling of commiseration and pity for beings that also seeks to rescue them from the sufferings associated with their difficulties.

8. The Meaning of "Resolute Faith in the Unsurpassable Dharma"

When it states that "one has resolute faith in supreme dharmas," this means that, with respect to the dharmas of the Buddha, one's power of faith has become completely penetrating.

9. The Meaning of "Bringing Forth the Vow"

As for making the vow in which one resolves, "After I have achieved my own liberation, I shall [return and] liberate beings," this vow is the very origin of all buddhas' Dharma.[29] If one abandons this vow, then one cannot succeed in achieving the realization [of buddhahood]. It is for this reason that one brings forth this vow.

a. Q: Why Do You Say, "After I Have Achieved Liberation"?

Question: Why do you not say, "I shall bring about the liberation of beings," but rather say instead, "After I have achieved my own liberation, I shall then [return and] bring about the liberation of beings"?

b. A: If One is Not Already Liberated, One Cannot Liberate Others

Response: If one has as not yet achieved one's own liberation, one cannot liberate others. This is just as when one has oneself sunken down into the mud. How could one then be able to rescue and extricate anyone else? This is also just as when one has been carried away by floodwaters and is thus incapable of rescuing others from drowning. It is for this reason that it says, "After I have achieved my own liberation, I shall then [return and] liberate others." This is as described in the following verse:

> If a person liberates himself from what is fearsome,
> he can then liberate those who take refuge in him.
> If one has not become liberated from doubt and regret,
> how could he liberate those taking refuge in him?
>
> If a person has not yet become good himself,
> he remains unable to influence others to become good.
> If one has not reached quiescent cessation himself,
> how then could he cause others to reach that quiescence?[30]

Therefore one first becomes thoroughly quiescent oneself and then later takes up the transformative teaching of others. This is also just as described in a verse from the *Dharmapada*:

> If one is able to establish himself
> in the station of what is good,
> afterward, one is able to establish other people
> in that same benefit that one has gained himself.[31]

It is commonly the case that beings first benefit themselves and only afterward are able to benefit others. And why is this? This is as described in the following verse:

> If one accomplishes one's own self-benefit,
> only then is one able to benefit others.
> If one forsakes oneself wishing to benefit others,
> one fails to be beneficial and later feels distress and regret.

It is for this reason that [the preceding verse] reads, "After I have achieved my own liberation, I shall [return and] liberate beings."

c. Q: For What Sort of Benefit and with What Sort of Resolve?

Question: It is in order to acquire what sort of benefit is it that one becomes able to accomplish this endeavor and enter the stage of certainty? Also, with what sort of resolve does one become able to bring forth this vow?

d. A: To Gain the Ten Powers and Enter the Stage of Certainty

Response: It is in order to acquire a buddha's ten powers that one becomes able to accomplishes this endeavor and it is in order to enter the stage of certainty that one becomes able to bring forth this vow.

1) Q: What Are the Ten Powers?

Question: What then are the ten powers of a buddha?

2) A: They Are as Follows

Response: [As for the ten powers, they are as follows]:[32]

The Buddha possesses a completely penetrating comprehension of the causes and effects involved in all dharmas. This is the first power.

He knows in accordance with reality the past, future, and present stations wherein one creates karma and undergoes retribution as the effect. This is the second power.

He knows in accordance with reality the characteristic aspects of all *dhyāna* absorptions and samādhis, their distinctions, their defilement and purity, and their entry and emergence. This is the third power.

He knows in accordance with reality the relative sharpness or dullness of all faculties possessed by beings. This is the fourth power.
He knows in accordance with reality the differences among beings inclinations. This is the fifth power.
He knows in accordance with reality all the world's many different sorts of realms.[33] This is the sixth power.
He knows in accordance with reality the paths that lead to all destinations. This is the seventh power.
He knows in accordance with reality all the circumstances of previous lives. This is the eighth power.
He knows in accordance with reality all circumstances involved in all births and deaths. This is the ninth power.
He knows in accordance with reality the matter of the cessation of the contaminants. This is the tenth power.

3) To Gain The Powers, One Makes the Vow and Becomes Irreversible

For the sake of acquiring ten powers of the buddha such as these, one brings forth the vow with great resolve and then directly enters the group of those who have reached the stage of certainty.

a) Q: Does Everyone Then Reach the Stage of Certainty?

Question: Is it generally so of everyone that, once they first bring forth the resolve, they then possess such a characteristic?

b) A: Some Do; Some Do Not

Response: There may be some people who claim that when one first brings forth the resolve, one then possesses such a characteristic. However, this is not actually the case. And why is this? This is a situation in which one should make distinctions. One should not set forth a fixed answer to this. Why? It should not be the case that, when all bodhisattvas first bring forth the resolve, they all then enter the stage of certainty.

In some cases, on first bringing forth the resolve, one *does* immediately enter the stage of certainty. In some cases, however, one gradually cultivates meritorious qualities. Take for example Śākyamuni Buddha. When he first brought forth the resolve, he did not immediately enter the stage of certainty. Rather, it was only after he had accumulated meritorious qualities and encountered Burning Lamp Buddha that he then entered the stage of certainty. Therefore, if you were to assert that all bodhisattvas directly enter the stage of certainty upon first generating the resolve, that would be an erroneous theory.

4) Q: If Some Do Not, Why Claim Certainty Relies on Resolve?

Question: If it is an erroneous theory, why do you claim that it is in reliance upon this resolve that one enters the stage of certainty?

5) A: Because This Is True of Some Bodhisattvas

Response: There are in fact bodhisattvas who, on first generating the resolve, then immediately gain entry into the stage of certainty. In such a case, it *is* in reliance upon this resolve that they become able to gain the first ground. It is on account of this particular category of persons that it is said that, on first generating the resolve, one may then immediately enter the stage of certainty.

a) Q: What is the Nature of This Initial Resolve?

Question: What is the nature of these bodhisattvas' initial resolve and Śākyamuni Buddha's initial generation of the resolve?

b) A: The Initial Resolve Is Characterized by These 41 Aspects

Response:

This resolve is not admixed with any of the afflictions;
This resolve is continuous and does not wish for any other vehicle;
This resolve is solid and cannot be overcome by any non-Buddhist;
This resolve cannot be destroyed by any of the many sorts of *māras*;
This resolve is always able to accumulate roots of goodness;
This resolve is able to know the impermanence of all conditioned things;
This resolve, even while remaining unmoving, is able to accumulate the dharmas of a buddha;
This resolve is free of the hindrances and abandons all wrong actions;
This resolve is established in stability because it is unshakable;
This resolve is peerless because it remains free of contradictions;
This resolve is like vajra because it possesses a penetrating comprehension of all dharmas;
This resolve is inexhaustible because it accumulates an inexhaustible amount of merit;
This resolve regards others equally because it sees all beings as equal;
This resolve remains free of "high" or "low" due to making no discriminations;
This resolve is pure because, by nature, it is free of defilement;
This resolve is stainless because its intelligence is characterized by radiant illumination;
This resolve remains free of defilement because it never relinquishes its resolute intentions;
This resolve is vast because its kindness is as expansive as empty space;
This resolve is magnanimous because it takes in all beings;
This resolve is unobstructed because it has arrived at unimpeded wisdom;

This resolve is universal in its reach because it never cuts off its great compassion;
This resolve is never cut off because it is able to practice correct dedication of merit;
This resolve is that toward which the multitude proceeds because it is praised by the wise;
This resolve is a fit object of admiring regard because even adherents of the Small Vehicle look up to it;
This resolve is difficult to observe, because no being is able to see it;
This resolve is difficult to destroy because it has been able to skillfully enter the Dharma of the Buddha;
This resolve serves as a dwelling because it is the place in which all sources of happiness abide;
This resolve is adorned because it possesses the provision of merit;
This resolve is skillfully selective because it possesses the provision of wisdom;
This resolve is completely generous because it takes giving as one of the provisions;[34]
This resolve is attended by great vows because it possesses the provision of moral virtue;
This resolve is difficult to hinder because it possesses the provision of patience;
This resolve is difficult to overcome because it possesses the provision of vigor;
This resolve is quiescent because it possesses the provision of *dhyāna* absorption;
This resolve is harmless because it possesses the provision of wisdom;
This resolve remains unimpeded by hatred because its mind of kindness is deeply seated;[35]
This resolve is deeply rooted because its mind of compassion is fully established;
This resolve abides in happiness because its mind of sympathetic joy is fully established;
This resolve is unmoved by either pain or pleasure because its mind of equanimity is fully established;
This resolve is the object of protective mindfulness because of the spiritual power of the Buddhas;
This resolve remains continuous because the lineage of the Three Jewels remains unsevered.

Countless meritorious qualities such as these adorn the initial resolve of those who abide in the stage of certainty. This is as extensively described in the Akṣayamati Chapter.[36]

i) The Meaning of "Not Admixed With Afflictions"

"This resolve is not admixed with any of the afflictions" refers to the resolve not being conjoined with any of the two hundred and ninety-four afflictions cut off on the path of seeing the truths (*darśana-mārga*) and on the path of meditation (*bhāvana-mārga*). Hence it is said that "it is not admixed."

ii) The Meaning of "Continuous, Not Wishing For Other Vehicles"

As for "this resolve is continuous and does not wish for any other vehicle," as it continues forth from the initial production of the resolve, it does not wish for the vehicles of the *śrāvaka* disciples or the *pratyekabuddhas*. It is because one remains motivated solely by the goal of reaching *anuttarasamyaksaṃbodhi* that it is referred to as "continuous" and as "not wishing for any other vehicle."

One should understand this forty-statement discussion in this manner.

(1) Q: Doesn't "Permanence" of Resolve Contradict Dharma?

Question: You are asserting that this resolve is permanently enduring. However, all conditioned dharmas are impermanent. This is as explained in the *Seals of the Dharma Sutra* wherein it states that the practitioner is to contemplate the world as empty, as devoid of anything that is permanent, and as containing nothing not subject to destruction. How then does this matter not involve a contradiction?

(2) A: You Misunderstand the Concept

Response: You pose this challenge because you fail to grasp the correct principle of this concept. It is not the case that any claim is being made herein for "permanency" of resolve. Although we spoke of constancy here, this was merely a reference to the fact that one who has initially generated the resolve and reached the stage of certainty is definitely "always able to accumulate roots of goodness." It is because one does not rest and does not desist from doing this that we refer here to such constancy.

10. The Meaning of "Birth In the Family of the Tathāgatas"

a. The Meaning of "Tathāgata"

[Returning again to the verses],[37] as for "being born into the family of the Tathāgatas," "the family of the Tathāgatas" is the family of the Buddhas. In "the Tathāgatas," (lit. "the Thus Come Ones"), the "thus" (*tathatā*) is a reference to reality whereas the "come" (*āgata*) is a reference to the ultimate point that is reached. It is because they have arrived at genuine reality that they are referred to as "Thus Come Ones."

What then is it that constitutes "genuine reality"? It is what is referred to as "nirvāṇa." It is because it involves no falseness or deceptiveness that this is referred to as "according with reality." This is as explained in the sutra where the Buddha tells a bhikshu, "The foremost among the truths of the Āryas is free of deceptiveness. This is nirvāṇa."[38]

Additionally, "thus" is a reference to being characterized by indestructibility. It is a reference to the so-called "true character of dharmas." "Come" is a reference to wisdom. One is referred to as a "Thus Come One" because, having arrived in the realm of the true character of dharmas, one possesses a penetrating comprehension of its meaning.

Also, it is emptiness, signlessness, and wishlessness that qualify as being "thus." When the Buddhas "come," they have arrived at these three gates of liberation while also then being able to cause beings to reach these gates. They are therefore referred to as "the Thus Come Ones."

Furthermore, "thus" is a reference to the four truths. It is because they see the four truths in all their modes that they are referred to as "the Thus Come Ones."

Moreover, "thus" refers to the six *pāramitās,* namely: giving, moral virtue, patience, vigor, *dhyāna* concentration, and wisdom. It is because they utilize these six dharmas to "come" and arrive at the ground of buddhahood that they are referred to as "the Thus Come Ones."

Additionally, it is in reference to their possession of the four bases of meritorious qualities consisting of truth, relinquishment, quiescence, and wisdom that they are referred to as "the Thus Come Ones." It is because they utilize these four dharmas to "come" and arrive at the ground of buddhahood that they are referred to as "the Thus Come Ones."

Also, all of the dharmas of a buddha are synonymous with "suchness" [and hence are "thus"]. It is because this suchness "comes forth" and extends to all buddhas that they are referred to as "the Thus Come Ones."

Then again, all of the bodhisattva grounds including the grounds of "Joyfulness," "Stainlessness," "Shining Light," "Blazing Brilliance," "Difficult-to-Conquer," "Direct Presence," "Far-Reaching," "Immovability," "Excellent Intelligence," and "Dharma Cloud" are synonymous with "suchness" (*tathatā*). It is because the bodhisattvas "come" and arrive at *anuttarasamyaksaṃbodhi* by way of these ten grounds that they are therefore known as "*Thus* Come Ones" (*tathāgata*).

Additionally, it is because they "come forth" by the eightfold path of the Āryas that accords with reality that they are referred to as "Thus Come Ones."

Also, it is because they "come forth" and arrive at buddhahood on the two "feet" of provisional means and wisdom that they are referred to as the "Thus Come Ones."

And it is because they went forth in "suchness," never to return again that they are referred to as "The Thus Gone Ones."

b. The Meaning of "the Family of the Tathāgatas"

"Tathāgatas" is a reference to all buddhas throughout the ten directions and the three periods of time. It is the family consisting of all of these buddhas that is referred to as the "the family of the Tathāgatas." It is because these bodhisattvas now travel along the path of the Tathāgatas and do so continuously and unceasingly that one speaks of their "birth into the family of the Tathāgatas."

Furthermore, it is because these bodhisattvas are certainly bound to become *tathāgatas* that one refers to their "birth into the family of the Tathāgatas." This is just as when someone possessed of the marks of a wheel-turning king is born into the family of a wheel-turning king. This person will certainly become a wheel-turning king. So too it is in the case of these bodhisattvas who, in this same way, are born into the family of the Tathāgatas. It is because they have brought forth this resolve that they will certainly become *tathāgatas*. This is what is meant by "birth into the family of the Tathāgatas."

Now, as for "the family of the Tathāgatas," there are those who assert that this is a reference to the four bases of meritorious qualities, namely truth, relinquishment, quiescence, and wisdom. It is because all of *tathāgatas* are born from these factors that they are collectively referred to as "the family of the Tathāgatas."

Then again, there are those who assert that it is based on *prajñāpāramitā* and skillful means that this is known as "the family of the Tathāgatas." This accords with the *Sutra on the Factors Assisting the Path* wherein it states:

> The perfection of wisdom is the peerless mother
> and it is skillful means that serves as the father.
> It is due to the act of begetting that one is known as a father,
> and due to raising and nourishing that one is known as a mother.

Throughout the world, it is the father and mother that are taken as the basis of the family. It is because these two factors are analogous to a father and mother that they are referred to as the "family."

There are also those persons who claim that goodness and wisdom are what constitute the family of the Buddhas. It is from these two dharmas that the Buddhas are born. This being the case, these two then constitute the very root of all good dharmas.

This accords with a statement in the scriptures that states, "When these two are practiced to completion, one becomes able to realize right Dharma. Goodness is the father and wisdom is the mother. It is with the coming together of these two that one then refers to 'the family of the Buddhas.'" This is as explained in the following verse:

> A bodhisattva takes the dharma of goodness as his father
> and takes wisdom as his mother.
> Every single one of the Tathāgatas
> is in every case born from these two.

There are yet others who claim that the *pratyutpanna* samādhi[39] and the great compassion constitute the family of the Buddhas and that it is from these two dharmas that all *tathāgatas* are born. Of these two, it is the *pratyutpanna* samādhi that serves as the father and the great compassion that serves as the mother.

Then again, one may say that the *pratyutpanna* samādhi serves as the father whereas it is the unproduced-dharmas patience that serves as the mother. This accords with a verse from the *Bodhisaṃbhāra* [*Śāstra*] that states:

> It is the *pratyutpanna* samādhi that serves as father.
> Great compassion and the unproduced [patience] serve as mother.
> Every single one of the Tathāgatas
> is born from these two dharmas.[40]

c. The Meaning of "Having No Transgressions or Faults," etc.

[Returning to the "grounds-entry" verse], as for "the family [of the Tathāgatas] having no transgressions or faults,"[41] this is because that family is pure. "Purity" here refers to the six *pāramitās*, the four bases of meritorious qualities,[42] skillful means, *prajñāpāramitā*, goodness, wisdom, the *pratyutpanna samādhi*, the great compassion, and all of the forms of patient acquiescence. It is because all of these dharmas are themselves pure and "free of any transgressions or faults" that one then refers to the "family" itself as "pure." It is because these bodhisattvas take these dharmas as the basis of their "family" that they qualify as being "free of any transgressions or faults."

They turn away from transgressions and faults. As for their "turning away from the worldly path and entering the supreme world-transcending path," this reference to "the worldly path" is just a reference to that very path in which common people course. "Turning away" refers to "desisting." As for the path of the common person, it is unable to ultimately take one to nirvāṇa, for one is bound therein to always come and go in *saṃsāra*. This is what is meant by "the path of the common person."

As for "world-transcendence," it is by virtue of the fact that, in reliance upon this path, one then succeeds in escaping from the three realms that it is therefore referred to as "the supreme world-transcending path."[43]

As for [that path being described in the verse as] "supreme," it is because it is sublime that one refers to it as supreme. As for "entering" [the supreme path], it is because one engages in right practice of the path that reference is made to "entering." It is in reliance upon this resolve that one enters the first ground, the ground referred to as "the Ground of Joyfulness."

d. Q: Why Is the First Ground Said To Be "Joyful"?

Question: Why is it that the first ground is said to be characterized by "joyfulness"?

e. A: Because of the Immense Significance of the First Ground

Response:

It is just as with one who gains the first fruit
and who is then ultimately bound to reach nirvāṇa.
When the bodhisattva gains this ground,
his mind is always abundantly joyful.

He then naturally succeeds in extending
the lineage of all the Buddhas, the Tathāgatas.
It is for this reason that a person such as this
acquires the designation as "one who is worthy and good."

As for its being "just as with one who gains the first fruit," this means that it is just as when someone gains the path of a stream enterer.[44] He succeeds thereby in completely shutting the gates leading to the three wretched destinies.[45] He has seen the Dharma, entered the Dharma, and gained the Dharma. He abides unshakably in the dharma of stability and is ultimately bound to reach nirvāṇa. Because he has severed the dharmas that are severed at the point of seeing the truths, his mind is filled with immense joyfulness, [for he realizes then that], even if he were to fall asleep or become indolent, he could not stray into some twenty-ninth realm of existence.[46]

[This first ground bodhisattva's circumstance] is also analogous to that of someone who has sliced a single hair into a hundred parts and then used but a single one of those hair segments to draw forth two or three drops from the great ocean's waters. [He realizes that] the suffering already brought to an end at this point is comparable to all of the waters of the great ocean, whereas what has not yet been brought to an end is comparable only to those two or three drops. [Because he realizes this], his mind is filled with great joyfulness.

After the bodhisattva has thus gained the first ground, he is then known as one who has been "born into the family of the Tathāgatas." At this point, he becomes one worthy of offerings and reverence from all devas, dragons, *yakṣas, gandharvas, asuras, garuḍas, kinnaras, mahoragas,* deva kings, Brahmā, kings, *śramaṇas,* the brahmans, all *śrāvaka* disciples, *pratyekabuddhas,* and others. Why? It is because his family is one that is free of any transgressions or faults.

He then "turns away from the worldly path and enters the world-transcending path." He then only delights in revering the Buddhas, in establishing himself in the four bases of meritorious qualities, and in gaining the flavor of the six *pāramitās.* Because he has prevented the severance of the lineage of all buddhas, his mind is filled with great joyfulness.

The entire quantity of this bodhisattva's remaining suffering is comparable to but two or three drops of water. Then, although there might remain a hundred thousand *koṭis* of kalpas before he gains *anuttarasamyaksaṃbodhi,* still, his remaining suffering is only like two or three drops of water when compared to that great ocean of suffering that he has already successfully brought to an end, namely that suffering that he has endured throughout beginningless lifetimes in *saṃsāra.* It is for these reasons that this ground is known as "the Ground of Joyfulness."

The End of Chapter Two

Chapter 3
The Characteristics of the Ground

III. Chapter Three: The Characteristics of the Ground

A. Q: What Are the Characteristics of the First Ground Bodhisattva?

Question: What are the characteristics of the bodhisattva who has gained the first ground?

B. A: He Immediately Acquires Seven Qualities (Verse)

Response:

The bodhisattva who abides on the first ground
has much that he is able to endure,
He is not fond of struggle or disputation,
and, for the most part, his mind is joyous and pleased.

He always delights in purity.
He has a compassionate mind and feels pity for beings.
He has no thoughts of hatred or anger,
and, for the most part, practices these seven things.

If a bodhisattva reaches the first ground, he immediately acquires these seven characteristics. "Having much that he is able to endure," refers to his ability to cultivate and accumulate measureless merit and roots of goodness in order to accomplish a difficult endeavor. He comes and goes in *saṃsāra* for countless kalpas as numerous as the sands of the Ganges as he instructs evil beings who are obdurate-minded and difficult to transform. Still, his mind does not retreat or withdraw. It is because he is able to bear taking on such endeavors as these that he is said to be "able to endure."

As for his being "free of struggle and disputation," although he is able to achieve great works, he still refrains from struggling with or opposing others as he does so.

As for his being "joyous," this is a function of his ability to bring about both physical pliancy and a peaceful, stable of mind. As for his being "pleased," his mind becomes buoyantly exultant when encountering ever more superior dharmas.

As for his "purity," he abandons all forms of defilement associated with the afflictions. There are those who explain that it is his resolute conviction that qualifies him as "pure." There are others who explain that it is solid faith that makes him pure.

This pure mind is in regard to the Buddha, Dharma, and Sangha Jewels, is in regard to the truths of suffering, origination, cessation, and the path, is in regard to the six *pāramitās,* is in regard to the ten grounds of the bodhisattva, and is in regard to the dharmas of emptiness, signlessness, and wishlessness. In short, in every case, his mind abides in pure faith with regard to all of the profound scriptures, with regard to the bodhisattvas, and with regard to all buddha dharmas that they practice.

As for "compassion" with regard to beings, he feels pity for them and strives to rescue and protect them. This compassion gradually increases and develops, thus transforming into the great compassion. There are those who explain that, in its presence within the mind of the bodhisattva, it may be referred to simply as "compassion," whereas, when this compassion actually reaches to other beings, it then qualifies as "the great compassion."

The great compassion is born in reliance upon ten types of causes and conditions. This is as extensively discussed in relation to the third ground.

As for "not hating," because this bodhisattva has not yet completely severed the fetters, it is said of him that, for the most part,[47] he practices goodness and his mind is seldom beset by animosity.

When a bodhisattva such as this abides on the first ground, because his mind is not prone to fearfulness or discouragement, he is therefore said to be able to have patience. It is because he is fond of quiescence that he is said "to not be fond of struggle or disputation."

It is because he is able to accord with [the path to] *anuttara-samyak-saṃbodhi* and the great compassion that it states "for the most part, his mind is joyous."

It is because he has abandoned the turbidity of all affliction-caused defilements that his mind is always pure in its relationship with the Buddha, Dharma, and Sangha Jewels, as well as with bodhisattvas.

Because his mind abides in peace and security and remains untroubled, it states here that "his mind is pleased."

It is because he feels profound pity for beings that he is said to be "compassionate."

It is because his mind always delights in practicing kindness that it is said to be "free of hatred."

These are the characteristics of the bodhisattva who dwells on the first ground.

1. Q: Why Only Say, "For the Most Part" He Has These Seven Traits?

Question: Why not say of the bodhisattva on the first ground that he "possesses" these seven traits rather than say of him that he has them "for the most part"?

2. A: Because He Still Hasn't Done Away with the Contaminants

Response: Because this bodhisattva has not yet completely done away with the contaminants,[48] there are times when he may be somewhat indolent and thus have temporary lapses in demonstrating these traits. It is because, for the most part, he *does* implement them that the text states "for the most part." On the first ground, he has already acquired these dharmas. On the subsequent grounds, they develop and increase.

3. Q: Is His Joyfulness Acquired by Him or Is It a Feature of This Ground?

Question: On the first ground, the Ground of Joyfulness, this bodhisattva for the most part experiences joyfulness. Is it because he has acquired meritorious qualities that he experiences joyfulness or is it rather because of it simply being an inherent dharma of this ground that one should experience joyfulness? Why is it that he experiences joyfulness here?

4. A: It Is Due to Mindfulness of Buddhas & the Stage of Certainty

Response:

He is always mindful of the Buddhas,
of the great dharmas of the Buddhas,
of those at the station of certain success, and of their rare practices.
It is because of this that he is for the most part joyful.

It is due to reasons for joyfulness such as these that, on the first ground, the bodhisattva's mind is mostly joyful.

As for his "being mindful of the Buddhas," he is mindful of Burning Lamp and the other buddhas of the past, is mindful of Amitābha and the other buddhas of the present, and is mindful of Maitreya and the other buddhas of the future. He "is always mindful" of them just as if they were appearing directly in front of him and realizes that, throughout the three realms of existence, there is no one able to be superior to them. It is for this reason that he is mostly joyful.

As for his being mindful of "the great dharmas of the Buddhas," to state it briefly, this refers to the forty dharmas exclusive to the Buddha.[49] The first is sovereign mastery in the ability to fly wherever one wishes. The second is sovereign mastery in the ability to perform boundless transformations. The third is sovereign mastery of the unimpeded faculty of hearing. The fourth is sovereign mastery in knowing in countless ways the minds of all beings. Dharmas of these sorts will be extensively discussed later in this work.

In his mindfulness of those bodhisattvas on "the station of certainty," he is aware that, once the bodhisattva receives his prediction of eventual realization of *anuttarasamyaksaṃbodhi,* he enters "the Dharma position" (*dharma-niyāma*) and acquires the unproduced-dharmas patience whereupon not even armies of thousands of myriads of *koṭis* of *māras* would be able to destroy or interfere with him. When one acquires the mind of great compassion and develops the dharmas of a great man, one does not stint even in sacrificing one's own body and life for, in order to realize bodhi, one is persistently diligent in practicing vigor. It is in this way that he is mindful of the bodhisattvas who have gained the stage of certainty.

As for his being mindful of "their rare practices," when he brings to mind the supremely rare practices of the bodhisattvas who have gained the stage of certainty, this causes his mind to be filled with joy. They are of a sort that no common person can match them and no *śrāvaka* disciple or *pratyekabuddhas* can practice them. They open forth and demonstrate the Buddha Dharma's unimpeded liberation and wisdom of all-knowledge. He is also mindful of all dharmas practiced on the ten grounds.

This is what is meant when it is said that, "for the most part, his mind is joyful." It is for these reasons that the bodhisattva who has succeeded in entering the first ground is said to be "joyful."

a. Q: What Is Unique about the First Ground Bodhisattva's Joyfulness?

Question: There are common persons not yet resolved on realizing the unsurpassable path and there may also be those who have already brought forth the resolve but have not yet reached the Ground of Joyfulness. When these persons are mindful of the Buddhas and the great dharmas of the Buddhas and also when they are mindful of the bodhisattvas who have gained the stage of certainty and their rare practices—these persons, too, experience joyfulness. What differences are there between the joyfulness of the bodhisattva who has reached the first ground and the joyfulness experienced by these other persons?

b. A: He Realizes He Will Definitely Become a Buddha

Response:

When the bodhisattva reaches the first ground
His mind is, for the most part, joyful.
Regarding the countless qualities of the Buddhas,
he realizes, "I too shall definitely attain them."

When the first-ground bodhisattva at the stage of certainty brings to mind the countless meritorious qualities of the Buddhas, he thinks,

"I shall definitely gain qualities such as these. Why? Because I have already[50] reached this first ground and have entered the stage of certainty."

Those others do not have this thought. It is for this reason that the bodhisattva on the first ground for the most part experiences joyfulness whereas this is not the case for the others. Why? Although the others are mindful of the Buddhas, they cannot think, "I will definitely become a buddha."

This circumstance is analogous to that of a wheel-turning prince born into the family of a wheel-turning king who completely manifests the signs of a wheel-turning king. When he brings to mind the meritorious qualities and venerable nobility of the wheel-turning kings of the past, he thinks, "Now I too have these signs and I too shall acquire just such power, wealth, and venerable nobility as theirs." His mind is then filled with great joy. If one does not have these signs of a wheel-turning king, he does not experience such joyfulness as this.

When the bodhisattva at the stage of certainty brings to mind the Buddhas and the great meritorious qualities, awesome deportment, and venerable nobility of the Buddhas, he thinks, "I have these qualities. I shall certainly become a buddha." He is then immediately filled with great joyfulness. The others have no such experience as this.

One whose mind has reached the stage of certainty has so deeply entered the Dharma of the Buddha that his resolve is unshakable. Additionally, when the bodhisattva on the first ground brings to mind the Buddhas, he reflects, "Before long, I too shall become one who benefits the entire world."

When he brings to mind the Dharma of the Buddha, he thinks, "I too shall acquire the body adorned with the major marks and minor characteristics, shall perfect the dharmas exclusive to the Buddha, and shall teach the Dharma in a manner adapted to the roots of goodness planted by beings and to the relative strength of their minds. Moreover, I have already acquired the flavor of good dharmas. Before long, just like the bodhisattva at the stage of certainty, I shall be able to roam about with the power of the spiritual superknowledges."

He also brings to mind the path practiced by the bodhisattva at the stage of certainty that is of a sort that no ordinary worldly being could believe. He then thinks, "I too shall practice it." Having reflected in this way, his mind is then filled with abundant joyfulness. This is not the case with those others. Why? Because this bodhisattva has entered the first ground, his resolve has become definitely fixed, his vows remain unshakable, and he seeks what should be sought.

This is analogous to the case of an elephant in musth which does what only an elephant in musth is able to do and other beasts are unable to do.[51] Therefore the idea that you implied [in the above question] is incorrect.

Additionally, it is because the bodhisattva who has reached the first ground has no fear that his mind experiences abundant joyfulness. If one is beset by fear, one is not joyful.

c. From Which Types of Fear Has This Bodhisattva Been Freed?

Question: From which types of fear has this bodhisattva been freed?

d. Fear of Not Surviving, Death, the Wretched Destinies, etc. (Verse)

Response:

He is free of the fear of not surviving,
the fear of death, the fear of the wretched destinies,
the fear of the Great Assembly's awesome virtue,
the fear of ill repute, and the fear of being disparaged.[52]

As for fear of imprisonment, shackles, and manacles,
and the fear of beatings or capital punishment,
given that he is free of a self or any possessions of self,
how then could he have any such fears as these?

1) Fear of Not Surviving

a) Why Does This Bodhisattva Not Fear Failing to Survive?

Question: Why is it that a bodhisattva dwelling on the first ground is free of the fear of not surviving?

b) Due to Great Merit, Endurance, Wisdom, and Easy Satisfaction

Response: It is because he possesses great awesome virtue, because he has the ability to endure whatever comes, because he possesses great wisdom, and because he is easily satisfied.

He thinks to himself, "I have engaged in much cultivation of merit. The clothes, food and drink, and other requisites of a person possessed of merit naturally and immediately come to him."

This is comparable to the circumstance at the beginning of previous kalpas when great men were requested to serve as kings by the government officials and the people. In the case of those who possessed only scant merit, even though they might have been born into the household of a king, they had to rely on their own personal strengths to sustain themselves. If they could not even provide sufficient clothing and food for themselves, how much the less might they be able to provide for the country?

The bodhisattva thinks to himself, "I have engaged in much cultivation of merit. Just as in the beginning of the kalpa when the king was able to naturally ascend to his position, so too shall it be with me, for I too shall be bound to once again acquire such circumstances. Hence I should not have any fear of not surviving."

Additionally, even though a person might have only scant merit, still, if he possesses the power to endure whatever comes, then he will diligently cultivate the means to be able to produce clothing and food for himself.

This is as set forth in the scriptures where it states, "There are three causes for acquiring material wealth. The first consists of the skillful means one has utilized in the present lifetime. The second consists of the power that others possess to bestow such things. The third consists of the causes and conditions relating to one's own merit."

He thinks: "I am able to endure difficult circumstances. Because I also have the power of skillful means in this present life, I should not have any fear of not surviving."

He thinks: "A wise person is able to ensure his own survival merely through instituting a few skillful means. I already possess a measure of wisdom adequate to enable pursuit of the Buddha path. Through the benefits arising from this wisdom I shall be able to survive. Therefore I should not have any fear of not surviving."

Moreover, the bodhisattva has this thought: "I dwell within the world. The world is characterized by the presence of gain and loss, slander and prestige, praise and blame, suffering and happiness. How could it be that these eight circumstances might ever not exist? I should not fear failing to survive simply because I do not acquire something."

Furthermore, it is because the bodhisattva is easily satisfied that he adapts to whatever comes his way, remaining at peace whether the circumstances be fine or foul, excellent or deplorable. Thus he realizes that he should not have any fear of not surviving. If one is not easily satisfied, even if he were to acquire enough material possessions to fill up the entire world, his mind would still be unsatisfied. This is as described here:

When a person is poverty-stricken,
he only seeks clothing and food.
Once he has obtained clothing and food,
he then also seeks to obtain what is fine.

Having gotten what is fine,
he then also seeks honor and nobility.
Once he has acquired honor and nobility,
he then strives to rule all lands.

If he gains complete dominion over all lands,
he then also seeks to become king of the devas.
The desires of those in the world
cannot be satisfied by wealth.

In the case of someone who is easily satisfied, if he obtains a little in the way of wealth or possessions, then he is able to provide for his own benefit in both the present and future lives. Because this bodhisattva delights in giving and because he is fully possessed of wisdom, he is abundantly able to generate the roots of goodness arising from non-covetousness.

If one does not delight in giving or if one engages in a multitude of evil actions, due to the causes and conditions of miserliness and delusion, one increases the roots of non-goodness produced by miserliness. The dharma of insatiability exists because of covetousness. Hence, because the bodhisattva has extensively developed roots of goodness associated with not being covetous, he is therefore easily satisfied. Because he is easily satisfied, he has no fear of not surviving.

2) Fear of Death

Also, as for "having no fear of dying," this comes from extensive creation of merit, from realizing one dies in each successive mind-moment,[53] from realizing it is unavoidable, from realizing that, throughout beginningless time, one has already practiced experiencing dying in the world, and from extensive cultivation of emptiness.

The bodhisattva reflects in this manner: "If a person has failed to cultivate merit, then he will fear death due to personally dreading descent into the wretched destinies in future lives. However, I have extensively cultivated all manner of merit. Hence, when I die, I will be reborn in a superior place. Therefore I should not fear death." This is as described here:

One awaits his death as if it were a dearly beloved guest
and then takes his leave as if going to a grand assembly.
Having accumulated an abundance of merit,
when one relinquishes this life, one has no fear.

He also has this thought:

> Death refers to that circumstance where, in whichever body one has taken on, one's very last thought is extinguished. That is what defines death. Since this extinguishing of thought is what constitutes death, then, because thoughts are ceasing in every successive mind-moment, every one of these circumstances should itself qualify as "death."

> If one fears death, then one should fear every single instance of this moment-after-moment extinguishing of thought. It is not the case that one should only fear the extinction of that very last thought.
>
> One should then also experience fearfulness with respect to the complete cessation of the immediately previous thought. Why? This is because there is no distinction between the immediately previous thought and one's very last thought as regards their vulnerability to being extinguished.
>
> If one were to say that it is because he fears falling into the wretched destinies that he dreads the perishing of the very last thought—a person possessed of merit should not fear falling into the wretched destinies. This is as mentioned earlier. I should simply accept this process of perishing that occurs with each successive mind-moment and hence should not have any fear of the death that is just the perishing of the very last thought.

He also has this additional thought:

> Throughout the course of beginningless existences in the world, I have come and gone in *saṃsāra,* undergoing death in measurelessly and boundlessly many *asaṃkhyeyas*[54] of ways. There is no place in which one is able to avoid dying.
>
> The Buddha declared that *saṃsāra* is beginningless. If a person were to stack up all of his bones left in death from but a single kalpa of his existences, they would exceed the height of the Himalaya Mountains. All of the deaths of this sort have not brought about any benefit for oneself, nor have they benefited others.
>
> Now, however, I have made the vow to follow the unsurpassable path. I have done this wishing to benefit myself while also benefiting others and also because practicing the path with a diligent mind brings immense benefits. Why then should I be frightened?

It is in this fashion that the bodhisattva is able to immediately relinquish the fear of death. Additionally, the bodhisattva has this thought:

> This dharma of death is one which I must now definitely accept. There is no one who is able to avoid it. How is this so? Even though all the great kings at the beginning of the kalpa such as King "Crown-Born," King "Joy-to-Behold," and King "Radiant Brilliance" all had the thirty-two marks of a great man as physical adornments, were led and followed by their "seven treasures,"[55] were revered and loved by both devas and men, were ruling over the four continents, and were practicing the ten good courses of karmic action, still, in each and every case, all of these great kings finally succumbed to death.
>
> Furthermore, the lesser *kṣatriya*[56] wheel-turning kings who use their own awesome power to rule over Jambudvīpa, whose physical

bodies are so handsome as to be comparable to devas, who enjoy unrestrained and unlimited enjoyment of sights, sounds, fragrances, flavors, and touchables, who cause everyone everywhere to submit to them, who do not retreat from anything, and who are so consummately skilled in archery—even all such kings as these who rule as kings over an entire continent—even they as well as all their citizens and retainers—none of them are able to avoid death.

Additionally, all of the rishis, *āryas*, Kāśyapa, *jiaojumo*,[57] and all of the others who have practiced the ascetic practices and gained the five types of spiritual superknowledges—these as well as those who created all of the classic scriptures—none of them are able to avoid death.

Additionally, all buddhas, *pratyekabuddhas*, and arhats, those whose minds have achieved sovereign mastery, who have abandoned the defilements, and who have realized [the fruits of] the path—all of them have been destroyed by the dharma of death. There are no beings at all who have been able to get past it.

Having brought forth the resolve to succeed in following the unsurpassable path, I should not fear death.

Then again, in order to destroy the fear of death, one brings forth the resolve and proceeds vigorously to dispel the fear of death in oneself while also assisting others in dispelling it. One therefore brings forth the resolve to cultivate the path. How then could one feel alarm and fearfulness regarding death?

The bodhisattva reflects upon impermanence in this way and thus immediately dispels the fear of death.

Additionally, the bodhisattva always cultivates the practice of the dharma of emptiness. Thus he should not fear death. This is as described in the following verse:

Apart from one who dies, there is no death.
Apart from death, there is no one who dies.[58]
It is because of death that one who dies is held to exist.
It is because of one who dies that death is held to exist.

As for it being death's occurrence that establishes "one who dies,"
prior to death, before it has occurred,
they have no fixed characteristics.
Hence there is neither any death nor anyone in whom it occurs.

If there were someone who dies apart from death itself,
then "the one who dies" ought to be self-established.
However, in truth, apart from the dying itself,
there is no "one who dies" [whose existence] is established.

Nonetheless, those in the world engage in discriminations, saying:
"This is death and this is the one who dies."
Hence they do not understand death or how one comes or goes.
Consequently, they can never avoid undergoing it.

For reasons such as these,
one who contemplates the [true] character of dharmas
is one whose mind remains unvarying
and who is never fearful of death.

3) Fear of the Wretched Destinies

As for "having no fear of the wretched destinies," because the bodhisattva always cultivates merit, he does not fear falling into the wretched destinies. He reflects to himself, "It is those persons who engage in karmic offenses who fall into the wretched destinies. This does not happen to those who cultivate merit. I do not allow any evil influences to enter even for the space of a single mind-moment and thus I am always bringing forth pure actions of body, speech, and mind. Therefore I have acquired a measureless and boundless number of meritorious qualities. Having developed such a great accumulation of meritorious qualities as this, how could I fear falling into the wretched destinies?"

Additionally, from the very time when the bodhisattva brings forth the resolve, because he does so for the sake of benefiting and bringing peace to all beings and because he is protected by his great kindness and compassion, he abides in the four foundations of meritorious qualities, gains a measureless number of meritorious qualities, and crosses beyond all the wretched destinies.

How is it that this is so? This resolve of his is superior to that of any *śrāvaka* disciple or *pratyekabuddha*. This is as stated in the *Pure Vinaya Sutra* in which Kāśyapa addressed the Buddha, saying, "It is rare indeed, O Bhagavat. You have so well explained how it is that, because of his resolve to realize all-knowledge, the bodhisattva is able to surpass all *śrāvaka* disciples and *pratyekabuddhas*."

One reflects, "Given that I have produced such a great amount of merit and have come to abide in such great dharmas as these, why should I have any fear of falling into the wretched destinies?"

One also thinks:

Throughout the course of beginningless time on up to the very present, I have been going and coming in *saṃsāra*, have fallen into all the wretched destinies, and have undergone measureless suffering and in doing so, it has not been to benefit myself or to benefit others. I now bring forth the unsurpassable great vow in order to fulfill the

> wish to benefit myself while also benefiting others. Throughout the past on forward to the very present, I have fallen into the wretched destinies without deriving any benefit from it. Now, even if I were to fall into the wretched destinies while striving to benefit other beings, that should not cause me to be fearful.

Moreover, the bodhisattva whose practice is genuine has this thought:

> Even if I was caused to fall into the Avīci Hells and undergo suffering for an entire kalpa after which I only then succeeded in getting out again, yet, by doing this, I was thus able to cause but a single person to produce a single good thought [and even if I had to continue in this way to cause him] to accumulate an immeasurable number of such good thoughts so that he eventually developed the capacity to undergo teaching influencing him to set forth in the Three Vehicles—and if in this same way, I was thereby able to instruct beings as numerous as the Ganges' sands to set forth in the Śrāvaka Disciple Vehicle, beings as numerous as the Ganges' sands to set forth in the Pratyekabuddha Vehicle, and beings as numerous as the Ganges' sands to set forth in the Great Vehicle, after which I only then was able to realize *anuttarasamyaksaṃbodhi*—even if this had to be the case, I should still not retreat and fall away from pursuing this course of action. How much the less should I [retreat from this] in the present circumstance wherein, by accumulating a measureless and boundless number of meritorious qualities, I am thereby able to leave the wretched destinies far behind?

When the bodhisattva ponders the matter in this way, how could he have any fear of falling into the wretched destinies?

Then again, this is as illustrated in the *Sutra on the Screaming Hells* wherein a bodhisattva replies to Māra, saying:

> If on account of giving,
> I were to fall into the Screaming Hells,
> yet all who received my gifts
> were thereby able to be reborn in the heavens—
>
> Even if this were to be the case, I should still
> always practice such giving
> if it results in beings dwelling in the heavens
> and in my enduring the sufferings of the Screaming Hells.

Through many different rationales such as these, the bodhisattva is able to deflect the fear of the wretched destinies.

4) Fear of Great Assemblies

As for "not having any fear in great assemblies," because he perfects the wisdom gained through learning, the wisdom gained through contemplative thought, and the wisdom gained through cultivation, and also because he abandons the faults involved in mere theorizing, when this bodhisattva establishes points of discourse, whatever he says is free of error. He is able to use reasoning, analogies, and conclusions that are neither excessive nor deficient, and that leave no room for doubt.

His words have nothing in them that contradicts what is meaningful and nothing in them that tends toward flattery or deception. They are direct, suffused with pliancy, and graced with all manner of adorning phrases. They are easy to understand, conducive to ease in retaining their meaning, and orderly in the sequence of their exposition. They are able to reveal the contents of his own case while refuting the theories of others. His speech is free of the four erroneous types of reasoning and is equipped with the four major types of correct reasoning. Using well-adorned types of discourse such as these, he is fearless when speaking before a great assembly.

5) Fear of Ill Repute and Fear of Being Disparaged

As for "having no fear of ill repute" and "having no fear of cursing and scolding," these are a consequence of having no craving for gain and offerings and due to maintaining pure physical, verbal, and mental conduct.

6) Fear of Imprisonment, shackles, manacles, or Beatings

As for "freedom from fear of imprisonment, shackles, manacles, or beatings," this is because one remains free of karmic offenses, because one feels kindness and sympathy for all beings, because one is able to endure all the many different sorts of sufferings and afflictions, and because one relies on karmic actions entailing their results and retributions. [Hence one reflects], "Because it is I who previously performed this act, I am now bound to undergo such retribution in return."

It is for reasons such as these that this bodhisattva has no fear of not surviving, nor does he have any of the other such sorts of fear.

e. Realizing Nonexistence of Self As the Basis of Fearlessness

Then again, he delights in contemplating all dharmas as having nothing constituting a self. Therefore he remains free of all fear, for all types of fear are born from the view that assumes the existence of a self. The view that assumes the existence of a self is in every case the root of all sufferings associated with worry about loss. Because this bodhisattva possesses sharp wisdom and because he penetrates deeply into the true character of all dharmas doing so in a manner that accords with reality, he remains free of any concept of a self. Since he has no self, how could he continue to be fearful?

1) Q: Why Does This Bodhisattva Have No Conception of a Self?

Question: How is it that this bodhisattva has no thoughts of a self?

2) A: He Delights in Emptiness and Sees the Body as Not Self (Verse)

Response: This is because he delights in the dharma of emptiness and because the bodhisattva contemplates the body as apart from any "self" or anything belonging to a self. This is as explained here:

The thought of "self" is caused by that of "mine."
That of "mine" is produced from that of "self."
Therefore, as for "self" and "mine,"
the nature of both of these is complete emptiness.

As for "self," it has the meaning of "subject."
As for "mine," this refers to whatever belongs to that subject.
If no "subject" exists,
whatever belongs to a subject is also nonexistent [as such].

If there is nothing that belongs to a subject,
then there is no subject, either.
As for "self," it is just the view imputing existence of a "self."
As for "a self's possessions," it is just the view imputing "mine."
Contemplating in accordance with reality, there is no "self."
In the absence of a self, there is no "nonself."

Because of "experiencing," "one who experiences" is produced.
In the absence of experiencing, there is no "one who experiences."
Apart from "one who experiences," there is no experiencing.
How then could it be established based on "experiencing"?

If it were so that "one who experiences" established "experiencing,"
then experiencing could not be established.
Because experiencing is thus not established,
then one cannot establish "one who experiences."

Because an "one who experiences" is empty [of inherent existence],
one cannot speak of it as constituting a self.
Because "experiencing" is empty [of inherent existence],
One cannot speak of it as something belonging to a self.

Therefore "self," "nonself,"
"both self and nonself,"
and "neither self nor nonself"—
These are all fallacious concepts.

"Mine," "not mine,"
"both mine and not mine,"
and "neither mine nor not mine"—
These too are fallacious concepts.

It is because the bodhisattva always delights in this way in the cultivation of emptiness and nonexistence of self that he abandons all types of fear. And why is this so? This is because the dharmas of emptiness and nonexistence of self are able to cause one to abandon all types of fear.

The bodhisattva who dwells on the Ground of Joyfulness is possessed of characteristics such as these.

The End of Chapter Three

Chapter 4
Purification of the Ground

IV. Chapter Four: Purification of the Ground

A. Q: How Should the 1st Ground Bodhisattva Cultivate Its Purification?

Question: In the case of the bodhisattva who has already gotten to the first ground, how should he go about cultivating its purification?

B. A: One Cultivates 27 Dharmas (Verse)

Response:

The power of faith becomes ever more superior
as one practices deeply the mind of great compassion.
One acts with kindness toward all types of beings
and tirelessly cultivates the mind of goodness.

One finds joyous delight in sublime dharmas,
always draws close to the good spiritual guide,
maintains a sense of shame, dread of blame, and reverence,
and makes one's mind gentle and harmonious.

One delights in contemplating dharmas and stays free of attachment,
single-mindedly strives to acquire abundant learning,
refrains from coveting offerings of benefits and support,
while staying far from treacherous cheating, flattery, and deception.

One does not defile the family of the Buddhas
and does not damage moral precepts or cheat the Buddhas.
One deeply delights in all-knowledge,[59]
and remains as unmoving as an immense mountain.

One always delights in cultivating and practicing
ever more superior sublime dharmas.
One delights in the world-transcending dharmas
and does not delight in worldly dharmas.

Even as one cultivates the Ground of Joyfulness,
one is able to cultivate what is difficult to cultivate.
Therefore one is always single-minded
in the diligent practice of these dharmas.

The bodhisattva is able to perfect
such supremely sublime dharmas as these.
It is this then that constitutes secure abiding
in the bodhisattva's first ground.

The bodhisattva relies on these twenty-seven dharmas in the purifying cultivation of the first ground.

1. "The Power of Faith Becomes Ever More Superior"

As for "the power of faith becomes ever more superior," "faith" refers here to definitely accepting, without doubts, what one learns and perceives. "Superiority" refers here to "exceptional supremacy."

a. Q: Of the Two Types of Superiority, of Which Do You Speak?

Question: There are two sorts of "superiority." In the case of the first, it refers to having a greater amount of something. In the case of the second, it refers to being of superior quality. Which is it that you now discuss?

b. A: Both "More" and "Better Quality"

Response: We speak here of both definitions. When the bodhisattva enters the first ground, because he experiences the flavor of the meritorious qualities, his power of faith becomes ever greater. Because of this power of faith, having assessed all buddhas' meritorious qualities and their measurelessly many extremely sublime aspects, he is able then to have faith in and accept them. Hence this mind [of faith] becomes both greater in its extensiveness and more superior in its quality.

2. "One Practices Deeply the Mind of Great Compassion"

As for "one practices deeply the mind of great compassion," it is because one's sympathetic mindfulness of beings penetrates to one's very marrow that its practice is described as "deep." It is because one seeks to realize the Buddha path for the sake of all beings that [the practice of compassion as] is described as "great."

3. "The Mind of Kindness"

As for "the mind of kindness," one always strives to benefit beings and promote their peace and security. There are three kinds of kindness. This should be more extensively discussed later on.

4. "Tirelessly Cultivating the Mind of Goodness"

As for "tirelessly cultivating the mind of goodness," the dharma of goodness is what one draws near to and cultivates, and it is what yields desirable results. As one cultivates dharmas such as these, one's mind does not fall into indolence. As for the causes and conditions comprising good dharmas, this refers to the dharmas comprising the four means of attraction, the ten courses of good karmic action, the six *pāramitās*, the ten bodhisattva grounds, and all of the meritorious qualities.

5. "One Finds Joyous Delight in Sublime Dharmas"

As for "one finds joyous delight in sublime dharmas," this means that, if one always reflects on them, cultivates them, and deeply experiences the flavor of these dharmas, after a long while, this produces happiness. This is just as when someone amidst flowers and forest groves takes pleasure in sights he finds lovely.

6. "Always Drawing Near to the Spiritual Guide"

As for "always drawing near to the good spiritual guide," the bodhisattva has four different types of good spiritual guides, a matter that shall be discussed extensively later on. As for the "good spiritual guides" that are intended here, it refers to buddhas and bodhisattvas. One always draws close to them with a mind that is correct and with which one is able to please them.

7. "A Sense of Shame" and "a Dread of Blame"

"A sense of shame and a dread of blame" refers to that mind that happily subjects itself to feeling self-consciously abashed.

8. "Reverence"

"Reverence" refers to bearing in mind someone else's meritorious qualities and revering him for that reason.

9. "Gentle and Harmonious"

"Gentle and harmonious" refers to having a mind that is congenially pleased in dwelling together with others.

10. "Delighting in Contemplating Dharmas"

In "delighting in contemplating dharmas," "dharmas" refers to the five aggregates, the twelve sense bases, the eighteen sense realms, emptiness, signlessness, wishlessness, and so forth. One always contemplates these dharmas with right mindfulness.

11. "Staying Free of Attachment"

In "staying free of attachment," "attachment" refers to the tendency of the mind to take refuge in the three realms of existence. This is where beings take refuge. There are those who explain that it is the five desires and all manner of erroneous views that constitute the places in which beings take refuge. Why is this? This is because the minds of beings always become bound up in attachment to them. The sharp wisdom of the bodhisattva is such that his mind has no such desire-based attachments.

12. "Single-Mindedness"

As for "single-mindedness," this means that one so esteems the Buddha's Dharma that one does not think of anything else.

13. "Striving to Acquire Abundant Learning"

"Striving to acquire abundant learning"[60] refers to the ability to exhaustively investigate, cultivate, study, and entirely comprehend the nine categories of scripture set forth by the Buddha, [realizing that] if one learns but little, one will never completely fathom them.

14. "Refraining from Coveting Offerings of Benefits and Support"

In "refraining from coveting offerings of benefits and support," "benefits" refers to the acquisition of food and drink, wealth, material possessions, and so forth. "Support" refers to others' reverential respect, ceremonial obeisance, arrangement of a place for one to rest and sit, welcoming one upon one's arrival, and escorting one off when one departs. The bodhisattva should be inclined to provide such assistance to other beings and should not covet and become attached to such things for himself.

15. "Staying Far from Cheating, Flattery, and Deception"

"Cheating" refers to deception in weights and measures and to dealing in clothing and other goods that are not genuine.

"Flattery" means one's mind is not upstanding and direct.

"Deception" refers to taking up dharmas associated with the five sorts of wrong livelihood:

a. The Five Types of Wrong livelihood

The first is feigning uniqueness;
The second is taking advantage of a close relationship;
The third is inducement through instigation;
The fourth is [manipulation] through praising and blaming;
And the fifth is seeking to gain benefits based on one's benefits.

1) Feigning Uniqueness

As for "feigning uniqueness," there are those persons who, because they covet benefit and support, may wear the patched robes of the forest hermitage dweller, may take up the practice of only accepting food obtained on the alms round, may take up the practice of limiting all food intake to that consumed in but a single sitting, may take up the practice of always sitting [and never lying down,] or may take up the practice of not taking any sort of beverage other than water after midday. They take on the practice of such *dhūta* austerities as these, thinking, "Others who have adopted these practices have been able to come by offerings and reverence. If I take up these practices, perhaps I too shall be able to obtain them." This alteration of one's outward appearance and demeanor for the sake of acquiring benefit and support is what is meant by "feigning uniqueness."

2) Taking Advantage of a Close Relationship

As for "taking advantage of a close relationship," there are those persons who, because they covet benefit and support, therefore visit the households of benefactors[61] and say to them, "You are to me just like and no different from my father, mother, brother, sister, or other close relative. If there is anything at all that you need, I will be able to assist you with it. If there's anything you need done, I will be able to see that it is done. No matter how far away I might be, I will be able to come and greet you. Actually, if I were to live right here, then that would really be the right course of action for us." Thus, because he seeks offerings, and because he has a covetous attachment to a benefactor, he resorts to particular phrasings that manipulate the minds of other people. Such behaviors as these exemplify what is meant by "taking advantage of a close relationship."

3) Inducement through Instigation

As for "inducement through instigation," there are those who pay no heed to incurring the karmic offense of covetousness, desire to obtain valuable possessions, and so indicate an interest in obtaining material possessions by saying such things as, "This bowl is a fine one," or "This robe is a fine one," or "This house is a fine one," or "This sitting mat[62] is a fine one," or "If I were to somehow obtain such a thing, I would be able to put it to use." They may then add the statement, "It is a rare person who is able to give spontaneously."

He may also go to some benefactor's home and speak in this fashion: "Your household's stew, rice, cakes, and meats are so fragrant and exquisite and your clothes are finer yet. If you were to make a regular practice of making offerings to me, based on the long-standing nature of our close relationship, I would certainly accept your gifts."

And so, in just this sort of fashion, he makes his desires apparent to others. This is what is meant by "inducement through instigation."

4) Manipulation through Praising and Blaming"

As for "manipulation through praising and blaming," there are those who, because they covet benefit and support, speak to a benefactor, saying, "You are the most extremely miserly person. You don't even make gifts to your father or mother, your brothers, your sisters, your wife, your children, or your relatives. Just who is it that might ever be able to receive anything at all from you?" Thereupon the benefactor, feeling ashamed and embarrassed, immediately gives him gifts.

He may then go to yet another household and speak in this fashion: "You have such merit that, indeed, you have not taken on this human rebirth in vain. Even arhats always come and go from your home so that you are able to sit down and converse with them." He does this thinking, "Perhaps the benefactor shall now reflect on this and think: 'Nobody else comes and goes from my home,' thereby concluding that this must certainly be referring to me."

These are examples of what is meant by "manipulation through praising and blaming."

5) Seeking to Gain Benefits Based on One's Benefits

As for "seeking to gain benefits based on one's benefits," there are those who take up some item of clothing, a bowl, a *saṃghāṭī* robe, a sitting mat, or other such requisite, hold them in hand, and then say to someone, "This item was given to me by the king," or "by the equal of a king," or "by others among the nobility." He speaks in this fashion, thinking, "Perhaps the benefactor will now be able to conclude, 'If he is one to whom even the king and members of the nobility make offerings, how much the less could someone like me fail to present gifts to this man?'"

It is because he seeks by means of this previously acquired benefit to gain additional benefits that this practice is referred to as "seeking to gain benefits based on one's benefits."

One should therefore leave these sorts of obsequious and fraudulent behaviors far behind.

16. "One Does Not Defile the Family of the Buddhas"

In "One does not defile the family of the Buddhas," just what sorts of things constitute "defilement of the family of the Buddhas"?

There are those who say that if someone who has brought forth the resolve to seek the unsurpassable path then later reverts to the *śrāvaka*-disciple or *pratyekabuddha* paths so that he is unable to remain in the world to see to the continuance of the lineage of the Three Jewels, this is what constitutes "defiling the family of the Buddhas." However, this is a wrong explanation of its meaning. How is this so? The person referenced herein is one who is still able to achieve liberation from *saṃsāra*. Moreover, he is able to achieve a state of realization of the [five] root faculties, [five] powers, [seven] limbs of enlightenment, and [eightfold] path that is free of the contaminants. Moreover, he is still "a son of the Buddha." How then can one assert that this amounts to "defiling the family of the Buddhas"?

As stated in a sutra: "The Buddha told the bhikshus, 'You are my sons who are born from my mind, are born from my mouth, and who are heirs to the Dharma.[63]'"

Furthermore, *śrāvaka* disciples claim that it is the [four] bases [of meritorious qualities] consisting of truth, relinquishment, quiescence, and wisdom that constitute the basis for abiding within the family of the Buddhas. How so? It is because all buddhas are born from these four factors. If one defiles these four dharmas, then this is what constitutes "defiling the family of the Buddhas."

Therefore, if a person acts in a false, miserly, covetous, manically deranged or foolish fashion, this is what constitutes "defiling the family of the Buddhas." If one is correct in his implementation of these four bases, then one does not "defile the family of the Buddhas."

There are others who claim that the six *pāramitās* constitute the bases for belonging to the family of the Buddhas, doing so because these are the dharmas that give birth to the Buddhas. Consequently they infer that, if one acts in a manner that contradicts these six sorts of endeavors, this is what constitutes "defiling the family of the Buddhas."

Then again, there are yet others who state that *prajñāpāramitā* serves as the mother of the Buddhas whereas skillful means serve as the father of the Buddhas. They hold that these are the factors that serve as the basis for belonging to the family of the Buddhas. They claim that, because these two dharmas give birth to all buddhas, if one transgresses against these dharmas, this constitutes "defilement of the family of the Buddhas."

17. "Not Damaging Moral Precepts" and "Not Cheating the Buddhas"

Then again, the verse itself explains what constitutes the marks of defilement and non-defilement, in particular referring to "not damaging the moral precepts" and "not cheating the Buddhas."

If one takes on the Buddha's moral precepts yet remains unable to guard and uphold them, it is this that constitutes "cheating the Buddhas" and "defiling the family of the Buddhas." How is this the case? It is because, when one takes on the moral precepts, one is born into the family of the Buddhas. If one then breaks the precepts, it is this, then, that constitutes "cheating the Buddhas" and it is this, then, that constitutes "defiling the family of the Buddhas."

a. Might a Bodhisattva at the Stage of Certainty Break Precepts?

Question: Is it possible that the bodhisattva who has reached the stage of certainty may have instances in which he breaks the moral precepts?

b. This Is Possible If He Has Not yet Cut off the Afflictions

Response: So long as one has not yet cut off the afflictions, this remains as a circumstance to be feared. Thus, when it has still not been long since he achieved entry into the stage of certainty, the bodhisattva may still have instances in which he breaks the precepts. This is as described in "the Dharma of Greatly Supreme Buddha"[64] wherein it states, "Nanda deliberately broke precepts. I declare that this possibility still remains as something to be feared." It is only on the basis of the sutras that there is this claim. Because one has faith in the words of the Buddha, one's mind believes and accepts this.

If, having taken on the moral precepts, one does not break them and does not cheat the Buddhas, it is this that qualifies as "not defiling the family of the Buddhas."

Then again, the moral precepts are synonymous with the three trainings, namely: the training in the moral precepts, the training of the mind [in *dhyāna* meditation], and the training in wisdom. If one breaks with these trainings, then this is "defiling the family of the Buddhas." If one takes on the precepts in a context that accords with the Dharma and yet later damages or breaks them, this is "cheating the Buddhas."

Thus, when one explains the matter in this fashion, each of these two phrases possesses a particular meaning and implication. As for "cheating the Buddhas," if one's making of vows has been merely an empty exercise and thus one does not carry them out in practice in a manner according to one's declarations, one thereby cheats and deceives beings. It is this, then, that constitutes "cheating the Buddhas."

Then again, if one fails to practice any of the dharmas in accordance with the way it was taught, this is "cheating the Buddhas."

18. "Deeply Delighting in All-Knowledge" and "Remaining Unmoving"

As for "deeply delighting in all-knowledge" and "remaining unmoving like a great mountain," in every vow that he makes, this bodhisattva seeks the goal of all-knowledge so that, no matter what causes and conditions he encounters, even if it entails having to undergo the sufferings of the Great Hells, his resolve is still never shaken. In this, he is just like Sumeru, the king of the mountains, that cannot be moved by the blowing of the winds.

19. "Always Cultivating Ever More Superior Dharmas"

As for "always cultivating ever more superior dharmas," from that very time when one first brings forth the resolve, one always strives to acquire supreme dharmas. Upon entering the first ground, one is even more involved in cultivating superior dharmas. One's resolve then continues insatiably onward in this manner.

20. "Delighting in World-Transcending Dharmas," "Not Worldly Ones"

As for "delighting in world-transcending dharmas" and "not delighting in worldly dharmas," "worldly dharmas" refers to endeavors that follow along and accord with worldly affairs and prolong one's involvement in *saṃsāra*. These include the six rebirth destinies, the three realms of existence, the five aggregates, the twelve sense bases, the eighteen sense realms, the twelvefold chain of causes and conditions, the afflictions, contaminated karmic actions, and so forth.

As for "world-transcending dharmas," this means that, whatever dharmas one puts to use are able to bring about transcendence of the three realms of existence. These include the five root faculties, the five powers, the seven limbs of enlightenment, the eightfold path, the four stations of mindfulness, the four right efforts, the four bases of psychic power, the gates of liberation consisting of emptiness, signlessness, and wishlessness, the moral precept codes, extensive learning, the roots of goodness consisting of non-greed, non-aversion, and non-delusion, the mind of renunciation, non-neglectfulness, and so forth.

Because this bodhisattva possesses sharp faculties, he does not delight in the false dharmas of the world. Rather, he delights only in true world-transcending dharmas.

21. "Cultivating What Is Difficult to Cultivate"

As for "Even as one cultivates the Ground of Joyfulness, one is able to cultivate what is difficult to cultivate," this "cultivation" is a reference to reaching an utterly penetrating unimpeded understanding. Just as when someone splits bamboo, the first section is difficult, but the rest are easy, so too, the first ground is difficult to cultivate, but after one has cultivated it, the rest are naturally easy to cultivate.

How is this the case? This is because, when the bodhisattva abides on the first ground, his strength has not yet become completely developed and his roots of goodness have not yet grown thick, for he has not yet cultivated the dharmas of goodness over a long time. Hence the eye sense faculty and the other sense faculties are all still prone to follow their respective sense objects and the mind has not yet become well controlled. Therefore the afflictions are still able to cause trouble for him. This is just as when someone's strength has not yet become fully developed, one finds it difficult to swim upstream, against the current.

Moreover, because Māra and Māra's minions create more of an obstacle on this ground, one is therefore compelled to use the power of skillful means and be diligent in the practice of vigor. It is for these reasons that this ground is said to be "difficult to cultivate."

So it is that, beginning with "the power of faith becomes ever more superior" as the foremost factor and "does not delight in worldly dharmas" as the last, one proceeds with the practice of these twenty-seven dharmas, carrying out one's cultivation of the bodhisattva's first ground, the Ground of Joyfulness.

It is therefore stated that the bodhisattva ought to always cultivate these dharmas. "Cultivation" refers here to single-mindedness and non-neglectfulness in always practicing them, in always contemplating them, and in getting rid of all transgressions and evils. It is for this reason that it refers here to "cultivation." This is just as when one maintains a walking path and thereby causes it to remain clean.

As for all of these dharmas, they are not cultivated solely on the first ground. Rather, one uses these dharmas on all the grounds.

22. Q: How Does One "Securely Abide" and Not Retreat?

Question: You have now completed the discussion of the skillful means and purification dharmas used to attain the first ground. How then does the bodhisattva "securely abide" in it so that he does not retreat from it and lose it?

23. A: By Always Practicing and Completely Developing These Dharmas

Response: This is a matter of always practicing and completely developing dharmas such as these consisting of "the power of faith becomes ever more superior," and so forth. This is what constitutes the basis for "secure abiding" in the first ground.

24. The Meaning of "Bodhisattva" and "Superior Dharmas"

Now, as for the "*bodhi*" of bodhisattva, this is a reference to the superior path. "*Sattva*" refers to [a being] that is possessed of resolute intentions. Hence it is because someone deeply delights in bodhi that he is referred to as a "bodhisattva." Then again, one may explain that "*sattva*" refers to "beings." Hence it is on the basis of a person's cultivating and accumulating [the bases for realization of] bodhi, doing so for the sake of other beings, that one is referred to as a "bodhisattva." "Superior dharmas," refers to dharmas such as "faith" and the others. It is because they enable a person to realize buddhahood that they are referred to as "superior dharmas."

The End of Chapter Four

Chapter 5
The Explanation of the Vows

V. Chapter Five: Explanation of the Vows

We have now finished explaining the skillful means that are used in entering the first ground and the dharmas that are used in its purification. It is because of his vows that the bodhisattva gains entry into all of the grounds. It is also due to completely developing the meritorious qualities associated with the [above-discussed dharmas beginning with] "the power of faith becoming ever more superior" that one is able to securely abide on one's ground. We shall now proceed with a differentiating discussion of these vows:

A. The First Bodhisattva Vow

I vow to make offerings to, supply the needs of,
and extend reverence to all buddhas.
I vow that in every case I shall protect and uphold
the Dharma of all buddhas.

This ["making of offerings"] is what constitutes the bodhisattva's first vow.[65] During the interim period between the time when one first brings forth the resolve up until the time one gains *anuttarasamyaksaṃbodhi,* one should make offerings to, supply the needs of, and extend reverence to all buddhas.

"Making offerings" refers to offerings of flowers, incense, strings of jewels, banners, canopies, lamplight, the erecting of stupas with shrines, and so forth. "Supplying needs" refers to providing them with robes, bedding, and necessities. "Reverence" refers to honoring them, treating them as important, making full reverential bows to them, welcoming them on arrival, seeing them off when leaving, placing the palms together, and serving them personally.

Then again, [it may be explained that] "making offerings" refers to using the dharmas of the Small Vehicle to teach beings, "supplying needs" refers to using the dharmas of the Pratyekabuddha Vehicle to teach beings, and "extending reverence" refers to using the dharmas of the Great Vehicle to teach beings.

These constitute the bases of the first vow.

B. The Second Bodhisattva Vow

As for [the second vow], "protecting and upholding the Dharma of all buddhas," the bodhisattva has this thought, "I should guard and protect the Dharma of all past, future, and present buddhas of the ten directions."[66]

Question: All buddhas of the past have already entered nirvāṇa and their Dharma has subsequently also become extinct. The buddhas of the future have not yet come forth and their Dharma does not yet even exist. They have not yet even initiated their turning of the wheel of Dharma, how much the less have they brought forth any other dharmas. How then could one succeed in protecting it? That which one might rightly be able to protect is the Dharma of the buddhas of the present, this because all of those buddhas are still present.

Response: The Dharma of all buddhas of the past, future and present is in every case of a single substance and of a single character. Hence, if one protects the Dharma of a single buddha, then this constitutes protection of the Dharma of all buddhas of the three periods of time. This is as stated in a sutra that reads, "The Buddha informed the bhikshus: 'The Dharma of Vipaśyin Buddha—the leaving of the home life, the taking on of the moral precepts, the wearing of the robes, the holding of the bowl, the *dhyāna* absorptions, the wisdom, the proclamation of Dharma, and their transformative teaching—it is all the same as mine.'" Thus the challenge you have posed is invalid. This [protection of the Dharma] is what constitutes the second of the vows.

Next, we have the following:

C. The Third Bodhisattva Vow

From that time when all buddhas depart from the Tuṣita Heaven
and come back to abide in the world,
on forward to the conclusion of their teaching
and their eternal entry into the realm [of nirvāṇa] without residue,

including when they abide in the womb, take birth,
leave the home life, proceed to the *bodhimaṇḍa*,
conquer Māra, achieve buddhahood,
and begin turning the wheel of the sublime Dharma—

From the time when I respectfully welcome them
and on through to the other occasions throughout their lives,
I vow that in all cases I shall completely
devote my mind to making offerings to them.[67]

This refers to that entire time beginning with the buddhas' withdrawal from the Tuṣita Heaven and descent into the world on up to their entry into the nirvāṇa without residue. During that entire interval, commencing with their entry into the womb, I shall arrange grand presentations of offerings to them, including as well those times when they are born, leave the home life, proceed to the *bodhimaṇḍa*, conquer Māra, the king of the demons, realize buddhahood, and turn the wheel of Dharma. I shall respectfully serve the Tathāgatas at these times.

As for "and on through to the other occasions throughout their lives," this refers to when they manifest great spiritual powers, abide in great assemblies of humans and devas, and engage in the extensive liberation of beings. [He vows]: "On such occasions, I shall make offerings to them of flowers, incense, banners, canopies, music, songs, verses, and praises. I shall leave behind the home life, take on the Dharma, and cultivate its practice in accordance with the way it has been taught. And I shall make offerings to the Buddhas of the foremost sorts of offering gifts." This is what constitutes the third vow.

D. The Fourth Bodhisattva Vow

Next, we have the following:

> I vow to engage in the transformative teaching of beings,
> causing them all to enter the paths.[68]

"Teaching" refers here to the teaching of good dharmas. "Transformation" refers to influencing them to abandon evil dharmas. [One resolves]: "Using these two types of dharmas I shall cause an incalculable number of *asaṃkhyeyas* of beings to abide in the paths of *śrāvaka* disciples and *pratyekabuddhas*." This is what constitutes the fourth of the vows.

E. The Fifth Bodhisattva Vow

Next, we have the following:

> I vow to enable all beings'
> complete realization of the Buddha's bodhi
> even where there are those tending toward *śrāvaka*-disciple
> or *pratyekabuddha* paths—[69]

In instances where these persons cultivating the paths of the *śrāvaka* disciples and the *pratyekabuddha*s have not yet entered the [right and fixed] Dharma position,[70] I shall teach and transform them, inducing them to instead proceed toward the path to buddhahood. Where there are those who have not taken up the paths of *śrāvaka* disciples or *pratyekabuddha*s, I shall teach and transform them in a manner that influences them to proceed toward the unsurpassable path to buddhahood. In instances where others have already begun to proceed toward the unsurpassable path to buddhahood, I shall reveal [aspects of Dharma], instruct, benefit, and delight them,[71] thereby causing their meritorious qualities to progressively increase. The fifth vow consists of adopting these means in the teaching and transforming of all beings.

F. The Sixth Bodhisattva Vow

Next, we have the following:

> Through resolute faith, I vow
> to cause all dharmas to enter [a state of] uniform equality.[72]

"All dharmas" is a general reference to all dharmas whatsoever, including:

Dharmas conducing to liberation and dharmas not conducing to liberation;
Dharmas subsumed within the limbs of enlightenment and dharmas not subsumed within the limbs of enlightenment;
Dharmas constituting provisions assisting the path and dharmas not constituting provisions assisting the path;
Dharmas subsumed within the paths of the Āryas and dharmas not subsumed within the paths of the Āryas;
Dharmas that should be cultivated and dharmas that should not be cultivated;
Dharmas to which one should draw near and dharmas to which one should not draw near;
Dharmas one should bring forth and dharmas one should not bring forth;
Dharmas that are produced and dharmas that are unproduced;
Dharmas of the present and dharmas not of the present;
Dharmas that are the product of causes and conditions and dharmas that are not the product of causes and conditions;
Dharmas constituting causes and conditions and dharmas not constituting causes and conditions;
Dharmas produced through meditative contemplation and dharmas not produced through meditative contemplation;
Dharmas that are coarse and dharmas that are subtle;
Dharmas associated with feeling and dharmas not associated with feeling;
Inward dharmas and outward dharmas;
Dharmas belonging to the inward sense bases and dharmas not belonging to inward sense bases;
Dharmas belonging to outward sense bases and dharmas not belonging to outward sense bases;
Dharmas subsumed within the five aggregates and dharmas not subsumed within the five aggregates;
Dharmas subsumed within the five appropriated aggregates and dharmas not subsumed within the five appropriated aggregates;

Dharmas subsumed by the four truths and dharmas not subsumed by the four truths;
Dharmas assisting the world and dharmas not assisting the world;
Dharmas dependent on covetousness and dharmas dependent on transcendence;
Dharmas associated with inverted views and dharmas not associated with inverted views;
Dharmas associated with transformations and dharmas not associated with transformations;
Dharmas associated with regret and dharmas not associated with regret;
Dharmas that are great and dharmas that are small;
Dharmas based in the feeling aggregate and dharmas not based in the feeling aggregate;
Dharmas subject to severance and dharmas not subject to severance;
Dharmas associated with knowledge and vision and dharmas not associated with knowledge and vision;
Dharmas associated with the contaminants and dharmas not associated with the contaminants;
Dharmas involving the bonds and dharmas free of the bonds;
Dharmas characterized by purity and dharmas devoid of purity;
Dharmas that are surpassable and dharmas that are unsurpassable;
Dharmas involving initial ideation (*vitarka*) and dharmas not involving initial ideation;
Dharmas involving mental discursion (*vicāra*) and dharmas not involving mental discursion;
Dharmas in which one can delight and dharmas in which one cannot delight;
Dharmas that are associated [with the mind] and dharmas not associated [with the mind];
Dharmas involving the making of discriminations and dharmas not involving the making of discriminations;
Dharmas associated with formative factors (*saṃskāra*) and dharmas not associated with formative factors;
Dharmas involving conditions and dharmas not involving conditions;
Dharmas involving sequence and dharmas devoid of sequence;
Dharmas that are visible and dharmas that are not visible;
Dharmas that may be opposed [as objective conditions] and dharmas that cannot be opposed [as objective conditions];
Dharmas that are visible and opposable [as objective conditions] and dharmas that are invisible and not opposable;

Dharmas possessing characteristic signs and dharmas that are signless;
Dharmas that can be implemented in practice and dharmas that cannot be implemented in practice;
Dharmas that are conditioned and dharmas that are unconditioned;
Dharmas that are dangerous and dharmas that are not dangerous;
Dharmas possessed of a foundation and dharmas not possessed of any foundation;
Dharmas conducive to transcendence and dharmas not conducive to transcendence;
Dharmas associated with beings and dharmas not associated with beings;
Dharmas of one who is suffering and dharmas of one who is not suffering;
Dharmas associated with the afflictions and dharmas not associated with the afflictions;
Dharmas associated with existence and dharmas not associated with existence;
Dharmas that are contrary and dharmas that are not contrary;
Dharmas associated with the karmic result of happiness and dharmas not associated with the karmic result of happiness;
Dharmas associated with the karmic result of suffering and dharmas not associated with the karmic result of suffering;
Dharmas produced through recollection and dharmas not produced through recollection;
Practice dharmas in which knowledge is foremost and practice dharmas in which knowledge is not foremost;
Practice dharmas in which faith is foremost and practice dharmas in which faith is not foremost;
Practice dharmas in which meditative contemplation is foremost and practice dharmas in which meditative contemplation is not foremost;
Practice dharmas in which vows are foremost and practice dharmas in which vows are not foremost;
Form dharmas and dharmas not associated with form;
Teaching dharmas and non-teaching dharmas;
Dharmas associated with transformationally created phenomena and dharmas unassociated with transformationally created phenomena;
Dharmas associated with roaming wherever one wishes and dharmas unassociated with roaming wherever one wishes;
Dharmas rooted in zeal and dharmas not rooted in zeal;

Dharmas in which the cause is goodness and dharmas in which the cause is not goodness;

Dharmas in which the cause is roots of goodness and dharmas in which the cause is not roots of goodness;

Dharmas that are fixed and dharmas that are unfixed;

Dharmas associated with the physical body and dharmas not associated with the physical body;

Dharmas associated with speech and dharmas not associated with speech;

Dharmas associated with the mind faculty and dharmas not associated with the mind faculty;

Dharmas arising through contact with opposable objects and dharmas not arising through contact with opposable objects;

Dharmas arising through mind faculty contact and dharmas not arising through mind faculty contact;

Evil dharmas and dharmas that are not evil;

Good dharmas and dharmas that are not good;

Dharmas that are able to initiate production and dharmas that are not able to initiate production;

Dharmas destroyed in each successive mind-moment and dharmas not destroyed in each successive mind-moment;

Dharmas that are accumulated and dharmas that are not accumulated;

Dharmas associated with the factors conducing to clear understanding[73] and dharmas not associated with the factors conducing to clear understanding;

Dharmas that are causal and dharmas that are not causal;

Dharmas associated with conditions and dharmas not associated with conditions;

Dharmas associated with causes and conditions and dharmas not associated with causes and conditions;

Dharmas produced through causes and dharmas not produced through causes;

Dharmas that are caused and dharmas that are not caused;

Dharmas associated with singular identity and dharmas associated with difference;

Dharmas associated with cessation and dharmas unassociated with cessation;

Dharmas associated with restraint of the sense faculties and dharmas not associated with restraint of the sense faculties;

Dharmas occurring in conjunction with the mind and dharmas not occurring in conjunction with the mind;

Mind dharmas and dharmas that are not mind;
Dharmas associated with the mind and dharmas unassociated with the mind;
The five dharmas associated with contact and dharmas that are not the five dharmas associated with contact;
Sixteen dharmas the acquisition of which is held in common and dharmas unassociated with the sixteen dharmas the acquisition of which is held in common;
Subtle dharmas and coarse dharmas;
Dharmas associated with dedication of merit and dharmas not associated with dedication of merit;
Good dharmas and dharmas that are not good;
Neutral dharmas;
Dharmas severed on the path of seeing the truths;
Dharmas severed on the path of meditation;
Dharmas that are not severed;
Dharmas of those still in training;
Dharmas of those already beyond training;
Dharmas neither of those still in training nor of those beyond training;
And all of the other incalculably many thousands of myriads of types of dharmas.

In every case one causes all of these dharmas to enter into the gates of emptiness, signlessness, and wishlessness so that they are realized to be uniformly equal and beyond duality. This is accomplished through the power of resolute faith. This is the sixth of the vows.

G. The Seventh Bodhisattva Vow

Next, we have the following:

Having vowed to purify the buddhalands,
I shall therefore extinguish all the various forms of evil.[74]

1. An Exhaustive List of the Characteristics of Evil and Impurity

"[The various forms of evil]" refers to killing beings, stealing, sexual misconduct, false speech, divisive speech, harsh speech, frivolous or lewd speech, greed, anger, wrong livelihood, consumption of intoxicants, and so forth. Wherever evils of these sorts are present, it is these places that are referred to as "impure."

Additionally, where a land includes the wretched destinies of the hells, animals, hungry ghosts, and such, these too are deemed to be "impure." Then again, it is also the case that "impurity" refers to circumstances in which beings have become covered over by such qualities as the following:

Absence of faith;
Indolence;
Mental scatteredness;
Stupidity;
Flattery;
Deviousness;
Miserliness;
Jealousy;
Rage;
Enmity;
Gravely erroneous views;
Pride;
Arrogance;
Pride based on estimations of greatness;
Pride based on the view of a self;
Deviancy-based pride;
Feigning uniqueness;
Manipulation of feelings of close relationship;
Inducement through instigation;
Manipulation through praising and blaming;
Seeking to gain benefits based on one's benefits;[75]
Esteeming worldly pleasures;
Negligence;
Absence of self-restraint;
Abundant desires;
Evil desires;
Deviant types of desire;
Sexual misconduct;
Failing to acknowledge [indebtedness to] one's father or mother, *śramaṇas*, or brahmans;
Failing to practice patience;
Breaking with the awesome deportment [required by the monastic moral code];
Making oneself difficult to remonstrate with;
Indulging in erroneous forms of initial ideation and secondary mental discursion;
Sensual desire;
Ill will;
[Lethargy and] sleepiness;
Agitated excitedness;
Or doubtfulness.[76]

Yet again, "impurity" is present in circumstances where there are manifestations such as the following:

Vicious birds and beasts;
An abundance of hostile bandits;
An absence of water or other things to drink;
Hunger;
Famine;
Disasters;
Pestilence;
Terror wrought by humans;
Terror wrought by nonhumans;
Rebellion from within [the state];
Pillaging invaders from beyond [the borders];
Excessive rains;
Drought;
Distress associated with [societal] decline;
Or all of the various sorts of suffering and affliction typical of the ending of minor kalpas.

Then again, "impurity" is also present in circumstances where beings are beset by manifestations such as:

A short life span;
A horribly ugly physical body;
Weakness;
An abundance of every sort of worry and suffering;
Insufficient courage or ability;
An abundance of sickness;
Inferior charismatic power;
A small retinue;
An evil retinue;
A retinue that is easily brought to ruin;
Small residences;
Or weak-willed, base, and deviant mendicants.

Also, "impurity" is present wherever there manifest among the householders or renunciates any of the wrong views and wrong practices exemplified by the following:

Seng-qu-yu-jia-you-lou-jia kings;
Na-bo-luo-ta-pi-qu-na-ping-sha kings;
Na-ji-liao rishis;[77]
Elephant rishis;

Those [whose path is merely] celibacy;
Those whose practice is that of "the superior disciple";
The sheep herders;
The "great-mind" practitioners;
The "patient ones";
The *qiao-tan-mo-jiu-lan-to-mo* "live ones";
The "deliverers";
The "swimmers";
The *po-luo-sha-jia-na-po-luo-duo-she* practitioners;
The "robe-wearers";
The "robeless ones";
Those wearing leather robes;
Those who dress in skins;
Those who dress in grass;
Those who dress in the lower robe;
Those who dress in horned-owl feathers;
Those who dress in tree bark;
Those who wash three times;
The "adapters";
Those who serve the king of the Brahma Heaven;
Those who serve the *kumāra* virgins;
Those who serve the *piśācī* ghosts;
Those who serve the golden-winged *garuḍa* bird;
Those who serve the *gandharvas*;
Those who serve King Yāma;
Those who serve Vaiśravana;
Those who serve the *guhyapāda* vajra spirits;
Those who serve the *bhūta* spirits;
Those who serve the dragons;
The naked *śramaṇas*;[78]
The white-robed *śramaṇas*;[79]
The dyed-robe *śramaṇas*;
The Maskarī Gośālīputra *śramaṇas*;[80]
The followers of Piluochizi;[81]
The followers of Jiazhanyannizi;[82]
The followers of Saqizhezi;[83]
Those practicing cow morality;
Those practicing deer morality;
Those practicing dog morality;
Those practicing horse morality;

Those practicing elephant morality;
Those whose morality consists in begging;
Those whose morality is that of the *kumāra* virgins;
Those whose morality is that of devas;
Those whose practice is the "superior" precepts;
Those whose moral code is defined by indulgence of sexual desire;
Those whose moral code is remaining pristinely immaculate;
Those who practice the "fire" morality;
Those who declare nirvāṇa to derive from the extinction of visually-perceived forms;
Those who declare nirvāṇa to derive from the extinction of sounds;
Those who declare nirvāṇa to derive from the extinction of smells;
Those who declare nirvāṇa to derive from the extinction of tastes;
Those who declare nirvāṇa to derive from the extinction of touchables;
Those who declare nirvāṇa to derive from the extinction of initial ideation and mental discursion;
Those who declare nirvāṇa to derive from the extinction of joy;
Those who declare nirvāṇa to derive from the extinction of pain and pleasure;[84]
Those who wear the water-robe headdress;
Those whose practice is rooted in purity of water;
Those whose practice is rooted in purity of food;
Those whose practice is rooted in purity of caste;
Those who carry about the mortar and pestle;
Those who are breakers of rocks;
Those who delight in bathing;
Those who float and then sink;
Those who abide out on the open ground;
Those who lie down on sharp thorns;
Those of a worldly nature;
Those who are "the Great Ones";
Those whose practice is rooted in the self;
Those who posit identity with forms;
Those who posit identity with sounds;
Those who posit identity with smells;
Those who posit identity with tastes;
Those who posit identity with touchables;
The earth-realizers;
The water-realizers;
The fire-realizers;

The wind realizers;
The space realizers;
The unity realizers;
The transformation realizers;
The eye-faculty realizers;
The ear-faculty realizers;
The nose-faculty realizers;
The tongue-faculty realizers;
The physical-body realizers;
The mind faculty realizers;
The spirit realizers.

All such instances of the many different sorts of wrong views and wrong practices on the part of householders and renunciates qualify as "impure."

Then again, "impurity" is involved wherever the lands are characterized by the following:

Precipitous terrain;
Abysses;
Steep coastlines;
Dense thickets;
Brambles and thorns;
Many sorts of obstacles;
Lands characterized by dustiness, dirtiness, muddiness, flooding, or quicksand pits;
Fearsome mountains with precipitous terrain and peaks;
Twisting defiles;
Deep obstructing inlets;
Rows of mountain peaks obstructing travel;
Towering cliffs;
Places that are difficult to ascend;
Saline waters;
Parched sands;
Terrains marked by stones, rubble, and rocks;
The various fruits characterized by merely weak flavor and deficient appearance and fragrance;
Unbeneficial herbs and plants possessing only scant and feeble potency;
A relative rarity of marvelous forms, sounds, smells, tastes, and touchables;

Only rare encounters with parks and groves, viewing towers, freely running streams, bathing ponds, small mountains and buttes to ascend for distant views, or other enjoyable places;

Provinces, counties, and villages that are not in favorable proximity to each other;

Lands full of desolate hills;

Scant populations;

Cities of inferior character where one frequently encounters poverty-stricken people bereft of merit;

Cities of inferior character;

Very few representatives of governing officialdom, magistrates, high ministers, members of the nobility, leaders among the merchant and professional classes, artists, craftsmen, and scholars;

Or extreme difficulties in coming by clothing, bedding, medicines, and conveniences providing enhancement of one's physical existence, and, in instances where they are obtainable, they are not particularly fine.

Places such as these qualify as impure. As a general statement, "impurity" is of two types. Those of the first type arise due to the beings' own causes and conditions. Those of the second type arise due to the causes and conditions of the karma of their actions.

In the case of those that arise due to beings' own causes and conditions, this is because of beings' faults and evils.

As regards that type of impurity that arises due to the causes and conditions of the karma of their karmic actions, these originate with the transgressions and evils of karmic actions. These two matters were already discussed earlier on.

Where one transforms these two types of circumstances, then there are beings with meritorious qualities and karmic actions that are meritorious. These two types of meritorious qualities constitute the bases for lands being referred to as "pure."

One should realize that this purifying of the lands is associated with the causes and conditions of bodhisattvas' original vows. Because the bodhisattvas are able to implement immense vigor many ways, what they vow to bring about is itself so measurelessly vast as to be impossible to fully describe. Consequently we shall now only provide a summary description explaining the main points of the matter. As for the remaining aspects, one should be able to understand them as of essentially the same sort.

2. A Description of the Characteristics of Pure Lands

As for a general description of the characteristics of pure lands, they include:

A bodhisattva who has thoroughly realized *anuttarasamyaksaṃbodhi*;
The complete presence of the dharmas associated with a buddha's meritorious qualities and powers;
The complete presence of the Dharma;
The complete presence of *śrāvaka* disciples;
The completeness of the bodhi tree;
A world that is adorned;
Beings that are well-endowed with good fortune;
The abundant presence of beings capable of achieving liberation;
The gathering of an immense congregation;
And completeness in the powers of a buddha.

"Thorough realization of bodhi" refers to the presence of ten enhancing factors:

First, the abandonment of asceticism.
Second, the absence of weak thoughts of renunciation.
Third, the rapid achievement of realization.
Fourth, the absence of anything sought from non-Buddhist gurus.
Fifth, the complete presence of bodhisattvas.
Sixth, the absence of demon adversaries.
Seventh, the absence of any of the entangling difficulties.
Eighth, the presence of immense deva congregations.
Ninth, the complete presence of rarely encountered phenomena.
And tenth, its occurrence at the perfect time.

"Abandonment of ascetic practices" means that, when the bodhisattva leaves the home life for the sake of realizing *anuttarasamyaksaṃbodhi*, he does not undertake ascetic practices.[85] In particular, this refers to practices such as going four days, six days, eight days, a half month, or even a month during which one eats as little as a single sesame seed, a single rice grain, or a single piece of fruit, drinks only water, or only ingests subtle energy. He does not resort to ascetic practices of this sort in striving to reach enlightenment. He sits peacefully in the *bodhimaṇḍa* and thereby realizes buddhahood.

"Absence of weak thoughts of renunciation" means that, when a bodhisattva is able to bring forth even a minor thought of renunciation, he immediately abandons the home life.

"Rapid achievement of realization" means that, once the bodhisattva has left the home life, he soon reaches *anuttarasamyaksaṃbodhi*.

"Refraining from seeking anything from non-Buddhist gurus" means that, once the bodhisattva has left behind the home life, even if there is a great non-Buddhist guru, one who has become very famous, still, he does not go to consult him, inquiring, "What dharma is it that you proclaim? What topics do you discuss? What is it that you set forth as beneficial?" Nor does he wander off in any of the four directions searching out [such gurus].

"The complete presence of bodhisattvas" means that, when the bodhisattva is on the verge of realizing buddhahood, all of the bodhisattvas throughout the great trichiliocosm as well as the bodhisattvas from other regions—they each take up offerings and they all come and surround him. Then, having waited until that buddha has realized buddhahood and emanated great radiance, they each present their offerings. They have heard the Dharma from the buddhas, have all become irreversible on the path, and have reached the stage of having but one life remaining prior to realizing buddhahood.

"Absence of demon adversaries" means that, when that bodhisattva is about to achieve buddhahood, there are no armies of Māra able to come forth and destroy him.

As for there being "the absence of any entangling difficulties," when the bodhisattva is about to attain the realization of buddhahood, there is not even the most infinitesimally minor degree of affliction that enters his mind.[86]

As for there being "immense congregations that convene," when the bodhisattva is about to gain buddhahood, the devas from the Heaven of the Four Heavenly Kings, the devas from the Trāyastriṃśa Heaven, and the devas from the Yāma Heaven, the Tuṣita Heaven, the Nirmāṇarati Heaven, the Paranirmita Vaśavartin Heaven, the Brahma Heaven, and the others up to and including the Akaniṣṭha Heaven—these, together with the dragons, the spirits, the *yakṣas*, the *gandharvas*, the *asuras*, the *garuḍas*, the *kinnaras*, the *mahoragas*, and all of the other sorts of spirits from all of the immeasurably many worlds throughout the ten directions—each of them takes up the most superior and marvelous of offerings and comes forth to make offerings to the bodhisattva. It is this that constitutes the convening of an immense congregation.

Then again, the *śrāvaka* disciples explain that, when all the devas abiding in ten world systems come forth, it is this that constitutes an immense congregation of devas.

As for there being "the complete presence of rarely encountered phenomena,"[87] when the Bodhisattva realizes buddhahood, rarely encountered phenomena occur: The earth moves and shakes in six ways; throughout the worlds of the ten directions' countless great trichiliocosms, all of the Māras' palaces deteriorate and no longer shine forth with radiance; the countless Sumeru mountains shake; the measurelessly vast seas are all roiled; throughout all worlds, the blossoms bloom out of season; a rain of powdered sandalwood incense descends; and there is a rain of the most renowned celestial flower blossoms.

As for "it occurs at a perfect time," this refers to a time when there is no pestilence, famine, war, or fleeing refugees. It is free of torrential rains and flooding. There are never any disasters. All the kings and other [authorities] govern in accordance with the Dharma. The people are at peace and their lives are long. There are no enemy insurgents, terrible birds and beasts, poisonous insects, or ghosts and spirits that harass and harm beings.

As for [complete presence of the dharmas associated with] "a buddha's meritorious qualities and powers," the awesome powers, meritorious qualities, wisdom, and immeasurably many profound dharmas of the buddhas of the past, the future, and the present are the same and no different. There are only [distinctions] in accordance with the causes and conditions of each buddha's original vows. Thus, in some cases, he may possess an immeasurably long life span. In other cases, if one but sees him, one immediately gains the stage of certainty. Or it may be that, upon hearing his name, one also becomes able in that way to gain the stage of certainty. Or it may be that when women see him, they are able to immediately gain the body of a man. Or it may be that on hearing his name, they are immediately able to transform that woman's body. It may be as well that, upon hearing his name, they are immediately able to go off to rebirth [in accordance with their wishes].

In some cases, he has measureless radiance that, when beings encounter it, they leave behind all impeding hindrances. In some cases, due to encountering such light, beings immediately enter the stage of certainty. It may also happen that, on encountering such light, they extinguish all suffering and afflictions.

As for the possession of "an immeasurably long life span," it may be that his life span extends in its duration to immeasurably many kalpas beyond counting, extending for a kalpa, a hundred kalpas, a thousand kalpas, a myriad kalpas, a *koṭi* of kalpas, or even a hundred thousand myriads of *koṭis* of *nayutas* of *asaṃkhyeyas* of kalpas. He may abide for such a long time in order to benefit beings and because of his pity for beings.

Although all buddhas possess the power to extend their life spans for an immeasurably long time, due to differences in their original vows, there are those who do dwell in the world for a long time and those who do not dwell in the world for a long time.

As for "being able to gain the stage of certainty on seeing [a buddha]," there are beings who, upon seeing a buddha, become immediately able to dwell on the ground of the *avaivartika's* [irreversibility] with respect to the attainment of *anuttarasamyaksaṃbodhi*. How is this the case? It is because, when these beings see the body of a buddha, their minds are filled with great delight, joy, and pure happiness. Their minds immediately become focused and acquire a bodhisattva samādhi of this sort. Due to the power of this samādhi, they achieve a penetrating understanding of the true character of all dharmas. They then become able to immediately enter the ground of certainty with respect to the attainment of *anuttarasamyaksaṃbodhi*. Due to their resolute intentions that have persisted during the long night [of previous lifetimes], beings of this sort have planted those roots of goodness whereby, upon seeing a buddha, they enter the stage of certainty.

This is because they have taken the mind of great compassion as foremost, because their goodness is sublime and pure, because they have sought to achieve a penetrating understanding of all the dharmas of a buddha, because they have sought to liberate all beings, and because the time has arrived for the perfection of these roots of goodness that they therefore succeed in meeting this buddha. Additionally, it is due to the particular causes and conditions of that buddha's original vows. It is because of the coming together of these two factors that this circumstance is then able to occur.

As for "entering the stage of certainty upon hearing the name of a buddha," a buddha may have made an original vow, declaring, "If there be anyone who so much as hears my name, then he shall immediately enter the stage of certainty." Hence, just as with the case of seeing a buddha, so too it is in this case of hearing a buddha's name.

As for a woman "being able to transform the woman's body as a result of having seen a buddha," if there be someone who single-mindedly wishes to change away from her female form and who has herself developed a profound renunciation for the troubles it involves, and who, based on the power of resolute faith has vowed to seek instead the physical form of a male—when a woman of this sort succeeds in seeing such a buddha, she immediately transforms and leaves behind the female body.

In the event that a woman does not have karmic causal conditions of this sort and also has not yet exhausted the karma that brings about birth in a female body, she will remain unable to encounter a buddha of this sort.

As for a woman "being able to transform and leave behind the female form upon hearing the name" of a given buddha, the causal conditions for this are just as explained with regard to achieving this by seeing a buddha.

As for "being enabled to go forth to rebirth" upon hearing the name of a buddha, if a person is possessed of much power arising from his resolute faith, if his roots of goodness have become completely developed, and if his karmic obstacles have already become exhausted, where this corresponds to the causes and conditions of the original vows of buddhas, when such a person hears the name of one of these buddhas, he will then be able to go forth to rebirth [in accordance with his wishes].

As for "measureless light," the illumination from the light of all buddhas is such that the distance it reaches accords with their wishes. The "measureless light" we speak of here is the illumination that they always emanate. Their always-emanated illumination is not limited to any given number of *yojanas* of distance whereby one might say of it that it extends universally in the eastern direction a given number of hundreds of thousands of myriads of *koṭis* of *yojanas*. It is not even amenable to calculation. This applies as well to its reach to the south, west, north, the four midpoints, the zenith, and the nadir. One may only know of it that it is measureless and no one knows its bounds.

As for "becoming able to get rid of all hindrances due to encountering this light," this is an effect brought about by the power of the original vows made by buddhas. Sensual desire, ill will, lethargy-and-sleepiness, excitedness-and-regretfulness, and doubtfulness—one gets rid of these hindrances.

When beings encounter such light, they immediately become able to abide in mindfulness of the Buddha. Due to this mindfulness of the Buddha, they then become mindful of the Dharma. Due to becoming mindful of the Dharma, they then become able to rid themselves of these hindrances.

When it is said that the contact of such illumination with the body brings about "the extinguishing of suffering and affliction," this refers to instances in which beings who have descended into the hell realms, animal realms, hungry ghost realms, and other nonhuman realms undergo the manifold sufferings and afflictions characteristic of these realms. Due to the power produced by a buddha's original vows and spiritual superknowledges, when that buddha's light touches their bodies, they immediately become able to abandon such sufferings.

As for there being "the complete presence of the Dharma," there is the complete presence of the Dharma of all buddhas. There is no such thing as [there being buddhas who] completely possess it as opposed to those who do not completely possess it. Because all buddhas are identical as regards the Dharma that they proclaim, the Dharma of each of them is therefore perfectly complete. It is solely a function of the causal conditions specific to their original vows that there are differences whereby their Dharma may remain for a long time or not remain for a long time. That's all.

What is meant by "the complete presence of the Dharma"? [When it is completely present], the Dharma includes:

Concise explanations;
Extensive explanations;
Explanations that are both concise and extensive;
Complete presence of the Śrāvaka Disciple Vehicle;
Complete presence of the Pratyekabuddha Vehicle;
Complete presence of the Great Vehicle;
Protection by the power of the spiritual superknowledges;
Prevention of ruination by non-Buddhist traditions;
Invulnerability to destruction by *māras;*
And long endurance in the world.

In "concise explanations" one uses but a few words and phrases that embrace an abundance of meanings. When those with sharp faculties hear it, they immediately become awakened.

In "extensive explanations," for the sake of those with dull faculties or those who delight in making distinctions, one presents a lengthy explanation of all of the causes and conditions associated with a single matter or single meaning.

In "explanations that are both concise and extensive," one both uses single statements to comprehensively include a wide range of meanings and also uses many different explanations to spread forth [the nuances of] a single meaning.

As for "complete presence of the Śrāvaka Disciple Vehicle, complete presence of the Pratyekabuddha Vehicle, and complete presence of the Great Vehicle," these are matters that shall be extensively discussed later on.

"Protection by the power of the spiritual superknowledges" refers to the use of the Buddha's spiritual powers in providing his protective mindfulness of this Dharma and it also refers to its being sealed with the seal of the Buddhas.

"The seal of the Buddhas" refers to [the Dharma's] association with the four great causal factors and its abandonment of the four black causes.

"Prevention of ruination by non-Buddhist traditions" refers to [the Dharma's countering of] all the deviant views of non-Buddhist *śramaṇas*, brahmans, and treatise masters by presenting [correct] teachings on arising, passing away, enjoyment, danger, and escape.[88]

Additionally, it refers to instigating awareness of all forms of goodness and explaining the causes and conditions that could bring about their ruination.

As for "invulnerability to destruction by *māras*," because the Buddhas possess a measureless and boundless number of meritorious qualities, wisdom, skillful means, and the powers of the spiritual superknowledges, even though *māras* are themselves possessed of powers, they still cannot destroy [the Dharma].

It is also because of the powers possessed by the bodhisattvas that the *māras* cannot destroy [the Dharma].

As for the Dharma's "long endurance," it may even be for so long as an entire kalpa or somewhat less than an entire kalpa, and in fact it may even extend for even longer to a hundred kalpas, a thousand kalpas, a myriad kalpas, ten myriads of kalpas, a hundred myriads of kalpas, a thousand myriads of kalpas, a myriad myriads of kalpas, for an immeasurable number of thousands of myriads of *koṭis* of *nayutas* of *asaṃkhyeyas* of kalpas, and so forth on up to a measureless and boundless number of kalpas during which it continues to endure.

As for "the complete presence of the Śrāvaka Disciple [Vehicle]," all buddhas are attended by a perfectly complete *śrāvaka*-disciple sangha. The fact that there are a lesser or greater number of distinctions between one instance and another instance is solely a reflection of the original vows of each respective buddha.

What then is it that is meant here by "complete presence"? This is to say that the Tathāgata's *śrāvaka*-disciple congregation is perfectly complete as regards observance of the moral prohibitions and accomplishment in the *dhyāna* absorptions, wisdom, liberation, and the knowledge and vision of liberation. They are identical in their equality, are pure, and are all possessed of sharp faculties. They benefit the bodhisattvas and are possessed of physical forms that are dignified and pure.

"Completeness in the observance of the moral prohibitions" means that they have abandoned any killing of beings, stealing, sexual misconduct, false speech, divisive speech, harsh speech, frivolous or lewd speech, consumption of intoxicants, wrong livelihood, and all of the other sorts of evil dharmas. Moreover, they have abandoned whatever is restricted by the *vinaya* and they are also able to completely develop their observance of the moral precepts so that is free of the contaminants.

As for "completeness in the *dhyāna* absorptions," this refers to such accomplishments as acquisition of the four *dhyānas*, the four immeasurable minds, the four formless absorptions, the eight liberations (*aṣṭā vimokṣa*),[89] [otherwise known as] the eight abandonments, the eight bases of mastery (*abhibhvāyatana*), and the ten universal meditation bases (*daśa kṛtsnāyatana*)[90]as well as the acquisition of the *dhyāna* absorptions free of the contaminants.

"Completeness in wisdom" refers to bringing the four types of wisdom to completion: that which arises through extensive learning; that which arises through meditative reflection; that which arises through cultivation and accumulation; and that which arises as the result of the karmic causes and conditions of previous lives.

"Completeness in liberation" refers to having gained liberation from all afflictions. Additionally, it refers to becoming liberated from all the hindrances.

In "completeness in the knowledge and vision of liberation," "knowledge" refers to the cognitive awareness of phenomena whereas "vision" refers to a complete understanding of those matters. Thus, in one's liberation, one gains a complete and utter knowledge and vision that is entirely free of doubts. Then again, one may also explain that "knowledge" refers to the knowledge of the destruction [of the contaminants], whereas "vision" refers to the seeing of the four truths.

As for "identical in their equality," all those who attain the fruit of a stream enterer are entirely equal. So too, all those [who attain the higher fruits of the path] on up to arhatship are just the same.

"Purity" refers to having completely developed the three types of purity, namely purity in physical actions, purity in verbal actions, and purity in mental actions.

"Sharp wisdom"[91] means that, when one merely hears a few words, one is able to gain a vast understanding through which one penetrates a meaning's import. Thus one is able to provide extensive presentations of concise [teachings], is able to provide concise presentations of extensive [teachings], and in an instance where the principle is subtle and obscure, one is able to render it easily understandable.

As for "benefiting the bodhisattvas," they remain mindful of the bodhisattvas, including even those who have only initially produced the resolve, and have no slighting arrogance toward them, this because they have a deep affection and respect for them. They always provide instruction in [the distinctions] between good and bad and explain for them the causes and conditions of the Buddha path's skillful means.

As for their having "physical forms that are dignified and pure," this means their bodies have an especially fine presence and their appearance is complete with the major marks and secondary characteristic signs. Consequently, those who observe them are filled with delight in the same way as when they behold a *pratyekabuddha*. Thus, in their walking forth, their advancing, stopping, sitting, lying down, sleeping, awakening, partaking of food and drink, bathing, donning the robe, and holding the bowl, their awesome deportment accords with the correct sequence and remains free of any defects or omissions. Thus, when a person observes this, his mind is then purified.

As for "completeness of the bodhi tree," the rest of all the great trees there such as the *sala* tree, the *tāla* tree, the *tiluojia* tree, the *duomoluo* tree, the *poqiuluo* tree, the *campaka* tree, the *aśoka* tree, the *suohejialuo* tree, the *fennamo* tree, the *namo* tree, the *nāga* tree, the *śirīṣa* tree, the *niequtuo* tree, the *āśvattha*, the *bolecha* tree, the *udumbara* tree, and so forth—no matter which of these great trees we speak of, when growing out on level land, they are tall, broad, perfect in the growth of their roots, trunk, branches, and leaves, and are perfect in their luster and luxuriant fullness. The coloration of their blossoms is fresh, bright, and free of any defects from damage.

His [bodhi] tree rises to a height of fifty *yojanas*. It is perfectly erect and level. It is lustrously smooth and free of any contorted branches. Its bark is fine and soft and its coloration is white, fresh, and clean. It has no thorns and is free of any internal decay. Additionally, it is not hollow and is free of any injury or gnawing by insects. Its roots are deep in their penetration, solid, and orderly in their interwoven plaiting. Its flowers gracefully adorn it, just as when one is graced by a floral garland and gemstone necklace.

Its branches and leaves are luxuriant and full in their growth and are comparable to a circular pavilion in their shape. It is orderly and sequential in the way that it spreads out and, in its gracefulness, it is more distinctive than anything made by man. Its leaves are green and fresh and comparable in color to jewels. Its branches are free of any distorting crisscrossing, yellowness caused by withering, or dried-out leaves, and it has no insects such as moths,[92] mosquitoes, midges, horseflies, or ants.

The ground below is pure and spread with golden sands. It emanates all manner of illumination and sends forth shining brightness all around. Sandalwood-scented waters are sprinkled over its grounds that are themselves level, soft, cool, and pleasing. Fine powders of ox-head sandalwood are spread over it. The devas always rain down *māndārava* flowers. The fragrance of burning aloe wood incense wafts all about. Five-colored celestial banners are suspended at intermittent intervals. A subtle breeze gently moves them, causing them to ripple and flutter in response to it. Birds and animals quietly roam about off to the sides, making no sounds.

To its left and right, devas are always sprinkling down flowers of the many marvelous and varied colors that naturally intersperse as they descend like strands of jewels like the golden flower garlands worn on the bodies of the dragons. A jeweled net hangs down from the larger branches on all four sides. The many sorts of jewels adorn it, making it appear like a purple-golden mountain. It stands there in awe-inspiring grandeur, distinctive and sublime, like Indra's canopy.

This is an effect brought about as a result of the Bodhisattva's hundreds of thousands of myriads of *koṭis* of *asaṃkhyeyas* of kalpas of cultivating and accumulating meritorious qualities deriving from the practice of goodness. The many different sorts of marvelous jewels have been used to create the appearance of the king of lions. On the crowns of four lions, there rests a broad and grand jeweled platform cushioned with celestial tapestries. The devas from the Heaven of the Four Heavenly Kings, the Trāyastriṃśa heaven, the Yāma Heaven, the Tuṣita Heaven, the Nirmāṇarati Heaven, the Paranirmita Vaśavartin Heaven, the Brahma Heaven, and so forth all the way up to the Akaniṣṭha Heaven—all of them appear riding along in their palaces composed of the many sorts of precious jewels consisting of such jewels as lapis lazuli, *musāra-galva*, carnelian, *mahānīla* sapphires, *indranīla* sapphires, vajra, and *sphaṭika*. They emanate an incomparable colored light that illuminates even to a great distance. They all assemble at the bejeweled tree, circumambulating it and presenting offerings.

Additionally, in accordance with their original vows, all of the congregations of bodhisattvas from the countless worlds throughout the ten directions, having prepared in abundance all of the various sorts of offerings, rain down the many sorts of precious gifts, including flowers, incense, banners, canopies, the many different sorts of music, and other such offerings. This is what is meant by "completeness of the bodhi tree."

As for "a world that is adorned," the bodhisattvas contemplate the most marvelous among all the pure lands throughout the ten directions and then make a great vow, "The land that I acquire through the cultivation of meritorious qualities shall even be superior to these. It shall be foremost and incomparable."

As for "the beings being well-endowed with good fortune,"[93] the beings there are fine in appearance, free of any sort of physical afflictions or calamities, and are not troubled by aging and sickness. Their life spans extend for a measureless number of *asaṃkhyeyas* of kalpas. In all cases, they are born there transformationally. Their bodies are free of the many sorts of defilement. They are possessed of the thirty-two major marks. They radiate measureless light. Their afflictions are merely subtle and slight and they are easily taught and led across to liberation.

As for being "complete in those capable of achieving liberation," during but a single sitting in which he teaches the Dharma, beings as numerous as the sands of the Ganges all simultaneously attain liberation. [This may be contrasted with the circumstance of] other buddhas for whom, in a single instance of proclaiming Dharma, they bring one or two people across to liberation. These beings have all planted roots of goodness in previous lives. Their fetters are but slight and scant, so much so that, when hearing an explanation, they awaken immediately.

As for "the gathering of an immense congregation," there are buddhas whose great assemblies fill up an area one *yojana* across, or in some cases, ten *yojanas*, or in some cases a hundred thousand myriads of *koṭis* of *yojanas*, or in some cases, they fill the worlds of an entire great trichiliocosm.

As for the "immense congregation" referred to here, it is one equal in scope to world systems as numerous as the sands in all the Ganges Rivers throughout the ten directions. This is what constitutes "an immense congregation." Moreover, the people in his assembly are only those who have accumulated merit. Also included in the congregations are all the devas, the beings in the eight divisions [of ghosts and spirits], and the bodhisattvas from the first through the tenth grounds. They have all come together there, with the sole exception of the buddhas themselves.

"Completeness in the powers of a buddha" refers to the forty dharmas exclusive to the buddhas that all buddhas practice. For each and every one of these dharmas, the places in which they have been practiced are all measurelessly and boundlessly many. This is the seventh vow.

H. The Eighth Bodhisattva Vow

Next, we have:

> When joining together with others in doing any single endeavor,
> I vow that there will be no enmity or contentiousness.[94]

In all merit-generating deeds a bodhisattva does, whether it be through the practice of giving, upholding moral precepts, patience, vigor, *dhyāna* meditation, or wisdom, whether it be through the four bases of meritorious qualities consisting of truth, relinquishment, quiescence, and wisdom, or whether it be through other endeavors in which, due to one's great vows, one pursues the attainment of buddhahood, one should make this vow: "In circumstances where others join with me in practicing the six *pāramitās* or the four bases of meritorious qualities, doing so with the aim of attaining buddhahood, I vow that I shall not create enmity or contention with others over the causes and conditions involved in such creation of merit." Why? The wise say that, among those jointly carrying out a single endeavor, the signs of enmity may develop. So, too, these sorts of circumstances appear in the world even now. It is in order to do away with such transgressions as these that one brings forth this great vow. This is the eighth vow.

I. The Ninth Bodhisattva Vow

Next, we have:

> I vow to practice the bodhisattva path
> and set turning the irreversible wheel,
> thereby enabling the dispelling of all afflictions
> and the entry into faith that is pure.[95]

"The wheel" is a reference to the wheel of Dharma. That it is "irreversible" signifies that there is no one who is able to interfere [with its continuing to turn]. The bodhisattva should bring forth a vow such as this: "I shall practice the path just as it has been taught and will certainly set turning the irreversible wheel of Dharma. I shall turn this wheel of Dharma to dispel beings' afflictions born of the three poisons, to cause them to turn away from *saṃsāra* and enter the domain of the Buddha, the Dharma, and the Sangha, and to cause them to accomplish their own purification through [the teaching of] suffering, origination, cessation, and the path." This is the ninth vow.

J. The Tenth Bodhisattva Vow

Next, we have:

> I vow that, in all worlds,
> I shall manifest the realization of bodhi.[96]

In whichever worlds that are appropriate as places for the appearance of the works of a buddha, one manifests the realization of *anuttarasamyaksaṃbodhi* in all of them, doing so for the sake of bringing peace and happiness to all beings and for the sake of leading all beings to nirvāṇa. It is due to the greatness of *anuttarasamyaksaṃbodhi* that its attainment is the only one [of a buddha's deeds] that is mentioned here. As for all the other deeds including entering the womb, taking birth, growing up in the home, leaving behind the home life, taking on the moral precepts, taking up the practice of austerities, conquering Māra's demon hordes, accepting the entreaties of the Brahma Heaven King, turning the wheel of Dharma, assembling an immense congregation, liberating beings on a vast scale, displaying great spiritual powers, and manifesting the great passing into final nirvāṇa, one should accomplish all such deeds as these in this same way.

One knows from this that, where one possesses immeasurable powers such as these whereby one is capable of benefiting an incalculable and boundless number of beings, one should not merely manifest the realization of buddhahood in but a single land. There are those who state that, within a single buddha's domain consisting of the four continents, it is the entirety of the continent of Jambudvīpa that constitutes that single buddha's buddha land and anything beyond that is a matter comprehensible only to a buddha. However, this is not actually the case. This is the tenth vow.

K. The Infinitely Vast Scope and Duration of the Ten Bodhisattva Vows

Next, we have:

> For all such bodhisattvas as these,
> it is the ten great vows that are foremost.
> They are as vast as empty space
> and exhaust even the bounds of the future.
> This extends to all of their other measurelessly many vows
> as well as to their distinguishing and explanation of each of them.

"Vows" is a reference to what the mind wishes for and what it is determined to definitely achieve. "Ten" is a reference to the existence of ten such gateways.

"They are as vast as empty space" refers to the fact that the regions taken as the objective focus of the vows are equal in their extensiveness to all of empty space. The scope of the vows is so very vast as this.

"Exhausting even the bounds of the future" means that the length of time during which these vows shall abide will exhaust the bounds of the future births and deaths of all beings.

There are others who claim that *anuttarasamyaksaṃbodhi* itself is what sets the bounds of future births and deaths. Or they may assert that, when buddhas enter the nirvāṇa without residue, it is this that constitutes the bounds of future births and death. Or they may say that, although the bodhisattva's vows may be endless, in fact, they end with the realization of buddhahood.

All of the great bodhisattvas throughout the worlds of the ten directions have made these vows. "All of their other measurelessly many vows" refers to the fact that, because all bodhisattvas perfect measurelessly many rare meritorious qualities, one could never exhaustively describe all the vows that they have made.

Next, we have:

> As the bodhisattva makes ten great vows such as these,
> [he does so in ways by which] they are ultimately enduring.

These ten great vows have ten ways in which they are caused to be ultimately enduring.

Question: What then are those ten ways?

Response:

> They are made until the end of realms of beings, of realms of worlds,
> of realms of empty space, of the Dharma realm,
> of the realm of nirvāṇa, of the realms in which buddhas are born,
> of the realms of all buddhas' knowledge—[97]
>
> Until the end of anything taken as an object of mind,
> the end of the knowledge associated with buddhas' range of actions,
> and of the permutations of their knowledge of worldly dharmas.

These are the ten ways they are ultimately enduring. [Hence these vows are made]:

First, until the end of the realms of beings;
Second, until the end of the realms of worlds;
Third, until the end of the realms of empty space;
Fourth, until the end of the Dharma realm;
Fifth, until the end of the realm of nirvāṇa;
Sixth, until the end of the realms in which buddhas are born;
Seventh, until the end of the realms of all buddhas' knowledge;
Eighth, until the end of everything that can be taken as an object of mind;
Ninth, until the end of the knowledge associated with all buddhas' range of actions;[98]
And tenth, until the end of the permutations of their knowledge of worldly dharmas.

These are the ten ways they are ultimately enduring.

Question: You speak of an ultimate "end." What is it that constitutes an ultimate "end"? You should distinguish what is meant by this.

Response:

> If the realms of beings were to come to an end,
> only then would my vows also come to an end.
> Just as it is with the ending of beings and the other things,
> so too it is with the ending of these vows.
> The meaning of "end" then is that there is no end,
> hence my roots of goodness are endless.

As for "if the realms of beings were to come to an end," this is to say: "If all beings became entirely extinct, my vows should then also cease." Thus, if even the realms of the world were to come to an end, if even the realms of empty space were to come to an end, if even the Dharma realm were to come to an end, if even the realm of nirvāṇa were to come to an end, if even the realms in which buddhas are born were to come to an end, if even the realms of all buddhas'[99] knowledge were to come to an end, if even the realms of conditions taken by all beings as objects of mind were to come to an end, if even the realms of the knowledge that fathoms the Buddha's Dharma were to come to an end, and if even the permutations of worlds, permutations of dharmas, and permutations of knowledge were to come to an end, then and only then would my ten vows finally come to an end.

However, as a matter of fact, these ten phenomena consisting of "the realms of beings" and so forth will never come to an end. Hence my merit and roots of goodness will never come to an end and will never cease.

As for the meaning of "will not cease," it refers to never ceasing even after a period of time that is immeasurable, boundless, inconceivable, and beyond calculation. It is because, throughout the ten directions, worlds of the sort that exist in this great trichiliocosm are measurelessly, boundlessly, and incalculably numerous that worlds are said to be boundless. It is because the beings within all of these worlds' three realms of existence and six rebirth destinies are boundlessly numerous that the realms of beings are said to be boundlessly many.

It is because the realms of the two types of empty space both within and beyond all these worlds are boundless that we refer here to the boundlessness of the realms of empty space.

It is because of the boundlessness of the conditioned dharmas contained within all these worlds' desire realms, form realms, formless realms, and uncontaminated realms that we refer here to the boundlessness of the Dharma realm.

Even if all beings attained nirvāṇa, still the realm of nirvāṇa would neither increase nor decrease. Therefore the realm of nirvāṇa is boundless.

Because the buddhas of the past throughout the ten directions were immeasurably and boundlessly many, because the buddhas of the present throughout the ten directions are immeasurably and boundlessly many, and because the buddhas of the future throughout the ten directions will be immeasurably and boundlessly many, the realms into which buddhas are born are therefore boundlessly many.

Because the buddhas' knowledge is measurelessly vast, indescribable, immeasurable, unequaled, equal to the unequaled, unrivaled, and incomparable, therefore the realms of all buddhas' knowledge are also measureless and boundless. This is just as stated by the Buddha when he told Ānanda, "The knowledge possessed by these *śrāvaka* disciples and by all buddhas is measureless." Therefore the realms of the knowledge possessed by the Buddhas are measureless and boundless.

The mind states produced by each and every one of all beings throughout the past were measurelessly and boundlessly many. All of these mind states had corresponding objective conditions serving as the bases of their arising. So too shall this be so of the mind states produced by the beings of the future. So too, the mind states produced by all the beings of the present era are measurelessly and boundlessly many. In every case, they have corresponding objective conditions that serve as the bases of their arising. Therefore the objective conditions taken as the object of those mind states are themselves also measurelessly and boundlessly many.

As for the powers of all buddhas, briefly speaking, they are manifested in the forty dharmas exclusive [to buddhas]. As for these forty exclusive dharmas, the range of implementation of each and every one of these dharmas is measureless and boundless. Because their range of implementation is measureless and boundless, so too then, their corresponding knowledge is also measureless and boundless. It is for this reason that it is stated here that the knowledge associated with the range of all buddhas' actions is itself measureless and boundless.

As for the permutations of worlds, the permutations of dharmas, and the permutations of wisdom, this "permutation" is a designation used to refer to the fact that each of these dharmas has transformational permutations.

As for the reference here to "worlds," worlds are of two types, namely the world that consists of lands and the world that consists of beings themselves. We speak here of the world of beings wherein all buddhas as well as all bodhisattvas guide beings by using the power of a measureless and boundless number of skillful means.

"Permutations of dharmas" refers to the use of measurelessly and boundlessly voluminous roots of goodness and merit in gathering together and acquiring all dharmas of a buddha.

As for "permutations of knowledge," one uses an incalculable number of good dharmas associated with the six *pāramitās* and ten grounds to gather together and acquire the knowledge of a buddha. Hence the permutations of knowledge are boundless. Because these three factors [of worlds, dharmas, and knowledge] are the same in their involvement of transformational permutations, they are therefore gathered together in a single pledge.

Because each and every [one of the ten great] vows of this bodhisattva is firm and solid, he establishes [for each of them] these ten pledges of endless duration, declaring those vows to be as spatially vast as empty space and as long-enduring as the bounds of future time. It is in this way that, using these condensed discussions and extensive discussions, we come to the end of this explanation of these ten vows' ultimately enduring duration.

The End of Chapter Five

Chapter 6
On Producing the Bodhi Resolve

VI. Chapter Six: On Producing the Bodhi Resolve

A. The Seven Bases for Producing the Bodhi Resolve

Question: The initial production of the resolve [to attain buddhahood] is the root of all vows. What then is meant by this "initial production of resolve"?

Response:

The initial resolve to attain bodhi
May involve three reasons or four reasons.

When beings initially produce the resolve to attain bodhi, this may find its origin in [one of] three reasons or else in [one of] four reasons.[100] Thus, when one combines them, there are a total of seven causes and conditions associated with producing the resolve to attain *anuttarasamyaksaṃbodhi.*

Question: What then are those seven?

Response:

In the case of the first, a Tathāgata
may influence one to bring forth the resolve to attain bodhi.
As for the second, observing that the Dharma is about to be destroyed,
one produces the resolve in order to guard and protect it.

In the case of the third, with respect to beings,
one feels great compassion for them and thus produces the resolve.
As for the fourth, there may be a bodhisattva
who instructs one in the production of the resolve to attain bodhi.

In the case of the fifth, one may observe the conduct of a bodhisattva
and also then consequently produce the resolve.
Or, alternatively, following upon an act of giving,
one may produce the resolve to attain bodhi [based on that].

Or else, having observed the marks of a buddha's body,
one may feel delight and then proceed to produce the resolve.
Thus it may be due to [any one of] these seven causes and conditions
that one produces the resolve to attain bodhi.

1. The Influence of a Buddha

In the case where a buddha "influences one to bring forth the resolve," a buddha uses the buddha eye to observe beings. He may then realize that a person's roots of goodness have become so completely ripe that he is capable of taking on this endeavor and that he will be able to realize *anuttarasamyaksaṃbodhi*. For a person such as this, the Buddha instructs him and enjoins him to bring forth the resolve, saying to him, "Son of good family, come forth. You may now bring forth that resolve by which you should bring suffering and afflicted beings across to liberation."

2. The Motivation to Protect the Dharma

Or then again there may be a person born into a dreadful era who, on observing that the Dharma is on the verge of destruction, then, for the sake of protecting it, brings forth the resolve, reflecting as follows:

> Alas! From a time in the past an immeasurable and boundless number of hundreds of thousands of myriads of *kotīs* of *asaṃkhyeyas* of kalpas ago on forth to the very present, there has only been:
>
> A single person;
>
> On two bases;
>
> Whose practice has transcended the three realms;
>
> Who has served as the great guide to the four truths of the Āryas;
>
> Who is that one who has known the fivefold treasury of Dharma;
>
> Who has gained liberation from the six destinies of rebirth;
>
> Who has taken possession of the great jewel of the seven kinds of right Dharma;[101]
>
> Who has deeply practiced the eight liberations;
>
> Who uses the nine categories of sutra text in teaching;
>
> Who has taken possession of the ten great powers;
>
> Who has described the eleven kinds of meritorious qualities;[102]
>
> Who has skillfully set forth the continuous cycle of the twelve causes and conditions;
>
> Who has explained the thirteen dharmas assisting realization of the path of the Āryas;
>
> Who has taken possession of the great jewel of the fourteen factors fundamental to awakening;
>
> Who has dispelled the fifteen kinds of craving;
>
> Who has both attained the realization of the sixteen mind states involved in unimpeded liberation and has also extricated beings from the sixteen kinds of hells;

Who has also mastered the seventeen physical dharmas;[103]
Who has completely perfected the eighteen dharmas exclusive [to the buddhas];
Who has skillfully distinguished the nineteen stations of persons who have gained the fruits [of the path];
And who has well known and distinguished the twenty kinds of faculties [consisting of five each] for those still in training, the arhats, the *pratyekabuddhas,* and all buddhas.[104]

This greatly compassionate one, this great lord of generals, this great lord of assemblies, this great king of physicians, this great guide, this great captain of the ship—only after a very long time then acquired this Dharma, and only after cultivating those ascetic practices so difficult to practice then acquired this Dharma. But now, it is on the verge of destruction. I should bring forth the resolve to attain *anuttarasamyaksaṃbodhi,* should plant thick roots of goodness, should thus attain buddhahood, and thus should cause the Dharma to abide for a long time, enduring even for countless *asaṃkhyeyas* of kalpas.

[Of this same sort are those who], while cultivating the bodhisattva path, strive with diligence and vigor to guard and uphold the Dharma of the incalculably many buddhas.

3. Compassion for the Suffering of Beings

Or, alternatively, there may be those who observe:

That beings, beset as they are by bitter afflictions, are pitiful;
That they have no one to rescue them, no refuge, and no one on whom they can rely;
That they flow along in *saṃsāra*'s dangerous and difficult wretched destinies;
That they are afflicted by great enemies, by all manner of fearsome insects and animals, by the terrors involved in births and deaths, by all manner of fearsome ghosts, and so forth;
That they are always beset by the piercing thorns of worry, sadness, pain, and distress;
That they fall into the deep pit of [sufferings associated with] separation from those they love and encounters with those they detest;
That the waters of joy and happiness are only very rarely encountered;
That they travel alone in the midst of intense cold and intense heat;
That they are stranded without shade in the vast wilderness and find it difficult to make their way across to liberation;
That beings in the midst of all this are possessed by every sort of terror and fear;

> And that they have no one to rescue them, protect them, or serve as guides for them.

Having observed that beings have entered in this manner into the dangerous and wretched destinies involved in *saṃsāra,* that they undergo all manner of suffering and affliction, such a person, because of the great compassion, may then bring forth the resolve to attain *anuttarasamyaksaṃbodhi* and may then proclaim, "I shall become a rescuer for those who have no one to rescue them. I shall become a refuge for those who have no refuge. I will become a support for those with no one to rely on.

Once I have gained liberation, I shall strive to liberate other beings as well. Once I have gained liberation, I shall then also liberate these beings. Once I have gained peace, I shall also bring peace to other beings."

4. The Instructive Influence of a Bodhisattva

Then again, there are also those persons who need only hear of this matter from others and then, due to thoughts of resolute belief[105] and other such factors, they produce the resolve to achieve the unsurpassed enlightenment and reflect:

> By always[106] and ceaselessly cultivating wholesome dharmas, I may reach the stage of certainty and realize the unproduced-dharmas patience.[107] Due to accumulating all manner of merit and due to the ripening of roots of goodness, I may then encounter buddhas or may encounter great bodhisattvas who are able to know the relative acuity or dullness of beings' faculties, are able to know from root to branch their deep-seated inclinations and the differences in their individual natures and aspirations, who thoroughly understand the use of skillful means, and who are under the protection of the *prajñāpāramitā.*
>
> Those [beings such as these] who are able to carry on the works of a buddha will realize that I have brought forth the vow. Then, because of the ripening of my roots of goodness, they may influence me to abide in the stage of certainty or the unproduced-dharmas patience.[108]

These bodhisattvas [to which he refers] are those who abide on the seventh, eighth, ninth, or tenth bodhisattva grounds. They are those who, like a buddha, thoroughly know the strengths of beings' minds and thereby teach them to produce the resolve.

5. The Aspiration to Emulate the Conduct of Bodhisattvas

But it is not solely through their possession of the power of resolute belief and other such factors that they are taught to bring forth the resolve. In addition, there are those persons who [bring forth the resolve] by observing other bodhisattvas practicing the path, cultivating all manner of roots of goodness, proceeding under the protection of the great compassion, and perfecting skillful means as they teach and transform beings. [They observe that]:

They accomplish an abundance of beneficial deeds without indulging any cherishing regard for their own bodies or lives;
They develop vastly extensive learning;
They become especially distinctive people in the world;
They become the most emblematically superior people;
They serve as a source of shade for weary and suffering beings;
They become securely established in the practices of giving, moral virtue, patience, vigor, *dhyāna* concentration, wisdom, a sense of shame, a dread of blame, straightforwardness in character, mental pliancy, and congeniality;
Their minds are pure;
And they deeply delight in good dharmas.

By observing persons such as these, they are inspired to reflect, "I too should practice what these people practice. I too should cultivate the vows and conduct that they cultivate. I should bring forth this vow for the sake of acquiring this Dharma." Having had this thought, they then bring forth the resolve to attain the unsurpassable enlightenment.

6. Inspiration Provoked by an Act of Giving

Yet again, there are those persons who engage in acts of great giving, acts whereby they present gifts to a buddha or to his sangha, or acts whereby they simply offer food, drink, or robes to a buddha. Due to such acts of giving, these persons may then call to mind those bodhisattvas of the past who were able to practice giving, bodhisattvas such as Velāma,[109] Viśvantara,[110] Sarvadā, and King Śibi. [Having called them to mind], they may then immediately bring forth the resolve to attain bodhi and then dedicate the merit from their act of giving to [their future attainment of] *anuttarasamyaksaṃbodhi.*

7. Inspiration Arising from Observing a Buddha's Physical Marks

Yet again, there may be those persons who directly observe or merely hear about the thirty-two marks of the Buddhas, namely such marks as:

The evenness of their soles;
The wheel-marks on the hands and feet;
The webbing at the roots of their fingers;
The softness of their hands and feet;
The fullness in seven places;

The slenderness and length of their fingers;
The breadth of their heels;
The straightness of their bodies;
Their high and even ankles;
The vertical swirling shape of their bodily hairs;
Their thighs resembling those of the *aiṇeya* antelope;
Their arms whereby the fingers reach even below the knees;
Their genital ensheathment like that of a stallion;
The gold color of their bodies;
The softness and thinness of their skin;
The placement of but a single hair in each and every pore;
Their white "hair mark" between their brows;
Their lion-like bodies;
Their round and large shoulders;
The fullness of the axillary region;
Their ability to distinctly know sublime flavors;
Their physical girth like that of the *nyagrodha* tree;
Their fleshy prominence atop the crown of their heads;
Their vast and long tongues;
Their voices possessed of the sound like Brahmā;
Their lion-like jaws;
Their forty teeth which are straight, white, and closely set;
Their blue eyes;
And their eyelashes like those of the king of the bulls.

[Having observed or heard of these marks of a buddha's body], they may then become delighted and think, "I too should strive to gain these physical marks and I too should strive to gain those dharmas gained by those who possess such physical marks." They may then immediately produce the resolve to attain *anuttarasamyaksaṃbodhi*.

Thus it may be because of any of these seven causes and conditions that one then brings forth the resolve to attain bodhi.

B. The Relative Probability of Success in these Seven Bases

Question: You stated that there are these seven reasons for a person's generation of the bodhisattva's resolve. Will they all result in success or is it instead the case that some will result in success but others will not?

Response: It is not necessarily the case that they will all result in success. They may result in success or they may not result in success.

Question: If that is so, you should explain this.

Response:

Of the seven reasons for generating the resolve,
where the Buddha has instructed one to produce the resolve,
where one produces the resolve in order to protect the Dharma,
and where one produces the resolve out of pity for others—

those who have the three motivations such as these
will certainly find success in this.
As for the other four types of motivation,
It is not certain that they will all be successful in this.

Among these seven reasons for generating the resolve, in a circumstance where a buddha has contemplated one's origins and then instructed one in a way that one is caused to produce the resolve, that will certainly result in success. This is because [buddhas] do not speak in vain.

So too is this true of those instances where [one's production of the resolve occurs] because one reveres and esteems the Dharma of the buddhas and one is motivated by the determination to protect it.

So too is this true of those instances where [one's production of the resolve occurs] because one has the mind of great compassion for beings. These three reasons for generating the resolve will definitely result in success, for the roots [of such resolve] are deeply anchored.

In instances where other bodhisattvas have provided instruction which has influenced one to produce the resolve, in instances where one has observed the practices of bodhisattvas and therefore produced the resolve, in instances where one has produced the resolve due to an act of great giving, and in instances where one has produced the resolve because of seeing or hearing about the physical marks of a buddha—for the most part, these four instances of generating the resolve do not result in success, though it may be that there are still those that do succeed. [When these do not result in success], it is due to the relative weakness of the foundations [of their practice].

The End of Chapter Six

Chapter 7
On Training the Mind

VII. Chapter Seven: On Training the Mind

A. Q: What Are the Bases of Success or Failure of One's Bodhi Resolve?

Question: According to the explanation in the previous chapter, there are three cases where production of the resolve [to attain buddhahood] will definitely result in success whereas, in the remaining four cases, it is not necessarily the case that they will result in success. Why is it that some of these result in success and why is it that some of these do not result in success?

B. A: Practicing Dharmas Resulting in Failure Entails Loss

Response: If a bodhisattva has brought forth the bodhi resolve yet practices dharmas conducing to loss of the bodhi resolve, this will not meet with success. If he practices the dharmas not conducing to losing bodhi resolve, this will certainly bring success. Hence this verse says:

> The bodhisattva should abandon
> any dharmas conducing to loss of the bodhi resolve
> and should single-mindedly cultivate
> those dharmas that prevent loss of bodhi.

By "abandonment," it is meant that one entirely extinguishes those dharmas that are bad and thus prevents them from entering one's mind. If they do enter, one swiftly extinguishes them. "Loss" refers to the forgetting, either in the present life or the future life, of one's resolve to realize bodhi whereupon one would no longer pursue it through cultivation of the practices. One must leave such dharmas far behind. If one is to succeed in avoiding losing those dharmas facilitating the realization of bodhi, and if one is to avoid forgetting the resolve to realize bodhi, then one should always pursue single-minded and diligent practice.

1. Q: Which Dharmas Result in Loss

Question: Which sorts of dharmas result in loss of the bodhi resolve?

2. A: There Are Four Such Dharmas (Verse)

Response:

> The first is failing to revere and esteem the Dharma.
> The second is possessing an arrogant mind.
> The third is false speech or being untruthful.
> The fourth is failing to revere spiritual guides.

Those possessed of any of these four dharmas—whether it be at the time of death in this present lifetime or whether it be in a subsequent lifetime—they will forget and lose their bodhi resolve. Thus they will become unable to realize, "I am a bodhisattva," and so they will no longer bring forth the vow. Thus the dharmas of bodhisattva practice will no longer manifest before them.

As for "failing to revere and esteem the Dharma," "Dharma" refers to the superior, middling, and lesser vehicles set forth by all buddhas. To take up what is essential here, it refers to all of those dharmas that all buddhas, all *tathāgatas,* have used in providing instruction. If, with respect to these dharmas, one does not revere them, does not make offerings to them, does not honor and esteem them, does not praise them, does not produce thoughts regarding them as rare, does not think of them as difficult to encounter, does not think of them as precious objects, or does not think of them as the means for the fulfillment of one's aspirations, these very dharmas [of disesteem] can bring about the loss of one's bodhi resolve.

As for an "arrogant mind," this refers to elevating the status of one's own mind and then claiming to have gained what one has not yet gained and claiming to have realized what one has not yet realized, claiming for instance that one has realized emptiness, signlessness, or wishlessness or the unproduced-dharmas patience, the six *pāramitās,* the ten bodhisattva grounds or any of the other dharmas that arise through cultivation. With regard to these dharmas, even though one has not yet attained them, one nonetheless claims to have attained them.

As for "false speech," there are instances that constitute *duṣkṛta* offenses, those that constitute *pāyantika* offenses, those that constitute *sthūlātyaya* offenses, those that constitute *saṃghāvaśeṣa* offenses, and those that constitute *pārājika* offenses.[111] There may be others who claim that there exists a sixth category of false speech. This refers to when one brings forth repentance with a mind that itself involves an instance of false speech.

Among the above five categories of false speech, the first is the lightest form of offense whereas the last is the most severe form of offense. The sixth category is the lightest of them all.

In the case of the *pārājika* offense, this is an instance where one does not in fact possess any of the superhuman dharmas but nonetheless tends to use various means to create the impression that he possesses such qualities, whether this impression be created through what is spoken by the mouth or what is signaled by the body.

As for the *saṃghāvaśeṣa* offense, this refers to an instance where, with respect to any one of those four circumstances [constituting *pārājika* offenses] for a bhikshu, whether through spoken words or physical signs, [a fully-ordained bhikshu or bhikshuni] commits a slander [of another bhikshu or bhikshuni] by [testifying to the existence of] any one of the bases [for a *pārājika* offense] when in fact there was no such basis [for such an accusation].

As for the *sthūlātyaya* offense, this refers to an instance where, wishing to slander someone, one brings forth either a plausible or baseless allegation, but that allegation is then not established [as truthful].[112]

As for the *pāyantika* offense, this refers to when one commits a slander in a circumstance involving a baseless *saṃghāvaśeṣa* allegation.

As for the *duṣkṛta* offense, this refers to any instance of false speech not subsumed among the other four categories of false speech.

As for those instances [of abandonment] where one is able to extinguish [bad dharmas] from one's own mind,[113] this refers to when, at the time when the precepts are being recited [each half month], one realizes that one has committed a minor offense but cannot bring oneself to declare it to anyone else, yet one nonetheless immediately repents of it in one's own mind.

Question: These types of "false speech" are exclusive to bhikshus and irrelevant to laity and yet this treatise is ostensibly intended to address both laity and monastics.

Response: Whenever anyone knows that some circumstance is actually this particular way and yet speaks of it in a manner that differs from what one knows to be the case, that is what we refer to in this treatise as generally constituting a lie. Due to distinctions in types of beings, distinctions in circumstances, distinctions in the time of commission, distinctions in five classes of transgressions, and distinctions in dwelling place, the transgression may be either minor or grave.

Also, although a given transgression may be relatively minor, when it is repeated for a long time, then it qualifies as grave and may cause one to lose the resolve to attain bodhi.

"Distinctions in types of beings" refers to instances involving lying transgressions committed by those with wrong views who have severed their roots of goodness or lying transgressions committed by others who are beset with heavy afflictions. These are grave transgressions.

"Distinctions in circumstances" refers for instance to untruthful claims to possess superhuman attainments and to those that create a schism in the monastic sangha.

As for "distinctions in the time of commission" if someone tells a lie when they are monastic, this is a grave transgression.

"Distinctions in five classes of transgressions," if one commits either a *pārājika* or a *saṃghāvaśeṣa* offense, these are grave transgressions.[114]

Distinctions according to the location: Lies committed by monastics at times of certification are grave transgressions.[115]

"Failing to revere good spiritual guides" refers to failing to have thoughts of reverence and awe toward them.

If one often engages in these four [behavioral] dharmas, then one is bound to lose the resolve to attain bodhi.

3. Q: Are There Only These Four or Are There More?

Question: Are there only these four dharmas by which one is able to lose the bodhi resolve or are there additional dharmas leading to the same outcome?

4. A: There Are Numerous Additional Cases (A Series of Verses)

Response:

If one is stingy with the most essential dharmas,
if one covets and delights in the Small Vehicle,
if one slanders bodhisattvas,
or if one slights those who practice *dhyāna* meditation—

"If one is stingy with the most essential dharmas," refers to circumstances where a teacher [of Dharma] understands an extremely profound and rare principle beneficial to many, yet, because he covets offerings and fears others might equal him [in his understanding of Dharma], he keeps that teaching secret, cherishes it as his own, and refrains from explaining it to others.

"If one covets and delights in the Small Vehicle" refers to circumstances in which, because one fails to realize and appreciate the flavor of the Great Vehicle, one instead covets and delights in [the paths taught by followers of] the Two Vehicles.[116]

In "if one slanders bodhisattvas," "slander" refers to [maliciously] ascribing an offense to one who has not committed an offense. The meaning of "bodhisattva" has already been explained. This refers to an instance where there has been no offense at all and yet this person falsely claims [that a particular bodhisattva] has committed an offense.

If [some bodhisattva practitioner] truly *has* committed a transgression and one then discusses the matter with others, although this itself constitutes a transgression, it is relatively light compared to the former case. What is the basis for this? The scriptures state that, whether or not any bodhisattva has committed a karmic offense, one should not discuss the matter in any case.

As for "if one slights those who practice *dhyāna* meditation," this refers to a case where, for the sake of cutting off afflictions, someone, either a layperson or a monastic, practices [*dhyāna* meditation] with diligence and vigor in order to block off the arising of any of the afflictions and in order to assemble dharmas supporting progress on the path to buddhahood. Such persons may not be skillful in doctrinal discourse, may be lacking in eloquence, or may have no esteem for the awe-inspiring deportment. Still, if some unwise person therefore slights or disparages them, he thereby commits a grave offense.

Next we have the following:

If one harbors enmity
toward a good spiritual guide
and also if one is possessed of flattering, devious thoughts
covetous of obtaining offerings and such,[117]

The meaning of "good spiritual guide" has already been explained. If one has thoughts of enmity toward this person when he is engaged in teaching and speaking on the Dharma, one thereby commits a grave karmic offense comparable to that of cherishing enmity toward one's own father or mother.

"Flattering" refers to the intention to ingratiate oneself with others. "Devious" refers to instances where one displays physical and verbal actions that create the [false] impression of having accomplished something. "Covetous of obtaining offerings and such" refers to seeking for and being attached to gaining benefit, pleasures, praise, or a fine reputation. It is because such dharmas damage one's straightforwardness of character, one becomes unable to develop deeply anchored roots of goodness. This is just as when a robe that has been dyed an ugly color cannot then be dyed a fine color.

Next, we have the following:

If one fails to become aware of the works of *māras*,
if one's bodhi resolve is inferior and weak,
or if one encounters karmic obstacles or Dharma obstacles,
then, too, one is bound to lose the resolve to attain bodhi.

As for "if one fails to become aware of the works of *māras*," if one remains unaware of the various works of *māras*, then one cannot control and overcome them. If one fails to control and overcome then, then one is bound to lose the resolve to attain bodhi.

a. Q: What Is Meant by "the Works of Māras"?

Question: What all is meant by "the works of *māras*"?

b. A: There Are Numerous Examples, As Follows: (List)

Response: [These are illustrated by the following examples]:

When, in explaining how one ought to take up the *pāramitās* of giving, moral virtue, patience, vigor, *dhyāna*, and wisdom or when explaining profound ideas included within the Great Vehicle, one does not readily delight in speaking about them or delights in speaking of them, but then becomes scattered and confused in discussing peripheral topics.

Whether one is involved in writing out, studying, setting forth explanations, discussing points of doctrine, or listening to and absorbing teachings, one becomes haughty, full of oneself, and one's mind becomes so scattered and disordered that one focuses one's thoughts on peripheral topics.

One mistakenly brings to mind frivolous or joking topics or becomes involved in mutually ridiculing dialogue resulting in the two people involved become disharmonious and unable to penetrate through to the actual meaning of the topic at issue.

One gets up from his seat and departs, thinking to himself, "There is no way that my capacities would be acknowledged here. Their minds are not pure and, what's more, they will not deign to engage in any discussion concerning my city, village, clan, or birthplace." Consequently one does not wish to listen to the Dharma, fails to realize its flavor, gets up from his seat, and then leaves.

One may relinquish the *pāramitās* discussed in the Great Vehicle and may even then seek all-knowledge through the scriptures of *śrāvaka* disciples and *pratyekabuddhas* that promote individual training and liberation.

When one is involved in writing out, studying, setting forth explanations, listening to absorbing teachings, and so forth, one may wish instead to delight in speaking of various other sorts of topics, thereby demolishing and scattering [discussions focused on] *prajñāpāramitā*, doing so through turning the discussion toward topics related to the country, one's village or city, parks and forests, matters to do with military commanders, matters to do with bandits, military armor or weaponry, hate and love, pain and pleasure, parents, siblings, men and women, wives and children, apparel, food and drink, bedding and cushions, medicines, or other things serving as supplementary aspects of one's life. Thus one's mind then becomes so scattered and disordered that one loses [the focus on] *prajñāpāramitā*.

It might also be that one speaks of matters involving greed, hatred, stupidity, adversaries, close relationships, when times were good, when times were bad, singing, dancing, performances, music, worrisome topics, playful joking and laughter, the classics, literature, poetry, ancient times, traditional stories, rulers of the state, emperors and kings, earth, water, fire, and wind, the five objects of desire, wealth and aristocratic birth, and also offerings and other such worldly matters that tend to delight one's mind.

Or it could be that a *māra* transforms himself into the appearance of a bhikshu or bhikshuni, causes one to encounter scriptures of the *śrāvaka* disciples or the *pratyekabuddha*s, and says, "You should study these scriptures and set aside what you were originally practicing."

Or it may be that those listening to explanations of Dharma do not delight in listening to or accepting the teachings. Alternatively, the Dharma teacher's mind may fall prey to indolence, or then again, each of the parties may have other conditions [to which they are drawn].

It may be that, although those who come to listen have a need to hear the Dharma, the teacher explaining it prefers instead to move on to some other place.

It might also be that, although the teacher delights in providing explanations, those listening desire to go somewhere else instead.

It may happen that someone explaining Dharma has an inordinate desire to receive offerings or that those listening do not feel any motivation to give.

Then again, it may be that those listening have faith-filled minds, delight in the Dharma, and wish to hear teachings on Dharma whereas the one who explains it does not enjoy speaking it for them. Alternatively, it may be that someone explaining Dharma delights in discussing it but those listening do not wish to hear it.

There may be times when discussions turn to the sufferings in the hells, whereupon [the Dharma teacher] may claim that nothing would be quite so fine as putting an utter end to suffering in this very life. He may then recommend that the most beneficial option would be to choose an early entry into nirvāṇa.

Or else, when the discussion turns to the measureless suffering and torments of the animal realm or turns to the many different sorts of faults associated with [rebirth in the realms of] the hungry ghosts and *asuras*, [the Dharma teacher] may explain that all realms of *saṃsāra* are beset by misery. He may then recommend, "It would be most beneficial for you to choose, in this very life, an early entry into nirvāṇa."

Or else he may praise the wealth and happiness of the world's aristocrats.

Or he may instead praise the meritorious qualities, bliss, and excellence of life in the form realm and formless realm [heavens], claiming then that great benefit can be realized by pursuing rebirth in those places.

Then again, he may praise the benefits associated with the qualities of the fruits of the path acquired by stream enterers and the others up to and including the arhats. He may then claim, "It would be most beneficial for you to gain these realizations in this very life."

It might be that the teacher delights in having a retinue of followers, but those who listen to Dharma do not wish to follow him. It might also be that the speaker of Dharma decides he wishes to go to some unsafe country afflicted with famine and civil disorder, telling those who listen to his teachings, "What use would there be in your following me to such countries?" Consequently they become disenchanted with the idea and decline to follow along with him.

It could also be that the speaker of Dharma esteems benefactors and repeatedly goes off to pay his respects to them, thereby causing those who listen to Dharma teachings to no longer be able to hear and absorb them.

Then again, he may cause listeners to produce doubts regarding the most profound Dharma, saying such things as, "That is not the Dharma proclaimed by the Buddhas in the sutras. However, the Dharma as I explain it corresponds to the Dharma set forth by the Buddha in the sutras. If a bodhisattva is able to practice this version of the Dharma, he will attain the realization of ultimate reality."

For all sorts of reasons such as these, the two parties may fail to abide in harmony. One should realize that any circumstances such as these are the work of *māras*. To sum it up, all situations in which obstacles arise to the prevalence of good dharmas—these are all the work of *māras*.

As for "if one's bodhi resolve is inferior and weak," this refers to circumstances wherein, due to the power of the afflictions, one's resolve to pursue the path becomes so weak and devoid of strength that the vow to attain *anuttarasamyaksaṃbodhi* becomes cut off forever.

As for "karmic obstacles," although[118] there are many different types of karmic obstacles, this refers to those capable of causing a person in quest of the Great Vehicle to turn back from that resolve.

"Dharma obstacles" here refers to delight in the practice of unwholesome dharmas and to dislike of emptiness, signlessness, wishlessness, and the other profound and sublime dharmas associated with the *pāramitās* and other such teachings.

Dharmas of the same sort as the above four[119] are able to bring about loss of the resolve to attain bodhi.

Next, we have the following:

> If one pledges a gift to a teacher, but deceives him,
> the karmic offense incurred is extremely grave.
> If someone is free of doubts
> but one then forcefully causes him to develop doubts and regrets—
>
> If one directs an extreme degree of intense hatred and anger
> toward someone who has resolute faith in the Great Vehicle,
> vilifying him and speaking in a way that gives him a bad reputation,
> spreading such talk broadly about in place after place—
>
> Or if, when participating in joint endeavors,
> one's mind is much given to flattery and deviousness—
> If one's actions resemble any of these four black dharmas,
> then one is bound to lose the resolve to attain bodhi.

As for "pledging a gift to a teacher" but then not giving it, this refers to something that, whether or not one has already pledged it, one should nonetheless bestow it on one's teacher and yet, even so, one ends up not giving it. Also, if in giving, one gives at the wrong time, gives at the wrong place, or gives in a manner not according with the Dharma, these are methods typical of the world's non-Buddhist traditions.

Within the Buddha's Dharma, it is from one's teacher that one obtains the Dharma of the sutras. If one is possessed of some measure of wealth, then, in order to make offerings to the Dharma, one gives to one's teacher. If one has nothing to give, then there is no fault in that.

As for "if someone is free of doubts, but one then forcefully causes him to develop doubts and regrets—," this refers to an instance where someone has not actually broken any precept but merely appears to have committed some minor transgression and yet one claims he has committed a major offense against the moral code. Whether someone has departed from standard deportment in regard to right livelihood or has committed some infraction with regard to right doctrinal views, one then causes him to give birth to doubts and regrets.

"Hatred toward someone [with firm belief] in the Great Vehicle" refers to directing hatred toward those who have taken up the practice of the Great Vehicle, the unsurpassable vehicle, the vehicle of the Tathāgata, the vehicle of the great men, the vehicle of those possessed of omniscience, doing so even with regard to those who have only just brought forth the initial resolve to pursue that path. One feels intense hatred toward these people, rebuking and ridiculing them, and spreading claims about them that give them a bad reputation that is then caused to circulate widely.

"Flattery and deviousness in the midst of joint endeavors" refers to failing to use a straightforward mind, resorting instead to devious means to establish close relations with monastic preceptors, monastic Dharma teachers,[120] and good spiritual guides, even going so far as to use flattery and deviousness to curry favor with those one has never met.

In "the four black dharmas," "black" refers here to something dirty and impure that is capable of causing one to lose one's resolve to attain bodhi. This is as described here:

> If one turns away from these five sets of four dharmas
> and cultivates wholesome actions in life after life,
> one will thereby prevent the loss
> of one's resolve to attain the unsurpassable bodhi.

Five sets of four dharmas make twenty dharmas. It is because of these that one loses one's bodhi resolve. If one turns away from these dharmas in one's cultivation of the practices, then, even across the course of lifetimes, one will not forget one's resolve to attain *anuttarasamyaksaṃbodhi.*

"Turning away from" refers to turning away from the above five sets of four dharmas, doing so as follows:

> By revering and esteeming the Dharma,
> by doing away with arrogance,
> by abandoning false speech,
> and by deeply revering and esteeming good spiritual guides.

As for the rest, one should understand them in this same manner.

C. Q: Which Dharmas Cause One to Make the Vows Again in Each Life?

Question: Through which dharmas might one cause increase and growth in one's vow to attain bodhi, doing so across the course of lifetimes while also additionally causing one later on to be able to bring forth the great vows yet again?

D. A: They Are as Follows: (Verse)

Response:

> Even at the cost of losing one's life
> or of losing the throne of a wheel-turning king—
> even in such instances as these—one still should not
> commit false speech or engage in flattery or deviousness.

One is able through this to cause the entire world,
including all the beings within it,
to develop thoughts of reverence
toward the community of bodhisattvas.

If there is anyone able to practice
such good dharmas as these,
in each successive lifetime, he will succeed in increasing
[the strength of] his vows to realize the unsurpassable bodhi.

Employing these dharmas, the bodhisattva increases [the strength of] his vows to attain bodhi and also becomes able yet again to bring forth these pure and great vows. If, due to telling the truth, one thereby dies or loses the position of the wheel-turning king or even loses a position as one of the deva kings, even then, he should speak the truth and should not engage in false speech. How much the less might one fail to tell the truth in matters of only minor consequence.

In addition, one abandons flattery and deviousness in interactions with one's own retinue and with outsiders as well.

Furthermore, one brings forth thoughts of reverence toward all bodhisattvas from the very moment they bring forth their initial resolve, honoring, esteeming, and praising them no differently than if they were buddhas.

One should also do whatever is in one's powers to influence others to abide in the Great Vehicle.

The End of Chapter Seven

Chapter 8
On the Avaivartika

VIII. Chapter Eight: On the Avaivartika

A. Q: What Are the Distinguishing Characteristics of an Avaivartika?

Question: These bodhisattvas are of two kinds: First, those who are *vaivartika* (reversible), and second, those who are *avaivartika* (irreversible). One should explain the characteristics that determine whether one is a *vaivartika* or an *avaivartika.*

B. A: There are Five Defining Dharmas, as Follows: (Verse)

Response:

He maintains a mind of equal regard toward beings,
does not envy the benefits and support obtained by others,
and, even at the cost of his own body and life,
does not speak of a Dharma master's transgressions.

He has resolute faith in the profound and sublime Dharma
and does not crave to be the object of others' reverence.
One who embodies these five dharmas
Is an *avaivartika.*

1. Maintaining a Mind of Equal Regard toward Beings

As for "maintaining a mind of equal regard toward beings," beings are those within the six rebirth destinies. One's mind remains free of discriminating judgments by which one might regard them as either superior, middling, or inferior. This is a defining quality of an *avaivartika.*

Question: As has been explained, one should bring forth a mind of supreme reverence for buddhas and bodhisattvas. As for the other beings, this is not the case. Moreover, it has been stated that one should draw near to buddhas and bodhisattvas, revere them, and making offerings to them. As for the other beings, they are not to be treated in this way. Why then do you claim here that one maintains a mind of equal regard toward all beings and refrains from any duality in this?

Response: Each of these statements is principled and such as one should neither doubt nor challenge.

As for "maintaining a mind of equal regard toward beings," there are beings who look upon the bodhisattva as if he were an enemy, those who look upon him as if he were a father or mother, and those who look upon him as a neutral person. It is because he maintains a mind of equal regard toward these three categories of beings as he benefits and strives to liberate them that he does not indulge any notions of differences among them. Hence you should not pose any challenge on this account.

2. Not Envying Benefits and Support Obtained by Others

As for "not envying the benefits and support obtained by others," in a case where someone else obtains robes, food and drink, bedding, medicines, dwellings, property, gold, silver, precious gems, villages, towns, states, cities, male and female attendants, and so forth, one does not feel envy toward them. Not only does one refrain from harboring any hostility toward them, one's mind is instead pleased by this.

3. Not Speaking of a Dharma Master's Transgressions

As for "He does not speak of a Dharma master's transgressions," in a case where someone is teaching the Great Vehicle dharmas of emptiness, signlessness, and wishlessness, the six *pāramitās,* the four bases of meritorious qualities, the bodhisattva's ten grounds, or any other such Great Vehicle dharmas, even if it would cost one his own life to do this, one still refrains from exposing any of that person's transgressions or negative aspects. How much the less might one create a bad situation for him.

4. Resolute Faith in the Profound and Sublime Dharma

As for "he has a resolute faith in the profound and sublime Dharma," "profound Dharma" refers to emptiness, signlessness, wishlessness, and all of the abstruse scriptures such as the *Prajñāpāraamitā,* the *Bodhisattvapiṭaka,* and other such scriptures. One maintains a single-minded resolute faith in this Dharma and has no doubts about it. Because one has obtained the flavor of the profound scriptures, one does not find this sort of delight in anything else.

5. Not Craving to Be the Object of Others' Reverence

As for "not craving to be the object of others' reverence," because one has reached a penetrating understanding of the true character of dharmas,[121] one sees no difference between esteem and disgrace, gain and absence of gain, and so forth.[122]

As for "embodying these five dharmas," they are those just listed above.

6. One Does Not Retreat from Complete Enlightenment

One does not retreat from *anuttarasamyaksaṃbodhi,* nor does one allow one's efforts in pursuit of it to deteriorate through indolence. These are the factors that characterize one who is an *avaivartika* (irreversible). The opposite qualities characterize one who is *vaivartika* (reversible).

C. Two Types of Reversible Bodhisattvas, Ruined Versus Progressing

Among those who are *vaivartika* (reversible) bodhisattvas, there are two types, those who fall into ruination and those who gradually develop and advance until they become *avaivartikas* (irreversible).

1. Q: What Are the Signs of a "Ruined" Reversible Bodhisattva?

Question: As for those described as having fallen into ruination, what are their characteristic qualities?

2. A: Seven Characteristics, as Follows: (Verse)

Response:

In a case where one has no determination and ability,
delights in inferior dharmas,
is deeply attached to fame and offerings,
or has a mind that is not upright and straight—

Where one feels a miserly cherishing toward others' households, [123]
does not have a resolute belief in the dharma of emptiness,
and only esteems all manner of verbal discourse—
These are the marks of one fallen into ruination.

a. Absence of Determination and Ability

In the case of "one who has no determination and ability," his countenance is lackluster in appearance and whatever awe-inspiring personal qualities he might have are only shallow and scant.

Question: It is not on the basis of a dignified physical appearance that one is an *avaivartika*. That being the case, what meaning is there in making such a statement?

Response: This is a meaningful statement and should not be a cause for doubt. I am saying that, because, inwardly, one possesses meritorious qualities, the body manifests a correspondingly awe-inspiring personal presence. This is not simply a case of claiming that, [independent of these causes], he has a handsome physical appearance and countenance.

As for "determination and ability," this is what may be referred to as the power of one with an awe-inspiring personal presence.

If a person is able to cultivate and accumulate good dharmas while ridding himself of bad dharmas and then develops strength in accomplishing this endeavor, he then becomes one who possesses this "determination and ability." Even though one might possess a body like that of a king of the devas and radiance comparable to the sun and moon, so long as one is unable to cultivate and accumulate good dharmas and entirely rid oneself of bad dharmas, one is still a person who is devoid of "determination and ability."

[On the other hand], even though one's physical appearance might be ugly and one might have the physique of a hungry ghost, if he is able to cultivate the good and get rid of the bad, he then becomes one who possesses "determination and ability."

It is for these reasons that the challenge you have posed here has no merit.

b. Delighting in Inferior Dharmas

As for "delighting in inferior dharmas," when compared to the Buddha Vehicle, with the exception of the Buddha Vehicle, all other vehicles are small in scope, inferior, and incapable of measuring up to it. It is for these reasons that they are referred to as "inferior," not because they are "bad" *per se*. Still, any other peripheral unwholesome factors would indeed also qualify as "inferior."

Whatever has been achieved by adherents of the Two Vehicles is relatively inferior when compared with the Buddha, that's all. Still, because they have entirely escaped the world and have entered the nirvāṇa without residue, this cannot be said to be "bad."

It is for reasons such as these that, if someone distances himself from the Buddha Vehicle and instead has a resolute belief in the Two Vehicles, this amounts to delighting in inferior dharmas. Although such people do delight in superior endeavors, because they have anchored their resolute faith in the teachings of the Two Vehicles and have abandoned the Great Vehicle, they are still referred to as "delighting in inferior dharmas."

Then again, "inferior" refers as well to matters that are themselves "bad," namely the five objects of desire,[124] annihilationism, eternalism, and the rest of the sixty-two wrong views, all of the doctrinal tenets typical of non-Buddhist traditions, and any preoccupations that would increase one's entanglement in *saṃsāra*. These are "inferior dharmas." It is due to practicing these sorts of dharmas that one is said to delight in inferior dharmas.

c. Being Deeply Attached to Fame and Offerings

Being "deeply attached to fame and offerings" refers to having deep-seated inclinations to focus one's thoughts on skillfully arranging ways to receive gifts of material wealth and other sorts of offerings and praises. It is due to failing to experience the flavor of the pure Dharma that one may then covet and delight in such matters.

d. Having a Mind That Is Not Upright and Straight

As for "the mind not being upright and straight," this refers to someone whose nature is given over to flattery and deviousness and who delights in being deceptive.

e. Feeling a Miserly Cherishing toward Others' Households

In the case of one who "feels a miserly cherishing toward others' households," this person, no matter which household he enters, whenever he witnesses others receiving offerings, reverence, or praise, he immediately becomes envious, saddened, and displeased. Because his mind is impure and because he is deeply habituated to conceiving of the existence of a self, he is covetous of and attached to offerings, has thoughts of jealousy, and harbors resentment toward others' benefactors.

f. Not Having a Resolute Belief in the Dharma of Emptiness

As for "not having a resolute belief in the dharma of emptiness," the buddhas have three ways in which they discuss the dharma of emptiness, namely the three gates to liberation. As for these dharmas associated with emptiness, this person does not believe in them, does not delight in them, and does not esteem them as precious. This is because his mind has not achieved a penetrating comprehension of them.

g. Only Esteeming All Manner of Verbal Discourse

As for "only esteeming all manner of verbal discourse," this means that one only delights in words and phrases, but cannot practice in accordance with them. One is only able in such a case to carry on verbal discourse, but still cannot develop a resolute belief in these dharmas to the degree that one realizes their true import and flavor.

h. These Are the Marks of One Fallen into Ruination

As for "these are the marks of one fallen into ruination," if someone has formerly brought forth the bodhi resolve but then displays signs such as these, one should realize that this is a bodhisattva who has fallen into ruination.

"Fallen into ruination" designates the quality of not being well trained or compliant. For instance, a poorly-bred, ill-tempered horse might appropriately be thought of as "ruined." It merely bears the name "horse" without having any of a horse's uses.

A bodhisattva fallen into ruination is just like this, bearing only an empty designation while not carrying on any genuine practice. If one wishes to avoid becoming a bodhisattva fallen into ruination, one should rid himself of bad dharmas and accord with the Dharma in a manner worthy of one's name.

3. Q: What Are the Traits of the Reversible Bodhisattva Who Succeeds?

Question: You stated that there are two kinds of bodhisattvas still on the grounds of the *vaivartika* (reversible) bodhisattva: First, the bodhisattva fallen into ruination and, second, someone who, after the consistent application of vigor, gradually becomes an *avaivartika* (irreversible) bodhisattva. Having already explained what is meant by "the bodhisattva fallen into ruination," you could now explain what is meant by the one who, after consistent application of vigor, gradually becomes *avaivartika* (irreversible).

4. A: He Has Five Qualities, as Follows: (Verse)

Response:

The bodhisattva does not apprehend the existence of any self
and also does not apprehend the existence of any being.
He does not engage in discriminations as he discourses on Dharma,
nor does he apprehend the existence of bodhi.

He does not see a buddha by his signs.
It is because of these five meritorious qualities
that he can be referred to as a great bodhisattva
who is bound to become an *avaivartika.*

If a bodhisattva implements these five meritorious qualities, he thereby proceeds directly to the stage of the *avaivartika.*

a. Not Apprehending the Existence of any "Self"

As for "not apprehending the existence of any self," this is due to having abandoned attachment to the existence of any self. When this bodhisattva searches among the inwardly related and outwardly related five aggregates, twelve sense bases, and eighteen sense realms, he cannot apprehend the existence of a self anywhere among them. He contemplates thus:[125]

If it were the case that the aggregates constituted a self,
then that "self" would be characterized by birth and destruction.
How could one, merely on the basis of feelings,
immediately create some entity that experiences feelings?

If a self were to exist apart from the aggregates,
one should be able to apprehend it apart from the aggregates.
But how could one take it that feelings
are something separate from what experiences feelings?

If it were the case that the self possessed the five aggregates,
that self would be something apart from the five aggregates
in the same way that it is commonly said in worldly parlance
that an ox is different from the ox-herder.

It is on the basis of the conjunction of different things
that this phenomenon is said to exist.
Therefore, if it were the case that some self possessed the aggregates,
that self would be something different from the aggregates.

If it were the case that the self existed within the aggregates,
then this is just like there being a person inside of a room
or like there being someone there on a couch, listening.
The self then should be something different from the aggregates.

If it were the case that the aggregates existed within a self,
this would be analogous to fruit being contained in a bowl
or like milk in which there are flies.
The aggregates then would be different from the self.

This is just as with a combustible not being the burning itself
even as burning cannot occur apart from a combustible.
Combustion does not possess its combustible
nor does combustion itself abide within what is combustible.

A self isn't identical with nor separate from the aggregates,
nor does a self possess the aggregates.
There is no self within the five aggregates
and there are no five aggregates within a self.

Similarly analogous are dye and that which is dyed,
the afflictions and whoever is affected by the afflictions,
a vase [and its clay], cloth [and its threads], and so forth.
All of these phenomena should be understood in this same way.

If someone asserts that the self exists as a fixed entity
or that dharmas are possessed of differentiating characteristics,
one should realize that such a person
has not realized the flavor of the Buddha's Dharma.

When the bodhisattva carries out such contemplations, he immediately abandons any view imputing the existence of a self. Because he abandons any view conceiving of the existence of a self, he becomes unable to apprehend the existence of any self at all.

b. Not Apprehending the Existence of Any "Being"

As for his being unable "to apprehend the existence of any being," the term "being" here refers to any entity other than this bodhisattva. Because he has abandoned any view clinging to the existence of a self, he contemplates thus: "If others truly had a self, then they would constitute an 'other.' It is based on the existence of a self that one is able to regard someone else as constituting an 'other.' However, in reality, when one seeks to find some 'self,' it cannot be apprehended. Because an 'other' cannot be apprehended, either, then there is neither any 'other' nor any 'self.'" It is in this manner that the bodhisattva remains unable to apprehend any [being that is] "other," either.

c. Not Engaging in Discriminations While Speaking on Dharma

As for, "he does not engage in discriminations as he discourses on Dharma," because this bodhisattva has a resolute belief in the non-duality of all dharmas, in the nonexistence of any distinctions among them, and in their being characterized by a singular character, he contemplates thus, "All dharmas arise from erroneous perceptions and discriminations. They are false and deceptive." This bodhisattva extinguishes all discriminations, becomes free of all distress, immediately enters into the unsurpassable supreme meaning's dharma of conditioned origination, and then no longer needs to rely upon the wisdom imparted by others.

The nature of reality is not something that exists,
nor is it the case that it does not exist,
nor does it both exist and not exist,
nor does it neither exist nor not exist.[126]

Nor does it abide in verbal expressions,
nor is it something apart from verbal expressions.
So it is that the meaning of ultimate reality
can never be expressed by resort to speech.

The speaker and the words that can be spoken—
—these are all characterized by quiescent cessation.
Whatsoever has the nature of quiescent cessation
is neither existent nor nonexistent.

No matter what one might wish to speak about
and no matter which means one might choose to speak,
how could there be someone who is wise and yet [still conceives]
of there being any "speaking" that takes place with some "speaker."

If the nature of all dharmas is emptiness,
then dharmas are devoid of any [inherently existent] nature.
Consequently whatever dharmas are empty [of inherent existence],
those very dharmas are ineffable.

One cannot fail to have words that one speaks,
hence we borrow words to speak about emptiness.
The true meaning is neither empty
nor non-empty,

nor both empty and not empty,
nor neither empty nor not empty.
It is not false nor is it true,
nor is it spoken, nor is it not spoken.

And yet, in truth, there is nothing that exists,
and yet it is not the case that nothing exists at all.
This constitutes the complete relinquishment
of the discrimination of anything at all as existent.

Causes as well as whatever arises from causes—
All such dharmas as these
are in every case characterized by quiescent cessation.
There is neither any seizing on them nor any relinquishing of them.

Without ash-soap, a robe cannot be made clean,
But still, ashes may have the contrary effect of staining a robe.
[So too], were it not for words, one could not proclaim the truth.
Still, if one uses words and speech, that too may have its faults.[127]

It is in this manner that the bodhisattva contemplates, develops resolute belief in, and then achieves a penetrating understanding whereby, in his discoursing on the Dharma, "he does not engage in discriminations."

d. Not Apprehending the Existence of Bodhi

As for being "unable to apprehend the existence of bodhi," because this bodhisattva possesses a resolute belief in the dharma of emptiness, his "apprehension" here is not of the same sort as the common person's apprehension of bodhi. He contemplates in this manner:

The buddhas have not apprehended bodhi
and those who are not buddhas do not apprehend it, either.
As for the fruits of the path and the other related dharmas,
in every case, this also applies in the same way to them.

Where there is a buddha, there is bodhi.
but to hold that a buddha has "apprehended" it is just eternalism.
Without a buddha, there is no bodhi,
but to hold that it cannot be apprehended is just annihilationism.

Apart from a buddha, there is no bodhi
and apart from bodhi, there is no buddha.
If they are singular, their difference cannot be established.
So how could there be any sort of conjoining of them?

In general, as regards all dharmas,
it is because they are different that they may be conjoined.
But bodhi is not something distinctly different from a buddha.
Therefore, in the case of these two, there is no conjoining.

In the case of a buddha and bodhi,
neither their difference nor their conjoining can be established.
There is no third alternative apart from these two.
How then could [such concepts] be validly established?

Therefore buddhas are characterized by quiescent cessation.
So too is bodhi characterized by quiescent cessation.
Because these two are characterized by quiescent cessation,
everything is characterized by quiescent cessation.

e. Not Seeing a Buddha by His Signs

As for "he does not see a buddha by his signs," this bodhisattva has a resolute belief in and an utterly penetrating understanding of the dharma of signlessness. He reflects thus:[128]

If everything is signless,
then everything is identical with whatever possesses signs.
Quiescent cessation is signless
and is identical with whatever is possessed of signs.[129]

If one contemplates the dharma of signlessness,
whatever is signless is [seen to be] the same as what possesses signs.
If one says that one is cultivating signlessness,
that is just a non-cultivation of signlessness.

Were one to relinquish all covetousness[130]
and designate that as constituting signlessness,
such seizing on this sign of having relinquished covetousness[131]
then becomes the very absence of liberation.

In general, it is because of the existence of grasping
that then, because of that grasping, there then is relinquishing.
There is someone who grasps and something that is grasped[132]—
It is on this basis that one then refers to "relinquishing."

As for the one who grasps, the grasping to which he resorts,
and also that dharma that is subject to being grasped—
whether as conjoined or separate, they all do not exist,[133]
for these are all synonymous with quiescent cessation.

If a dharma's signs are established on the basis of causes,
this is just something devoid of any [inherently existent] nature.
Whatever is devoid of any [inherently existent] nature—
this is just something devoid of any [inherently existent] signs.

If a dharma has no [inherently existent] nature—
this is just something that is signless.
How can one assert that it has no [inherently existent] nature?
It is precisely because it is signless.[134]

If one uses [such terms as] "existence" and "nonexistence,"
"both" and "neither" should be permissible as well,[135] for,
although one may speak thus, so long as one's mind is not attached,
one thereby remains free of any fault in doing so.

Where has there ever first existed some dharma
that, afterward, was not destroyed?
Wherever there has first existed some fire
that, afterward, was then extinguished,
the quiescent cessation of these existent signs
is identical to the quiescent cessation of whatsoever is signless.

Therefore, as for these words about quiescent cessation
as well as the one who speaks about quiescent cessation,
from the beginning, too, they have not been quiescent[136]
nor have they been non-quiescent,
nor have they been both quiescent and non-quiescent,
nor have they been neither quiescent nor non-quiescent.

Because this bodhisattva has such a penetrating comprehension of the wisdom of signlessness, he is free of any doubts or regrets. He does not see a buddha in terms of the signs of his physical form, nor does he see a buddha in terms of feelings, perceptions, formative factors, or consciousness.

Question: How is it that he does not see a buddha by the signs of his physical form? And how is it that he does not see a buddha in terms of feelings, perceptions, formative factors, or consciousness?

Response: It is not the case that physical form is a buddha, nor is it the case that feelings, perceptions, formative factors, or consciousness are what constitute a buddha.[137]

Nor is it the case that a buddha exists apart from physical form, nor is it the case that he exists apart from feelings, perceptions, formative factors, or consciousness.

Nor is it the case that a buddha possesses physical forms, nor is it the case that a buddha possesses feelings, perceptions, formative factors, or consciousness.

Nor is it the case that a buddha exists within physical form. Nor is it the case that a buddha exists within feelings, perceptions, formative factors, or consciousness.

Nor is it the case that physical form resides within a buddha. Nor is it the case that feelings, perceptions, formative factors, or consciousness reside within a buddha.

The bodhisattva who does not seize on any signs of these five aggregates succeeds in reaching the ground of the *avaivartika*.

D. Q: What Are the Characteristic Signs of an Avaivartika?

Question: Now that we already know that one who acquires these dharmas is an *avaivartika*, what characteristic signs does the *avaivartika* possess?

E. A: The Avaivartika Has Numerous Characteristics, as Follows:

Response:

The *Prajñāpāramitā* has already extensively explained
the characteristic signs of the *avaivartika.*

If, in contemplating the ground of the common person, the grounds of the *śrāvaka* disciple, the ground of the *pratyekabuddha,* and the ground of a buddha, a bodhisattva does not engage in duality-based perceptions, does not engage in discriminating thoughts, and has no doubts or regrets, one should realize that this is an *avaivartika.*

Whenever an *avaivartika* speaks, it is beneficial in some way.

He does not contemplate others' relative strengths and shortcomings or good and bad aspects.

He does not long to hear the discourses of non-Buddhist *śramaṇas.*

What should be known, he immediately learns. Whatever should be seen, he then sees.

He does not revere or serve others' deities, nor does he make offerings to them of flowers, incense, banners, or canopies. Nor does he venerate or serve the gurus of those other traditions.

He does not fall into the wretched destinies nor, when reborn, does he take on a female body.

He always cultivates the ten courses of good karmic action himself while also teaching them to others, thereby causing them to practice them.

He always uses good dharmas in revealing [truths], instructing, benefiting, and delighting others. Even in his dreams, he never relinquishes the ten courses of good karmic action and never engages in any of the ten courses of bad karmic action.

The roots of goodness that he plants through physical, verbal, and mental actions are all done in order to facilitate beings' peace and happiness and their liberation [from *saṃsāra*]. He shares with other beings the karmic rewards that result from his endeavors.

Whenever he hears discussions of profound dharmas, he does not develop either doubts or regrets.

He tends to be one of relatively few words. His discourse is beneficial and peaceful, agreeable and pleasing, soft and pliant.

He sleeps but little and, whether going or coming, moving along or stopping, his mind is not scattered. He is refined in his deportment and his thoughts are stable and resolute.

His body is free of parasites. His robes and mat are clean and unstained. He is pure in both body and mind and he is serene and uninvolved in extraneous matters.

His mind is free of flattery and deviousness nor does it tend toward miserliness or jealousy.

He does not prize offerings, robes, food and drink, mats, medicines, or other physical necessities.

He has no tendency to engage in disputation over profound dharmas. He listens single-mindedly to explanations of the Dharma and always wishes to be in front [wherever it is taught].

Through the merit gained in these various ways, he succeeds in perfecting his practice of the *pāramitās*.

He excels over others in mastery of the world's cultural skills and arts.

He contemplates all dharmas in accordance with the nature of dharmas.

Even if Māra, the Evil One, were to manifest an apparition of the eight great hells while transformationally appearing before him as a bodhisattva, saying, "If you do not relinquish the resolve to attain bodhi, you will be reborn here"—even when witnessing such a terrifying circumstance as this, his mind would still refuse to relinquish its resolve.

Should Māra, the Evil One, then also say, "The sutras of the Mahāyāna were not spoken by the Buddha"—even when hearing this declaration, his resolve would remain unchanged. He continues to rely on the characteristic aspects of the Dharma and does not follow others.

He is not terrorized by the sufferings of *saṃsāra*. Even were he to hear of bodhisattvas who finally fell back and retreated [from the bodhi resolve] after *asaṃkhyeyas* of kalpas of cultivating and accumulating roots of goodness, his resolve would still not sink away as a result.

Also, were he to hear of a bodhisattva that had retreated to become an arhat, even then, he would still not retreat from his resolve to acquire the *dhyāna* absorptions, proclaim the Dharma, and liberate others [from *saṃsāra*].

He is always able to become aware of and recognize all actions of *māras*. Even if he were to be informed that omniscience is empty, that the Great Vehicle's ten grounds are empty, that the beings amenable to liberation [from *saṃsāra*] are empty, and that all dharmas are nonexistent and like empty space—were he to be told such things by someone attempting to throw his mind into confusion, someone wishing thereby to influence him to turn back due to weariness and diminishing intensity of effort—this bodhisattva would still respond by redoubling his practice of vigor and his deep practice of kindness and compassion.

Whenever he wishes to enter the first *dhyāna,* second *dhyāna,* third *dhyāna,* or fourth *dhyāna* meditation states, though he may do so, he nonetheless refrains from taking rebirth in those corresponding *dhyāna* [heavens], but rather returns and takes up dharmas suitable for practice within the desire realm.

He crushes and expels any potential arrogance, does not prize the praise of others, and keeps his mind free of the hindrance of hatred.

In lives spent as a householder, he remains unstained by the five objects of desire, merely taking them on with a mind of renunciation just as one would take medicine when beset with disease.

He does not live by wrong livelihoods and does not live in a manner that disrupts others' lives.

It is only for the sake of bringing peace and happiness to beings that he might abide in the role of a householder.

Traceless vajra-wielding dharma protectors[138] always follow him, serving and protecting him and ensuring that he cannot be harmed or interfered with by any human or nonhuman being.

All of his faculties are normally intact and free of defect. He does not use magical spells or noxious elixirs to subdue people or harm beings.

He is not fond of disputation and does not elevate himself or degrade others.

He does not perform divinations to determine auspiciousness or misfortune.

He is not fond of discussing manifold topics, topics such as: kings, ministers and the people, the state and its frontier lands, wars and battles, weaponry, clothing, possessions, alcoholic beverages and cuisine, matters associated with women, historical happenings, or maritime matters. He does not delight in discussing any matters such as these.

He does not attend, watch, or listen to singing, dancing, or music.

He only wishes to discuss the meaning of the *pāramitās* and only wishes to discuss dharmas related to the *pāramitās,* seeking thereby to cause those listening to gain increased benefit from this.

He abandons all disputation and always wishes to see the Buddha. If he hears of there now being a buddha in some other region, he wishes to take rebirth there. He is always reborn in a country central [to the presence of Dharma]. He never entertains doubts in himself whereby he wonders, "Am I or am I not an *avaivartika*?" He knows with complete certainty that he is an *avaivartika.*

He recognizes the various works of the *māras,* but does not accord with them. [His resolve is so solid that], even after he has taken rebirth, he does not then generate any aspiration to follow the paths of *śrāvaka* disciples or *pratyekabuddhas*. Even if Māra, the Evil One, were to manifest before him in the body of a buddha, telling him, "You must attain arhatship. I shall now speak the Dharma for you so that you may immediately achieve arhatship right here," even then, he would refuse to believe or accept this.

He does not spare even his own body or life in his efforts to preserve the Dharma and always practices vigor.

When explaining the Dharma, he is free of doubt or uncertainty and does so in a manner that is free of any deficiencies or errors.

It is factors such as these that constitute the characteristic signs of an *avaivartika*. One should realize that whoever is able to perfect these signs is an *avaivartika*. It might also happen that one encounters those who have not yet completely developed these signs. What sort of individual is this? This individual will, before long, ascend to the ground of the *avaivartika*. He is one who, after having cultivated and accumulated roots of goodness on later grounds and after having developed ever deeper roots of goodness, shall then acquire these characteristic signs of the *avaivartika*.

The End of Chapter Eight

Chapter 9
On the Easy Practice

IX. Chapter Nine: On the Easy Practice

A. Q: How Difficult! Is There an Easier Path to the Avaivartika Ground?

Question: Given that this *avaivartika* bodhisattva's initial endeavors are such as previously discussed, one aspiring to reach the ground of the *avaivartika* would have to practice all manner of difficult practices for a long time and only then be able to reach it. [This being the case], he might become prone then to fall down onto the grounds of the *śrāvaka* disciples or *pratyekabuddhas*. If that were the case, this would be for him an immensely ruinous calamity. As stated in the Dharma of *The Provisions Essential for Bodhi* (*Bodhisambhāra Śāstra*):[139]

If one were to fall onto the ground of the *śrāvaka* disciples
or onto the ground of the *pratyekabuddhas*,
this amounts to "death" for a bodhisattva,
for he then loses all beneficial effects [of his bodhisattva practice].

If one faced the prospect of falling into the hells,
he would not become filled with such fear as this.
If one were to [contemplate] falling onto the Two Vehicles' ground,
then this would bring about great terror.

If one were to fall into the hells,
he could still ultimately succeed in reaching buddhahood.
If one were to fall onto the grounds of the Two Vehicles, however,
this would ultimately block the realization of buddhahood.

In the scriptures, the Buddha himself
explained matters such as these, stating that
this is just as with a person who covets a long life span:
If he is faced with decapitation, he is then filled with great fear.

The bodhisattva is also just like this.
If [confronted with the prospect of] the *śrāvaka* disciples' ground
or the *pratyekabuddhas*' ground,
he should react with great terror.

Therefore, if, as a skillful means, the Buddhas have mentioned the existence of an easily-practiced path by which one might rapidly succeed in arriving at the ground of the *avaivartika*, then please explain it for me.

B. A: How Weak & Inferior! But, If You Want That, I Will Explain

Response: Statements such as you have just made are symptomatic of a weak, pusillanimous, and inferior mind devoid of the great resolve. These are not the words of a heroic man possessed of determination and ability.

How is this so? If a person has brought forth the vow to strive for the realization of *anuttarasamyaksaṃbodhi*, during that interim period in which he has not yet gained the *avaivartika* stage, he must not be sparing of even his own body or life. Rather he should strive with vigor both day and night, acting with the same urgency to save himself as someone whose turban has just caught fire. This is as stated in the *Bodhisambhara Śāstra*:

So long as the bodhisattva has not yet succeeded in reaching
the ground of the *avaivartika*,
he should always diligently practice vigor,
acting with the urgency of one whose turban has caught fire.

Taking up the heavy burden
for the sake of striving to attain bodhi,
he should always act with diligent vigor,
refraining from developing an indolent mind.[140]

Even were one to seek the *śrāvaka* disciples' vehicle
or the *pratyekabuddha*'s vehicle,
thus seeking only to perfect one's own benefit,
even then, one should always diligently practice vigor.

How much the more should this be so in the case of the bodhisattva,
one who strives to liberate both himself and others.
Compared to these men of the Two Vehicles,
he should be a *koṭi's* number of times more vigorous than they are.[141]

In speaking of the practice of the Great Vehicle, the Buddha described it thus: "As for generating the vow to attain buddhahood, it is a challenge heavier than lifting all of the worlds in a great trichiliocosm."

As for your saying, "This dharma of the *avaivartika* ground is so extremely difficult to accomplish that one can only reach it after a long time" and "If there were only some easily-traveled path by which one could swiftly reach the *avaivartika* ground," these are the words of those who are weak and inferior. These are not statements of a great man possessed of determination and ability. Still, if you definitely do wish to hear of this skillful means, then I shall now explain it for you.

1. The Practice of Calling on Ten Buddhas, One in Each Direction

The Dharma of the Buddha has measurelessly many gateways. This is just as with the world's various routes among which there are those that are difficult and those that are easy. When taking overland routes, the traveling may involve suffering, whereas in the case of water routes where one boards a boat, it may instead be pleasurable.

So too it is in the case of the bodhisattva path. In some instances, one is diligently devoted to the practice of vigor, whereas in others that involve faith and skillful means, one adopts an easy practice by which one swiftly arrives at the station of the *avaivartika*. This is as described in the following verse:

In the East, there is Meritorious Qualities Buddha.
In the South, there is Candana Qualities Buddha.
In the West, there is Measureless Light Buddha.
In the North, there is Emblematic Qualities Buddha.

In the Southeast, there is Sorrowless Qualities Buddha.
In the Southwest, there is Giver of Jewels Buddha.
In the Northwest, there is Floral Qualities Buddha.
In the Northeast, there is Three Vehicles' Practices Buddha.[142]

Toward the Nadir, there is Brilliant Qualities Buddha.
Toward the Zenith, there is Vast Multitude of Qualities Buddha.
Bhagavats such as these
now abide throughout the ten directions.

If a person wishes to swiftly reach
the ground of irreversibility,
he should, with a reverential mind,
take up and maintain the practice of invoking these buddhas' names.

If a bodhisattva wishes in this very body to succeed in reaching the ground of the *avaivartika* and then attain *anuttarasamyaksaṃbodhi*, then he should bear in mind these buddhas of the ten directions and invoke their names. This is just as explained in the "Avaivartika Chapter" of the *Sutra Spoken in Response to the Questions of the Youth Precious Moon*,[143] in which the Buddha told Precious Moon:

> Off in the East, going beyond a number of buddha lands equal to the sands in a measureless, boundless, and inconceivable number of Ganges Rivers, there is a world system named Sorrowless. Its ground is level and composed of the seven precious things. Strands of purple powdered gold are woven throughout that realm and rows of jeweled trees serve as adornments there.
>
> There are no destinies of the hells, animals, hungry ghosts, or *asuras*, nor are there any places beset by difficulties. It is pure, free of any filth, and also free of gravel, ceramic shards, stones, mountains, hillocks, deep pits, and dark ravines. The devas always rain down flowers that cover its ground.

That world now has a buddha named Meritorious Qualities Tathāgata, Worthy of Offerings, of Right and Universal Enlightenment, Perfect in Knowledge and Conduct, Well Gone One, Knower of the Worlds, Unsurpassable One, Tamer of Those to Be Tamed, Teacher of Devas and Humans, Buddha, Bhagavat. He is respectfully surrounded by an assembly of great bodhisattvas. His body's characteristic radiance and appearance are like a great flaming gold mountain and like a great aggregation of precious jewels.

For the sake of everyone in that great assembly, he extensively proclaims the right Dharma that is good in the beginning, middle, and end, that is eloquently presented and meaningful. Whatever he proclaims is free of admixture, perfect in its purity, accordant with reality, and free of error.

What is meant by "free of error"? It is free of any error with respect to the [four great elements of] earth, water, fire, and wind, is free of any error with respect to the desire realm, the form realm, and the formless realm and is free of error with respect to [the five aggregates of] form, feelings, perceptions, formative factors, and consciousness.

Precious Moon, from the time this buddha achieved buddhahood until the present, sixty *koṭis* of kalpas have passed. Moreover, in that buddha's country, there is no difference between the day and the night. It is only by reference to the enumeration of days, months and years of Jambudvīpa that one describes his lifetime in terms of a particular number of kalpas.

The light from that buddha always illuminates that world. In the course of a single discourse on Dharma, he causes a measureless and boundless number of thousands of myriads of *koṭis* of *asaṃkhyeyas* of beings to abide in the unproduced-dharmas patience. Twice this number of people are thereby caused to abide in the first, second, and third type of patience.

Precious Moon, the power of that buddha's original vows is such that, if there are any beings in other regions who have planted roots of goodness under a previous buddha, he need only be touched by this buddha's light in order to immediately attain the unproduced-dharmas patience.

Precious Moon, if there is a son or daughter of good family who but hears this buddha's name and is then able to have faith and accept him, such a person will immediately achieve irreversibility with respect to the attainment of *anuttarasamyaksaṃbodhi.*

The circumstances related to the other nine buddhas are just like this. Now we shall explain the names of those Buddhas as well as the names of their lands.

As for "Meritorious Qualities Buddha," his qualities are associated with pure goodness and the possession of peace and happiness. They are unlike the meritorious qualities of devas, dragons, and spirits which delude and trouble beings.

As for "Candana Qualities Buddha," in the South, off at a distance from here of buddha lands as numerous as the sands in incalculably and boundlessly many Ganges Rivers, there is a world named Delightful. The name of the buddha there is Candana Qualities. He is right now proclaiming the Dharma that is as fragrant and cooling as *candana*.[144] The fame of that buddha's name is heard afar, circulating and spreading about like the fragrance of incense. It extinguishes the heat from the fire of beings' three poisons and thereby causes them to experience refreshing coolness.

As for "Measureless Light Buddha," off in the West, at a distance from here of buddha lands as numerous as the sands in incalculably and boundlessly many Ganges Rivers, there is a world named "Excellence." That buddha is named Measureless Light. He is at this very time proclaiming the Dharma. The light from that buddha's body and the brilliant illumination from his wisdom reach an incalculable and boundless distance.

As for "Emblematic Qualities Buddha," off in the North, at a distance from here of buddha lands as numerous as the sands in incalculably and boundlessly many Ganges Rivers, there is a world known as "Immovable." Its buddha is known as Emblematic Qualities. He is right now proclaiming the Dharma. That buddha's meritorious qualities are lofty and prominently displayed, appearing like a banner.

As for "Sorrowless Qualities Buddha," in the Southeast, off at a distance from here of buddha lands as numerous as the sands in incalculably and boundlessly many Ganges Rivers, there is a world named "Lunar Brilliance." The buddha who abides there is named Sorrowless Qualities. He is even now proclaiming the Dharma. That buddha's spiritual qualities are such that they cause all of the devas and men there to be free of any sort of sorrow.

As for "Giver of Jewels Buddha," in the Southwest, off at a distance from here of buddha lands as numerous as the sands in incalculably and boundlessly many Ganges Rivers, there is a world named "Multitude of Signs." The buddha who abides there is known as Giver of Jewels. Even now he is proclaiming the Dharma. That buddha always bestows on beings the jewels of the uncontaminated root faculties, powers, limbs of enlightenment, the path, and so forth.

As for "Floral Qualities Buddha," in the Northwest, off at a distance from here of buddha lands as numerous as the sands in incalculably and boundlessly many Ganges Rivers, there is a world known as "Multitude of Sounds." The Buddha who abides there is known as Floral Qualities. Even now, he is proclaiming the Dharma. That buddha's physical body is like a marvelous flower and his meritorious qualities are incalculably numerous.

As for "Three Vehicles Practices Buddha," in the Northeast, off at a distance from here of buddha lands as numerous as the sands in incalculably and boundlessly many Ganges Rivers, there is a world known as "Peaceful and Secure." The buddha who abides there is known as Three Vehicles' Practices Buddha. Even now, he is proclaiming the Dharma. That buddha always explains the practices of the *śrāvaka* disciples, the practices of the *pratyekabuddhas,* and the practices of the bodhisattvas. There are those who state that it is because he explains the superior, the middling, and the lesser levels of vigor that he is named Three Vehicles' Practices.

As for "Brilliant Qualities Buddha," in the Nadir, off at a distance from here of buddha lands as numerous as the sands in incalculably and boundlessly many Ganges Rivers, there is a world known as "Expansive." The buddha who abides there is known as Brilliant Qualities. Even now he is proclaiming the Dharma. "Brilliant" refers to the light that shines from his body, the light of his wisdom, and the light that shines from his jeweled tree. These three kinds of brilliance always illuminate that world.

As for "Vast Multitude of Qualities Buddha," in the Zenith, off at a distance from here of buddha lands as numerous as the sands in incalculably and boundlessly many Ganges Rivers, there is a world known as "Many Moons." The buddha who abides there is known as Vast Multitude of Qualities. Even now he is proclaiming the Dharma. It is because the meritorious qualities of that buddha's disciples are vast that he is known as Vast Multitude of Qualities.

Now, as for these buddhas of the ten directions, beginning with Meritorious Qualities Buddha and concluding with Vast Multitude of Qualities Buddha, if a person single-mindedly invokes their names, he will thereby immediately succeed in gaining irreversibility with respect to the attainment of *anuttarasamyaksaṃbodhi.* This is as described in a verse:

If there is a person who is able to hear
the utterance of all these buddhas' names,
he will immediately acquire countless meritorious qualities,
just as was explained for Precious Moon.

I bow in reverence to these buddhas
presently abiding throughout the ten directions.
Whosoever invokes their names
immediately attains irreversibility.

Off in the East, in the realm known as Sorrowless,
that buddha named Meritorious Qualities
has a form resembling a mountain of gold.
The reach of his fame is boundless.

If a person so much as hears his name,
he immediately attains irreversibility.
With palms pressed together, I now bow in reverence to him
and pray that worries and afflictions may be entirely dispelled.

Off in the South, in the realm known as Delightful,
there is a buddha named Candana Qualities.
His countenance is as pristine as the full moon
and the radiance of his light is measureless.

He is able to bring about the extinguishing of beings'
fiery afflictions produced by the three poisons.
If one but hears his name, he then attains irreversibility.
I therefore bow down in reverence to him.

Off in the West, in a realm known as Excellence,
there is a buddha known as Limitless Light.
The light from his body and the brilliance of his wisdom
are boundless in the range of their illumination.

If there be anyone who but hears his name
he will immediately attain irreversibility.
I now bow down in reverence to him,
praying that I may put an end to the limits imposed by *saṃsāra*.

Off in the North, in a realm known as Immovable,
there is a buddha named Emblematic Qualities.
His body is replete with the many signs and minor characteristics
with which he is personally adorned.

He utterly defeats the hordes of Māra, the enemy,
and skillfully teaches both humans and devas.
Those who hear his name attain irreversibility.
I therefore bow down in reverence to him.

Off in the Southeast, in a world known as Lunar Brilliance,
there is a buddha named Sorrowless.
His illumination surpasses that of the sun and moon.
Those who encounter it are thus able to extinguish their afflictions.

He always explains the Dharma for the sake of the multitude,
thus ridding them of all inward and outward sufferings.
The buddhas of the ten directions praise him.
I therefore bow down in reverence to him.

Off in the Southwest, in a realm known as Multitude of Signs,
there is a buddha named Giver of Jewels.
He always uses all manner of Dharma jewels
to engage in extensive universal giving.

All the devas bow down in reverence to him
so that their jeweled crowns are brought low at his feet.
I now, bowing in reverence with all five extremities,
take refuge in the Bhagavat, Giver of Jewels.

Off in the Northwest, in a realm known as Multitude of Sounds,
there is a buddha named Floral Qualities.
That world is graced with an abundance of jeweled trees
that send forth sounds expounding the sublime Dharma.

He always uses the flowers of the seven limbs of enlightenment
to bestow adornments on those beings.
His mid-brow white hair tuft mark is like the moon.
I now bow down in reverence to him.

Off in the Northeast, in a world known as Peaceful and Secure,
one that is composed of all manner of jewels,
there is a buddha named Three Vehicles Practices
whose body is adorned with the measureless marks.

The light from his wisdom is measureless.
It is able to dispel the darkness of ignorance
and cause beings to become free of worry and afflictions.
I therefore bow down in reverence to him.

Off toward the Zenith, in a world known as Many Moons,
adorned with the many types of jewels,
attended by a congregation of greatly virtuous *śrāvaka* disciples
and bodhisattvas who are incalculable in number,

there is a lion among the Āryas
named Vast Multitude of Qualities.
He is feared by all the *māras.*
I therefore bow down in reverence to him.

Off toward the Nadir, there is world known as Expansive
in which there is a buddha named Brilliant Qualities.
His physical marks are far more marvelous
even than a mountain of *jambūnada* gold.

He always uses the sun of his wisdom
to open the blossoms of beings' roots of goodness.
His land of jewels is extremely vast.
From afar, I bow down in reverence to him.

In the past, countless kalpas ago,
there was a buddha named Oceanic Meritorious Qualities.
These buddhas of the present era
all made their vows under him.

His life span was incalculably long
and the reach of his light's illumination was endless.
His country was extremely pure.
Those hearing his name became definitely bound for buddhahood.

These [buddhas] who now abide in the ten directions
are completely equipped with the ten powers.
I therefore bow down in reverence to them,
these most venerable ones among all humans and devas.

2. Q: Can One Instead Call on Other Buddhas and Bodhisattvas?

Question: Is it the case that one may only be able to reach irreversibility with respect to *anuttarasamyaksaṃbodhi* through hearing these ten buddhas' names and bearing them in mind? Or is it the case that there are yet other buddhas' and other bodhisattvas' names through which one may succeed in reaching the station of the *avaivartika*?

3. A: Yes, There is Amitābha as Well as Other Such Buddhas

Response:

There is Amitābha and also other such buddhas
as well as the great bodhisattvas.
If one invokes their names and single-mindedly bears them in mind,
one will also thereby attain irreversibility.

In addition, there is Amitābha as well as other buddhas to whom one should also respectfully bow down in reverence and utter their names. I shall now set forth their names in full:

Limitless Life Buddha, King of Sovereign Mastery in the World Buddha, Lion Mind Buddha, Dharma Mind Buddha, Brahman Signs Buddha, World Signs Buddha, Sublimity of the World Buddha, Kindness and Compassion Buddha, World King Buddha, King Among Men Buddha, Moon-like Virtues Buddha, Precious Virtues Buddha, Qualities of the Marks Buddha, Great Marks Buddha, Jeweled Canopy Buddha, Lion Mane Buddha, Destroyer of Ignorance Buddha, Flower of Wisdom Buddha, Tamālapattra Candana Fragrance Buddha, and Upholder of Great Meritorious Qualities Buddha.

There are also: Rain of the Seven Precious Things Buddha, Excellent Bravery Buddha, Enmity Transcendence Buddha, Great Adornment Buddha, Signlessness Buddha, Jewel Treasury Buddha, Summit of Virtue Buddha, Tagara Fragrance Buddha, Candana Incense Buddha, Lotus Fragrance Buddha, Adorned Path Buddha, Dragon Canopy Buddha, Rain of Flowers Buddha, Scatterer of Flowers Buddha, Floral Radiance Buddha, Solar Voice Buddha, Eclipsing the Sun and Moon Buddha, Lapis Lazuli Treasury Buddha, Brahman Sound Buddha, and Pure Radiance Buddha.

There are also: Treasury of Gold Buddha, Sumeru Summit Buddha, King of the Mountains Buddha, Masterful Voice Buddha, Pure Eyes Buddha, Lunar Radiance Buddha, Mount Sumeru Likeness Buddha, Sun and Moon Buddha, Acquirer of Multitudes Buddha, Flower-born Buddha, Proclaimer of the Brahman Sounds Buddha, Lord of the Worlds Buddha, Lion-like Practice Buddha, Sublime Dharma Mind Lion's Roar Buddha, Pearl Canopy Coral Appearance Buddha, Dispeller of the Darkness of Delusion and Desire Buddha, Water Moon Buddha, Multitude of Flowers Buddha, Opener of Wisdom Buddha, and Retainer of Various Jewels Buddha.

There are also: Bodhi Buddha, Flower Transcendence Buddha, Radiance of True Lapis Lazuli Buddha, Outshining Sunlight Buddha, Retainer of Great Qualities Buddha, Realizer of Right Wisdom Buddha, Heroic Strength Buddha, Beyond Flattery and Deception Buddha, Dispensing with Planting Roots of Evil Buddha, Great Fragrance Buddha, Path Splendor Buddha, Water Light Buddha, Roamer in Oceanic Clouds of Wisdom Buddha, Virtue Summit Flower Buddha, Floral Adornment Buddha, Solar Voice Buddha, Lunar Supremacy Buddha, Lapis Lazuli Buddha, Brahmā-like Voice Buddha, and Light Buddha.[145]

There are also: Treasury of Gold Buddha, Mountain Summit Buddha, Mountain King Buddha, Sound King Buddha, Dragon Vigor Buddha, Stainless Buddha, Pure Countenance Buddha, Lunar Countenance Buddha, Sumeru Semblance Buddha, Candana Fragrance Buddha, Awesome Strength Buddha, Blazing Lamp Buddha, Difficult to Overcome Buddha, Precious Virtue Buddha, Joyous Sound Buddha, Radiance Buddha,[146] Dragon Supremacy Buddha, Defilement Transcendence Light Buddha, Lion Buddha, and King Among Kings Buddha.

And there are also Supremacy of Powers Buddha, Floral Garden Buddha,[147] Fearless Brilliance Buddha, Fragrant Summit Buddha, Universally Worthy Buddha, Universal Flower Buddha, and Precious Signs Buddha.

These buddhas, *bhagavats,* abide now in pure worlds throughout the ten directions. One should invoke the names of all of them and bear them in mind.

a. Amitābha's Original Vows and a Praise Verse

The original vows of Amitābha are of this sort: "If any person bears me in mind, invokes my name, and takes refuge in me, he will immediately enter the stage of certainty with respect to attaining *anuttarasamyaksaṃbodhi.*"

One should therefore always remain mindful of him. I set forth his praises here with a verse:

He possesses boundless illumination and wisdom
and his body is like a mountain of gold.
Paying homage to him with body, speech, and mind, I now
place my palms together and bow down in reverence to him.

His marvelous golden-colored light
everywhere streams into all worlds,
increasing in its brilliance in response to each being.
I therefore bow down in reverence to him.

If, when life's end comes, a person
succeeds in being reborn in that land,
he immediately acquires countless meritorious qualities.
I do therefore take refuge in him.

Whoever is able to bear in mind this buddha
possessed of measureless powers and awe-inspiring qualities
will immediately enter the stage of certainty.
I do therefore always bear him in mind.

That land is such that if, at the end of one's life,
one should otherwise undergo all manner of suffering,
even so, one will not then fall into those terrible hells.
Therefore, taking refuge in him, I now bow down in reverence.

If a person gains rebirth in his land,
he will never again fall into the three wretched destinies
or into the realms of the *asuras.*
Taking refuge in him, I now bow down in reverence.

Though his body is similar to that of humans and devas,
it resembles the summit of a mountain of gold.
This is the place to which all supreme [qualities] return.
I therefore bow down in reverence to him.

Those who have been reborn in his land
gain the powers of the heavenly eye and ear
that reach unimpededly throughout the ten directions.
I bow down in reverence to the one honored among the Āryas.

All the beings in his land
perform supernatural transformations, know others' thoughts,
and are endowed with the knowledge of past lives as well.
Therefore, taking refuge in him, I bow down in reverence.

Those who are reborn in his land
have no conception of either "I" or "mine."
They do not have thoughts conceiving of "others" or "self."
I therefore bow down in reverence to him.

He has stepped beyond the prison of the three realms.
His eyes are like the petals of a lotus.
The assembly of *śrāvaka* disciples there is measurelessly vast.
I therefore bow down in reverence to him.

All the beings in his land
are in nature gentle and harmonious
and they naturally practice the ten good deeds.
I bow down in reverence to this king of the many *āryas*.

It is from such goodness that his pure light is produced
that, in the number of its rays, is measureless and boundless.
He is foremost among those who stand on two feet.
I do therefore take refuge in him.

If a person vows to become a buddha
and then bears in mind Amitābha,
when the time is right, he will appear for his sake.
I do therefore take refuge in him.

Through the power of that buddha's vows
the bodhisattvas of the ten directions
come to make offerings and listen to the Dharma.
I therefore bow down in reverence to him.

All the bodhisattvas in his land
are endowed with all the major marks and secondary characteristics
by which they thereby adorn their own bodies.
Taking refuge in him, I now bow down in reverence.

Three times every day,
all those great bodhisattvas
make offerings to the buddhas of the ten directions.
I therefore bow down in reverence.

If a person who has planted roots of goodness
retains doubts, then the flower will not open.
If one's mind of faith is pure,
the flower will open and one will then see the Buddha.

For many different reasons,
the buddhas of the present throughout the ten directions
praise the qualities of that buddha.
Taking refuge in him, I now bow down in reverence.

His land is especially majestic in its adornment,
surpassing in its excellence the palaces of all the devas.
Its qualities are especially profound and abundant.
I therefore bow down in reverence at the feet of the Buddha.

The Buddha's feet carry the sign of the thousand-spoked wheel.
They are soft and, in appearance, resemble the blossoms of a lotus.
Those who see them are all filled with delight
and bow down their heads in reverence at the feet of the Buddha.

The light from the white hair tuft between his brows
appears like a pristinely shining moon,
enhancing the radiance displayed by his countenance.
I bow down in reverence at the feet of the Buddha.

When he originally sought out the path to buddhahood,
he performed all manner of distinctive and marvelous works.
These are just as described in the sutras.
I bow down in reverence to him.

That which is proclaimed by that buddha
eliminates the roots of karmic offenses.
His eloquent discourse brings benefit to many.
I now bow down in reverence to him.

By resorting to such eloquent discourse,
he rescues beings from all maladies arising by clinging to pleasures.
He has already liberated such beings and now liberates yet more.
I therefore bow down in reverence to him.

The devas bow down in reverence
to he who is the most honored of all humans and devas.
Their seven-jeweled crowns are brought low and touch his feet.
I do therefore take refuge in him.

The Sangha of all the Worthies and the Āryas
as well as the multitudes of humans and devas
all join in taking refuge in him.
Therefore I too bow down in reverence to him.

One who boards his ship of the eightfold path,
will be able to cross beyond that sea so difficult to cross,
delivering himself to liberation while liberating others as well.
I bow in reverence to he who has achieved sovereign mastery in this.

If, for countless kalpas, the Buddhas
proclaimed their praises of his meritorious qualities,
they would still be unable to come to the end of them.
I take refuge in he who has become such a purified person.

In this same manner, I now proclaim
the praises of his boundless qualities.
I pray that, due to the causes and conditions of this merit,
the Buddha may therefore always bear me in mind.

By whatever merit I have created in the present or previous lives,
whether it be but little or much,
I pray that my mind will become forever purified
in the very presence of the Buddha.

As for the supremely marvelous qualities that may be acquired
through the causes and conditions of such merit as this,
I pray that all of the many varieties of beings
shall all become able to acquire them as well.

4. Also, the Seven Buddhas of the Past as Well as Maitreya

One should also bear in mind Vipaśyin Buddha, Śikhin Buddha, Viśvabhū Buddha, Krakucchanda Buddha, Kanakamuni Buddha, Kāśyapa Buddha, and Śākyamuni Buddha, as well as Maitreya, the future Buddha. One should bear them all in mind and bow down in reverence to them. I set forth their praises here in verse:

The Bhagavat Vipaśyin
abides beneath an *aśoka* bodhi tree,[148]
having perfected all-knowledge
and all of the subtle and marvelous meritorious qualities.

Having rightly contemplated the world,
his mind has succeeded in gaining liberation.
I now, with all five extremities, bow down in reverence,
taking refuge in that unsurpassable Honored One.

The Bhagavat, Śikhin Buddha,
sat in the *bodhimaṇḍa*
beneath a *puṇḍarīka* bodhi tree
where he then achieved the complete realization of bodhi.[149]

His physical appearance is incomparable.
It resembles a mountain of flaming purple gold.
I now take refuge in the Honored One
who is unsurpassed by anyone in the three realms of existence.

Viśvabhū Bhagavat
sits beneath the *śāla* tree
where he naturally acquired the penetrating comprehension
of all forms of sublime wisdom.

Among all humans and devas,
he is the foremost and without peer.
I do therefore take refuge in the Honored One
who is the most supreme among them all.

Krakucchanda Buddha
succeeded in attaining
anuttarasamyaksaṃbodhi
beneath the *śirīṣa* tree.[150]

He perfected the great wisdom,
and became forever liberated from *saṃsāra*.
I now take refuge and bow in reverence
to that supreme and incomparable Honored One.

Kanakamuni,
the great Ārya and unsurpassable Honored One,
attained the perfect realization of buddhahood
beneath the *udumbara* tree

and reached the penetrating comprehension
of all the measurelessly and boundlessly many dharmas.
I do therefore take refuge in him,
that foremost and unsurpassable Honored One.

Kāśyapa Buddha, the Bhagavat,
with eyes like a pair of lotus blossoms,
achieved the perfect realization of buddhahood
beneath the *nyagrodha* tree.

Throughout the three realms, there is nothing he fears.
His gait is like that of the king of the elephants.
I now take refuge in him, bowing down in reverence
to that insuperable Honored One.

Śākyamuni Buddha,
beneath the *aśvattha* tree,[151]
conquered Māra, the enemy,
and perfected the unsurpassed enlightenment.

His countenance is like the full moon,
pure and free of any blemish.
I now bow down in reverence
To that heroically brave and supreme Honored One.

Maitreya, the buddha of the future,
sitting beneath the *nāga* tree,
shall attain the perfect realization of the vast resolve
and then naturally realize buddhahood.

His meritorious qualities are so extremely solid and durable
that no one is able to surpass them.
I do therefore take refuge in him,
that incomparable king of the sublime Dharma.

5. Also, by Calling on Ten Other Buddhas

Additionally, there are: Supreme in Meritorious Qualities Buddha, Universal Illumination Buddha, Victorious over Adversaries Buddha, Marks of the Sovereign[152] Buddha, King of the Marks Buddha,[153] King of Measureless Qualities' Brilliance and Sovereign Mastery Buddha, Unimpeded Medicine King Buddha, Jeweled Traveler Buddha, Precious Flower Buddha, Peacefully Abiding Buddha,[154] and Mountain King Buddha. One should remain mindful of them as well, respectfully bowing in reverence to them. I set forth their praises here in verse:

In the world known as Invincible,
there is a buddha named Supreme in Meritorious Qualities.
I now bow down in reverence to him
as well as to his Dharma Jewel and his Sangha Jewel.

In a world known as Joy in Whatever One Wishes,
there is a buddha named Universal Illumination.
I now take refuge in him
as well as in his Dharma Jewel and his Sangha Jewel.

In the world known as Universal Excellence,
there is a buddha named Victorious over Adversaries.
I now take refuge in him and bow down in reverence to him
as well as to his Dharma Jewel and his Sangha Jewel.

In the world known as Accumulation of Goodness and Purity,
there is a buddha named Marks of the Sovereign's Banner.
I now bow down in reverence to him
as well as to his Dharma Jewel and his Sangha Jewel.

In the world known as Accumulation of Stainlessness,
there is a buddha named Measureless Qualities' Brilliance
whose sovereign mastery extends throughout the ten directions.
I therefore bow down in reverence to him.

In the world known as Undeceptive,
there is a buddha named Unimpeded Medicine King.
I now bow down in reverence to him
as well as to his Dharma Jewel and his Sangha Jewel.

In the world known as Present Accumulation,
there is a buddha named Jeweled Traveler.
I now bow down in reverence to him
as well as to his Dharma Jewel and his Sangha Jewel.

In the Beautiful Sound World, there is Precious Flower Buddha.
[So too,] Peacefully Established and Mountain King Buddhas.
I now bow down in reverence to them
as well as to the Dharma Jewel and the Sangha Jewel.

All of these *tathāgatas* now abide
off in the regions to the East.
With a respectful mind, I spread their praises and,
taking refuge in them, bow down in reverence to them.

I only pray that the Tathāgatas
will bestow their deep kindness and sympathy
and thus manifest their bodies before me
so that I might be allowed to personally[155] see them all.

6. Also, by Calling on All Buddhas of the Three Times

Additionally, one should exhaustively and comprehensively bear in mind and respectfully bow in reverence to all buddhas of the past, the future, and the present. I set forth their praises here in verse:

All buddhas of the past
conquered the many *māras*, their adversaries
and, using the power of great wisdom,
provided vast benefit to beings.

The beings who existed in those eras
were entirely devoted to making offerings to them all,
showed them reverence, and proclaimed their praises.
I therefore bow down in reverence to them.

The incalculably many buddhas of the present
throughout the worlds of the ten directions
are so measurelessly and boundlessly many
as to surpass the number of sands in the Ganges River.

Out of kindness and pity for beings,
they always turn the wheel of the sublime Dharma.
I do therefore accord them respect,
take refuge in them, and bow down my head to them in reverence.

The buddhas of the future
shall appear with bodies resembling mountains of gold
that emanate measureless illumination
and display the self-adornment of their many characteristic signs.

They shall appear in the world and liberate beings,
after which they shall then enter nirvāṇa.
To all such *bhagavats* as these,
I do now bow down in reverence.

7. Also, by Calling on the Great Bodhisattvas

Additionally, one should bear in mind the great bodhisattvas, namely: Good Intentions Bodhisattva, Good Eyes Bodhisattva, Moon Hearer Bodhisattva, King Śibi Bodhisattva, Universally Supreme Bodhisattva, Knower of the Great Earth Bodhisattva, Great Medicine Bodhisattva, Kapotagṛha Bodhisattva, Arenemin Bodhisattva, Summit Born King Bodhisattva, Delightful View Bodhisattva, Uttara Bodhisattva, Sarvadāna Bodhisattva, Long Life King Bodhisattva, Kṣānti Bodhisattva, Velāma Bodhisattva, Flashing Light Bodhisattva, Moon Covering Bodhisattva, Brilliant Leader Bodhisattva, Dharma Leader Bodhisattva, Perfecting Benefit Bodhisattva, and Maitreya Bodhisattva.

In addition, there are: Vajragarbha Bodhisattva, Vajra Leader Bodhisattva, Treasury of Non-defilement Bodhisattva, Vimalakīrti Bodhisattva, Dispeller of Doubts Bodhisattva, Undefiled Virtue Bodhisattva, Net-like Brilliance Bodhisattva, Immeasurable Brilliance Bodhisattva, Great Brilliance Bodhisattva, Akṣayamati Bodhisattva, Mind King Bodhisattva, Boundless Mind Bodhisattva, Sun Sound Bodhisattva, Moon Sound Bodhisattva, Beautiful Sound Bodhisattva, Beautiful Voice Bodhisattva, Great Voice Bodhisattva, Solid Vigor Bodhisattva, Ever Solid Bodhisattva, and Solidly Generated Bodhisattva.

There are also: Adornment King Bodhisattva, Ever Compassionate Bodhisattva, Never slighting Bodhisattva, Dharma Superior Bodhisattva, Dharma Mind Bodhisattva, Dharma Joy Bodhisattva, Dharma Leader Bodhisattva, Dharma Accumulation Bodhisattva, Generator of Vigor Bodhisattva, Wisdom Bodhisattva, Pure Awesome Virtue Bodhisattva, Nārāyaṇa Bodhisattva, Good Meditation Bodhisattva, Dharma Meditation Bodhisattva, Bhadrapāla Bodhisattva, Dharma Benefit Bodhisattva, Lofty Virtue Bodhisattva, Lion Traveler Bodhisattva, Joyous Faculties Bodhisattva, and Supreme Jewel Moon Bodhisattva.

There are also: Virtue Free of Falseness Bodhisattva, Dragon Virtue Bodhisattva, Mañjuśrī Bodhisattva, Wonderful Sound Bodhisattva, Cloud Sound Bodhisattva, Supreme Mind Bodhisattva, Illuminating Brilliance Bodhisattva, Brave Assembly Bodhisattva, Supreme Assembly Bodhisattva, Awesome Deportment Bodhisattva, Lion Mind Bodhisattva, Superior Mind Bodhisattva, Beneficial Intentions Bodhisattva, Augmented Mind Bodhisattva, Precious Brilliance Bodhisattva, Wisdom Summit Bodhisattva, Peak of Eloquence Bodhisattva, Possessed of Virtue Bodhisattva, Avalokiteśvara King Bodhisattva, and Dhāraṇī Mastery King Bodhisattva.

There are also: Great Sovereign Mastery King Bodhisattva, Sorrowless Virtue Bodhisattva, Not Seen in Vain Bodhisattva, Beyond the Wretched Destinies Bodhisattva, Universally Brave and Strong Bodhisattva, Dispeller of Darkness Bodhisattva, Merit Jewel Bodhisattva, Floral Awesome Virtue Bodhisattva, Gold Necklace Brilliant Virtue Bodhisattva, Beyond the Aggregates and Hindrances Bodhisattva, Unimpeded Mind Bodhisattva, Pure in All Actions Bodhisattva, Equal Vision Bodhisattva, Unequaled Vision Bodhisattva, Wandering Joyfully in Samādhi Bodhisattva, Sovereign Mastery in Dharma Bodhisattva, Dharma Marks Bodhisattva, Brilliant Adornment Bodhisattva, Great Adornment Bodhisattva, and Jeweled Summit Bodhisattva.

There are also: Jeweled Mudrā Hand Bodhisattva, Ever Raised Hand Bodhisattva, Ever Lowered Hand Bodhisattva, Ever Piteous Bodhisattva, Ever Joyful Bodhisattva, Joy King Bodhisattva, Possessed of Eloquent Voice Bodhisattva, Sound of Thunder in Space Bodhisattva, Upholder of the Jeweled Torch Bodhisattva, Valiant Giving Bodhisattva, Imperial Net Bodhisattva, Horse Light Bodhisattva, Empty and Unimpeded Bodhisattva, Jeweled Supremacy Bodhisattva, Celestial King Bodhisattva, Demon Crusher Bodhisattva, Lightning Virtue Bodhisattva, Sovereign Mastery Bodhisattva, Summit Sign Bodhisattva, and Beyond Transgressions Bodhisattva.

And there are also: Lion's Roar Bodhisattva, Cloud Shade Bodhisattva, Able to Conquer Bodhisattva, Mountainous Marks Banner Bodhisattva, Fragrant Elephant Bodhisattva, Great Fragrant Elephant Bodhisattva, White Fragrant Elephant Bodhisattva, Ever Vigorous Bodhisattva, Never Resting Bodhisattva, Sublime Birth Bodhisattva, Floral Adornment Bodhisattva, Avalokiteśvara Bodhisattva, Mahāsthāmaprāpta Bodhisattva, Water King Bodhisattva, Mountain King Bodhisattva, Indra's Net Bodhisattva, Jewel Giving Bodhisattva, Crusher of Demons Bodhisattva, Adorner of Lands Bodhisattva, Golden Topknot Bodhisattva, and Pearl Topknot Bodhisattva.

One should bear in mind all such bodhisattvas and bow down to them in reverence as one seeks to attain the ground of the *avaivartika*.

The End of Chapter Nine

Chapter 10
Getting Rid of Karma

X. Chapter 10: Getting Rid of Bad Karma

A. Q: Is Buddha Mindfulness All One Must Do to Become Irreversible?

Question: Is it the case that, in order to become an *avaivartika*, one need only bear in mind Amitābha and those other buddhas while also bearing in mind the others, the bodhisattvas [mentioned above]? Or are there other additional skillful means [that must be used]?

B. A: One Should Also Repent, Entreat, Rejoice & Dedicate Merit

Response: For one who seeks to become an *avaivartika,* it is not the case that one must only remain mindful of them, utter their names, and make reverential obeisance to them, and that is all there is to it. In addition, one should, in the presence of the buddhas, perform repentances, entreat them, rejoice [in their meritorious deeds], and dedicate one's own merit.

1. How Does One Perform These Endeavors?

Question: How does one go about carrying out these endeavors?

2. "Repentance" Is Performed as Follows:

Response:

There is nothing not exhaustively known by
the countless buddhas of the ten directions,
Now, in the presence of them all,
I reveal all of my black and evil deeds.

Three times three, nine kinds in all,[156]
all of them have arisen from the three types of afflictions.
Whether committed in the present body or in prior births,
I repent of all of these karmic offenses.

If I should otherwise be bound to undergo karmic retribution
in the three wretched destinies,
I pray that [my offenses] may instead be repaid in this very body
so that I will not enter the wretched destinies to undergo retribution.

"The buddhas of the ten directions" refers to all of the buddhas of the present whose life faculty has become completely perfected but who have still not yet entered nirvāṇa. "Ten directions" refers to the four directions, the four midpoints, the zenith, and the nadir. "Buddhas" refers to those who, with regard to all things that should be known, know them all without exception.

"Reveal" means that, in the presence of all buddhas, one reveals all of one's karmic offenses, leaving none hidden, [while also resolving] to not commit them ever again. [In so doing, one's resolve becomes] like a dike that holds back the waters.

As for "black and evil deeds," because one has not had the bright light of wisdom, one has often committed many types of evil deeds, in some cases practicing unwholesome dharmas, and in some cases involving oneself in obscured morally indeterminate dharmas.[157]

"Three times three, nine kinds in all" refers to creation of evil karma on the part of body, mouth, and mind that brings about negative retribution in the present life, negative retribution in the next rebirth, and negative retribution in subsequent lives. [This retribution may arise through] directly committing the deed oneself, instructing others to commit it, or by rejoicing that others have committed it.

As for "all arisen from three types of afflictions," the "three types of afflictions" refers to [those actions] connected to the desire realm, the form realm, or the formless realm, whether promoting the affliction of desire, the affliction of hatred, or the affliction of delusion, and whether involving a supreme degree of affliction, a middling-degree of affliction, or a lesser-degree of affliction.

As for "whether it be that committed in the present body or in prior births, I repent of all of these karmic offenses," this means that one repents of all of the many kinds of evil deeds committed in this present life and former lives, repenting of them all without exception.

[With regard to "the three wretched destinies,"] there are the hells, namely the eight hot hells and the ten cold-and-ice hells. There are the animals, including those that are earth-born, water-born, legless, two-legged, or many-legged. And there are the hungry ghosts, in particular those who feed upon spittle, vomit, rinsings, pus-and-blood, excrement and urine, and other such things.

[The intent here is to state]: "If my karma is such that I should undergo retribution in these three wretched destinies, I pray that I will instead be allowed to undergo that retribution in this very body. If it is to be undergone in a subsequent rebirth's body, may I not be compelled to undergo it in the hells, among hungry ghosts, or in the animal realm."

Also, the Buddha himself explained the dharma to be used in repentance, indicating that, if a bodhisattva wishes to repent of karmic offenses, he should utter his repentance as follows:

Facing the Buddhas of the present time throughout the worlds of the ten directions, namely those who have realized *anuttarasamyaksaṃbodhi,* turned the Dharma wheel, rained down the Dharma rain, sounded the Dharma drum, blown the Dharma conch, planted the Dharma banner, and who have, through the giving of Dharma, fulfilled the needs of beings, benefited the many, brought peace and security to the many, taken pity on the world, and abundantly benefited devas and humans—I now, with body, mouth, and mind, make full reverential prostrations at the feet of the buddhas of the present, the buddhas who know, who see, who are the eyes of the world, and who are the lamps for the world.

[I hereby reveal] all of the karmic offenses I have created throughout the course of beginningless births and deaths due to being driven along by greed, hatred, and delusion, including:

Sometimes failing to recognize the Buddhas, failing to recognize the Dharma, or failing to recognize the Sangha;
Sometimes failing to distinguish between offense-generating karma and meritorious karma;
Sometimes abundantly creating the many sorts of karmic offenses through actions of body, speech, and mind;
Sometimes, with evil intentions, drawing the blood of a buddha;
Sometimes contributing to the destruction of right Dharma;
Sometimes bringing about the destruction of the Sangha;
Sometimes murdering arhats;
Sometimes engaging in the ten courses of bad karmic action;
Sometimes instructing others to engage in them;
Sometimes subjecting others to speech that displeases them;
Sometimes cheating and deceiving others with altered weights and measures;
Sometimes afflicting beings with immoral behavior;
Sometimes failing in filial piety toward parents;
Sometimes stealing belongings from stupas;
Sometimes stealing possessions from the Sangha of the four directions;
Sometimes destroying or transgressing against [the teachings of] sutras or moral-precept codes originally set forth by the Buddha;
And sometimes disobeying monastic preceptors or monastic Dharma teachers.[158]
Sometimes, when people have set their resolve on realization of the Śrāvaka Disciple Vehicle or the Pratyekabuddha Vehicle,

or have set their resolve on realization of the Great Vehicle, due to having a mind covered over by hatred or jealousy, I have used evil speech to vilify and slight them.

And sometimes, in the presence of buddhas, I have uttered abusive speech, have claimed right Dharma to be non-Dharma, and have claimed non-Dharma to be right Dharma.

Now, in the presence of the buddhas of the present, those who know, who see, and who have become realized, I entirely reveal all of these karmic offenses, not daring to conceal any of them, and I vow, from this point on, that I shall not dare to commit them again.

If I have committed karmic offenses through which I should fall into the hells, into the animal realm, into the hungry-ghost realm, or into the *asura* realm,[159] or if I ought not encounter the three objects of reverence,[160] but rather should be reborn in the midst of the [eight] difficulties,[161] I pray that I may [instead be allowed to] undergo retribution for these karmic offenses in this present life.

Just as all the bodhisattvas of the past who sought realization of buddhahood did themselves repent of offenses created through bad karma, in the very same manner, I too reveal all of my offenses, repent of them, do not dare to conceal any of them, and vow not to commit them again.

Just as all the bodhisattvas of the present who seek realization of buddhahood do repent of offenses created through bad karma, in the very same manner, I too reveal all of my offenses, repent of them, do not dare to conceal any of them, and vow not to commit them again.

Just as all of the bodhisattvas of the future who shall seek realization of buddhahood shall repent of offenses created through bad karma, in the very same manner, I too reveal all of my offenses, repent of them, do not dare to conceal any of them, and vow not to commit them again.

Just as all of the past, future, and present bodhisattvas seeking realization of buddhahood did repent, do repent, and shall repent of offenses created through bad karma, in the very same manner, I too repent of offenses created through bad karma, do not dare to conceal any of them, and vow not to commit them again.

3. Q: How Does One Go about "Entreating"?

Question: Having already explained the method for repentance, how does one go about "entreating"?

4. A: "Entreating" Is Performed as Follows:

Response:

Whenever any of the buddhas of the ten directions
now attain buddhahood,

> I request them to turn the wheel of Dharma
> and bring peace and happiness to all beings.
>
> Whenever any of the buddhas of the ten directions
> are about to relinquish their life spans,
> I now make full reverential prostrations to them,
> and entreat them to remain for a long time.

As for "turning the wheel of Dharma," this refers to the proclamation of the four truths of the Āryas in three turnings, thereby revealing their twelve aspects:

> This is the truth of the existence of suffering. This is the origination of suffering. This is the extinguishing of suffering. This is the path leading to the extinguishing of suffering. This is what is meant by the four aspects of the first turning.
>
> This truth of the existence of suffering should be known. This origination of suffering should be cut off. This extinguishing of suffering should be realized. This path leading to the extinguishing of suffering should be cultivated. This is what is meant by the four aspects of the second turning.
>
> This truth of the existence of suffering has been known. This origination of suffering has been cut off. This extinguishing of suffering has been realized. This path leading to the extinguishing of suffering has been cultivated. This is what is meant by the four aspects of the third turning.

As for the four aspects, within the four truths, they correspond to the development of the eyes, the knowledges, the clear knowledges, and the awakenings.[162]

There are those who explain that the Śrāvaka Disciple Vehicle, the Pratyekabuddha Vehicle, and the Great Vehicle are what constitute "the Dharma wheel" and that it is the explanation of the meaning of the Three Vehicles that constitutes the "the turning of the Dharma wheel."

As for "bringing peace and happiness to all beings," the pleasures associated with the five objects of desire do not constitute peace and happiness. Rather, it is entry into the Three Vehicles for the sake of achieving pure peace and happiness in the present and future lifetimes—this is what is meant by peace and happiness.

This person entreats the Buddhas to turn the wheel of Dharma to cause all beings to receive the bliss of nirvāṇa and, so long as they have not yet gained entry into nirvāṇa, to cause them to receive the types of happiness available in the world. It is for this reason that "peace and happiness" are mentioned here.

As for this matter of a "life span," it is due to the causes and conditions involved in undergoing karmic retribution that the continuity of one's life faculty is sustained. It is comparable to an apparition created through a magical conjuration that continues to be sustained in correspondence with [the magician's] mental actions. When those mental actions cease, [that conjuration] is then extinguished.[163]

"Entreat" refers to the most ultimately sincere prayerful beseeching. The Buddhas regard all beings [equally], great and small, without treating them differently. Therefore one sets forth this earnest request, hoping that they will accede to one's wishes and refrain from relinquishing their life spans and instead remain in the world for *asaṃkhyeyas* of kalpas in order to liberate beings.

Then again, the Buddha himself described the method to be used in entreating the Buddhas, indicating that the bodhisattva should speak as follows: "I bow down in reverence to all buddhas of the present throughout the ten directions." Then, at that time when they have just realized *anuttarasamyaksaṃbodhi* but have not yet begun to turn the wheel of Dharma, [he is to say]:

> I now beseech you, praying that you will turn the wheel of Dharma, sound the Dharma drum, blow the Dharma conch, plant the Dharma banner, establish the great Dharma rituals, and ignite the great Dharma torch, using these means of Dharma giving to fulfill the needs of beings so that there will be many who are benefited and many who are made happy. Have pity on the world and bestow abundant benefit on devas and humans. It is for these reasons that I now present this entreaty.

This is what is meant by "entreating." As for entreating the buddhas who have turned the wheel of Dharma to then "remain for a long time," in that case as well, one should address all buddhas of the present throughout the ten directions at just that time when those buddhas are about to relinquish their life spans, saying, "I beseech you to remain for a long time so that there will be many who are benefited and many who are made happy. Have pity on the world and bestow abundant benefit on devas and humans."

5. Q: What is meant by "Rejoicing"?

Question: Having already explained "repentance" and "entreating," what is meant by "rejoicing"?

6. A: "Rejoicing" Is Performed as Follows:

Response:

All of the merit produced by giving,
observance of moral precepts, and *dhyāna* practice—

all of it arising through body, speech, and mind,
all of it created throughout the past, the future, and the present,

all of it created by those who cultivate the Three Vehicles,
by those who have fulfilled the practice of any of the Three Vehicles,
and all of the merit created by common people—
I rejoice in accordance with all of it.

As for "the merit produced by giving," it is created through relinquishing the dharma of miserliness.

As for "the merit arising from observance of moral precepts," this is created through being able to subdue the body and speech.

"*Dhyāna* practice" refers to developing all of the *dhyāna* concentrations.

As for "that arising through body and speech," this refers to acts arising because of the body or speech such as giving, observance of the moral precepts, welcoming others when they come, escorting them off when they leave,[164] and other such actions.

As for "that arising through the mind," this refers to the *dhyāna* concentration states[165] as well as to kindness, compassion, and so forth.[166]

As for "all of it created in the past, the future, or the present," this is referring to all merit produced by all beings throughout the three periods of time.

As for "those who cultivate the Three Vehicles," this refers to those who aspire to success in the Śrāvaka Disciple Vehicle, the Pratyekabuddha Vehicle, and the Great Vehicle.

As for "those who have fulfilled the practice of any of the Three Vehicles," this refers to those who have perfected the cultivation of either the Arhat Vehicle, the Pratyekabuddha Vehicle, or the Buddha Vehicle.

"All" means every single instance, exhaustively, excluding none.

"Common people" refers to those who have not yet realized the four truths.

With respect to "merit," there may be two types of actions which may be involved here, namely good actions or unobscured morally indeterminate actions.[167]

"Rejoicing in accordance with it" refers to circumstances where, when others engage in meritorious actions, one's mind is filled with delight and one praises that deed as good.

7. Q: What Is Meant by "Dedication"?

Question: Since you have already explained "repentance," "entreating," and "rejoicing," what is meant by "dedication"?

8. A: Dedication Is Performed as Follows:

Response:

May all of the merit that I have acquired
be gathered together,
and then, for the sake of all beings,
may it be rightly dedicated to attaining buddhahood.

"I" refers to oneself. "All of the merit," whether produced through physical actions, produced through verbal actions, produced through mental actions, produced through giving, through upholding the moral precepts, through cultivation of *dhyāna* meditation, through rejoicing, or through entreating—all such goodness as this as well as any other goodness—all of these are what constitute "all of the merit."

As for "may it all be gathered together," this refers to a reflection whereby one envisions all of the merit being gathered together and assessed in a manner whereby one becomes aware of its expansiveness.

"All beings" refers to all beings throughout the three realms of existence.

"Rightly" refers to performing this dedication of merit in a manner corresponding to the way it is done by all buddhas. It is that dedication that aligns itself with reality. It is dedication directed toward bodhi. This "dedication directed toward bodhi" involves dedicating all merit toward the realization of *anuttarasamyaksaṃbodhi.*

Again, these two matters of "rejoicing" and "dedication" were explained by the Buddha himself who spoke of them as follows:

> Where there is a bodhisattva *mahāsattva* who wishes to engage in rejoicing and in dedication, he should bring to mind all of the roots of goodness and merit of all buddhas, those who have cut off continuous abiding in the three realms of existence, who have extinguished all conceptual elaborations, who have dried up the mud of the afflictions, who have destroyed their piercing thorns, who have thrown off the heavy burden, who have accomplished their own benefit, who have obtained right knowledge and liberation, whose minds have achieved sovereign mastery, and who have put an end to the fetters of existence.
>
> So too, he should bring to mind all of the measurelessly, boundlessly, and inconceivably many *asaṃkhyeyas* of buddhas in each and every one of the measurelessly, boundlessly, and inconceivably many *asaṃkhyeyas* of worlds throughout the ten directions while also bringing to mind all the roots of goodness and merit of all of these buddhas from the time they come forth [into the world] to the time they enter nirvāṇa, from the time they first brought forth their resolve to realize buddhahood to the time they actually realize buddhahood

on to that time when they enter the nirvāṇa without residue, and on to all of the remaining time before the Dharma they bequeath finally comes to an end.

He should bring to mind the roots of goodness associated with [bodhisattvas' practice of] the six *pāramitās* as well as the roots of goodness of those who have received the prediction that they are bound to become *pratyekabuddhas*.

He should also bring to mind the roots of goodness of the *śrāvaka* disciples, whether they are the product of giving, of upholding moral precepts, or of cultivation of *dhyāna* meditation, including in this the uncontaminated roots of goodness those in training and those beyond training.[168]

He should also [bring to mind the roots of goodness] associated with all buddhas' measureless meritorious qualities related to moral precept observance, meditative absorptions, wisdom, liberations, knowledge and vision of liberation, great kindness, and great compassion, including as well that related to all buddhas' proclamation of Dharma, for there are those people who have consequently brought forth faith and understanding in these dharmas, who have then undertaken training in them, and who have then acquired the benefit of these dharmas. Hence he should bring to mind all the roots of goodness planted by these people in relation to these dharmas.

He should also include all the roots of goodness of all common people as well those of all the devas, dragons, *yakṣas*, *gandharvas*, *asuras*, *garuḍas*, *kinnaras*, and *mahoragas* who, on being able to hear the proclamation of Dharma, then brought forth thoughts of goodness. He should also include here even [those roots of goodness planted] by animals who heard the Dharma and then brought forth thoughts of goodness. And he should also include here the roots of goodness planted by beings [who gathered together] when the Buddhas were about to enter nirvāṇa.

All of these roots of goodness and all of this merit are brought together and assessed, excluding none, and are, then and there, made the object of the most superior rejoicing, of the most sublime rejoicing, of the most excellent rejoicing, of unsurpassable rejoicing, of incomparable rejoicing, and of rejoicing that is equal to the unequaled.

Having rejoiced in all of this, one then takes all of the merit arising from this rejoicing and dedicates it to the realization of *anuttarasamyaksaṃbodhi*. In precisely the same manner, one does this with respect to the merit associated with all buddhas of the future and all buddhas of the present.

One's mind rejoices in all merit created by all these buddhas of the three periods of time, rejoicing as well in all merit produced by others due to the influence of all these buddhas. One then dedicates the merit [produced by this rejoicing] to the realization of *anuttarasamyaksaṃbodhi.*

Therefore we have a verse here that states:

One should repent of karmic offenses in this manner.
As for entreating, rejoicing in merit, and
dedicating merit to the unsurpassable path,
all of these should be carried out in this manner as well.

Just as taught by the Buddhas,
I repent of karmic offenses, entreat,
rejoice, and also dedicate merit,
all in this very same manner.

Throughout the course of the beginningless time in which one has dwelt in the world, one has committed an immeasurable number of karmic offenses that obstruct one's path to buddhahood. One should repent of these offenses in the presence of all buddhas of the ten directions and, in this same way, one should also present entreaties to all buddhas, rejoice in others' merit, and dedicate one's merit accordingly, [reflecting], "Just such repentance as does accord with what is known, seen, and permitted by the Buddhas—it is in accordance with this that I repent of my own karmic offenses." One's entreaties to all buddhas and one's dedications of merit should also be performed in this way. If one repents, entreats, rejoices, and then dedicates one's merit in this manner, this is what is meant by "right dedication."

9. Q: Which Ways of Performing These Accords with the Buddhas?

Question: Just what is meant by "repentance, entreating, rejoicing, and dedicating merit that accord with what is known, seen, and permitted by the Buddhas"?

10. A: Whichever Ways Accord with This Passage from Scripture

Response: "Repentance" and "entreating" are as previously explained. As for "rejoicing in merit" and "dedicating merit," they should accord with the following statements in the large edition of the *[Great Perfection of Wisdom] Sutra:*[169]

> Subhūti addressed the Buddha, saying, "O Bhagavat, as for the aforementioned 'supreme rejoicing' brought forth by the bodhisattva after comprehensively considering and assessing all the merit and roots of goodness of all past, future, and present buddhas, of all their disciples, and of all other beings—O Bhagavat, precisely what is meant by this 'supreme rejoicing'?"

The Buddha then told Subhūti, "It is when, with respect to all dharmas of the past, the future, and the present, a bodhisattva does not seize on them, does not retain them in mind, does not perceive them, does not apprehend them, and does not make discriminations about them, even as he is still able to reflect in this way:

> All of these dharmas are supposed to exist merely due to perceptions and mental discriminations regarding the coming together of many conditions. In reality, none of these dharmas is ever produced nor do any of them have any place from which they come forth. There is not even a single dharma among them that has ever been produced, is now being produced, or ever will be produced. Nor are there any of them that have ever been destroyed, are now being destroyed, or ever will be destroyed. The character of all dharmas is precisely of this sort.
>
> It is in accordance with the character of dharmas that I rejoice and, having rejoiced, it is then also in accordance with the true character of all dharmas that I dedicate all merit to *anuttarasamyaksaṃbodhi.*

"It is precisely this that constitutes the most supreme rejoicing and dedication.

"Furthermore, Subhūti, a son or daughter of good family striving to follow the path to buddhahood who wishes to refrain from slandering the Buddha should dedicate their roots of goodness in this way and they should think as follows:

> Just as, using the buddha mind, the buddha wisdom, and the buddha eye, all buddhas know and see from root to branch and in terms of substance and signs on which bases this merit and these roots of goodness exist—so too do I also accord with all buddhas' knowledge and vision as I rejoice. And just as all buddhas have permitted it, so too do I also dedicate these roots of goodness.

"If a bodhisattva dedicates merit in this manner, then he will thereby refrain from slandering the buddhas. Thus he will remain free of fault by acting in this way. Dedicating merit with deep-seated aspirations and resolute faith, doing so in a manner that accords with reality—this is what is meant by 'great dedication' and 'perfectly complete dedication.'

"Furthermore, Subhūti, a son or daughter of good family should dedicate roots of goodness and merit in the following manner: This dedication should be done in a way that conforms to the moral precept observance, meditative absorptions, wisdom, liberation, and knowledge and vision of liberation possessed by worthies and *āryas.*

Those dedications are not anchored in the desire realm, are not anchored in the form realm, are not anchored in the formless realm, and are not situated in the past, the future, or the present. Just as those qualities are not anchored anywhere within the three realms, just so should this dedication of merit not be anchored there, either. Nor should the bases for the dedication of merit be anchored in any such way, either.

"If a bodhisattva is able in this way to gain aspirations and resolute faith that accord with reality, this is what is meant by dedication that is free of error, dedication that is free of the poisons, and dedication that accords with the nature of dharmas.

"If, however, in performing dedications of merit, a bodhisattva were to seize on any signs or were to have any fond attachment to them, this would constitute wrong dedication.

"Therefore, all bodhisattvas and *mahāsattvas* should understand the character of dharmas as it is known by buddhas. When one dedicates merit in a manner that accords with the character of dharmas, one becomes able to reach *anuttarasamyaksaṃbodhi*. This is what is meant by 'right dedication.'"

The End of Chapter Ten

Chapter 11
Distinctions with Regard to Merit

XI. Chapter 11: Distinctions with Regard to Merit

A. Q: How Should One Repent, Entreat, Rejoice, and Dedicate Merit?

Question: In what way should one carry out repentance, entreating, rejoicing, and dedication? How many times during the course of the day and night should one perform these actions?

B. A: With Reverence and Pressed Palms, Three Times Each Day & Night

Response:

With the right knee touching the ground
and with the right shoulder bared,
place the palms together and, with reverential mind,
do these three times each day and night.

Because these actions are emblematic of reverential behavior, one touches the right knee to the ground, bares the right shoulder, and presses one's palms together. This observance should be carried out at the beginning of the night as one simultaneously pays reverence to all buddhas, repents, entreats, rejoices, and dedicates merit. One does so yet again in this same way in the middle of the night and again at the end of the night.

One proceeds in this same way at the beginning of the day, again in the middle of the day, and again at the end of the day, doing so altogether six times in the day and night, doing so while single-mindedly bringing to mind all buddhas, envisioning them as if they were manifesting right before one's very eyes.

C. Q: What Karmic Result Ensues from Doing This?

Question: What karmic result ensues from acting in this way?

D. A: If One Did This but Once, the Merit Would Be Incalculably Great

Response:

If one were to practice this but a single time
and the associated merit were to have physical form,
not even world systems as numerous as the Ganges' sands
would be capable of holding it all.

If one were to carry out this procedure even once and if the resulting merit was given physical form, that merit would be so immense that it could not be contained even in a measureless, boundless, and inconceivable number of great trichiliocosms equal the number of sands in the Ganges River. This is as described in the "Getting Rid of Karmic Offenses" chapter of *The Three Branches Sutra*:[170]

> The Buddha told Śāriputra, "Even if a son or daughter of good family made an offering to the Buddhas of a quantity of the seven precious things sufficient to fill up the worlds of great trichiliocosms equal in number to the sands of the Ganges, that merit would still be superseded by the amount of merit created by some other person who entreated the Buddhas to turn the wheel of Dharma."

Moreover, in the "Rejoicing and Dedication" chapter of *The [Mahā] prajñāpāramitā [Sūtra]*, the Buddha said:[171]

> It is good indeed, good indeed, Subhūti, that you are able to carry on the work of the Buddha by explaining to the bodhisattvas this dharma of dedicating [merit]. Suppose a bodhisattva were to engage in the following reflection:
>
> > Just as all buddhas know and see from root to branch and in terms of substance and signs which causes and conditions serve as the bases for the existence of this merit and these roots of goodness, so too, as I engage in this dedication [of merit], I also accord with what the buddhas know and see.
>
> This person [who carries out dedications in this manner] thereby acquires an immense amount of merit. By way of analogy, even if beings as numerous as those in the worlds of great trichiliocosms as numerous as the Ganges' sands were all to achieve perfect adherence to the ten courses of good karmic action, still, the merit gained by that bodhisattva [mentioned above] would be, in its magnitude, the most superior, the most sublime, and the most excellent. It would be matchless, unequaled, and equal to the unequaled.
>
> But, Subhūti, set aside this example of all beings in the worlds of great trichiliocosms as numerous as the Ganges' sands achieving perfect adherence to the ten courses of good karmic action. Even if beings as numerous as those in the worlds of great trichiliocosms as numerous as the Ganges' sands were all to acquire the four *dhyānas*, when compared to the merit arising from all of this, his merit would still be the most superior, the most sublime, and the most excellent.
>
> So too would this also be the case with regard to the merit that those beings would gain if they acquired the four immeasurable minds, if they acquired the four formless-realm absorptions, if they acquired the five spiritual superknowledges, or if they realized the fruit of the path of the stream enterer, the fruit of the path of the *sakṛdāgāmin*, the fruit of the path of the *anāgāmin*, the fruit of the path

of the arhat, or if they achieved the realization of the *pratyekabuddha*'s path. In those cases as well, comparatively speaking, the merit derived from dedications of merit made in accordance with the Dharma would be the most superior, the most sublime, and the most excellent.

But, Subhūti, set aside this example of all the beings in the worlds of great trichiliocosms as numerous as the Ganges' sands achieving [all of these accomplishments up to and including] the realization of the *pratyekabuddha*'s path.

Suppose instead that, on the one hand, there were a number of beings in the worlds of great trichiliocosms as numerous as the Ganges' sands who all brought forth the resolve to attain *anuttarasamyaksaṃbodhi* while, on the other hand, there were a number of beings equivalent to those in the worlds of great trichiliocosms as numerous as the Ganges' sands. If one of those bodhisattvas [who had brought forth the resolve], relying on a mind that still seizes upon signs, were to make offerings to all those beings of clothing, food and drink, bedding, and medicines, doing so for kalpas as numerous as the Ganges' sands, using every sort of happiness enhancing gift while making offerings to them, paying reverence to them, and also praising them. Supposing that each and every one of those bodhisattvas all acted in this very same manner, what do you think, Subhūti? Would all of these bodhisattvas gain a great deal of merit because of this, or not?

[Subhūti replied:]

O Bhagavat, they would gain an extremely great amount. Such an amount of merit as this would be beyond the reach of any calculation or analogy. If such a quantity of merit were to be given physical form, it could not be contained even within worlds as numerous as the Ganges' sands.

The Buddha told Subhūti:

Good indeed, good indeed, Subhūti. [Even so], the merit of this bodhisattva guarded and protected by the *prajñāpāramitā* who performs the dedication of roots of goodness in a manner conforming to the nature of dharmas—that merit is such that the merit gained by all of those aforementioned bodhisattvas whose giving involved seizing on signs could not equal even a hundredth of it, a thousandth of it, one ten-thousandth of it, or even one billionth of a *koṭi*'s part of it. This comparison would even be beyond the reach of calculation or analogy. And why is that? It is because the giving practiced by those aforementioned bodhisattvas involved mental discriminations seizing on signs.

> [Because of this], their merit remains confined entirely within the sphere of what is measurable and calculable.

Also, the "Dedication" of the *[Mahā]prajñāpāramitā [Sūtra]* records that, in speaking to the devas of the Pure Abodes Heavens, the Buddha said the following:

> Let us set aside this case of there being on the one hand beings as numerous as those in the worlds of great trichiliocosms as numerous as the Ganges' sands who had brought forth the resolve to attain *anuttarasamyaksaṃbodhi* while on the other hand there is another group of beings as numerous as those in the worlds of great trichiliocosms as numerous as the Ganges' sands and then each and every one of these bodhisattvas [in the former group] made offerings to all these beings [in the latter group], giving clothing, food and drink, bedding, medicines, and other means of sustenance, freely making such offerings for a number of kalpas as numerous as the Ganges' sands, but doing all of this giving with minds attached to signs.
>
> Devas, [consider instead a case where, on the one hand, there are] all these beings in the worlds of great trichiliocosms as numerous as the Ganges' sands who had brought forth the resolve to attain *anuttarasamyaksaṃbodhi* while on the other hand there was yet another group of beings in the worlds of great trichiliocosms as numerous as Ganges' sands who had also brought forth the resolve to attain *anuttarasamyaksaṃbodhi.*
>
> If one of that latter group of bodhisattvas made offerings to every one of that former group of bodhisattvas, making offerings of clothing, food and drink, bedding, medicines, and means of sustenance, doing so for kalpas as numerous as the Ganges' sands, but doing so with mental discriminations seizing on signs even as, in addition, in this same manner, every one of all of the rest of those bodhisattvas [in this latter group] made offerings to all those bodhisattvas [in the former group], giving clothing, food and drink, bedding, medicines, and means of sustenance, freely making such offerings for kalpas as numerous as the Ganges' sands while also paying reverence to them and uttering their praises, but with all of this giving also involving seizing on signs.
>
> [Now consider yet another case, as follows:] If a bodhisattva guarded and protected by the *prajñāpāramitā* were to consider the roots of goodness of all buddhas of the past, future, and present, including that associated with their qualities of moral precept observance, meditative absorption, wisdom, liberation, and knowledge and vision of liberation, [and the roots of goodness] associated with these same five qualities as acquired by the *śrāvaka* disciples, and

also [the roots of goodness of] common people—if he were to consider all these roots of goodness planted in the past, present, and future, considering them all together, and assessing them all without excluding any—if with respect to all that merit he were to then perform the most supreme, the most sublime, the most excellent rejoicing, unequaled rejoicing, rejoicing that is equal to the unequaled and inconceivable—and if he were then to dedicate the merit arising from that rejoicing to *anuttarasamyaksaṃbodhi*, reflecting, "May this merit of mine enable the realization of buddhahood,"—if one were to compare the former merit involving seizing on signs with this latter stock of merit, it could not equal even a hundredth part, a thousandth part, a ten-thousandth part, or even the smallest fraction of a *koṭi*'s part. The comparison is such that it would be beyond the reach of calculation or analogy. Why is this so? This is because the giving done by that former group of bodhisattvas involved mental discriminations seizing on signs.

Furthermore, suppose that on the one hand there was a group of beings as numerous as those in all worlds in great trichiliocosms as numerous as the Ganges' sands who had brought forth the resolve to attain *anuttarasamyaksaṃbodhi* and who practiced good physical karma, good verbal karma, and good mental karma, while [on the other hand] there was yet another group of beings as numerous as those in all the worlds in great trichiliocosms as numerous as the Ganges' sands who had also brought forth the resolve to attain *anuttarasamyaksaṃbodhi*, [doing so with such solidity of resolve that], even if they were scolded, reviled, and cursed for kalpas as numerous as the Ganges' sands, they would still be able to endure this for kalpas as numerous as the Ganges' sands even as they continued with physical and mental vigor to rid themselves of every form of indolence and focus their minds in *dhyāna* concentration free of scattered thoughts, but doing so while still seizing on signs. The merit of those [described in both these latter cases], would still not compare with that of the single bodhisattva who carried out his dedication of merit in a manner conforming to the nature of dharmas, for his merit would be superior.

Therefore, regarding your earlier question as to what benefit results from these practices [involving repentance, entreating, rejoicing, and dedication], one gains a mass of merit of such magnitude as this. Therefore, if someone wishes to gain such an immeasurable, boundless, and inconceivable mass of merit, he should practice this repentance, entreating, rejoicing, and dedication, not sparing even his own body and life and not caring about receiving offerings or enjoying fame, but rather always diligently devoting himself to these practices both by day and by night.

E. Q: Why Have You Not Discussed the Merit Arising from Repentance?

Question: You have still only described the merit derived from entreating, rejoicing, and dedication of merit. Why have you not discussed the merit involved in repentance?

F. A: The Merit Arising from Repentance Is the Greatest

Response: Among all of these sources of merit, the merit associated with repentance is the greatest. Because one is thereby able to get rid of the offenses constituting one's karmic obstacles, one therefore becomes able to skillfully practice the bodhisattva path and practice entreating, rejoicing, and dedication of merit, doing so in a manner that is conjoined with and no different from the realization of emptiness, signlessness, and wishlessness.

Additionally, repentance is comparable to some wish-fulfilling jewel through which one is able to obtain whatever one wishes. As the Buddha said:

> If someone wishes to be reborn within a great brahman-caste family, within a great *kṣatriyan*-caste family, or within a great *vaiśya*-caste clan, he should repent of his karmic offenses, concealing none of them, and vowing not to repeat them.
>
> If someone wishes to be reborn in the Heaven of the Four Heavenly Kings, in the Trāyastriṃśa Heaven, in the Yāma Heaven, in the Tuṣita Heaven, in the Nirmāṇarati Heaven, or in the Paramirmita Vaśavartin Heaven, in those cases as well, he should carry out the repentance of karmic offenses, concealing none of them, and vowing not to repeat them.
>
> If someone wishes to be reborn in the Brahma Heaven or anywhere on up to the station of neither perception nor non-perception, this person too should repent of karmic offenses in this very same way, concealing none of them, and vowing not to repeat them.
>
> If someone wishes to gain the fruit of the stream enterer, the fruit of the *sakṛdāgāmin*, the fruit of the *anāgāmin*, or the fruit of arhatship, he too should carry out this repentance of karmic offenses.
>
> If someone wishes to gain the three clear knowledges,[172] the six types of psychic power, or the powers of sovereign mastery associated with the *śrāvaka* disciple path, or if he wishes to reach the far shore of perfection in the meritorious qualities associated with the *śrāvaka* disciple path, in these cases too, he should carry out repentance of karmic offenses in this manner.
>
> If someone wishes to become a *pratyekabuddha*, in this case too, he should carry out repentance of karmic offenses in this manner.
>
> If someone wishes to gain the wisdom of omniscience, inconceivable wisdom, unimpeded wisdom, or unsurpassable wisdom, in

these cases too, he should carry out repentance of karmic offenses in this manner, concealing none of them, and vowing not to repeat them.

Therefore, one should realize that repentance has great karmic effects.

G. Q: How Can You Say That Repentance Gets Rid of Karmic Offenses?

Question: You claim that repentance allows one to eliminate the karmic offenses that create karmic obstacles. However, another sutra states: "The Buddha told Ānanda, 'If one intentionally commits a karmic act, one is certainly bound to undergo its retribution.'"

Additionally, the Abhidharma states, "The causes and conditions involved in karmic acts are not empty. Their retributions are neither lost nor extinguished."

Furthermore, it states in the sutras that beings all belong to their karma, that they all exist on the basis of their karma, that they depend upon and abide within their karma, that beings follow their karma, and that everyone individually undergoes their own corresponding karmic retribution, whether that be present-life retribution, retribution undergone in the next life, or retribution undergone in subsequent lives.[173]

Also, in *The Karmic Retribution Sutra*, King Yāma says to beings, "Tut! You beings! These karmic offenses of yours were not created by your parents, by devas, by *śramaṇas*, or by brahmans. You created them yourselves and so you should undergo retribution for them yourselves."

Furthermore, in "The Verse of the Worthies and Āryas," it says:

The true Dharma is like vajra.
The general of karmic power remains unconquerable.
Even though I have now already attained buddhahood,
I would still be bound to undergo retribution for bad karma.

Additionally, the Buddha said:

The great seas and the famous mountains,
the hills, the trees, the forests,
the earth, the water, fire, wind, and such,
as well as the sun, the moon, the stars and constellations—

Once they reach the time of the kalpa's burning,
all without exception will come to an end.
Karma, however, even for countless kalpas,
always abides and never is lost.

You have encountered the one replete with all the marks,
the omniscient one, the teacher of men.

As for the karmic offenses committed in the past,
his resulting retributions have already been repaid.

Now, although you have succeeded in meeting the Buddha,
in ending the defilements, and in attaining the fruits of the Ārya,
because of residual causes and conditions,
slivers of wood are still able to penetrate the body.

Therefore one should not claim that repentance gets rid of karmic offenses.

H. A: Although Not Eliminated Entirely, They Are Greatly Reduced

Response: I did not claim that if one repents, then offense karma is entirely extinguished so that there is no resulting karmic retribution. I said that if one repents of one's karmic offenses, then [their retribution] may be lightened and undergone in a short period of time. Therefore, a verse on repentance says, "If I should fall into the three wretched destinies, I pray that I might instead undergo [the retribution] in a human body."

Additionally, in *The Sutra on the Wisdom Seal of the Tathāgata,* it states that the Buddha informed Maitreya, saying:

Bodhisattvas who, with deep-seated aspirations, delight in [the prospect of attaining] *anuttarasamyaksaṃbodhi* may still have karmic offenses whereby they should otherwise undergo retribution in the wretched destinies. When these karmic offenses have become lighter, they may then be bound in later lifetimes:

To receive an ugly physical form;

To be much afflicted by sickness;

To have no awe-inspiring personal presence;

To be born into a lower-class family, into a poor family, into a family in which wrong views are dominant, or into a family supporting itself with a deviant livelihood;

To be born into a place contrary to their wishes or a place beset with many worries;

To be born into a country that becomes destroyed, a village that becomes destroyed, a family compound that becomes destroyed, or a circumstance where whatever they love becomes destroyed;

To be unable to encounter a good spiritual guide;

To never be able to hear the Dharma;

To be unable to receive any means of support, or, if they acquire it, it is coarse, inferior, and always inadequate for self-sustenance;

To have the ability to inspire the faith and respect of those who are of inferior or base character, but to never be able to inspire the faith and respect of great men;

To have it happen that, whenever they cultivate the accumulation of merit, they encounter a multitude of hindrances and end up being unsuccessful in the attempt;

To have all of their faculties be dim and dull;

To have it be that, whenever they practice *dhyāna*, their mind is subject to confusion;

To be unable to gain the qualities of an awakened mind free of contaminants;

To be unable to understand the correct import of the Dharma of the sutras;

And so forth, including even experiencing nightmares, thereby undergoing [in these various ways] the retribution [that would otherwise entail descent into] the wretched destinies.[174]

Additionally, the Buddha stated:[175]

If a person has a minor karmic offense, he may be able to undergo the retribution in this present life, but if that karmic offense increases in its magnitude, he will be bound to fall into the hells.

What is meant by this statement that a small karmic offense in the present life might increase in magnitude to the point that one is then bound to fall into the hells? It could be that someone fails to cultivate [the actions of] the body, fails to cultivate observance of the moral precepts, fails to cultivate qualities of mind, fails to cultivate wisdom, and also remains bereft of great intentions. This is a person who, if he commits even a minor karmic offense, may become bound to fall into the hells.

What is meant by the statement that this person with a karmic offense entailing retribution in the present life may avoid falling into the hells provided that his karmic offenses do not increase in magnitude? This refers to someone of this sort who cultivates [the actions of] the body, cultivates observance of the moral precepts, cultivates qualities of mind, cultivates wisdom, and also possesses great intentions unconstrained by hindrances. If someone of this sort has karmic offenses, but they do not increase in their magnitude, their retribution will occur in the present life.

Suppose for example that someone mixed a pint of salt into a small container of water. He would then find it to be undrinkable. But if another person casts a pint of salt into a large pond, he would not find its water the least bit salty, how much the less would he find it undrinkable. What is the reason for this? It is because the volume of water is great while that of the salt is but little. So too it is with karmic offenses.

Accordingly, we have the following verses:

When a pint of salt is thrown into an immense pond,
its flavor remains no different,
However, if one instead mixes it into a small container of water,
the harshness of the salt makes the water undrinkable.

This is analogous to there being a person with a great stock of merit
who has but few karmic offenses
and who is not bound to fall into the wretched destinies,
but rather undergoes mild retribution under other conditions

while there is another person with only a scant amount of merit
who has committed but few karmic offenses that,
because his mental resolve is but narrow and small,
is caused by those karmic offenses to fall into the wretched destinies.

If someone's physical vitality (lit. "fire") is weak in its strength,
when he eats but a little of something difficult to digest,
although this person doesn't die,
his body undergoes much suffering.

If someone's physical vitality is strong,
when he eats but a little of something difficult to digest,
such a person never dies from it
and undergoes only a minor amount of suffering.

If the vitality of one's goodness, merit, and wisdom is weak,
and he has committed but few bad karmic offenses,
there is nothing to save him from these karmic offenses,
and hence they are able to cause his descent into the hells.

In the case of someone possessed of great merit,
even though he may have done bad things involving karmic offenses,
they may not compel him to fall into the hells,
for he may instead undergo only mild present-life retribution.

Take for example the case of Aṅgulimāla.
Although he murdered many people
and also wished to harm his mother and the Buddha,
he still attained the path of arhatship.

The principle of undergoing only mild retribution in this present life is also illustrated by Ajātaśatru who killed his father, the King, a man who had already attained enlightenment. Through causes and conditions having to do with the Buddha and Mañjuśrī, this grave karmic offense resulted in only relatively mild retribution.

[This principle is also illustrated by] the case of "Poisonous Snake Man." When he was born, it rained blood. Afterward, as he grew up, if he wished to kill some person, he only needed to glare at him, whereupon they would immediately fall dead. If he so much as blew his breath on someone, then too, they would fall dead. Because of this, the people of the time called him "Breath Blower."

When this man's life was about to come to an end, Śāriputra went to his abode, whereupon he became angry and glared at Śāriputra. Even so, this did not cause Śāriputra to fall dead. He then blew his breath onto Śāriputra, but that did not cause him to fall dead, either. Rather, the radiance of Śāriputra's body simply shone ever brighter.

When this happened, his mind immediately became pure and he gazed at Śāriputra, scanning him up and down seven times. Based on these causes and conditions, after he died, he was born seven times up in the heavens and seven times back in the human realm and became bound to become a *pratyekabuddha* at that time when the human life span extends to forty thousand years. Then his body will become the color of gold, whereupon the people of that time will mistake him for a mass of gold and will attempt to hack away chunks of it. His life will then immediately come to an end and he will enter nirvāṇa.

This is also illustrated by the case of King Aśoka who, having used his troops to subdue the continent of Jambudvīpa, was responsible for killing eighteen thousand palace courtiers [in those conquered domains]. However, because, as a child in a previous life, he had gifted the Buddha with a lump of clay, he was later moved to erect eighty thousand stupas, always listened to and accepted the Dharma taught to him by great arhats, and later attained the enlightenment of the stream enterer. This is yet another instance of being able to undergo mild retribution while still abiding in a human body.

In instances where one undergoes [retribution for] karmic offenses in this way, it is when one has practiced many meritorious deeds while also being possessed of a vast and immense resolve. Then, because one has accumulated all manner of merit, he does not fall into the wretched destinies.

Therefore, as for the challenge that you presented earlier [with regard to the teaching that], if one repents of karmic offenses, they will then be completely extinguished so that there is no resulting karmic retribution—[that challenge] is erroneous. Furthermore, if one claims that karmic offenses cannot be extinguished at all, then one would be unable to believe the Buddha's statement in the Vinaya that, if one repents, one may thereby get rid of one's offenses. This matter is not as you have claimed. Therefore, one should indeed repent of the karmic offenses that create karmic obstacles.

The End of Chapter Eleven

Chapter 12
Distinctions with Regard to Giving

XII. Chapter 12: Distinctions with Regard to Giving

A. With More Merit & Mental Pliancy, the Bodhisattva Develops Faith

As for the bodhisattva who is able in this manner to carry out repentance, entreating, rejoicing, and dedication:

As the power of his merit increases,
and his mind also becomes more pliant,
he then develops faith in the Buddhas' meritorious qualities
and in the great conduct of the bodhisattvas.

Because of his repentance, entreating, rejoicing, and dedication, the power of this bodhisattva's merit increases and his mind becomes well-trained and possessed of pliancy. Thus he becomes able to have faith in and accept what the common person has no faith in, namely the Buddhas' measureless and supremely pure meritorious qualities. He is also able to place faith in and accept the rare and difficult endeavors accomplished by the great bodhisattvas' as they carry out their pure and great practices.

Now, again, a verse:

B. The Bodhisattva's Sympathy for Beings Leads to Compassion for Them

Beings who are all afflicted with suffering
do not possess this profound and pure Dharma.
He feels pity and sadness for them
and so brings forth a mind of deep compassion for them.

Having developed faith in the measureless, extremely profound, and supremely pure meritorious qualities of the buddhas and bodhisattvas, the bodhisattva feels pity and sadness for all beings who have none of these meritorious qualities. Because they hold every sort of wrong view, they only experience the many different types of suffering. Consequently, he brings forth a mind of deep compassion for them.

C. The Bodhisattva Is Then Motivated to Rescue Beings from Suffering

He is mindful of all these beings
that are mired in the mud of suffering, and thinks,
"I should rescue them by extricating them from this,
thereby causing them to abide in a state of peace and security."

Having brought forth the mind of compassion, this bodhisattva thinks, "All of these beings are always afflicted by greed, hatred, and delusion and because of that they undergo all manner of physical and mental suffering. I shall rescue them by extricating them from that, thereby causing them to leave behind the deep mud of physical and mental suffering. Then they will finally become free of the misfortunes of birth, aging, sickness, and death and become able to abide in the peace and security of nirvāṇa's bliss."

He therefore brings forth a deeply compassionate mind for these suffering beings. If, because of this mind of compassion, he seeks for their sakes to bring about whatever they wish for, thereby causing them to find happiness, this is what is known as the mind of loving kindness.

D. Due to Kindness & Compassion, He Devotes Himself to Giving

When, in this manner, the bodhisattva
deeply accords with the mind of kindness and compassion,
he cuts off all covetous cherishing
and devotes himself to giving with diligence and vigor.

It is in this manner that the bodhisattva seeks to realize buddhahood and to liberate beings afflicted by sufferings. As for the "accordance" [engaged in by this individual] who is mindful in this way, this refers to his accordance with kindness and compassion and to his refraining from according with any other states of mind. "Deep kindness" refers to that which extends universally to all beings and involves a degree of mindfulness of them that penetrates to the very marrow of his bones.

"All" refers to every inward and outward thing, to all gold, silver, precious jewels, the state, its cities, his wife and children, and so forth. "Covetousness" refers to the insatiable desire to obtain something. "Cherishing" refers to affectionate attachment on account of which one does not wish to give up something to someone else. "Cut off" refers to abandoning these two bad influences.[176]

If one accords with this, then one thereby throws open the gates of *dāna pāramitā* (the perfection of giving). Therefore, one should always engage in its single-minded and diligent practice, not allowing any room for negligence. And how does one go about accomplishing this? The bodhisattva thinks to himself, "I will now strive to benefit beings however I am able." And so it is that he brings forth a solid resolve to practice giving.

1. The Bodhisattva Is Willing to Give Everything to Beings

As for all of those things he possesses,
whether living or not living,

including even the throne of a wheel-turning or heavenly king,
there are no instances of their being requested but not given.

This is still the case even with sons and daughters
as well as the clan's wives and consorts of which he is fond,
these who in their youthfulness have extremely fine appearances
and are skillful in their ability to render service to others,

Whose respectful and acquiescent minds are pliant and congenial,
whom he lovingly bears in mind with utmost depth of feeling,
cherishing them even more than his own life—
If someone seeks to have them, he is able to give them all.

This is so even with the flesh and blood of his own body,
his own marrow, his hands and feet,
his head, eyes, ears, nose, and so forth.
He is even able to sacrifice his entire body.

This bodhisattva fixes his mind on giving. As regards whatever outward things he owns, whether sentient or insentient, there is never any case where someone seeks to have them and yet he fails to make a gift of them.

"Not living things" refers to all such things as gold, silver, and precious jewels even up to and including the position of a wheel-turning king or the position of a king among the devas.

"Living things" refers to sons or daughters or to the youthful wives and consorts of the nobility and the best of the clans. Though they are of fine appearance, gentle and agreeable, respectful, and thoroughly acquiescent and even though he feels the most extremely affectionate cherishing for them, greater even than what he feels for his own life, he is still able to give them away to others.

In doing so, he is like "Comprehensive Giving Bodhisattva"[177] who was able to give away all outward possessions including his wife and children. This bodhisattva was able to give even the flesh and blood from his own body, his head, his eyes, his hands and feet, his ears, and his nose, and he was also able to cut into his own flesh, expose the bones, break the bones, and extract his own marrow.

In this, he is also like Sadāprarudita Bodhisattva who would even give his entire body. One cherishes nothing more than one's own body and yet he, too, was able to give like Sarvadāna.

In this, he is also like the bodhisattva who, when he was a rabbit, gave his body as a gift to a rishi.[178]

And, in doing so, he is also like King Śibi who gave up his body to substitute for [and save the life of] a pigeon.

2. Q: Is His Giving Done for Merit or Due to Kindness and Compassion?

Question: Is this bodhisattva able to perform such difficult acts of giving because of his discriminating knowledge of the value of different types of giving and their corresponding karmic rewards, or does he instead give simply because of the mind of kindness and compassion that he has brought forth?

3. A: He Knows, Has Faith, May Have the Heavenly Eye & So Gives All

Response:

> If one practices giving of this sort,
> then one will gain karmic results of this very same sort.
> Inwardly, one gives up his limbs and such
> while also giving away even all of one's outward possessions.

"Inward possessions" refers to one's own head, eyes, hands, feet, and so forth. "Outward possessions" refers to one's wife, children, gold, silver, jeweled objects, and so forth. This bodhisattva understands giving in accordance with reality in a manner whereby, making distinctions with regard to each case, he realizes, "When this is achieved, then this will be the corresponding karmic result."

In addition, he has faith in what is taught in the sutras and may also be able to use the heavenly eye to know such matters.

a. Q: As You Said He Knows Them, Please Explain These Karmic Results

Question: You just said that he knows the karmic results obtained by giving his body or limbs or by giving away his outward possessions. Could you now speak of the karmic results that may be obtained from this?

b. A: Akṣayamati Bodhisattva's Explanation Is As Follows:

Response: In Chapter Thirty of the *Precious Summit Sutra,* "On the Meaning of Dāna Pāramitā,"[179] Akṣayamati Bodhisattva states that the bodhisattva makes the following aspirational vows:

> May giving food to the hungry result in my receiving five things as karmic results: First, long life; second, courage; third, happiness; fourth, strength; and fifth, physical beauty;
>
> May providing drinks to those needing something to drink first result in being able when abiding in the human realm to have fragrant and delicious beverages, and then, afterward, being able to dispel the thirst-like cravings associated with the afflictions;
>
> May giving vehicles to those needing vehicles result in gaining happiness through whatever one wishes, in perfecting the four bases of psychic power, and later on, in attaining success in the paths of the Three Vehicles;

May providing clothing to those in need of clothes bring about the karmic result of then being able to wear the robes of a sense of shame and a dread of blame;
May giving lamplight to those in need of lamplight result in gaining the light of the buddha eye;
May giving music to those wishing for music result in complete acquisition of the heavenly ear;
May giving powdered incenses and perfumes to those needing powdered incense and perfumes result in gaining a body free of unpleasant odors;
May giving juices to those needing juices result in obtaining flavorful tastes;
May providing homes to those in need of homes result in becoming a place of refuge and a source of rescue and protection for all beings;
May providing life-sustaining things to beings result in acquiring the meritorious qualities assisting the attainment of bodhi;
May the giving of medical treatment and medicines result in becoming free of aging, sickness, and death, and in always being able to abide in happiness and security;
May the providing of servants result in perfect wisdom that is masterfully and freely implemented;
May giving gold, silver, coral, mother-of-pearl, and carnelian result in complete acquisition of all thirty-two marks;
May giving all manner of adornments result in gaining the eighty secondary characteristics;
May giving elephants, horses, and carriages result in complete acquisition of the Great Vehicle;
May giving gardens and groves result in complete acquisition of the bliss of *dhyāna* meditation;
May providing male and female [servants] for others result in gaining the *anuttarasamyaksaṃbodhi* that one so cherishes;
May giving granaries and treasuries result in gaining the complete treasury of Dharma;
May bestowing royal dominion over a country, over a Jambudvīpa continent or over the four continents result in becoming a Dharma king exercising sovereign mastery in the *bodhimaṇḍa;*
May the giving all manner of happiness enhancing amusements result in acquiring Dharma bliss;
May giving away one's feet result in gaining the feet of Dharma with which one is able to arrive at the *bodhimaṇḍa;*
May giving away one's hands result in gaining the jewel-bestowing hands with which one is able to give everything;

May giving away one's ears and nose result in gaining the perfect physical body;
May giving away one's eyes result in gaining the unimpeded Dharma eye;
May giving up one's head result in gaining the omniscience of he who is especially revered throughout the three realms;
May giving one's flesh and blood result in influencing all beings to achieve solid practice;
May the giving of one's marrow result in gaining the indestructible vajra body.

It is in this manner that karmic rewards ensue from opening the gates to the practice of giving.

c. The Karmic Results of Other Sorts of Giving

The karmic results derived from other sorts of giving should be readily deducible, as follows:

By giving bedding, one may gain the couch of liberation that comes with the peace and security of the Three Vehicles;
By providing a place for sitting [meditation], one may gain the indestructible abode in the *bodhimaṇḍa* beneath the bodhi tree;
By providing someone with a wife, one may gain the pleasures of Dharma joy;
By providing roads, one may be able to enter the right path for the sake of beings who are lost on the road of *saṃsāra;*
By giving rafts, one becomes able to cross beyond the flood of desire, the flood of existence, the flood of views, and the flood of ignorance;
By giving one's bones, one gains solidity in moral precept observance, solidity in meditative concentration, solidity in wisdom,[180] solidity in liberation, solidity in the knowledge and vision of liberation, and solidity in [dedication to liberating] beings;
By providing others with a following, one becomes able to assemble a retinue consisting of a countless and boundless number of *asaṃkhyeyas* of devas who are endowed with merit and who are all identically possessed of pure minds and inviolable loyalty;
By conferring admiring accolades on others, when one speaks on the Dharma, one elicits the delight and praises of devas, dragons, *yakṣas, gandharvas, śramaṇas,* and brahmans;
By giving volumes of the sutras, one enables the nine categories of canonical texts to remain for an immeasurably long period of time;
By giving the Dharma, one becomes able to gain a penetrating understanding of all dharmas.

Because it enables the accumulation of all of the meritorious qualities, this bodhisattva delights in the practice of giving in this manner. He understands how it is that giving is made pure and understands as well the measure of the karmic results that ensue from the practice of giving. Therefore:

d. He Avoids Wrong Giving and Gives In Accordance with Emptiness

As for giving wealth obtained contrary to Dharma and so forth,
as well as all those sorts of giving that are censured by the wise,
he remains free of any such forms of giving, and instead
gives only in ways that are conjoined with emptiness and such.[181]

Giving that is "contrary to Dharma" involves wealth obtained through bad actions. "Wealth" refers to life-supporting possessions. To sum it up, because the bodhisattva realizes that giving involving wealth obtained through bad actions is not pure, he does not engage in any of these sorts of giving that are contrary to Dharma. He refrains from participating in any of them, including especially such forms of giving as might be censured by the wise. Hence, when the bodhisattva engages in the practice of giving, he only gives in ways that are conjoined with the wisdom that fathoms emptiness and with the other sorts of associated qualities.

1) Q: Will You Please Discuss These Two Types of Giving?

Question: As for these two types of giving: that sort of giving which involves wealth obtained contrary to Dharma and that sort of giving which is conjoined with the wisdom that fathoms emptiness, one should present here a broad-ranging discussion elucidating the associated distinctions.

2) Akṣayamati Bodhisattva Explains Them as Follows:

Response: These two types of giving are discussed in the treatment of *dāna pāramitā* that is contained within the "Akṣayamati Bodhisattva Assembly" chapter, as below:[182]

a) The Types of Impure Giving

First, let us consider the distinctions involved in giving-associated merit, specifically as follows:

Bodhisattvas do not give wealth acquired in a manner that is contrary to Dharma. They do not engage in any giving that has the effect of aggravating other beings. No giving is done out of fearfulness. No giving is done due to some type of attachment. There are no instances where someone makes a request and yet they fail to give. There is no giving that fails to accord with what one has already pledged. There is no giving done wherein, because one is stingy with what is fine, one instead gives an inferior item;

There is no giving not rooted in earnest intentions, no giving intended to curry favor, no giving of anything that is counterfeit, no giving that produces damaging effects, no giving done with perverse intent, no giving done with a deluded mind, no giving done with mixed motivations, no giving involving an absence of resolute conviction,[183] and no giving done out of weariness;

There is no giving involving personal favoritism, no giving with the expectation of self-benefit, no giving seeking to focus [exclusively] on "fields of merit," and no giving that slights other beings as inadequate "fields of merit";[184]

There is no giving with a mind that distinguishes between those who uphold the moral precepts versus those who transgress against the moral precepts or that distinguishes between those who are seen as superior versus those who are seen as inferior;

There is no giving done out of a desire for fame, no giving done with the intent to elevate oneself, no giving done in a way that treats others as inferior, no giving because of intensely painful regret, and no giving that is done out of remorse;

There is no giving done [only as] a response to cries of urgency, no abusive giving, no giving promoting the dharma of spontaneous [acausal] occurrence,[185] no giving done simply to gain the resulting karmic rewards, no giving done out of hatred, and no giving that causes others to be left wanting;

There is no giving involving annoyance toward the supplicant, no giving involving slighting or dallying with the recipient, no deceptive giving, no giving just to save face, no giving done by tossing a donation, no giving not done with focused mind, and no giving of gifts not presented with one's own hands;

There is no failure to always give, no desisting from giving, no halting of giving, no giving as a means of struggling for superiority, no giving of merely insignificant and trivial things, and no giving involving an invitation to take whatever one wishes when one is offering only trivial things;

There is no giving not matching one's powers to give, no giving that considers some to not be fields of merit,[186] no giving of merely trivial things that is accompanied by inferior intentions, no giving accompanied by arrogance because of the abundance of one's gifts, and no giving that involves unprincipled actions;

There is no giving done with the intention of gaining rebirth in pleasurable places, no giving reliant upon the largesse of wealthy and noble clans, no giving done to gain rebirth in the heavens of the Four Heavenly Kings, Śakra, or Brahmā, no giving in pursuit of the Śrāvaka Vehicle or the Pratyekabuddha Vehicle, no giving in quest of becoming a king or a prince, and no giving with only a view to [favorable effects to be gained in] this present lifetime;

There is no self-satisfied [termination of one's] giving, no giving not dedicated to realization of all-knowledge, no impure giving, no giving at the wrong time, no giving of knives or poisons, no giving intended to aggravate or dally with beings, and no giving censured by the wise.

It is in this manner that one opens up and reveals what constitutes the gateway of giving. The other sorts of impure giving are such that one should be able to deduce what they are, as follows:

The bodhisattva does not give cast-off things. There is no giving demonstrating a hatred or abhorrence of nirvāṇa, no giving of easily acquired and abundantly available things, no giving calculated to manipulate kindness, no giving done just to repay kindnesses, and no giving done to elicit some reward in return;

There is no giving to ensure protection, no giving in quest of auspicious occurrences, no giving motivated by pride, no giving only to accord with customs of the clan, no perfunctory giving simply as a response to having received something, no failing to give for one's entire life, and no giving occasioned by defiled thoughts;

There is no giving done for sport, no giving done simply at the behest of a good spiritual guide, no giving done but lightly, no giving done with an unbridled mind, no giving because one has experienced loss, no giving simply as a response to having been praised by someone, no giving done because one has been rebuked, no giving done as a prayer for auspicious developments, no giving in praise of performing miracles, and no giving done to make a show of one's faith;

There is no giving because one has become fearful, no giving done with the intent to deceive, no giving to gain a following, no giving that does not serve to lead others [toward goodness], no giving done to lead others along, no giving done in the absence of faith, no giving that asserts the nonexistence of causes and conditions, no merely frivolous giving, and no giving done to make a display of one's exceptional qualities;

There is no giving to elicit one's own praises, no giving that does not accord with what is sought, no giving done to reduce the significance of someone else's giving, no giving of what does not please, no giving of something that will not be put to use, no giving out of disrespect, no inferior giving, no giving because of the occurrence of strange signs, no giving to restrain or suppress others, no giving of things obtained through intimidation, and no giving done with impure intentions;

There is no giving done with doubting thoughts, no giving intended to mentally crush a supplicant, no giving of forbidden things, no giving done out of discrimination, no giving of alcoholic beverages, no giving of tools of war, no giving of things seized from others, no giving that causes others to have doubts, and no giving done to induce intimacy;

There is no giving that serves to announce the faults of others, no giving in pursuit of something one cherishes, no giving influenced by hatred, no giving influenced by delusion, no giving rooted in fallacious conceptual proliferation,[187] and no giving not done for the sake of bodhi.

i) Q: Is the Bodhisattva Entirely Free of All Such Giving?

Question: [As for the types of giving just listed], from giving of wealth sought in ways contrary to Dharma to giving not done for the sake of bodhi, does the bodhisattva engage in any of them or not? Were he to engage in none of them, then he would be at fault for not seeking out fields of merit, for not making distinctions among beings, for not acknowledging kindnesses, for not repaying kindnesses, for not presenting gifts in accordance with clan customs, or for not giving things in accordance with national customs. If he does in fact engage in such giving, why do you claim here that there are no instances of this?

ii) A: No, but Such Giving Is Not Included in the Perfection of Giving

Response: It is not necessarily the case that the bodhisattva is completely free of all of these sorts of giving from giving of wealth that is acquired in ways contrary to Dharma to giving not done for the sake of bodhi. There may be times when he engages in some of them. However, these sorts of giving are not included within *dāna pāramitā*. It is because they cannot be instrumental in the perfection of *dāna pāramitā* that they are characterized here as being absent.

a) Giving Conjoined with Emptiness, Signlessness, or Wishlessness

Now, as for what is meant by [the above stanza's reference to] "giving conjoined with emptiness and other such meritorious qualities," this is as described in the *Akṣayamati Bodhisattva Sutra*, in the "Dāna Pāramitā" chapter, as follows:[188]

Because the giving done by the bodhisattva is conjoined with the mind that fathoms emptiness, it is endless;
Because this giving involves the cultivation of signlessness, it is endless;
Because this giving is preserved and protected by the practice of wishlessness, it is endless;
Because this giving is subsumed within roots of goodness, it is endless;
Because this giving accords with the characteristics associated with liberation, it is endless;
Because this giving is able to defeat all *māras,* it is endless;
Because this giving involves no admixture with the afflictions, it is endless;
Because this giving becomes ever more superior in its benefits, it is endless;
Because this giving is done with definite resolve, it is endless;
Because this giving facilitates accumulation of the dharmas constituting the limbs of bodhi, it is endless;
Because this giving is rightly dedicated, it is endless;
Because this giving brings about acquisition of the fruits of the liberation attained in the *bodhimaṇḍa,* it is endless;
Because this giving knows no bounds, it is endless;
Because this giving is inexhaustible, it is endless;
Because this giving is never cut off, it is endless;
Because this giving is vast, it is endless;
Because this giving is indestructible, it is endless;
Because this giving is invincible, it is endless;
Because this giving leads one to all-knowledge, it is endless;
Because this giving cuts off the defilement involved in giving wealth obtained in ways contrary to Dharma and other such forms of giving, and because it leads to the complete development of the realization of emptiness and the other associated meritorious qualities, it is therefore endless.

b) Impure Giving Versus Pure Giving

As for "the giving of wealth obtained in ways contrary to Dharma and other such forms of giving" these types of giving constitute "defiled giving." Whichever types of giving are conjoined with defilement are instances of impure giving whereas whichever types of giving are conjoined with emptiness and the other [associated meritorious qualities]—those are instances of pure giving.

Additionally, this topic of purity versus impurity in the practice of giving is one that now merits further discussion.

i) Four Types of Giving According to the Agents of Its Purification

The sutras state that there are four types of giving, as follows:[189]

There is giving that is purified by the giver and that is not purified by the receiver;
There is giving that is purified by the receiver and that is not purified by the giver;
There is giving that is purified by the giver and that is also purified by the receiver.
There is giving that is not purified by the giver and that is also not purified by the receiver.

Where the giver performs good actions of body, speech, and mind but the receiver has performed bad actions of body, speech, and mind, this is an instance of giving that is purified by the giver and that is not purified by the receiver.

Where the giver performs bad actions of body, speech, and mind and the receiver performs good actions of body, speech, and mind, this is an instance of giving that is purified by the receiver and that is not purified by the giver.

Where the giver performs good actions of body, speech, and mind and the receiver also performs good actions of body, speech, and mind, this is an instance of giving that is purified by the giver and that is also purified by the receiver.

Where the giver performs bad actions of body, speech, and mind and the receiver also performs bad actions of body, speech, and mind, this is an instance of giving that is not purified by the giver and that is also not purified by the receiver.

One should also make distinctions of this sort with regard to whether or not covetousness, hatred, and delusion have been cut off.

(1) The Bases for Presence or Absence of Purification

Additionally, in connection with these four types of giving, there are bases for distinguishing presence or absence of purification:

First, purification may be accomplished by the giver;
Second, purification may be accomplished by the receiver;
Third, purification is accomplished by both of them.

These classifications are determinants of purification. Also:

First, purification is not accomplished by the giver;
Second, purification is not accomplished by the recipient;
Third, they do not both purify [the act of giving].

These classifications are determinants of failure to accomplish purification [of the act of giving].

In these instances, when the giver possesses meritorious qualities, the act of giving derives its qualification as "pure" from the giver. When the receiver possesses meritorious qualities, the act of giving derives its qualification as "pure" from the receiver. When both the giver and the receiver possess meritorious qualities, the act of giving derives its qualification as "pure" from both the giver and the receiver.

When the giver commits karmic offenses, the act of giving derives its qualification as "impure" from the giver. When the receiver commits karmic offenses, the act of giving derives its qualification as "impure" from the receiver. When both the giver and the receiver commit karmic offenses, the act of giving derives its qualification as "impure" from both the giver and the receiver.

As for what constitutes the possession of meritorious qualities on the part of the giver, what constitutes possession of meritorious qualities on the part of the receiver, what constitutes commission of karmic offenses on the part of the giver, and what constitutes the commission of karmic offenses on the part of the receiver, these have already been discussed.

(1) Q: Of These Four, Which Should Be Practiced?

Question: Of the approaches to giving that you have described as contained within these four types of giving, which ones should the bodhisattva practice?

(2) A: Practice Two That Are Pure and Avoid Selfish Motives

Response:

Among the four types of giving,
one practices the two types involving pure giving.
In doing so, one does not seek fame or self-benefit
and one also does not seek to obtain any karmic fruits from this.

These types of giving consist of four types of which three contain bases of purity and three contain bases of impurity.[190] He does not practice any type of impure giving and does practice two types of pure giving: First, giving that is purified by the giver but is not purified by the receiver, and, second, giving where the giving is purified by both [the giver and the receiver].

One should always be vigorously devoted to the practice of these two types of pure giving. Why? Because this bodhisattva does not hope for any associated karmic fruits from this. Were one to hope for some sort of karmic fruits [from performing this act], then one would be inclined to seek out a pure receiver.

"Purity" is defined here by the giver and the receiver both being graced by meritorious qualities whereby the minds of each of them are pure. "Impurity" is defined by the presence in the giver of a miserliness. This accords with the Buddha's declaration that, in the practice of giving, miserliness constitutes a defilement. Although the other afflictions also constitute bases of impurity, here it is miserliness that constitutes the most serious [form of defilement].

(2) Q: How Can One Possessed of Desires Practice Pure Giving?

Question: If the bodhisattva should engage in diligent practice of these two types of giving, that wherein the giving is purified by the giver [but not by the receiver] and that wherein the giving is purified by both the giver and the receiver, since miserliness constitutes a defilement on the part of the giver and a major defilement of the act of giving, if the bodhisattva has not yet transcended desire and hence cannot yet cut off miserliness, how then could he succeed in practicing these two types of pure giving?

(3) A: Do Not Accumulate Things That Engender Miserliness

Response:

If some possession is capable of causing the arising of miserliness,
then one should refrain from accumulating such things.

If a bodhisattva realizes that some possession, whether living or not, causes the arising of miserly thoughts, then he should not accumulate such things. As a consequence [of refraining from accumulating such things], whenever he gives something, he will always be free of miserliness.

(a) Q: How Can One Accomplish This with One's Own Body?

Question: Outward possessions are such that one might refrain from accumulating them. But how does one accomplish this in relation to one's own body?

(b) A: Consider One's Body to Be Like a Medicine Tree

Response:

In order to always be of benefit to beings,
understand the body as like a medicinal tree.

In order to provide benefit to beings, one should possess a firm belief that one's body is like a medicinal tree that beings may use as medicine, taking roots, trunk, branches, leaves, blossoms, fruit, and so forth, each to cure a particular disease. In such a case, they may take whatever they wish without [the tree] preventing them from doing so in order to protect itself.

The bodhisattva is just like this. In order to be of benefit to beings, he is able to relinquish his body, thinking in this way: "If beings take whatever they need of my head, eyes, hands, feet, limbs, spine, abdomen, arms, ears, nose, teeth, tongue, blood, flesh, bones, marrow, and so forth, I shall be able to give them up, perhaps even giving them my entire body."

It is in this manner that one subdues one's mind as one cultivates and accumulates roots of goodness and remains protected by the adoption of skillful means in one's practice of *dāna pāramitā* (the perfection of giving).

E. The Bodhisattva's Dedication of the Merit Arising from His Giving

In ways that are general in character and specific in character,
one is always able to dedicate all acts of giving that one performs.

This bodhisattva is able to understand and pursue two sorts of dedication in relation to the two types of pure giving. The first is that which is of a general character and the second is that which is of a specific character.

As for dedications that are of a general character, one dedicates the merit from all of one's giving to *anuttarasamyaksaṃbodhi*. As for dedication of a specific character, this is as described in the above treatment of the karmic fruits resulting from acts of giving.

Then again, in the case of dedication of a general character, it is done for the sake of bringing peace, happiness, and benefit to all beings. As for dedication of a specific character, it is done for the sake of influencing beings without faith to gain faith, for the sake of influencing those who have broken the precepts to succeed in upholding the precepts, for the sake of influencing those of but little learning to develop extensive learning, for the sake of influencing those who are indolent to become vigorous in their efforts, for the sake of influencing those whose minds are scattered to gain *dhyāna* concentration, for the sake of influencing deluded beings to gain wisdom, and for the sake of influencing the miserly to develop minds inclined toward generosity.[191] And so it is that there are many different sorts of specifically-directed dedications.

Additionally, with regard to dedication of a general character, one dedicates the merit associated with the six *pāramitās* to *anuttarasamyaksaṃbodhi*, whereas, with regard to dedication of a specific character, when one gives outward things, one prays that all beings will gain the most supreme happiness. When giving one's limbs, one prays that all beings will gain the perfect body of a buddha.

1. Q: How Many Types of Right and Wrong Dedication are There?

Question: In the practice of giving, how many kinds of dedication are there? And how many kinds of dedication does one not practice?

2. There Are 4 Pure Objectives of Dedication and 3 Not Practiced

Response: The first category, those done for the sake of pure objectives, consist of four types of dedication. There are three types of dedication that one does not practice. The bodhisattva's giving may be dedicated to four types of pure objectives.

a. The Three Types of Dedication One Does Not Practice

The three objectives toward which one does not dedicate merit are as follows:

One does not dedicate merit for the sake of becoming a king.
One does not dedicate merit for the sake of sensual pleasures.
And one does not dedicate merit for the sake of gaining any of the grounds of a *śrāvaka* disciple or a *pratyekabuddha*.

Now, as for "not dedicating merit for the sake of becoming a king," this restriction of the objective of becoming a king is also intended to restrict dedications done to acquire the power and sovereign freedom of the nobility.

As for "not dedicating merit for the sake of acquiring sensual pleasures," this refers, aside from the above-mentioned nobility, to all others who partake of wealth's enjoyments and indulge themselves in the pleasures of the five types of desire.

As for "not dedicating merit for the sake of gaining any of the grounds of a *śrāvaka* disciple or a *pratyekabuddha*," this restricts entry into the Small Vehicle's nirvāṇa without residue but it does enable one to become securely established in the Great Vehicle in which, after a long time, one eventually enters the nirvāṇa without residue.

b. The Four Types of Dedication Done for the Sake of Pure Objectives

Now, as for the four types of dedication done for the sake of pure objectives, the merit from a bodhisattva's giving:

Is dedicated for the sake of purifying buddha lands;
Is dedicated for the sake of purifying one's realization of bodhi;[192]
Is dedicated for the sake of purifying one's teaching of beings;
And is dedicated for the sake of purifying one's realization of all-knowledge.[193]

The bodhisattva should adopt skillful means such as these in making dedications so as to not diminish the effectiveness of his giving and so as to cause it to become powerful.

1) Q: Which Dharmas Diminish Its Benefit and Which Increase It?

Question: Through which dharmas does one diminish the effectiveness of one's giving and through which dharmas does one cause the benefits of one's giving to increase?

b) A: There Are Four Causes of Diminishment, as Follows:

Response:

If one gives but fails to dedicate the merit,
if one has no skillful means,
if one seeks rebirth in an inferior station of existence,
or if one draws close to bad friends—

If one's giving takes place under such conditions,
then its effectiveness will thereby be diminished.

[This means]:

If one gives, but fails to dedicate the merit to *anuttarasamyaksaṃbodhi*—

If, because one is pursuing worldly happiness, one seeks rebirth in an inferior station of existence—

If one has no skillful means by which one can freely bring forth the karmic fruits of giving and *dhyāna* concentration—

Or if one draws near to [bad] friends who obstruct one's progress in the Great Vehicle—

Then, because of [any of] these four dharmas, [the effectiveness of] one's giving will be diminished.

c) For Increase, Stop These Four and Adopt Three Types of Thought

If one abandons these four, the power of one's giving will increase.
Also, one should adopt three types of thought as one gives.
In this, the bodhisattva accords with the words of the Buddha
while also not seeking to gain any karmic rewards [from giving].

If one abandons the above four dharmas, then the effectiveness of one's giving will be able to increase. [One does so as follows]:

First, one dedicates one's merit to *anuttarasamyaksaṃbodhi;*

Second, one adopts appropriate skillful means in carrying out dedications of merit;

Third, one seeks to reach the station of a Dharma king;

Fourth, one draws near to good spiritual guides.

Also, in one's practice of giving, one should use three types of Dharma-based thought, as follows:

First, because one feels pity for all beings, one bases one's giving on the resolve to attain bodhi;

Second, in one's practice of giving, one does not depart from the Dharma of the Buddha;

Third, in one's practice of giving, one does not seek any karmic rewards.

F. One Gives for the Sake of Causing 3 Dharmas and Seeking 2 Dharmas

Moreover:

> It is for the sake of bringing about three dharmas
> that one engages in the practice of giving
> and it is also for the sake of seeking two dharmas
> that one should engage in the practice giving.

It is for the sake of bringing about three dharmas that the bodhisattva engages in the practice of giving:

First, to acquire the Dharma of a Buddha;

Second, to bring about the proclamation of the Dharma;

Third, to cause all beings to abide in unsurpassable happiness.

Additionally, it is because one wishes to seek two dharmas that one practices giving: First, to acquire great wealth, and second, to perfect the practice of *dāna pāramitā*. Why? If the bodhisattva is endowed with great wealth, then:

He will leave behind the suffering of poverty;

He will not take others' wealth;

He will not seek to earn interest;

He will have nobody to whom he is indebted;

And he will have no worries about the repayment of debts.

When one possesses much wealth and one's assets are adequate, then:

One is able to see to one's own clothing and food while also being able to give out of kindness, thereby benefiting one's relatives, one's clan, and one's good spiritual guides;

One's retinue will be happy, one's household will prosper for their minds will always be as delighted as if they were always participating in a celebratory gathering;

One will be able to practice great giving, one's retinue will not slight him, and people will look up to him with respect;

Everyone will be inclined to believe and accept one's words;

One will be relied upon by the many;

When others come, one will be looked up to as a mentor;

On entering an assembly, one will have nothing to fear;

One will always delight in bathing, smoothing famous fragrances onto the body, wearing fine new clothes, and being adorned by a full array of ornaments;

One will become able to behold fine physical forms, to hear agreeable sounds, to smell marvelous fragrances, to always eat the most supremely exquisite flavors, [and to experience] subtle tactile sensations;

One will become indomitable by adversaries and will become well-liked by good spiritual friends.

These are instances of karmic rewards for goodness as experienced in the human body. Moreover:

One will become respected and admired, one will always be praised as wonderfully good, and others will forget one's disgraceful lapses;

Although one may be been born into a lower-class household, one will have the marks of a great man;

Although one might have no skill in speech, one will become a skillful speaker;

Although one might not be learned, one will acquire extensive learning;

Although one might be deficient in wisdom, one will become a wise person;

If one is already a person of fine appearance, one will develop a doubly outstanding appearance;

If one was formerly from a great clan, one will rise to a doubly revered social station;

If one is already a skillful speaker, one will become a doubly skillful speaker;

If one was already learned, one will become doubly learned;

If one was already wise, one will become doubly wise;

Wherever one sits or lies down, it will be on a precious bejeweled couch;

Whether asleep or awake, one will be peaceful and secure and surrounded by an abundance of attendants;

One's house will be made from the many sorts of jewels and one will be completely free to roam about at will;

One will be regarded as a personage worthy of the highest esteem;

If one has need of any scriptures or books, one will readily obtain whichever ones he seeks;

One's power and position will ensure that one has easy access to the king and one will be borne in mind by all of the nobility;

Physicians will voluntarily come and one will always have those who are close and trustworthy, attending as appropriate to the vicissitudes [of one's health];

If one catches some disease, it will be only minor and mild;

Whatever one's disease, it will be easily cured;

One will leave far behind any fears with respect to either present or later lives;

One will ultimately forever abandon any fear of one's life not continuing on and one will always be rescued and protected;

There will be many people close to one who will feel immensely blessed with good fortune;

One will be sincerely and joyously celebrated by those of like mind;

Whenever anyone extends even a small kindness to one, that person will be repaid magnanimously and whenever anyone afflicts one with even a minor evil deed, that person will encounter a major personal disaster;

Young women from one's own clan who are possessed of fine appearance and complete adornments will voluntarily seek to serve as retainers;

Whoever is seeking to reach agreements will take refuge in one [as a source of resolution];

If one falls into some bad action, that action will usually be only minor;

If one expends even a small effort [in some endeavor], one will immediately receive great benefit as a result;

One will have an abundance of good spiritual friends whereas those who dislike one will grow ever fewer;

One will not be susceptible to accidental encounters with venomous snakes, poison, negligence, evil people, or other such occurrences;

All of one's kindly and respectful actions will tend to be returned in kind;

Whenever one experiences some kind of good fortune, everyone will join in sympathetic rejoicing;

If one experiences some sort of anguishing misfortune, everyone will join in sympathetic commiseration;

Everyone will join in assisting one's guidance, vying to provide one with whatever is good and auspicious while influencing one to avoid whatever is contrary to Dharma and to abide securely in good dharmas;

The works that one accomplishes will be grand and none who witness them will fail to be delighted by them;

If one is able to abide together with those of identical aims, one will find satisfaction in that and will not aspire for worldly wealth, noble birth, acclamation, or benefit;

If one comes to abide in a position of power, people will devote their thoughts to assisting one and doing away with anything that might cause anguishing misfortune;

On observing the wealth and high social stature of others, one entertains no aspirations to assume them for himself;

The people sing the praises of one's virtues but do not propagate reports of one's errors;
Although one might be from a family of inferior social stature, one will acquire the reputation of a great personage;
One never displays a disapproving expression and, whenever one observes someone else's appearance, one does not adopt a pretentious demeanor;
If one becomes a brahman,[194] one will garner great karmic rewards from his works within the temples of the deities. When studying the scriptures, one gains their genuine benefits and, having gained them, one is able to bestow them on others;
If one becomes a *kṣatriya*,[195] one succeeds in his endeavors, is renowned for his skill in archery, is consummate in one's abilities, and is well able to gain the results taught in the classics on ruling the world;
If one becomes a *vaiśya*,[196] one is well able to grow whichever crops one wishes;
If one becomes a merchant, one is well able to gain the profit one seeks;
If one becomes a *śūdra*,[197] whatever work one does becomes abundantly successful in a way that matches one's wishes.

1. Q: You Said One Doesn't Seek Rewards. Isn't This Contradictory?

Question: Earlier, you claimed that the bodhisattva does not have the motivation to seek karmic rewards from his practice of giving, and, beyond that, that he is not motivated by a desire for wealth and high social status. Now, however, you state that one gives in quest of great wealth. How are these statements not contradictory?

2. A: No, Because This Wealth Is Gained & Used Only to Benefit Beings

Response: They are not contradictory. It is with reference to cases where one seeks to acquire wealth and enjoyment of pleasures for oneself that it was said that one should not seek for wealth. Now, however, we speak of seeking wealth solely to benefit beings. It is for that reason that it was stated that one seeks wealth out of an aspiration to engage in great giving. This is not a case of seeking wealth and pleasures for oneself. Hence we discuss here the causal factors within such karmic results.

If a bodhisattva fails to come by great wealth, then, even though he has a resolute belief in giving, he still has no wealth that he can use in giving. Therefore you should not raise such a challenge.

G. One Also Gives to Cut Off Two Dharmas and Gain Two Dharmas

Additionally, it is for the sake of cutting off two types of dharmas that one should practice giving. What are those two? The first is miserliness and the second is covetousness. These two dharmas are the most extreme sorts of defilement that may sully one's practice of giving.

Then again, it is for the sake of gaining two types of dharmas that one practices giving, namely the knowledge of cessation and also the knowledge of nonproduction.

H. One Also Gives to Increase Three Types of Wisdom

Also, [giving is done] in order to increase three types of wisdom:

First, the wisdom that serves to achieve self-benefit;[198]
Second, fundamental wisdom;
Third, the wisdom arising from extensive learning.

I. Others Say That Giving Is Practiced to Increase Two Dharmas

There are yet others who say that one should give in order to bring about the increase of two dharmas: First, goodness. Second, wisdom.

J. In Summary, the Bodhisattva Should Practice Four Kinds of Giving

To present a general summation here, the bodhisattva should engage in four kinds of giving in order to subsume within his practice all of the different types of good dharmas, as follows:

First, giving that originates in a mind that perceives everyone as equal;
Second, giving that transcends opposites;
Third, giving that is dedicated to attaining bodhi;
Fourth, giving characterized by the presence of a thoroughly quiescent mind.

It is in order to completely perfect *dāna pāramitā* in this manner that the bodhisattva diligently practices the giving of material wealth.

The End of Chapter Twelve

Chapter 13
Distinctions with Regard to the Giving of Dharma

XIII. Chapter 13: Distinctions with Regard to the Giving of Dharma

A. Dharma Giving Is Supreme and the Wise Should Practice It

The bodhisattva should cultivate the giving of material wealth in the above-discussed manner and should also cultivate the giving of Dharma, doing so in accordance with this statement:

> Of the many sorts of giving, the giving of Dharma is supreme.
> Thus the wise should cultivate its practice.

Of all of the kinds of giving, the foremost, the most superior, and the most sublime is the giving of Dharma. This is the type of giving that the wise should practice.

B. Q: Why Do You Say Only the Wise Should Practice Dharma Giving?

Question: Why do you say that [only] the wise should engage in the practice of giving Dharma?

C. A: Erroneous Interpretations Do Not Benefit Anyone

Response: If those who are not wise pursue the giving of Dharma, they will set forth erroneous interpretations. By setting forth erroneous interpretations they will fail to benefit themselves and will also fail to benefit others.

1. Q: What Do You Mean by "Erroneous Interpretations"?

Question: What is meant here by "erroneous[199] interpretations"?

2. A: Wrong Ideas of Spurious Origin (Four Cases from Scripture)

Response: When the Buddha was on the verge of entering nirvāṇa, he told Ānanda:

> From this day forward, one should rely upon the sutras. Do not rely on persons. Ānanda, what is meant by relying on the sutras and not relying on persons?[200]
>
> If a bhikshu comes and speaks thus: "In his presence, I have heard this from the Buddha, and in his presence, I have received this from the Buddha. It is Dharma, it is good, and it is as taught by the Buddha," neither accept nor reject the words of this bhikshu, but rather, having listened carefully, one should search for what has been said in the sutras and in the moral code.
>
> If it is not included in the sutras, is not included in the Vinaya, and it also contradicts the true character of dharmas,[201] one should

reply to this bhikshu, saying, "Perhaps this dharma is one that was not spoken by the Buddha. Perhaps the Venerable One has mistakenly accepted it as such. Why? This dharma is not included in the sutras and is not included in the Vinaya, either. What's more, it contradicts the true character of dharmas. Therefore this is non-Dharma, not good, and not taught by the Buddha." Having realized this, one should then immediately reject this.

Now suppose some other bhikshu comes and speaks thus: "There is a large sangha in which I reside wherein there is a senior monk, one who understands the sutras and who is skillful in explaining the moral code. In his presence, I have heard this from him, and in his presence, I have received this from him. It is Dharma, it is good, and it is as taught by the Buddha."

Again, neither accept nor reject the words of this bhikshu, but rather, having listened carefully, one should search for what he has said in the sutras and in the moral code. If it is not included in the sutras, is not included in the Vinaya, and it also contradicts the true character of dharmas, one should reply to this bhikshu, saying, "Venerable One, that sangha of bhikshus—regarding their understanding of the character of dharmas and the character of what constitutes goodness—perhaps they have spoken of these things in a manner that is contrary to Dharma and contrary to goodness. Perhaps the Venerable One has mistakenly accepted it. Why? This dharma is not included in the sutras and is not included in the Vinaya, either. What's more, it contradicts the true character of dharmas. Therefore this is non-Dharma, not good, and not spoken by the Buddha." Having realized this, one should then immediately reject this.

Suppose yet another bhikshu comes and speaks thus: "There are many bhikshus where I abide who preserve the sutras, preserve the Vinaya, and preserve the *mātṛkās*."[202] In their presence, I have heard this from them, and in their presence, I have accepted this from them. It is Dharma, it is good, and it is as taught by the Buddha."

Neither accept nor reject the words of this bhikshu, but rather, having listened carefully, one should search in the sutras and in the moral code for what he has said. If it is not included in the sutras, is not included in the Vinaya, and it also contradicts the true character of dharmas, one should reply to this bhikshu, saying, "Venerable One, that sangha of bhikshus—regarding their understanding of the character of dharmas and the character of what constitutes goodness—perhaps they have spoken of these things in a manner that is contrary to Dharma and contrary to goodness. Perhaps the Venerable One has mistakenly accepted it. Why? This dharma is not included in the sutras and is not included in the Vinaya, either. What's more, it contradicts the true character of dharmas. Therefore this is non-Dharma, not good, and not taught by the Buddha." Having realized this, one should then immediately reject this.

Suppose yet another bhikshu comes and speaks thus: "There is a senior bhikshu where I abide, one who understands much, one who is aware of much, and one whom people revere. In his presence, I have heard this from him, and in his presence, I have received this from him. It is Dharma, it is good, and it is as taught by the Buddha."

Neither accept nor reject the words of this bhikshu, but rather, having listened carefully, one should search for what he has said in the sutras and in the moral code. If it is not included in the sutras, is not included in the Vinaya, and it also contradicts the true character of dharmas, one should reply to this bhikshu, saying, "Venerable One, that sangha of bhikshus—regarding their understanding of the character of dharmas and the character of what constitutes goodness—perhaps they have spoken of these things in a manner that is contrary to Dharma and contrary to goodness. Perhaps the Venerable One has mistakenly accepted it. Why? This dharma is not included in the sutras and is not included in the Vinaya, either. What's more, it contradicts the true character of dharmas. Therefore this is non-Dharma, not good, and not taught by the Buddha." Having realized this, one should then immediately reject this.

These four cases illustrate what is meant here by "erroneous interpretations." It is therefore said that the wise do not rely upon erroneous interpretations, but rather practice pristinely pure Dharma giving.

D. Q: How Does One Know That Dharma Giving Is Supreme?

Question: How is it that one knows the giving of Dharma is the foremost among all forms of giving?

E. A: The Sutras Say So

Response: The sutras state that there are two types of giving, the giving of material wealth and the giving of Dharma, and that, among those two types of giving, it is the giving of Dharma that is superior.

F. A Sutra Explains Propriety in Speaking Dharma as Follows:

Furthermore:

In *The Sutra of the Resolute King,*[203]
there are praises of Dharma giving's merit
and explanations of propriety in the speaking of Dharma.
One should always cultivate and practice in accordance with these.

If the bodhisattva wishes to bestow Dharma on beings, he should follow and cultivate in accordance with the passages in *The Sutra of the Resolute King* that praise the meritorious qualities possessed by a teacher of Dharma and that set forth the correct ceremonial procedures involved in speaking Dharma. It stipulates the following:

1. Four Qualities of a Qualified Dharma Speaker

The speaker of Dharma should incorporate four dharmas in his practice. What are those four?

First, he is to be one possessed of vast and extensive learning while also being well able to bear in mind [the meaning of] all the phrases and passages [of the scripture at hand];

Second, he is to be resolutely and skillfully cognizant of the marks of production and extinction as they manifest in all worldly and world-transcending dharmas;

Third, having acquired the wisdom arising from *dhyāna* concentration, he accords with the Dharma set forth in the sutras while also remaining free of any contentiousness;

Fourth, neither adding anything to nor taking anything away [from the Dharma set forth in the sutras], he practices in accordance with what is proclaimed therein.

2. Four Correct Behaviors When Ascending the High Seat to Teach

There are four additional dharmas that are to be observed when the speaker of Dharma occupies the lion throne. What are those four?

First, when about to ascend to the high seat, one should first respectfully pay reverence to the great assembly in attendance and then afterward ascend to that seat;

Second, in audiences including women, one should contemplate impurity [of the body];

Third, in one's deportment and bearing, one maintains the appearance of a great man. As one spreads forth the sound of Dharma, one's countenance appears harmonious and pleased, inspiring all in attendance to accept [one's words] with faith. One does not teach non-Buddhist scriptures and one's mind remains fearless;

Fourth, in the face of harsh words and challenging questions, one should practice patience.

3. Four More Correct Behaviors for When One Sits on the High Seat

There are four additional dharmas pertaining to sitting in the high seat. What are those four?

First, one brings forth the motivation to be of abundant benefit to beings;

Second, one does not conceive of the idea of a self in connection with any being;

Third, one does not conceive of the words as synonymous with the dharmas [that they describe];

Fourth, one vows, "May any being who hears me speak on Dharma thereby gain irreversibility in the path to *anuttarasamyaksaṃbodhi.*"

4. Another Four Correct Behaviors When Sitting on the High Seat

There are another four dharmas pertaining to sitting in the high seat. What are these four?

First, one is well able to abide securely within the gateway of *dhāraṇī* practice[204] and in resolute faith in the Dharma;

Second, one is skilled in realization of the *pratyutpanna* samādhi, diligent in the practice of vigor, and pure in observance of the moral precepts;

Third, one sees no happiness inhering in any place of rebirth, does not covet offerings, and does not seek to obtain any sort of karmic reward;

Fourth, one's mind is free of any doubt regarding the three gates to liberation.

5. Eighteen More Qualifications For One Who Sits on the High Seat

Additionally:

One is well able to bring forth deep samādhis;

One is completely adherent to the awesome deportment;

One has a strong memory;

One's thoughts are imbued with stable wisdom;

One refrains from joking and teasing;

One refrains from acting with a frivolous demeanor;

One refrains from shamelessness;

One refrains from falling into delusion and confusion;

One's discourse remains free of error;

One's sense faculties remain well-guarded;

One does not covet fine flavors;

One is careful to maintain proper deportment with one's arms and legs;

One does not forget what one has chosen to bear in mind;

One enjoys practicing the *dhūta* austerities;[205]

One is well able to make distinctions regarding worldly and world-transcending dharmas;

One's mind is free of doubts and regrets;

One's discourse is inexhaustible in its phrasing and in its command of scriptural passages;

And one seeks to promote the security and benefit of the audience and also refrains from finding fault with them.

If one is in possession of dharmas of this sort, then one should occupy the lion throne.

6. Four More Dharmas To Be Observed When Sitting on the High Seat

There are yet four more dharmas in this connection:

First, one does not slight oneself;
Second, one does not slight audience members;
Third, one does not slight the topic that is being discussed;
Fourth, one does not [teach Dharma] for the sake of obtaining offerings or support.

G. A Scriptural Citation Regarding the Buddha's Teaching of Dharma

[Nāgārjuna introduces another passage from scripture]:

The Buddha spoke to Ānanda, saying, "On which dharmas should the speaker of Dharma speak? Ānanda, whichever dharma one may discuss—it cannot be demonstrated, it cannot be described, it is signless, and it is unconditioned."

"O Bhagavat, if this is the case, how can they be discussed?"

"Ānanda, this Dharma is extremely profound. When the Tathāgata expounds [on Dharma], he uses an expedient device that involves four factors:

First, the sound of his voice;
Second, names;
Third, verbal discourse;
Fourth, principles.

Additionally, there are four causal circumstances associated with his speaking about the Dharma for others:

First, it is done for the sake of liberating beings who are amenable to being liberated;

Second, in doing so, he only deals in designations associated with forms, feelings, perceptions, formative factors, and consciousnesses;

Third, he uses all sorts of phrases and sentences to benefit beings;

Fourth, although, in speaking, he uses such names, [their referents] still cannot be apprehended.

This is just as when there is a basin of clean, unsullied oil in which an observer can see an image of his own face. Ānanda, have you ever seen or heard of any wise man, virtuous woman, or disciple of an *ārya* who was able to claim, 'I have seen a real person right there in a basin of oil'?"

"O Bhagavat, I have neither heard nor seen any wise man, virtuous woman, or disciple of an *ārya* who has claimed, 'I have seen a real person in a basin of oil.' Why is that so? One who is wise would know ahead of time that even the basin of oil was not [intrinsically] existent. How much the less might he claim the existence of a person there. It is solely by resort to artificial naming that one may claim the existence of a basin of oil in which one sees a person's image."

"Ānanda, the Tathāgata is just the same in this respect. It is only through reliance upon names that there is an artificial existence of anything of which he speaks.

Ānanda, there are four causes and conditions involved in the Tathāgata's speaking about the Dharma for others:

When beings hear this, their minds experience peace and happiness and they plant the causes for attaining nirvāṇa.

The sound of the Tathāgata's proclamation of Dharma pervades the worlds of the ten directions. When beings hear this, their minds are delighted, they abandon the wretched destinies, and they gain rebirth in the Tuṣita Heaven.

In the sounds of the Tathāgata's voice, there is nothing that is either masculine or feminine. Men do not seize on any feminine aspects and women do not seize on any masculine aspects.

The sound of the Tathāgata's voice does not cause distress to beings nor does it interfere with [the correct representation of] any dharma. It is resorted to solely in order to make manifest the nature of the sounds."

H. Conclusion: In Dharma Giving, One Should Practice Accordingly

The speaker of Dharma should practice in accord with these ideas [discussed above] and should perform the giving of Dharma in compliance with these practices. As for the karmic results that accrue to the giver and the receiver, these should be extensively discussed later on.

The End of Chapter Thirteen

Chapter 14
The Characteristics of the Refuges

XIV. Chapter 14: The Characteristics of the [Three] Refuges

A. Distinctions Regarding Material Giving versus Dharma Giving

The giving of material wealth and the giving of Dharma were already explained above. Now, we shall make further distinctions in this regard:

> The "white-robed ones," the householders,[206]
> should extensively practice the giving of material wealth.
> The dharmas associated with the rest of the good practices
> shall now be explained as well.

1. Laity Excel at Material Giving & Monastics Excel at Dharma Giving

Of these two types of giving, the householder should practice the giving of material wealth. Those who have left the home life should practice the giving of Dharma. Why is this? It is because, in the giving of Dharma, the layperson is unable to match those who have left the home life. This is because those who listen to and accept the Dharma have only shallow and scant faith in a householder's [ability to teach Dharma].

2. Monastics Are Better Trained to Practice Dharma Giving

Moreover, whereas the householders possess greater resources of material wealth, it is the monastics who have studied, recited, and deeply understood the dharmas of the sutras to the point that, in the midst of assemblies, they are fearless in explaining them for others. The householders are unable to match them in this. Additionally, they do not match the monastics' ability to inspire a reverential frame of mind in the listener. Also, in instances where one might wish, through expounding the Dharma, to overcome [doubts in] the minds of others, [the householders] are unable to match the monastics. This is as described [in this verse]:

> If one first cultivates the Dharma oneself
> and then later engages in the teaching of others.
> Then and only then can one utter these words:
> "You should accord with what I myself practice."

This is an endeavor that is fitting for those who have left the home life. It is not something that the householder carries out in practice. It is also said that:

If one personally practices what is not good,
how can one influence others to engage in goodness?
If one personally fails to attain quiescence,
how can one cause others to attain quiescence?

Hence, if one personally practices goodness,
one can influence others to practice goodness.
If one personally attains quiescence,
one can cause others to attain quiescence.

Good dharmas and quiescence are matters that should be practiced by those who have left the home life. Also, monastics have a superior ability to inspire reverence in those who listen to the Dharma.

3. The Hazards to Monastics of Devotion to Material Giving

Furthermore, if those who have left the home life practice the giving of material wealth, then this prevents their own development of the other forms of goodness. They are also thus prevented from practicing renunciation in a forest hermitage where they dwell off in a wilderness forest or marshland. If those who have left the home life take pleasure in the giving of material wealth, that will completely interfere with their pursuit of such cultivation.

It is the nature of these sorts of endeavors that, if one practices the giving of material wealth, one must certainly go into the villages and involve oneself in the endeavors of the layperson. In such instances, there will be much talk.[207]

If one does not take up such work, then there will be no means by which one can obtain such material wealth. If one is involved in coming and going from the villages, then one will be exposed to seeing and hearing the sights and sounds therein. Thus one's sense faculties will become difficult to restrain and one will become prone to give rise to the three poisons.[208]

Moreover, one's mind will become only shallowly engaged in the practice of moral virtue, patience, vigor, *dhyāna* absorption, and wisdom.[209]

Also, when one takes up the endeavors of the laity, defilements arise in relation to offerings and support that entail the production of afflictions such as craving, anger, miserliness, and jealousy. It is solely by resort to the power of contemplative practice that one is able to restrain such mental inclinations. [Absent the power of such contemplative practice], those who are weak may fail to restrain themselves and may then go so far as to encounter death itself or a painful calamity comparable to death.

"Death" refers here to becoming so covetously attached to the objects of the five types of desire that one relinquishes the moral precepts and returns to the lay life. Or one may find one is even able to allow oneself to transgress the moral precepts and incur numerous grave offenses. This is what is meant by "encountering a painful calamity comparable to death."[210]

It is for these reasons that one praises the giving of Dharma as the province of those who have left the home life while praising the giving of material wealth as the province of the householder. This being so, there are extensive discussions of the householder bodhisattva's practice of giving material wealth.

B. Taking Refuge in the Three Jewels

The other sorts of good conduct should now be discussed. The bodhisattva who has brought forth the resolve [to attain buddhahood] should first take refuge in the Buddha, take refuge in the Dharma, and take refuge in the Sangha. The merit that is gained from taking the Three Refuges should then all be dedicated to the realization of *anuttarasamyaksaṃbodhi*. Additionally:

> Taking refuge in the Buddha, the Dharma, and the Sangha
> is a matter that the bodhisattva should comprehend.

The bodhisattva should understand well and in accordance with reality this matter of taking refuge in the Buddha, taking refuge in the Dharma, and taking refuge in the Sangha.

1. Q: What Is Meant by Taking Refuge in the Buddha?

Question: What is meant by taking refuge in the Buddha?

2. A: The Primary Aspects of Taking Refuge in the Buddha

Response:

> Do not relinquish the resolve to attain bodhi,
> do not damage the Dharma that one has received,
> do not abandon the mind of great compassion,
> and do not covet other vehicles [to liberation].
>
> If one acts in this fashion, then this is what is meant by
> taking refuge in the Buddha in accordance with reality.

"The resolve to attain bodhi" refers to bringing forth the determination to seek buddhahood without ever desisting from it, without ever letting it cease, and without ever relinquishing this determination.

As for "do not damage the Dharma that one has received," this refers to the fact that the bodhisattvas have each taken on the practice of the moral precepts as components of the dharmas of goodness that they delight in. Consequently, there are circumstances where one particular practice should be taken up whereas yet another practice should be avoided. Thus, if a particular practice corresponds to any of the *pāramitās*, to any of the four bases of meritorious qualities,[211] or to any of the many other different sorts of good dharmas such as these, for the sake of benefiting beings, one accepts and upholds it, cultivates it, and does not allow it to deteriorate or to become deficient.

As for "the mind of great compassion," one wishes to liberate beings who are afflicted by suffering. In order to pursue the attainment of buddhahood, even in a dream, one never abandons the great compassion.

As for "do not covet other vehicles [to liberation]," because one possesses a deep resolute faith in the path to buddhahood, one does seek to take up the vehicles of *śrāvaka* disciples or *pratyekabuddhas*.

One should realize that it is through the possession of dharmas such as these that one "takes refuge in the Buddha in accordance with reality."

3. Q: What Is Meant by Taking Refuge in the Dharma?

Question: What is meant by taking refuge in the Dharma?

4. A: The Primary Aspects of Taking Refuge in the Dharma

Response:

Draw near to those who speak the Dharma.
Single-mindedly listen to and accept the Dharma.
Be mindful of it, uphold it, and then expound upon it.
This is what is meant by taking refuge in the Dharma.

"Those who speak the Dharma" refers to those who explain, set forth, and proclaim the profound Dharma of the Buddha, offering instruction as to what is good and what is evil while also cutting away all one's doubts. One always repeatedly draws near to them, going forth to wherever they may dwell, making offerings and displaying reverential respect as one single-mindedly listens to and accepts [the Dharma]. One uses the power of memory to retain it and does not forget it. One reflects upon it, assesses it, and accords with its import.

Afterward, one expounds upon it for others, doing so in a manner that accords with the way one has been led to understand it. Then one dedicates the merit arising from this gift of Dharma to the attainment of buddhahood. This is what is meant by "taking refuge in the Dharma."

5. Q: What Is Meant by Taking Refuge in the Sangha?

Question: What is meant by taking refuge in the Sangha?

6. A: The Primary Aspects of Taking Refuge in the Sangha

Response:

In the case of *śrāvaka* disciple practitioners
who have not yet entered the Dharma position,[212]
induce them to bring forth the unsurpassable resolve
by which they are caused to acquire the ten powers of a buddha.

One first uses the giving of material resources to attract them
and afterward resorts to the giving of Dharma.
One maintains deep faith in the Sangha that attains four fruitions[213]
and does not discriminate among members of that noble community.

One may strive to gain the *śrāvaka* disciples' meritorious qualities
while still not opting for realization of their liberation.
This is the meaning of taking refuge in the Sangha.
Moreover, one should maintain mindfulness of three matters.[214]

"*Śrāvaka* disciple practitioners" refers to those who achieve success in the Śrāvaka Disciple Vehicle. "Who have not yet entered the Dharma position" refers to those who have not yet reached the stage of absolute irreversibility on the *śrāvaka* disciple path. One may still influence such persons to bring forth the resolve to attain buddhahood so that they will then be able to acquire the ten powers.

In the case of those who have already entered the Dharma position, one can never influence them to bring forth the unsurpassable resolve. Even supposing that some of these were to be caused to bring forth such an aspiration, they would still not succeed [in bringing it to realization].

This is as stated by the venerable Subhūti in the *[Mahā]prajñāpāramitā [Sūtra]* where he said, "Those who have already entered the "right Dharma position" are unable to bring forth the unsurpassable resolve. Why is this the case? Such persons have already created an obstacle to further transmigration in *saṃsāra*."[215] Thus they will never again come and go within *saṃsāra*.

[To induce those who have not yet entered the Dharma position] to bring forth the unsurpassable resolve, one first uses the giving of material resources. "To attract them," refers to bestowing the requisites of robes, food and drink, bedding, and medicine to attract them.

In the case of those who have left the home life, one attracts them by giving them robes, food-and-drink, bedding, medicines, and various incenses including unguent incenses. As for householders, one uses means of attraction that cause them to feel a sense of close friendship through which they tend to trust and accept one's words. Afterward, one engages in Dharma giving that causes them to gain the fruits of bringing forth the unsurpassable resolve.

"Sangha" refers to those who have gained the four preliminary stages as well as those who have actually attained the four corresponding fruits [of the path].

"Community" refers to those who have taken on the characteristic features of the monastic in accordance with the Buddha's Dharma. They completely uphold the moral precepts, yet may not have attained the fruits [of the path] or the corresponding preliminary stages. One does not make discriminating distinctions among members of the Sangha such as these.

It is because they have abandoned the bondage of sensual desire that they are known as "noble" members of the Sangha. They maintain resolute belief in emptiness, signlessness, and wishlessness while still not indulging in conceptual elaboration rooted in the making of discriminating distinctions. When one relies on members of the Sangha of this sort, this is what is meant by "taking refuge in the Sangha."

As for "One may strive to gain the meritorious qualities of the *śrāvaka* disciples while still not opting for realization of their liberation," one knows that these members of the Sangha are accomplished in the upholding of the moral precepts, that they are accomplished in the *dhyāna* absorptions, that they are accomplished in wisdom, that they are accomplished in liberation, that they are accomplished in the knowledge and vision of liberation, that they possess the three clear knowledges and six superknowledges, that their minds have gained sovereign mastery, that they possess great awe-inspiring qualities, and that that they have forsaken the pleasures of the world and have escaped Māra's realms.[216]

One knows that they do not experience joy due to attaining profit, fine reputation, praise, or pleasure and that they do not experience distress due to loss, disrepute, derision, or pain.[217] One knows they always practice six kinds of equanimity[218] and knows that they have gained the eight liberations in accordance with the Buddha's instructions.

One knows that there are those who practice the path, that there are those who have achieved liberation, that there are those who practice the singular path, that they have demolished the two kinds of afflictions,[219] that they well understand the three realms of existence, that they have a well-developed penetrating understanding of the four truths, that they have thoroughly done away with the five hindrances,[220] that they have come to peacefully abide in the six dharmas of harmony and respect, that they have become accomplished in seven dharmas of non-retreat,[221] that they possess the eight realizations of great men, that they have abandoned the nine types of fetters, and that they have gained the ten powers of the *śrāvaka* disciples.

It is those who have perfected meritorious qualities such as these who are referred to as the Buddha's *śrāvaka* disciple sangha. One may strive to acquire meritorious qualities such as these even as one still does not seek to attain their type of liberation. Why? This is because one maintains deep-seated aspirations and resolute belief[222] in the unimpeded liberation of the Buddha.

This [preceding discussion explains] what is meant by "taking refuge in the Sangha."

Then again, if on hearing the passages, sentences and words of the Dharma, one immediately brings to mind the dharma of the true character [of dharmas],[223] this is what is meant by "taking refuge in the Dharma."

If upon seeing a member of the *śrāvaka*-disciple sangha, one immediately brings to mind the community of all bodhisattvas who have brought forth the resolve to attain bodhi, this is what is meant by "taking refuge in the Sangha."

If on viewing an image of the Buddha, one immediately becomes mindful of the true Buddha, this is what is meant by "taking refuge in the Buddha."[224]

7. The Meaning of Mindfulness of the Buddha, Dharma, and Sangha

a. The Meaning of Mindfulness of the Buddha

1) Q: What Is Meant by "Mindfulness of the True Buddha"?

Question: What is meant by "mindfulness of the true Buddha"?

2) A: "Mindfulness of the True Buddha" as Set Forth in a Sutra

Response: This corresponds to the discussion of the meaning of the mindfulness-of-the-Buddha samādhi as found in the *Akṣayamati Bodhisattva Sutra* wherein it states:[225]

> As for "mindfulness of the true Buddha," it is not based on physical form, is not based on characteristic signs, is not based on birth, is not based on caste,[226] is not based on clan, is not based on the past, future, or present, and is not based on the five aggregates, twelve sense bases, or eighteen sense realms.
>
> It is not based on seeing, hearing, sensing, or cognizing,[227] is not based on the mind or mind consciousness, is not based in practice associated with conceptual elaboration, is not based on production, extinction, or abiding, is not based on either grasping or relinquishing, is not based on bearing in mind discriminating distinctions, is not based on dharma characteristics, is not based on individual characteristics, is not based on a unitary characteristic, and is not based on differentiating characteristics.

It is not based on the mental factors associated with the mind's cognition of objective phenomena,[228] is not based on what is either inward or outward, is not based on any seizing on characteristics by either primary ideation (*vitarka*), or mental discursion (*vicāra*), is not based on either what is taken in or what is produced, is not based on physical appearances, is not based on any aspects of deportment that one might cultivate, is not based on moral precepts, *dhyāna* absorption, wisdom, liberation, or the knowledge and vision of liberation, and is not based on the ten powers, four fearlessnesses, or any other dharmas of the Buddha.

As for "mindfulness of the Buddha that accords with reality," it is immeasurable, is inconceivable, has no practice, has no knowing, has no self or anything belonging to a self, has no recollection, and has nothing it bears in mind. It does not engage in discriminations regarding the five aggregates, twelve sense bases, or eighteen sense realms. It has no shape, is unobstructed, and has no initiation, no abiding, and no non-abiding. It does not abide in forms, and does not abide in feelings, perceptions, formative factors, or consciousness.

It does not abide in the eye or visual forms and does not abide in eye consciousness. It does not abide in the ear or sounds and does not abide in ear consciousness. It does not abide in the nose or fragrances and does not abide in olfactory consciousness. It does not abide in the tongue or flavors and does not abide in gustatory consciousness. It does not abide in the body or touchables and does not abide in tactile consciousness. It does not abide in the mind faculty or dharmas and does not abide in mind consciousness.

It does not abide in any objective conditions. It does not give rise to any characteristic signs. It does not involve the production of any movement of mind, of any recollective thought, of any discriminations, or of any other such phenomena. Nor does it involve the production of any seeing, hearing, sensing, or cognition.

It accords in its practice with all the characteristic features of right liberation. It does not involve any continuity of thought but does involve the cessation of all mental discriminations. It demolishes all forms of affection and anger.

It confutes (lit. "ruins") all normative characteristics of causality. It does away with [conceptions of what is temporally] past, future, or intermediate. It perceives with utter clarity the nonexistence of any [duality of] object and subject.

Because it is motionless, it is free of [any attraction to] joyfulness. Because it declines to indulge the delectable, it is free of [any attraction to] bliss.[229]

Because its fundamental character is that of quiescence, it remains free of the heat [of mental agitation].

Because the mind has no endeavors in which it is involved, it is liberated.

Because appearances are devoid of any existent form, there is no body. Because one does not indulge them, there are no feelings. Because there are no perceptions, there are no fetters. Because there are no actions, there is nothing that one does. Because there is no knowing, there is no consciousness.[230]

Because there is no grasping, there is no engagement in actions. Because there is no relinquishing, it is not the case that one does not act.

Because there is no dwelling [in any dharma], there is no abiding. Because it is empty [of inherent existence], there is no coming. Because there is no arising, there is no departing.

Because one does not covet, does not become attached to, does not seize upon, does not indulge, does not "ignite," and does not extinguish any recollective thought, any mental dharmas or any other sort of dharmas, from the very beginning on forward to the present, there has never been any production [of dharmas] nor have there ever been any marks of their production. They are all entirely subsumed within the nature of dharmas that extends beyond the path [defined by the duality of] the eye, visual forms, and [their intervening] empty space.

Characteristics such as these define what is meant by "true mindfulness of the Buddha."

b. The Meaning of "Mindfulness of the Dharma"

Also, as for mindfulness of the Dharma, the Dharma of the Buddha is well spoken. One gains results from it in this very life. [Its benefits] are not limited to some fixed time. This is amenable to one's own contemplation and investigation. It is excellent in its ability to lead one to attainment of the path. It is such that the wise can inwardly realize. It is good in the beginning, good in the middle, and good in the end. Its words are good. Its meaning is good. It is completely pure in its goodness and free of any admixture [with anything not good]. It is perfect in its purity.

It is able to cut off covetousness, able to cut of hatred, able to cut off delusion, able to do away with prideful thoughts, able to do away with all [erroneous] views, able to do away with doubt and regret, able to do away with arrogance, and able to do away with all craving.

It breaks [one's attachment to] whatever one is inclined to take refuge in. It cuts short the path of continuance [in *saṃsāra*]. It puts an end to craving, leads to the abandonment of sensual desires, and leads to quiescence and nirvāṇa.

Characteristics such as these illustrate what is meant by "mindfulness of the Dharma." [It is characterized] by emptiness, signlessness, and wishlessness. It is unproduced and undestroyed, ultimately quiescent, incomparable, and devoid of any [phenomenal] manifestation. These ideas are just as set forth in the discussion of the meaning of "mindfulness of the Buddha."[231]

Additionally, "mindfulness of the Dharma" is of three types. The descriptions from "the Dharma of the Buddha is well spoken" to "it is completely pure in its goodness" are all references to the path. From "it is able to cut off covetousness" to "it leads to quiescence and nirvāṇa" are all references to nirvāṇa. From "emptiness" and so forth on up to "incomparable, and devoid of any [phenomenal] manifestation," is all a reference to the very essence of the Dharma.

c. The Meaning of Mindfulness of the Sangha

Also, regarding "mindfulness of the Sangha," this is as explained earlier in the discussion of the meritorious qualities of the Sangha.

C. A Concluding Statement on the Three Refuges

In one's mindfulness of these Three Jewels, one develops a definite resolve. When one uses such mindfulness as one strives to attain buddhahood and then takes up the practice of giving, this is what is meant by "taking refuge in the Buddha."

When one endeavors to preserve and protect the Dharma and thus takes up the practice of giving, this is what is meant by "taking refuge in the Dharma."

When, based on this practice of giving, one dedicates the merit, resolving that, once one has realized buddhahood, one will bring together a sangha community consisting of both bodhisattvas and *śrāvaka* disciples, this is what is meant by "taking refuge in the Sangha."

The End of Chapter Fourteen

Chapter 15
The Five Moral Precepts

XV. Chapter 15: The Five Moral Precepts

A. The Lay Bodhisattva Cultivates Goodness and Avoids Bad Actions

It is in this [above-discussed] manner that the lay bodhisattva becomes able to cultivate the karmic deeds of a good person while leaving far behind the karmic deeds of a bad person. In this connection, there is a verse:

> One cultivates and brings forth the karmic deeds of a good person,
> Accumulating wealth for one's use in a way consistent with Dharma.
> Whatever one is capable of, one takes that on as a grave duty.
> That of which one is not capable—one refrains from taking it on.[232]

As for "the karmic deeds of a good person," to sum it up, the karmic deeds of a good person involve abiding in what is good and beneficial for oneself while also being able to facilitate the benefit of others.

As for "the karmic deeds of a bad person" these bring about descent into decline and anguish for oneself while also bringing about decline and anguish in others.

"Accumulating wealth for one's own use in a way consistent with Dharma" refers to not killing, not stealing, and neither deceiving nor cheating others. One devotes one's energies to accumulating wealth and then puts it to use in a way that accords with the Dharma by making offerings to the Three Jewels, by rescuing those fallen into misfortune, by aiding the old and the sick, and by carrying out other such deeds.

Whatever one can take on and can adhere to in practice—one regards that as a grave responsibility. As for what one would be unable to adhere to in practice, one does not take that on.

As for the works of the bodhisattva, whether it be those of this life or those of future lives, whether it be those concerned with self-benefit or those concerned with benefiting others, these are as discussed earlier and they are endeavors that definitely must be brought to a state of successful completion. If there are endeavors that one realizes one cannot yet carry out in practice, then one does not take these on.

B. One Relinquishes Self Benefit, Benefits Others & Repays Kindness

Furthermore:

One neither sorrows nor rejoices over worldly dharmas.
One is able to relinquish one's own benefit,
while always acting diligently for the benefit of others.
Being deeply grateful for others' kindnesses, one repays them doubly.

"Worldly dharmas" refers to profit and loss, ill repute and esteem, praise and blame, and pain and pleasure. One's mind remains free of any tendency to become either dejected or joyful in response to any of these dharmas.

In "relinquishing one's own benefit," and "acting diligently for the benefit of others," the bodhisattva sets aside self-benefit to devote the good works he does to facilitating what is good for others, doing so even for those he has not yet befriended and even for those with whom he has no causal affinities.

C. Q: Relinquishing Self-Benefit to Benefit Others Is Wrong

Question: As for [your recommending] "relinquishing self-benefit in order to work diligently for the benefit of others," this is wrong. As stated by the Buddha, "Although one might accomplish greatly beneficial works for others, one should not relinquish attention to one's own self-benefit."

This idea is reminiscent of the saying that: "One may have to sacrifice a person for the success of a clan, may have to sacrifice a single clan for the success of a village, may have to sacrifice a village for the success of a country, may have to sacrifice a country for the success of oneself, or may have to sacrifice oneself for the sake of right Dharma."

One first accomplishes self-benefit
and then, afterward, benefits others.
If one sacrifices self-benefit to benefit others,
later on, one will experience sorrow and regret.

If one relinquishes self-benefit to benefit others
while thinking to oneself that this constitutes wisdom,
this is something that in the context of the world
amounts to the foremost sort of stupidity.

D. A: No. This Is Good Even in Worldly Terms & Also Benefits Oneself

Response: Even from the worldly standpoint, seeking to bring about good for the benefit of others is regarded as good and as the mark of solid resolve. How much the more so is this true of the bodhisattva whose practice transcends worldly concerns. If one benefits others, that is just benefiting oneself. This is as described here:

Regarding matters pertaining to others, the bodhisattva
is neither inferior nor weak in the quality of his determination.

For whoever has brought forth the resolve to attain bodhi,
benefit of others is just benefit of oneself.

The meaning of this has already been extensively discussed in the first chapter. Therefore, your statements on this matter are wrong.

As for "being deeply grateful for others' kindnesses, one repays them doubly," whenever others do good things for the bodhisattva, he should repay them liberally and also be deeply grateful for their kindnesses. This is the mark of a good person. Additionally:

One gives wealth to the poor
and bestows fearlessness on the fearful.
One engages in meritorious deeds of these sorts
until they become solidly and durably established.

As for "giving wealth to the poor," there are those who, in previous lives, did not plant the causes of merit. Hence they now do not have the means to provide for their scarcity of life-sustaining necessities. As befits one's capacities, one gives aid to such people.

As for "bestowing fearlessness on the fearful," in all sorts of cases where beings are frightened, whether that be due to fear of enemies, fear of hunger, fear of floods, fire, cold, heat, or some other cause of fear—in the midst of these many fears, the bodhisattva instructs and guides these people, sees to their security and happiness, and thereby causes them to become free of fear.

Meritorious qualities such as these [are caused to become] the most solid and enduring. Finally:

For those beset with sorrow, one strives to rid them of their sorrows.
Regarding those lacking in strength, one practices patience and abandons arrogance, great arrogance, and so forth.[233]
One acts with deep reverence toward those who are venerable.
One always draws close to those who are learned and consults with the wise on matters of good and evil.
One always maintains right views with respect to one's own practice.
In one's relations with beings, one does not flatter them, deceive them, or make false declarations of affection.
One is insatiable in quest of goodness and one pursues the acquisition of immeasurably vast learning.
All of one's endeavors are accomplished with solid resolve.
One always carries on one's endeavors in the company of good people.
One maintains a mind of great compassion toward those who are evil.

Regarding both those who are good spiritual friends and those who are not good spiritual friends, one establishes a solid conception of them all as being one's good spiritual friends.

One maintains a mind of equal regard toward beings and refrains from stinginess in the dispensation of essential Dharma [teachings].

One expounds [the Dharma] for others in a manner consistent with what one has heard.

One realizes the import and flavor of all the Dharma teachings that one has heard.

Regarding the entertaining and pleasurable matters associated with the five types of desire, one contemplates them all as merely transitory.

One contemplates having a spouse (lit. "a wife") and children as comparable to abiding in the hells.

One contemplates the things required to sustain one's life as a source of weariness and suffering.

One contemplates matters having to do with carrying on a business as freighted with worry and distress.

One contemplates whatever one might seek to obtain as tending to destroy one's roots of goodness.

One contemplates abiding in the life of a householder as comparable to living in a prison.

One contemplates relatives, clan, and friends as comparable to jailers.

One contemplates one's persistent day-and-night thinking by inquiring, "What benefit is gained by this?"

One contemplates this non-enduring body as the basis for acquiring the body that does endure.[234]

One contemplates wealth that is not durable as capable of bringing forth the wealth that does endure.[235]

E. One Should Steadfastly Observe the Five Moral Precepts

Additionally:

> One's mind should steadfastly abide in observance of
> the five moral precepts of the layperson's Dharma.

The lay bodhisattva who relies on the Three Refuges as he practices the above meritorious qualities should steadfastly abide in the five moral precepts. The five moral precepts constitute the comprehensively encompassing standard for the layperson's Dharma.

One should abandon all thoughts of killing and maintain compassionate pity for beings.

One should know when enough is enough and not covet the possessions of others even to the point where one will not even take a blade of grass that has not been given.

One abandons sexual misconduct and become weary of and averse to the affairs of one's private chambers. One guards against and distances oneself from any outside sensual involvements and so does not gaze at others inappropriately. One is ever mindful of the body as something productive of repulsive outflows and thereby brings forth thoughts of renunciation while also fully realizing that the five types of desire all ultimately conduce to suffering.

If desire for one's wife comes to mind, one should dispel and relinquish it. One should always contemplate the body's unloveliness[236] and nurture a fear of becoming someone driven along by the fetters. Hence one should abandon desire and not be attached to its objects. Always remaining aware of the world as suffering and nonself, one should bring forth this prayerful aspiration: "Oh when will I finally succeed in no longer giving rise to thoughts of desire?" How much the less would one actually engage in such physical actions.

One abandons false speech, takes pleasure in speaking truthfully, and refrains from deceiving others. One's speech reflects what is known by the mind and one's thoughts are a reflection of serene wisdom. What one says to others accords with what one sees, hears, senses, and knows. One naturally abides in a way so determined by the Dharma that, even at the cost of one's life, one would not speak in ways that mislead others.

Alcohol is the gateway to neglectfulness and a multitude of bad actions. One should always stay far from it and never let it pass one's lips. One will thereby refrain from acting crazy and deranged, will not become inebriated and confused, will not become agitated, will not become seized by fears, will not act shamelessly, and will not engage in inappropriate sorts of joking. Rather, one will always be able to single-mindedly distinguish between what is good and what is disgraceful.

Now, there may be times when this bodhisattva delights in giving everything and thus is moved to think, "To those who want food, I shall provide food, and for those who seek drink, I shall provide drink." If, as a consequence, one does provide alcohol, in doing so, one should reflect: "Now, this is an occasion in the practice of *dāna pāramitā* when one gives whatever is sought. Later, I will use skillful expedients to teach and coax them into abandoning alcohol altogether and into developing the mindfulness and wisdom that shall cause them to refrain from any such negligence."

Now, how can this be? It is because the essence of *dāna pāramitā* lies in fulfilling the wishes of others. Hence, in circumstances of this sort, the lay bodhisattva's provision of alcoholic beverages does not constitute a karmic offense.[237]

One dedicates the merit from upholding the five moral precepts to one's future realization of *anuttarasamyaksaṃbodhi*. One guards and upholds the five precepts in the same manner that one would guard precious jewels and in the same manner that one protects one's own body and life.

1. Q: Does This Bodhisattva Only Observe These Precepts?

Question: Does this bodhisattva only observe these five moral precepts while not upholding any of the other sorts of good actions?

2. A: Uphold The 5 Precepts & Also Practice the Other Good Actions

Response:

The bodhisattva should steadfastly abide
in these five general moral precepts.
The other [wholesome] actions of body, speech, and mind
should all also be practiced as well.

We have already discussed the meaning of the layperson's five precepts. Having taken on these five moral precepts, one should steadfastly abide in their observance and, in addition, should cultivate the rest of the three types of good karmic deeds. Additionally, as for those dharmas that the lay bodhisattva should practice, [there are the following practices]:

a. He Should Explain Dharma for Beings & Proceed to Teach Them

As befits those beings whom one should benefit,
one explains the Dharma and thus teaches and transforms them.

This bodhisattva is able to give to all beings in ways appropriately addressing any deficiencies they may have. No matter what country one lives in and no matter whether one is in a city, in a village, in the forest, or beneath some tree, one explains Dharma and teaches the beings there in accordance with whatever might benefit them. As it is said, one explains dharmas conducive to faith for those bereft of faith, explains propriety in etiquette for those who are disrespectful, explains dharmas conducive to extensive learning for those deficient in learning, explains the dharma of giving for those who are miserly, explains the dharma of harmoniousness and patience for those who are full of hatred, explains the dharma of vigor for those who are indolent, explains the stations of right mindfulness for those of chaotic mind, and speaks in a way conducive to wisdom for those who are foolish or deluded. In addition:

b. One Should Provide Beings with Whatever They Are Deficient In

In accordance with whatever one finds to be deficient,
one should supply all such things in sufficient measure.

All beings have that in which they are deficient. One should provide all such things in sufficient measure. There are those people who, although wealthy, still have ways in which they are deficient. This may even be true of kings, for they too should have those things in which they are deficient. Hence, even though it was previously explained that one bestows wealth on the poor, it is now further stated that one provides in sufficient measure whatever beings are deficient in. Additionally:

c. The Bodhisattva Teaches All Sorts of Evil Beings

There are all sorts of evil beings
who, in various ways, bring about troublesome circumstances
through flattery, deviousness, or unbridled arrogance,
through cursing, slighting, cheating, or deceiving,

or by turning their backs on kindnesses, leaving them unrequited.
Though the stupid and the base are difficult to instruct and transform,
because the bodhisattva's mind feels pity and sadness for them,
he valiantly redoubles his vigor [in teaching them].

d. When Evil Beings Disturb Him, He Must Not Think In These Ways:

Evil beings use many different sorts of evil behavior to attack and disturb the bodhisattva. Even in the midst of this, the bodhisattva's resolve does not withdraw in disgust. He should not think in these ways:

Who would be able to train such evil people as these?

Who would be able to instruct them?

Who would be able to exhort them, causing them to be liberated from *saṃsāra* so that they might reach nirvāṇa?

Who would be able to go and come in *saṃsāra* in the company of such beings?

Who would be able to work together harmoniously with them?

As for all these evil deeds and such unprincipled behavior, who would be able to endure it?

My resolve is exhausted. I cannot engage in joint endeavors with them anymore.

I am going to leave them all far behind and never again participate in joint endeavors with them.

What's more, I am unable to even remain together with them at all.

> These people, the most evil among the evil—there is no way I can have any interactions with them.
> What is the use of any further involvement with people such as these?

e. He Should Redouble His Resolve & Act Like a Great Physician

The bodhisattva knows and sees that it is difficult to rid beings of their evil karmic offenses. He should instead reflect in this manner:

> These sorts of evil people are not few. It is through the application of vigor that they may be influenced to abide in dharmas such as they will delight in. For their sakes, I should intensify my resolve and exert myself to the utmost in diligent practice. I should redouble my practice in a million-fold application of vigor so that, later on, I will acquire great powers by which I will then be able to transform through teaching these most evil among evil beings who are so very difficult to awaken. I should be like the great king of physicians who, by resorting to some small circumstantial method, can cure beings' severe illnesses.

It is in this way that the bodhisattva does away with the disease of the afflictions and is then allowed to abide in whichever meritorious qualities he wishes. [He reflects]:

> I should feel doubly strong pity for these extremely evil beings who are burdened by grave karmic offenses and so I should bring forth profoundly great compassion for them, doing so like that especially fine physician who is abundantly endowed with kindheartedness as he cures the many sorts of illnesses. For those who are seriously ill, he brings forth deep pity and then diligently invents skillful means by which he can seek out an especially fine medicine for them.

It is in this manner that the bodhisattva should feel pity for all beings beset by the disease of the afflictions. Thus, even for the most evil among the evil and those beset with the most serious afflictions, he still feels profound pity. Hence he is diligent in creating means through which, by intensifying his resolve, he is able to cure them. And why?:

f. Failing in This, He Would Be Worthy of the Buddhas' Censure

No matter where the bodhisattva abides,
if he fails to initiate the transformative teaching of beings,
thus allowing them to fall into the three wretched destinies,
he is deeply deserving of the censure of the Buddhas.

And so it is that the bodhisattva, no matter in what country he abides, and no matter whether he is in the city, a village, in the mountains, or beneath some tree—wherever he has the power through which to be able to benefit and teach beings—if he instead withdraws from them in disgust, resents their covetous attachment to the pleasures of the world, and thus becomes unable to initiate their transformative teaching, he thereby allows them to fall into the wretched destinies. This bodhisattva thereby becomes deeply deserving of the censure of all buddhas now abiding throughout the ten directions before whom he ought to feel deeply ashamed and embarrassed, [knowing that they would demand to know], "Oh, how could you let such petty reasons cause you to abandon such a great endeavor?"

Therefore, if the bodhisattva does not wish to become someone deserving of the rebuke and censure of the Buddhas, even when faced with all sorts of deceitful and extremely evil beings, he should not let his resolve sink away. Rather he should benefit them in whatever way suits his power to help them. He should use all manner of expedient means and diligent resolve to begin their transformative teaching.

In this respect, he is like a brave military general. If the general's troops encounter catastrophic losses, he is the one who will then be severely reprimanded by the king. Since the soldiers themselves had no way of knowing [how to avoid this defeat], the king would not reprimand them.

The End of Chapter Fifteen

Chapter 16
On Realizing the Faults of the Householder's Life

XVI. Chapter 16: On Realizing the Faults of the Householder's Life

A. The Bodhisattva Should Know the Faults of the Householder's Life

As the bodhisattva trains in this manner, he should realize the serious faults of the householder's life. Why? If he realizes those serious faults, he might then abandon the householder's life and enter the path. Moreover, he might then be able to instruct others, make them aware of the faults of the household life, and thereby inspire them to leave the home life and enter the path.

B. Q: What Are the Faults of the Householder's Life?

Question: What are the faults of the householder's life?

C. A: They Are Well Described in This Passage from a Sutra

Response: As stated in a sutra, the Buddha informed Ugradatta:[238]

> The home life destroys all roots of goodness. The household is a deep forest of thorns from which it is difficult to escape. The household is a circumstance that destroys the dharmas of purity. The household is the dwelling place of all manner of bad ideation and discursion.[239] The household is the dwelling place of the foolish common person[240] unrestrained in corrupt and evil actions. The household is the place in which one dwells when carrying out every sort of unwholesome endeavor. The household is the gathering place of bad people. The household is the dwelling place of greed, hatred, and delusion. The household is the dwelling place of all forms of suffering. The household is the place where one entirely uses up all the roots of goodness established in previous lives.
>
> When the foolish common person abides in this household, he does what should not be done, says what should not be said, and practices what should not be practiced. When he dwells herein, he slights his parents as well as his teachers and elders. He does not respect the venerable fields of merit, the *śramaṇas*, or the brahmans.
>
> The life of the householder involves causes and conditions conducing to craving, sorrow, grief, suffering, afflictions, and the many sorts of tribulations. The home life is the circumstance in which one encounters the sufferings of harsh speech and scolding, wherein one becomes vulnerable to blades and cudgels, to being bound up and imprisoned, to being beaten, or to being subjected to [punitive]

amputations.[241] One fails to plant whichever roots of goodness one has not yet planted and those roots of goodness one has already planted become vulnerable to destruction.

[The householder's life] is able to cause the common person involved in these desire-related causal circumstances to fall into the wretched destinies. Causal circumstances related to hatred or delusion may also precipitate descent into the wretched destinies. [So, too], causal circumstances related to fearfulness may result in one's falling into the wretched destinies.[242]

The householder's life is a circumstance in which one does not maintain the aggregate (*skandha*) of the moral precepts, abandons the aggregate of meditative absorption, does not contemplate the aggregate of wisdom, does not acquire the aggregate of the liberations, and does not bring forth the aggregate of the knowledge and vision of liberation.

One is born into this householder's life, a circumstance in which parents lovingly dote on their sons, and in which one indulges affection for one's wife and children, for one's retinue, and even for one's carriages and horses. This situation encourages the proliferation of desires to the point where they become insatiable.

[The desires associated with] the householder's life are as difficult to fulfill as the ocean is as it swallows up every tributary that flows into it.

[The desires associated with] the household are as insatiable as a fire in its burning up of firewood.

The life of the householder involves ceaseless ideation and mental discursiveness that are just as continuous as the winds that blow through empty space.

The life of the householder conduces to misfortune in one's future existences just as surely as does delectable food laced with poison [surely leads to one's death].

The life of the householder, by its very nature, is linked to suffering and, in that, it is comparable to having enemies posing as close relations.

Being a householder is an obstruction, for it is able to block one's access to the path of the Āryas.

The householder's life is beset with discord arising from disputation and many different causes and conditions involving mutual opposition and conflict.

The householder's life involves much hatred associated with scolding and much censure over what is desirable versus what is detestable.

The household is impermanent. Even though it may have endured for a long time, it is bound for destruction.

The household is beset by many forms of suffering as one strives to acquire clothing, food, and so forth and then does whatever is necessary to preserve and protect them.

The householder's life is a circumstance involving much mutual doubting, just as when abiding in close proximity to thieves.

One's household is not intrinsically "mine." It is solely through inverted views and covetous attachment that, by resort to conventional designations, one claims "it exists."

The circumstance of the householder is like that of an actor who, although he may use all different sorts of makeup and costumes to present the appearance of a member of the aristocracy, before long, in but an instant, all of those adornments disappear and he resumes his role as someone who is poor and of inferior social status.[243]

The household is ever-changing. Once its components have come together, they are bound to fall apart and disperse.

A household is like a magical conjuration. It depends upon the mere aggregation of components and thus is devoid of any reality.

The household is like a dream. After a while, all of one's wealth and high social status are bound to be lost.

The household is like the morning dew. After a short while, it disappears entirely.

[The happiness derived from] the householder's life is like a mere drop of honey. Its flavor is extremely weak.

The household is like a thicket of thorns. As a person enjoys the taste of the objects of the five types of desire, poisonous piercings inflict injuries.

The household is analogous to a needle-beaked insect. Unwholesome ideation and discursive thought always gnaw at and consume the people within it.

Life as a householder sullies the purity of one's life. One becomes predisposed by it to engage in much cheating and deception.

The life of a householder is plagued by anxiety and worries. Thus one's mind is often muddled and confused.

The house becomes the common property of many others and it is vulnerable to destruction by [agents of] the king, thieves, floods, fires, and evil relatives.

The householder's life is freighted with many defects. It involves the commission of numerous erroneous actions. This being the case, an elder who is a lay bodhisattvas should well realize the faults of the householder's life.

D. Also Practice Giving, Uphold Precepts, and Contemplate Almsmen

Next we have:

The bodhisattva should know
the serious faults of the householder's life.
He should draw close to the practice of giving
and skillfulness in observing moral precepts, delighting in these.

Whenever one sees any almsman,
he should bring forth five threefold contemplations.

The lay bodhisattva should know in this way the tribulations of the householder's life. He should adopt in practice the excellence of giving and observance of moral precepts. "Giving" refers here to relinquishing the covetous mind. "Observing moral precepts" refers to purity of physical and verbal actions. "Skillfulness" refers to skillful restraint of the sense faculties. "Delighting in these" refers to like-mindedness and exultant happiness [in the adoption of these practices].

1. Five Threefold Contemplations Whenever Seeing an Almsman

"Five threefold contemplations" refers to five different threefold contemplations one should take up whenever encountering an almsman.

The first of the threefold contemplations is as follows:

Contemplating [the almsman] as a good spiritual guide.[244]
Contemplating [the acquisition of] great wealth in future lives.[245]
Contemplating [one's giving] as assisting the realization of bodhi.[246]

There is yet another threefold contemplation, as follows:

Contemplating the conquering of miserliness.
Contemplating the relinquishing of everything.
Contemplating striving for the acquisition of all-knowledge.[247]

There is yet another threefold contemplation, as follows:

Contemplating in accordance with the teachings of the Tathāgata.
Contemplating refraining from seeking any karmic result.[248]
Contemplating the defeat of Māra.[249]

There is yet another threefold contemplation, as follows:

Contemplating those who come for alms as one's own retinue.[250]
Contemplating the importance of not abandoning the dharmas comprising "the means of attraction."[251]
Contemplating the relinquishing of what has been wrongfully acquired.

There is yet another threefold contemplation, as follows:

Contemplating dispassion.[252]
Contemplating the cultivation of kindness.
Contemplating non-delusion.

We should now explain this fifth of these five threefold contemplations:

Because an almsman has come, a bodhisattva may be able to diminish the three poisons. Through relinquishing some possession as a gift one may thereby bringing forth the contemplation of dispassion.[253]

Through providing causes and conditions for the happiness of the supplicant, one's thoughts of hatred become but scant. This is cultivation of the contemplation of kindness.

If the [merit from] this act of giving is dedicated to success in the unsurpassable path, this diminishes one's deluded mind states. This is the contemplation of non-delusion.

One should understand the meaning of the other contemplations in accordance with the above explanations.

2. It Is Due to Almsmen That One Is Able to Perfect the Six pāramitās

Furthermore:

> It is because of the almsman
> that the bodhisattva perfects the six *pāramitās*.
> For this reason, one should feel great joy
> on seeing someone who has come to seek alms.

The six *pāramitās* consist of giving, moral virtue, patience, vigor, *dhyāna* concentration, and wisdom. It is because of the almsman that one becomes able to bring them to a state of completion. It is because he gains such benefit that, whenever a bodhisattva sees from afar that a supplicant is coming, his mind is filled with great delight and he thinks, "A walking field of merit has arrived here of his own accord. It is because of just such people as these that I shall be able to perfect the six *pāramitās*." Now, how might this be so? [Consider the following]:

When one's mind feels no miserly cherishing for the object one gives, this is *dāna pāramitā*, [the perfection of giving].

When one gives for the sake of attaining *anuttarasamyaksaṃbodhi*, [the utmost, right, and perfect enlightenment], this is an instance of practicing *śīla pāramitā*, [the perfection of moral virtue].[254]

When one is able to refrain from feeling hatred toward the mendicant, this is an instance of practicing *kṣānti pāramitā*, [the perfection of patience].

When, as one is carrying out the act of giving, one refrains from reflecting on one's own resulting material scarcity while also not retreating from one's resolve, this is an instance of practicing *vīrya pāramitā*, [the perfection of vigor].[255]

If, in giving to an almsman, at that very time when one is presenting the gift, one's mind remains fixed [in its resolve] and does not entertain any regretfulness, this is an instance of practicing *dhyāna pāramitā,* [the perfection of meditative concentration].

By not apprehending [any inherent existence in] any dharma as one carries out an act of giving, by not seeking any karmic reward from it, and by remaining free of any attachment in this, thereby doing so after the manner of a worthy or an *ārya,*[256] when one then dedicates that act of giving to *anuttarasamyaksaṃbodhi,* one's giving then becomes an instance of practicing *prajñā pāramitā,* [the perfection of wisdom].

3. One Knows the Benefits of Giving and the Faults of Miserliness

Furthermore:

As for the karmic results ensuing from giving the gift,
he is able to know all of its various forms.
He also knows the various faults associated with
keeping it at home due to miserliness.

As for the merit acquired from the giving of the gift that has been given as well as all the serious faults associated with keeping the gift due to miserliness, the bodhisattva completely comprehends all of these matters.

a. Q: What Are the Merits of Giving and Faults of Keeping the Gift?

Question: If one gives it, what sort of merit is gained by that? And if one instead keeps it at home, what fault or blame is there in that?

b. A: Using True Wisdom, the Bodhisattva Understands as Follows:

Response: The bodhisattva uses true wisdom to understand this matter in the following manner, [reflecting]:

After this gift has been given away, it is still mine [in terms of its ongoing karmic rewards]. However, if it is instead kept at home, it is not [rightfully] mine.

Once the gift has been given, it endures.[257] However, if it is instead kept at home, it will not endure.[258]

After the gift has been given, future-life happiness will follow from that. However, if it is instead kept at home, it will provide happiness only for a brief period of time.

Once the gift has been given away, there is no longer any need to be anxious about preserving and guarding it. However, if it is instead kept at home, one will continue to feel protective concern for it.

If one has already given away the gift, one's thoughts of affection for it become scant. However, if it is instead kept at home, one increases one's affection for it.

Once the gift has been given, one becomes free of [any thought of it as] "mine." However, if it is instead kept at home, it is [still thought of as] "mine."

Once the gift has been given, there is no [conception of] anyone to whom it belongs. However, if it is instead kept at home, there is [the conception of] someone to whom it belongs.

Once the gift has been given, one is free of concerns about it. However, if it is instead kept at home, one entertains many fears about it.

Once the gift has been given, it assists progress on the path to bodhi. However, if it is instead kept at home, it assists progress on the path of Māra.

Once the gift has been given, [the benefit from having given it] is endless. However, if it is instead kept at home, it remains finite [in its capacity to provide benefit].

Once the gift has been given, one continues to experience happiness from it. However, if it is instead kept at home, one continues to experience suffering [from one's concerns about it].

Having given the gift, one relinquishes afflictions. However, if it is instead kept at home, it increases one's afflictions.

Having given the gift, one gains great wealth and happiness. However, if it is instead kept at home, one does not gain great wealth and happiness.

Having given the gift, one has done the deed of a great man. However, if it is instead kept at home, one has done the deed of a petty man.

Having given the gift, one is praised by the Buddhas. However, if it is instead kept at home, one is praised only by fools.

4. Contemplate Relatives and Possessions as Like Mere Illusions

Furthermore:

Regarding one's wife, children, and retinue
as well as one's good spiritual friends,
one's giving of wealth, and one's animals, too—
one should contemplate them all as mere illusory conjurations.

It is one's karma consisting of all of one's actions
that serves as their conjuring magician.

Regarding his wife, children, and so forth, the householder bodhisattva should contemplate them as mere illusory conjurations. They are just like phenomena manifesting as illusory conjurations that merely deceive a person's eyes. It is the karma of one's actions that serves as their conjurer.

As for phenomena such as one's wife, sons, and so forth, they will all disappear before long. This is as explained in the sutras where the Buddha told the bhikshus, "All of one's actions are like an illusory conjuration that deceives and deludes foolish people for there are no genuinely-existent phenomena present there at all."

One should realize that it is because of karma that these phenomena exist. Once that karma has finally become exhausted, then they all disappear. Hence they are all like illusory conjurations. Thus one should reflect on them as follows:

5. One Should Reflect on Them All as the Results of Karma

I am not a possession of theirs,
nor are they possessions of mine.
Those things and myself all belong to karma
and exist in accordance with karmic causes and conditions.

If one carries on right contemplation in this manner,
one should not create any bad karma.

[The bodhisattva reflects in the following manner]:

My father, mother, wife, children, relatives, fellow villagers, friends, slaves, maidservants, servant boys, guests, and such—none of them are able to save me, to be a refuge for me, or to serve as my ultimate resort. They are neither my self nor a possession of my self.

Not even the five aggregates, twelve sense bases, or eighteen sense fields constitute either a self or anything that is owned by a self. How much the less could this be so in the case of my parents, my wife, my children, or those other individuals?

Neither am I capable of serving as a savior for them, of serving as a refuge for them, or of serving as an ultimate resort for them. I too belong to my own karma and am thereby bound to accord with my karma in what I experience. They too belong to their own karma and are thereby bound to accord with their karma in what they experience.

In this connection, regarding this matter of experiencing good and bad karmic retributions, there are three bases for evaluating and assessing [this idea]:

First, it has meaningful significance.
Second, we see this in the sutras' explanations.
Third, we see this in presently manifest circumstances.

[This being the case], one should not perform even the slightest bad physical, verbal, or mental karmic deed [even when it is done] for the sake of one's parents, wife, or children.

6. Use the Following Threefold Contemplations of One's Spouse

Furthermore:

Regarding a spouse,[259] the bodhisattva
should bring forth three threefold contemplations
in addition to which there are another three that are threefold,
after which there are yet more sets of three that are threefold as well.[260]

The lay bodhisattva should take up the threefold contemplations, as below:[261]

The first three are as follows: One's spouse is impermanent, bound to be lost, and bound for destruction.

There are three more contemplations: One's spouse is a companion for enjoyment and laughter now, but not a companion in future lives, a companion with whom to share meals, but not a companion in the undergoing of karmic retributions, and is a companion in times of happiness, but not a companion in [future] times of suffering.

There are three more contemplations: One's spouse is an object for the contemplation of the body as unlovely,[262] as malodorous and filled with filth, and as loathsome.

There are three more contemplations: One's spouse is to be contemplated as an adversary, as a source of injurious anguish, and as one who stands in mutual opposition [to one's aims].

There are three more contemplations: One's spouse is to be contemplated as a *rākṣasa*, a *piśācī*, and as physically ugly.

There are three more contemplations: One's spouse is to be contemplated as a cause for falling into the hells, as a cause for falling into the animal realm, and as a cause for falling into the realm of hungry ghosts.

There are three more contemplations: One's spouse is to be contemplated as a heavy burden, as a cause of decline, and as fearsome.

There are three more contemplations: One's spouse is to be contemplated as not-self, as of no certain loyalty, and as merely borrowed.

There are three more contemplations: One's spouse is to be contemplated as the cause for generating bad physical karma, as the cause for generating bad verbal karma, and as the cause for generating bad mental karma.

There are three more contemplations: One's spouse is to be contemplated as the basis for thoughts of lust, as the basis for thoughts of hatred, and as the basis for thoughts of annoyance.

There are three more contemplations:[263] One's spouse is to be contemplated as manacles, as chains, and as a cangue.

There are three more contemplations: One's spouse is to be contemplated as an obstacle to maintaining the moral precepts, as an obstacle to *dhyāna* concentration, and as an obstacle to wisdom.

There are three more contemplations: One's spouse is to be contemplated as a deep pit, as a net-trap, and as a corral-trap.

There are three more contemplations: One's spouse is to be contemplated as a natural disaster, as a plague, and as causing the anguish of decline.

There are three more contemplations: One's spouse is to be contemplated as associated with karmic offenses, as a black-eared kite,[264] and as a disastrous hailstorm.

There are three more contemplations: One's spouse is to be contemplated as symbolic of illness, as symbolic of aging, and as symbolic of death.

There are three more contemplations: One's spouse is to be contemplated as Māra, as the abode of Māra, and as fearsome.

There are three more contemplations: One's spouse is to be contemplated as emblematic of worry, as emblematic of anguish, and as emblematic of weeping.

There are three more contemplations: One's spouse is to be contemplated as a large jackal or wolf, as the *makara* sea monster, and as a huge leopard.

There are three more contemplations: One's spouse is to be contemplated as a black venomous serpent, as the Sakhalin sturgeon,[265] and as the force of violent pillaging.

There are three more contemplations: One's spouse is to be contemplated as not a savior, as not a refuge, and as not a shelter.

There are three more contemplations: One's spouse is to be contemplated as associated with failure, as associated with retreat, and as associated with physical exhaustion.

There are three more contemplations: One's spouse is to be contemplated as a thief, as a jailer, and as one of the minions in hell.

There are three more contemplations: One's spouse is to be contemplated as detention, as bondage, and as a fetter.

There are three more contemplations: One's spouse is to be contemplated as like mire, as like a flood, and as like being adrift.

There are three more contemplations: One's spouse is to be contemplated as fetters, as a lock, and as glue.

There are three more contemplations: One's spouse is to be contemplated as a fierce conflagration, as a spinning wheel of knives, and as a flaming torch.

There are three more contemplations: One's spouse is to be contemplated as of no benefit, as a thicket of thorns, and as noxious poison.

There are three more contemplations: One's spouse is to be contemplated as on a burial mound, as obscuring radiance, and as symbolic of desirous attachment.

There are three more contemplations: One's spouse is to be contemplated as symbolic of resentment, as symbolic of whips and cudgels, and as symbolic of swords and lances.

There are three more contemplations: One's spouse is to be contemplated as symbolic of rage, as symbolic of disputatiousness, and as symbolic of being beaten with a cudgel.

There are three more contemplations: One's spouse is to be contemplated as symbolic of proximity to what one detests, as symbolic of separation from what one loves, and as symbolic of quarrelsomeness.

To sum up what is essential: One's spouse is to be contemplated as symbolic of every sort of malodorousness, repulsiveness, and impurity, as symbolic of every sort of ruin and corruption, and as symbolic of all sorts of bad karmic roots.

Therefore, having visualized such contemplations of one's spouse and children, the lay bodhisattva should bring forth feelings of renunciation, leave behind the householder's life, cultivate goodness, and do good deeds. If one is unable to leave behind the householder's life,[266] one should at least refrain from creating any sort of bad karma in one's relationship with one's spouse.

7. Use Wisdom to Reduce Bias Toward One's Own Children

Additionally:

If one cherishes a preferential affection for one's children,
one should then use the power of wisdom to relinquish it, and,
based on [such feeling for] one's children, practice equal regard for all
by which one then extends universal kindness to all beings.

If the lay bodhisattva realizes that he cherishes an especially great partiality toward his own children, he should then use the power of wisdom to reflect upon it and relinquish it. One who is possessed of the power of wisdom should reflect in this manner:

It is only once the bodhisattva develops a mind of equal regard for all that he then attains *anuttarasamyaksaṃbodhi*. If one's mind discriminates between those who are regarded as superior and those who are regarded as inferior, then he will have no attainment of bodhi. This *anuttarasamyaksaṃbodhi* is acquired through [realization of] the one characteristic, that of signlessness. It is not attained through discriminating on the basis of different characteristics.

Now, I am seeking the realization of *anuttarasamyaksaṃbodhi*. If the mind of affection that I maintain toward my own children is preferentially greater than for others, then this is an instance of retaining discriminations as to who is regarded as superior and who is regarded as inferior. This does not qualify as "equal regard for all." It is just a case of making discriminations based on different characteristics and it is not a case of perceiving a singular unitary character.

If I allow this to happen, then I will remain very far from *anuttarasamyaksaṃbodhi*. Therefore I should not bring forth a mind of preferentially greater affection for my own children.

8. Take up This Threefold Contemplation of One's Children

One should then take up a threefold contemplation regarding one's own children:

First, "They are for me like thieves, for, although the Buddha has taught that one is to feel equal kindness for all, because of my preferentially greater affection for them, this has been destroyed, resulting in my failure to maintain equal regard for everyone."

Second, "They bring about the harm inflicted by thieves, for it is because of these children that roots of goodness have been destroyed and a life of great wisdom has been obstructed."

Third, "It is because of these children that I have gone against the middle-way practice of the path and do not practice in accordance with the path."

9. Use The Following Thoughts to Develop Equal Regard for All

Then, due to [having contemplated] one's children, one immediately takes up the practice of being equally kind toward all beings. One should then reflect in this manner:

"My children have come from some other place and I too have come from some other place. My children will go off to some different location and I too shall depart to some different location. I do not know where they shall go and they do not know where I shall go. They do not know where I have come from and I do not know where they have come from. These children are not my possessions. Why for no reason do I just suddenly develop these bonds of affection?" This is as described here:

They and I do not know of each other
from where we have come or where we shall go.
In what respect then are they and I such "close relatives"
that we conceive of each other as "mine"?

Additionally, [one should reflect]: "Throughout the course of *saṃsāra*'s beginningless cycle of births and deaths, all beings have previously been my children. I too have been their child. In this sphere of conditioned dharmas, there is no fixed relationship whereby this one is my child or that one is someone else's child. Why? While traveling through the six destinies of rebirth, beings take turns in serving as either the father or the child of the other." This is as described here:

> Ignorance covers over the eye of wisdom.
> Time and time again, during the course of our births and deaths,
> we have gone and come, each having much that we have done,
> as each has taken turns in serving for the other as father or child.
>
> One becomes attached through desire for the pleasures of the world,
> remaining oblivious to the existence of the supreme endeavor.
> Time and time again, adversaries become each other's friends,
> and, time and time again, friends become each other's adversaries.

[One continues to reflect, as follows]:

> Therefore I should adopt expedient means that compel me to refrain from feeling thoughts of either hatred or love. Why? If one has those one considers to be "good friends," then one will always seek in many different ways to benefit them, whereas, if one has those one considers to be "adversaries," one will always bring forth many different sorts of thoughts that cause one to refrain from benefitting them. Hence, if one retains these thoughts of hatred or love, then one will remain unable to gain a penetrating understanding of the uniform equality of all dharmas.
>
> After death, those whose minds discriminate between those who are superior and those who are inferior are bound to be reborn in a place where wrong [practice] is prevalent, whereas, those who adhere to right practice are bound to be reborn in a place where right practice is prevalent.
>
> Therefore, I should refrain from cultivating wrong practices. If one practices uniformly equal regard toward other beings, then one will be bound in the future to attain all-knowledge[267] where the uniform equality [of all things is realized].

The End of Chapter Sixteen

Chapter 17
On Entering the Temple

XVII. Chapter 17: On Entering the Temple

A. One Should Be Able to Relinquish Whatever One Is Attached to

In this way, the lay bodhisattva should refrain from generating thoughts of attachment, thoughts imputing the existence of a self, or thoughts imputing the existence of anything belonging to a self. Why is this so? As for whatever has become such an object of affectionate attachment that one finds it difficult to relinquish, to accord with the Dharma, one should relinquish it. If one can give it away, then this is the means for getting rid of this fault. Bodhisattvas who are able by this means to remain free of thoughts of attachment or miserliness are capable of abiding as householders.

B. Q: If One Is Attached to Something, What if Someone Asks for It?

Question: It might happen that the lay bodhisattva has things for which he feels a miserly cherishing and to which he is affectionately attached. When someone comes wishing to receive them as a gift, what should he do?

C. A: Exhort Oneself to Abandon Miserliness and Relinquish It

Response:

Regarding those things to which one is attached,
whenever someone comes seeking to obtain them,
one should exhort and persuade his mind
to simply relinquish them, for he must not indulge miserliness.

As for possessions toward which a bodhisattva feels a covetous cherishing, if a beggar were to come urgently seeking to obtain it from him, saying, "If you give this thing to me, you will quickly attain buddhahood," the bodhisattva should immediately exhort and persuade himself to go ahead and give it to him, reflecting as follows:

> If I fail to relinquish this possession just now, this thing is certainly bound in due course to depart far from me anyway. Once I am at the point of death, this thing will not accompany me when I go. If this is so, then this possession is characterized by the inevitability of its departure.
>
> Now, for the sake of *anuttarasamyaksaṃbodhi* and for the sake of perfecting *dāna pāramitā* (the perfection of giving), I shall give it

away. Later, when I am on the verge of death, my mind will be free of regrets. The sutras state that if one dies with a mind free of regrets, one will be reborn in a good place. This amounts to a great benefit. How then could I fail to relinquish this?

D. If One Is Still Unable to Relinquish It, One May Politely Decline

If, even after having exhorted oneself in this manner, one still retains a miserly cherishing for the possession, then, politely declining, he should speak to the beggar, saying:

I am now still only new in my training.
Hence my roots of goodness are not yet well established.
Thus my mind has not yet achieved sovereign mastery in this.
I hope that, later on, I will be able to give to you.

One should politely decline the beggar's entreaty, saying, "Do not become angry with me. I have only recently brought forth the resolve and my roots of goodness are not yet fully developed. Thus I have not yet gained adequate strength in the methods of the bodhisattva's practice. As a consequence I am not yet able to relinquish this possession. Later, once I have gained strength in this and my roots of goodness have become completely developed, my resolve will then be solid enough that I will be able to give it to you."

E. If a Divided Sangha Stops Functioning, One Should Try to Mediate

Additionally:

If it happens that the community, failing to abide in harmony,
is about to suspend the Dharma activities prescribed in the sutras,
the bodhisattva should do whatever lies within his powers
to implement skillful means that will prevent their termination.

It could happen that, due to the circumstances associated with some matter, the monastic community becomes involved in disputes so severe that it splits into factions, thus causing its Dharma activities to be abandoned. In such a case, the lay bodhisattva should apply diligent thought to implementing some skillful method to restore the relationship between the factions, doing so with a mind free of partisan favoritism. One may use gifts of valuables, [mediating] discussion, or reverential entreaty to somehow cause the factions to become reunited.

The situation could have been caused by deficiencies in clothing or food, by someone with wrong views obstinately creating obstacles, by the speaker of Dharma seeking donations or support, or by the audience failing to be respectful. In such circumstances, the lay bodhisattva should use whichever skillful means are appropriate, perhaps doing so by contributing valuables, or perhaps doing so by speaking to those involved with a humbled mind and sincere entreaties, thus somehow preventing their abandonment of Dharma activities.

If the abandoning of Dharma activities is prevented, this amounts to lighting the lamp of the Buddha's Dharma and making an offering to all buddhas of the ten directions and the three periods of time.

F. On Abstinence Days, the Lay Bodhisattva Takes the Eight Precepts

Additionally:

> On the abstinence days, take the eight moral precepts
> and draw near to those pure in the moral precepts.
> Because of the good causes and conditions created by the precepts,
> be deeply sincere in observing them with fond regard and reverence.

As for the abstinence days, they are the eighth, the fourteenth, the fifteenth, the twenty-third, the twenty-ninth, and the thirtieth days of the lunar month. One additionally observes the three days of personal restraint. To determine these three days of personal restraint, one counts forward fifteen days for each day of restriction, starting with the winter solstice, [doing this three times] until one comes to the forty-fifth day thereafter.

On each of these inauspicious days, there are many more ghosts and spirits going about inflicting wanton violence. Because common people of the world observed these as days to be on their guard [against improper behavior], they made a practice of not eating after midday on such occasions. The Buddha took this circumstance as a basis for teaching them the practice of "the single-day precept observance," since they could thereby create merit and make the devas happy when they descended [from the heavens] to monitor the quality of people's behavior in the world. As a consequence, the devas would be inspired to be protectively mindful of those who observe this practice.

The lay bodhisattva would take even the most minor matters as bases for increasing beneficial actions. How much the more so then would he be sure to avoid failing to accord with these previously ordained days of abstinence? Therefore one should take up the practice of the single-day abstinence dharma. If one does so, one not only garners self-benefit by doing this but also thereby becomes able to benefit others.

1. Q: How Should One Practice This Abstinence Dharma?

Question: How is it that this abstinence dharma is to be observed?

2. A: Solemn Vow to Uphold the Eight Precepts as Follows:

Response: One should utter the following words:[268]

Just as all the Āryas have forever abandoned killing, have cast aside the knife and cudgel, are always free of hatred, are possessed of a sense of shame and dread of blame, and treat beings with kindness and compassion, I, so-and-so, for one day and one night, shall also abandon killing, shall cast aside the knife and cudgel, shall remain free of hatred, shall be possessed of a sense of shame and dread of blame, and shall also treat beings with kindness and compassion, adopting this dharma in emulation of the Āryas.

Just as the Āryas have forever abandoned taking anything not given, are pure in their physical actions, and are content with whatever they receive, I now, for one day and one night, shall also abandon theft and taking what is not given, and shall pursue pure livelihood, adopting this dharma in emulation of the Āryas.

Just as the Āryas have forever cut off sexual indulgence and have abandoned such worldly pleasures, I now, for one day and one night, shall also cut off sexual indulgence, shall abandon such worldly pleasures, and shall purely cultivate celibate *brahmacarya*, adopting this dharma in emulation of the Āryas.

Just as the Āryas have forever abandoned false speech and always practice true speech and speech that is right and direct, I now, for one day and one night, shall also abandon false speech and shall also practice true speech and speech that is right and direct, adopting this dharma in emulation of the Āryas.

Just as the Āryas have forever abandoned the consumption of intoxicants,[269] this because intoxicants are the basis for falling into neglectfulness, I now, for one day and one night, shall also abandon intoxicants, adopting this dharma in emulation of the Āryas.

Just as the Āryas have forever abandoned singing, dancing, making music, wearing flowers, perfumes, necklaces, and other bodily adornments, I now, for one day and one night, shall also abandon singing, dancing, making music, wearing flowers, perfumes, necklaces, and other bodily adornments, adopting this dharma in emulation of the Āryas.

Just as the Āryas have forever abandoned the use of large high-and-wide beds, preferring instead small beds and sitting cushions made of straw, I now, for one day and one night, shall also abandon large high-and-wide beds, preferring a small bed and sitting cushions made of straw, adopting this dharma in emulation of the Āryas.

And just as the Āryas have forever abandoned meals after midday and have abandoned actions and eating done at the wrong times, I now, for one day and one night, shall also abstain from eating after midday, abandoning actions and eating done at the wrong time, adopting this dharma in emulation of the Āryas.

This is as described in the following lines:

> Killing, stealing, sexual indulgence, and lying,
> consuming intoxicants and also wearing flowers and perfumes,
> wearing necklaces, singing, dancing, and so forth,
> also high beds and eating after midday—
>
> These are behaviors that the Āryas have abandoned.
> Hence I too now act accordingly,
> dedicating these causes and conditions for the creation of merit
> to everyone's joint success in the attainment of buddhahood.

As for "drawing near to bhikshus pure in observing the moral precepts," the lay bodhisattva should draw near to those bhikshus who are completely able to guard and uphold the precepts of moral purity, who have thoroughly developed the meritorious qualities, and who defend against and distance themselves from the many sorts of evil.

As for "because of the good causes and conditions created by the precepts," in addition, one should draw near to bhikshus who observe the moral precepts, whose physical and verbal actions are pure, and whose mental actions are direct, good, and free of the many sorts of evil.

As for being "deeply sincere in treating them with fond regard and reverence," with respect to the above-referenced bhikshus whose minds are direct, whose actions are imbued with goodness, who uphold the moral precepts, and who have thoroughly developed the meritorious qualities, one should extend supreme reverence toward them that is accompanied by deeply sincere thoughts of fond regard.

3. Q: Should One Treat Bad Monks with Disdain and Anger?

Question: If the lay bodhisattva is to bring forth a fond and reverential attitude toward the bhikshus who uphold the moral precepts and who have thoroughly developed the meritorious qualities, should he then adopt a disdainful or angry attitude toward bhikshus who break the moral precepts?

4. A: Do Not Adopt a Disdainful or Angry Attitude toward Them

Response:

> If one encounters someone who breaks the moral precepts,
> one should not adopt a disdainful or angry attitude toward them.

Supposing that a lay bodhisattva were to encounter a bhikshu who breaks the precepts and engages in corrupt practices, whose deportment is defective, whose cultivation is defiled, who conceals his own faults, and who, while failing to observe celibate *brahmacarya,* nonetheless claims to observe celibate *brahmacarya,* even then, one should not behave toward this bhikshu with slighting disdainfulness or angry thoughts.

5. Q: If Hatred Is Wrong, What Attitude Is Most Appropriate?

Question: If one is to refrain from feeling hatred toward him, then just what sort of attitude should one adopt?

6. A: Feel Pity for Him and Condemn His Afflictions Instead

Response:

One should bring forth thoughts of pity toward him,
making it the afflictions themselves that one condemns.

If a lay bodhisattva encounters a precept-breaking bhikshu, he should not feel hatred or adopt a slighting and disdainful attitude toward him. Rather he should feel pity for him and think of ways to benefit him, reflecting:

> How terrible! This man has been able to encounter the sublime Dharma of the Buddha. He has succeeded in leaving behind the destinies of hell-dwellers, animals, hungry ghosts, form and formless-realm devas, and those reborn in borderlands [distant from Dharma]. Being complete in his faculties and hence neither deaf, dumb, or dim-witted, he has encountered the sublime Dharma of the Buddha through which one may distinguish what is good from what is disgraceful and through which one's mind may still retain right views and understand what is meaningfully principled.
>
> This human body is so difficult to come by. It is just as in the case of the one-eyed tortoise out on the great sea who, emerging from the depths, happens by chance to poke his head up through a knothole in a floating plank. Even when compared to the rarity of this, the opportunity to gain a human rebirth is doubly difficult to acquire.
>
> Having heard the Dharma of the Buddha through which one can extinguish all forms of evil, become liberated from all suffering and afflictions, and succeed in reaching right wisdom, one relinquishes all of one's life-supporting possessions however extensive they may be and then severs forever one's relations with one's relatives and clan, having no one for whom one retains any further sentimental attachment. Regardless of whether one is from the common classes or from an elevated caste, because one has faith in the Buddha's words, one is able to leave behind the home life.
>
> One constantly hears of the moral transgressions associated with breaking the moral precepts, of the associated self-loathing, of becoming someone rebuked and censured by the wise, of coming to have a bad reputation that circulates widely, and of being constantly beset by doubts and regrets. Then, at death, one is bound to

plummet into the wretched destinies. Even having heard of these circumstances, one nonetheless still persists in breaking the moral precepts.

It is through practice of the ten courses of good karmic action that one then gains a human rebirth. Even so, one remains unable to put them to skillful use in accordance with Dharma so as to secure his own self-benefit.

What a shame! The power of the three poisons is so extremely terrible that they constantly assail beings and remain difficult to successfully abandon.

In all sorts of ways, the Buddhas rebuke the evil actions caused by the evil bandits of the afflictions.

If, in accordance with reality and in a principled fashion, one contemplates the matter in this way, [one realizes] one should not slight and disdain those people who have broken the moral precepts. One also reflects as follows:

> If I am not completely able to abandon thoughts of anger and condescending disdain, I should consider that, given that the Dharma of the Buddha is as vast as a great sea, it could be that there are exceptional circumstances of which I am unaware.

This accords with the passage in the Mahāyāna's *Sutra of the Resolute King* wherein it is recorded that the Buddha told Ānanda:[270]

> It could be that there are bhikshus of dull faculties who are obstructed by their mental dimness, whose minds are not completely clear, and who do not possess a penetrating comprehension of the true character of dharmas. They may forever be bearing in mind dharmas associated with the perception of existence or with the perception of nonexistence whereupon they then seize on perceptions of existence whereby they produce perceptions of male versus female, produce perceptions of obstacles associated with transgressions, produce perceptions of defilement, or produce perceptions of purity.
>
> The production of these sorts of perceptions is a function of dull faculties. If someone's mind is not completely clear, then he is bound to commit transgressions. Ānanda, if, within the sphere of all dharmas, someone remains unable to well understand their character, then this is a case of failing to completely comprehend them.
>
> From the very beginning on forward to the present, there has never been any fundamental substance, nature, or characteristic of any dharma that could be apprehended. This sort of person fails to realize such things. When one produces perceptions such as these, then he becomes indistinguishable from the followers of non-Buddhist traditions.

Ānanda, within all the dharmas I have explained, there are exceptional circumstances that are consistent with complete clarity and purity. In these circumstances, there is no such thing as a "transgression" or a "transgressor."

Ānanda, the commission of transgressions is characterized by the existence of doubts and regrets, by stupidity, and by benightedness. The commission of transgressions involves the production of perceptions of the existence of a being, perceptions of the existence of a self, perceptions of the existence of a living entity, or perceptions of the existence of a person. In all cases, it is because of the fallacious view that a "self" exists in association with the body that one speaks of some "transgressor." But, within my Dharma, no such "person" exists at all.

If it were the case that, within my Dharma, there was some fixed and genuinely-existent self, being, living entity, person, body-associated self, or other such thing, I would not declare that, within my Dharma, there are exceptional circumstances and it is not the case that there are no such exceptional circumstances. From the beginning on through to the present, my Dharma has always been pure and completely clear.

Furthermore, Ānanda, if it were definitely the case that transgressions existed and that there was some being who takes on those transgressions, then it would be the case that the body is identical with some "soul." But [positing any such view] would amount to falling into the eternalist fallacy by the dictates of which no path to buddhahood could even exist.

Then again, if the body were distinct from some "soul," then [positing any such view] would amount to falling into an annihilationist view. In that case too, no path to buddhahood could exist. In much the same manner, all of the sixty-two false views might be posited as consistent with bodhi, but these cases are all wrong.

Therefore, Ānanda, in the midst of the Great Assembly, I roar the lion's roar and, possessed of the fearlessnesses, declare that within my Dharma, there are exceptional circumstances and it is not the case that there are no such exceptional circumstances. From its very origin on through to the present, it has always been pure and completely clear.

Ānanda, if moral transgressions had any sort of definite existence, then there could never be any nirvāṇa. If that were so, then I would not state that, within of my Dharma, there may be exceptional circumstances.

Ānanda, in truth, my Dharma has been pure and completely radiant from its very inception on forward to the present. Consequently my disciples are able to subdue their minds so that they are stable and free of doubts and regrets. They become free of the evil of moral transgressions and become pure in their practice of the path.

Having reflected in this manner, the bodhisattva should refrain from maintaining a hostile attitude toward those who break the moral precepts. He should also reason in this manner:

> Those who have taken on these precepts will definitely succeed in coming to abide in *anuttarasamyaksaṃbodhi.* How is this so? I have heard that even bodhisattvas who have reached the right and definite position (*samyaktva niyāma*) still have had occasions on which they have committed moral transgressions. Take for instance that case from one hundred thousand kalpas ago when a bodhisattva slandered an arhat who had already extinguished all contaminants, saying of him that he was an arhat in name only.
>
> I have also heard of that bodhisattva thirty-one kalpas prior to the present one who, although he had already reached the right and definite position, nonetheless stabbed a stream enterer with a spear. Additionally, I have heard of that case during this current Auspicious Kalpa where a bodhisattva slandered Krakucchanda Buddha,[271] saying to him, "How could one of you bald pates ever succeed in attaining buddhahood?"
>
> It would be hard to understand [the actual circumstances of] beings such as these. Hence, what would be the use in my knowing in this situation what constitutes gain versus loss or right versus wrong? They will each individually undergo the consequences of what they have each individually done. How is that any of my business? If I wish to pursue actual knowledge of their circumstances, it could result in injury to myself through my making judgments regarding other beings. This is the sort of thing that the Buddha himself would not permit.

This accords with the testimony of the sutras wherein it states, "The Buddha told Ānanda, 'If a person makes judgmental assessments regarding others, he will thereby bring injury on himself. It is I alone who can make such assessments. [Only] beings who are my equal may also make such assessments.'"[272] This is as described in the following lines:[273]

> A covered pitcher may still be empty
> while an uncovered pitcher may be empty as well.
> Other covered pitchers may themselves be full
> as, so too, may uncovered pitchers be full.

One should realize that, throughout the world,
there are these four different types of people.
Matters of awesome deportment and possession of merit,
whether existent or not, are very much the same as this.

If one is not possessed of all-knowledge,
how could one make judgments about others?
How could one merely observe another's deportment
and yet then know the level of their virtue?

It is right wisdom and the possession of a wholesome mind
that define the characteristic qualities of a worthy person.
By merely observing someone's outward deportment,
how could one know what lies within?

There are those who, inwardly, possess merit and wisdom,
even as, outwardly, they reveal no awesome deportment.
As they wander about, there is no one who recognizes them.
In this, they are like hot coals hidden by ashes.

If one assesses inward qualities on the basis of externals
and hence develops an attitude of slighting condescension,
one brings ruin on oneself as well as on one's own roots of goodness
so that, at the end of one's life, one falls into the wretched destinies.

Those displaying outward pretenses of awesome deportment
and parading about as if they were worthies or *āryas*
even as they only possess impressive rhetoric
are like the sounds of thunder that fail to bring rain.

As for the places to which someone else's mind proceeds,
one may be mistaken about them, for they are hard to know.
Therefore one must not make false assessments
with regard to any being.

It is only someone possessed of all-knowledge
who can fully know their minds' mind states
and the subtle and secret places to which they may proceed.
Hence, with regard to judging other beings,

the Buddha said, "It is only those who are my equals
who can pass judgment on other beings."
If the Buddha himself spoke in this manner,
who then could have the ability to pass judgment on others?

If one merely observes someone's outward deportment
and thereby presumes to assess his inner virtue,
one will ruin one's own roots of goodness
just as a flooding river may collapse its own banks.

If one is mistaken about such things,
one creates immense karmic obstacles.
Therefore, with regard to these people,
one should not bring forth an attitude of slighting disdain.

Therefore the lay bodhisattva should refrain from adopting an attitude of slighting arrogance or anger toward those who may have broken the moral precepts. What's more, regarding this matter of upholding the moral precepts or breaking the moral precepts, a layperson does not dwell together with these people. What basis then might he have for acquiring knowledge of such matters?

[One should reflect], "If I strive to make such clear distinctions with regard to these matters, then I am bound to create the obstacle of transgressions and, because of such karmic obstacles, I shall be bound to undergo every sort of suffering for thousands of myriads of kalpas." This is as stated in *Sutra on the Inaction of Dharmas*.[274]

Additionally, in a Mahāyāna sutra,[275] the Buddha told Ugra, the Elder, "Thus the lay bodhisattva should feel pity for any bhikshu who has broken the precepts, [reflecting as follows]: 'This man's defilement is such that he engages in what is evil and engages in what is unwholesome. Why? This man has donned the Dharma robes of the Tathāgata, the well-extinguished lord of the Āryas, yet he has not made his mind pliant and has not been able to subdue his sense faculties. Hence he engages in such self-destructive conduct.'"

Moreover, one of the Buddha's sutras states, "One does not slight those who have not yet become accomplished in learning. These are not a person's moral transgressions so much as they are transgressions committed at the behest of the afflictions themselves. It is because of these afflictions that this person has engaged in such unwholesome behavior."

Also, within the Buddha's Dharma, there are exceptional circumstances. This person may actually be able to rid himself of these moral transgressions. Then, with right mindfulness as the cause and condition, he may be able to enter the Dharma position. If he does indeed gain entry to the right and definite position, then he will eventually abide in *anuttarasamyaksaṃbodhi*.

Then again, as stated by the Buddha himself, "It is only through the possession of wisdom that one can then defeat the afflictions." He additionally stated, "One should not make false assessments of others. If one makes such assessments, he thereby wreaks injury on himself. It is only one in possession of the wisdom of a buddha who is able to completely understand these matters." [Hence one should reflect],

"Matters of this sort are not such as I can know." One should then refrain from adopting an angry and condescending attitude toward those who may have broken the precepts.

Moreover:

G. On Entering a Temple, One Should Be Respectful and Make Offerings

When a bodhisattva enters a temple,
he should observe all the protocols of deportment,
should act respectfully and bow down in reverence,
and should make an offering to the bhikshus.

When this lay bodhisattva is about to enter a Buddhist temple, right before entering, he should bow down outside the temple door in a five-point prostration and should then reflect, "This is the dwelling place of good people. It is the dwelling place of those who practice emptiness, the dwelling place of those who practice signlessness,[276] the dwelling place of those who practice wishlessness, the dwelling place of those who practice kindness, compassion, sympathetic joy, and equanimity,[277] and it is the dwelling place of those who practice in right conduct and right mindfulness."

If one encounters bhikshus perfect in deportment, serene in gaze, and restrained in wearing the robe and holding the bowl, bhikshus who bear observation in the way they sit, lie down, walk, stand, awaken, retire, drink, eat, speak, and remain silent, bhikshus who also bear observation in the appearance of their countenance and in their going forth and coming to a halt—if one encounters bhikshus who cultivate the four stations of mindfulness practiced by the Āryas, who uphold the moral precepts purely, who recite and study the Dharma of the sutras, and who are refined in their contemplations and devoted to sitting in *dhyāna* meditation—having observed them, with respectful solemnity and reverential mind, one should bow down in reverence to them. Then, drawing nearer, one should greet them and reflect thus:

H. One Should Reflect on the Merit of Becoming a Monastic

Even were I for kalpas in number as a Ganges' sands
to always perform great acts of giving at the shrines of the devas
and never cease or neglect this practice,
that would still not compare to becoming a monk but a single time.

This bodhisattva should then reflect:

> If, in pursuing wealth in accordance with the Dharma, I were to always perform great acts of giving for a number of kalpas equal to the sands in the Ganges, all the merit derived from that giving would still not even equal that from merely generating the resolve to leave

behind the householder's life, how much the less could it equal the merit of actually doing so?

How could this be so? [This is so because]:

I. Ninety-Nine Reflections on the Advantages of Monastic Life

The householder's life is possessed of countless serious faults whereas a monastic can perfect countless meritorious qualities.

The householder's life is overrun with confusion and disturbance whereas the monastic's life is carefree and serene.

The householder's life belongs to the sphere of defilement whereas the monastic's life has nothing to which it belongs.

The household is the place for committing bad actions whereas the monastic life is the place for good actions.

If one pursues the householder's life, then one becomes stained by all manner of defilement whereas the monastic abandons every sort of defilement.

The householder becomes mired in the mud of the five types of desire whereas the monastic abandons the five types of desire.

For the householder, it is difficult to pursue a pure livelihood whereas it is easy for a monastic to pursue right livelihood.

The householder is subject to the incursions of many adversaries whereas the monastic is free of incursions by adversaries.

The householder is encumbered by many troublesome obstructions whereas the monastic remains free of troublesome obstructions.

The household is the place beset by sorrows whereas the monastic life is the place of joyfulness.

The household is the gateway to the wretched destinies whereas the monastic life is the gateway to benefit.

The household life is one of bondage whereas the monastic's life is one of liberation.

The householder is subject to various forms of fear whereas the monastic is free of fear.

The householder possesses whips and cudgels whereas the monastic has no whips or cudgels.

The householder owns a sword and spear whereas the monastic has no swords or spears.

The householder is subject to the heat of regretfulness whereas the monastic is free of the heat of regretfulness.

Because the householder seeks many things, he is subject to sufferings whereas the monastic is happy because he seeks nothing.

The householder tends toward frivolous agitation whereas the monastic is bound for tranquility.

The householder is worthy of pity whereas the monastic has nothing for which he could be pitied.

The householder is subject to worry and sorrow whereas the monastic is free of worry and sorrow.

The householder is of lowly social station whereas the monastic is one who is lofty and prominent.

The householder is burning up with a raging fire whereas the monastic extinguishes it.

The householder's life is lived for others whereas the monastic is able to act in his own self-interest.

The householder has but little power whereas the monastic has abundant power.

The householder enters the gateway of defilement whereas the monastic enters the gateway to purity.

The householder grows an ever larger thicket of thorns whereas the monastic crushes the thicket of thorns.

The householder achieves success in lesser dharmas whereas the monastic achieves success in the great Dharma.

The householder engages in what is unwholesome whereas the monastic cultivates what is good.

The householder is bound to have regrets whereas the monastic is bound to become free of regrets.

The householder fills up an ocean of tears, milk, and blood whereas the monastic dries up the ocean of tears, milk, and blood.[278]

The household life is censured and considered base by buddhas, *pratyekabuddhas*, and *śrāvaka* disciples whereas the monastic life is praised by buddhas, *pratyekabuddhas*, and *śrāvaka* disciples.

The householder tends to be discontented whereas the monastic tends to be easily contented.

The householder causes Māra to be delighted whereas the monastic causes Māra to feel sorrowful.

The householder is bound for later ruination whereas the monastic is bound to become free of ruination.

The householder is one who is easy to defeat whereas the monastic is one who is difficult to defeat.

The householder is like a slave whereas the monastic is like a lord.

The householder is bound to remain forever in *saṃsāra* whereas the monastic will ultimately reach nirvāṇa.

The householder has fallen into a pit whereas the monastic has escaped from a pit.

The householder abides in darkness whereas the monastic emerges into bright light.

The householder remains unable to subdue his own sense faculties whereas the monastic is able to subdue his sense faculties.

The householder tends toward haughtiness and grandiosity whereas the monastic abides in humility and modesty.

The householder's life tends toward what is coarse and inferior whereas the monastic's life is one of venerable nobility.

The householder has origins from which he comes whereas the monastic has no origins from which he comes.[279]

The householder has many duties whereas the monastic has but few duties.

The householder attains only minor karmic fruits whereas the monastic is bound to attain great karmic fruits.

The householder tends to fall into flattery and deviousness whereas the monastic cultivates a straightforward character.

The householder has an abundance of sorrows whereas the monastic has an abundance of joy.

The householder's life is like being shot with an arrow whereas the monastic's life is like [being able to] extricate that arrow.

The household life is like being afflicted with a sickness whereas the monastic life is like becoming cured of that sickness.

Because the householder practices dharmas associated with evil, he ages swiftly whereas, because the monastic practices good dharmas, he tends to be youthful and strong.

The householder courses in neglectfulness synonymous with death whereas the monastic possesses the life of wisdom.

The householder tends to indulge in deception whereas the monastic behaves in a manner that is genuine.

The householder has many things for which he seeks whereas the monastic seeks but few things.

The householder sips a broth mixed with poisons whereas the monastic drinks the elixir of immortality.[280]

The householder suffers harm from numerous external encroachments whereas the monastic is free of any such harms brought about by external encroachments.[281]

The householder is bound for a ruinous decline whereas the monastic has no such ruinous decline.

The householder's life is like fruit from a poisonous tree whereas the monastic's life is like fruits suffused with sweet-dew nectar.

The householder is bound to remain associated with whatever he detests whereas the monastic abandons the suffering of association with whatever he detests.

The householder is beset with the suffering of separation from what he loves whereas the monastic remains in close proximity to what he loves.

The householder is burdened with heavy delusions whereas the delusions of the monastic are only slight.

The householder fails to carry on with a life of pure conduct whereas the monastic lives a life of pure conduct.

The householder's life destroys one's resolute intentions whereas the monastic succeeds in his resolute intentions.

The householder is beyond rescue whereas the monastic has acquired the means to be rescued.

The householder is bound for solitude and poverty whereas the monastic does not fall into solitude and poverty.

The householder has no shelter whereas the monastic does indeed have shelter.

The householder has no place of refuge whereas the monastic does indeed have a place of refuge.

The householder abides in the midst of much hatred whereas the monastic is possessed of an abundance of kindness.

The householder carries a heavy burden whereas the monastic has relinquished that burden.

The householder is beset with endless responsibilities whereas the monastic has none of those responsibilities.

The householder's life is characterized by encounters with karmic transgressions whereas the monastic's life is characterized by encounters with fortuitous karma.

The householder is subject to distressing afflictions whereas the monastic becomes free of distressing afflictions.

The householder's life is one beset by heat whereas the monastic life has no such heat.[282]

The householder's life involves disputation whereas the monastic is free from disputation.

The householder is involved in defiling attachments whereas the monastic is free of defiling attachments.

The householder tends toward arrogance whereas the monastic becomes free of arrogance.

The householder esteems wealth whereas the monastic esteems meritorious qualities.

The householder is subject to disastrous harm whereas the monastic puts an end to disastrous harm.

The householder is subject to decrease and loss whereas the monastic enjoys increasing advantage.

The householder's life is easily come by whereas the monastic's life is one which is so rarely encountered that one may take it on but once in thousands of myriads of kalpas.
The householder's life is easy to practice in whereas the monastic's life involves difficult practices.
The household simply goes along with the current whereas the monastic moves against the current.
The householder's life is one of drifting in a flood whereas the monastic's is one of riding on a raft.
The householder floats along on a torrent of afflictions whereas the monastic has a bridge by which he passes beyond them.
The householder's life takes place on the near shore whereas the monastic's life is concerned with reaching the far shore.
The householder's life is one of being tied up in bondage whereas the monastic's life is one of separation from bondage.
The householder harbors enmity whereas the monastic relinquishes enmity.
The householder is bound to follow the laws of officialdom whereas the monastic follows the law of the Buddha.
The householder's life is characterized by mishaps whereas the monastic's life is one that has become free of mishaps.
The household life has suffering as its karmic fruits whereas the monastic life has happiness as its karmic fruits.
The householder tends to develop an agitated demeanor whereas the monastic possesses awe-inspiring dignity.
Householder companions are easily come by whereas monastic companions are only rarely found.
The householder takes a wife as his companion whereas the monastic takes a solid resolve as his companion.
The householder is entrapped in a corral whereas the monastic escapes from the corral.
The householder tends to esteem inflicting troubles on others whereas the monastic esteems benefiting others.
The householder tends to esteem the giving of wealth whereas the monastic esteems the giving of Dharma.
The householder holds up the banner of Māra whereas the monastic holds up the banner of the Buddha.
The householder has some place he goes back to whereas the monastic demolishes all places of refuge.
The householder is concerned with the growth of his body whereas the monastic is one who abandons the body.

The householder plunges into the deep undergrowth whereas the monastic escapes the deep undergrowth.

Additionally:

J. One Should Develop a Deep Yearning to Become a Monastic

Moreover, in regard to becoming a monastic,
one's mind should feel a deep yearning admiration.

As this lay bodhisattva thus ponders the meritorious aspects of becoming a monastic, he should feel a yearning admiration for it, wondering:

Oh, when will I myself finally be able to leave behind the home life and acquire such meritorious qualities?

Oh, when will I myself be able to leave behind the home life and carry out in correct sequence the dharmas of the *śramaṇa* wherein, one participates in the poṣada recitation of the moral precepts, joins in the rains retreat, and freely sits in the order of seniority

Oh, when will I be able to don the Dharma robes of the Āryas who are imbued with their cultivation of the moral precepts, meditative concentration, wisdom, liberation, and the knowledge and vision of liberation?

Oh, when will I be able to maintain the deportment of the Āryas?

Oh, when will I be able to abide peacefully, meditating in a quiet forest?

Oh, when will I be able to carry the alms bowl and go out on the alms round, either being given something or not being given anything, either being given much or only a little, either being given delectable food or bad food, either being given cold food or hot food, thus proceeding in sequential order along the alms round, thereby coming by what is needed merely to sustain the body, accepting alms merely as one might apply ointment on an ulceration or as one might apply grease to the axle of a cart?

Oh, when will I become free of distress and joyfulness over the eight worldly dharmas?

Oh, when will I be able to restrain the six sense faculties in the same manner as one might confine some dog, deer, fish, snake, monkey, or bird? Just as a dog enjoys a village, a deer enjoys mountains and marshes, a fish enjoys ponds, a snake is fond of his den, a monkey enjoys a jungle, and a bird enjoys flying in the air, the eye, ear, nose, tongue, body, and mind always enjoy forms, sounds, smells, tastes, touchables, and dharmas as objects of mind.[283] The sense faculties are not things that common people of shallow wisdom and weak resolve are able to subdue. It is only one possessed of wisdom, solid resolve, and right mindfulness who is able to control the rebels of the six senses so that they are prevented from doing harm to one's sovereign mastery and fearlessness.

Oh, when will I be able to delight in *dhyāna* meditation, delight in recitation and study of the sutras' dharmas, delight in cutting off afflictions, delight in cultivating good dharmas, and delight in donning rag robes, going forth with the body well covered, recalling then that, formerly, when I was a layperson, I was for the most part neglectful, but, now, in order to bring about self-benefit and the benefit of others, I should be diligently vigorous?

Oh, when will I be able to follow the dharmas of the path practiced by bodhisattvas?

Oh, when will I too become one who can serve as an unsurpassable field of merit for those in the world?

Oh, when will I be able to quit being a slave of familial affection?

And when will I be able to be freed from this prison of the household?

This is as stated here:

K. Three Aspirational Thought When Bowing at a Stupa or Temple

Whenever one bows down in reverence at any stupa or temple,
inspired by the Buddha, one should bring forth three thoughts.

Having already been inspired to feel a yearning to go forth into homelessness, whenever this lay bodhisattva enters the grounds of a stupa or temple and bows down in reverence, he should bring forth three thoughts. And what are these three? They are as follows:

Oh, when will I become one worthy to receive the offerings of devas, dragons, *yakṣas, gandharvas, asuras, kinnaras, mahoragas,* humans, and nonhumans?

Oh, when will I be able to produce the *śarīra* relics imbued with spiritual powers that, distributed throughout the world, bestow benefit on beings?

I now bring forth the deep resolve to practice the great vigor by which I shall attain *anuttarasamyaksaṃbodhi.* Then, after serving as one of the buddhas, I shall enter the nirvāṇa without residue.

Additionally:

L. On Meeting Any Monk, Serve, Follow Instructions, and Assist

Whenever meeting any of the bhikshus,
offer to serve in a manner appropriate to whatever he is doing,
quietly obey all instructions he might offer,
and be unstinting in providing any requisites he needs.

After this lay bodhisattva bows down in reverence at any stupa site, he seeks to visit the bhikshus, including those who teach Dharma, those who uphold the moral-precept codes, those who study sutras, those who study *mātṛkās,* those who study the bodhisattva canon, those who dwell in a forest hermitage, those who wear robes made of cast-off rags, those who obtain their sustenance from the alms round, those who eat but once each day, those who only sit and never lie down, those who do not drink broths after midday, those who possess only the three-part robe,[284] those who wear only robes sewn from coarse cloth, those who take their rest wherever they stop to sit, those who dwell only at the base of a tree, those who dwell in charnel fields, those who dwell only out on open grounds, those who have but little that they wish for, those who are easily satisfied, those who dwell in seclusion, those who sit in *dhyāna* meditation, and those who exhort and instruct others.

One should offer up one's service to each bhikshu in a manner appropriate to whichever practice he focuses upon. For instance:

If one goes to the dwelling place of a bhikshu who studies *abhidharma,* then, in accordance with those dharmas and their nature and characteristics, whether they be dharmas associated with the mind or whether they be unassociated compositional-factor dharmas, one should inquire into any related points about which one has doubts. Having inquired, one should then proceed to study them.

If one meets an expert on the moral-precept codes, one should inquire about the causes and conditions involved in the commission of moral transgressions, about the relative severity of moral transgressions, about the means for extinguishing moral transgressions, and about the *avadāna* stories.[285] Having inquired about these matters, one should then study and practice accordingly.

If one meets someone specializing in study of sutras, one should inquire into the meanings contained within the *Āgama Sutra* collections, practice accordingly, and become learned himself.

If one meets someone specializing in study of *mātṛkās* associated with the *Sutra on Benefiting the Many,* the *Udānas,* the *Assalāyano,* and the *Dharmapada,* one should then study such sutras.

If one meets someone specializing in the bodhisattva canon, one should inquire about the six *pāramitās* and also the matter of using expedients and then, having thus inquired, one should study and practice accordingly.

If one meets someone abiding in a forest hermitage, one should study those dharmas related to practice in seclusion.

If one meets someone practicing *dhyāna* meditation, one should study his *dhyāna* meditation methods.

As for the other types of bhikshus, on meeting them, one should inquire into whatever they have chosen to practice and then study and practice accordingly, doing so without disobeying any instructions they provide.

As for the matter of guarding one's speech, when meeting bhikshus, one should thoroughly restrain oneself from talking, remaining serenely silent. Giving due regard to issues of time and place and considering the circumstance at hand, one should ensure that one's mind does not stray into confusion and that one speaks but few words.

Additionally, as regards the place in which the speaker of Dharma resides, in accordance with whatever those bhikshus and others there have grown short of, according to one's own capacity to do so, one should supply them with such things, whether they be robes, bowls, sitting cloths,[286] or other life-supporting requisites, not being stinting in one's generosity in providing any of them.[287]

Why should one do this? A bodhisattva should provide even for people who are bad, how much the more so should one provide for bhikshus, those who are possessed of meritorious qualities. In assisting them, one should not even be sparing of one's own flesh, how much the more readily then should one provide them with the outward possessions that serve as causes and conditions supporting their progress on the path.

Additionally:

M. Avoid Causing Afflictions in Those Not Receiving One's Gifts

When one engages in giving,
do not instigate afflictions in others.

When one carries out an act of giving, if one gives to but a single person, it might well be that another person, not having received anything, becomes angry. This is a matter that one should skillfully assess in one's practice of giving. Do not influence others to become afflicted with anger. Why must one take care in this?

The careful consideration one accords those with common minds
should surpass even that which one reserves for arhats.

When this lay bodhisattva provides clothing, drink and food, medicines, and bedding for bhikshus, making offerings to them, welcoming them and escorting them off, bowing in reverence, and drawing personally close to them, he should be even more solicitous about the needs of those still possessed of a common person's mind than he would be in his deferential treatment of an arhat.

And why should this be so? Arhats do not differ in their mental response to gain and loss, ill repute and esteem, praise and blame, or pain and pleasure. But because a common person is subject to feelings of craving, hatred, miserliness, and jealousy, he is able in these circumstances to commit transgressions because of which he may fall into the hell realms, the animal realms, or the hungry-ghost realms.

Consequently one should be extremely careful to be protective of those with a common person's mentality. Thus, when a bodhisattva offers his services, he does so in a manner intended to benefit all beings. His giving is not done merely for the sake of his own happiness, is not done for the sake of acquiring karmic rewards for himself in future lives, and is not done merely as if it were some business transaction.

Additionally:

N. Giving as an Opportunity to Encourage Highest Bodhi Resolve

Due to having given some sort of material wealth,
one may then be able to draw forth others through Dharma giving.
In accordance with whatsoever is desired, one bestows benefit,
and then instructs others in bringing forth the unsurpassable resolve.

Even as one pursues one's own benefit, whether it be through the giving of robes, through the giving of bowls, or through the many other various sorts of giving of material wealth, if bhikshus such as these have not yet entered the [right and definite] Dharma position and have not yet attained the fruits of that path, this lay bodhisattva should encourage the bhikshus he benefits to bring forth the vow to attain *anuttarasamyaksaṃbodhi*. Why? Having drawn them forth through the giving of wealth, he may then be able to draw them forth through the giving of Dharma. It may well be that, due to their fondness and respect for the benefactor who has made gifts to them, they will be inclined to believe and accept what he says to them.

Additionally:

O. Do Whatever Is Necessary to Preserve and Protect the Dharma

For the sake of protecting and preserving the Dharma,
one should remain unstinting even if it means sacrificing one's life.
One should strive to cure bhikshus who have fallen ill
even to the point where one makes a gift of one's own body.

Even to the point of sacrificing his own life in order to preserve and protect the Dharma, this lay bodhisattva should be diligently vigorous in overcoming those who detest the Dharma of the Buddha, whether they be from among the sixty-two types of non-Buddhist traditions or whether they be from among the retinues of Māra.

Among the disciples of the Buddha, there may be those who deviate in their practice through spurious distortion of the Buddha's Dharma. [The influence of] such people should be overcome in a manner consistent with Dharma. This constitutes the protecting and preservation of the Dharma. Furthermore, with increased thoughts of faith and respect, one should make offerings of the four requisites to those who are learned speakers of the Dharma. This too constitutes the protection and preservation of the Dharma.

If one studies, recites, explains, or transcribes sutras, *vinaya* texts, *abhidharma* texts, *mātṛkās*, or canonical bodhisattva texts while also instructing others in their study, recitation, explanation, and transcription, due to these causes and conditions, the Dharma will remain for a long time, providing benefit to everyone.

To laypeople and monastics alike, one should extol and speak in praise of the benefits of the Dharma's enduring for a long time while also describing the extreme evil bound to ensue in the event of the Dharma's rapid demise. One should also bear in mind that the Tathāgata, from the distant past on forward to the present, practiced the bodhisattva path, carried out all kinds of difficult practices, and only then succeeded in acquiring this Dharma.

For these reasons, with diligent resolve, one should be vigorous in using it to show, instruct, benefit, and delight both laypeople and monastics, thereby perhaps instigating them to become enlightened or perhaps instigating them to reach the station of the *avaivartika*.[288]

To summarize the causes and conditions subsumed in the protection of the Dharma, they amount to enabling others' acquisition of the means for universal peace and happiness while also enabling one's own cultivation of [the Dharma] in accordance with the manner in which it was proclaimed. All of these ideas define what is meant by protecting and preserving the Dharma.

Additionally, it is the Dharma of the lay bodhisattva to see to it that any sick bhikshu gets medical treatment. This bodhisattva should be willing even to sacrifice his own life to cure that illness, not being the least bit stinting in his efforts. This is a matter of the greatest importance. The monastics should seek this essential service from the laity, instigating them to personally look after whoever is sick, supplying them with medical care and medicines.

Additionally:

P. When Giving, Have No Regrets or Selfish Motives & Dedicate Merit

One gives with a resolute mind
and, having given the gift, one remains free of any regrets.

Whether this bodhisattva is doing some deed for the sake of protecting and preserving right Dharma, or whether he is personally looking after someone fallen ill, responding in a manner appropriate to the circumstance, he bestows offerings with a mind free of any regrets. It is this that qualifies as pure giving.

If one gives without seeking for any resulting karmic rewards, if one gives without distinguishing, "This one should be able to be a recipient whereas that one should not be a recipient," and if one gives only with thoughts of pity and the motivation to be beneficial in one's actions, these are the factors that define pure giving. This is as described below:

If one gives with a compassionate mind,
this is what qualifies as giving that is pure.
He does not say of this one, "He is a field of merit,"
and does not say of that one, "He is not a field of merit."

If someone is to take up the practice of giving,
he remains free of any selfish motivation as a basis for giving.
If one does this for the sake of acquiring some karmic reward,
then this just amounts to seeking to earn interest.

Therefore, having pledged to give,
one proceeds with a mind free of regret or resentment.
Even the most minor amount of merit thus derived
is all dedicated to realization of the unsurpassable path.

All of the merit produced by the causes and conditions of giving should be entirely dedicated to *anuttarasamyaksaṃbodhi*. One should not seek to derive from it any benefit or bliss in present or future lifetimes and should not seek to thereby gain the fruits of the Small Vehicle. It is solely for the sake of beings that one seeks the realization of *anuttarasamyaksaṃbodhi*.

As for my earlier statement that discussion of the additional lay bodhisattva practices would follow—that explanation has now been concluded. These practices were all selected from their various locations throughout the Great Vehicle sutras. In order to accord with the Dharma taught in the sutras, the bodhisattva abides in these very practices and thereby swiftly attains *anuttarasamyaksaṃbodhi*. The treatment of the second bodhisattva ground shall be mostly devoted to the practices of the monastic bodhisattva. Now, however, we shall proceed to a discussion of the jointly shared practices taken up by both lay and monastic bodhisattvas.

The End of Chapter Seventeen

Chapter 18
The Jointly Shared Practices

XVIII. Chapter 18: The Jointly Shared Practices

A. Q: Would You Please Discuss the Jointly Shared Practices?

Question: You stated earlier that you would discuss the practices jointly shared by both lay and monastic bodhisattvas. You could now begin that discussion.

B. A: The Jointly Shared Practices Are as Follows: (List)

Response: They are:

Patience;
Dharma giving;
Dharmas patience;[289]
Contemplation;
Not distorting the Dharma;
Maintaining reverential esteem for the Dharma;
Refraining from presenting any obstacle to Dharma;
Making offerings in support of the Dharma;
Resolute faith;[290]
Cultivation of emptiness;
Not being covetous or envious;
Acting in accordance with one's own words;
Giving lamp light;
Giving musical performances;
Giving means of transport;
Right vows;
Thought imbued with the means of attraction;
Benefiting and comforting beings;
Maintaining a mind of equal regard toward everyone.

These are the essential dharmas jointly practiced by both lay peo-ple and monastics. Hence there is this verse which says:

1. Patience, Dharma Giving, Dharmas Patience, and Contemplation:

Practicing patience results in a well-formed, handsome body.
The giving of Dharma results in knowledge of previous lifetimes.
By dharmas patience, one acquires the *dhāraṇīs*.[291]
Contemplation results in the procuring of wisdom.
By never distorting any dharma
one always acquires right recollective mindfulness.

a. Patience

As for "practicing patience results in a well-formed, handsome body," this means that, if one is able to endure harsh speech, curses, hate-filled oaths, being bound and tied, being assailed with knives and staves, being tortured, and being beaten and whipped, being able to endure all of this without any quavering or variation in one's state of mind—the karmic result procured through such patience is that, whether one is reborn among humans or devas, one always obtains a well-formed body. Then, later on, when one becomes a buddha, one's major marks and minor characteristics are incomparable in their perfection.

b. Dharma Giving

As for "the giving of Dharma results in knowledge of previous lifetimes," this means that those who practice the giving of Dharma become able to know the events that have occurred throughout the course of countless past kalpas. The giving of Dharma refers to explaining all of the many different distinctions present in the teachings of the Śrāvaka Disciple Vehicle, the Pratyekabuddha Vehicle, and the Buddha Vehicle, providing explanations of the associated meanings and principles. Although there are thirty-five different karmic rewards resulting from the giving of Dharma, the most essential among them is the gaining of the knowledge of past lifetimes. The causes and conditions associated with the speaking of Dharma bring about the severance of doubts held by others. Consequently the corresponding karmic result is that one comes to know previous lifetimes.

c. Dharmas Patience

As for "by dharmas patience, one acquires the *dhāraṇīs*," "dharmas" refers here to those dharmas that are associated with emptiness, signlessness, and wishlessness, with the six *pāramitās*, with the grounds through which the bodhisattva progresses, and with the dharmas practiced by all bodhisattvas. One so thoroughly comprehends and clearly understands them that one's mind becomes able to acquiesce in them and uphold them in practice. This is what is meant by "dharmas patience."

If one practices this patience, then one gains the means for "comprehensive retention" (*dhāraṇīs*) as a result. "Comprehensive retention" refers to the ability to never forget the significance of any of the scriptures one has ever heard or recited even after hundreds of thousands of myriads of kalpas.

d. Contemplation

In "contemplation results in the procuring of wisdom," "contemplation" refers to the judicious assessment of good dharmas and the making of right distinctions regarding their significance. As a consequence, one becomes able to attain their benefits in both present and future lifetimes.

e. Not Distorting the Dharma

As for the idea that by "not distorting [the Dharma]," one's mind acquires "right mindfulness," "refraining from distortion" refers to being straightforward and free of flattery. If one cultivates this dharma, then one gains the ability to maintain solid mindfulness in the midst of all dharmas.

Additionally:

2. Esteem for Dharma, Nonobstruction, Offerings & Resolute Faith

If one esteems the Dharma, the Dharma will be solidly enduring.
If one does not create obstacles, one will be protected.
Through offerings in support of the Dharma, one meets the Buddhas.
Through resolute faith, one sheds all difficulties.

a. Esteem for the Dharma

"If one esteems the Dharma, the Dharma will be solidly enduring" means that if one maintains veneration, esteem, and reverence for the Dharma, then the Dharma will be solidly enduring. "Solidity in the Dharma" refers to the fact that, whatever dharma one accepts and upholds in practice, that will all naturally become so solid and enduring that one can never be shaken or turned back in its practice. Later on, when one becomes a buddha, one will have many bodhisattvas and *śrāvakas* as disciples. Having come to abide in these solidly maintained dharmas, no one will ever be able to obstruct one in the practice of the dharmas one has received. Additionally, "solidity" refers here to the ability of the Dharma to abide for a long time.

"If one does not create obstacles, one will be protected," means that, no matter whether it is with regard to someone's speaking Dharma or someone's being able to hear the Dharma, one refrains from perversely creating obstacles to their being able to do so. As a consequence, later on, when one attains buddhahood, both the devas and the people of the world will jointly serve as protectors of one's Dharma.

If while one has still not yet attained buddhahood one is ever able to protect and preserve the right Dharma of the Buddhas, and if, after the Buddha's passing into nirvāṇa, one strives to protect his Dharma legacy, one will then be able to encounter the next buddha when he appears in the World.

For these reasons, bodhisattva and *śrāvaka* disciple practitioners alike should all exert themselves to the utmost in thoroughly preserving and protecting the Dharma.

b. Offerings in Support of the Dharma

In "through offerings in support of the Dharma, one meets the Buddhas," "offerings" refers to demonstrations of reverential respect in all endeavors related to the Dharma. For instance, in a Dharma congregation where there will be the giving of Dharma, with a reverential mind, one makes offerings to those who speak on the Dharma, sets up a Dharma seat for them, establishes places for *dhyāna* meditation, and provides decorative adornments for the place where the lectures on Dharma will take place. Because of such earnest intentions and fondness in making offerings for the sake of Dharma, one will be able to encounter the Buddhas.

c. Resolute Faith

In "through resolute faith, one sheds all difficulties," "faith" refers to the arising of profound zeal and aspiration with respect to all good dharmas. It is because of this dharma that one becomes able to abandon the eight difficulties.

It is through the "resoluteness" [of one's faith] that one becomes able to extinguish all karmic offenses. Thus, through the power of one's resolve, one freely comprehends the import of all good dharmas. This is comparable to when, in cultivating the ten universal bases (*kṛtsnāyatana*), one becomes freely able to comprehend them in accordance with one's wishes.[292]

If one has abundant power of resolute faith, one can then extinguish the measureless karmic evil one has created due to karmic transgressions throughout beginningless time in *saṃsāra*. This accords with the earlier discussion in the chapter on repentance of karmic transgressions.

Additionally:

3. Emptiness, Non-Greed, Congruent Actions & Words, Lamp Light

Through cultivating emptiness one avoids neglectfulness.
By avoiding covetousness, one succeeds in whatever is beneficial.
Through actions faithful to one's words, one extinguishes afflictions.
Through the giving of lamp light, one acquires the heavenly eye.

a. Cultivation of Emptiness

In "through cultivating emptiness, one avoids neglectfulness," "cultivation" is of two types, namely cultivation involving realization and cultivation consisting of practice. Due to the power associated with cultivating emptiness, one believes that all conditioned dharmas are false and deceptive, yet still does not abide in emptiness. One realizes then that all dharmas are not fixed entities. Consequently, one always naturally focuses and restrains one's mind so that one does not fall into neglectfulness.

b. Not Being Covetous or Envious

In "by avoiding covetousness, one succeeds in whatever is beneficial," "covetousness" refers to bringing forth thoughts desirous of appropriating others' possessions. If one rids oneself of this condition, then whatever one seeks to accomplish will meet with success and whatever one wishes for, those wishes will all be fulfilled.

c. Acting in Accordance with One's Own Words

As for "through actions faithful to one's words, one extinguishes afflictions," if one immediately carries out what one has said one will do, then one will succeed in severing afflictions. If, in all that one does, one always acts in a manner consistent with one's pronouncements, then the karmic propensities associated with the afflictions[293] that have always imbued one's mind in life after life up to the present—these will all be entirely extinguished. One will thereby transform the nature of one's evil habitual karmic propensities associated with the afflictions.

d. Giving Lamp Light

As for "through the giving of lamp light, one acquires the heavenly eye," if one lights lamps as offerings to buddhas, *śrāvaka* disciples, and *pratyekabuddhas* and also makes such offerings wherever there are their stupas, images, or *śarīra* relics, because of these actions, one will acquire the heavenly eye as a karmic result.

Additionally:

4. Music, Means of Transport, Right Vows, the Means of Attraction

Through offerings of music, one gains the heavenly ear as a result.
By giving means of transport, one gains the bases of psychic power.
Through right vows, one reaches a pure land.[294]
Through the means of attraction, one's sangha will be complete.

a. Giving Musical Performances

As for "through offerings of music, one gains the heavenly ear as a result," it is by making offerings of musical performances to the Buddha on the occasion of great Dharma assemblies[295] that one gains the heavenly ear as a karmic result.

b. Giving Means of Transport

In "by giving means of transport, one obtains the bases of psychic power," "means of transport" refers to carriages, sedan chairs, elephants, horses, and the like. There are others who state that one may also gain the bases for psychic power through the giving of shoes, slippers, and such.

c. Right Vows

As for "through right vows, one reaches a pure land," one may take rebirth in a pure land in a manner corresponding to one's vows, thereby becoming able to go to a pure land where everything is made of gold, silver, crystal, coral, amber, mother-of-pearl, carnelian, and countless other precious things.

d. Thought Imbued with the Means of Attraction

"Through the means of attraction, one's sangha will be complete," means that, if a bodhisattva perfects the practice of the four means of attraction, he will acquire a perfectly complete sangha. Thus, by attracting beings through giving, pleasing words, beneficial actions, and joint endeavors, later, when one becomes a buddha, one will have a perfectly pure sangha consisting of countless bodhisattvas and *śrāvaka* disciples just as is the case with Amitābha Buddha who has just such a twofold sangha perfect in its purity. As for [those bodhisattvas'] "perfection in vows," this is as discussed earlier in the treatment of the ten vows.

Additionally, there are these lines:

5. Benefiting and Comforting Beings and Equal Regard for All Beings

Through benefiting beings,
one becomes loved and respected by all.
By preserving a non-dual mind holding all in equal regard,
one is able to become one who is supremely victorious.

Whatever the bodhisattva does in all physical, verbal, and mental actions is for the sake of benefiting beings and causing them to acquire peace and happiness. As a consequence, beings all revere and respect him. If the bodhisattva maintains equal regard for all beings whether they be adversaries, close friends, or those who are neutral in their relationship with him, and if he refuses to forsake any being, the karmic result of this will be that he will become supremely victorious. "Victorious" here refers to the ability to triumph over greed, hatred, delusion, and all of the other afflictions and bad dharmas. One who is able to succeed in this is known as a "buddha."

a. Q: How Can One Differentiate a Buddha from Other People?

Question: People all have eyes, ears, nose, tongue, mouth, and so forth. There are no differences between them in this regard. That being the case, how then might one be able to know which among them is a buddha?

b. A: A Buddha Possesses the Thirty-Two marks

Response: A buddha possesses the thirty-two major physical marks of a great man. One should realize that those possessed of these marks are buddhas. Both laypeople and monastics should be able to distinguish and completely recognize the thirty-two marks, coming to know with respect to this particular physical mark which particular dharma brought about its acquisition and coming to know with respect to this particular dharma which particular sort of action brought about its acquisition. One should also understand these corresponding actions. And why? If one wishes to develop a particular meritorious quality, one should know its corresponding physical mark and if one wishes to acquire a particular physical mark, one should know the corresponding actions by which it is acquired.

1) Q: How Can One Understand Such Matters?

Question: By what means would one be able to understand matters such as these?

2) A: Each of the Thirty-Two marks Has Three Distinctions

Response:

> In the chapter on the marks of dharmas,
> each one of the marks has three distinctions.

In the Abhidharma's chapter on the thirty-two marks, each and every one of the physical marks has three types of distinctions. One should know all of these.[296]

a) Q: What Is Meant by Each Mark Having Three Distinctions?

Question: What is meant by "each and every one of the marks has three different distinctions"?

b) A: This Refers to Each Mark's Substance, Fruition, and Karma

Response:

> The first explains the substance of each mark.
> The second explains the karmic effects associated with each mark.
> And the third explains the karmic actions producing each mark.

i) A List of the "Substance" of Each of the Thirty-Two Marks

The physical mark consisting of a "wheel" emblem on the hands and on the feet is a matter that has already been discussed. Wheel-turning kings also have these marks. Bodhisattvas also have these marks. Other people may have this physical mark as well. However, these cases are not the same, that's all.

As for this wheel mark on the hands and the feet, the palms of the hands and the soles of the feet have a mark consisting of a thousand-spoked wheel that is so perfect and utterly clear in its detail that it looks like an inscribed pattern.

[As for that mark whereby the Buddha's] feet are so stable in their stance when standing up that he does not move at all, this is "the mark of securely planted feet."

The mark consisting of proximal [finger and toe] webbing as soft and thin as that of a royal goose marked by lines so utterly clear as to be made from real gold thread—this is "the mark of having webbed fingers and toes."

Softness and tenderness [of hands and feet] like the down of the tala palm[297] or the skin of a baby wherein they are more rosy in hue than the rest of the body—this is "the mark of soft hands and feet."

Fullness in seven places: the palms of both hands; the soles of both feet; the surface of the neck; and the two subaxillary regions—this is what is meant by "the mark of fullness in seven places."

Long fingers that are slender and straight—this is "the mark of long fingers."

Long and broad heels are "the mark of broad heels."

The body being seven cubits in height and in no way crooked—this is "the mark of a large and erect body."

Prominent elevation of the top of the feet—this is "the mark of high arches."

Body hair grown upwards in a clockwise spiral—this is "the mark of upwardly spiraling body hair."

Legs gradually increasing in thickness after the manner of an *aiṇeya* antelope—this is "the mark of antelope-like legs."

The two hands being able to touch the knees even when standing erect—this is "the mark of long arms."

Having the male organ retracted after the manner of the thoroughbred horse or elephant—this is "the mark of genital ensheathment."

Having the most pure sort of golden radiance—this is "the mark of the golden hue."

Having skin that is soft, that appears as if it was made from refined gold, and that cannot be smudged by dirt—this is "the mark of fine skin."

Each and every bodily pore has but a single hair grown from it—this is "the mark of having but a single hair in each pore."

Having a white hair mark between the brows that is the color of white agate—this is "the mark of the white hair tuft."[298]

Having an upper body broad and massive like that of a lion—this is " the mark of the lion-like torso."

Having large rounded shoulders—this is "the mark of large round shoulders."

Having the area below the axilla flat and full—this is "the mark of subaxillary fullness."

Because the tongue is invulnerable to injury by wind, cold, or heat, it is able to skillfully distinguish all flavors in a manner unmatched by any other person. This is "the mark of being aware of each and every flavor."

Having a body as thick and wide as the trunk of the *nyagrodha* tree[299]—this is "the mark of a round body."

Having the round *uṣṇiṣa* bulge atop the crown upon which the hair grows in a clockwise spiral—this is "the mark of the fleshy prominence atop the crown."

Having a tongue as red as a red lotus that is broad, long, and thin—this is "the mark of broad and long tongue."

Having a voice like the king of the Brahma Heavens and the *kalaviṅka* bird—this is "the mark of a Brahmā-like voice."

Having a jaw that is round and as broad as a mirror—this is "the mark of the lion-like jaw."

Having teeth that are as white as white agate or the *kunda* jasmine blossom—this is "the mark of white teeth."

Having teeth that are not uneven or skewed—this is "the mark of straight teeth."

Having teeth that are close-set and free of gaps—this is "the mark of perfect teeth."

Having teeth well matched above and below—this is "the mark of forty teeth."

Having bright and clear eyes in which black and white areas are distinctly delineated and there are no reddening surface veins—this is "the mark of blue eyes."

Having eyelashes that are not mismatched above and below, that blink in unison, and that are neither too long nor too short—this is "the mark of eyelashes like the king of bulls."

ii) The 32 Marks' Karmic Actions and Eventual Karmic Effects

Through respectfully welcoming and escorting away those who are venerated and through making sustaining offerings to those who are at stupas and temples, doing so in places where there are Dharma assemblies, and where Dharma is spoken—it is because of doing these things that one acquires hands and feet that have the wheel mark.

Due to having [planted the karmic causes that result in] this mark, one who is a layperson is destined to become a wheel-turning king who acquires a large population of subjects. If one who has this mark instead leaves the home life and studies the path, he will acquire a retinue consisting of many disciples.

Through continuing to solidly uphold all dharmas one has received without ever forsaking them, one acquires the mark of solidly planted feet. Due to having [planted the karmic causes that result in] this mark, one becomes one who cannot be the least bit moved by anyone at all.

Through always cultivating the four means of attraction, namely giving, pleasing words, beneficial actions, and joint endeavors, one acquires the mark of proximal webbing of fingers and toes. Due to having [planted the karmic causes that result in] this mark, one quickly attracts a community of other people.

Through giving fragrant, sweet, delectable, and soft foods and beverages to others, including giving them to those that are venerated, providing them with everything they need, one comes to possess the mark of soft and tender hands and feet while also obtaining the mark of fullness in seven places. Due to having [planted the karmic causes that result in] these marks, one mostly receives fragrant, sweet, delectable, and soft foods and beverages, is rescued from life-threatening circumstances, and acquires a life span of increased duration.

Also, through taking on the moral precept of abstaining from killing beings, one acquires the mark of slender and long fingers and toes, the mark of fullness of the heels, and the mark of the large and erect body. Due to having [planted the karmic causes that result in] these marks, one's life span is bound to be long-lasting.

Through increased and unfailing development of the good dharmas one has taken on, one acquires the mark of high arches and the mark of having bodily hairs that grow upwardly in a clockwise spiraling fashion. Due to having [planted the karmic causes that result in] these marks, none of the meritorious qualities that one has developed recede or disappear.

Through being able to offer unstinting instruction in special skills and classic texts and through making gifts of shoes, slippers, and such, one acquires the mark of legs that gradually increase in the thickness of their shape in a manner similar to those of the *aiṇeya* [antelope].[300] Due to having [planted the karmic causes that result in] this mark, one rapidly learns whatever one cultivates or studies, doing so in a manner that accords with one's wishes.

Through unstintingly and completely granting the requests of those who come seeking something, one acquires the mark of long arms. Due to having [planted the karmic causes that result in] this mark, one is able to gain personal power, is able to engage in immensely generous giving, and is able to skillfully establish harmony among others.

Through not allowing estrangement to occur among other beings or among one's relatives, and through being able to cause those who have become estranged to be reunited, one acquires the mark of male genital ensheathment. Due to having [planted the karmic causes that result in] this mark, one acquires many disciples.

Through giving fine and perfectly clean clothing, bedding, halls, and dwellings, one acquires the mark of the golden hue as well as the mark of thin and fine skin. Due to having [planted the karmic causes that result in] these marks, one acquires fine and perfectly clean clothing, bedding, halls, and dwellings.

Through being well able to look after and protect those worthy of one's offerings whether they be monastic preceptors, monastic Dharma teachers,[301] one's parents, one's elder and younger siblings,[302] or those worthy of veneration and esteem, one acquires the mark of a single clockwise spiraling bodily hair in each hair pore and the mark of the mid-brow white hair tuft adorning one's countenance. Due to having [planted the karmic causes that result in] these marks, one becomes someone who has no peer.

Through using speech imbued with a sense of shame and dread of blame, speech that is compliant with the circumstances, and speech that is pleasing, one acquires the mark of having a lion-like torso and the mark of having large and round shoulders. Due to having [planted the karmic causes that result in] these marks, whoever sees one never tires of looking at one.

Through providing medical care, medicines, food, and drink to those who are sick while also personally seeing to their care, one acquires the mark of fullness in the subaxillary region as well as the mark of being able to clearly distinguish each and every flavor. Due to having [planted the karmic causes that result in] these marks, one's body is only seldom assailed by sickness.

Through the giving of parks, groves, sweet fruit, bridges, luxuriantly thriving trees, ponds, wells, food and drink, flowers, incenses, necklaces, and buildings, by building stupas, merit halls,[303] and such, and also through bringing forth many things as gifts at such times as offerings are made to the assembly—through doing these things, one acquires the mark of a body resembling the trunk of the *nyagrodha* tree as well as the mark of having the fleshy *uṣṇīṣa* prominence atop one's crown. Due to having [planted the karmic causes that result in] these marks, one is readily honored and regarded with the highest esteem.

Through cultivating the practice of truthful speech and gentle speech during the long night [of previous lifetimes], one acquires the mark of the broad and long tongue as well as the mark of having the Brahmā-like voice. Due to having [planted the karmic causes that result in] these marks, one has the voice replete with five excellent qualities. Those five excellent voice qualities are:

One's voice is easily understood;
A listener can never get enough of listening to this voice;
Its sound is deep and far-reaching;
Its sound is pleasing to the ear of the listener;
And its sound does not easily fade away.

Through practicing truthful speech and non-frivolous speech during the long night [of previous lifetimes], one acquires the mark of the lion-like jaw. Due to having [planted the karmic causes that result in] this mark, one's words are definitely trusted and accepted.

Through never slighting someone after making an offering to them and through being freely generous in making offerings, one acquires the mark of white teeth and the mark of straight teeth. Due to having [planted the karmic causes that result in] this mark, one acquires a pure, harmonious, and like-minded retinue.

Through truthful speech during the long night [of previous lifetimes] and through abstaining from slander, one acquires the mark of forty teeth and the mark of closely set teeth. Due to having [planted the karmic causes that result in] these marks, one acquires a unified retinue that is invulnerable to being impeded or destroyed.

Through having sincere intentions, through thinking fondly of others, through looking upon beings with a harmonious expression free of desire, hatred, or delusion, one acquires the mark of blue eyes as well as the mark of eyelashes like the king of bulls. Due to having [planted the karmic causes that result in] these marks, everyone who sees one is moved to feelings of fondness and respect.

The End of Chapter Eighteen

Chapter 19
The Fourfold Dharmas

XIX. Chapter 19: The Fourfold Dharmas

A. One Should Cultivate the Causes for Gaining the 32 Marks

The bodhisattva should single-mindedly cultivate the above-discussed actions by which one acquires the thirty-two marks. Cultivating the actions that lead to acquisition of the thirty-two marks is an endeavor rooted in wisdom. Therefore:

1. Fourfold Dharmas Causing Either Loss or Gain of Wisdom

The bodhisattva should utterly abandon
the four dharmas leading to lessening and loss of wisdom
He should always cultivate and practice
the four dharmas leading to the acquisition of wisdom.

a. Four Dharmas Causing Loss of Wisdom

There are four dharmas able to bring about the lessening and loss of wisdom that the bodhisattva should abandon. There are also four dharmas leading to the acquisition of wisdom that one should always cultivate. What are the four dharmas leading to loss of wisdom? They are:

The first is failing to revere the Dharma or one who speaks the Dharma.

The second is being secretive and miserly in the teaching of essential dharmas.

The third is presenting an obstacle to someone fond of Dharma and thereby harming their motivation to listen to the speaking of Dharma.

The fourth is harboring an arrogant attitude and consequently elevating oneself while looking on others as inferiors.

b. Four Dharmas Causing Attainment of Wisdom

What are the four dharmas leading to acquisition of wisdom? They are:

First, one reveres the Dharma as well as those who speak the Dharma.

Second, one explains Dharma for others as one has heard it and as one has studied and recited it, doing so with a pure mind and without seeking to receive offerings.

Third, knowing that the realization of wisdom occurs through extensive learning, one diligently and unremittingly applies oneself to one's study, doing so as urgently as if one were putting out a fire in his own turban.

Fourth, one accepts and upholds in practice, in a manner faithful to how it was taught, whatever Dharma one has learned, never forgetting it. In so doing, one esteems actions that are consistent with the words and does not esteem words alone.

These are the four. If one does not damage his roots of goodness, he will be able to abandon the four dharmas leading to loss of wisdom while being able to practice the four dharmas leading to acquiring wisdom. Consequently, one who strives to increase his wisdom acts in accord with the following verse:

2. Fourfold Dharmas Causing Decrease or Increase of Good Roots

As for the four dharmas that devour one's roots of goodness,
the bodhisattva should utterly abandon them.
As for the four dharmas that increase one's roots of goodness,
the bodhisattva should cultivate and practice them.

a. Four Dharmas That Decrease One's Roots of Goodness

What then are those four dharmas that assail and devour one's roots of goodness? They are:

The first is the harboring of arrogance while coveting worldly matters.

The second is, while being attached to offerings, coming and going from the households.

The third is giving rise to hatred and jealousy through which one slanders bodhisattvas.

The fourth is that, on hearing scriptures one has not previously heard, one refuses to believe or accept them.

b. Four Dharmas That Increase One's Roots of Goodness

What then are the four dharmas conducing to the increase of one's roots of goodness? They are:

First, one strives insatiably to acquire any scriptures that one has not yet heard, in particular those that deal with the six *pāramitās* and those that belong to the bodhisattva canon.

Second, one rids oneself of any arrogance toward other beings, adopting instead an attitude of humility and deferential regard for even to the lowest of the lowly.

Third, whatever wealth one gains is gained only in accordance with Dharma and is sought only to the degree that it satisfies one's needs. Thus one abandons all types of wrong livelihood while delighting in the practice of the four lineage bases of the Āryas.[304]

Fourth, one does not ridicule others' transgressions, whether real or not, and one does not focus on the shortcomings of others. Hence, if there happens to be something within the sphere of Dharma that one has not yet thoroughly understood, one must not harbor a mental opposition to it. Rather one should take the testimony of the Buddha as the basis for certifying its validity. [Thus, one should reflect], "Given that the Buddha is possessed of all-knowledge, his dharmas are countless. He speaks of them in ways that are appropriate to any given circumstance. These are not matters about which I have direct knowledge."

And so it is that one increases one's roots of goodness.

3. Fourfold Dharmas That Increase or Stop Flattery and Deviousness

In addition, there are four dharmas perfectible only by those without flattery or deviousness. Therefore:

The bodhisattva should utterly abandon
four dharmas characterized by flattery and deviousness.
He should always cultivate and practice
four dharmas characterized by a straightforward mind.

a. Four Dharmas Involving Flattery and Deviousness

Both lay and monastic bodhisattvas should utterly abandon four dharmas involving flattery or deviousness. This is a matter analogous to the difficulty of extricating a crooked tree from a dense forest. In this same manner, there are disciples of the Buddha in the world who, although they have entered the Dharma of the Buddha, they are nonetheless unable to depart from the dense forest of *saṃsāra*. What then are these four dharmas? They are:

First, one harbors doubts about, does not place faith in, and is unfixed in one's resolve regarding the Buddha's Dharma.

Second, one maintains an arrogant and hate-filled attitude toward other beings.

Third, one's mind is beset by covetousness and jealousy when witnessing benefits accruing to others.

Fourth, the defaming rumors emanating from one's slander of bodhisattvas spread about everywhere.

These are the four.

b. Four Dharmas Characteristic of a Straightforward Mind

What then are the four dharmas characterized by a straightforward mind? They are:

First, if one commits some offense, one immediately reveals it, conceals none of it, extinguishes it through the confession of transgressions, and then proceeds along the path that is free of regrets.

Second, even if, by telling the truth, one would lose the royal throne as well all manner of valuable treasures, one still refuses to utter a falsehood. [What's more], no words disparaging of others ever pass one's lips.

Third, if somebody assails one with harsh speech, curses, ridicule, disparagement, mocking, slanders, bondage, confinement, whipping, beating, torture, or other such offensive behavior, one only blames his own previous-life actions and does not fault others. Because one has faith in karmic retribution, one's mind remains free of anger or resentment.

Fourth, one peacefully abides in the meritorious quality of faith. It is very difficult to maintain resolute faith in the sublime Dharma of the Buddhas. But because one's mind is pure, one is able to maintain faith in it and accept it all.

4. Fourfold Dharmas of Ruined Bodhisattvas & Those Well-Trained

The bodhisattva fallen into ruin engages in the four sorts of flattery and deviousness. The well-trained bodhisattva has four straightforward practices to which he adheres. Consequently, if the bodhisattva wishes to refrain from engaging in actions characterized by flattery and deviousness and instead wishes to carry forth his practice with a straightforward mind, he should accord with the following lines:

One should abandon four kinds of dharmas
practiced by a bodhisattva fallen into ruin.
One should cultivate four kinds of dharmas
practiced by the well-trained bodhisattva.

a. Four Dharmas Practiced by a Bodhisattva Fallen into Ruin

What are the four dharmas practiced by a bodhisattva fallen into ruin? They are:

First, even though he may be learned, he nonetheless gives himself over to frivolous joking and thus fails to practice in compliance with the Dharma.

Second, he responds to transformative teaching with frivolous rationalizations and fails to respect or comply with instructions provided by monastic preceptors or monastic Dharma teachers.[305]

Third, he is unable to remain worthy of the offerings bestowed by the faithful. He does away with vigilant restraint of his behavior and yet still continues to accept offerings.

Fourth, he does not revere bodhisattvas who are gentle and good, but instead maintains an arrogant attitude toward them.

These are the four.

b. Four Dharmas Practiced by the Well-Trained Bodhisattva

What then are the four dharmas practiced by the well-trained bodhisattva? They are:

First, he is always happy to hear Dharma that he has not heard before and, having heard it, he is able to practice in accordance with what is taught. He relies on Dharma, relies on its meaning, and relies on practicing in accord with how it was taught.

Second, he accords with the import [of the teachings], is not misled by words and expressions, and is agreeable and easy to instruct. In matters related to serving as a teacher, he carries on those responsibilities with conscientious purposefulness.

Third, he is unfailing in observance of the moral precepts and in cultivation of meditative concentration while also maintaining a pure livelihood.

Fourth, in his relations with well-trained bodhisattvas, he brings forth respectful thoughts, acts congenially, and treats them with high regard. Thus he does away with any tendencies toward arrogance and focuses on their meritorious qualities.

5. Fourfold Bodhisattva Mistakes versus Good Paths of Conduct

There are also four types of mistakes a bodhisattva may be vulnerable to committing, all the while seeking in these contexts to focus on the shortcomings of other bodhisattvas. These behaviors are the defining features of a bodhisattva fallen into ruin. If, on the other hand, he is able to draw close to four paths of goodness, these serve to define the bodhisattva who is well-trained. This is as described in a verse:

The bodhisattva should utterly abandon
four types of bodhisattva mistakes.
The bodhisattva should cultivate
four paths of bodhisattva conduct.

a. Four Kinds of Bodhisattva Mistakes

What are the four kinds of bodhisattva mistakes? They are:

First, if one were to teach extremely profound Dharma to beings who are not adequate vessels to receive it, this would be a mistake.

Second, if one were to teach Small Vehicle doctrines to those who delight in profound and magnificent dharmas, this would be a mistake.

Third, if one were to act with condescending arrogance or disrespect toward someone engaged in right practice of the path who, with wholesome mind, observes the moral precepts, this would be a mistake.

Fourth, if with regard to someone who is not yet adequately developed and cannot yet be trusted one were to nonetheless trust him, or if one were to attract a bad person [into the community] who is a breaker of precepts and take him to be a good person worthy of friendship, this would be a mistake.

b. Four Paths of Good Bodhisattva Conduct

What are the four paths of bodhisattva conduct? They are:

First, one treats all beings with a mind of equal regard.

Second, one uses the good Dharma to teach everyone.

Third, one teaches Dharma equally to all beings.

Fourth, one behaves with right conduct toward all beings.

6. Four Dharmas Indicative of an Imitation Bodhisattva

If one always commits the four kinds of bodhisattva mistakes, fails to delight in judicious reflection on all dharmas, and fails to diligently cultivate good dharmas, then one is an imitation bodhisattva. Therefore:

Among all of the bodhisattva dharmas,
there are four that are indicative of imitation bodhisattvas.
The Buddha said of such dharmas
that one should utterly abandon each and every one of them.

What then are those four? They are:

First, one covets and esteems offerings and does not regard the Dharma as precious.

Second, one acts solely for the sake of fame and accolades and does not strive to acquire meritorious qualities.

Third, one seeks one's own happiness and is not mindful of other beings.

Fourth, one seeks to attract and delights in having a retinue of followers and does not delight in renunciation.

These are the four.

a. Q: How Can One Abandon Imitation Bodhisattva Dharmas?

Question: How is one able to abandon the dharmas of an imitation bodhisattva?

b. A: Cultivate Four Qualities of the Initial Bodhisattva Practices

Response: One who is a bodhisattva should cultivate the meritorious qualities associated with the initial bodhisattva practices. If one does this, he will then be able to abandon the dharmas of imitation bodhisattvas. Therefore, if a bodhisattva wishes to abandon the dharmas of imitation bodhisattvas, he should act in accordance with the following verse that states:

1) The Four Qualities of the Initial Bodhisattva Practices

With regard to the four meritorious qualities of the initial practices,
one should be energetically diligent in causing them to arise.
Once they have arisen, cause them to increase.
Having caused them to increase, continue to guard them.

What then are these four? They are:

First, one develops a resolute belief in the dharma of emptiness and yet still believes in karmic retribution.

Second, one delights in the dharma of nonself and yet still brings forth the mind of great compassion for all beings.

Third, one's mind resides in nirvāṇa and yet one's practice abides within *saṃsāra.*

Fourth, one practices giving wishing to facilitate beings' development [in the path] and not because one seeks any karmic reward in return.

2) To Develop The Qualities, Draw Near to a Good Spiritual Guide

If someone wishes to produce, increase, and guard the four meritorious qualities associated with the initial bodhisattva practices, he should draw near to a good spiritual guide.[306] This is as described in this verse:

a) Fourfold Good and Bad Spiritual Friends

The bodhisattva should draw near
to four kinds of good spiritual friends
and he should also utterly abandon
four kinds of bad spiritual friends.

The bodhisattva who delights in [the prospect of realizing] *anuttarasamyaksaṃbodhi* should draw near to, pay reverence to, and make offerings to four kinds of good spiritual friends and should remain distant from four kinds of bad spiritual friends.

i) The Four Kinds of Good Spiritual Friends

What then are the four kinds of good spiritual friends? They are:

First, one contemplates anyone who comes seeking something as a worthy friend, for he is thereby able to assist one in realizing the unsurpassable path.

Second, one contemplates anyone who speaks Dharma as a good spiritual guide, for he is able to assist one in achieving the wisdom that arises from extensive learning.

Third, one speaks in praise of monastics, contemplating them as good spiritual guides, for they are able to assist in the growth of all roots of goodness.

Fourth, one contemplates the Buddhas, the Bhagavats, as good spiritual guides, for they are able to assist one in successfully developing all of the dharmas of a buddha.

ii) The Four Kinds of Bad Spiritual Friends

What then are the four types of bad spiritual friends? They are:

First, those who have resolved to seek success in the Pratyekabuddha Vehicle and delight in having but few desires and few tasks to attend to.

Second, bhikshus seeking success in the Śrāvaka Disciple Vehicle who [merely] delight in sitting in *dhyāna* meditation.

Third, those fond of studying the non-Buddhist Lokāyata scriptures,[307] decorous literature, poetry, and polemical sophistry.

Fourth, those who, if one draws close to them, esteem the acquisition of worldly benefits, not the acquisition of benefits associated with the Dharma.

Given the above, the bodhisattva should draw near to the four kinds of good spiritual friends while remaining distant from the four types of bad spiritual friends. If the bodhisattva can remain distant from the four kinds of bad spiritual friends while drawing near to the four kinds of good spiritual friends, then he will acquire four vast treasuries, will go entirely beyond all dharmas associated with the works of Māra, will produce measureless merit, and will exhaustively accumulate all good dharmas.

3) Four Questions on the Good Effects of Good Spiritual Friends

Questions:

What are the dharmas constituting the bodhisattva's vast[308] treasuries?

What is meant by being able to go entirely beyond all dharmas associated with the works of Māra?

What are the dharmas by which one is able to produce measureless merit?

And what all is meant by being able to accumulate all good dharmas?

a) Answer #1: The Meaning of the Four Vast Treasuries

Response:

All bodhisattvas are possessed of four
vast treasuries of the sublime Dharma.
Of the four that facilitate accumulation of all good dharmas,
the resolve to attain bodhi is foremost among them.

What then are the four? They are:

First, one is able to meet the Buddha.

Second, one is able to hear [teachings on] the six *pāramitās*.

Third, one's mind remains free of the obstacle of hostility toward teacher of Dharma.

Fourth, because one is not neglectful, one's mind delights in dwelling in a forest hermitage.

These are the four vast treasuries.

b) Answer #2: The Meaning of Going Beyond the Works of Māra

As for "being able to go beyond all [works of] Māra," there are four dharmas in this connection. What are the four? They are:

First, one never abandons one's resolve to attain bodhi.

Second, one's mind remains free of the obstacle of hostility toward any being.

Third, one becomes aware of and knows all views.

Fourth, one's mind remains free of arrogance toward any bodhisattva.

These are the four.

c) Answer #3: The Meaning of Producing Measureless Merit

As for the dharmas by which one acquires measureless merit, there are four additional dharmas in this connection. What are the four? They are:

First, in one's giving of Dharma, one has nothing that he hopes for in return.

Second, one brings forth the mind of great compassion for bad people who break the moral precepts.

Third, in teaching other beings, one brings forth [the resolve to attain] the unsurpassable bodhi.

Fourth, in dealing with beings of base character, one practices patience.

These are the four.

d) Answer #4: The Meaning of Accumulating All Good Dharmas

As regards the accumulation of all good dharmas, this refers to four dharmas. And what are those four? They are:

First, when abiding in the solitary leisure of a recluse, one avoids adopting affected or eccentric practices.

Second, in the practice of the four means of attraction, one does not seek anything in return for one's kindness.

Third, in protecting and preserving right Dharma, one will not be sparing of even one's own body and life.

Fourth, when planting roots of goodness, one takes the resolve to attain bodhi as the foremost priority.

These are the four. Ideally, one should take up an extensive explanation of each and every one of these sets of four dharmas. However, because the text could become tediously complex, we do not present extensive discussions,[309] but now instead use verses to provide concise explanations that accord with what the Buddha has taught.

7. Eight Twofold Dharmas the Bodhisattva Must Completely Abandon

If a bodhisattva wishes to acquire the treasuries of the bodhisattvas, if he wishes to go beyond all the works of Māra, and if he wishes to accumulate all good dharmas, he should completely abandon all of the following things:

The two hollow attachments and the two types of bondage,
the two types of hindrances and the two defiling dharmas,
the two ulcerous sores as well as the two types of abysses,
the two causes of being burned and the two illness dharmas.

If the bodhisattva wishes to gain access to the bodhisattva treasuries and the other sorts of meritorious qualities, then he should utterly abandon all of these twofold dharmas.

a. The Two Hollow Attachments

What is meant by "the two hollow attachments"? The first is that of indulging a covetous attachment to ideas related to the Lokāyata scriptures. The second is adding decorative ornamentation to one's robe and bowl.

b. The Two Types of Bondage

As for "the two types of bondage," the first is the bondage of being attached to views. The second is the bondage of coveting fame and profit.

c. The Two Hindrance Dharmas

Of the "the two hindrance dharmas," the first is that of forming close relationships with members of the laity and the second is that of remaining distant from good people.

d. The Two Defiling Dharmas

As for "the two defiling dharmas," the first is that of simply enduring and accepting one's own afflictions. The second is that of delighting in carrying on friendships with benefactors.[310]

e. The Two Ulcerous Sores

Of "the two ulcerous sores," the first is that of focusing on the transgressions of others. The second is that of concealing one's own transgressions.

f. The Two Abyss-Like Dharmas

As for "the two abyss-like dharmas," the first is that of contributing to the damage and destruction of right Dharma. The second is that of accepting offerings even as one breaks the moral precepts.

g. The Two Dharmas Leading to Being Burned

Of "the two dharmas leading to being burned," the first is that of continuing to wear the monastic's *kaṣāya* robe even when possessed of a defiled mind. The second is that of [continuing under such circumstances] to accept sustaining offerings from those who are pure in their observance of the precepts.

h. The Two Types of Illnesses

Monastics may be prone to developing "the two types of illnesses" that are difficult to cure. The first is that of possessing such overweening pride[311] that one thinks he can simply subdue his own mind [without availing himself of a teacher or the appropriate Dharma antidotes]. The second is that of obstructing and destroying the resolve of someone seeking to [cultivate the practices of] the Great Vehicle.

If the bodhisattva is able to completely abandon dharmas such as these, there are additional dharmas by which he may swiftly attain *anuttarasamyaksaṃbodhi*. [If he avails himself of them], he can then swiftly attain it. He may also acquire those that are praised by all buddhas, *pratyekabuddhas*, and arhats.

1) Q: Which Dharmas Lead to Bodhi & Which Earn Āryas' Praise?

Question: Which dharmas are those that lead to rapid attainment of *anuttarasamyaksaṃbodhi*? And which of them are praised by all buddhas, *pratyekabuddhas*, and arhats?

2) A: The Four Truths' Practices and Four Additional Dharmas

Response:

If one is able to practice the characteristic practices of the four truths,
one will swiftly attain the bodhi of the Buddha.
Also, if one practices four additional dharmas,
he will be praised by the three classes of *āryas*.

a) The Four Dharmas Characteristic of Cultivating the Truths

What are the practices that are characteristic of cultivating the four truths? They are:

First, because one seeks to develop all good dharmas, one is energetically vigorous.

Second, one listens to, accepts, studies, and recites the Dharma of the sutras and then practices in accordance with their teachings.

Third, having renounced the three realms of existence as comparable to a site of human slaughter, one always seeks the means to avoid and transcend them.

Fourth, in order to benefit and bring peace and happiness to all beings, one strives to benefit one's own mind.

The "truth" [of "the four truths"] refers to being genuine and non-deceptive. Because [the four truths] lead to the attainment of *anuttarasamyaksaṃbodhi*, they are not false.

b) The Four Dharmas Praised by the Three Classes of Āryas

Next, there are four dharmas that are praised by the three classes of *āryas*. What are those four? They are:

First, even if abstaining from it will cost one's life, one will not do any bad deed.

Second, one always practices the giving of Dharma.

Third, one remains single-mindedly focused whenever receiving teachings on Dharma.

Fourth, if one produces a defiled thought, one is immediately able to correctly contemplate the defiled thought and the causes and conditions that initiated the defiled thought, [reflecting], "As for these 'roots of defilement,' just what about them is designated as 'defiled'? What is it that becomes 'defiled'? In what circumstances does it arise? And precisely who is it that that generates this defilement?"

As one carries on right reflection in this way, one realizes that these factors are all false, devoid of any genuine substantiality, and devoid of any intrinsic existence of their own. Because one possesses a definite and resolute belief in the emptiness of all dharmas, because no dharmas whatsoever exist intrinsically, and because one carries on such right contemplation of the causes and conditions of defilement, one does not bring forth any sort of evil karmic action. As for all the other afflictions, one also contemplates them in this same manner.

The bodhisattva's acquisition of these dharmas that elicit the praises of the great men is a consequence of his abandoning all bad karmic actions rooted in the afflictions. His mind then completely develops the relinquishing mind. This is as described below:

8. The Bodhisattva's Relinquishing Mind & Freedom from Weariness

Having completely developed the relinquishing mind,
one seeks to bestow both worldly and world-transcending benefit.
As one seeks to bestow these forms of benefit,
one's mind remains free of any weariness.

This bodhisattva completely develops the dharma of relinquishing. His desire to practice Dharma giving and to practice the giving of material wealth is due to his motivation to benefit beings. Whether he is striving to bring about worldly benefit or world-transcending benefit, so long as he has not yet succeeded, his mind still remains free of any weariness or any inclination to retreat.

[The bestowal of] "worldly benefit" entails a thorough understanding of the world's classical texts, cultural arts, professional skills, the implementation of clever expedients, and so forth. [The bestowal of "world-transcending benefit" entails [providing instruction in the practice of] the dharmas of the [five] root faculties, [five] powers, [seven] limbs of enlightenment, and [eightfold] path [as practiced by those who have become] free of the contaminants. This is as described here:

a. The Bodhisattva Doesn't Weary of Providing Two Kinds of Benefit

As one seeks in this manner to bestow the two kinds of benefit,
one's mind remains free of weariness and neglectfulness.
Through staying free of weariness and neglectfulness,
one becomes able to acquire all of the profound dharmas.

It is due to seeking it from within the classical works
that one is able to acquire wisdom.
One thereby develops a perfectly complete knowledge of the world's most superior and foremost dharmas.

In "remaining free of weariness and neglectfulness," "weariness and neglectfulness" refer to feelings of loathing. If in one's studies one remains free of loathing, then one's mind will remain free of weariness. If one remains free of weariness, then one will always be free of weariness as one seeks to acquire the dharmas found within the scriptures, the arts, medicine, professional skills, and the codes of propriety. If one remains free of weariness in these pursuits, then one will acquire wisdom and will perfect a deep knowledge of the dharmas appropriate for use in the world.

"Dharmas of the world" refers here to the local customs determining what is appropriate in any given situation for adapting to the minds of those in the world. One becomes well able to understand the dharmas necessary to maintain order in the world. One thereby becomes able to understand what is appropriate in addressing beings possessed of superior, middling, and inferior capacities. In guiding them, one accords with whatsoever is appropriate. One becomes skillful in understanding worldly affairs while also maintaining a mind deeply imbued with a sense of shame and a dread of blame.

As for "in guiding them, one accords with whatever is appropriate," this refers to the fact that, in addressing the needs of beings of superior, middling, and inferior capacity, each of them has what is most appropriate for use in instructing them.

As for "a sense of shame and a dread of blame," "shame" refers to a feeling of mortification regarding one's own actions whereas "dread of blame" refers to the potential for feeling mortified by [the critical judgments of] others.

There are those who hold that it is because of one's actions that one feels a sense of shame and that it is because of seeing others that one feels a dread of blame. Within the sphere of worldly dharmas, having a dread of blame is the primary priority. This is as described in a sutra [that says], "There are two dharmas of pristine purity that guard the world, namely a sense of shame and a dread of blame." This is as described in a verse:

> Whenever there are people possessed of a dread of blame,
> they understand the Dharma, karmic transgressions, and merit.
> As for those devoid of a dread of blame, good people avoid them,
> for there is no evil that they will not do.

b. Q: Why Are Bodhisattvas Taught to Understand Worldly Dharmas?

Question: Why do you so assiduously counsel bodhisattvas to develop a good understanding of the dharmas appropriate for use in the world?

c. A: Knowledge of the World Enables Dharma Teaching Expedients

Response: If the bodhisattva is knowledgeable about the dharmas of the world, it will be easy for him to gain access to beings in a way that is mutually pleasing. He will thereby be able to teach them and guide the development of their minds in a way that causes them to abide in the Great Vehicle.

If one does not understand the dharmas of the world, then he will be incapable of teaching even a single person. Therefore the dharmas of the world serve as an expedient path for teaching beings.

9. One Must Have a Sense of Shame, Dread of Blame, and Respect

The bodhisattva who understands the dharmas of the world in this way has a mind that is well equipped with a sense of shame and dread of blame. This is as described here:

When subjected to bad actions, remain respectful and generous.
How much the more so in dealing with those that benefit oneself.
One possessed of a dread of blame and an inclination to be respectful
refrains from slighting or deriding those who are good.

Because this bodhisattva has a well-developed dread of blame, even in dealing with badly-behaved people, he is still able to behave respectfully, bestow offerings, welcome those who arrive, escort those who depart, and extend greetings. How much the more so would this be the case when dealing with good people possessed of meritorious qualities.

Because one is possessed of the two mental attitudes of a dread of blame on the one hand and respectfulness on the other, in dealing with those who are worthy and good but deficient in knowledge, one does not adopt a slighting or arrogant attitude toward them. One reflects: "There are those who are possessed of meritorious qualities, yet conceal their presence in the world just as ashes conceal hot coals. They should not be slighted merely because they feel disdain for such worldly concerns. If I were to slight them for such minor reasons, I would be guilty of a karmic offense."

Additionally:

10. The Bodhisattva Must Never Retreat from Completing His Works

In whatever endeavor one takes up,
although it may be difficult, one still completes it.
This being so, even in endeavors undertaken in the world,
they are still characterized by never retreating.

No matter what endeavors this bodhisattva takes up, whether that be building a stupa or a temple, arranging for a great Dharma assembly, or rescuing someone who has committed some crime—in all such difficult endeavors in the world, one's mind refuses to desist or retreat from the task. So long as any given endeavor has not yet been completed, it is essential to use the power of all sorts of expedients as well as the power of physical, verbal, and mental persistence to successfully complete the task.

It is not only with respect to endeavors related to the Dharma of the Buddha that one refuses to turn back in retreat, for even in worldly endeavors, one maintains this characteristic of refusing to turn back in retreat.

a. Q: How Can the Bodhisattva Succeed in Completing His Works?

Question: Based on which causes and conditions is one able to succeed in such endeavors?

b. A: He Has Patience, Makes Offerings, and Follows Teachings

Response: If one is possessed of the power of patient endurance, he will be able to successfully complete his endeavors. This is as described here:

> Having developed this power of great patient endurance,
> one becomes deeply committed to making offerings to the Buddhas.
> Whatever teachings have been taught by the Buddhas,
> one is able to accept and uphold all of them.

Having developed this power of patient endurance, the bodhisattva uses this power to make offerings to the Buddhas, to bow to them in reverence, and to freely offer up, as appropriate, robes, food, drink, and so forth.

Additionally, whatever the Buddha has taught one to do, whether that be upholding the moral precepts, cultivating *dhyāna* concentration, subduing one's own mind, or contemplating all dharmas in accordance with ultimate reality—one uses the power of patient endurance in all of these endeavors.

This is just as when one obtains a sharp knife. He should then use it for beneficial purposes and should not use it for unbeneficial purposes. As it is said:

11. Right Practice of Ten Dharmas Enabling 1st Ground Purification

> It is through faith, compassion, kindness, and relinquishing,
> through the capacity for tireless patient endurance,
> through also being able to understand the significance [of teachings],
> through serving as a guide for the minds of other beings,
>
> through keeping a dread of blame enabling supreme endurance,
> through making momentous offerings to the Buddhas,
> and through abiding in what the Buddha has taught—
> it is through right practice of these ten dharmas
> that one becomes able to purify the first of the grounds.
> These then are what constitute the bodhisattva path.

It is due to the bodhisattva's ability to carry out these practices, beginning with faith and concluding with abiding in the Buddha's teachings, that he is able to purify the first ground.

a. Faith

These ten dharmas all take faith as what is foremost. "Faith" refers to the mind's reaching a definite resolve with respect to the causes and conditions of the Dharma of the Buddhas, one that is enhanced by one's delight in it.

How does this come to be the case? It is because this bodhisattva's mind is pure in nature that he is able to develop such a deeply rooted power of faith.

b. Compassion

Having acquired this power of faith, he then brings forth the mind of compassion toward beings, reflecting as follows: "The Dharma of all Buddhas takes the great compassion as its very foundation. I now single-mindedly delight in the Dharma of the Buddha. Therefore, when in the midst of beings I should bring forth the mind of compassion."

As this compassion of his gradually increases, it develops into the great compassion.

c. Kindness

Having developed the great compassion, one then brings forth thoughts of kindness toward other beings, reflecting as follows: "I should benefit other beings in a manner consistent with my capacity to do so. If I do this, then this would become the practice of kindness based on genuine compassion."

d. Relinquishing

When one benefits beings, one is immediately able to practice relinquishing to the degree that one can give away all of his inward or outward possessions, reflecting as follows: "If I dispense with my possessions in this manner, doing so out of a wish to benefit beings and make them happy, this shall become genuine kindness. In addition, these beings will then become well-disposed to trust and accept my words."

e. Tirelessly Patient Endurance

One then becomes able to endure all manner of distressing situations in order to acquire valuable possessions with which to fulfill one's desire to practice such relinquishing. One then reflects in this manner: "If in doing this I were to become weary, then there would be nothing gained from my pursuit of wealth by involving myself in the means for mastering the world's various skills, arts, classical texts, and agriculture techniques. Therefore I should be tireless in learning the world's skills, arts, classical texts, agricultural techniques, and other such things."

f. The Ability to Understand the Meaning of Teachings

Through such a capacity for patient endurance, one is able to understand the meaning and significance [of what one studies], whereupon one reflects as follows: "The flavor of worldly classics and texts derives from the meaningful ideas contained within them. If one becomes well able to understand the conceptual flavor of such classics, one is thereby able to gain a penetrating comprehension of all worldly dharmas."

g. Serving as Guide for Beings' Minds

If one becomes able to completely comprehend them, one can then serve as a guide for other beings of superior, middling, and inferior capacities.

h. A Sense of Shame and Dread of Blame

One then reflects as follows: "If one has no sense of shame or dread of blame, he will be unable to inspire delight in other beings. In order to cause them to be delighted, I should act with a sense of shame and dread of blame."

One then reflects as follows: "If I have no capacity for patient endurance, then I will not be able to bring about either worldly or world-transcending benefit. It is through the capacity for patient endurance that one can serve as a guide for all beings and cause them all to be delighted. It is because their minds are delighted that they will then trust and accept my words. Because they believe and accept my words, I can diligently implement skillful means by which I can serve as a guide for them."

i. Making Offerings to the Buddha

One also reflects as follows: "If beings make offerings to the Buddha, then they will gain much benefit from this." Then, wishing to influence beings to make offerings to the Buddha, one immediately adopts this practice oneself by making offerings to the Buddha, his images, and his *śarīra* relics.

j. Abiding in the Buddha's Teachings

Because those beings believe and accept whatever one does, they then emulate one's practice of making offerings to the Buddha and thereby establish the causes and conditions for being reborn in the human and celestial realms and for abiding in the Dharma of the Three Vehicles.

It is in this manner that the bodhisattva sequentially develops his practice of these ten dharmas by which he is then able to purify the first bodhisattva ground.

The End of Chapter Nineteen

Chapter 20
Mindfulness of the Buddhas

XX. Chapter 20: Mindfulness of the Buddhas

A. On Finishing 1st Ground Practices, the Bodhisattva Sees Buddhas

When the bodhisattva dwelling on the first ground
has completed what is to be practiced,
due to the power of his roots of goodness, he will naturally
be able to see several hundred buddhas.[312]

When, in this [above-discussed] manner, the bodhisattva subdues his own mind, he develops a deep love for the path to buddhahood. He then completely fulfills the first-ground practices in accordance with the way he learned them. Then, due to the power of his roots of goodness and merit, he is naturally able to see the present-era buddhas of the ten directions right before his very eyes.

1. Q: Is There Any Other Way to Be Able to See the Buddhas?

Question: Is it solely through the power of roots of goodness and merit that one is then able to see buddhas or is there some other method by which one can do so?

2. A: On Entering the Pratyutpanna Samādhi, One Sees the Buddhas

Response:

There is a deep samādhi that the Buddha
explained for the sake of Bhadrapāla.
If one acquires this samādhi treasure,
one becomes able to see the Buddhas.

Bhadrapāla was a lay bodhisattva well able to practice the *dhūta* austerities. It was for the sake of this bodhisattva that the Buddha spoke the *Pratyutpanna Samādhi Sūtra.*[313] The *pratyutpanna* samādhi is one in which one sees the Buddhas right before one's very eyes. When the bodhisattva accesses this magnificently precious samādhi, even though he might not yet have gained the heavenly eye and heavenly ear, he is nonetheless able to see the buddhas of the ten directions and he is also able to listen to the Dharma of the sutras being taught by those buddhas.

3. Q: How Can One Acquire This Samadhi?

Question: What means should one use to acquire this samādhi?

4. A: Envision the Buddhas with the 32 Marks and 80 Characteristics

Response:

One should bring to mind the Buddhas,
envisioning them as residing in a great assembly,
replete with all thirty-two major marks
and eighty secondary characteristics adorning their bodies.

a. Recollection of the Buddhas' Qualities and Accomplishments

In cultivating this samādhi, the practitioner brings to mind the Buddhas with the thirty-two major marks and eighty secondary characteristics gracing their bodies, with bhikshus close by, with devas making offerings, and with a grand and reverential assembly surrounding them. With focused mind, one envisions each of the major marks of those buddhas.

One also recollects the Buddhas as those who are possessed of great vows, recollects their perfection of the great compassion and the fact that it has not been cut off, recollects their perfection of the great kindness through which they bring profound peace to beings, recollects their practice of the great sympathetic joy and their fulfillment of beings' aspirations, and recollects their practice of equanimity through which they have abandoned aversion and craving and do not abandon beings.

One also recollects their practice of the truthfulness basis of meritorious qualities by which they are never deceptive, recollects their practice of the relinquishment basis of meritorious qualities by which they have rid themselves of the miserliness defilement, recollects their practice of the thoroughgoing [quiescence][314] basis of meritorious qualities by which their minds maintain a state of thoroughgoing quiescence, and recollects their practice of the wisdom basis of meritorious qualities through which they have acquired great wisdom.[315]

One recollects too their perfect practice of *dāna pāramitā* by which they have become the lords of Dharma giving, their perfect practice of *śīla pāramitā* by which their observance of the moral precepts is pure, their perfect practice of *kṣānti pāramitā* by which their capacity for patient endurance is analogous to that of the earth, their perfect practice of *vīrya pāramitā* by which their vigor is preeminent, their perfect practice of *dhyāna pāramitā* by which they have destroyed all hindrances to meditative absorption, and their perfect practice of *prajñā pāramitā* by which they have destroyed all obstacles to wisdom.

b. Recollection of the 32 Marks of the Buddhas

One recollects too:

Their mark of having the wheel insignia on the hands and feet, emblematic of their ability to turn the wheel of Dharma;

Their mark of securely planted feet, emblematic of their standing securely in every dharma;

Their mark of proximal webbing on fingers and toes, emblematic of the extinguishing of all afflictions;

Their mark of seven places of fullness, emblematic of their complete fulfillment of merit;

Their mark of soft and tender hands and feet, emblematic of their harmonious manner of proclaiming the Dharma;

Their mark of slender and long fingers and toes, emblematic of their cultivation and accumulation of every sort of good and sublime dharma during the long night [of previous lifetimes];

Their mark of having broad heels and wide eyes, emblematic of their vast learning;

Their mark of having a large and erect body, emblematic of their proclamation of the great and upright Dharma;

Their mark of having high arches, emblematic of their being lofty in all things;

Their mark of having upwardly spiraling bodily hairs, emblematic of their ability to cause beings to abide in the supreme and sublime dharma;

Their mark of having legs gradually growing in thickness like those of the *aiṇeya* antelope;

Their mark of long arms reaching past the knees, their arms appearing like golden gate bars;[316]

Their mark of the stallion-like retracted male organ, emblematic of their possession of the treasury of Dharma jewels;

Their mark of the golden-hued body emanating light of countless colors;

Their mark of fine and thin skin, emblematic of their proclamation of subtle and sublime Dharma;

Their mark of one hair per hair pore, emblematic of their revealing of the single-mark Dharma;

Their mark of the [mid-brow] white-down tuft adorning the countenance, due to which beings happily and tirelessly gaze at the Buddha's face;

Their mark of a lion-like upper torso, emblematic of the Buddha, like the lion, being one who is fearless;

Their mark of round and large shoulders, emblematic of their ability to make skillful distinctions regarding the nature of the five aggregates;

Their mark of fullness in the subaxillary region, emblematic of their possession of a full measure of good roots;

Their mark of distinguishing every flavor, emblematic of their having perfectly tasted the flavor of quiescence;

Their mark of having a square-set body, emblematic of having crushed the fear of births and deaths;

Their mark of the fleshy prominence atop the crown, emblematic of their heads never having to be lowered in reverence [to someone superior];

Their mark of the large tongue the color of real coral that is even able to cover the face;

Their mark of the Brahmā-like voice and the physical mark that reaches even to the Brahma Heaven;

Their mark of the lion-like jaw;

Their mark of the broad shoulders, these being emblematic of their ability to demolish [the views held by] non-Buddhist traditions;

Their mark of even teeth, emblematic of their practice of pure *dhyāna* meditation;

Their mark of their teeth being of even height, emblematic of their minds' equal regard for all beings;

Their mark of closely set teeth, emblematic of their abandonment of the desires;

Their mark of having forty teeth, emblematic of their perfection of the forty dharmas exclusive to buddhas;

Their mark of blue eyes, emblematic of their looking on beings with minds imbued with kindness;

Their mark of having eyelashes like those of the royal bull, with the lashes long and in no way disarrayed;

Their obtaining of a rare physical form that beings look on without ever tiring of holding it in their gaze;

Their having bodies adorned with these thirty-two marks;

c. Recollection of Other Qualities of the Buddhas

Their having the eighty minor characteristics like inlaid adornments on their bodies, emanating brilliant radiance;

Their complete fulfillment of merit;

Their transcendently supreme and awesome powers;

Their wide-spread illustrious esteem;

Their bodies' incense-like fragrance produced by purity in observing the moral precepts;

Their invulnerability to being moved by worldly dharmas;

Their ability to remain undefiled by any arising of afflictions;

Their ability to remain unsullied by others' verbal abuse;
Their ability to roam and sport through use of their spiritual powers;
The ability of the Buddhas to be so intensely magnificent in the manifestation of their awe-inspiring powers that no one would dare obstruct them;
Their freely exercised sovereign mastery in using wisdom to proclaim the Dharma that is like the roaring of a lion;
Their ability to dispel the darkness of delusion by marshaling the power of vigor;
Their use of magnificent brilliance to everywhere illuminate the heavens and the earth;
Their utter invincibility in debate;
Their being such that everyone looks up to them and no one can look down on them;
Their constancy in regarding all beings with kindness;
Their possession of mindfulness as vast as the great oceans;
Their meditative absorption that is like Mount Sumeru [in its unshakability];
Their possession of patience comparable to the earth's [ability to endure anything];
Their ability to bring about growth in the merit planted by beings that is analogous [to the growth-enhancing capacity of] water's moisture;[317]
Their ability to bring forth roots of goodness in beings that, in its power, is like the rising of the wind;
Their ability to ripen beings that is like fire's ability to cook things;
Their possession of wisdom as boundless as empty space;
Their universal raining down of the great Dharma [rain] that is like [the rain that pours down from] immense dense clouds;
Their ability to remain unstained by worldly dharmas that is like lotus blossoms' [ability to rise from mud and yet remain unsullied by it];
Their ability, like lions pouncing on deer, to decisively refute [the doctrines of] non-Buddhist masters;
Their ability to bear a heavy burden that is like that of the great king of the elephants;
Their ability to lead a great congregation of followers that is like that of the great king of bulls;
Their possession of a retinue of pure followers that is like [the retinue of] a wheel-turning king;
Their utter supremacy in the world that is like that of the lord of the Mahābrahma Heaven;

Their ability to inspire fondness and delight that is like that of a bright moon in the clear night sky;
Their universal illumination that is able to burn as brightly as the brilliantly shining sun;
Their bestowal on beings of the causes and conditions for peace and happiness that is like [the generosity of] a humane father;
Their acting out of pity toward beings, protecting them in whatever way is appropriate, that is like the actions of a lovingly kind mother;
Their purity of conduct that is like [the purity of] the real gold in the heavens;
Their possession of the power of great strength that is like that of Indra in the heavens;
Their diligence in benefiting those in the world that is like that of a world-protecting lord;
Their ability to cure the disease of the afflictions that is like [the curative power of] a king of physicians;
Their ability to rescue one from disastrous circumstances that is like that of close relatives;
Their ability to accumulate a store of meritorious qualities that is like an immense treasury;
Their possession of immeasurably vast moral virtue;
Their possession of boundless meditative absorptions;
Their ineffable wisdom;
Their unequaled liberation;
Their knowledge and vision of liberation that is the equal of the unequaled;
Their incomparability in all things;
Their supremacy over everyone in the world due to which they are recognized as foremost among men;
And their perfection of great dharmas by which they are recognized as great men.

It is in this way that the bodhisattva engages in recollective contemplation of all buddhas in accordance with their possession of the qualities characteristic of the great men. [So, too, he recollects]:

d. Recollection of More Special Qualities & Abilities of Buddhas

That these buddhas have cultivated these meritorious qualities for a countless, boundless, inconceivable, and incalculable number of hundreds of thousands of myriads of *koṭis* of kalpas during which they have been well able to guard their physical, verbal, and mental karma;

That they are well able to completely sever all doubts with respect to the five categorical repositories of dharmas: past dharmas, future dharmas, present dharmas, unconditioned dharmas, and ineffable dharmas;

That, without falling into any error, they employ the four modes of reply: the definitive reply, the distinguishing reply, the counter-questioning reply, and the reply that sets aside the question;[318]

That they skillfully explain the dharmas of the thirty-seven enlightenment factors, namely: the faculties, the powers, the limbs of enlightenment, the path, the stations of mindfulness, the right efforts, and the foundations of psychic power;[319]

That they are well able to distinguish [each link comprising the chain of] cause-and-effect, namely: ignorance, actions, consciousness, name-and-form, the six sense faculties, contact, feeling, craving, grasping, becoming, birth, and aging-and-death;

That they are free of any attachment to the eye or visual forms, to the ear or sounds, to the nose or fragrances, to the tongue or flavors, to the body or touch, or to the mind or dharmas [as objects of mind];

That they skillfully expound the nine types of passages contained in the Dharma of the sutras, namely: sutras; *geyas;* prophetic teachings or expositions; *gāthās*; *udānas*; *nidānas*; [short] discourses beginning with "Thus [spoke the Buddha]..."; *vaipulyas*; and unprecedented events;

That they are not influenced by any of the negative influences such as: greed, hatred, delusion, arrogance, the view that conceives of the existence of true personhood, extreme views, wrong views, seizing upon views; seizing on rules and regulations, or doubts;

That they are not assailed by such afflictions as absence of faith, absence of a sense of shame, absence of a dread of blame, flattery, deviousness, frivolousness, neglectfulness, indolence, somnolence, animosity, miserliness, or jealousy;

That they have known and seen the truth of suffering, have cut off its origination, have realized cessation, have cultivated the path, have abandoned what is to be abandoned, have seen what is to be seen, have done what is to be done, have utterly destroyed the foes,[320] and have perfectly fulfilled their vows;

That they are venerated in the world, are as fathers to the world, and are lords of the world, are well come, are well gone, are possessed of the well-cultivated mind, are consummately skilled in meditative stillness, are well-realized in the realization of cessation, and are well liberated;

That, as they abide in countless and boundless worlds throughout the ten directions in worlds as numerous as the sands in the

Ganges, [one envisions them] as if they were appearing directly before one's very eyes.

e. Contemplative Recollection of the 80 Secondary Characteristics

The bodhisattva should also envision in contemplation all of the buddhas as graced with their eighty secondary characteristics,[321] recollecting:

That their nails are copper-colored is emblematic of their practice of pure dharmas;

That their nails are prominent and large is emblematic of birth into the great clan;

That their nails are glossy and smooth is emblematic of a deep affection for beings;

That their fingers are round, tapered, and long is emblematic of the depth and duration of their practice;

That their fingers are fully fleshed is emblematic of fully developed roots of goodness;

That their fingers are tapered and long is emblematic of sequential accumulation of all dharmas of a buddha;

That their veins are hidden and invisible, but they do not hide the lineage of [the quality of their conduct in] body, mouth, and mind;

That there are no thick knots in their veins is emblematic of their having broken up the knots of afflictions;

That their ankle bones are flat and inconspicuous is emblematic of their not hiding away the Dharma;

That their feet are not misaligned in their track is emblematic of their liberation of the multitudes who have fallen into deviant conduct;

That their gait is like that of the lion is emblematic of their being the lions among men;

That their gait is also like that of the king of elephants is emblematic of their being the elephant kings among men;

That their gait is also like the king of geese is emblematic of their flying high, like the wild goose;

That their gait is also like the king of bulls is emblematic of their being the most revered of all men;

That, when walking, they turn around to the right, is emblematic of their skillful proclamation of the right path;

That their posture is not hunched or crooked is emblematic of the fact that their minds are never crooked;

That their bodies stand solid and erect in their posture is emblematic of their praise of solidity and durability in upholding the moral precepts;

That their bodies gradually grew large is emblematic of their sequential exposition of Dharma;

That all parts of their bodies are large and majestic is emblematic of their ability to skillfully explain the great and sublime meritorious qualities;

That their bodies are perfectly developed is emblematic of their perfection in the Dharma;

That their strides are of equal length is emblematic of their equal-minded regard for all beings;

That their bodies are pristine in their cleanliness is emblematic of the purity of their three types of karma;

That their skin is fine and soft is emblematic of the naturally pliant character of their minds;

That their bodies remain free of all dust and dirt is emblematic of their good views that have abandoned all defilement;

That their bodies do not shrink through wasting [even in old age] is emblematic of their minds' always remaining unsinkable;

That their bodies are boundless and immeasurable is emblematic of the immeasurability of their roots of goodness;

That the flesh of their bodies is taut and finely textured is emblematic of their eternal severance of [karmically-compulsory] later incarnations;

That all of their joints are smooth in their articulations is emblematic of their skillful explication of the twelve causes and conditions and their perfectly clear distinguishing of each of them;

That the hue of their bodies is not dark is emblematic of their knowledge and vision being free of any darkness;

That their waists are full all around is emblematic of their disciples' possession of fully developed conduct;

That their bellies are clear [of blemishes] and of fresh and immaculate appearance is emblematic of their being well able to completely know the serious faults of *saṃsāra;*

That their bellies do not protrude is emblematic of their having crushed the mountain of arrogance;

That their bellies are flat and do not show is emblematic of the fact that their proclamation of Dharma is directed equally toward everyone;

That their umbilici are round and deep is emblematic of their penetrating comprehension of extremely deep dharmas;

That their umbilici have a rightward swirl is emblematic of their disciples' compliance with instruction;

That their bodies are in every way graceful in their refinements is emblematic of the thoroughgoing purity of their disciples;

That their awesomeness in deportment is utterly immaculate is emblematic of the incomparable purity of their minds;

That their bodies are free of blemishes is emblematic of their being completely free of any black dharmas;

That the softness of their hands is superior even to that of *tūla*-cotton silk is emblematic of the experience of those receiving their instruction who feel as if their bodies have become as light as a wisp of down;

That the lines on their palms form a deep pattern is emblematic of the profoundly dignified nature of their awesome deportment;

That the lines on their palms are long is emblematic of their contemplative regard for the long-term future of those receiving their Dharma teaching;

That the pattern on their palms is lustrous and smooth is emblematic of their relinquishing of the affection of relatives and of their acquisition of the fruits of the great path;

That their countenances remain free of any long-faced expression is emblematic of the presence of exceptional circumstances in the moral precepts they establish;

That their lips are as red as *bimba* fruit is emblematic of their looking on the entire world as merely like an image reflected in a mirror;

That their tongues are soft and pliant is emblematic of their initial use of gentle speech in liberating beings;

That their tongues are thin and wide is emblematic of the purity and abundance of their meritorious qualities;

That their tongues are crimson red is emblematic of their Dharma's ability to cause common people to understand what they find difficult to understand;

That their voices are like thunder is emblematic of their not fearing the boom of a thunderclap;

That their voices are harmonious and gentle is emblematic of their proclamation of soft and gentle Dharma;

That their four central incisors are rounded [in their visible profile] and straight is emblematic of their proclamation of the Dharma of the straight path;

That their four central incisors are all sharp is emblematic of their liberation of those beings who are possessed of sharp faculties;

That their four central incisors are immaculately white is emblematic of their being foremost in purity;

That their four central incisors are evenly and equally set is emblematic of their standing on the level ground of the moral precepts;

That the profile of their rows of teeth gradually taper to those that are smaller [in height] is emblematic of the graduated sequence in their explanation of the dharma of the four truths;

That they have noses that are high and straight-ridged is emblematic of their standing atop the high mountain of wisdom;

That their nasal apertures are clear and clean is emblematic of the purity of their disciples;

That their eyes are wide and laterally long is emblematic of their wisdom's qualities of being vast and far-reaching;

That their eyelashes are not sparse or in disarray is emblematic of their skill in their differential assessment of beings;

That the whites and pupils of their eyes are as fresh and pristine as the petals of a blue lotus blossom is emblematic of their being such that even devas and heavenly maidens are moved to gaze upon them fondly and bow down in reverence before them;

That their eyebrows are high and long is emblematic of the far-reaching spread of their fame;

That the hair of their eyebrows is smooth and glossy is emblematic of their thoroughgoing knowledge of the dharmas of mental pliancy;

That their ears are equal in their appearance is emblematic of the equality of all who listen to the Dharma;

That their faculty of hearing is undamaged is emblematic of their ability to liberate any being possessed of an undamaged mind;

That their foreheads are flat and of fine appearance is emblematic of their having skillfully abandoned all views;

That their foreheads are unrestricted in their wide breadth is emblematic of their having broadly refuted [the claims of] non-Buddhist traditions;

That their heads are in all respects perfectly developed is emblematic of their having thoroughly perfected [the goals of] their great vows;

That their hair is the color of the black bee is emblematic of their having transformed the pleasures associated with the five types of desire;

That their hair is dense and fine is emblematic of their having already put an end to the fetters;

That their hair, so pleasing in its appearance, is soft in texture is emblematic of their pliant and sharp wisdom's ability to know well the flavor of dharmas;

That their hair is not in disarray is emblematic of their words never being disordered;
That their hair is smooth and glossy is emblematic of their always being free of any sort of coarse speech;
That their hair has a marvelous fragrance is emblematic of their use of the fragrant blossoms of the seven branches of bodhi to teach and guide beings in whatever way is appropriate.
That their mark of virtue, peace, and joy appears in their hair.
And that their mark of virtue, peace, and joy also appears on the palms of their hands and on the soles of their feet.

f. Envisioning the Buddhas in an Assembly, Teaching, on the Lion Seat

1) Envisioning the Buddhas as They Sit on the Lion's Seat

It is in this manner that a bodhisattva should envision the Buddhas residing in the midst of a great assembly, speaking on right Dharma, and sitting on the lion seat. The lion seat has feet made from *vaiḍūrya* inset with various jewels, a headrest made from real coral with marvelous red pearls, and a canopy made of hammered gold. It is draped with all sorts of soft, silky, and lustrous heavenly robes and is supported by bejeweled lions whose bodies are made of purple gold. Their eyes are amber and their tails are mother-of-pearl. They have carnelian tongues, four white-diamond tusk-teeth, hair made of real white silver, and long, full manes. That seat rests upon these four lions. They form [the base of] the throne that has armrests made from royal elephant tusks and a footrest made of the many sorts of jewels.

The Buddhas receive there the reverential obeisance of the devas, dragons, *yakṣas, gandharvas, asuras, garuḍas, kinnaras,* and *mahoragas*. The Buddhas appear in this way on this throne. They wear the *saṃkakṣikā*[322] and the *nivāsana*,[323] neither too high nor too low, so that they cover the three regions of the body and are neatly arranged and straight all around. They wear a light-colored *saṃghāṭī* robe,[324] with the strips composing it clearly visible, neither too high nor too low, and not misaligned.

2) Envisioning the Audience as the Buddhas Teach Dharma

They abide in the midst of an audience adorned by the presence of the eight kinds of great *āryas*,[325] surrounded by a great assembly of humans and devas. When in attendance there, the dragons and golden-winged *garuḍa* birds all listen together to the teaching of Dharma, remaining free of any thoughts of mutual hostility.[326]

Everyone in the entire assembly is imbued with a deeply sincere sense of shame and dread of blame as, with reverential affection for the Buddha, they all listen single-mindedly to the discourse of the

Buddha, accept and uphold it, reflect upon it, and practice in accordance with what is taught. Because their minds are focused as they listen and because their thoughts are pure, they are able to block any interference by the hindrances. Everyone in the great assembly gazes insatiably up at the Tathāgata, with all the hairs raised on their bodies, with their eyes filled with tears, with their minds afire with intensity, or with hearts filled with great joy.

Wherever people have become like this, one knows that their minds have become purified. They remain there motionless and silent, serenely still, and as if having entered *dhyāna* absorption. Their minds are free of either love or hatred and remain undistracted by any extraneous matters. They have thoughts of great compassion[327] by which they feel kindness and pity for beings, wishing to rescue them all. Their minds do not descend into flattery or deviousness, but rather have become utterly quiescent and pure as they distinguish what is good from what is bad. They have an immensely strong determination from which they neither fall away or shrink back and they do not regard themselves as superior or others as inferior.

3) Envisioning the Manner in Which They Teach Dharma

The Buddhas are all observed abiding in such great assemblies, teaching Dharma that is easy to understand and easy to completely fathom. [Their audiences] listen with insatiable delight. Their voices are deep, are not subject to fading [even at a distance], are gentle, and are pleasing to the ear. Originating in the belly, through the interaction of the throat, tongue, nasopharynx, dental palate, teeth, and lips, the air is caused to become sounds and sentences that may be soft and pleasing to the ear, may be as powerfully strong as the earth-quaking thunder emanating from huge, dense rain clouds, may be like those fierce winds off the great ocean that drive up the surf, or may be like the voice of the devas in the Mahābrahma Heaven. With voices such as these, they lead forth and guide those beings that are capable of being liberated.

They have abandoned any modes of expression associated with scolding that may involve contortion of the brow, the countenance, or the lips. Their speech is neither deficient in any way nor unnecessarily long and redundant. There is no doubt in what they proclaim and their words will certainly be beneficial. Their speech is entirely free of any deceptive statements, any statements vulnerable to refutation, or any other such statements. It is entirely free of these faults and it is heard equally well by those far and near.

The Buddhas are freely able to answer the four types of challenging questions. They explain the four truths, thereby causing beings to gain the four fruits of the path. They establish points of meaning and make statements supported by reasons. They are completely equipped with all of the methods used in speaking. In the many different sorts of matters that they discuss, their meaning is easy to completely comprehend. Whatever they proclaim is entirely clear and never intentionally cryptic or convoluted. Their speech is neither too fast nor too slow. The beginnings and conclusions of each discourse are mutually compatible and invulnerable to anyone's challenges.

4) Envisioning the Effects of the Buddhas' Teaching of Dharma

With speech such as this, they spread forth and proclaim the Dharma which is good in the beginning, middle, and end, imbued with meaning, beneficial, devoted solely to Dharma, and, in all respects, perfect.[328] It is able to cause beings to gain karmic rewards in in this very lifetime. Their discourse is not meaningful only for a time, is such that one can test it for oneself, and is such that will lead to the fulfillment of one's aspirations. Those possessed of profound and sublime wisdom realize it within themselves. It can extinguish in beings the raging fire set ablaze by the three poisons. It is able to rid one of all karmic offenses committed by body, speech, and mind, and it is also well able to open up and reveal the essence of moral virtue, the meditative absorptions, and wisdom.

It begins with mere naming that in turn provokes realization of meaning that then in its own turn causes one to be filled with joy. From this joy, there then arises bliss, and from this bliss, there then arises meditative concentration. From this meditative concentration, there arises a wise knowing in accordance with reality, and from this wise knowing in accordance with reality, one then develops renunciation. Due to having developed this renunciation, one becomes able to destroy the fetters, and due to having destroyed those fetters, one then gains liberation.

In this very manner, this Dharma is caused to unfold in a sequence whereby:

It is well able to open forth and reveal the four bases [of meritorious qualities]: truth, relinquishment, quiescence, and wisdom;

It is able to reveal for beings the means by which they are caused to perfectly fulfill the *pāramitās* of giving, moral virtue, patience, vigor, meditative concentration, and wisdom;

It is able to cause beings to sequentially enter and proceed through the Ground of Joyfulness, the Ground of Stainlessness, the ground of Shining Light, the Ground of Blazing Brilliance, the Difficult-to-Conquer Ground, the Ground of Direct Presence, the Far-Reaching

Ground, the Ground of Immovability, the Ground of Excellent Intelligence, and the Ground of the Dharma Cloud;

It is able to make clear distinctions with regard to the Śrāvaka Disciple Vehicle, the Pratyekabuddha Vehicle, and the Great Vehicle;

It is able to provoke realization of the fruits of the path gained by the stream enterer, once returner, non-returner and arhat;[329]

And it is able too to cause complete success in gaining wealth and happiness in the realms of humans and devas.

This is what constitutes the treasury of meritorious qualities that provides all of the foremost forms of benefit.

5) Instruction on This Type of Contemplative Mindfulness

It is in this manner that one uses right thought in the recollective mindfulness of all buddhas. One abides in a peaceful and quiet place, rids oneself of sensual desire, ill will, dullness and drowsiness, doubtfulness, regret and agitation, and single-mindedly carries on focused mindfulness in which one refrains from generating thoughts that obstruct or cause one to lose meditative absorption. One employs this sort of mind in one's focused mindfulness of the Buddhas. If one's mind sinks, one should raise it up again. If one's mind becomes scattered, one should draw it back into a focused state. One then sees the entire great assembly as if it were always right before one's very eyes.

6) The Importance of Praising the Major Marks and Secondary Signs

When one has not yet managed to enter concentrated meditative absorption, one should always praise the two types of phenomena that consist of the Buddha's major marks and secondary characteristics, using verses to celebrate the qualities of the Buddhas and to cause one's mind to become well trained in this.

a) Verses in Praise of the Buddhas' 32 Marks

Accordingly, there are these lines of verse as follows:

Referring to the marks and characteristics of the Bhagavats
and the karmic causes and conditions by which they acquired them,
I shall use these marks and their corresponding karmic actions
to set forth the praises of these great *āryas*:

The thousand-spoked wheel mark on the feet
is associated with a pure retinue and with giving.
It is because of these causes and conditions
that the many worthies and *āryas* surround them.

The mark of the stable stance of the feet
arises from upholding without fail all goodness one has taken on.
It is because of this that the legions of Māra's armies
are unable to succeed in destroying them.

Their fingers and toes join with proximal webs
and their bodies have the mark of purple-golden coloration.
Because of their skillful practice of the means of attraction,
the great assembly naturally bows in deferential reverence.

Their hands and feet are extremely soft
and the body has the mark of fullness in the seven places.
It is due to giving food that accords with others' wishes
that they are naturally given many offerings.

They have long fingers, broad heels,
and the body has the mark of being large and upright.
This results from abandoning the causes and conditions of killing
and may lead to a life span lasting even up to a kalpa in length.

The hairs of the body grow in an upward and rightward spiral
and the feet have the mark of high arches.
By always advancing in good endeavors,
they thereby acquired the dharma of irreversibility.

They have the gradually tapering legs of the *aiṇeya* antelope
due to always delighting in study and recitation of scriptures.
It is through speaking the Dharma for others
that they rapidly realized the unsurpassable path.

As for having long arms that reach below the knees,
this is due to never being miserly in giving
anything one possesses to whoever seeks to acquire them.
Thus they can teach and guide others in ways suited to their wishes.

Genital ensheathment reflects a treasury of meritorious qualities
associated with skillfully reconciling those who are estranged.[330]
As a result, they acquire a great congregation of humans and devas
and use the pure wisdom eye to create their sons.[331]

Their thin skin that radiates golden light
is associated with giving marvelous apparel and halls.
As a consequence, they acquire an abundance of fine robes
as well as pristine quarters, buildings, and viewing terraces.

The single hair in each pore
and the white hair tuft between the eyes
are associated with serving as a supreme protector.
Hence they are revered throughout the three realms of existence.

They have an upper body like that of a lion
with the two shoulders rounded and full.
These result from always using speech that is pleasing to others.
As a consequence, there is no one who opposes them.

The marks of subaxillary fullness and cognition of all tastes
stem from providing medical care and medicines for the sick.
As a consequence, devas and men all revere and love them
and their bodies remain ever free of disease.

The roundness of the mid-body and the crown's fleshy *uṣṇīṣa* sign
reflect the merit of giving with a harmonious and delighted mind.
As a consequence of exhorting and teaching even the stubborn,
they reign as sovereignly masterful kings of Dharma.

As for the voice like that of a *kalaviṅka* bird,
the broad tongue, and the voice like a Great Brahma Heaven deva,
they are from the speaking of words that are both gentle and true.
They therefore acquire the Great Ārya's eight voice qualities.[332]

Having first brought contemplative thought to bear
and then afterward spoken words of definite truthfulness,
they acquired the lion-like mark.
Hence all who see them trust them and defer to them.

That their teeth are white, straight, and close-set
is because they have always refrained from slighting
those who have previously given offerings.
Hence the minds of those in their retinue are agreeable and unified.

Above and below, they have a total of forty teeth
that, being close-set, have no gaps.
These result from never slandering and not lying.
Hence their disciples' [loyalty] cannot be destroyed.

The pupils and whites of their eyes are clearly delineated
and they have the mark of eyelashes like those of a royal bull.
These are caused by kindly thought and an amicable view of others.
Consequently all observers look on them with a tireless gaze.

Even though a wheel-turning king
who rules over four continents
possesses these major marks and secondary characteristics,
their radiance still cannot compare with that of a buddha.

I pray that the power of the merit from my setting forth praises
of the major marks and the secondary characteristics
may be able to cause everyone
to have purified minds as well as everlasting peace and happiness.

d) Verses in Praise of the Buddhas Secondary Characteristics

The bodhisattva should also engage in contemplative mindfulness of the buddhas by way of their eighty secondary characteristics. Accordingly, there are these lines of verse, as follows:

All buddhas possess the marvelous secondary characteristics,
eighty in number, with which their bodies are adorned.
You should all delight in them
and listen intently as I describe them.

The Bhagavats have round and slender fingers,
nails that are purplish red in hue,
convex in profile, smooth, and glossy,
characteristics of having everything in measureless abundance.

Their veins lie flat, their ankle bones are invisible,
their feet are not skewed in their track,
their gait is like that of the king of lions,
and they are incomparably awe-inspiring to all observers.

When walking, the entire body turns to the right.
They are serene in manner and refined in their deportment.
The parts of their squarely set bodies are orderly in their posture
and their dignified grace inspires fondness and happiness.

Their bodies are firm in tone, but extremely soft.
The articulations of their joints are quite visibly distinct.
When walking, they do not travel in a meandering manner.
All of their sense faculties are fully and perfectly developed.

The flesh on their bodies is extremely taut, finely textured,
freshly radiant, and especially immaculate.
Their physical posture is especially upright, refined,
and devoid of any feature subject to dispraise.

The belly is round, but does not visibly bulge.
The navel, though deep, does not appear to be an orifice.
Its creases manifest as a rightward spiraling swirl.
Their deportment is extremely pure.

The body is free of any blemishes
and the hands and feet are extremely soft.
The lines in the palms are deep and long,
continuous, straight, and lustrous.

The tongue is slender, the face is not too long.
The central incisors are white, rounded, slender, and sharp.
The hue of the lips is like that of the *bimba* fruit.
Their voice is as deep as the king of the wild geese.

The nose is prominent in profile and the eyes are bright and clear.
The eyelashes are close-set and fine, but not in disarray.
The brow is elevated, has eyebrow hair that is soft,
and it is straight and not crooked.

The hair of the brows, being even and straight,
is emblematic of being well aware of the faults in any dharma.
The hair of the brows is smooth and glossy,
a feature emblematic of skillfully liberating and aiding beings.

The ears are full, long, even in shape,
undamaged, and especially pleasing to the eye.
The forehead is broad and straight.
All of the head's features are perfectly formed.

The hair is fine, dense, never in disarray,
the color of the king of the black bees,
clean, pleasantly fragrant, immaculate,
and possessed of three of the marks.

e) Summation on Importance of Such Recollective Contemplation

This has been the description of the eighty secondary characteristics. Because these eighty secondary characteristics are interspersed with and serve to adorn the thirty-two major marks, if one fails to take up contemplative mindfulness of both the thirty-two marks and the eighty secondary characteristics in one's praises of the Buddha's body, then one may lose forever the causal factors conducing to well-being and happiness in the present and future lives.

The End of Chapter Twenty

Chapter 21

Forty Dharmas Exclusive to Buddhas (Part 1)

XXI. Chapter 21: Forty Dharmas Exclusive to Buddhas (Part 1)

A. Introduction to the Forty Dharmas Exclusive to Buddhas

It is in the above-discussed manner that the bodhisattva uses the thirty-two major marks and eighty secondary characteristics in his contemplative mindfulness of the Buddha's physical body. Now one should proceed to mindfulness of the dharmas exemplifying the Buddha's meritorious qualities, namely:

One should also use the forty exclusive dharmas
in one's contemplation of the Buddhas,
for the Buddhas are their Dharma body
and are not merely associated with their physical bodies.

Although the Buddhas possess countless dharmas not held in common with any other persons, there are forty dharmas that, if borne in mind, will cause one to experience joyful happiness. And why [should one bear them in mind]? It is not the case that the Buddhas are their form bodies, for they are rather to be identified with the Dharma body. This accords with this scriptural testimony: "You should not contemplate the Buddha merely in terms of his form body, for it is on the basis of Dharma that one should carry on such contemplation."

As for the forty dharmas exclusive to the Buddhas, they are as follows:[333]

1) Sovereign mastery of the ability to fly;
2) [The ability to manifest] countless transformations;
3) Boundless psychic powers of the sort possessed by *āryas*;
4) Sovereign mastery of the ability to hear sounds;
5) Immeasurable power of knowledge to know others' thoughts;
6) Sovereign mastery in [training and subduing] the mind;
7) Constant abiding in stable wisdom;
8) Never forgetting;
9) Possession of the powers of the vajra samādhi;
10) Thorough knowing of matters that are unfixed;
11) Thorough knowing of matters pertaining to the formless realm's meditative absorptions;
12) The completely penetrating knowledge of all matters associated with eternal cessation;

13) Thorough knowing of the non-form dharmas unassociated with the mind;[334]
14) The great powers *pāramitā;*
15) The [four] unimpeded [knowledges] *pāramitā;*
16) The *pāramitā* of perfectly complete replies and predictions in response to questions;
17) Invulnerability to harm by anyone;
18) Their words are never spoken without a purpose;[335]
19) Their speech is free of errors and mistakes;
20) Complete implementation of the three turnings [of the Dharma wheel] in speaking Dharma;
21) They are the great generals among all *āryas;*
22–25) They are able to remain unguarded in four ways;[336]
26–29) They possess the four types of fearlessness;
30–39) They possess the ten powers;
40) They have achieved unimpeded liberation.

These are the forty dharmas exclusive to the Buddhas. We shall now discuss them more extensively, as below:

B. 1) Sovereign Mastery of the Ability to Fly

As for "sovereign mastery of the ability to fly" all buddhas fly with sovereign mastery, entirely as they wish, and with a manner and speed that are limitless and unimpeded. How is this so? If the Buddha wishes to raise one foot and then the other, walking through space in just such a fashion, then he is immediately able to do so. If he wishes to simply step into space and depart in this manner or if he wishes to simply stand motionlessly in space and depart in this way, he is immediately able to do so.

If he prefers to just sit there peacefully in the full lotus posture and depart like that, then he is also able to leave that way. If he wishes instead to lie down peacefully and then depart, he is able to leave in that way as well.

If he decides to stand upon a precious lotus blossom extending to the very boundaries of empty space, one with a blue *vaiḍūrya* stem, real coral petals, pistils of yellow gold, wish-fulfilling pearls for its pedestal, and countless sorts of surrounding phenomena, one that appears like the sun on first rising—departing in just such a fashion—then he does just that.

Or if, alternatively, he wishes to create through spontaneous psychic transformation a palace like the palaces of the sun or moon, like the supremely marvelous palace of Indra, or like those of the Yāma Heaven devas, the Tuṣita Heaven devas, the Nirmāṇarati Heaven devas, the Paranirmita Vaśavartin Heaven devas, the Brahma Heaven kings, or like the palaces of any of the other devas, and if he then wishes to create any such palaces, sit down within them, and then depart in that fashion [in one of those flying palaces], then he is immediately able to do precisely that.

Then again, if he prefers to use any of the many other means [for flying from one place to another], then he is freely able to depart however he chooses. Hence it is said, "He is able to completely fulfill whatever wishes he makes." Consequently, with but a single step, the Buddhas can pass beyond great trichiliocosms as numerous as the sands of the Ganges.

There are those who claim that the Buddha is able to move beyond some particular number of hundreds of thousands of lands in but a single mind-moment, whereas there are yet others who claim that, if anyone [supposed he could] know that the Buddha could depart such a distance with but a single step and in but a single mind-moment, then that would be [to infer that the Buddha's abilities] could be limited. But the sutras declare that the powers of the Buddhas surpass all limits. One should therefore realize that the sovereign power of the Buddhas to freely fly through empty space is limitless and boundless.

So how is this the case? Given that one of the great *śrāvaka* disciples using his sovereign mastery of the psychic powers is able in a single mind-moment to pass beyond a hundred *koṭis* of Jambudvīpas, Avara-godānīyas, Pūrva-videhas, Uttara-kurus, Four Heavenly Kings Heavens, Trāyastriṃśa Heavens, Yāma Heavens, Tuṣita Heavens, Nirmāṇarati Heavens, Paranirmita Vaśavartin Heavens, and Brahma Heavens—and given that there are a particular number of mind-moments in the wink of an eye and given that one might aggregate enough of these mind-moments to comprise a whole day, seven whole days, a whole month, a whole year, and so forth, on up to a full hundred years, and if in only a single day, such a *śrāvaka* disciple might pass through fifty-three *koṭis* plus two million, nine hundred and sixty-six thousand, that large a number of great trichiliosms, any Buddha would still be able in a mere mind-moment to exceed that number of great trichiliocosms passed through by such a *śrāvaka* disciple in the course of a full hundred years.

Then again, if one were to allow the passage of a single kalpa for each and every grain of sand in the Ganges—and if there was a great *śrāvaka* disciple foremost in psychic powers who, across the course of a life span of kalpas as numerous as the Ganges' sands, passed through in each successive mind-moment just such a number of world systems [as described above]—and if he were to do this for a number of mind-moments equivalent to a day, month, or year, doing so with the free exercise of all of his powers even to the exhaustion of such a number of great kalpas—all of those lands passed through by that great *śrāvaka* disciple during that entire time could still be passed through by a buddha in but a single mind-moment. The Buddhas may freely fly from one place to another with just such a speed as this.

In this, they cannot be obstructed by the iron-ring mountains, the ten jeweled mountains, the stations of the Four Heavenly Kings, the stations of the Trāyastriṃśa Heavens, the stations of the Yāma Heavens, Tuṣita Heavens, Nirmāṇarati Heavens, Paranirmita Vaśavartin Heavens, Brahma World Heavens, Brahma Assembly Heavens, Great Brahma Heavens, Lesser Light Heavens, Limitless Light Heavens, Light-and-Sound Heavens, Lesser Purity Heavens, Measureless Purity Heavens, Universal Purity Heavens, Vast Fruition Heavens, Non-Perception Heavens, Not Vast Heavens, No Heat Heavens, Delightful Vision Heavens, Sublime Vision Heavens, or the Akaniṣṭha Heaven.

[Nor can their flight be obstructed by] the great winds, by the great floods, or by the fires that occur at the end of the kalpa. Nor can it be obstructed by any heavenly dragon, *yakṣa, gandharva, asura, kinnara, mahoraga,* deva, Māra, Brahmā, *śramaṇa,* brahman, or anyone possessed of all the psychic powers. It is therefore said of the Buddhas that they are unimpeded in their ability to fly.

Additionally, by virtue of the sovereign mastery of their flight, they are able to exercise that ability in any manner they wish, by sinking into or emerging from the earth, or by passing through the obstructions presented by stone cliffs, mountains, and such. The Buddha is superior in this ability to any of the other *āryas.* Also, the Buddha is able to make his normal standing body reach in its height on up to the Brahma Heavens. *Śravaka* disciples are unable to match this. There are all manner of differences of this sort.

C. 2) [The Ability to Manifest] Countless Transformations

As for the Buddhas' sovereign mastery in "the ability to manifest transformations," in the matter of manifesting phenomena, they have immeasurable power to do this. The capacity to manifest transformations as possessed by the other classes of *āryas* is both measurable and bounded whereas the Buddhas' capacity to manifest transformations is measureless and unbounded.

The other *āryas* are able, in but a single mind-moment, to manifest a single transformation body whereas the Buddhas are able, in but a single mind-moment, to manifest countless phenomena in whatever way they wish.

This is as described in the *Sutra on the Great Spiritual Powers*: "The Buddha may send forth from his navel a lotus blossom with transformation buddhas sitting atop it that then, in an orderly fashion, fill up all of space on up to the Akaniṣṭha Heaven. The many sorts of transformations created by the Buddhas take all sorts of different forms and all sorts of different shapes and are all created in but a single mind-moment."

Also, *śrāvaka* disciples are able to perform transformations within a thousand lands whereas the Buddhas are able to freely perform transformations within a countless and boundless number of lands and are additionally able to do much more than this, for the Buddhas have gained the solid transformation samādhi. Also, the transformations performed by but one of the Buddhas' bodies are able to occur in worlds as numerous as the sands of the Ganges.

Additionally, a buddha is able in a countless and boundless number of worlds of the ten directions to manifest a buddha being born, taking on a body, dropping to the earth, taking seven steps, leaving the home life, studying the path, defeating Māra's armies, achieving enlightenment, and turning the Dharma wheel. All of these phenomena are created in but a single mind-moment. All of these transformation buddhas are themselves also able to carry out the work of the Buddhas. And the transformation-generated phenomena created by all of those buddhas are themselves countless and boundless.

D. 3) Boundless Psychic Powers of the Sort Possessed by Āryas

Also, the Buddhas have "boundless psychic powers of the sort possessed by *āryas*." As for "the psychic powers possessed by *āryas*," this refers to phenomena such as: radiating light from their bodies that may manifest as raging fire and also pouring forth rains; transforming their length of life however they wish, either lengthening it or shortening it; being able in a single thought to go to the Brahma Heaven; being able to perform transformations of various phenomena, being able to shake the great earth whenever they wish; or being able to ceaselessly radiate light capable of illuminating countless worlds.

Also, "psychic powers possessed by *āryas*" are referred to as such because they are incomparably different from those possessed by common people, because of their being boundless, and because of their going beyond all limits. Although common people may possess some ability to perform transformations of various phenomena, their power to do so is so minor as to be beneath mention here.

A *śrāvaka* disciple may be able to split a thousand lands and then cause them to join back together again, may be able to lengthen his life span to a kalpa or somewhat less than a kalpa in duration and then be able to shorten it, but after having shortened it, he will be unable to make it long again. He may be able in a single mind-moment to go to the brahma worlds of a thousand lands, may be able to freely perform transformations in a thousand lands, may be able to shake the earth in a thousand lands, may be able to ceaselessly radiate light from his body that can illuminate a thousand lands, and, even if his body is destroyed, he may retain the presence of his spiritual powers and their ability to perform transformations just as before, doing so in a thousand lands.

The lesser *pratyekabuddha* is able to perform a myriad transformations in a myriad lands. The middling *pratyekabuddha* is able to perform a million transformations in a million lands. A great *pratyekabuddha* is able to perform the sorts of transformations cited above, doing so throughout all lands in a great trichiliocosm.

The Buddhas, the Bhagavats, are able to perform transformations in worlds more numerous than the Ganges' sands wherein they send forth fire and water from their bodies. They are even able to grind to fine dust worlds as numerous as the Ganges' sands and then cause them to be restored. They are able to abide for a life span of countless kalpas, are able to shorten that life span, and having shortened it, they are then able to lengthen it again. They are able to abide for an immeasurably long period of time. They are able to freely perform transformations such that, in the space of but a single mind-moment, they are able to go to countless and boundless worlds as numerous as the sands in the River Ganges.

They are able to cause their usual body, when standing, to reach all the way up to the Brahma Worlds. They are also able to perform a transformation whereby countless and boundless *asaṃkhyeyas* of worlds are all caused to be transformed into gold, or into silver, or into *vaiḍūrya*, coral, mother-of-pearl, or carnelian. To sum up the essential point, they are freely able in accordance with their wishes to cause them to be transformed into a countless number of precious things.

They are also able in accordance with their wishes to transform the waters of the great oceans in worlds as numerous as the Ganges' sands into milk, ghee, yogurt, or honey. They are also able in but a single mind-moment to transform incalculably many mountains into real gold.

They are also able to shake the heavenly palaces of the desire realm and form realm heavens of countless and boundless worlds. They are also able in but a single mind-moment to cause gold-colored radiance to so universally illuminate an immeasurably great number of worlds that the light from all those suns and moons and heavenly palaces of the desire realm and the form realm no longer appear at all.

Although a buddha may have already passed into nirvāṇa, afterward, he is still freely ever able in all those worlds to remain for however long he wishes, ceaselessly implementing his spiritual powers.

E. 4) Sovereign Mastery of the Ability to Hear Sounds

As for "sovereign mastery in the ability to hear sounds," the Buddhas have sovereign mastery in their ability to hear sounds however they please. Even if there were countless hundreds of thousands of myriads of *koṭis* of musical sounds being simultaneously played and hundreds of thousands of myriads of *koṭis* of beings simultaneously speaking—whether those sounds are far or near, the Buddhas are freely able to hear whichever sounds they please.[337]

If one were to cause all beings in great trichiliocosms as numerous as the Ganges' sands to simultaneously create any given number of hundreds of thousands of myriads of *koṭis* of kinds of music that filled up all those worlds, and if at the same time all beings in worlds as numerous as the Ganges' sands were to fill up all those worlds with the voice of Brahmā, if any buddha wished to hear only one single sound from among all those sounds, then that buddha would be freely able to hear that single sound while not hearing any other sound.

In the case of the sounds heard by *śrāvaka* disciples, if someone possessed of great spiritual powers were to block any given sound, then they would not be able to hear it. In the case of sounds heard by buddhas, even though there might be someone possessed of great spiritual powers seeking to block their hearing some sound, the Buddhas are nonetheless able to hear it.

A *śrāvaka* disciple may be able to hear any sound within a thousand lands. The Buddhas, the Bhagavats, are able to hear even the most subtle sounds even from a distance spanning countlessly and boundlessly many world systems.

A *śrāvaka* disciple possessed of great spiritual powers and abiding in the Brahma World Heavens is able to issue such a great sound that it is capable of pervasively filling a thousand lands. As for the Buddhas, the Bhagavats, it matters not whether they are abiding here or in the Brahma World Heaven, or are instead in yet some other place—their voices are still able to fill up countlessly and boundlessly many world systems. If they wish to cause a particular being to hear the most subtle sound across a distance of countlessly and boundlessly many worlds, they can cause him to hear it and if they wish to prevent someone from hearing a sound, then that person will indeed be unable to hear it at all. Consequently, it is only the Buddhas who have gained sovereign mastery with regard to the hearing of sounds.

F. 5) Immeasurable Power of Knowledge to Know Others' Thoughts

As for "measureless power of sovereign mastery in the ability to know others' thoughts," the Buddhas, the Bhagavats, are completely aware of all the thoughts of all beings of the present existing throughout countlessly and boundlessly many worlds. Others may develop the ability to know someone else's thoughts, but only as represented by the words [contained in others' thoughts]. The Buddhas, however, know others' thoughts in terms of the associated meanings of the words [contained in others' thoughts].

Moreover, others remain unable to know the thoughts of beings in the formless realm, but the Buddhas are able to know them. Although others may possess the ability to know someone else's thoughts, if anyone possessed of great powers wishes to block that ability, then they will no longer be able to know others' thoughts.

Supposing that all beings had developed psychic powers to the same degree as Śāriputra, Maudgalyāyana, or a *pratyekabuddha*. Now suppose that they used all of their collective spiritual powers to block anyone from knowing someone's thoughts. In such a case, a buddha would still be able to break their spiritual powers and would still succeed in knowing that person's thoughts.

Additionally, a buddha is able to use his spiritual powers to completely know any being's superior, middling, and inferior thoughts, his defiled thoughts, and his pure thoughts. Moreover, he is able to know with regard to each thought, the condition taken as the object of that thought, is able to know also the sequential progression of each thought as it moves from one objective condition to another, and is able to comprehensively know all of the conditions associated with any given thought. Also, he is able to know any being's thoughts in accordance with their true character.

It is on these bases that the Buddhas are acknowledged to have immeasurable powers to completely know the thoughts of others.

G. 6) Sovereign Mastery in [Training and Subduing] the Mind

As for the Buddhas' "*pāramitā* of being foremost in training and subduing the mind," they well know all of the *dhyānas*, samādhis, and liberations and well understand entry into them, abiding in them, and emerging from them. Whether a buddha is immersed in meditative absorption or not, should he wish to focus his mind on a single object, then he is freely able to focus upon it for however long he wishes and then is able to change from this object to focusing on some other condition, freely abiding in that focus for however long he wishes.

If the Buddha, abiding in his normal thoughts, wishes to cause others to remain unaware of his thoughts, then they would be unable to know them. Even if all beings had perfected the ability to know others' minds to a degree comparable to the ability to know others' thoughts as possessed by a king of the Great Brahma Heaven, a great *śrāvaka* disciple, or a *pratyekabuddha*, and they all then caused a single person to acquire their collective abilities in this, and this person then wished to know the normal thought of a buddha, so long as that buddha did not permit it, that person would still be unable to acquire that knowledge.

This is as described in the *Sutra on the Seven Expedients*: "The practitioner:

> Well knows the signs of meditative absorption;
> Well knows the signs of abiding in meditative absorption;
> Well knows the signs of emerging from meditative absorption;
> Well knows the signs of stable and secure meditative absorption;
> Well knows the signs of the stations of practice in meditative absorption;
> Well knows the signs of the development of meditative absorption;
> And well knows what is and is not appropriate to the dharmas of meditative absorption."[338]

This is what is meant by the Buddhas' "*pāramitā* of being foremost in training and subduing the mind."

H. 7) Constant Abiding in Stable Wisdom

As for the Buddhas' "constant abiding in stable wisdom," the Buddhas' stable wisdom is constant and unshakable and their mindfulness is always maintained in their minds. And why is this the case? It is because they first know and then act, because they freely dwell on whichever object they choose while having no doubt in their actions, because they have cut off all afflictions, and because they have gone utterly beyond the realm[339] of movement itself.

This is as the Buddha told Ānanda:

> The Buddha, in this one evening, gains *anuttarasamyaksaṃbodhi* and proceeds then to teach the path to the ending of suffering to everyone in the world, whether they be a deva, Māra, Brahmā, a *śramaṇa*, or a brahman, and then, in the end, finally enters the nirvāṇa without residue.
>
> During the interim, the Buddha, with respect to every feeling, is aware of its arising, is aware of its abiding, is aware of its birth and

is aware of its cessation. With respect to all perceptions,[340] all tactile contact, all ideation, and all mental discursion, he is aware of their arising, aware of their abiding, aware of their birth, and aware of their cessation.

Māra the Evil One,[341] constantly and without resting, followed along after the Buddha both day and night for seven years yet was never in all that time able to come upon any shortcomings of the Buddha and was never able to observe an instance of the Buddha's mindfulness not abiding in a state of stable wisdom. This is what is meant by the Buddha's constant abiding in the practice of stable wisdom.

I. 8) Never Forgetting

As for the dharma of "never forgetting," because the Buddhas have gained the dharma of irreversibility, have reached a penetrating understanding of the five categorical repositories of dharmas,[342] and have acquired the unsurpassable Dharma, the Buddhas never forget.

With respect to all that the Buddhas have realized beneath the bodhi tree and have then subsequently acquired up to the time when they enter the nirvāṇa without residue, no matter whether it be a deva, Māra, Brahmā, a *śramaṇa,* a brahman, or some other *ārya,* there is no one who is able to cause the Buddhas to forget anything at all.

This is as described in the *Sutra on the Seal of Dharma*: "As for that which is realized at the *bodhimaṇḍa,* this is known as the genuine realization and there is no dharma superior to it."

This is also as described in the *Horripilation Sutra*: "Śāriputra. If anyone could claim truthfully that they do not have any aspect of Dharma that they forget, I would be the one who could make that claim. How is this so? I alone do not forget anything whatsoever."

This is what is intended when it is said that the Buddhas never forget Dharma.

J. 9) Possession of the Powers of the Vajra Samādhi

As for "the vajra samādhi," the vajra samādhi of all the Buddhas, the Bhagavats, is one of the exclusive dharmas, [so named]:

Because it cannot be destroyed by anything;
Because there is no place where it can be obstructed;
Because it is associated with right and universal knowledge;
Because it destroys all hindrances to Dharma;
Because it is able to equally penetrate [all dharmas];
Because it brings about the power to acquire the benefit of all meritorious qualities;
And because it is the most supreme of all *dhyāna* samādhis.

As for its being called "the vajra samādhi" because there is nothing that can destroy it, it is like the precious vajra gem that cannot be crushed by anything at all. This samādhi is just like this. There is no dharma capable of destroying it. It is therefore known as "the vajra samādhi."

Question: Why is it that it cannot be destroyed?

Response: This is because there is nothing anywhere that obstructs it. It is just as with Indra's vajra that meets no obstruction anywhere. This samādhi is just like that.

Question: Why is this samādhi said to have nothing anywhere that obstructs it?

Response: Because it possesses a right and utterly penetrating comprehension of all dharmas. All buddhas, abiding in this samādhi, are able to utterly penetrate all of the dharmas subsumed within the five categorical repositories of dharmas: all dharmas of the past, of the present, of the future, those that transcend the three periods of time, and those that are ineffable dharmas. It is for this reason that it is said to meet with no obstruction anywhere.

If it were the case that, while abiding in this samādhi, all buddhas still did not have an utterly penetrating comprehension of all dharmas, then that would be a case of still having obstructions. But, in truth, this is not the case. It is therefore said to not be obstructed by anything whatsoever.

Question: How is it that this samādhi brings about a penetrating comprehension of all dharmas?

Response: It is because this samādhi is able to open up all obstructive dharmas, namely the obstacle of the afflictions, the obstacles to meditative absorption, and the obstacles to knowledge. Because it is able to open up all obstructions, it is therefore said to bring about an utterly penetrating comprehension of all dharmas.

Question: How is it that this samādhi is able to open up all obstructions whereas other samādhis remain unable to do so?

Response: This samādhi is well able to penetrate three[343] dharmas:

> Because it is able to destroy the mountain of afflictions so that nothing remains of them;
>
> Because it brings about the right and universal comprehension of all dharmas;
>
> And because it brings about the thoroughgoing attainment of the liberation of the indestructible resolve.

It is for these reasons that this samādhi is said to be able to open up all obstructions.

Question: How is it that this samādhi is able to equally penetrate these three dharmas?[344]

Response: This is because, when one abides in this samādhi, one gains the power by which one is then able to acquire every sort of meritorious quality. None of the other samādhis possess this sort of power. It is for this reason that this samādhi is able to "equally penetrate" [all dharmas].

Question: How is it that, abiding in this samādhi, one gains the power by which one is then able to acquire every sort of meritorious quality?

Response: This samādhi is the foremost among all meditative absorptions. It is because of this that, abiding in this samādhi, one is able to gain every sort of meritorious quality.

Question: How is it that this samādhi is foremost among all samādhis?

Response: This samādhi is foremost among all meditative absorptions because it is produced through the possession of measurelessly and boundlessly many roots of goodness.

Question: How is it that this samādhi is produced through the possession of measurelessly and boundlessly many roots of goodness?

Response: This samādhi is possessed only by those who are equipped with all-knowledge. It has not been acquired by anyone else. Hence it is known as "the vajra samādhi."

The End of Chapter Twenty-One

Chapter 22
Forty Dharmas Exclusive to Buddhas (Part 2)
Challenges to the Reality of Omniscience

XXII. Chapter 22: Forty Dharmas Exclusive to Buddhas (Part 2)

A. Q: Your Claim That Omniscience Exists Is False for these Reasons

Question: You claim that only those possessed of all-knowledge possess the vajra samādhi and no one else has it. If this samādhi was only possessed by someone who has all-knowledge and no one else possessed it, then this samādhi does not even exist. Why? Because there is no one who possesses all-knowledge.

And why is this? It is because the dharmas that might be known are measureless and boundless whereas the knowledge that might know them is measurable and bounded. It should not be the case that this measurable and bounded knowledge could know measurelessly many phenomena.

For instance, on the present-day continent of Jambudvīpa, the number of beings dwelling in its waters and on its lands are beyond count. Also, consider the three categories of beings, whether male, female, or neither male nor female, those still in the womb, the children, the young and strong, the frail and old, and also the dharmas associated with their suffering, happiness, and so forth. Also, consider all of the mind and mental dharmas of the past, future, and present, as well as all good and bad karmic actions accumulated in the past, present, and future, all the karmic retributions undergone in the past, present, and future, all the births and deaths of the myriad creatures, and also all of Jambudvīpa's mountains, rivers, springs, ponds, grasses, trees, dense forests, roots, stems, branches, leaves, blossoms, and fruit. The things that can be known are limitlessly many.

The same is true for the other three continents. And just as this is the case with these four continents, it is also the case throughout all of the worlds of the great trichiliocosm. And just as this is the case with all of the worlds of the great trichiliocosm, so too is it also the case for all things that can be known in all other worlds.

As for the number of the worlds, that matter alone is measureless, boundless, and difficult to know. How much the more so is this the case for all of the sentient and insentient beings and all other categories of things on the Jambudvīpa continents in all those worlds.

For these reasons, one should realize that the things that can be known are countless and limitless and, because of that, it cannot be that there is anyone at all who is possessed of all-knowledge.

Suppose that one were to claim that the knowledge [of someone who is omniscient] is possessed of such great power that, because it is unimpeded with respect to those dharmas it cognizes, it is able to pervasively know all those dharmas in just the same manner as empty space is able to reach everywhere in its universal pervasion of all things. Suppose too that one were to claim that, because of this, it ought to be the case that there truly is such a thing as an omniscient person. If one were to make such a claim, this still could not be so, for even if knowledge could possess such a great power as this, even such great knowledge as this would still remain unable to know itself in just the same way that one's fingertip remains unable to touch itself. Therefore, there is no such thing as all-knowledge.

If, [in response to this], one were to claim that there is yet some other knowledge possessed of the capacity to know this knowledge, this could not be the case, either. And why not? That is because this proposition would then fall into the fallacy of infinite regression. Knowledge either knows itself or is known by something other. They cannot both be true.

If, as you say, this knowledge is somehow possessed of measureless power, because of the fact that it still remains unable to know itself, one really cannot claim that it is possessed of measureless power. Therefore there is no such thing as some knowledge possessed of the ability to know all dharmas.

If there is no such thing as some knowledge possessed of the ability to know all dharmas, then there could not be anyone possessed of all-knowledge. And why is this the case? It is because anyone possessed of all-knowledge [could only be so by] availing himself of just such a [nonexistent] knowledge that knows all dharmas.

Furthermore, the dharmas that can be known are measureless and boundless. Even if one were to employ the combined knowing capacity of a hundred thousand myriads of *koṭis* of wise men, they would still be unable to exhaustively know them all. How much the less could a single person do so. Therefore there is no such thing as any single person who is able to know all dharmas and there is no such thing as "all-knowledge."

If one were to claim that it is not on the basis of comprehensively knowing every mountain, river, being, or non-being that we speak of someone possessed of all-knowledge, but rather it is simply on the basis of exhaustively knowing all scriptures that one speaks of someone possessed of all-knowledge, this is also wrong. How so? It is because, within the sphere of the Buddha's Dharma, one does not speak of the concepts treated in the Vedas and other such scriptures. If the Buddha really were, [in this sense of the term], a man possessed of all-knowledge, then he should make use of the Vedas and other such scriptures, but in truth, he does not use these, and so, because of this, the Buddha is not an all-knowing man.

Moreover, the scriptures comprising the four Vedas are themselves measurable and limited in their scope and, even so, there is not even anyone capable of exhaustively knowing those scriptures, how much the less could there be anyone who exhaustively knows all the scriptures in existence. Therefore there is no such thing as a person possessed of "all-knowledge" [even in this limited sense of the term].

Moreover, there are scriptures that are able to cause the proliferation of desire and that devote themselves to such things as dance and music and such. If a person possessed of all-knowledge were to become knowledgeable with respect to these matters, then he would be subjected to the arising of desire. Scriptures of these sorts constitute the causes and conditions for the arising of desire. Where there is a given cause, there must necessarily be the corresponding result [ensuing from it]. If a person possessed of all-knowledge does not know these matters, then he could not be validly referred to as someone possessed of all-knowledge.

Furthermore, there are scriptures that are able to influence a person to become full of hate and to take delight in deceiving others, specifically such works as those classics concerned with ruling the world. Were one to become knowledgeable about such matters, then one would come to be possessed of hatred. How is the case? It is because, where there is such a given cause, then there must necessarily be the corresponding result ensuing from it. And were one to not know such matters, then one could not be validly referred to as possessed of all-knowledge. One should therefore realize that there really is no such thing as a person who is possessed of all-knowledge.

Additionally, it is not necessarily the case that a buddha could exhaustively know matters pertaining to the future. Take for instance my present challenge to the plausibility of there being anyone who is omniscient. The Buddha has no scriptural record of having predicted that in the future there would be this particular man of this particular caste from this particular clan in this particular place who would on these particular grounds challenge the plausibility of there being anyone who might be omniscient. If one were to claim that the Buddha exhaustively knows such things, why did he not speak of this matter? If he is the one who spoke these scriptures, then those scriptures should have a record of such matters, but he did not speak of these matters. Therefore one knows that he was not omniscient.

Moreover, if the Buddha exhaustively knew future matters, then he should have known in advance that, after Devadatta left home to become a monk, he would then create a schism in the Sangha. If he had knowledge of that, then he should not have allowed Devadatta to become a monk. Also, the Buddha did not know that Devadatta would use a stick to pry loose a boulder [that would roll down and draw blood from the Buddha's foot]. If the Buddha had known of this matter in advance, then he should not have been walking in that place.

Additionally, the Buddha failed to know in advance that Ciñca, the brahman woman, would slander him by accusing him of having had sexual relations with her. If the Buddha had known of this in advance, then he should have told the bhikshus that, in the future, there would be just such an occurrence.

Also, there was the case of the *brahmacārin* who, because he was jealous of the Buddha, killed a *brahmacārin* woman named Sundarī in another place and then buried her in a trench in the vicinity of the Jeta Grove. The Buddha did not know of this matter. If he had known of this, then he should have sought among the brahmans to [find a way to] see that her life would be saved.

The Buddha went to that place beneath which Devadatta was about to set loose the falling boulder and he also failed to announce in advance the incidents having to do with the brahman woman and the *brahmacārin* woman. Because he did not know of these matters, one should realize that the Buddha did not exhaustively know the future. Therefore he could not possibly have been omniscient.

Furthermore, the Buddha once entered a brahman village seeking food on the alms round but then had to leave with an empty bowl. He was unable then to know in advance that Māra would so turn the minds of the villagers against him that he would be unable to obtain anything to eat. If the Buddha had known of this matter, then he should not have entered that brahman village. Therefore one knows that the Buddha did not exhaustively know how matters would transpire in the future.

Moreover, because King Ajātaśatru wished to harm the Buddha, he released a drunken elephant used to guard the treasury.[345] Because the Buddha did not know of this matter, he entered the city of Rājagṛha on his alms round. If he had known of this matter in advance, then he should not have gone into the city. Therefore he did not have knowledge of future matters. Because he did not have knowledge of future matters, he therefore could not have been omniscient.

Additionally, the Buddha did not know of the causal circumstances involved in Agnidatta's invitation to the Buddha. Consequently he immediately accepted that invitation and then led the bhikshus to the state of Verañjā. Because this brahman had forgotten his prior issuance of that invitation, he caused the Buddha to eat only horse fodder. If the Buddha had known of this matter in advance, then he should not have accepted that invitation on account of which he spent the entire three months [of the rains retreat] surviving only on horse fodder. We know therefore that the Buddha did not have knowledge of future matters. Because he did not have knowledge of future matters, he therefore could not have been omniscient.

Also, because the Buddha accepted Sunakṣatra as a disciple, he could not have had knowledge of future matters. This man possessed an obdurately evil mind, made himself difficult to teach, and did not believe the words of the Buddha. If the Buddha had known of this, how could he have accepted him as a disciple? Because he accepted him as a disciple, then he could not have known future matters. Because he did not have knowledge of future matters, he therefore could not have been omniscient.

Furthermore, if the Buddha had been omniscient, then, in order to prevent inevitable future instances of moral transgressions, he would have formulated his moral precepts in advance. Because he had no prior knowledge of the causal circumstances that eventually led to the formulation of each particular moral precept, it was only after someone had committed such a transgression that he then subsequently laid down these moral regulations. This being the case, he could not have known of future matters. Because he did not have knowledge of future matters, he therefore could not have been omniscient.

Moreover, in the Dharma set forth by the Buddha, it is solely on the basis of seniority in years of monastic ordination that, within the community, one sits more toward the front and is accorded reverence and obeisance [by those of fewer years of seniority]. One is not acknowledged as of greater eminence merely on the basis of one's venerable age, one's noble birth, the stature of one's clan, one's meritorious qualities, the level of wisdom one has developed, the degree of learning one has achieved, the particular *dhyāna* absorptions one has entered, the fruits of the path one has gained, the fetters one has cut off, or the spiritual powers one has acquired.

If the Buddha had really been someone possessed of all-knowledge, then he would have accorded eminence, higher priority in the receipt of offerings, and stature in receipt of reverential obeisance on the basis of one's venerable age, one's noble birth, the stature of one's clan, one's meritorious qualities, the level of wisdom one has developed, the degree of learning one has achieved, the particular *dhyāna* absorptions one has entered, the fruits of the path one has gained, the fetters one has cut off, and the spiritual powers one has acquired. If the Buddha had made stipulations of this sort, then that would qualify as having established a well-regulated community.

Regarding the matter of years of monastic ordination seniority, this is the principle by which a practitioner of the path ordained for only five years is enjoined to accord reverential obeisance to a monk ordained for six years.

As for the issue of nobility of birth caste, the world has four classes of beings: *brahmans, kṣatriyas, vaiśyas,* and *śūdras. Śūdras* are enjoined to revere *vaiśyas, kṣatriyas,* and *brahmans. Vaiśyas* ought to pay obeisance to *kṣatriyas* and *brahmans. Kṣatriyas* are supposed to pay reverential obeisance to *brahmans.*

As for the status of clans, there are the artisan clans, the business-and-trade clans, the merchant clans, the clans led by those of senior status, the clans of great officials, royal clans, and so forth. Among them, the members of lesser-status clans are supposed to revere members of the eminent clans. This being the case, when those from poor and base clans leave the home life to become monks, they should be enjoined to pay reverence to monks from wealthy and noble clans.

With respect to meritorious qualities, whoever has broken moral precepts should be enjoined to revere and bow in formal obeisance to those who uphold the moral precepts. Those who strictly observe the moral precepts should not be bowing in reverence to anyone who has broken the moral precepts.

Those who do not practice the twelve *dhūta* austerities[346] should bow in reverence to those who are practitioners of the twelve *dhūta* austerities. Those who are not perfectly complete in their practice of the *dhūta* practices should bow in reverence to those who are perfect in their practice of the *dhūta* austerities.

As for the matter of wisdom, people devoid of wisdom should bow in reverence to those possessed of wisdom. With regard to learning, those of shallow learning should bow in reverence to those who have achieved a high level of learning. Those who do not recite many scriptures should bow in reverence to those who are able to recite many sutras from memory.

As for the fruits of the path, the stream enterer should bow in reverence to the *sakṛdāgāmin* and it should proceed in this fashion on up to [the circumstance where realizers of the first three fruits of the path are enjoined to] bow in reverence to the arhat. As for all of the common people, they should bow in reverence to anyone who has gained any of the fruits of the path.

Those who have severed fewer of the fetters as well as those who have not yet severed any of the fetters should all bow in reverence to those who have severed many of the fetters.

Regarding the matter of spiritual powers, if one has not yet acquired any of the spiritual powers, he should then be bowing in obeisance to whomever has already acquired spiritual powers.

If the Buddha had skillfully set forth such sequentially ranked protocols regarding the making of offerings and the according of reverence, then his proclamations on these matters would be of a superior order. But, in truth, he did not do so. One can therefore know that the Buddha was not omniscient.

Furthermore, the Buddha was not even able to know all matters having to do with the present. If you were to ask me how I know that the Buddha did not have knowledge of present-era matters, then I would now inform you as follows:

There were beings whose fetters were but slight, who had no karmic obstacles, who were free of the eight difficulties, who were capable of practicing deep dharmas, and who were able to be successful in the cultivation of right Dharma, and yet the Buddha did not realize this. After the Buddha had attained enlightenment and was first on the verge of proclaiming the Dharma, he gave rise to the following doubt:

> The Dharma that I have gained is extremely profound, recondite, far-reaching, sublime, quiescent, difficult to know, difficult to comprehend, and such as only the wise might be able to realize inwardly. The beings in this world are attached by their desires to worldly matters. That there might be any among them who might be able to cut off their afflictions, extinguish craving, and develop renunciation—this would be the rarest of possibilities. If I were to expound the Dharma, beings would fail to comprehend it. Such an endeavor would be but a useless experiencing of wearisome hardship.

And so the Buddha generated just such a doubt even though there were in fact beings whose fetters were but slight, who had no karmic obstacles, who were free of the eight difficulties, who were capable of practicing deep dharmas, and who were able to be successful in the cultivation of right Dharma. Because the Buddha was unable to know of the existence of such beings, one should therefore know that the Buddha failed to know matters having to do with the present time.

The Buddha also thought as follows: "Previously, when I was practicing ascetic austerities, the five bhikshus made offerings to me and supported me. It is only appropriate that I first benefit them. Where are they now?" After he had this thought, a deva informed him, "They are now in Benares, in the place known as 'Deer Park.'"

Because of this, one knows that the Buddha did not even know of matters having to do with the present. If he failed to know of matters having to do with the present, then we can know from this that the Buddha could not have been omniscient.

Furthermore, after he had attained enlightenment, the Buddha accepted the invitation to expound on Dharma and then had this thought, "As I now proceed to proclaim the Dharma, who is it that ought to be the first to hear it?" He then had another thought, "Udraka Rāmaputra—this is a man of sharp wisdom, one who might easily become enlightened."

By this time, that man had already died and yet the Buddha nonetheless went in search of him. A deva then informed him, "His life came to an end just last night." The Buddha thought again and, having reflected, he decided he wanted to liberate Ārāḍa Kālāma. A deva then told him, "This man died seven days ago."

If the Buddha had been omniscient, he should have known beforehand that these men had already died, but in truth he did not know these events had happened. Because the Buddha did not know about past matters, he could not have been omniscient.

The methods employed by an omniscient man would be such that he should strive to bring about the liberation of those capable of achieving liberation while also setting aside those incapable of success in this.

Moreover, in place after place, the Buddha spoke in terms revealing the presence of doubts on his part. Take for example the city of Pāṭaliputra that he said was bound to be destroyed by one of three causes: by flood, by fire, or by a conspiracy between insiders and outsiders. If the Buddha had really been omniscient, then he should not have had instances where his speech was marked by the presence of doubts. One knows therefore that he could not have been omniscient.

Additionally, the Buddha inquired of the bhikshus, "What matter have you all come together to discuss?" He asked questions of this sort. If he were omniscient, then he should not have asked about matters of this sort. Because he was compelled to ask others [in order to know of these matters], then he could not have been omniscient.

Also, the Buddha engaged in self-praise while deprecating others. This is as described in the sutras, "The Buddha told Ānanda, 'I alone am foremost, without a peer, unequaled by anyone.'"[347]

He told the bhikshus, "The Nirgranthas and others of that sort are base and evil people who have perfected the five types of deviant dharmas. The Nirgranthas and such have no faith, have no sense of shame, have no dread of blame, and are people of but little learning who are indolent and possessed of only scant mindfulness and shallow wisdom."

He also discussed all manner of impermissible endeavors engaged in by *brahmacārins*, by Nirgranthas, and by the disciples and other followers of the non-Buddhist traditions.

Self-praise and deprecation of others is a behavior of which even common people of the world are ashamed. How much the more so should this be the case for someone who is omniscient. Because the Buddha engaged in behaviors of this sort, he could not have been omniscient.

Furthermore, comparing beginnings and endings, one finds that the Buddhist scriptures are self-contradictory. Take for instance the statements in the sutras in which, on the one hand, the Buddha claims, "Bhikshus, I am one who has newly discovered the path." Then, on the other hand, he claims, "I have attained that path which has previously been attained by all buddhas of antiquity."

Even wise worldly people abandon any tendency to contradict themselves through chronological inconsistencies. How much the less should it be that a monastic possessed of all-knowledge could stumble into such chronological self-contradictions. Because the Buddha fell into chronological inconsistencies, one should realize that he could not possibly have been omniscient. Therefore your claim that the vajra samādhi is only acquired by omniscient men is wrong, this because there is no such thing as an omniscient person. Nor can one establish any case for the existence of some sort of omniscience samādhi.

B. A: Wrong. As I Shall Now Explain, The Buddha Truly Is Omniscient

Response: You should not speak this way. The Buddha truly is omniscient. And how is this so? In general, all dharmas are comprised of five categorical repositories of dharmas, namely: past dharmas, future dharmas, present dharmas, dharmas that transcend the three periods of time, and ineffable dharmas. It is only a buddha who completely knows all these dharmas in accordance with reality.

I shall now respond to your earlier challenge that asserts, because knowable dharmas are measureless and boundless, there are no omniscient people. Insofar as knowable dharmas might be measureless and boundless, the corresponding knowledge is also measureless and boundless. There is no fault in claiming that it is by means of measureless and boundless knowledge that one may know measureless and boundless dharmas.

As for your earlier assertion that knowing should somehow also involve a knowledge that knows [itself] and that this would entail the fallacy of infinite regress, I shall now respond, as follows:

It should be the case that dharmas are known by one's cognition. This cognition is similar to what is referenced when the world's common people describe themselves in this way: "I am a knowledgeable person," "I am someone with no knowledge," "I am someone possessed of only a coarse type of knowledge," or "I am someone who possesses subtle knowledge."

One should realize from these circumstances that it is with one's own cognitive ability that one knows [the character of one's own] knowledge. This being the case, there is no fallacy of infinite regress involved here. This is just a case of using one's own present cognitive ability to know one's past knowledge. It is in this way that one can exhaustively know all dharmas without any omissions.

Also, this is just like when someone counts others [in addition to oneself], thus reaching [for instance a total of] ten [people in all]. The capacity to know is just like that. For knowing to thereby know both itself and others is thus a concept free of any fault. This is also analogous to when a lamp is able to illuminate both itself and other things as well.

As for your contention that even the aggregated knowing capacity of a hundred thousand myriads of *koṭis* of wise people could not exhaustively know all dharmas, how much the less might a single person be able to know them—this is wrong. How is this so? An omniscient person is able to know the many things. Although there may be some additional multitude of people, if they have no cognitive ability, they won't know much of anything.

This is comparable to a situation in which there was a group of a hundred thousand blind men. [Even together], they still could not get hired as guides, but just one single person with good eyes might well be able to serve as a guide. Consequently, as regards your challenge to [the plausibility of omniscience on the part of] a single person, even in a situation where many knowers might be involved, they would still have no knowledge at all compared to the Buddha's capacities in this regard. Therefore your position as stated is erroneous.

As for your contention that, because the Buddha does not discuss the Vedas and other such non-Buddhist scriptures, he must therefore not be omniscient—I shall now respond to that as follows:

The Vedas are entirely lacking in the dharma of [liberation achieved through] skillful realization of nirvāṇa.[348] They contain only all manner of conceptual elaboration. Since what the Buddhas proclaim is all entirely devoted to the skillful realization of nirvāṇa, even though the Buddha is already well aware of the contents of the Vedas and other such scriptures, the Buddha does not discuss such things because those [Vedic] teachings have no capacity to lead anyone to the skillful realization of nirvāṇa.

Question: The Vedas *do* contain discussions of the skillful realization of nirvāṇa. Before the arising of this world, all was darkness and nothing whatsoever existed. In the beginning there existed a great man who appeared like the rising of the sun. If one was able to see him, then one could be liberated from the difficulty of being subject to dying.

[The Vedas] contain yet more guidance on these matters. They state that, because one's person is but small, then one's spiritual soul is correspondingly small. However, if one's person is great, then one's spiritual soul will be correspondingly great in scope, for the body is the home of the spiritual soul that always abides within it. If one uses wisdom to untie the bonds restraining one's spiritual soul, one will then gain liberation. Therefore one should realize from this that the Vedas *do* contain teachings leading to liberation through attainment of nirvāṇa.

Response: This is simply not so. Why not? The Vedic scriptures are tied up with the four inverted views. The world is impermanent and yet they posit the existence of a separate and permanent world. They claim that only one or two sacrifices to their deva [is insufficient and] conduces to falling away from it, but with a third sacrifice, one will not be subject to falling away from it. This scenario involves the inverted view that falsely ascribes permanence to what is itself impermanent.

The world is a place of suffering and yet the Vedas claim the existence of a sphere of eternal bliss. This is just an instance of the inverted view that falsely ascribes bliss to what is inherently bound up with suffering.

The Vedas also claim that one's soul may transform into one's son and be subject through prayer to an extended lifetime of a hundred years. But a "son" is another person, so how could it constitute a self? This is just an instance of the inverted view that falsely ascribes selfhood to what is not actually a self.

They also claim that one's body is possessed of the foremost level of purity and so incomparable in this respect that not even the purity of gold, silver, or precious gems can approach the purity of the body. This is just an instance of the inverted view that falsely ascribes purity to what is devoid of purity.

If one holds inverted views, then [one's views] are devoid of reality. [If such teachings] are devoid of reality, how could they possess [a path to] nirvāṇa? Therefore the Vedas are devoid of any good methods for attaining nirvāṇa.

Question: The Vedas assert that whoever is able to know the Vedas becomes purified and possessed of peace and security. How then can you state that they have no good methods for attaining nirvāṇa?

Response: Although the Vedas assert that whoever knows the Vedas will gain peace and security, this is not ultimate liberation. Rather, this is but an envisioning of liberation projected onto another body. This claim bases itself on the idea that existence in the long-life heavens constitutes liberation. Therefore the Vedas truly contain no means to achieve liberation.

Furthermore, the teachings in the Vedas generally embody three types of concepts: The first involves chants and prayers. The second involves the utterance of praises. The third involves the principles of their dharma.

"Chants and prayers" refers to praying, "May I be caused to obtain a wife and sons, cows, horses, gold, silver, and precious jewels."

"Utterance of praises" refers to statements such as, "Oh, you, the spirit of fire with your black head, your red neck, and your yellow body—you abide eternally in the five great elements of living beings."

"Principles of their dharma" refers to teachings stating that one should do this and abstain from doing that.

Just as with their [erroneous teaching that] fire was first received from the Pleiades, so too, in truth, their methods of using chants and prayers and utterances of praises are all devoid of [any means to achieve] nirvāṇa's liberation. How is this so? Covetous attachment to worldly pleasures, [offerings of] burning ghee, spells, and incantations—these are all devoid of genuine wisdom. Since these do not cut off the afflictions, how could [the Vedas] have [the means to achieve] liberation?

Question: The dharmas in the Vedas have come forth from antiquity and are deserving of the foremost degree of faith. As for your contention that they have no good methods by which one might reach nirvāṇa, they are therefore not fit to be believed, this is wrong. Why?

Whereas the Buddha's Dharma has only recently emerged into the world, the Vedas have come down from long distant antiquity and have always prevailed in the world. Therefore, given that ancient dharmas are deserving of belief and newly arisen dharmas are not deserving of belief, your claim that the Vedas are devoid of any good methods by which one might realize nirvāṇa—this is wrong.

Response: Their relative antiquity is no justification for faith. Ignorance tends to come first whereas right knowledge comes only later. Erroneous views emerge first whereas right views emerge later. One cannot have faith in ignorance and erroneous views simply because they happened to emerge first nor can one deem right knowledge and right views to be unbelievable simply because they emerged later. This is analogous to there first being mud and only later lotuses, first being disease and only later a cure. Matters of these sorts are not worthy of being valued simply because they happened to appear first. Therefore, as for your contention that, because the Vedas came first and the Buddha's Dharma came later, the latter is unworthy of belief, this is a fallacy.

Furthermore, Dīpaṃkara Buddha and the other buddhas of the past all came into the world earlier. Their Dharma principles emerged in antiquity whereas the Vedas actually came forth only later. If you insist on relying on chronological primacy and long history as your bases for according esteem, then the Buddhas and their Dharma should be most highly valued.

Question: You claim it is because the Vedas have no good methods for reaching nirvāṇa that they are therefore not discussed in the Buddha's Dharma. But if the Buddha had really already known they are unable to lead to nirvāṇa, why did he bother to become knowledgeable about them? If in fact he was not *already* knowledgeable about them, he could not have been omniscient. Both stances are faulty.

Response: Your claim is wrong. The Buddha knew from early on that the Vedas have no good methods for reaching nirvāṇa. It is for this reason that he neither discussed them nor practiced what they teach.

Question: If it really was because the Buddha already knew there is no benefit to be had through the Vedas that he therefore instructed others not to cultivate their teaching, what was the point in his acquiring knowledge about them?

Response: People possessed of great knowledge should thoroughly distinguish between the correct path and the erroneous path. It is because one wishes to cause countless beings to go beyond dangerous and bad paths that one takes up the practice of the right path. This is analogous to a guide who skillfully distinguishes between errant paths and the right path.

The Buddha is just the same in this respect. Since he himself had already succeeded in escaping the dangerous path of birth, aging, and death and also wished to cause other beings to escape from it as well, he knew well the genuine eightfold path of the Āryas and also knew the dangerous and bad paths of the Vedas and other such teachings. It was in order to facilitate others' abandonment of deviant and bad paths and in order to encourage their practice of the correct path that, [with regard to the Vedas], he merely became knowledgeable about them, but did not discuss them.

This is analogous to the situation with farmers who plant their fields and then, with the arrival of autumn, reap a harvest that may also happen to include a few useless weeds. The Buddha is like this as well. For the sake of achieving success in the unsurpassable path, he cultivates assiduously and vigorously and consequently gains the path of bodhi while incidentally gaining knowledge of the Vedas and other such erroneous paths. Hence there is no fault on his part in any of this.

As for your previous statement claiming that no single person can completely know the four Vedas, this challenge of yours is false. People of the world each have the power of memory. There are those who, in a single day, can only recite five verses from memory, whereas others can recite one or two hundred verses from memory. If a particular person who cannot even recite ten verses from memory then holds the opinion that nobody could be able to recite from memory a hundred or more than a hundred verses, this would be an untruthful claim. It is because people such as yourself are unable to completely know the Vedas that you then claim nobody knows them.

If someone observes that some other person was unable to ford a particular river and then claims that nobody can cross that river, this person's statement on the matter does not qualify as correct speech. Why not? It is because there will naturally be some other person possessed of great strength who can indeed cross that river. This case is just like that. Even if one supposes that other [ordinary people] would be unable to entirely know [the Vedas], what fault is there in stipulating that someone possessed of all-knowledge would know them?

Furthermore, the *pisuo*[349] rishis all study the Vedas and ought themselves to be able to reach all-knowledge. Thus if there are these persons who have completely studied the Vedas, how can you say that nobody can have all-knowledge?

I shall now respond to your [above-stated] claim that there are scriptures which [by their explication of the causes and conditions conducing to desire] are capable of causing one to feel desire or hatred. If one wishes to have a long life, he should abandon causes and conditions conducive to death. The Buddha, too, in this same way, wished to influence beings to cut off their desires and hatreds. This required that he know the causes and conditions that initiate the arising of desire and hatred.

Additionally, as for your contention that, if one is able to know the classical texts concerned with generating desire or hatred, one will then become afflicted with desire and hatred—this is a baseless claim. Although the Buddha had knowledge of these texts, because he did not use them or implement their practices, he was without fault in this respect. So too, if a person merely knows the causes and conditions that precipitate death, this does not entail his dying [as a result]. Only if he were to implement the causes and conditions that precipitate death would he then die as a result. This case is just the same as that one.

I shall now address your contention that, if one does not know future matters, then one does not qualify as omniscient. This does not constitute as a valid challenge. We already know of instances involving challenges to the plausibility of omniscience. As stated in the sutras: "The Buddha told the bhikshus, 'The common person bereft of wisdom has three characteristics: He contemplates what he should not contemplate, discusses what he should not discuss, and does what he should not do.'"[350]

Everything of relevance is already comprehensively mentioned in that statement. You common people of this future time are all included in it. As it would have no particular benefit, what would be the point in his having distinguished and mentioned names and such [related to future events]?

If one were to claim [that there is a contradiction] if the Buddha knew there would be these challenges, yet failed to reply to them in advance, there would really have been no need for this, for, in this presently existing fourfold assembly there are already those well able to cut off doubts in their responses to challenges [such as this]. We now already have those well able to refute challenging inquiries. What then would be the point in [the Buddha himself] responding in advance to such things? Right now, among the bhikshus you encounter in the present day, there are already those well able to refute the tenets posited by brahmans. Therefore there is no need [for the Buddha] to have responded in advance to such challenges.

Furthermore, there have already been prior responses to such challenges that are scattered in various places throughout the many sutras. Because people are unable to completely know the Dharma of the Buddha, they do not know where those passages are located.

I shall now address your challenge on the matter of the Buddha's having allowed Devadatta to leave the home life and become a monk. As for your opinion that, if the Buddha allowed Devadatta to leave the home life, he could not have been omniscient, this statement is wrong. When Devadatta left the home life to become a monk, it was not the Buddha who was involved in allowing him to become a monastic.

Question: Even if it was someone else who allowed him to become a monastic, why did the Buddha allow this to happen?

Response: The doing of good and the doing of evil each have the season in which they occur. It was not necessarily the case that, having left home, he would immediately embark on doing evil. After Devadatta left home to become a monk, he had all of the meritorious qualities that are associated with upholding the moral precepts. Therefore there was no fault in [permitting] his leaving the home life.

Additionally, for twelve years, Devadatta was pure in his observance of the moral precepts and also became able then to recite from memory sixty-thousand lines from the treasury of Dharma. The karmic reward from this is such that, in the future, [such cultivation] will not have been in vain. In fact, it will definitely benefit him later on.

I will now reply to your statement regarding Devadatta's prying loose of a boulder [in an attempt to murder the Buddha]. Because all buddhas have already perfected the dharma of not killing, nobody in any world can ever rob them of life.

Question: If the Buddha had actually perfected the dharma of not killing, why did the boulder shatter and [allow a piece of it] to come down [and strike him in the foot]?

Response: The Buddha had planted karmic causes associated with damage to the body for which he was bound to undergo this fixed retribution. He manifested the appearance of having to undergo it in order to demonstrate to beings that karmic retributions cannot be escaped. It was for this reason that he voluntarily came to that place.

I shall now respond to your contention that there was some problem in the Buddha's not having spoken in advance about the incident involving that woman, Ciñcā. There is nothing in that woman, Ciñcā's, disparaging of the Buddha that can serve as a causal basis for impugning his qualification as omniscient. If the Buddha had announced in advance, "In the future, that woman, Ciñca, will come forth and slander me," then that woman, Ciñca, would not in fact have come forth as she did. Furthermore, it was due to the karmic causes and conditions associated with the Buddha's having slandered others in a previous lifetime that he was now definitely bound to undergo [the corresponding retribution]. [351]

I shall now address your challenge as to how it could have been that the Buddha failed to prevent the incident that occurred when Sundarī entered the Jeta Grove.[352] This incident does not constitute a reason for impugning the Buddha's qualification as omniscient. The Buddha does not have some power by which he is able to cause every being's life to be an entirely happy one. Also, the Buddhas have all left behind disputation, do not elevate themselves, and are not attached to [making others] uphold moral precepts, consequently he did not act to prevent this incident.

Additionally, it was because of the ripening of karma from a previous life that he was definitely bound to undergo that seven days of slander. Moreover, when beings observed that the Buddha was neither perturbed over hearing himself slandered nor joyful when his innocence was made clear, they brought forth the resolve to follow the unsurpassable path, uttering this vow, "We too shall acquire just such a pure mind as this." Therefore there was no fault [in the Buddha's having acted as he did].

I shall now respond to your contention that, because the Buddha entered a brahman village and then left with an empty bowl, he was therefore not omniscient.[353] The Buddha [did not go to that village] for the sake of food and drink, [but rather because] he had contemplated the minds of the people there. It was only after he entered the village that Māra changed the villagers' minds.

Question: This is a matter about which the Buddha should have become aware in advance, thinking, "If I go into this village, Māra will change these peoples' minds."

Response: The Buddha in fact *did* know about this matter in advance [and entered that village anyway] in order to bring great benefit to those beings. It is not solely on the basis of receiving alms food from them that the Buddhas benefit beings and facilitate their liberation. There were those who welcomed him there with pure minds, bowed in reverence to him, and looked up to him with congenial gazes. All of these things already served great benefit. Why should it be an essential requirement that he be given food and drink? There are many different sorts of methods by which he was able to be of benefit to beings. Thus it was not in vain that he entered that village.

I shall now respond to your statement about the Buddha's having gone up the road on which there was a drunken elephant.[354] Although the Buddha already knew of this matter, there was a reason he deliberately went there. It was because this drunken elephant was definitely at a point where he could be brought across to liberation. The Buddha was also intent on preventing his falling into the karmic offense of harming a buddha.

Additionally, this elephant's body had the appearance of a black mountain. When the population there saw this elephant bow down its head in reverence to the Buddha, they all brought forth thoughts of reverence. It was for these reasons that the Buddha deliberately went up that road. Also, there was no error involved in the Buddha's having entered that road to encounter that elephant. Only if some unfortunate incident had transpired would you have a basis for bringing up this challenge.

As for your challenge regarding the Buddha's having gone to Verañjā, that was simply a case of having to undergo retribution for karmic deeds committed in a previous life.[355]

I shall now address your statement on the issue of the Buddha's having accepted Sunakṣatra as a disciple.[356] The Buddha has no need to guard against errors in actions of body, speech, mind, or livelihood.[357] It was because he is utterly without fear that he permitted Sunakṣatra to become a disciple.

Also, because this man always dwelt in close proximity to the Buddha, he was thus able to observe the display of all manner of spiritual powers and also saw the arrival of devas, dragons, *yakṣas, gandharvas, asuras,* kings, and others, all coming to make offerings to the Buddha and to pose respectful questions to him on all manner of extremely profound and essential dharmas. Hence his mind was thereby able to become purified. Because he was able to achieve purification of mind, this was a causal basis for his [eventual] benefit. Therefore, even though he was an evil man, the Buddha nonetheless accepted him as a disciple.

Question: This man had many evil thoughts about the Buddha. Therefore the Buddha should not have permitted him to become a disciple.

Response: Even if the Buddha had not accepted him as a disciple, the man still would have had those evil thoughts. Therefore there was no fault in the Buddha's permitting him to become a disciple.

I shall now respond to your challenge as to why the Buddha did not formulate the moral precepts in advance of [his disciples'] commission of the corresponding transgressions. The Buddha did in fact formulate moral precepts in advance. He set forth the eightfold path of the Āryas that consist of right views, right thought, right speech, right action, right livelihood, right effort, right mindfulness, and right meditative concentration. Because he did describe this path leading to the attainment of nirvāṇa, he in fact had already formulated all of the precepts.

Furthermore, the Buddha described the three trainings wherein one thoroughly trains in moral virtue, thoroughly trains in [focusing] the mind, and thoroughly trains in wisdom. One should then realize from this that he had in fact already set forth all of the moral precepts.

Additionally, the Buddha told the bhikshus that they should definitely not do any sort of evil. Does this not constitute prior formulation of moral precepts?

Also, the Buddha spoke of the path of the ten courses of good karmic action, namely abandoning killing, stealing, sexual misconduct, divisive speech, harsh speech, false speech, frivolous speech, covetousness, ill will, and wrong views. Does this not constitute prior formulation of moral precepts?

Twelve years earlier, the Buddha described in a single verse the *upoṣadha* dharma,[358] namely:

To refrain from doing any sort of evil deed,
to respectfully engage in every sort of good deed,
and to purify one's own mind—
This is the teaching of all Buddhas.[359]

One should therefore realize that the Buddha in fact *did* formulate the moral precepts in advance.

Also, the Buddha stated that one should abandon even all of the most minor causes and conditions associated with evil, as stated in these lines:

Abandon all evil actions of the body.
Also abandon all evil speech,
abandon all evil actions of the mind,
and utterly abandon all other forms of evil.

On the basis of statements such as these, one should realize that the Buddha had already formulated the moral precepts in advance. Additionally, the Buddha had already described in advance the dharmas through which one guards against transgressions, as stated in these lines:

To guard the body is good indeed.
To be able to guard one's speech is also good.

To guard one's mind is good indeed,
and to guard against all errors is good as well.[360]
The bhikshu guards against all errors
and thereby succeeds in abandoning all evil.

One should realize on the basis of these statements that the Buddha in fact *did* formulate the moral precepts in advance. Moreover, the Buddha also described in advance the characteristics of goodness, as stated in these lines:

Do not allow hands or feet to carelessly commit transgressions.
Restrain your words and take care in actions done.
One should take pleasure in guarding and focusing the mind.
It is on these bases that one is rightfully called a bhikshu.[361]

One should realize on the basis of statements such as this that the Buddha in fact *did* formulate the moral precepts in advance.

Furthermore, because the Buddha described the dharmas by which one is a *śramaṇa,* one should realize he did in fact formulate the moral precepts in advance. There are four dharmas by which one is a *śramaṇa*: First, one does not respond in kind to hate-filled actions. Second, one remains silent in the face of scolding. Third, one is able to endure even being beaten with staves. And fourth, one maintains patience with those who have dealt one harm.

Moreover, the Buddha taught the four stations of mindfulness, namely the contemplation of the body, the contemplation of feelings, the contemplation of thoughts, and the contemplation of dharmas, doing so because they constitute the abode of the path to nirvāṇa. Hence one should realize that he *did* formulate the moral precepts in advance.

The Buddha would not even permit the most subtle form of evil, how much the less would he condone any sort of evil karma in one's physical actions or speech. For reasons such as these, one should realize that he did indeed formulate the moral precepts in advance.

This is analogous to a king's establishment of laws in which one is forbidden to do evil deeds. When, later on, there are transgressions against those laws, it is according to the relative gravity of the crime that corresponding punishments are imposed. The Buddha is just the same in this respect. He first made general statements describing the moral precepts. Later on, when offenses occurred, he described the specific characteristic factors by which the given action constituted an offense.

Where there were those who committed evil deeds, they were instructed and caused to repent. He instructed that, for a given offense, a given corresponding form of penance was to be performed or that either temporary expulsion or complete expulsion was stipulated so that the miscreant could not dwell together with the community, and so forth. It was only with the establishment of these sorts of cases that we came to have the subsequent formulation of moral precepts.

I shall now address your contention that superior position in the monastic community should be accorded on the basis of age, nobility of birth caste, status of one's clan, and so forth. In the dharmas of the path, issues of age, nobility of birth caste, status of one's clan, and so forth afford no benefit. How is this so? It is on the basis of being born into the Dharma of the Buddha that one qualifies as being born into nobility and into a fine clan. Seniority is determined on the basis of the number of years one has received the higher ordination and this is the rationale for being referred to as an elder.

As for your opinion that those who are merely older in years should be given priority in the receipt of offerings, is it not the case that those who first left the home life and received the ordination precepts are better regarded as of greater eminence?

Furthermore, from the time one receives the ordination precepts onward, there are no longer any distinctions on the basis of one's caste and such. It is only when bhikshus receive the precepts of the higher ordination that they then qualify as having been born into the family of the Buddhas. It is at this point that one loses any name associated with prior birth into a greater or lesser clan and everyone then belongs to this one single family.

As for your statements on upholding the precepts—those who first left the home life to become monastics and who have observed the moral precepts for the longest time and then proceed to uphold those moral precepts for a long time—it is because of their years of seniority in this that they should be accorded a superior position within the monastic community. This is as set forth in the original formulation of the moral precept code.

I shall now address your contention that those who are most strictly observant in their upholding of the moral precepts should not bow in reverence to those who have broken the moral precepts. Those who truly have broken the moral precepts should not even be allowed to dwell together with the community, how much the less should they receive reverential obeisance or offerings.

It is on the basis of their claim to be a bhikshu that one pays reverence to them according to their order of seniority. This is similar to when one bows in reverence before a deity's image made of clay or wood, doing so as a means of bearing in mind that actual deity.

The Buddha decreed that those of fewer years seniority should revere those who are seated in a superior position within the monastic order. It is through according with the Buddha's instructions in this that one acquires karmic merit.

I shall now respond to your statement that the according of reverence should be based on one's practice of the *dhūta* austerities. In this matter of those who take up the *dhūta* practices, there are five general types of practitioners among which it is difficult to make clear distinctions:[362]

First, there are those who are deluded and who, due to an absence of right knowledge, are driven by desire to practice these difficult dharmas;

Second, there are those possessed of only dull faculties who wish to acquire benefits as a result;

Third, there are those with evil intentions focused on deceiving others;

Fourth, there are those who are mentally ill;

And fifth, there are those who [take them up], thinking, "The dharmas of the *dhūta* austerities are praised by all buddhas, worthies, and *āryas* because they accord with the path to nirvāṇa."

Among these five classes of practitioners of the *dhūta* austerities, it is difficult to distinguish which are genuine and which are false.

Now, as for this matter of one's level of learning, just as with the *dhūta* austerities, it is difficult to distinguish clearly among those who have acquired abundant learning. How is this so? It could be that it is on the basis of delighting in the path that one has accrued much learning. Or perhaps it is only for the sake of receiving offerings that one has accrued much learning. It is difficult to make clear distinctions in matters such as these.

Additionally, in the Dharma of the Buddha, it is practice in accordance with one's words that is accorded esteem. One does not accord esteem merely on the basis of having engaged in much study or having become able to recite many scriptures. Also, according to the statements of the Buddha himself, if one practices but a single sentence of Dharma and is thereby able to derive self-benefit from that, this itself qualifies as abundant learning.

So too it is with this matter of wisdom. If one remains unable to implement a level of practice consistent with one's level of discourse, of what use is this wisdom? Consequently, it is not on the basis of one's degree of wisdom that one determines who is accorded a superior position in the monastic order.

This is analogous to the current way of doing things in the world. Although a younger brother may indeed be more learned or more wise, the elder brother is still not enjoined to pay him reverence. Therefore, after this same fashion, it is not on the basis of one's level of wisdom that one gains priority in the receipt of offerings or reverence. So it is then that, even though one may indeed have accrued much learning or wisdom, one should still accord reverence on the basis of who first received the ordination precepts. Were one to accord priority in the receipt of offerings to those of greater learning or a higher level of wisdom, this would inevitably result in discord within the community.

As for the other [criteria you propose for priority in according reverence], namely realization of the *śramaṇa's* fruits of the path, severance of fetters, and acquisition of spiritual powers, those are the most difficult matters to know. Whether or not this person has attained a fruit of the path, whether he has cut off more fetters or fewer fetters [than this other person], and whether or not he has acquired spiritual powers—one cannot use such matters as the basis for superior position in the monastic order. Consider for instance those who have realized the same fruits of the path, cut off the same fetters, and acquired the same spiritual powers. Who among them should be accorded superior position in the monastic order? Consequently, it is by far the best to simply accord with the Buddha's instructions on these matters.

I shall now address your contention that the Buddha himself was beset by doubt about whether he should expound the Dharma.[363] The Buddha had no doubts at all even with regard to the most profound sorts of dharmas, how much the less might he have had doubts with regard to whether or not he should expound the Dharma. The Buddha never said that he would entirely forego his teaching of the Dharma. He merely indicated a preference for continuing to abide in serenity, refraining from becoming involved in numerous endeavors. There was no fault in his having simply waited till later to begin expounding the Dharma.

Also, the non-Buddhist partisans would say, "If the Buddha is such a great *ārya* that he remains silent and declines to involve himself in conceptual elaboration, what use could he have for assembling a following and offering to give teachings?" Then again, once he started teaching, this would inevitably turn into an endless endeavor. It was as if he was weighing the utility of proceeding to teach the Dharma and assemble a group of disciples when this could appear outwardly as if it were a mark of covetous attachment.

Due to these factors, the Buddha reflected, "Though my Dharma is extremely deep, the wisdom and skillful means that might be employed in teaching it would be measureless and boundless. Still, those who are actually amenable to gaining liberation are but few." Consequently, he thought to himself, "It would be better to remain silent." It was also to defend against the potential for mocking deprecation by non-Buddhist partisans that he instead influenced the Brahma Heaven King to [first] request the proclamation of Dharma. The Brahma Heaven King and others then immediately addressed the Buddha, saying, "Beings are surely worthy of pity. There are among them those of sharp faculties and but few fetters who would be easy to teach and bring across to liberation."

Because of this, the Buddha acceded to the request of the Brahma Heaven King and others. It was as if someone who had just found a great treasury of jewels felt he should reveal their presence to others. In this same way, when *āryas* themselves gain the benefits of the Dharma, they feel they should also use it to benefit others.

I shall now address your contention that, because the Buddha expressed a wish to speak the Dharma for Ārāḍa Kālāma and others and therefore had not realized they had already died, [this contradicts the plausibility of his being omniscient]. The Buddha had not brought to mind the issue of whether or not they had already died, but rather was only considering the fact that, because these men's fetters were but scant, they would be capable of being instructed and brought across to liberation. It is in correspondence with the point upon which one's thought is focused that a corresponding knowledge arises. It was as a consequence of this that the Buddha first said this to himself and a deva then appropriately informed him.[364]

Also, since earlier on, when the Buddha had just abandoned the home life, he had gone to those men, [Ārāḍa Kālāma and Udraka Rāmaputra], and had spent time with them, the devas and other people could have entertained doubts in which they thought the Buddha had perhaps received the sublime Dharma from them and had then become enlightened in another location. Because the Buddha wished to cut off any doubts that they might have had, he immediately exclaimed, "Oh, those men—they have for so long suffered such misfortune as this. How can it be that they have still not heard this sublime Dharma?"

By inferring the implications of this idea, one can deduce the nature of the matter of the five bhikshus. It was because the Buddha had only brought to mind the causes and conditions associated with their capacity to gain liberation that he had not yet considered precisely where they were currently dwelling. Afterward, once he had thought about where they were dwelling, he then knew where they were.

Therefore one should not look upon these issues as refuting the plausibility of there being an omniscient person.

I shall now address your stated doubt with regard to the causes for the destruction of the city of Pāṭaliputra. The precise causes and conditions by which this city would meet its destruction were still unfixed. To make a fixed pronouncement on the unfolding of unfixed causes and conditions would itself be a fault.

Also among the forty exclusive dharmas listed earlier, I stated that all buddhas are thoroughly cognizant of dharmas that are unfixed. In response then, I do not accept this challenge as valid.

I shall now address your contention about the Buddha's querying the bhikshus as to the contents of their conversation by asking, "So, what are you all gathered together to discuss?" It was because the Buddha was about to hold forth on some aspect of Dharma that he initiated the discussion by asking a question of this sort. It could have been that, because he wished to formulate another of the moral prohibitions, he directed them to talk about what they were discussing. Because he took all sorts of such instances as occasions for speaking Dharma, the Buddha's posing a question was free of any fault [in relation to the issue of his omniscience].

Furthermore it is a commonplace in the world, even when one is already well aware of what is happening, for one to go ahead and ask a question. For instance, on observing someone eating, one may ask, "Oh, so you're eating, are you?" Or, for instance, on a particularly cold day, one may ask, "Isn't it cold?"

In this same way, even though he already knew, the Buddha would nonetheless pose a question. Being but a means of conforming to convention, this is entirely free of fault.

I shall now address your judgment that anyone who praises himself and criticizes others could not possibly be an omniscient person. The Buddha entertained no desires with respect to himself and so was not the least bit covetous of receiving offerings. He did not hate other men and was not possessed of overweening pride. As for the reason for his having declared himself to be foremost among everyone in the world, it was because there were beings who were amenable to faith and possessed of acutely sharp faculties who, if they cast aside bad spiritual guides and took the Buddha as their teacher, they could then gain that peace and security that would see them through the long night [of subsequent rebirths]. It was for this reason that the Buddha did in fact praise his own personal qualities.

Additionally, there were those who, although they sought the path to the supreme bliss, were still indolent and unable to bring forth vigorous effort. Consequently the Buddha declared, "In this matter of gaining the most supreme benefit, one must not be indolent. I am the supreme spiritual guide in this world, the one who well proclaims right Dharma. It is only fitting then that you become assiduous and vigorous, for it is only then that you may gain the fruits of the path." And so it was that, for reasons such as these, the Buddha did indeed praise his own personal qualities. It was not out of a wish to be accorded esteem, nor was it out of a wish to slight and deprecate others.

In cases where the Buddha rebuked evil men, it was for the sake of inducing them to get rid of evil dharmas. It was not because he detested other beings. In some cases, there were those seeking to achieve benefit through Dharma, people whose minds were pure and of straightforward character, but who were locked in relationships with bad spiritual guides. In order to induce them to abandon these bad teachers, the Buddha would sometimes criticize and rebuke them. Even before he had achieved buddhahood, [in earlier lifetimes] he even sacrificed his own brain and the very marrow of his bones as gifts to others. How much the less could it be that, once he had already attained buddhahood, he would be inclined to berate and scold others?

I shall now respond to your contention that there were chronologically contradictory tenets in the Buddha's Dharma. There are no contradictions present in the Dharma of the Buddha between what came at the beginning and what followed later on. It is only because you and your cohorts do not understand the concepts involved in the Buddha's Dharma that you have the opinion that it is inherently contradictory.

This path leading to the realization of nirvāṇa had not been either proclaimed or realized by anyone during the entire time between Kāśyapa Buddha's nirvāṇa on forward to the present. It was for this reason that the Buddha declared, "I am he who has newly attained the path." In other places, he also said, "I have attained the ancient path." The path is that which was previously realized by Dīpaṃkara Buddha and the other buddhas of the past, namely the eightfold path of the Āryas that is able to lead one to nirvāṇa. It is because, in all these cases, it is but a single path relying on but a single set of causes and conditions that it is referred to it as "the ancient path." One should realize from this that the Buddha did obtain all-knowledge.

Question: As for the so-called "all-knowledge," precisely what is it that constitutes all-knowledge? Is it really on the basis of knowing absolutely everything that it is referred to as "all-knowledge"?

Response: "All-knowledge" refers to knowing all that can be known. "What can be known" refers to the five categorical repositories of dharmas, namely all past, future, and present dharmas, the dharmas that transcend the three periods of time, and the ineffable dharmas. That which is used in knowing these five categories of dharmas is cognition. Hence it is both cognition and those things that it knows that are referred to as the "all" [in the term "all-knowledge."]

Question: As for this contention that it is both the faculty of cognition and those things it knows that together comprise the "all" [of all-knowledge], this is wrong. How so? This is but a singular dharma, this because that cognition that is capable of knowing is itself knowable as when people of the world speak of this person's cognitive ability as sharp whereas that person's cognitive ability is dull.

Response: Well, if as you state that "all" is itself just a singular entity, then it should be that those polar opposites such as "hot" and "cold" are but one thing. And so too it should be that "bright" and "dark," "suffering" and "happiness," and all polar opposites should in each case be but a single thing. But this is not the case. Therefore, one cannot claim that "all" is but a singular entity.

Question: That idea to which you are clinging is itself possessed of this same fault. If the faculty of cognition is one thing, then [that which it knows, namely] "suffering," "happiness," and so forth—those should all also be but singular entities, but in truth, they are not.

Response: I never claimed that everything that can be known is, [in aggregate], but one single thing. Now that idea to which *you* are clinging is indeed that everything [that can be known] *is* somehow, [in its collective aggregate], but a single thing. Therefore, [what I am saying] is not the same as that faulty concept you are proposing.

Furthermore, since you claim that [both of] these positions are equally at fault, that idea to which you are clinging is faulty. In a case where someone accepts that the idea he is proposing is faulty, his position is thereby refuted. Now, when you understand that the idea to which you have been clinging is faulty, you should not continue to claim that someone else is the party whose position is faulty. Hence, as for your contention that what I have set forth here is somehow possessed of the same fault that characterizes your position—this is wrong.

Moreover, if you claim that the two dharmas consisting of the faculty of cognition on the one hand and that which is known on the other are somehow but a single entity, then one should be able to use any particular knowable dharma to know phenomena like vases and robes and such, but in truth it is solely the faculty of cognition that can be used in the knowing of all things.

If you are going to claim that phenomena like vases and robes and such are no different from the faculty of cognition—this vase and robe and so forth—they are entirely unable to know any phenomenon at all. It immediately follows that it ought to be the case that they are different [from the faculty of cognition] and it is truly the case that one uses the faculty of cognition to know everything.

Because your position is faulty in these ways in place after place, you cannot thus claim that the constituent phenomena forming the "all" of all-knowledge are all collectively but a single thing.

So, again, the faculty of cognition and that which is known, these two things—they are what constitute the "all" of "all-knowledge," this because they together constitute all dharmas. It is because of the Buddha's knowing of all of these dharmas that he is known as the Tathāgata and is renowned as one who is possessed of all-knowledge. This omniscient man became possessed of all-knowledge because of the *vajra* samādhi. Therefore the *vajra* samādhi is indeed something that can be established. As for your initial contentions that the *vajra* samādhi cannot be established and that "all-knowledge" is also not something that can be established, these contentions are both wrong.

The End of Chapter Twenty-Two

Chapter 23[365]

Forty Dharmas Exclusive to Buddhas (Part 3)

XXIII. Chapter 23: Forty Dharmas Exclusive to Buddhas (Part 3)

A. 10) Thorough Knowing of Matters That Are Unfixed

As for knowing well the unfixed dharmas, the Tathāgata's wisdom has achieved power within the sphere of all dharmas even at that point when they have not yet arisen, have not yet come forth, have not yet reached completion, have not become definitively fixed, and have not yet become clearly distinguishable. This is as stated in the *Sutra on the Buddha's Distinguishing of Karma* wherein it states:

> The Buddha told Ānanda, "There are people who practice good deeds with the body, who practice good deeds through speech, and who practice good deeds with the mind, and yet, when their lives come to an end, they then fall into the hells. There are yet other people who practice evil deeds with the body, who practice evil deeds through speech, and who practice evil deeds with the mind, and yet, when their lives come to an end, they are nonetheless reborn in the heavens."
>
> Ānanda addressed the Buddha and asked, "Why do events occur in this way?"
>
> The Buddha replied, "It may have been that the causes and conditions associated with previous life karmic offenses or meritorious deeds had already ripened, whereas the karmic offenses or meritorious deeds of the present life had not yet ripened. Or, alternatively, when approaching the end of life, they gave rise to either right views or erroneous views that precipitated either wholesome or evil thoughts, this because the power of the thoughts produced as one approaches the moment of death—their power is immense."[366]

Additionally, in the *Śuka Sutra*, it states:

> Śuka, son of a brahman, addressed the Buddha and asked, "Gotama, why is it that the brahman laity are in some cases able to cultivate meritorious deeds and roots of goodness in a manner superior to that of some of those who have left the home life and become monastics?"
>
> The Buddha replied, "For these sorts of matters, I do not present a fixed reply. There may be cases in which someone who has left behind the home life does not cultivate goodness and, as a consequence, in this endeavor, he does not equal the efforts of a given

householder. This is a case in which a householder is able to cultivate goodness in a manner superior to that of a particular monastic."

Furthermore, the *Great Nirvāṇa Sutra* states that the city of Pāṭaliputra is bound to be destroyed by one of three circumstances: by flood, by fire, or by a conspiracy between insiders and outsiders.

Also, [another example of an unfixed statement] arose because of a *brahmacārin* named Patikaputra about which the Buddha said:

> As for this naked ascetic, the *brahmacārin* named Patikaputra, if he fails to relinquish this statement, these thoughts, and these wrong views, then it will be impossible for him to come and appear before me. He will either be trapped by a broken rope or prevented from leaving by a broken body. In any case, he will never be able to arrive here in the presence of the Buddha.

Additionally, in the *Sutra on the Analogy of the Raft*, the Buddha said:

> This Dharma of mine is extremely deep. It is by resort to expedients that I enable even those who are shallow to easily reach an understanding of it. If there be anyone possessed of a straightforward mind who is willing to practice in accordance with the teachings, he will gain one of two kinds of benefit from this, either the cessation of the contaminants in this present lifetime or, in the event that he doesn't achieve the cessation of the contaminants, he will still succeed in attaining the path of the non-returner (*anāgāmin*).[367]

Also, in the *Ekottara Āgama*'s *Shejiali Sutra*,[368] the Buddha told Ānanda:

> As for whosoever deliberately undertakes the requisite karmic actions, none among them will fail to gain the karmic rewards and thus achieve success in the path, whether that be through receiving the results of present-life karma in this present life, whether that be through receiving them in the next birth, or whether that be through receiving them in subsequent lives.[369]

In addition, we also have this statement in the *Ekottara Āgama*'s *Afuluo Sutra*:[370] "The Buddha told the bhikshus, 'When evil people die, they may become animals or they may fall into the hells. Good people will be reborn either in the heavens or among humans.'"

Also, in the *Prince Fearless Sutra*, it states:

> Prince Fearless addressed the Buddha, saying, "Does the Buddha not have instances in which what he proclaims is able to cause others to become angry?"
>
> The Buddha replied, "Prince, this is an unfixed matter. It may happen that the Buddha, motivated by pity, will influence someone to become angry with the intended result that they will thereby

> plant the causes and conditions for goodness. This is analogous to a wet-nurse having to use a crooked finger to clear an infant's mouth of some dangerous object. Although it may inflict injury, it is done in order to prevent a calamity."[371]

There is also the statement recorded in the Abhidharma: "Beings fall into three groups. From the [karmically] indefinite group, they may fall into the definitely deviant group or the definitely righteous group."[372]

There are several thousand or even myriads of similar such types of unfixed phenomena that are cited within the four repositories of the Dharma.[373]

Question: If a person's wisdom is unfixed and characterized by indefinite thought that takes a given circumstance to perhaps be this way or perhaps not be this way, then this is not someone who is omniscient. One who is omniscient would not make two different statements [with regard to a single matter], but rather would instead be able to make definitive pronouncements, pronouncements that are utterly clear. Because of this, "thoroughly knowing unfixed matters" cannot be referred to as a dharma exclusive to the Buddha.

Response: Unfixed matters are such that they may either be this way or not this way. It is because they develop in accordance with a multiplicity of causes and conditions that one should not make definite pronouncements about them.

Moreover, were one to offer definite answers regarding indefinite phenomena, then that itself would indicate that one is *not* omniscient. Consequently, in assessing unfixed phenomena, it is essential to employ the knowledge of unfixed matters. Hence there is this exclusive dharma referred to as "the knowledge of unfixed matters."

Additionally, if one were to claim definitive knowledge with respect to all dharmas, then one would fall into the erroneous determinist fallacy. If all dharmas really were already definitely fixed, then all that one does would not require any human effort and skillful means to bring it about. This idea is as set forth here:

> If good or bad experiences were already definitely determined,
> then the character of a person's efforts should be fixed as well.
> There would be no need for any of the causal factors
> involved in the skillful means that one uses in one's cultivation.

Moreover, it is already manifestly clear that if one fails to take care with regard to one's personal behavior, then one will bring about manifold sufferings, whereas, if one is guarded with respect to one's personal behavior, then one will enjoy peace and benefit as a result of doing so.

Also, this is just as in all sorts of endeavors involved in carrying on one's livelihood wherein, on the one hand, one is required to endure a good deal of weariness and suffering to later acquire a reward in the form of all manner of wealth and happiness, whereas, on the other hand, someone else is able to simply remain still and silent in this present life, doing nothing whatsoever, only to then reap karmic rewards. So it is that there are these unfixed circumstances. It is because they are cognizant of these unfixed circumstances that we can know that the Buddhas possess the knowledge of what is unfixed.

Question: Whether or not you personally take care and whether or not you make a direct personal effort, these unfixed circumstances will still occur. On the one hand there are those who skillfully defend against untoward developments and yet still end up being subjected to intense anguish while on the other hand there are those who do not defend against such exigencies at all and yet do not encounter any intense anguish at all. Also, there are those who, in their diligence, undergo much weariness and pain, but still do not obtain the fruits of their efforts, whereas there are others who are not the least bit diligent and make no particular effort and, even so, they still manage to gain fruits [otherwise] associated with making an effort. These matters are all unfixed.

Response: Your statement simply serves to cooperate in the establishment of my position regarding unfixed matters. If these unfixed matters do indeed exist, then this wisdom that is cognizant of whatsoever is unfixed should exist. I never claimed that if someone failed to guard against untoward events they would always be subjected to suffering. Nor did I ever claim that, without the expenditure of effortful action, one would necessarily be able to enjoy fruitful results. There are those people who, despite making an effort, are still blocked from the enjoyment of happiness by karmic obstacles originating in earlier lifetimes. I never claimed that all cases were necessarily this way. Therefore the challenges that you have posed on this topic are wrong.

This is what is meant [when it is said] with regard to unfixed circumstances that it is the Buddhas alone who possess complete knowledge of what is unfixed.

B. 11) Thorough Knowing of Formless Absorption Phenomena

As for knowing the formless realm stations, *śrāvaka* disciples and *pratyekabuddhas* know a lesser portion of the beings and dharmas associated with the formless realm stations of existence whereas the Buddhas, the Bhagavats, have a perfectly complete knowledge of the beings and dharmas associated with the formless realm stations of existence.

Regarding these formless realm stations of existence, the Buddhas know:

That a certain number of beings are born into this station;

That a certain number of beings are born into that station;

That a certain number of beings are born into the station associated with the first formless absorption;

That a certain number of beings are born into the second station;

That a certain number of beings are born into the third station;

That a certain number of beings are born into the fourth station;

That a certain number of beings have dwelt there for a particular amount of time since they were born there;

That a certain number of beings, after a particular period of time, will fall away from that realm;

That a certain number of beings will enjoy a maximum life span of a particular amount of time;

That a certain number of beings will have a definitely fixed life span;

That a certain number of beings will enjoy a life span the length of which is not definitely fixed;

That a certain number of beings will be born here after their lifetimes in the desire realm have come to an end;

That a certain number of beings will be born here after their lifetimes in the form realm have come to an end;

That a certain number of beings will return to be reborn here after their lifetimes in this formless realm have come to an end;

That a certain number of beings will be born here directly after their lives in the human realm come to an end;

That a certain number of beings will be reborn here directly after their lives in the heavens have come to an end;

That, when the lives of these particular beings end here, they will then take birth in the desire realm, that they will then take birth in the form realm, or that they will then take birth in the formless realm;

That, when the lives of these particular beings end here, they will then take birth in the celestial realm rebirth destiny, that they will then take birth in the human realm rebirth destiny, that they will then take birth in the *asura* realm rebirth destiny, or that they will then take birth in the rebirth destinies of the hell realms, the animal realms, or the hungry ghost realms;

That these particular beings will enter nirvāṇa in that particular place;

That a particular group of beings are all merely common people;
That a particular group of beings are *ārya* disciples of buddhas;
That a particular group of beings are [buddhas'] disciples who are common people [that have not yet become *āryas*];
That a particular group of beings will achieve success in the Śrāvaka Disciple Vehicle;
That a particular group of beings will achieve success in the Pratyekabuddha Vehicle;
That a particular group of beings will all achieve success in the Great Vehicle;
That a particular group of beings will fail to achieve success in the Śrāvaka Disciple Vehicle;
That a particular group of beings will fail to achieve success in the Pratyekabuddha Vehicle and will also fail to achieve success in the Great Vehicle;
That a particular group of beings will develop their practice to the point of reaching nirvāṇa;
That a particular group of beings will fail to develop their practice to the point where they reach nirvāṇa;
That a particular group of beings will pursue a superior level of practice;
And that a particular group of beings are all disciples of a particular buddha.

The Buddhas also know:

That this particular meditative absorption is one in which one is exposed to delectably blissful experiences;[374]
That in this particular meditative absorption there will be no exposure to delectably blissful experiences;
[That this particular meditative absorption] is wholesome or is merely neutral;
That in this particular meditative absorption one may successfully sever a certain number of fetters;
And that this particular meditative absorption is superior, is middling, or is inferior.

To summarize, only the Buddhas, by employing their knowledge of all modes are able to clearly distinguish which of these formless-realm meditative absorptions are greater or lesser, which are deeper or shallower, which involve mental dharmas, which involve dharmas not associated with the mind, which are acquired as resultant effects [of previous karma], which are not acquired as resultant effects [of previous karma], and so forth. This is what is meant when it is said that the

Buddhas thoroughly know the stations of existence corresponding to the formless meditative absorptions.

C. 12) The Knowledge of All Matters Related to Eternal Cessation

As for [the completely penetrating knowledge of all] dharmas pertaining to cessation, the Buddhas possess a penetrating knowledge of the *pratyekabuddhas* and arhats who have entered nirvāṇa either in the past or present eras. This is as recorded in the sutras where it states:

> Bhikshus, ninety-one kalpas prior to this "Worthy Kalpa" (*bhadrakalpa*), Vipaśyin Buddha appeared. After thirty-one kalpas, there followed two more buddhas, the first of whom was Śikhin and the second of whom was Viśvabhū. Then, in this Worthy Kalpa, Krakucchanda, Kanakamuni, and Kāśyapa Buddha emerged.[375]

Just such great knowledge and vision regarding all buddhas of the past should be discussed [more extensively] herein in relation to this sutra.[376] It also reaches to those *śrāvaka* disciples who have entered the nirvāṇa without residue and extends also to the *pratyekabuddha* named "Success," to the one named "Floral Insignia," to the one named "Seer of Dharma," to the one named "Dharma Basket," to the one named "Delightful Vision," to the one named "Stainless," to the one named "Free of Gain," and to the other such *pratyekabuddhas* as well. So it is that the Buddhas possess a completely penetrating knowledge of those who have entered the nirvāṇa without residue.[377]

Additionally, in cases where they have not yet entered final nirvāṇa, but rather still abide in the nirvāṇa with residue, the Buddhas possess a penetratingly comprehensive knowledge with regard to the utter ending of all conditions associated with taking birth. [These matters] also pertain to their penetrating knowledge of [the phenomena associated with] cessation.

This is as recorded in the sutras wherein it states, "The Buddha told Ānanda, 'I entirely know with respect to this person that he no longer has even the slightest darkness. This person has definitely put an end to these particular inward dharmas. When this person reaches the end of this life, he will enter nirvāṇa.'" This too is included in what is meant by "having knowledge of cessation."[378]

Also, regarding other people's penetrating comprehension of the four truths, he is able to know their circumstances. This too is included in what is meant by "having knowledge of cessation."

As it is said in the sutras, "Why should I not simply resort to expedients to cause this person in this very place to gain the liberation associated with ending the contaminants?"

And as the Buddha told Ānanda, "You delight in *dhyāna* concentration and delight in cutting off the fetters." These circumstances too are associated with what is meant by having a completely penetrating knowledge of cessation.

This is also as illustrated in the Buddha's statement to Śāriputra, "I know nirvāṇa, know the path leading to the realization of nirvāṇa, and know those beings who will arrive at the realization of nirvāṇa."[379]

Such sutras as we have cited herein should all be discussed at greater length. The ideas cited above are indicative of what is meant by all buddhas possessing the penetrating comprehension of all matters having to do with cessation.

D. 13) Thorough Knowing of Non-Form Dharmas Unrelated to Mind

As for thorough knowing of the non-form dharmas unassociated with the mind, roots of goodness associated with the moral precepts influence all of those non-form dharmas unassociated with the mind such as the moral regulations requiring wholesome actions and the moral regulations prohibiting bad actions. *Śrāvaka* disciples and *pratyekabuddhas* are unable to possess a completely penetrating comprehension of such matters. The Buddhas, however, are so well able to penetratingly comprehend them that these become as manifestly clear to them as if they were right before their very eyes. This is because they have perfected the foremost power of wisdom with respect to dharmas unassociated with the mind.

Question: Moral regulations requiring wholesome actions and moral regulations prohibiting bad actions are form dharmas. Why do you refer to them as "non-form" dharmas?

Response: Moral regulations requiring wholesome actions and moral regulations prohibiting bad actions are of two kinds, namely those involving actions and those not involving actions. Those involving actions are within the sphere of form dharmas whereas those not involving actions are "non-form" dharmas. As for those non-form dharmas not involving actions, employing his exclusive power of knowing, the Buddha is able to have a clear and present knowledge of them whereas others are compelled to rely upon inferential knowledge to understand them.

Question: Are the Buddhas only able to thoroughly know the non-form dharmas unassociated with the mind while not being able to thoroughly know the dharmas associated with the mind?

Response: If one already possesses a penetrating comprehension of the unassociated dharmas, then there is no need even to bring up the associated dharmas. It is as if we were speaking of an archer able to pierce a single fine feather [floating through the air]. One would have no need in such a case to inquire if his arrow might be able to hit something large.

Furthermore, *śrāvaka* disciples and *pratyekabuddhas* are able to employ their sixth consciousness to know but seven among the seven hundred unassociated dharmas, namely: first, names; second, characteristic marks; third, meanings; fourth, impermanence; fifth, production; sixth, nonproduction; and seventh, crossing on beyond. The Buddhas, however, are able to employ their sixth consciousness to know every one of them. The Buddhas also know the marks of the four truths as well as the mundane dharmas. It is for these reasons that it is said that the Buddhas thoroughly know the non-form dharmas unassociated with the mind.

E. 14) The Great Powers Pāramitā

As for the powers *pāramitā*, [the Buddhas] gain the power of the knowledge of all modes with respect to all knowable dharmas without exception and are assisted in this by the ten powers, the four fearlessnesses, and the four bases of meritorious qualities. Also, it is due to having gained the ten powers that the Buddhas are therefore able to perfect the powers *pāramitā*. This power is increased in the sixteenth mind-moment [involved in achieving the direct seeing of the path]. All-knowledge is always present in the person of the Buddha until he attains the nirvāṇa without residue. It is because of this that he gains the unimpeded knowledge of all dharmas.

F. 15) The Four Unimpeded Knowledges Pāramitā

As for the *pāramitā* of the [four] unimpeded knowledges (*pratisaṃvid*), they are unimpeded knowledge with respect to: dharmas (*dharma-pratisaṃvid*), meaning (*artha-pratisaṃvid*), language (*nirukti-pratisaṃvid*), and eloquence (*pratibhāna-pratisaṃvid*). [The Buddhas] possess an unlimited penetrating comprehension of these four dharmas that is unimpeded in its implementation. As described in the sutras:[380]

> The Buddha told the bhikshus, "There are four of the Tathāgata's disciples who have perfected the foremost power of mindfulness, power of wisdom, and power of endurance so consummately that they are like a skilled archer who can shoot any single tree leaf without difficulty. Even if these disciples were to all come forth and pose challenging questions on the four stations of mindfulness, setting aside the time required for drink, food, toilet, and sleep, I could always and incessantly respond to their questions for a hundred years during which the Tathāgata would always reply with inexhaustible eloquence and wisdom."

Here the Buddha, with his characteristically scant wish to do so, discussed his own implementation of these knowledges. Supposing that there were a number of great trichiliocosms as numerous as all the atoms in all four continents of all worlds in a great trichiliocosm, supposing also that all those world systems were filled with beings all of whom were the likes of Śāriputra and the *pratyekabuddhas,* and suppose too that all these beings employed their perfected knowledges and eloquence to pose difficult questions to the Tathāgata on the four stations of mindfulness, doing so to the exhaustion of lifetimes extending to a number of kalpas as numerous as all the aforementioned atoms—the Tathāgata would still be able to reply to their questions on the meanings involved in the four stations of mindfulness, expounding on their meaning without redundancy and with inexhaustible eloquence.[381]

Now, as for the unimpeded knowledge with respect to dharmas, [the Buddhas] are well able to distinguish all details involved in the designations of dharmas with an unimpededly penetrating comprehension.

As for the unimpeded knowledge with respect to meaning, they are able to bring to bear an unimpededly penetrating comprehension of the meanings associated with those dharmas.

In the case of their unimpeded knowledge with respect to language, the Buddhas are able to accord with the languages and phrases through which the various sorts of beings are caused to understand those meanings, doing so with an unimpededly penetrating comprehension.

Regarding their unimpeded knowledge as it applies to eloquence, during that entire time in which they are answering questions, they are skillful and clever in speaking on Dharma and they are able to carry on in this fashion endlessly. Whatever topic all other worthies and *āryas* are unable to treat exhaustively, it is only the Buddhas who can reach the limits of that topic.

It is on these bases that we speak of the *pāramitā* of the unimpeded knowledges.

G. 16) The Pāramitā of Perfectly Complete Replies and Predictions

Regarding the *pāramitā* of perfection in the answering of questions, the Buddha is well able to answer in all situations involving the posing of difficult questions. And why is this so? It is because, in the four types of responses, he remains utterly free of erroneous or disordered presentations, because he well knows the conceptual meanings, because he has perfected the *pāramitā* of preserving the undamaged meaning, and because he delights in a profound knowing of the natures of all beings, what they themselves practice, and what they themselves find pleasing. This is illustrated by the instance in which Śāriputra addressed the Buddha, saying:

> Bhagavat, when the Buddha discourses on the good Dharma, many are the beings who, upon hearing this, then gain realizations. Having gained such realizations, their minds become free of all craving. And because they become free of all craving, they no longer have anything in the world that they indulge. And once they no longer have anything at all that they indulge, their minds achieve a state of inward cessation.

The Buddha exhaustively knows, without exceptions, the unsurpassable aspects of the good Dharma. There is no one who is superior to him in this regard.

Question: You spoke of the four types of replies. What are those four?

Response:

> First, the definitive reply.
> Second, the distinguishing reply.
> Third, the counter-questioning reply.
> And, fourth, the reply that sets aside the question.

In the case of the definitive reply, this is illustrated by the instance where a bhikshu asked the Buddha, "Bhagavat, is it or is it not the case that there could be some form that is eternal and unchanging? Bhagavat, is it or is it not the case that there could be any feelings, perceptions, formative factors, or consciousnesses that are permanent and unchanging?"

The Buddha replied, saying, "Bhikshu, there is no form that is permanent and unchanging. There are no feelings, perceptions, formative factors, or consciousnesses that are permanent and unchanging."

Cases such as these illustrate the "definitive reply."

The distinguishing reply is illustrated by the instance where Potaliputta,[382] the Brahmacārin, inquired of Samiddhi,[383]asking: [384] "In instances where a person deliberately performs actions of body, speech, or mind, what sorts of karmic retributions ensue therefrom?"

Samiddhi responded with a definitive reply, saying, "In instances where persons deliberately perform actions of body, speech, or mind, they are bound to undergo retributions involving suffering and anguish."

But this should have involved a distinguishing reply. This *brahmacārin* later came and asked the Buddha about this matter, to which the Buddha replied, saying, "Potaliputta, in instances where someone deliberately performs actions of body, speech, or mind, this karma may result in undergoing painful retributions, in undergoing pleasurable retributions, or in undergoing retributions that are neither painful nor pleasurable. Pain-inducing actions result in undergoing painful retributions. Pleasure-inducing actions result in undergoing pleasurable retributions. Actions that are neither pain-inducing nor pleasure-inducing result in undergoing karmic retributions that are neither painful nor pleasurable."

Scriptural passages such as these illustrate instances of the distinguishing reply.

The counter-questioning reply is illustrated by that instance in which the *brahmacārin* named Śreṇika inquired of the Buddha and the Buddha replied, "I shall now return the question to you whereupon you may reply in accordance with your own idea on this matter. Śreṇika, what do you think? Do physical forms constitute the Tathāgata, or not? Or is it that feelings, perceptions, formative factors, or consciousnesses constitute the Tathāgata?"

He replied, "No, Bhagavat. They do not."

[The Buddha then asked him], "Is the Tathāgata apart from form, feelings, perceptions, formative factors, or consciousnesses, or not?"

He replied, "No, Bhagavat. He is not."

These types of passages from scripture should be more extensively discussed. They illustrate what is meant by the counter-questioning reply.

As for the reply that sets aside the question, this applies to the response to questions regarding the fourteen classic erroneous views, namely:

Is the world eternal?
Is the world non-eternal?
Is the world both eternal and non-eternal?
Is the world neither eternal nor non-eternal?
Is the world bounded?
Is the world unbounded?
Is the world both bounded and unbounded?
Is the world neither bounded nor unbounded?
Does the Tathāgata exist after his nirvāṇa?
Does the Tathāgata not exist after his nirvāṇa?
Does the Tathāgata both exist and not exist after his nirvāṇa?
Does the Tathāgata neither exist nor not exist after his nirvāṇa?
Is the body identical with a spiritual soul (*jīva*)?
Is the body different from a spiritual soul?

As stated above, even in an instance where all beings possessed the wisdom and eloquence of the *pratyekabuddha* and they inquired of the Buddha on these four matters, the Buddha would in all cases adapt to their needs in answering their questions, offering replies that are neither excessive nor deficient. It is for these reasons that the Buddhas are said to possess the *pāramitā* of perfection in the answering of questions.

H. 17) Invulnerability to Harm by Anyone

There is no one whatsoever who can harm the Buddha. This is because he has gained that dharma by which one cannot be killed. There is no one who can cut off any part of the Buddha's body. He has sovereign mastery over whether he will live or die. This is as stated in scripture, wherein it states: "Were one to seek some method by which to inflict harm on the Buddha—there simply is no such possibility at all."

Question: Is the life span of a buddha fixed or is it unfixed?

Response: There are those who claim that it is unfixed. But if a buddha's life span were actually fixed, what difference then would there be between his case and that of all others who have fixed life spans? Still, in truth, the life span of a buddha is not fixed. That there is no one who can harm a buddha—now *that* is extraordinary. There are those who say that the life span of a buddha is fixed. However, whereas others whose life spans are fixed are indeed subject to having hands, feet, ears, and nose sliced off, the Buddha [is unique in that he] is entirely free of any such vulnerability.

Question: How is it that the Buddhas have this exclusive dharma of being invulnerable to being harmed?

Response: The inconceivability of the Buddhas can be understood by resort to analogy. Suppose for instance that all beings throughout the worlds of the ten directions were to have a given amount of power. Now, if a single *māra* could possess a certain amount of power, also suppose that each and every one of those beings throughout the ten directions was caused to possess powers like those of Māra, the Evil One. Even if all of those beings then joined in wishing to inflict harm on the Buddha, they would still be unable to move even a single hair on the Buddha's body. How much the less might they actually succeed in harming the Buddha.

Question: Well, if that is the case, how then could Devadatta have succeeded in injuring the Buddha?

Response: This question was already answered earlier. The Buddha wished to show beings the character of the three poisons. Even though

Devadatta had previously upheld the moral precepts and cultivated goodness, because he was attached to receiving offerings, he then committed immensely evil deeds.

[The Buddha] also allowed this to happen to enable [beings] to realize that the mind of the Buddha does not vary in the way it regards any human or deva. His having compassion and pity for Devadatta on the one hand and Rāhula[385] on the other was the same as his equal regard for his own left and right eyes.

The Buddha always spoke of the mind of uniformly equal regard for everyone. He revealed his equality of regard at this time. When the devas and people observed this, they were struck by the extraordinary nature of this and thus felt even stronger resolute faith.

In addition, because of this, the devas of the long-life heavens could see that the Buddha was still bound to undergo retribution for bad karmic actions done in previous lives. Had he not undergone it now, they might have thought that bad actions could be free of corresponding karmic retributions. Because the Buddha wished to cut off their wrong views, he thereby revealed his own undergoing of this karmic retribution.

Furthermore, the Buddha's mind is no different in the presence of pain or pleasure. His mind is free of any concept of a self. This is because it is ultimately empty. Because his sense faculties have all been made pliant and imperturbable by change, he has no need to use expedients to separate from pain and enjoy pleasures. This is as described in the Bodhisattva canon where it states: "It was merely as an expedient that the Buddha manifested as subject to this experience." One should infer the broader implications of this.

The above points illustrate what is meant by the Buddha's exclusive dharma of being invulnerable to being killed or harmed.

I. 18) Their Words Are Never Spoken without a Purpose

In speaking on the Dharma, their words are never empty. All words spoken by the Buddhas have a corresponding intended effect. Therefore, when the Buddhas speak on Dharma, their words are never empty. And how is this so? Before the Buddhas begin to speak on Dharma, they first contemplate from root to branch where beings' minds abide and whether their fetters are thick or only scant. Thus they know the origins of their meritorious qualities in previous lives, observe the nature and strength of their karmic roots, and know:

Where and when beings [will encounter] obstacles;

Whether they are susceptible to liberation through gentle teaching methods;

Whether they are susceptible to liberation through harsh teaching methods;
Whether they are susceptible to liberation through a combination of gentle and harsh teaching methods.[386]
Whether they need only a little bit of instigation to gain liberation;
Whether they require extensive distinguishing instructions to gain liberation;
That there are those who gain liberation through [teachings on] the aggregates, the sense bases, the sense realms, or the twelve links of conditioned co-production;
Whether they may gain access [to liberation] through the gateway of faith or through the gateway of wisdom;
That this person should gain liberation through the teaching of a buddha;
That this person should gain liberation through the teaching of a *śrāvaka* disciple;
That this person should gain liberation through some other set of conditions;
That this person should be able to gain success in the Śrāvaka Disciple Vehicle;
That this person should be able to gain success in the Pratyekabuddha Vehicle;
That this person should be able to gain success in the Great Vehicle;
That this person has long practiced habitual greed, habitual hatred, and habitual delusion;
That this person has practiced habitual greed and hatred;
And that this person has practiced habitual greed and delusion.

In this way, they distinguish and determine with regard to each and every situation:

That this person has fallen into an annihilationist view;
That this person has fallen into an eternalist view;
That this person is for the most part attached to the view that seizes on the existence of a real self in association with the body [or any of the other four aggregates];[387]
That this person is most often habitually attached to extreme views;
That this person is most often habitually attached to the views that seize upon either prohibitions or on opinionated views;
That this person is for the most part habitually arrogant;
That this person is for the most part habitually inclined toward feelings of inferiority and the tendency to flattery and deviousness;
That this person's mind is mostly inclined toward doubt and regret.

That this person has developed a fondness for refined literary expressiveness;
That there are those who prize refinement in meanings and principles;
That there are those who delight in profundities;
That there are those who enjoy topics that are merely superficial;
That, in previous lifetimes, this person has accumulated the Dharma provisions requisite to success in the path;
That this person is accumulating the Dharma provisions for the path in this present lifetime;
That this person has only accumulated roots of goodness conducive to enjoying karmic rewards [from previous meritorious actions];
That this person has only accumulated roots of goodness associated with thorough understanding;
That this person should be able to rapidly become enlightened;
And that this person will require a long time before he can become enlightened.[388]

The Buddha first engages in investigative contemplation and assessment of individual circumstances and then, according with whichever approach is appropriate to instigate someone's liberation, he then speaks Dharma for them and thereby brings about their liberation.

It is as a consequence of this that every instance of the Buddha's speaking of Dharma is free of any merely empty discourse. This is as described in a sutra: "The Bhagavat first knows and sees and only then speaks Dharma. It is not the case that he speaks Dharma without first knowing and seeing."

J. 19) Their Speech Is Free of Error

Regarding the absence of errors and mistakes [in their speech], when the Buddhas speak Dharma, they do not commit any errors or make any mistakes. "Absence of errors" refers to there being no instances in which the meaning of what they say is contradictory. "Absence of mistakes" means they make no mistakes with regard to meanings.

It is because they do not make mistakes with regard to causes and conditions as they relate to the path that they are said to not make mistakes. It is because they do not commit errors with regard to causes and conditions as they relate to the fruits of the path that they are said to not commit any error.

It is because they are not deficient that they are said to not make mistakes and it is because they are not excessive that they are said to not commit any error.

This is accomplished through their possession of a penetrating comprehension of the four unimpeded knowledges, through their constant harmonization of mindfulness and stable wisdom, and through their utter abandonment of views associated with annihilationism, eternalism, acausality, erroneous causality, or other such wrong views.

In the Dharma that they speak, there is no cause by which people become perplexed. In whatsoever they say, there are no faults involving inconsistencies between what is set forth in the beginning and in the end.

Scriptures accordant with these concepts should be discussed more extensively herein. As it says in one of the sutras: "Bhikshus. When I speak Dharma for you, it is good in the beginning, good in the middle, and good in the end. The phrasings are good and the meanings are good. It possesses a singular purity free of any debasing admixture and it is perfectly complete in its proclamation of *brahmacarya*."[389]

K. 20) Complete Use of the Three Turnings in Speaking Dharma

As regards the matter of [the Buddha's] speaking of Dharma involving rarities, whomever they undertake to teach is immediately enabled to realize the fruits of the path. This is a rarity.

Whenever they provide a reply or offer a prediction, their statements are always genuine and do not differ [from actual circumstances]. This too is a rarity.

The Buddha has the path as the subject of his discourse. This path as it is proclaimed by the Buddha is not admixed with afflictions and is able to bring about the severance of the afflictions. This too is a rarity.

Whenever the Buddha speaks, benefit ensues from it and it never involves mere empty words. This too is a rarity.

Whenever a person applies mental diligence and vigor to the cultivation of the Buddha's Dharma, he can cut off the unwholesome dharmas and bring about increase in the good dharmas. This too is a rarity.

There are three additional rarities: the rarity of displaying spiritual powers, the rarity of foretelling the content of others' thoughts, and the rarity of being able to accomplish the transformational teaching of others. It is on the basis of these three sorts of rarities in the proclaiming of Dharma that the Buddha's discourse on Dharma is said to be characterized by rarities.[390]

L. 21) They Are the Great Generals Among All Āryas

Regarding [the Buddha's] eminence as the most superior spiritual guide among all the Āryas, buddhas know what the minds of beings course in, know what they delight in, know whether their fetters are deep or shallow, know whether their faculties are sharp or dull, and know whether their wisdom is superior, middling, or inferior. It is because they know these matters well and know them with penetrating comprehension that they are the most superior spiritual guides among all the Āryas.

They are also able to well know the characteristics of the four truths, and to well know all the general and specific characteristics of all dharmas.

It is also because, when they speak on the Dharma, their words are not empty and because, when they speak on the Dharma, they commit no errors and make no mistakes that they are therefore the most superior spiritual guides among all the Āryas.

Question: But the other four groups are also able to speak on the Dharma and thus refute the teachings of the non-Buddhists and thereby cause them to enter into the Dharma of the Buddha. Why then does one only speak of the Buddha as the most superior spiritual guide?

Response: This should be explained by an analogy. Suppose all beings possessed the wisdom powers of a *pratyekabuddha*. If all of these beings did not receive the intentional assistance of the Buddha and yet wished somehow to bring about the liberation of but a single person, this would be a complete impossibility. When all of these persons spoke Dharma, they would still be unable to cause the severance of a tiny fraction of even one of the formless realm fetters.

If, on the other hand, the Buddha wished to bring about the liberation of some being and then proceeded to say something, even those burdened with the erroneous views of the non-Buddhists, the dragons, the *yakṣas*, and the various other sorts of beings who do not understand the language of the Buddha—these would all still be caused to understand. Then all of these would in turn be able to teach countless other beings. And so this proceeds even to the point that, today, whenever those within the community of *śrāvaka* disciples cause beings to abide in the four fruits of the path, they are all emblematically representative of the Tathāgata as the most superior of all spiritual guides.

It is for these reasons that the Buddha is known as the most superior spiritual guide, and it is for these reasons that this is regarded as an exclusive dharma not held in common with the other *āryas*.

M. 22–25) They Are Able to Remain Unguarded in Four Ways

As for the four unguarded dharmas, the Buddhas are unguarded in their physical actions, are unguarded in their verbal actions, are unguarded in their mental actions, and are unguarded with respect to the means for sustaining life. And why is this? These four matters are not protected from others' [knowledge]. They do not think, "Regarding my [actions of] body, speech, and mind, and my [means of sustaining] life—I fear that others might come to know about them."

And why is this? This is because, during the long night [of previous lifetimes], they have cultivated every sort of pure karmic deed and have always well seen, well known, and well severed every one of the dharmas associated with the afflictions. And this is because they have perfected every sort of peerless root of goodness, because they have so well practiced whatever dharma is amenable to practice, because they have reached the point where there is nothing about them the least bit worthy of criticism, and because they have utterly perfected the *pāramitā* of equanimity.

Now, on this matter of their "equanimity," when their eyes view form, they relinquish any thoughts of either distress or delight. And so it goes [with the other sense faculties and objects] up to and including the mind faculty's engagement with dharmas [as objects of mind]. In this connection, one would ideally also discuss here citations from such scriptures as the *Poheti* and *Uttara* sutras.[391]

N. 26–29) They Possess the Four Types of Fearlessnesses

Now, as for the four types of fearlessness....

Question: There is a single dharma known as "fearlessness." How is it that we here have four of them?

Response: It is because there are four matters in which there is an absence of doubt or fear that we therefore speak of four of them, as follows:[392]

First, as the Buddha told the bhikshus, "I myself here utter these truthful words: 'I am a man possessed of all-knowledge.' If anyone here, whether he be a *śramaṇa*, brahman, deva, Māra, Brahmā, or other person possessed of worldly knowledge were to challenge this statement in a manner consistent with Dharma, claiming that I do not indeed possess a direct knowledge of this Dharma, I would not then experience in this challenge even the slightest sign of fearfulness, and it is because of not experiencing any such sign that I have become established in security and fearlessness in this regard." This is the first type of fearlessness. It is a result of exhaustively knowing all dharmas in accordance with reality.

As for the second type of fearlessness, the Buddha said, "I myself here utter these truthful words: 'I have brought all of the contaminants to an end.' If any *śramaṇa*, brahman, deva, Māra, or Brahmā were to claim that these contaminants have not indeed been brought to an end, I would not then experience in this challenge even the slightest sign of fearfulness.[393] It is because of not experiencing any such sign that I have become established in security and fearlessness in this regard." This is the second type of fearlessness. It is a result of having thoroughly cut off all afflictions and having also cut off the habitual propensities associated with past afflictions.

As for the third [type of fearlessness], [the Buddha said], "I have proclaimed which dharmas constitute obstacles to realization of the path. If anyone herein, whether he be a *śramaṇa,* brahman, deva, Māra, Brahmā, or other person possessed of worldly knowledge were to challenge this statement in a manner consistent with Dharma, claiming that, even though one might avail oneself of these dharmas, they would not be able to cause an obstacle to the path, I would not then experience in this challenge even the slightest sign of fearfulness. It is because of not experiencing any such sign that I have become established in security and fearlessness in this regard." This is the third type of the fearlessness. It is a result of having thoroughly known those dharmas that constitute obstacles to the achievement of liberation.

As for the fourth [type of fearlessness, the Buddha said], "Whoever practices the path I have proclaimed, practicing it in accordance with the way I have explained the Dharma, will succeed in reaching the end of suffering. If any *śramaṇa,* brahman, deva, Māra, Brahmā, or other person possessed of worldly knowledge were to challenge this statement in a manner accordant with Dharma, claiming that, although one might practice a dharma such as this in a manner consistent with the way it has been explained, one would be unable to reach the path that brings about the end of suffering, I would not then experience in this challenge even the slightest sign of fearfulness. It is because of not experiencing any such sign that I have become established in security and fearlessness in this regard." This is the fourth type of fearlessness. It is a result of thoroughly knowing the path leading to the extinguishing of suffering.

All four of these types of fearlessness are referred to as "fearlessnesses" because they all involve leaving behind such characteristic signs as fearfulness, terror, or horripilation. They are also termed "fearlessnesses" because they are able to maintain within the Great Assembly an awe-inspiring power of virtue extraordinary in its excellence. They are also called "fearlessnesses" because they so well know how to respond to all sorts of questions. Here, one should extensively discuss citations from *The Sutra on the Convocation of the Devas.*[394]

Question: If the Buddhas are indeed possessed of all-knowledge, then they should be fearless in relation to all dharmas. Why is it then that we speak only of these four types [of fearlessness]?

Response: These serve to raise the major essential topics in order to introduce the most important instances. All other instances are similar to these.

O. 30–39) They Possess the Ten Powers

As for the ten powers of the Buddha, "power" refers to the inexhaustible energetic strength that assists them and makes them invulnerable to interference by anyone. Although there are ten designations in this regard, in truth, this involves a single type of knowledge that, because it takes ten different circumstances as objective conditions, [these ten exemplary manifestations] are known as "the ten powers."

Because the knowledge of the Buddha takes all things as its objective conditions, it should be that there are countless powers. But it is because these ten powers are adequate to bring about the liberation of beings that we only speak of "the ten powers." Through merely introducing these ten powers, one can then know the others by inference.

1. The First Power

The first power is [the Buddha's] definite and completely penetrating knowledge with respect to all dharmas of what does and does not constitute the cause. This is the first power. [This was the basis for, as cited earlier], the Buddha's having said [in reference to the *brahmacārin* named Patikaputra], "If this crazy person does not relinquish these claims, does not relinquish these perverse views, and does not relinquish these thoughts, then, as for his being able to arrive here in the presence of the Buddha—this is an utter impossibility."

[This is also the basis for] the Buddha's having said to Ānanda:

> It is utterly impossible that two buddhas might arise in the world at the same time. However, it is indeed possible for a single buddha to come forth into the world."[395] This was said solely with respect to the circumstance of a single buddha emerging in a single world. In truth, in all of the countless and limitless worlds throughout the ten directions, there are countless hundreds of thousands of myriads of *koṭis* of buddhas simultaneously emerging throughout those worlds.
>
> Additionally, the sutras state: "It is impossible that bad physical, verbal, and mental karmic actions might have excellent and desirable results. However, it is indeed possible that good physical, verbal, and mental karmic actions may have excellent and desirable results."[396]

Here one should extensively discuss related scriptural citations from among the five categorical repositories of Dharma.

2. The Second Power

The second power is [the Buddha's] knowing in accordance with reality and with distinguishing clarity the place, the circumstances, and the karmic retributions associated with all past, future, and present karmic deeds along with all the dharmas that are involved in experiencing [those retributions].

If the Buddha wishes to know with regard to any being their past karmic deeds and their past karmic retributions, he is able to immediately know them. So too, he is immediately able to know:

With respect to past karmic deeds, their retribution in the present;
With respect to past karmic deeds, their retribution in the future;
With respect to past karmic deeds, their retribution in the past;
With respect to past karmic deeds, their retribution in both the past and the future;
With respect to past karmic deeds, their retribution in both the past and the present;
With respect to past karmic deeds, their retribution in both the future and the present;
With respect to past karmic deeds, their retribution in the past, the future, and the present;
With respect to present karmic deeds, their retribution in the present;
With respect to present karmic deeds, their retribution in the future;
With respect to present karmic deeds, their retribution in both the present and the future;
And with respect to future karmic deeds, their retribution in the future.

There are all manner of such distinctions regarding the dharmas involved in undergoing karmic retributions. There are four dharmas categorizing such karmic retributions, namely:

Undergoing blissful experiences in the present followed by undergoing suffering in future lifetimes;
Undergoing suffering in the present followed by undergoing blissful experiences in future lifetimes;
Undergoing blissful experiences in the present followed by blissful experiences in the future;
And undergoing suffering in the present followed by undergoing suffering in the future as well.[397]

As regards [the Buddha's knowing] "the place," this refers to his knowing for any karmic deed the time and place [of its occurrence] as well as the precise place in which this retribution will be undergone.

As regards [the Buddha's] knowing "the circumstances," this refers to knowing the corresponding causes and conditions, knowing the three corresponding types of bad karmic roots, knowing whether the deed was primarily performed by oneself, or knowing whether the deed occurred for the most part through the instigation of someone else. The Buddha entirely knows all such causes and conditions associated with good and bad karmic deeds.

As regards [the Buddha's knowing] "the karmic retributions," he knows that all karmic deeds have their corresponding karmic retributions. For instance, good karmic deeds may result in being reborn in a good place or in attaining nirvāṇa, whereas bad karmic deeds may result in being reborn in any of the wretched destinies.

The Buddha knows entirely with respect to all these karmic deeds their roots, their branches, their associated causes and conditions, and whether they were done at one's own behest or at the behest of others. It is because this power of knowledge does not diminish that it is referred to as a "power."

3. The Third Power

The third power is the Buddha's knowing in accordance with reality the *dhyānas*, the meditative concentrations, the liberations, and the samādhis, together with their corresponding marks of defilement and purity.

"*Dhyānas*" refers to the four *dhyānas*. "Meditative concentrations" refers to the four formless-realm meditative concentrations, the four immeasurable minds, and other such states, all of which are referred to as "meditative concentrations." "Liberations" refers to the eight liberations. As for "samādhis" all of the other meditative concentrations aside from the *dhyānas* and the liberations are referred to as "samādhis."

There are others who claim that the three gates to liberation, meditative concentrations still characterized by initial ideation (*vitarka*) and discursive thought (*vicāra*), meditative concentrations characterized by the absence of initial ideation and the presence of discursive thought, and meditative concentrations devoid of both initial ideation and discursive thought—these may all be referred to as "samādhis."

There are yet others who claim that "meditative concentrations" are relatively minor [meditative states] whereas "samādhis" are relatively major. Therefore, one may refer to all meditative concentrations realized by any buddha or bodhisattva as constituting a "samādhi."

All four of these constituent categories are subsumed within all explanations of "*dhyāna pāramitā*."

As for "defilement," this refers to [meditative states characterized by] the experience of delectably pleasurable (*āsvādana*) sensations whereas "purity" refers here to not indulging delectably pleasurable sensations.

Then again, "defilement" may refer to any meditative concentration still characterized by the contaminants (*āsrava*) whereas "purity" may refer to any meditative concentration characterized by the absence of the contaminants.

As for the distinctions among the samādhis, liberations, and so forth, [the Buddha] knows with distinguishing clarity these sorts of *dhyāna* meditation states.

4. The Fourth Power

The fourth power is [the Buddha's] knowing in accordance with reality the relative superiority or inferiority of the faculties of other beings and other personages.

"Other beings" refers to common persons. "Other personages" refers here to the stream enterer and the other classes of worthies and *āryas*. There may be others who interpret "beings" as a reference not only to common persons, but also even to those practitioners still involved in the learning stages, this because all of these have still not succeeded in putting an end to all of the contaminants. For them, "other personages" is a reference reserved for arhats and such, this because they have utterly ended all afflictions.

Yet others point out that both "beings" and "other personages" are but a single category and it is only the designations themselves that differ.

As for their "faculties," in this context they refer to faith, vigor, mindfulness, concentration, and wisdom and *not* to the sense faculties such as the eye and so forth [as the word might otherwise signify].

"Superior," as it applies to these faculties, refers to faculties that are fiercely sharp and which have the capacity to enable the attainment of enlightenment. "Inferior," on the other hand, refers to [faculties] that are dim, dull, and inadequate to enable one to take up [the practice of] the path.

The Buddha knows the relative superiority and inferiority of these two types of faculties and knows these matters in accordance with reality and in a manner free of any sort of error.

5. The Fifth Power

The fifth power is [the Buddha's] knowing in accordance with reality that in which the minds of other beings and other personages delight. "That in which they delight" refers to whatever endeavors they esteem and are inclined to engage in. For instance, there are those people who esteem wealth and worldly pleasures, whereas there are others who deeply esteem karmic merit and the practice of good dharmas. The Buddha knows all of these matters in accordance with reality.

6. The Sixth Power

The sixth power is the Buddha's knowing in accordance with reality the different types of natures of beings in the world as well as the countless [distinctions among those] natures. "Different types of natures" refers to the myriad variations in these natures. "Countless natures" is a reference to the countless distinctions in each and every one of these types of natures. As for the term "nature," it is because one's mind has always habitually practiced [particular sorts of endeavors] and has always delighted in practicing and cultivating them throughout one's past lives right up until the very present—it is for this reason that they therefore form the basis of one's "nature." The Buddha knows in accordance with reality these two categories of natures, the good and the bad.

7. The Seventh Power

The seventh power is [the Buddha's] knowing in accordance with reality the paths leading to all destinations. As for "the paths leading to all destinations," those are the means by which one may succeed in acquiring all meritorious qualities. These paths are referred to as "the paths leading to all destinations."

These include, for instance, the five-factor samādhi,[398] the fivefold awareness samādhi,[399] the eightfold path of the Āryas, all dharmas subsumed by the path of the Āryas, or the four bases of psychic power, the latter as cited in a sutra that says: "If a bhikshu cultivates the four bases of psychic power, there is no benefit that he will not acquire."

There are others who claim that this may also refer to the four *dhyānas*, as cited in a sutra that says: "When a bhikshu gains the four *dhyānas*, his mind comes to abide with stability and purity in a single place in which he then succeeds in ridding himself of all afflictions and in destroying all obstacles. It then becomes well-regulated so that it becomes serviceable and no longer subject to movement or distraction."

8. The Eighth Power

The eighth power is the [Buddha's] immediate ability to know past-life matters whenever he chooses to direct his awareness to events from previous lives. If the Buddha wishes to recall any of the countless and limitless lifetimes of either himself or all other beings, he then knows all of these matters entirely. There are no instances in which he is unable to know some particular matter even beyond a number of kalpas equal to the number of sands in the Ganges River.

He knows where this person was born, what his name was, whether he was of noble or lowly caste, what he drank and ate, how he sustained his life, whether he experienced suffering or happiness, the types of endeavors in which he engaged, the karmic retributions that he underwent, what his mind engaged in, and from whence he originally came. He knows all such matters.

9. The Ninth Power

The ninth power is the [Buddha's] ability to see with the heavenly eye purified beyond the power of man's eyes the beings of the six destinies taking on bodies in accordance with their karmic deeds.

A *śrāvaka* disciple possessed of great powers uses the heavenly eye to see the lands contained within a small chiliocosm and also sees when the beings therein are born and when they die.

A lesser *pratyekabuddha* sees the lands of a thousand small chiliocosms and sees when the beings therein are born and when they die.

A *pratyekabuddha* possessed of middling powers sees the lands contained in a hundred myriads of small chiliocosms and sees when the beings therein are born and when they die.

A *pratyekabuddha* possessed of great powers sees the lands contained in a great trichiliocosm and sees the destinies to which they proceed when they die and are reborn.

The Buddhas, the Bhagavats, see a countless, boundless, and inconceivable number of worlds and also see when the beings therein are born and when they die.

10. The Tenth Power

As for the tenth power, it is the [Buddha's] ending of all contaminants, including the contaminant of sensual desire, the contaminant of [craving for] existence, and the contaminant of ignorance, these together with the utter ending of all afflictions or affliction-associated energetic propensities. This is the tenth power.

P. 40) They Have Achieved Unimpeded Liberation

As for unimpeded liberation, there are three types of liberations. The first is the liberation from the obstacles of the afflictions. The second is the liberation from the obstacles to meditative concentration. The third is the liberation from the obstacles to [the knowledge of] all dharmas. Among these, an arhat who has achieved liberation through wisdom gains liberation from the obstacles of the afflictions. Both the doubly-liberated arhat and the *pratyekabuddha* succeed in achieving both the liberation from the obstacles of the afflictions and the liberation from the obstacles to the *dhyāna* concentrations.

It is only the Buddhas who have completely achieved all three of these liberations, namely liberation from the obstacles of the afflictions, liberation from the obstacles to acquisition of the *dhyāna* concentrations, and the liberation from the obstacles to [the knowledge of] all dharmas. It is because he brings together all three of the liberations that the Buddha is designated as having achieved unimpeded liberation. This [unimpeded liberation] always accompanies the mind all the way up to the point of entry into the nirvāṇa without residue.

Q. Summary Discussion of the Dharmas Exclusive to the Buddha

These forty dharmas exclusive to the Buddhas provide a general introduction to an entryway into the dharmas of the Buddha. They are discussed here because this allows beings to thereby acquire an understanding of them. However, those [exclusive dharmas] that remain undiscussed herein are innumerable and boundless. Specifically, these include the following:

1) [The Buddha] never departs from wisdom.
2) He never errs in knowing the right time.
3) He has extinguished all habitual karmic propensities.
4) He has gained the meditative concentration *pāramitā*.
5) All of his meritorious qualities are possessed of extraordinary supremacy.
6) He has perfected the *pāramitā* of always according in his actions with what is appropriate to the circumstances.
7) No one is able to view the very top of [the light rays radiating from] the crown of his head.
8) No one is his equal.
9) No one is able to surpass him.
10) He is superior to all beings in the world.
11) His attainment of the path is not learned from anyone else.
12) He never turns away from the Dharma.
13) Whoever else might claim to be a buddha is forever unable to enter the presence of the Buddha.
14) He has perfected the dharma of never retreating.
15) He has acquired the great compassion.
16) He has acquired the great kindness.
17) He is the foremost among all whose teachings one may accept in faith.

18) He is the foremost among those [who are worthy of] fame and offerings.
19) No guru who is a contemporary of the Buddha is equal to the Buddha.
20) No guru gains a community of disciples equal to that of the Buddha.
21) The supreme refinement of his appearance causes all who see him to be delighted.
22) Whoever is sent forth as an emissary of a Buddha cannot be harmed by anyone.
23) No one is able to injure anyone whom the Buddha has set out to liberate.
24) From the very moment he first brings forth a thought, he is able to sever all thought-related fetters.
25) He never misses the right time [to provide appropriate instruction to] beings who are capable of achieving liberation.
26) In the sixteenth [mind-moment involved in the acquisition of] wisdom, a buddha attains *anuttarasamyaksaṃbodhi.*
27) He is the foremost among the world's fields of merit.
28) He emanates measureless radiant light.
29) His actions differ from those of anyone else.
30) He possesses the [physical] marks that are associated with a hundredfold generation of merit.[400]
31) He has measureless and boundless roots of goodness.
32) When he enters the womb—
33) When he is born—
34) When he achieves buddhahood—
35) When he turns the wheel of the Dharma—
36) When he relinquishes the possibility of the long life span—
37) And when he enters nirvāṇa—[on all these occasions], he is able to cause all the worlds throughout the great trichiliocosm to shake.
38) [On all of the above occasions], he sets quaking the countless palaces of the *māras,* causing them to lose their awesome power and be struck with terror.
39) [When he achieves buddhahood], the world-protecting heavenly kings, Śakra, ruler of the devas, the Yāma Heaven King, the Tuṣita Heaven King, the Nirmāṇarati Heaven King, the Paranirmita Vaśavartin Heaven King, the Brahma Heaven King, the devas of the Pure Abodes, and the other devas—they all simultaneously assemble and request the turning of the Dharma wheel.
40) The Buddha's body is as solid as the body of Nārāyaṇa.[401]

41) When the moral precepts have not yet been formulated, he is the one who first formulates the moral precepts.
42) Whenever he takes up any endeavor, his power in accomplishing this is superior to that of any man.
43) During the entire time the Bodhisattva is residing in his mother's womb, she loses all thoughts of defiling attachment for men.
44) His power is such that he is able to bring about the rescue and liberation of all beings.

There are measurelessly and innumerably many dharmas such as these that are exclusive to the Buddha. Because it would interfere with the explanation of other matters, there is no need to present an extensive discussion of them here. Although these dharmas as found in the Dharma of the Śrāvaka Disciples do resemble dharmas of the Buddha, due to dissimilarities in the degree of superiority or inferiority, there are distinct differences [in how they are described].

Moreover, to summarize, all of the dharmas of the Buddhas are measureless, limitless, inconceivable, of the foremost degree of rarity, and such that no other being is able to have them in common [with any buddha]. Even if all the countless beings in the worlds of all the great trichiliocosms throughout the ten directions possessed wisdom comparable to the king of the Great Brahma Heaven, comparable to a great *pratyekabuddha,* or comparable to Śāriputra, and one were somehow able to collect all this wisdom together in a single person—even if that one person then wished to approach the most minutely small fraction of these forty dharmas exclusive to the Buddhas—this would still be an utter impossibility. He could not even measure up to but one part in a hundred thousand myriads of *koṭis* of parts of just a single one of those dharmas.

The Buddhas possess the power of just such an immeasurable and limitless number of meritorious qualities. And why is this so? It is because they have securely established themselves in the four bases of meritorious qualities for a countless number of great kalpas during which they have deeply practiced the six *pāramitās* and have become well able to completely equip themselves with all dharmas practiced by the bodhisattva. Because [these dharmas] are not held in common with any other beings, so too, the fruits resulting [from their practice] are not held in common with any beings, either.

The End of Chapter Twenty-Three

CHAPTER 24
Verses Offered in Praise

XXIV. CHAPTER 24: VERSES OFFERED IN PRAISE

A. THE IMPORTANCE OF PRAISES TO MINDFULNESS-OF-THE-BUDDHA PRACTICE

Now that, in this way, we have reached the end of this explanation of the forty dharmas exclusive to the Buddhas, one should take the aspects emblematic of these forty exclusive dharmas and use them in one's own practice of mindfulness of the Buddha. One should also use verses to praise the Buddha, doing so as if one were standing directly before him, speaking to him. If one proceeds in this manner, then one may succeed in entering the mindfulness-of-the-Buddha samādhi. Accordingly, there are verses, as follows:

B. THE PRAISE VERSES

1. VERSES IN PRAISE OF THE FORTY DHARMAS EXCLUSIVE TO THE BUDDHAS

Oh, greatly vigorous lord of the Āryas—
Now, in the presence of the Buddha,
I shall praise with reverential mind
these forty dharmas possessed only [by buddhas].[402]

As for his supernatural powers and travel through flight,
their power when enacted is utterly limitless.
Among the psychic powers of the other *āryas,*
there are none at all that can equal these.

Among the *śrāvaka* disciples, he holds sway with sovereign mastery,
using his measureless knowledge of others' thoughts.
Thus he is well able to train their thoughts
by according with their minds as he appropriately responds to them.

His mindfulness is as expansive as the great ocean
while also being tranquil and calmly secure.
In all the world, there is no dharma
able to cause him to become perturbed.

The jewel of the vajra samādhi
that is praised by all buddhas—
he has acquired it and it resides within in his heart
just as the Worthies embrace the straightforward mind.

He thoroughly knows the unfixed dharmas
and the matters associated with the four formless absorptions
that are so subtle they are difficult to distinguish.
He exhaustively knows them all without exception.

Regarding whether a being has already died in the past,
dies now in the present, or will die at some point later in the future,
it is solely the Bhagavat, and he alone,
whose wisdom is able to fully comprehend such things.

He knows well all matters related
to the formless dharmas unassociated with the mind
that everyone else throughout all worlds
remains entirely unable to know.

The Bhagavat's great awesome powers,
his measureless meritorious qualities,
and his boundless wisdom
are all unmatched by anyone at all.

In the four types of responses to questions,
he is so preeminent that he has no peer.
As for all the challenging questions that beings present,
he replies to them all with utter ease.

If anywhere in any world
there is someone wishing to harm the Buddha,
this circumstance never comes to pass,
for he has gained the dharma by which he cannot be slain.

If at any point throughout the three periods of time
there is anything that he says,
those words are definitely not set forth in vain,
but rather always bring great fruits as a result.

Of all the dharmas that he proclaims,
none of them are not especially rare.
He is never in error as regards their significance,
how much the less might he ever err in words and phrases.

For the three types of *ārya* disciples
that differ as either superior, middling, or inferior,
and include the eight classes in four pairs,[403] and the others,
he is the foremost great spiritual guide.

In actions of body, speech, and mind, and in sustaining his life,
he is ultimately and always pure
and hence, in all of these,
he never again needs to act in a guarded way.

When he himself proclaims his possession of all-knowledge,
his mind remains utterly free of any doubt or fear
such that he might think, "If someone comes and challenges me,
I fear there may be something I do not know."

When declaring his characteristic of having ended the contaminants,
thus reaching the utmost elimination of the contaminants,
his mind remains utterly free of any doubt or fear
that there might be residual contaminants that are not yet ended.

When proclaiming his knowledge of the obstructive dharmas,
he has no doubt at the prospect of being challenged
that, though one might indulge in these dharmas,
they might not actually then constitute an obstacle.

As for the eightfold path of the Āryas that he has proclaimed,
his mind is free of any doubt or fear
that someone might rightly claim of this eightfold path
that it is unable to lead one to reach liberation.

He knows in accordance with reality that this is a cause,
this is its result, and this other factor does not constitute [a cause].
It is for these reasons that he is said to be omniscient
and that his fame spreads immeasurably far.

All actions carried out throughout the three periods of time,
the fixed retribution associated with these actions,
and their unfixed karmic results—
He thoroughly knows all of these different matters.

As for all coarse, subtle, deep, and shallow phenomena
within all of the *dhyāna* absorptions and samādhis,
he is able to entirely know them all.
In the realm of *dhyāna* absorptions, no one is his equal.

He first knows with regard to the faculties of beings,
their distinctions as either superior, middling, or inferior,
knows what they delight in, and knows their individual natures,
whereupon, adapting to what is fitting, he teaches them the Dharma.

He cultivated the path and gained its benefits
while also teaching and guiding others.
It is in this manner that the community of disciples
gains the wholesome benefit that accords with reality.

His knowledge of past lives is measurelessly vast
and the vision of his heavenly eye has no bounds.
Among all humans and devas,
no one is able to know their limits.

He abides in the vajra samādhi,
having extinguished the afflictions and karmic propensities,
and also knows the utter ending of the human contaminants.
Hence this is known as the power of having ended the contaminants.

The obstacle of afflictions, the obstacles to *dhyāna* absorptions,
and the obstacles to the knowledge of all dharmas—
he has gained liberation from all three obstacles
and hence is known as one who has gained unimpeded liberation.

The forty exclusive dharmas
have measureless meritorious qualities
of which no one could present an expansive explanation.
I have hereby now concluded this general explanation.

Even if, for an entire kalpa, the Bhagavat
spoke in praise of these dharmas of the Buddhas,
he would still be unable to completely describe them.
How much the less might I do so in the absence of such wisdom.

2. Verses Praising the Four Bases of Meritorious Qualities

The shade of the Bhagavat's great kindness
has been thoroughly gathered together through countless deeds.
It is because of the four bases of meritorious qualities
that he has gained the Buddha's measureless Dharma.

As for these four supreme bases of meritorious qualities
of which the Bhagavat has spoken with praise—
I shall now return to these
in setting forth praises of the Tathāgata.

He is completely endowed with the thirty-two marks,
each mark of which requires a hundredfold generation of merit.
As for the eighty marvelous secondary characteristics,
who residing in the three realms could possibly possess them?

Were one to multiply by a hundred all the karmic rewards
produced by the merit created by all the beings
residing within a great trichiliocosm,
each of the marks has just such a quantity of merit [as its cause].

It would require just such a quantity of merit
as well as its associated karmic rewards,
multiplied yet another hundred times
to produce a buddha's mid-brow white hair mark.

It would require for each and every one of thirty marks
all of their corresponding merit and karmic rewards,
multiplied yet again a thousand more times,
to produce the fleshy *uṣṇīṣa* sign atop a buddha's crown.

The meritorious qualities of the Bhagavat
are such that they could never be measured.
Any attempt to do so would be like someone using a ruler
to measure the endless expanse of empty space.

From the moment he brought forth the great resolve
for the sake of bringing about the liberation of all beings,
he persevered for countless kalpas with solid resolve.
It was because of this that he then achieved buddhahood.

Intensely diligent in his zeal to achieve the fulfillment
of such a magnanimous vow,
throughout an immeasurably great number of kalpas,
he has cultivated all the difficult ascetic practices.

Just as with all buddhas of the ancient past
who taught these four bases of meritorious qualities,
only after countless kalpas were they then perfected
so that now he has succeeded in securely abiding within them.

a. Verses Praising the Truth Basis of Meritorious Qualities

Their foundation lies in preservation of the actual truth,
for which he relinquished even his own body and loved ones,
his riches, treasures, and the happiness associated with wealth.
It is through this that he achieved its complete fulfillment.

Throughout measurelessly many kalpas,
in every instance, he has first thoroughly contemplated
the dharmas that are seen, heard, sensed, and known,[404]
and then, afterward, has explained them for the sake of others.

Where others had not observed (some aspect of Dharma) and such,
as well as in situations where they were beset by doubts,
he was then able to explain these matters in accordance with reality.
Those whom he benefited in this way were measurelessly many.

He would not discuss the confidential matters of others.
Even if resented or ridiculed for this, he still refused to betray them.
His thoughts always dwelt in a state of stable wisdom
as he adapted his teachings to lead others to peace and security.

As for the foremost and most genuinely sublime truth,
nirvāṇa is truly supreme,
for all else, in every case, is false.
The Bhagavat has achieved[405] its complete fulfillment.

b. Verses Praising the Relinquishment Basis of Meritorious Qualities

[He made gifts of] beverages, food, bedding, and such,
halls, buildings, marvelous residences, viewing terraces,
highly prized elephants, horses, and vehicles, and also
relinquished female companions of especially fine appearance.

[He gave away] gold, silver, pearls, jewels, and such,
villages, cities, and towns,

entire states, and exalted official positions,
and gave away [his dominion over] the four continents as well.

[He relinquished] cherished sons, beloved wives,
his limbs, his head, and his eyes,
and made gifts by slicing off his flesh, removing bones and marrow,
or even giving away his entire body.

Doing so out of pity for beings,
he gave them all, having none that he continued to cherish.
He did so aspiring to go beyond *saṃsāra*
and not out of some quest to secure his own bliss.

All of the stars and constellations throughout empty space,
and all the grains of sand in this entire earth—
when the Tathāgata was still a bodhisattva,
the number of times he gave in such ways exceeded even these.

He never resorted to actions contrary to Dharma
as he sought out wealth to be used in giving.
He never engaged in giving unaccompanied by knowledge and
never engaged in giving that was invasive or distressing to others.

He never gave bad things as gifts
because he coveted some other fine thing [in return].
He never gave with an ingratiating deviousness
and never engaged in forceful giving because of coveting something.

He never gave with a hate-filled or doubting mind,
never did so with perverse intent or with derisive laughter,
never did so out of disgust or disbelief,
and never gave with the face turned away, or in other such ways.

He had no discriminating mind [by which he judged],
"This one is worthy and that one is unworthy."
Because he only relied on the mind of compassion,
it was with equal regard for everyone that he practiced giving.

He did not slight other beings,
considering them to not qualify as fields of merit.
On seeing *āryas*, his mind was reverential.
On seeing those who have broken the precepts, he felt pity for them.

He did not elevate himself above others,
treat others as mere inferiors,
engage in giving for the sake of praise,
give in expectation of rewards, or give in other such ways.

He never gave with regrets or with worry-filled misgivings
and never gave with thoughts of disdain or disrespect.

He never gave with a mind affected by irritability or hostility
and never gave simply as a protocol-dictated formality.

He never gave with a disrespectful mind,
never gave by simply tossing the gift on the ground,
never gave deliberately seeking to cause distress,
and never gave out of a jealousy-driven struggle for supremacy.

He would never tease a supplicant,
never failed to present a gift with his own hands,
did not slight the recipient with a merely paltry gift,
and did not give excessively in order to enhance his own esteem.

His giving was never motivated by intentions associated with
either the Śrāvaka Disciple Vehicle or the Pratyekabuddha Vehicle.
His giving was never limited to concern for only a single lifetime
and he never engaged in giving done at the wrong time.

For countless kalpas, the Bhagavat
practiced every form of rare giving,
always doing so for the sake of the unsurpassable path
and not merely in order to seek his own happiness.

Throughout the duration of all buddhas' Dharma,
he became a monastic, practiced renunciation,
cultivated the Dharma of all buddhas,
and proclaimed the Dharma for the sake of all humans and devas.

He taught just such a dharma of giving as this
that is supreme among all types of giving,
just as, among all the stars and the moon,
it is the light of the sun that is supreme.

Such supremacy in the relinquishment basis [of meritorious qualities]
surpasses that of any deva or human,
just as it is the Bhagavat
who is superior to everyone in the world.

He was therefore able to perfect
such supreme practice of the relinquishment basis.
His fame shall endure for countless kalpas,
flowing on and spreading ceaselessly.

c. Verses Praising the Quiescence Basis of Meritorious Qualities

For countless kalpas, the Bhagavat
preserved and upheld the precepts of moral purity
and opened the gates of the *dhyāna* absorptions
for the sake of acquiring the deep quiescence basis.

He began by abandoning five characteristics[406]
and later practiced the eight liberations.
He entered and purified the three samādhis,
and also dwelt in the three liberations.

The Bhagavat well distinguishes
the sixty-five kinds of *dhyānas*.
There is no *dhyāna* whatsoever
that he has not formerly produced.

Even when abiding in these meditative absorptions,
he did not indulge in their delectably pleasurable states.
Due to the various meditative absorptions,
the Bhagavat gained three types of spiritual superknowledges.

He used these in the liberation of beings
and so became supreme in all things.
For countless kalpas, with a mind of equal regard,
the Bhagavat widely spread his kindly transformative teaching.

An *asaṃkhyeya* of beings
was thereby caused to abide in the Brahma World Heavens
because he was able to use skillful means
in thoroughly teaching the *dhyāna* absorptions.

While still a bodhisattva, the Bhagavat
for incalculably many lifetimes, always
remained free of any entanglement in the affliction of covetousness.
Thus he was able to come and go in the world.

Of those who succeeded in encountering him in the past,
countless such beings thereby achieved rebirth in the heavens.
As for that quiescence that
all bodhisattvas of the past were able to practice,

when still a bodhisattva, the Bhagavat
also practiced, doing so in a manner no different from theirs.
Thus, as regards the realization of quiescence,
that supreme basis [of meritorious qualities], it was entirely fulfilled.

d. Verses Praising the Wisdom Basis of Meritorious Qualities

All those forms of wisdom
possessed by the Bhagavat while he was still a bodhisattva—
He relied on such wisdom in his quest for bodhi
so that, as a karmic result, he has now developed this wisdom.

Just as people rely on the earth for the production
of all the food that it supplies,
[so, too], as in life after life, the Bhagavat
relinquished the ten courses of dark and bad actions

and always practiced the path of the ten good actions,
these [deeds] were all due to the power of wisdom.[407]

He renounced the five desires and the five hindrances
and thus acquired all the various *dhyāna* absorptions.
He accomplished this for the number of lifetimes in countless kalpas
and did not acquire this from others.
This is excellent indeed, O Great Honored One of the Āryas.
All of this was due to the power of wisdom.

It is because of the Bhagavat that beings,
countless in number, have taken rebirth in the six heavens.
So too has he enabled them to reach the Brahma World.
All of this was due to the power of wisdom.

Throughout the course of his births and deaths, the Bhagavat,
even when confused and perturbed by sufferings and pleasures,
never lost the resolve to attain bodhi.
All of this was due to the power of wisdom.

Throughout the course of *saṃsāra,* the Bhagavat
did not delight [in worldly existence] and yet still always remained.
He delighted in nirvāṇa, yet did not seize on its [final] realization.
All of this was due to the power of wisdom.

When sitting peacefully there in the *bodhimaṇḍa,*
he overcame Māra and his armies
and proceeded to liberate all the classes of beings.
All of this was due to the power of wisdom.

When he originally strove in quest of bodhi,
he accumulated countless provisions for the path.
If merely hearing of them causes one to be confused and perturbed,
how much the less might one be able to take on their practice.
That the Bhagavat was able to patiently endure such things
was in every case due to the power of wisdom.

That, in lifetime after lifetime, he was able to naturally know
the classic texts as well as all the arts and skills
while also being able to teach them to others
was in every case due to the power of wisdom.

He drew close to countless buddhas
and from them all drank the sweet-dew nectar of their teachings,
He consulted them and inquired about the many different topics
and then also pursued additional distinguishing [clarifications].

He was never the least bit miserly
with the wisdom of the sutras' Dharma,

but rather offered it even to servants, youths, and menials,
allowing them to freely receive his fine explanations.
Because of this, [the fame of] the Bhagavat's
supreme wisdom basis [of meritorious qualities] spreads on afar.

Throughout his former lifetimes, as the Bhagavat
pursued his quest for the realization of bodhi,
he practiced the great kindness and compassion
toward all beings.

Relying on the foremost wisdom,
he always marshaled his great strength
to take up and do all the countless kinds
of rare and difficult endeavors.

3. Concluding Praise Verses

In all of the many worlds,
he exhaustively contributed all his efforts for countless kalpas.
One could never come to the end of them through verbal description,
nor could one even reach it through mathematical calculation.

All of his endeavors of such sorts
surpass those done by any human or deva.
Even in all the many worlds,
there is nothing comparable to his extraordinary marvels.

The fruits reaped through such great deeds
reach complete fulfillment in the realization of all-knowledge.
He is the king of those able to destroy *saṃsāra*
and dwells securely in the place of the Dharma king.

The End of Chapter Twenty-Four

Chapter 25
Teachings to Aid the Mindfulness-of-the-Buddha Samādhi

XXV. Chapter 25: Teachings Aiding Mindfulness-of-the Buddha Samādhi

A. Initial Instructions on the Mindfulness-of-the Buddha Samādhi

The bodhisattva should rely on these
forty exclusive dharmas
in his mindfulness of the Buddhas' Dharma body,
for the Buddhas are not their form bodies.

These [preceding] verses have sequentially and summarily explained six categories of meanings associated with the forty exclusive dharmas.[408] In doing so, the practitioner therefore first takes up the mindfulness of the Buddha's form body and then takes up the mindfulness of the Buddha's Dharma body.

Why is this the case? The bodhisattva who has only recently brought forth the resolve [to attain buddhahood] should first take up the practice of mindfulness of the Buddha in reliance on the thirty-two marks and eighty secondary characteristics [of the Buddha's form body], doing so in the manner described earlier.

Then, as one's practice progressively penetrates more deeply, one will develop a middling degree of strength in that practice. One should then rely on the Dharma body in his mindfulness of the Buddha.

Then, as one's mind progressively penetrates yet more deeply, one will then achieve a supreme degree of power in the development of this practice. At that point, one should then take up mindfulness of the Buddha in accordance with the true character of [all dharmas][409] and remain free of any sort of attachment in doing so.

One must not become deeply attached to the form body.[410]
One also refrains from becoming attached to the Dharma body.
One should thoroughly realize that all dharmas
are as eternally quiescent as empty space.

As this bodhisattva develops a superior degree of power [in this practice], he refrains from developing a deep attachment to the Buddha on the basis of either the form body or the Dharma body. Why not? Through one's resolute belief in the dharma of emptiness, one understands that all dharmas are like empty space.

Empty space is defined by the absence of obstruction. The causal circumstances associated with obstruction include phenomena like

Mount Sumeru, Yugaṃdhara Mountain, the rest of the ten jeweled mountains, the Iron Ring Mountains, Black Mountain, Stone Mountain, and the others. There are all sorts of other such causal bases for the existence of obstructions.

Why is this [a point at issue]? Because this person has still not yet gained the heavenly eye, if he brings to mind buddhas abiding in the worlds off in the other directions, the various mountains will block them from his view. Consequently, The bodhisattva who has only recently brought forth the resolve [to attain buddhahood] should use the sublime characteristics described by the ten names as bases for his mindfulness of the Buddha. This is as described in these lines:

> The bodhisattva who has only recently brought forth the resolve
> uses the sublime features described by the ten names
> in practicing mindfulness of the Buddhas that is free of fault,
> seeing them just as if they were images in a mirror.

As for "the sublime features described in the ten names," those ten names are:

> Tathāgata;[411]
> Worthy of Offerings;
> The Right and Universally Enlightened One;
> Perfect in the Clear Knowledges and Conduct;
> Well Gone One;
> Knower of the Worlds;
> Unsurpassable Trainer of Those to Be Tamed;
> Teacher of Devas and Humans;
> Buddha;
> Bhagavat.

As for "free of fault," the phenomena that one contemplates are beheld as empty and like space itself. Thus [one's contemplation] is free of any fault with regard to the Dharma. And how is this so? It is because all dharmas, from their very origin on forward to the present, have been unproduced and quiescent. Just as this is true [with respect to these dharmas], so too is this also true of all other dharmas.

By taking these names as the object [of his contemplation], this person develops his practice of the dharma of *dhyāna* meditation. Having done so, he is then able to take these characteristic signs themselves as the object of his contemplation.

At this time, this person then immediately acquires these signs in his practice of the dharma of *dhyāna* meditation and experiences what is referred to as the direct personal experience of an especially extraordinary bliss. One should realize that when this occurs, one has acquired the *pratyutpanna* samādhi. Because of developing this samādhi, one is then able to see the Buddhas.

As for "as if they were images in a mirror," once the bodhisattva has developed this samādhi, it is as if one is seeing one's own face in a clean, brightly-lit mirror or like seeing the image of one's own body in a clear, still pool of water.

Initially, whichever buddha one first brings to mind, it is that very image that one sees. After one has seen this image, if one wishes to see buddhas in other regions, then, in accordance with whichever region one brings to mind, one obtains an unimpeded vision of those very buddhas. Hence, regarding this person:

> Although he does not yet possess the spiritual superknowledges
> by which he could fly to visit them,
> he is nonetheless able to see those buddhas
> and has an unimpeded ability to listen to their Dharma.

For this bodhisattva who has only recently brought forth the resolve [to attain buddhahood], neither Mount Sumeru nor any other mountain can present an obstacle and, even though he has not yet acquired any of the spiritual superknowledges, the heavenly eye, or the heavenly ear, and even though he has not yet developed the ability to fly from this country to that country, through the power of this samādhi, even while still abiding in this country, he is able to see the Buddhas, the Bhagavats, abiding in the other regions and is able to hear the Dharma as they are speaking it. Through always cultivating this samādhi, he becomes able to see all of the buddhas throughout the ten directions just as they really are.

B. Four Dharmas Capable of Bringing Forth This Samādhi

Question: Through which dharmas is one able to bring forth this meditative absorption and how can one acquire it?

Response:

> One draws close to the good spiritual guide,
> brings forth nonretreating vigor,
> develops extremely solid and durable wisdom,
> and develops the power of unshakable faith.

It is through utilizing these four dharmas that one is able to bring forth this samādhi.

As for "drawing near to the good spiritual guide," someone able to instruct a person in the acquisition of this samādhi qualifies here as "the good spiritual guide." One should bring forth reverential respect and assiduous diligence and, in drawing near [to the good spiritual guide], one must not allow any indolence, diminishment in motivation, or relinquishing of effort to take place. If one acts accordingly, one will then be able to hear the teaching of the deep meaning of this samādhi.

Sharp wisdom, wisdom characterized by penetrating comprehension, and undiminishing wisdom are what qualify as "solid and durable" [wisdom]. One's faculty of faith is deeply and firmly established, so much so that, no matter whether it be a *śramaṇa* or a brahman or a celestial *māra* or Brahmā or anyone else in the world—none of them could cause it to quaver even slightly. This is what is meant by an unshakable power of faith. It is these very four dharmas described here that are able to bring forth this samādhi.

C. Four More Dharmas Capable of Bringing Forth This Samādhi

Furthermore:

> With a sense of shame, dread of blame, cherishing reverence,
> and offerings to those who proclaim the Dharma
> presented as if they were given to the Bhagavats themselves,
> one thereby becomes able to bring forth this samādhi.

As for "with a sense of shame, dread of blame, and cherishing reverence," one brings forth a profound sense of shame and dread of blame in relation to those who teach the Dharma. With sincere reverence and affectionate delight, one makes offerings to them as if they were the Buddhas themselves. In this way, these four dharmas are able to produce this samādhi.

D. Four More Dharmas Capable of Bringing Forth This Samādhi

Another preliminary set of fourfold dharmas is as follows:

First, for a period of three months, one strives to refrain from sleeping and, with the exception of using the toilet and eating and drinking, one refrains from sitting down;

Second, for that period of three months, one avoids, even for the duration of a finger snap, indulgence in any thought seizing on the existence of a self;

Third, for that entire three months, one strives to always walk and never rest;

Fourth, for that entire three months, when also engaged in the giving of Dharma, one refrains from seeking offerings from others.

These are the four. There are four more such dharmas, as follows:

E. Four More Dharmas Capable of Bringing Forth This Samādhi

First, one becomes able to see the Buddhas;

Second, one reassures and encourages others to listen to the teaching of this samādhi;

Third, one is never envious or jealous of anyone who is putting the resolve to attain bodhi into practice;

Fourth, one is able to accumulate the dharmas of the bodhisattva path.

These are the four. There are four more such dharmas, as follows:

F. Four More Dharmas Capable of Bringing Forth This Samādhi

First, one makes buddha images that may also include painted images;

Second, one should carefully write out copies of the sutra that discusses this samādhi and then encourage others who have a resolute faith in it to study and recite it aloud once they have obtained it;[412]

Third, teach those of overweening pride[413] to abandon their overweening pride[414] and then influence them to pursue the attainment of *anuttarasamyaksaṃbodhi;*

Fourth, one should devote oneself to the protection and preservation of the right Dharma of all buddhas.

These are the four. There are four more such dharmas, as follows:

G. Four More Dharmas Capable of Bringing Forth This Samādhi

First, one avoids speaking;

Second, both lay and monastic practitioners are to refrain from dwelling together with others;

Third, one always anchors one's mind on the characteristic sign that has been chosen as the object of one's mental focus;[415]

Fourth, one delights in dwelling far apart from others, in a location that is vacant, serene, and silent.

These are the four. The first of the fivefold sets of associated dharmas is as follows:

H. Five More Dharmas Capable of Bringing Forth This Samādhi

First, abiding in the unproduced-dharmas patience (*anutpattika-dharma-kṣānti*), one renounces all conditioned dharmas, does not delight in any of the destinies of rebirth, refuses to accept any of the non-Buddhist dharmas, and remains so disgusted with all worldly desires that one does not even bring them to mind, how much the less might one draw physically close to them;

Second, even as one's mind always cultivates and practices countless dharmas, it remains in a state of one-pointed concentration;

One remains free of the obstacle of hatred toward any being and one's mind always accords with the practice of the four means of attraction;

Third, one becomes able to perfect kindness, compassion, sympathetic joy, and equanimity while also refraining from exposing others' transgressions;

Fourth, one becomes able to accumulate a multitude of dharmas proclaimed by the Buddha while also being able to carry them out in accordance with the way they were taught;

Fifth, one purifies one's physical, verbal, and mental actions as well as one's views.

These are the five. There are five more associated dharmas, as follows:

I. Five More Dharmas Capable of Bringing Forth This Samādhi

First, one delights in according with the practice of giving as praised in the sutras, doing so without miserly thoughts. One delights in speaking on profound dharmas, withholds nothing due to stinginess, and also remains able to dwell in those very dharmas oneself;

Second, one abides in patience, mental pliancy, and delight when abiding in close proximity to others and, if subjected to harsh speech, scolding and cursing, whippings, beatings, being tied up, or other such experiences, one simply attributes it to one's own karmic conditions and does not hate others for doing this;

Third, one always delights in listening to teachings that explain this samādhi, in reading and reciting them, in thoroughly understanding them, in explaining them for others, and in causing them to circulate and spread ever more widely even as one diligently practices and cultivates [this samādhi];

Fourth, one's mind remains free of any jealous feelings toward others, one refrains from elevating oneself and looking down on others, and one strives to rid oneself of the hindrance of drowsiness;

Fifth, one maintains a mind of pure faith in the Buddha Jewel, the Dharma Jewel, and the Sangha Jewel, offers up deeply sincere service to those of senior, middling, and lower station, always remembers and never forgets even the smallest kindnesses of others, and always abides in truthful speech.

These are the five. In addition, there are the following lines:

J. The Guidelines for Lay and Monastic Cultivation of This Samādhi

As for those samādhi dharmas
in which monastic bodhisattvas train,
householder bodhisattvas
should also know these dharmas.

1. Twenty Guidelines for Lay Cultivators of This Samādhi

If a householder bodhisattva wishes to cultivate this samādhi, [he should observe the following twenty guidelines]:

1) One should proceed with a mind of deep faith;
2) One should not seek any sort of karmic reward;
3) One should give up all personal and extra-personal things;
4) One should take refuge in the Three Jewels;
5) One should uphold the five moral precepts purely and in a manner free of any transgression or deficiency;
6) One should perfect the practice of the ten courses of good karmic action while also influencing others to abide in these dharmas;
7) One should cut off all sexual desire;
8) One should repudiate the five types of desire;
9) One should refrain from any feelings of jealousy toward others;
10) One should not nurture an affectionate attachment for either one's spouse or one's children;
11) One should always maintain an aspiration to leave the householder's life to become a monastic;
12) One should always take on and observe the layperson's precepts of abstinence;[416]
13) One's mind should delight in the opportunity to abide within the precincts of a temple;[417]
14) One should be well possessed of a sense of shame and a dread of blame;
15) One should bring forth thoughts of reverential respect toward bhikshus who are pure in upholding the moral precepts;
16) One should not act in a miserly way with the Dharma;
17) One should maintain a mind of deep affection and reverence toward those who teach the Dharma;
18) One should think of teachers of Dharma as if they were one's father, mother, or great teaching master;
19) One should respectfully present all manner of delightful gifts as offerings to the Dharma teaching masters;
20) One should feel gratitude for the kindnesses that have been bestowed upon one and one should repay those kindnesses accordingly.

If a householder bodhisattva abides in meritorious qualities such as these, he will then be able to learn this samādhi.

2. Sixty Guidelines for Monastic Cultivators of This Samādhi

As for [the guidelines appropriate to] a monastic bodhisattva's cultivation of dharmas pertaining to this samādhi, they are as follows:

1) One remains free of any defect as regards observance of the moral precepts;
2) One maintains uncorrupted observance of the moral precepts;
3) One maintains unsullied observance of the moral precepts;
4) One maintains pure observance of the moral precepts;
5) One maintains undiminished observance of the moral precepts;
6) One does not seize on the moral precepts themselves [as constituting the very essence of moral virtue];
7) One does not rely on the moral precepts [alone as the sole component of one's practice];
8) One realizes that the moral precepts cannot finally be apprehended at all [as inherently existent entities];
9) One never retreats from one's observance of the moral precepts;
10) One upholds the moral precepts in the manner that is praised by the Āryas;
11) One upholds the moral precepts in the manner that is extolled by the wise;
12) One accords with the *prātimokṣa* precepts;
13) One perfects the bases for the awe-inspiring deportment;
14) One remains immensely fearful of committing even the most minor transgression of the precepts;
15) One purifies the actions of body, speech, and mind;
16) One maintains purity in right livelihood;
17) One completely upholds all of the moral precepts;
18) One maintains resolute belief in the extremely profound dharmas;
19) One is able to patiently acquiesce in the dharma of the non-apprehension [of any dharma whatsoever] and is able to not be frightened even by the dharmas of emptiness, signlessness, and wishlessness;
20) One remains diligent in bringing forth vigor [in one's practice];
21) One always maintains ever-present mindfulness;
22) One maintains a mind of solid faith;
23) One is well possessed of a sense of shame and a dread of blame;
24) One does not covet offerings;
25) One remains free of jealousy toward others;
26) One abides in the meritorious qualities associated with practicing the *dhūta* austerities;
27) One abides in the subtleties of Dharma practice;
28) One takes no delight in speaking the coarse language of the world;

29) One avoids gathering in groups for [idle] conversation;
30) One knows to repay kindnesses one has received;
31) One acknowledges those who bestow kindnesses and those who repay kindnesses;
32) Toward one's monastic preceptors and monastic Dharma teachers, one brings forth thoughts of sincere reverence and appreciation for the rarity of being able to encounter them;[418]
33) One does away with any arrogance one might be harboring;
34) One overcomes the self-cherishing mind;
35) Because a good spiritual guide can only rarely be encountered, one strives with diligence to look after his needs;
36) With regard to the source from which one first learned about this Dharma, whether by obtaining a sutra text from someone or by hearing someone recite it, one thinks of them with the same regard as one would maintain for one's own father or mother, one's good spiritual guide, or a great teaching master, and with regard to them, one also feels a sense of shame, dread of blame, affection, and reverence;
37) One always delights in dwelling in a forest hermitage;
38) One does not delight in dwelling in a city or village;
39) One does not covet the opportunity to frequent the homes of benefactors[419] and good spiritual friends;
40) One does not maintain a stinting covetousness for one's own physical survival;
41) One remains ever mindful of death;
42) One does not hoard offerings;
43) One does not indulge any defiling attachment for possessions;
44) One remains free of cravings;
45) One guards and preserves right Dharma;
46) One is not attached to one's robes or bowl;
47) One does not hoard leftover things;
48) One prefers to eat only food that has been obtained on the alms round;
49) On the alms round, one moves along seeking alms according to the proper sequence;[420]
50) One always maintains a sense of shame and dread of blame and always feels remorse [for one's past transgressions];
51) One refrains from hoarding gold, silver, precious jewels, or money and also avoids indulging in unwholesome remorsefulness;[421]
52) One's mind remains free of entangling defilements;
53) One always puts the mind of kindness into practice;

54) One cuts off all feelings of anger;
55) One always puts the mind of compassion into practice;
56) One cuts off affectionate attachments;
57) One always seeks ways to benefit and bring peace to the entire world;
58) One always feels pity for all beings;
59) One always delights in [meditative] walking;
60) One does away with lethargy and sleepiness.

The monastic bodhisattva who abides in dharmas such as these should cultivate and practice this samādhi. Additionally:

3. Fifty Dharmas Supporting Cultivation of This Samādhi

One should also train in this same manner
in the other dharmas pertaining to the cultivation of samādhi.

In order to be able to bring forth this *pratyutpanna* samādhi, one should also cultivate the other supportive dharmas. And what are these? They are:

1) One takes the Buddha's kindness as one's objective focus and always mindfully contemplates him as if he were directly before one;
2) One does not allow one's mind to become scattered;
3) One anchors one's attention directly before one;
4) One guards the gates of the sense faculties;
5) With respect to food and drink, one is easily satisfied;
6) One always cultivates samādhi in both the first and last watches of the night;
7) One abandons the obstacle of the afflictions;
8) One brings forth all of the *dhyāna* absorptions;
9) In one's practice of *dhyāna* meditation, one does not indulge in the delectably pleasurable meditation states;
10) One demolishes through separation the appearance of attractive forms;[422]
11) One acquires the sign of unloveliness;[423]
12) One does not desire the five aggregates;
13) One does not become attached to the eighteen sense realms;
14) One does not indulge any defilement in relation to the twelve sense bases;
15) One does not presumptuously rely on one's [superior] caste origins;
16) One destroys any arrogance;
17) One's mind always remains empty and quiescent in relation to all dharmas that one encounters;

18) One imagines all beings as one's close relatives;
19) One does not seize on the moral precepts themselves [as constituting the very essence of moral virtue];
20) One does not make discriminating distinctions regarding the meditative absorptions;
21) One should diligently pursue abundant learning;
22) One does not become arrogant because of this abundant learning;
23) One remains free of doubts with respect to any of the dharmas;
24) One does not oppose the Buddhas;
25) One does not act in a manner that is contrary to the Dharma;
26) One does not do anything that contributes to the destruction of the Sangha;
27) One always goes to pay one's respects to worthies and *āryas*;
28) One distances oneself from foolish common people;
29) One delights in discussion of world-transcending topics;
30) One cultivates the six dharmas of mutual harmony;[424]
31) One always cultivates the five bases of liberation;[425]
32) One rids himself of the nine bases for generating the affliction of anger;[426]
33) One cuts off the eight dharmas associated with indolence;[427]
34) One cultivates the eight types of vigor;[428]
35) One always contemplates the nine signs [of the deterioration of the corpse];[429]
36) One has realized for himself the eight realizations of great men;[430]
37) One perfects all of the *dhyāna* concentrations and samādhis;
38) One has no covetous attachment to these *dhyāna* concentrations and realizes they have no apprehensible reality;[431]
39) When listening to Dharma, one does so with a focused mind;
40) One demolishes the perception of the five aggregates [as inherently existent phenomena];
41) One does not abide in the perception of phenomena [as inherently existent];
42) One is deeply fearful of *saṃsāra*'s births and deaths;
43) One contemplates the five aggregates as like enemies;[432]
44) One contemplates the sense bases as like an empty village;
45) One contemplates the four great elements as like venomous serpents;
46) One brings forth the contemplation of nirvāṇa as quiescent, secure, and happy;[433]
47) One contemplates the five desires as worthy of being spat upon and one's mind delights in escaping from them;

48) One never opposes the teachings of the Buddha;
49) One has no disputes or quarrels with any other being;
50) In teaching beings, one influences them to dwell securely in all of the meritorious qualities.

K. The Benefits of Cultivating This Pratyutpanna Samādhi

In addition:

The bodhisattva should understand
the benefits that result from such a samādhi.

The bodhisattva should also understand the benefits that result from practicing this *pratyutpanna* samādhi.

Question: What are the resulting benefits gained by cultivating this samādhi?

Response: One obtains the resulting benefit of becoming irreversible with respect to the unsurpassable path. Additionally, as for what the sutra says about these resulting benefits, we have the following:[434]

> The Buddha told Bhadrapāla Bodhisattva, "By way of analogy, suppose there was a person who was able to crush to dust all the earth in all worlds in a trichiliocosm and was also able also to crush to dust all the grasses, trees, flowers, leaves, and everything else throughout all of the worlds in a great trichiliocosm.
>
> "Bhadrapala, let us consider now that each and every one of those motes of dust were to constitute one world in which a single buddha dwells and suppose then that one filled to overflowing just such a number of worlds with sublimely marvelous precious jewels and presented all of these jewels as an offering to them.
>
> "Bhadrapāla, what do you think? By performing such an act of giving, would this person gain a great deal of merit or not?"
>
> "Indeed, O Bhagavat, he would reap a great deal."
>
> The Buddha said, "Bhadrapāla, I will now tell you truthfully that if there was a son of good family who heard of this samādhi in which all buddhas appear before one and he were then to be neither startled nor frightened by hearing of it, the merit he would reap from that alone would be immeasurably vast. How much the more so would this be the case if he were to have faith in it, accept it, uphold it, read [teachings in which it is explained], recite them, and explain them for others. How much the more so yet would this be the case if he were to actually cultivate it with concentrated mind even for the time it takes to tug a single squirt of milk from the udder of a cow.
>
> "Bhadrapāla, let me tell you: Even this person's merit would surpass one's ability to measure it. How much the more so would this be so in the case of someone who was actually able to succeed in acquiring this samādhi."

The Buddha continued, telling Bhadrapāla, "If a son or daughter of good family who receives, upholds, reads, recites, and explains [teachings on this samādhi] for others were on the verge of falling into the fires arising at the end of the kalpa, those fires would immediately become extinguished.

"Bhadrapāla, whosoever sustains this samādhi—supposing that he were to encounter some difficulty with officialdom, or supposing that he were to encounter hostile thieves, lions, tigers, wolves, fearsome beasts, fearsome dragons, any of the venomous serpents, or any other such threat, whether from *yakṣas, rākṣasas, kumbhāṇḍas, piśācis,* and such, or from humans, nonhumans, or any other sort of entity—that any of those entities might succeed in physically harming him, taking his life, or causing him to break the precepts—this would be an utter impossibility.

So too would this also be the case with respect to those who might be reading, reciting, or teaching this to others. In those cases too they would remain free of any destructive affliction, with the sole exception of instances where they were already bound to undergo compulsory karmic retributions.[435]

"Furthermore, Bhadrapala, when a bodhisattva accepts, upholds, reads, or recites the sutra on this samādhi, if he happens to contract some sickness of the eye, ear, nose, tongue, mouth, or teeth, some disease instigated by wind or cold, or any other such disease, that he might then lose his life because of any of these diseases would be an utter impossibility with the sole exception of instances where he was already bound to undergo compulsory karmic retributions.

"Also, Bhadrapāla, if a person were to accept, uphold, read, or recite the sutra on this samādhi, the devas themselves would protect him. So too would he be protected by the dragons, *yakṣas, mahoragas,* humans, nonhumans, the Four Heavenly Kings, Śakra, ruler of the devas, the Brahma Heaven King, and the Buddhas, the Bhagavats. They would all join in remaining protectively mindful of this practitioner.

"Furthermore, this person would be one of whom the devas would all be affectionately mindful, and so too would this be so for other such beings up to and including the Buddhas themselves who would also remain affectionately mindful of this practitioner.

"Additionally, this person would be one whom the devas praise, and so too, he would be one whom other beings up to and including all buddhas would praise as well.

"Also, this bodhisattva would be one whom the devas would all wish to see coming to visit them, and so too with the others on up to the Buddhas themselves who would all wish to see him coming to visit them.

"Furthermore, the bodhisattva who accepts and upholds the sutra on this samādhi will naturally become able to hear whichever other sutras he has not yet heard.

"Additionally, this bodhisattva who gains this samādhi will become able to acquire all of these beneficial experiences even in his dreams.

"Bhadrapāla, were I to attempt to describe the merit of this bodhisattva who accepts, uphold, reads, and recites the sutra on this samādhi, doing so even for an entire kalpa or somewhat less than a kalpa, I would still be unable to come to the end of it. How much the less would this be possible in the case of someone who actually succeeds in perfecting this samādhi.

"Bhadrapāla, if some man with strong body and speed like the wind ran for a hundred years without resting, always proceeding to the east, south, west, north, the four midpoints, above, and below, what do you think? Would anyone be able to know the number of miles he traveled in all those regions throughout the ten directions?"

Bhadrapāla replied, "That would be an incalculable number. Except for the Tathāgata, someone like Śāriputra, or an *avaivartika* [bodhisattva], nobody would be able to know such a number."

"Bhadrapāla, suppose that, on the one hand, there was a son or daughter of good family who filled up with real gold all the area traveled by that man and then give it all away as gifts. Suppose too that, on the other hand, there was someone who merely heard of this samādhi and then engaged in four types of rejoicing and dedication of merit to *anuttarasamyaksaṃbodhi* and the constant pursuit of abundant learning, [doing so by reflecting as follows]:

> Just as all buddhas of the past when practicing the bodhisattva path rejoiced in this samādhi, so too do I now rejoice in it;
>
> Just as the bodhisattvas of the present now rejoice in this samādhi, so too do I now rejoice in it;
>
> Just as all future buddhas during their practice of the bodhisattva path shall rejoice in this samādhi, so too do I now rejoice in it;
>
> And in just that fashion as this samādhi was practiced by all past, future, and present bodhisattvas, so too do I now also rejoice in all of that, and just as they all did so for the sake of pursuing abundant learning [essential to the path], so too do I now rejoice in this samādhi for the sake of the quest for such abundant learning.

"Bhadrapāla, if one were to attempt to compare the previously described merit with the merit from this rejoicing, it could not approach a hundredth part or even one part in a hundred thousand myriads of *koṭis* of parts. The futility of this comparison simply could not be adequately described through any form of calculation or analogy. The benefits resulting from this samādhi are just so immeasurable and boundless as this."

L. This Samādhi's Various Stations and Levels of Cultivation

In addition:

As for the stations in which one may abide in this samādhi
as well as the distinctions pertaining to lesser, middling, and greater,
the many different characteristics such as these
should all be taken up for a discussion of their meaning.

The stations in which one may abide in this samādhi as well as its lesser, middling, and greater characteristics—all such things should be distinguished and known and these matters should then be explained.

Regarding "the stations in which one may abide in it," this samādhi may be acquired in the first *dhyāna*, the second *dhyāna*, the third *dhyāna*, or the fourth *dhyāna* and one may acquire strength in it while in the first *dhyāna*.

It may be that someone who is "lesser" is able to bring forth this samādhi. Here, "lesser" may refer to the fact that a person is possessed of only a lesser degree of strength [in this practice]. "Lesser" may also refer to abiding [in the samādhi] for a shorter period of time. "Lesser" may also refer to the practitioner's seeing a relatively smaller number of buddha worlds. Distinctions regarding "middling" and "greater" may be made in just the same way.

M. Various Qualitative Variations in How This Samādhi Manifests

In discussing this samādhi, one may speak of it as:

Sometimes involving the presence of ideation (*vitarka*) and the presence of discursion (*vicāra*);
Sometimes involving the absence of ideation and the presence of discursion;
Sometimes involving the absence of ideation and the absence of discursion;
Sometimes involving the presence of joy (*prīti*);
Sometimes involving the presence of bliss (*sukha*);
Sometimes involving neither suffering nor bliss;
Sometimes involving the presence of breathing;
Sometimes involving the absence of breathing;
Sometimes definitely being of a wholesome nature;
Sometimes involving the presence of the contaminants;
Sometimes involving the absence of the contaminants;

Sometimes connected with the desire realm;
Sometimes connected with the form realm;
Sometimes connected with the formless realm;
Sometimes not connected with the desire realm;
Sometimes not connected with the form realm;
And sometimes not connected with the formless realm.

N. Various Abhidharmic Classifications of This Samādhi

This samādhi;

Is a mental dharma;
Is [a dharma] associated with the mind;
Is a dharma that occurs along with the mind;
Is a non-form [dharma];
Is a non-manifest [dharma];
Is able to take an object;
Is not karma [*per se*];
Is associated with karmic activity;
Is coexistent with karmic activity;
Is not the result of karmic actions from a previous life except when it is the result of a particular cause;[436]
Can be cultivated, can be known, and can be realized;
Can be realized both with the body and by means of wisdom;
Can be subject to severance or may be invulnerable to severance;
Should be severed when contaminants are present;
And is invulnerable to severance when free of the contaminants.

Similar distinctions of this sort may also made with respect to the knowledge and vision associated with this samādhi. Also, it is not necessarily conjoined with the seven limbs of enlightenment.[437] Ideally, all of these distinctions should be discussed herein.

O. The Practitioner's Offerings, Roots of Goodness, and Teaching

Furthermore, it is through the cultivation of this samādhi that one may succeed in seeing the Buddhas. Accordingly, it is said that:

After one has succeeded in seeing the Buddhas,
one proceeds with diligent resolve to present offerings [to them].
As one's roots of goodness are thus able to grow,
one becomes able to rapidly teach beings.

"Making offerings" refers to having a pure mind imbued with reverence and delight as one brings to mind the countless meritorious qualities of the Buddha. When one praises him in various ways, this constitutes the making of verbal offerings. When one makes formal reverential bows and presents flowers, incenses, and other such things, this constitutes the making of physical offerings.

Because of these actions, one's karmic merit grows ever greater just as a seed starts to grow when it is planted in earth and receives moisture from the rain. "Rapidly teaching" refers to influencing beings to abide in the Three Vehicles. It is in this way that the bodhisattva brings about the growth of his roots of goodness.

P. The Practitioner's Use of the Four Means of Attraction

Through availing oneself of the first two dharmas of attraction,
one is able to attract beings [to the Dharma].
One resorts to the latter two dharmas of attraction
for those not yet fully able to believe and accept [Dharma teachings].

"The first two" refers to "giving" and to "pleasing words" whereas "beneficial actions" and "joint endeavors" constitute "the latter two dharmas" [of the four means of attraction]. Because this bodhisattva who abides on the first ground is as yet unable to completely comprehend everything, [there may be certain aspects of the teaching] that he can only accept on faith.

Q. The Practitioner's Dedication of Roots of Goodness

He then takes all of his roots of goodness
and dedicates them to the realization of buddhahood.
This is comparable to when others smelt gold
and then refine it, whereupon it thereby becomes amenable to use.

It is through being smelted by the fire of wisdom that, in all the endeavors undertaken by the bodhisattva, his roots of goodness ripen and then finally become amenable to use.

The End of Chapter Twenty-Five

Chapter 26
The Analogy Chapter

XXVI. Chapter 26: The Analogy Chapter

A. The Bodhisattva Should Study, Cultivate, and Reach the Grounds

This bodhisattva should learn of the characteristic features
of the grounds and then attain the fruits of their cultivation.
It is in order to attain all aspects of the grounds
that he is therefore diligent in the practice of vigor.

"Characteristic features" refers here to their appearances. It is due to [learning about them] that one is then able to know them. "Attain" refers here to bringing them to a state of complete development. It is because of this dharma [of "complete development"] that one refers to completely developing this dharma.

"Cultivation" refers to [the two types of cultivation, namely] cultivation associated with acquisition and cultivation associated with practice. As for always bearing in mind "the fruits," it is from the cause that one achieves the accomplishment of an endeavor that is referred to as its "fruits."

This bodhisattva who aspires to acquire the practices specific to the ten grounds should learn well to their characteristic features and then acquire the fruits of their cultivation. "Learning" refers to hearing [these teachings] from buddhas, bodhisattvas, and one's superiors.

"It is in order to gain all aspects of the grounds," means that it is for the sake of successful acquisition of the aspects of these grounds that one diligently practices vigor. The characteristic aspects of the first ground that are of concern here are as described earlier in this text:

B. Seven Practices Characteristic of the First Ground Bodhisattva

The bodhisattva who abides on the first ground
has much that he is able to endure.
He is not fond of struggle or disputation,
and, for the most part, his mind is joyous and pleased.

He always delights in purity.
He has a compassionate mind and feels pity for beings.
He has no thoughts of hatred or anger,
and, for the most part, practices these seven things.[438]

Thus, the seven dharmas consisting of the capacity for endurance, non-disputation, being joyous and pleased, purity, compassion, an absence of hatred in the mind, and such—these are all characteristic features of the first ground. It is the complete development of these seven dharmas consisting of the "capacity for endurance" and so forth that define their "acquisition." Furthermore, these seven dharmas comprising the characteristics of "capacity for endurance" and so forth—they are all acquired on the first ground. This is as described in verse, as follows:

C. Eight Accomplishments Associated with Entering the First Ground

Having densely planted one's roots of goodness,
having thoroughly practiced the practices,
having well accumulated all the provisions,
having made offerings to all buddhas,

having become protected by the good spiritual guide,
having completely developed the resolute intentions,
having become compassionately mindful of beings,
and having resolute belief in the unsurpassable Dharma—[439]

Once one has become completely equipped with these eight dharmas,
at one's own behest, one should bring forth a vow, saying,
"After I have accomplished my own liberation,
I shall return and liberate other beings."

For the sake of gaining the ten powers,
one enters the congregation of those at the stage of certainty.[440]
Then one is born into the family of the Tathāgatas
that is free of any transgressions.

One immediately turns away from the worldly path
and enters the supreme path that goes beyond the world.
It is because of this that one gains the first ground.
This ground is referred to as "the Ground of Joyfulness."[441]

Therefore, one should understand that the definite resolve one has developed for the sake of attaining bodhi is what constitutes the essence of one's cultivation in gaining the first ground. From that initial bringing forth of the resolve all the way to one's attainment of the samādhi in which all buddhas manifest before one—all of the meritorious qualities thoroughly described as pertaining to that intervening period are what are able to bring forth all of these meritorious qualities. And after they have arisen, their cultivation, accumulation, and growth are what define the first ground.

As for "the fruits of their cultivation," we have previously already emphasized in place after place that, when one acquires however much merit, one is not to dedicate that merit for the sake of reaching the grounds of either *śrāvaka* disciples or *pratyekabuddhas*. Now we should state this yet again. When the bodhisattva acquires the fruition of the first ground, he is able to acquire several hundreds of meditative concentrations and other such results.

As for the "aspects" of the first ground, this refers to all the many dharmas that jointly establish the first ground. This is what is meant here by "all aspects." This is analogous to the yeast, rice, and other ingredients that, when mixed together, are able to make wine. These are what constitute the causes and conditions for the making of wine. So too it is with all the dharmas that are able to contribute to the establishment of the first ground. These are what constitute the "aspects" of the first ground. These are as follows:

D. The Essential Aspects of the Bodhisattva's First Ground Cultivation

The power of faith becomes ever more superior
as one perfects the mind of great compassion.
One feels kindness and pity for all types of beings
and tirelessly cultivates the mind of goodness.

One finds joyous delight in sublime dharmas,
always draws close to the good spiritual guide,
maintains a sense of shame, dread of blame, and reverence,
and makes one's mind gentle and harmonious.

One delights in contemplating dharmas and stays free of attachment,
single-mindedly strives to acquire abundant learning,
and refrains from coveting offerings of benefits and support,
while staying far from base cheating, flattery, and deception.

One does not defile the family of the Buddhas
and does not damage moral precepts or cheat the Buddhas.
One deeply delights in all-knowledge[442]
and remains as unmoving as an immense mountain.

One always delights in cultivating the practice
of ever more superior sublime dharmas.
One delights in the world-transcending dharmas
and does not delight in worldly dharmas.

Even as one cultivates the Ground of Joyfulness,
one is able to cultivate what is difficult to cultivate.
Therefore one is always single-minded
in the diligent practice of these dharmas.

The bodhisattva is able to perfect
such supremely sublime dharmas as these.
It is this then that constitutes secure abiding
on the bodhisattva's first ground.[443]

Question: What use is there for the bodhisattva in learning of these characteristic features of the first ground and other related matters?

Response: This bodhisattva should thoroughly know the skillful means associated with the characteristic features of the first ground and the other associated dharmas. Therefore he should learn about them.

Question: Should the bodhisattva come to thoroughly know only the skillful means associated with these dharmas or should he also thoroughly know other associated skillful means as well?

Response: He should not only thoroughly know the skillful means associated with all of these dharmas but should also thoroughly know the skillful means associated with other dharmas.

Question: If that is the case, then could you perhaps set forth a summary discussion [of these additional topics]?

Response:

E. Additional Factors That the Bodhisattva Must Learn

There are dharmas able to assist [in acquisition of] the ground.
There are dharmas running counter to [acquisition of] the ground.
There are dharmas able to give rise to the ground.
There are dharmas able to destroy the ground.

There are the characteristic features and fruits of each ground.
There are those things gained as one abides on each ground.
There are aspects of each ground that facilitate its purification.
There are things gained in advancing from one ground to another.

There are things that increase as one abides on each ground.
There are factors through which no one can cause one's retreat.
From the point where the bodhisattva [begins to] purify the grounds
to the point he reaches the ground of the countlessly many buddhas,

when engaged in all these endeavors,
he should thoroughly know the associated skillful means,
should inquire of those who are skilled in such matters,
and should rid himself of arrogance.

As for "dharmas assisting acquisition of the first ground," these include such factors as faith, moral virtue, learning, relinquishing, vigor, mindfulness, and wisdom. It is dharmas of this sort along with the other dharmas that accord with the first ground that constitute what is meant here by "assisting dharmas."

"Dharmas running counter [to acquisition of the ground]" include disbelief, breaking of precepts, having but little learning, covetousness, indolence, chaotic thoughts, absence of wisdom, and any other dharmas that fail to accord with the first ground and do not assist its acquisition.

As for "dharmas able to destroy the ground," these include any that might cause one to retreat from and abandon cultivation of this ground, any that might obstruct it, and any that might cause it to not manifest. These would be comparable in their effect to the utter destruction of the myriad things that occurs at the very end of the kalpa.

What are the dharmas said to have the ability to rob one of the resolve to attain bodhi? This is a matter that has already been explained [earlier in this text].

As for "dharmas able to give rise to the ground," this refers to those that are able to bring forth the first ground and those that are able to bring about successful establishment in the first ground. These are the dharmas preventing one from being robbed of the resolve to realize bodhi. These were explained earlier as well.

The meanings of "characteristic features," "acquisition of fruition," and "the aspects of the ground" were explained above.

As for "dharmas facilitating purification," if one uses these dharmas, one will be able to purify the first ground. As previously explained,[444] they are as follows:

The bodhisattva who abides on the first ground
has much that he is able to endure.
He is not fond of struggle or disputation,
and, for the most part, his mind is joyous and pleased.

He always delights in purity.
He has a compassionate mind and feels pity for beings.
He has no thoughts of hatred or anger,
and, for the most part, practices these seven things.

It is by resort to dharmas such as these seven that one is able to purify the first ground.

"Advancing from one ground to another," refers for example to when one advances from the first ground to the second ground, and from the second ground to the third ground. So too it is with the rest [of the grounds]. [That one is able to proceed] from the first ground to the second ground is due to acquiring ten types of mind including refraining from deviousness, and so forth. [And that one is able to proceed] from the second ground to the third ground is due to acquiring the ten types of mind through which one acquires resolute faith, and so forth. It is due to acquiring just such various sorts of mind and various types of dharmas that one is then able to advance from one ground to the next ground.

As for "things that increase as one abides on each ground," this includes for example the fact that the first ground is characterized by much cultivation of the perfection of giving (lit. *dāna pāramitā*), the second ground is characterized by much cultivation of the perfection of moral virtue (lit. *śīla pāramitā*) and an increase in the strength of faith and other such dharmas, and the third ground is characterized by much cultivation of abundant learning and increasing strength in giving, moral virtue, faith, and other such dharmas. The same process occurs on each of the other grounds as well.

Regarding "factors through which no one can cause one's retreat," this refers to the capacity that develops as one dwells on this ground through which no *śramaṇa* or brahman, and no celestial *māra*, Brahmā, or anyone else in the world can possibly cause one to turn back from it. Why [can't they cause one to turn back]? It is because one has gained the power of great meritorious qualities, because one has deeply penetrated to the very bottom of the nature of all dharmas, and because one has developed great resolute faith.

As for "from the point where the bodhisattva [begins to] purify the grounds to the point he reaches the ground of the countlessly many buddhas," refers to the fact that, if the bodhisattva finishes the complete purification of all the grounds, he will then succeed in reaching the Buddha Ground.

"When engaged in all of these endeavors," in every case, "he should thoroughly know the associated skillful means."

Regarding "inquiring of those who are skilled in such matters" it is on the basis of having completely perfected one's cultivation of right Dharma that one qualifies as "one who is skilled in such matters."

As for what is meant here by "right Dharma," in summary, this refers to:

First, faith;
Second, vigor;
Third, mindfulness;
Fourth, meditative concentration;
Fifth, wisdom;
Sixth, moral virtue in body, speech, and mind; and
Seventh, freedom from desire, hatred, and delusion.

Regarding "ridding himself of arrogance," when one regards oneself as superior to those who truly *are* superior, this is known as "great arrogance." When one regards oneself as superior to those who are one's equals and thus elevates oneself in one's own mind, this is what is known as "arrogance." When, with regard to those compared to whom one is in fact vastly inferior one instead regards oneself as being only slightly inferior, this is what is known as "arrogance even in inferiority."

F. The Benefit of Knowing These Dharmas and Their Skillful Means

Question: You have stated that one should come to thoroughly know the skillful means associated with all of these dharmas. Assuming that one does gain all of these skillful means, of what use are they?

Response:

If the bodhisattva thoroughly knows with regard to all the grounds
their characteristic features and their acquisition,
so long as he has not yet attained buddhahood,
he will never turn back from the first ground.

"Characteristic features" refers to the seven [above-listed] dharmas that assist advancement through the grounds. "Acquisition" refers to [avoidance of] the eight [above-listed] dharmas that run counter to acquisition of the grounds.[445] The eight dharmas that destroy cultivation are those one should not practice. If the bodhisattva thoroughly knows these dharmas, so long as he has not yet attained buddhahood, he will never turn back.

G. An Analogy for a Bodhisattva's Knowledge of the 10 Grounds Path

Question: As for this bodhisattva who well knows all of these dharmas but will never retreat so long as he has not yet attained buddhahood, what sort of analogy would serve to describe his circumstance?

Response:

It is as if there was a guide possessed of immense powers
who knew well the characteristics of the good road
and knew how best to get from this place to that place,
knew what was appropriate when encountering a turn in the path,

knew the provisions and implements to be taken on the trip,
knew how they were all to be adequately prepared,
knew how in the midst of that dangerous road
one ensures that the group can remain safe and secure

and succeed in reaching the great city,
being able all the while to cause everyone to escape calamities.
[Success in this] would be because of this great guide,
because of his being well able to know the path,

because of his knowing well the changes in the terrain,
and due to having completely prepared the provisions for the path.
The bodhisattva thoroughly knows the path,
the good and bad aspects in this place and that place

so that he can himself cross beyond the dangers of *saṃsāra*
while also leading many other beings across,
thereby causing them to arrive at a safe and secure place
in the city of unconditioned nirvāṇa,

enabling them all to avoid the many anguishing calamities
encountered within the wretched destinies.
The power of a bodhisattva's skillful means
is the result of his ability to thoroughly know the path.

As for "the characteristics of the good road," this refers to knowing where there is abundant firewood, forage grasses, and water, knowing where there are no bandits, lions, wolves, tigers or any other sorts of fearsome beasts or venomous insects, knowing where it is neither too cold nor too hot, knowing where there are no fearsome mountains, crevasses, abysses, precipitous river gorges, hazardous ravines, deep thorny underbrush, jungles, or deep coves blocking the path, knowing where there are no steep ascents and plummeting descents, knowing where the path is level, straight, flat, direct in its connections, and having but few forks in the road, and knowing where it is wide, able to accommodate many people, and frequented by many travelers. It refers as well to knowing where traveling is not inordinately wearisome or exhausting, and to knowing where there is an abundance of flowers, fruit, and things one can eat. It is just such circumstances as these that define what is meant by "the characteristics of the best road." Whatever features are opposite to these characteristics are signs of a bad road.

"This place" refers to a location where the band of travelers stops, eats, and rests. "That place" refers to a different place that is reached after departing from this place, or it may also refer to the different places passed through between two overnight stops. "Turn in the path" refers to where one sees that there is a fork in the path. As for [the path that] "reaches the great city," it is this path that should be traveled, whereas all other paths must be avoided.

"Provisions" refers to supplies that are eaten along the road such as balls made of wheat and honey.

The "immense powers" [as possessed by this guide] refers to great strength, the possession of abundant resources in wealth, and a thorough understanding of the methods required to maintain order.

"Adequate preparation" refers to gathering together an abundance of food and drink so that they will encounter no shortages.

"Safety" refers to ensuring that there will be no frightful experiences involving encounters with bandits.

"Security" refers to ensuring that there will be no sickness, intensely painful incidents, or ruinous calamities.

"Great city" refers here to being able to reach a great city accommodating a large population.

This great guide thoroughly understands all of the signs along the road and is himself personally free of any troublesome difficulties while also being well able to prevent the entire group from encountering any troublesome difficulties. This is a result of his thorough familiarity with the path. There are no encounters with intense cold or heat, hunger or thirst, bandits, fearsome beasts, poisonous insects, fearsome mountainous terrain, treacherous rivers, deep chasms or other such calamities. And why is this? This is because he thoroughly knows all of the good and bad signs along the entire road.

This comparison is used as an analogy for one's progression through the Ground of Joyfulness and the rest of the ten grounds, for it is comparable to when someone who has embarked on a path refrains from resting and thereby becomes able to reach a great city. So too, the bodhisattva travels in this way through the ten grounds and thus succeeds in arriving at the Buddha Dharma's entry into the great city of nirvāṇa.

This route is comparable to that good road along which there is an abundance of firewood, forage grasses, water, and such. As a consequence, the traveler does not encounter shortages in those things. "Forage grasses" refers to that situation wherein someone traveling by horse does so on a road where, because there are excellent fields of grass along the way, the horse's strength remains robust. The meritorious qualities associated with the path of the ten grounds are just like this.

Because the four supreme bases [of meritorious qualities] consisting of truth, relinquishment, quiescence, and wisdom facilitate the arising of all the meritorious qualities, they are analogous here to those forage grasses. How is this so? If a person esteems truthfulness in his endeavors, then he delights in speaking in a manner that accords with the truth. One should draw near to those who speak the truth. One sees that truthfulness is beneficial and thus delights in according with truth in his endeavors. Hence he deeply abhors false speech, renounces false speech, sees the faults inherent in false speech, and does not wish to even hear it. Due to causes and conditions such as these, one acquires the supreme basis of truthfulness. The other three supreme bases [of meritorious qualities] consisting of relinquishment and the rest should be similarly understood.

Just as, in traveling that good road, in order to reach the great city, it is essential that the elephants, horses, cattle, donkeys, and such obtain foraging grass through which they are provided with strength, so too it is that the bases of truthfulness, relinquishment, quiescence, and wisdom enable one to reach the Buddha Dharma's entry into the great city of nirvāṇa.

"Firewood" is analogous here to the wisdom associated with extensive learning, [the wisdom associated with] contemplation, and [the wisdom associated with] cultivation by which one is able to perfect the works of great wisdom. Just as firewood is able to cause a fire to burn and also cause it to become fiercely intense, so too is the wisdom of learning, contemplation, and cultivation able to produce the great wisdom that one is then able to cause to grow. In just the same manner as fire is able to burn, is able to cook, and is able to provide illumination, so too is the fire of wisdom able to burn up the afflictions, ripen one's roots of goodness, and illuminate the four truths of the Āryas. Just as fire is analogous to wisdom, firewood is analogous to the various dharmas that are capable of generating wisdom.

"Abundant water" refers to there being numerous flowing rivers and canals one can freely use to satisfy everyone's needs in a way that mere springs, wells, and ponds could not sufficiently serve.

Then again "abundant water" is analogous to when people board boats and then follow the current until they reach a great city. The water contained in wells, springs, reservoirs, and ponds is simply unable to serve in this capacity. As stated in the sutras:

> Faith serves as the great river and merit serves as its banks. Just as a river is able to relieve heat, quench thirst, rinse away filth, and produce power [for waterwheels and such], faith in good dharmas is similarly able to extinguish the fire of the three poisons, rinse away the filth of the three types of bad actions, quench the thirst associated with the three realms of existence, and contribute power to good dharmas undertaken for the sake of nirvāṇa.

Just as that good road has an abundance of roots and medicinal herbs along its course by which the traveler will not encounter shortages of those things, so too it is with the path of the ten grounds.

In this case, "roots" signifies whatever is cherished by [virtue of] one's resolute intentions. Just as when roots are established, sprouts, a trunk, branches, leaves, and an abundance of fruit grow forth, so too, when one's resolute intentions cherish the path, they then bring about the growth of right recollective mindfulness, great vows, and the other meritorious qualities.

"Medicinal herbs" here signifies the *pāramitās*. Just as the medicinal herbs are able to extinguish all manner of toxins, the medicinal herbs of the *pāramitās* are able in this same manner to extinguish the poisons of greed, hatred, and delusion and do away with the sickness associated with the afflictions.

[When one possesses these *pāramitās*] it is analogous to when one travels a good road and makes sure not to lose his passport.[446] He is then able to travel safely along the road.[447] Just as when a traveler who has not lost his passport is able to go wherever he wishes without being obstructed by anyone, so too, on the path of the ten grounds, so long as one does not lose his passport, the roots of goodness gathered while ascending through the grounds are able to freely assist the increase and growth of the roots of goodness that one currently possesses.

One is then also able to teach those beings who presently abide in the paths of *śrāvaka* disciples, *pratyekabuddhas,* and devas of the desire realm and form realm, thereby influencing them to abide in the path to buddhahood. Then, no matter whether it be Māra or some proponent of a non-Buddhist tradition, one cannot be interfered with or disturbed by anyone. This is what is meant by "not losing one's passport."

Just as that good road is free of mosquitoes, horseflies, and the various sorts of poisonous insects, the path of the ten grounds is free of the sounds of sorrow, worry, weeping, and crying. Just as that good road is free of difficulties wrought by bandits, so too is the path of the ten grounds free of the five hindrances' gang of evil thieves. This is just as described by the Buddha when he told the bhikshus, "The thieves in this village are the so-called "five hindrances."[448] Just as thieves start by stealing peoples' possessions, but then later move on to murder, so too it is with the thieves of the five hindrances. They start by stealing one's roots of goodness, but then later cut off the life of one's wisdom with the result that one falls into negligence and finally dies.

Just as that road is free of lions, tigers, wolves, and the various other sorts of fearsome beasts, so too is the path of the ten grounds free of hatred, anger, fighting, and disputation. Just as lions and the other sorts of fearsome beasts enjoy tormenting and harming other beings, so too do hatred, anger, and such arise in order to afflict others in this same way. Just as those fearsome beasts eat flesh and drink blood, so too do hatred, hostility and such consume the flesh of the wisdom that arises from abundant learning. And so too do they drink the blood of the wisdom that arises from cultivation and the other [forms of wisdom][449] in this same manner.

And just as that good road is free of terribly extreme cold and heat, so too, because on the path of the ten grounds one does not fall into the hells of cold and ice, it is free of terribly extreme cold. And because one does not fall into the hot hells, it is free of terribly extreme heat.

Just as that good road is free of deep chasms and other such difficulties, so too is the path of the ten grounds free of the difficulties inherent in the ascetic practices of the non-Buddhist traditions such as:

Coating the body with ashes;
Plunging into ice;
Pulling out one's hair;
Bathing three times each day;
Standing on one foot;
Eating one meal the first day, then one meal every two days, and so forth until one goes a month on only one meal;
Taking a life-long vow of silence;
Always holding up one arm;
Always practicing endurance by subjecting one's body to the five kinds of fire;
Lying down on beds of nails:
Plunging into fire;
Plunging into water;
Throwing oneself off of high cliffs;
Burning one's body by standing in a deep cauldron of cattle excrement;
Going straight off in one direction without avoiding any difficulties one might encounter;
Always wearing wet clothes;
Lying down in water;
Or subjecting oneself to any of the other sorts of physical or mental sufferings.

None of these lead to right wisdom. Because [the path of the ten grounds] is free of such things, it is said to be free of difficulties.

Just as that road is free of deviating pathways, so too it is with the path of the ten grounds. It is because it is free of evil actions of body, mouth, or mind that it is said to be free of deviating pathways.

Just as that road is free of thorny underbrush, so too it is with the path of the ten grounds. It is because it is free of the thorny underbrush of karmic obstacles that it is said to be free of thorny underbrush. Just as when thorns pierce one's feet, one is then prevented from traveling along that road, so too, the thorny underbrush of karmic obstacles impede one's ability to practice the Dharma of the Buddha and thus reach nirvāṇa.

Just as that road is straight and direct, so too it is with the path of the ten grounds. It is because it is free of any ingratiating flattery, deviousness, cheating, or deception that it is said to be straight and direct.

Just as that road has but few forks in it, so too it is with the path of the ten grounds, for it has but few variant paths. How is this so? Those who have set out along the path of the Great Vehicle travel but little on the pathways of *śrāvaka* disciples and *pratyekabuddhas*. Hence there is but little involvement with variant paths. Where there may be cases in which a bodhisattva travels along in the path of those two vehicles, one should realize that he has not yet established himself on the grounds of a bodhisattva. Because he has not yet entered the right and fixed position,[450] he engages in those peripheral practices.

Just as that good path is free of jungles that obstruct the way, so too it is with the path of the ten grounds. It is free of the jungles of evils associated with the five objects of desire.

Question: Why did you not just state that it is free of *all* jungles associated with the five objects of desire, but instead only stated that it is free of the jungles of "evils" [associated with the five objects of desire]?

Response: For one who has set out in the Great Vehicle, the causes and conditions of one's merit conduce to possession of the foremost objects of the five desires. Consequently one cannot say that they are utterly nonexistent. It is just that those associated with evil are nonexistent.

Moreover, in the case of a deep jungle, it is difficult to enter, difficult to pass through, and possessed of a multitude of difficult obstructions. The objects of the five desires as encountered by the bodhisattva are not of this sort. He is not like the foolish common person who creates all manner of transgressions in association with the objects of the five desires. Because this is the case, it was only stated here that [the path of the ten grounds] is free of [such evil] jungles.

Just as that road is wide, accommodating of many people, and not conducive to mutual interference, so too is the path of the ten grounds able to accommodate many people, for the countless hundreds of thousands of myriads of *koṭis* of beings could all bring forth the resolve to embark upon this unsurpassable path and there would still be no mutual interference among these hundreds of thousands of myriads of *koṭis* of beings. In fact, all beings could bring forth the resolve to attain *anuttarasamyaksaṃbodhi* and they could all still travel together along this path and there would still be no mutual interference.

Just as that road is one along which many people travel, so too it is with the path of the ten grounds. When they were still cultivating the bodhisattva path, past and present buddhas as numerous as the sands of the Ganges all traveled along this path.

Just as that good road admits of travel without weariness or exhaustion, so too it is with the path of the ten grounds, for this path is associated with abundant bliss produced through cause and effect. For instance, bliss is enjoyed when one is often born into the realms of humans and devas and then enjoys one's karmic rewards there. Because [the practitioner] delights in the abandonment of desire, he then experiences joy and bliss, the bliss of *dhyāna* concentration, the bliss that is free of joy, and the bliss experienced in abiding in this present moment. Because one acquires these various sorts of bliss, one is free of weariness or exhaustion.

Just as that path has along its course an abundance of flowers, fruit, and roots, so too does the path of the ten grounds also possess an abundance of roots, flowers, and fruit. "Roots" refers here to the three types of good roots. "Flowers" refers to the flowers of the seven limbs of bodhi. This is as stated in the sutras where it says, "The seven types of flowers are the seven limbs of bodhi." "Fruit" refers to the four fruits of the *śramaṇa*.

Because one is free of any of these faults that would obstruct the attainment of meritorious qualities as one courses along this good path, one is said to have abandoned evil.

Just as that guide knows with respect to that road that one should stop and eat here, that one should spend the night here, and that one should then stop for the night there, so too it is with a bodhisattva as he travels through the ten grounds wherein he knows in which place one may stop for the night and knows in which place one may eat.

"Where one may stop for the night" refers to those places where buddhas of the present now dwell. "Where one may eat" refers to where one can cultivate the practice of good dharmas.

Just as eating is able to benefit all of one's faculties and also assists the fulfillment of one's life span, so too it is with good dharmas. They are able to increase faith and the rest of those faculties[451] while also assisting the fulfillment of one's wisdom life.

"Spending the night in another place" is a reference to going from the dwelling place of that buddha to the dwelling place of yet another buddha. Also, one may interpret "another place" as signifying the places in between this buddha's land and that buddha's land.

"Knowing well where to make a turn in the road" refers for example to when a guide recognizes that a road has become unsafe and so then takes a turn. So too it is with a bodhisattva. He knows that this particular path takes one into the realm of the *śrāvaka* disciples, that this other path takes one into the realm of the *pratyekabuddhas,* and that this other path takes one to the realization of buddhahood. Having realized this, he relinquishes the paths of *śrāvaka* disciples and *pratyekabuddhas* and thenceforth travels solely along the path to buddhahood.

Just as that good road has much to eat and drink along the way, so too the path of the ten grounds provides sustenance through the abundant practice of giving, moral virtue, and cultivation of the *dhyāna* concentrations.

Just as that guide has great power because he has abundant wealth and is well able to use the means for maintaining order, so too does the bodhisattva also have great power because he has wealth and the means for maintaining order.

"Wealth" here refers to the seven kinds of wealth, namely: faith, [adherence to] moral precepts, a sense of shame, a dread of blame, relinquishing, learning, and wisdom.

"Means for maintaining order" refers to the ability to defeat all challenges from any *māra* or from any of the various sorts of *śramaṇas*, brahmans, or non-Buddhist treatise masters. This is what is meant by "awesome strength."

Just as that great city is deemed to be safe and secure because it is free of bandits, pestilence, the causes of violent death, and the many different sorts of distress, so too is the great city of nirvāṇa deemed to be safe and secure, this because it is free of *māras*, non-Buddhists, the contaminants, greed, hatred, neglectfulness, death, sorrow, grief, suffering, anguish, and lamentation.

Just as that great city, because it has an abundance of food and drink, is deemed to be bountiful, so too is the city of nirvāṇa deemed to be bountiful because it has an abundance of deep *dhyāna* absorptions, liberations, and samādhis.

Just as that great city, because it is able to accommodate many people, is said therefore to be a great city, so too is the city of nirvāṇa deemed to be great because it is able to accommodate many beings. If one could cause all beings to enter the nirvāna without residue through their nonacceptance of any dharmas [as inherently existent], the nature of nirvāṇa would still neither increase nor decrease.

Just as that guide is deemed to be a guide because he is able to lead many groups of people to safety and security by showing them the good road, so too is a bodhisattva also deemed to be a great guide, for he is able to lead forth beings, showing them the Dharma of the Buddha, showing them nirvāṇa, and guiding them out from the hazardous road of *saṃsāra* so that they successfully reach nirvāṇa.

And just as that guide, because he so well knows the signs all along that road, is able to ensure that he himself as well as the rest of his group do not encounter any calamities, so too it is with the bodhisattva.

Because he himself does not course in desire, ill will, or the other hindrances, because he does not practice bad ascetic practices, because he does not fall into the deep pit of aging and death, and because he also does not fall into the hot hells, the cold hells or the realms of the hungry ghosts, he is deemed to be one who does not encounter calamities himself while ensuring that his followers do not encounter calamities, either.

It is for these reasons that the verse says that it is due to knowing well the signs along the path that [the guide] does not encounter any calamities himself, nor do any of the others encounter calamities, either.

The End of Chapter Twenty-Six

Chapter 27
A Summarizing Discussion of the Bodhisattva Practices

XXVII. Chapter 27: A Summarizing Discussion of Bodhisattva Practices

A. A Brief Presentation Intended to Finish the First Ground Discussion

We have now come to the end of the general explanation
of the bodhisattva's Ground of Joyfulness
The bodhisattva who abides herein
often becomes a monarch who rules over Jambudvīpa.

He is ever distant from the defilements of greed and desire,
and never fails in his recollection of the Three Jewels.
His mind always aspires to become a buddha
and to rescue and protect all beings.

The first ground is known as the Ground of Joyfulness. We have come to the end of its general explanation. All of the measureless and boundless dharmas of all buddhas take this very ground as their foundation. Were one to take up an expansive discussion of it, that too would become measureless and boundless. Hence we speak here of a "summarizing" explanation.

The bodhisattva who abides on this ground will often serve as a powerful wheel-turning monarch reigning over the entire continent of Jambudvīpa. Due to having cultivated the causes and conditions for this ground in previous lives, he has a resolute belief in the practice of giving and is free of the defilement of miserliness. Because he is always gives to the Three Jewels, he never fails in his recollection of the Three Jewels. He always bears in mind his resolve to become a buddha and to rescue and protect all beings. Good thoughts such as these are always in his mind.

Additionally:

If he aspires to leave behind the home life
and then diligently practices vigor,
he is able to acquire several hundred meditative concentrations,
and is able to see several hundred buddhas.

He is able to shake a hundred worlds,
and his ability to travel [to other worlds] is also of this sort.
If he wishes to emanate radiant light,
he is able to illuminate a hundred worlds.

He creates transformation bodies of several hundred kinds of people
and can remain for a life span of a hundred kalpas.
He is able to selectively investigate several hundred dharmas
and is able to manifest a hundred transformation bodies,

He is able to transformationally create a hundred bodhisattvas
that manifest as his retinue.
Those of sharp faculties can exceed these numbers
through relying on the Buddha's spiritual powers.

Having already explained the first ground's characteristic features,
its fruits, its powers, and the dharmas used in its purification,
We shall now also present an explanation
of the second ground, the Ground of Stainlessness.

"Fruits" refers to the acquisition of several hundred meditative absorptions, the ability to see several hundred buddhas, and so forth. "Powers" refers to the ability to manifest as several hundred [kinds of] beings, and so forth. The meanings implicit in the rest of the verse have already been explained. Hence we shall not proceed with an explanation of the rest of the verse but rather shall now discuss the second ground, the Ground of Stainlessness.

B. Q: Before Finishing, Please Summarize the Bodhisattva Path

Question: You wish to present an expansive discussion of the dharmas practiced by the bodhisattva. There are still many [additional] meanings pertaining to the first ground. It is to be feared that, if the discussion becomes ever more expansive, those attempting to study this will become prone to indolent thoughts that could impair their ability to study and recite this. Therefore, for the sake of those unable to [memorize and] recite a more [extensive explanation], you should now [instead] present a summarizing explanation of the dharmas practiced by the bodhisattva.

C. A: A Series of Statements Summarizing the Bodhisattva Practices

1. Practice All Bodhisattva Dharmas & Abandon All Transgressions

Response:

All dharmas of the bodhisattva—
these dharmas should all be practiced.
All forms of evil should be relinquished.
This is what constitutes the summarizing explanation.

Dharmas such as those explained in preceding chapters are able to produce and are able to instigate growth in the dharmas pertaining to the [bodhisattva] grounds. Also, if dharmas such as those explained in previous chapters have been explained elsewhere, one should cause all of those dharmas to arise as well. One should abandon all endeavors involving bodhisattva transgressions. This is what constitutes the summarizing explanation of what the bodhisattva should practice. This is as taught in the *Dharmapada*:

> To refrain from doing any manner of evil,
> to respectfully perform all varieties of good,
> and to carry out the purification of one's own mind—
> This is the teaching of all Buddhas.

2. Be Single-Minded and Non-Neglectful in Practicing Good Dharmas

There is one dharma that subsumes the path to buddhahood and that is what the bodhisattva should practice. And what is that singular teaching? It is what is referred to as being single-minded and non-neglectful in the cultivation of good dharmas. As the Buddha told Ānanda: "It is due to not being neglectful that I attained *anuttarasamyaksaṃbodhi*." This is as described here:

> It is through non-neglectfulness that one becomes a buddha,
> one who is unmatched by anyone anywhere in the world.
> If one is simply able to refrain from neglectfulness,
> what endeavor could one fail to achieve?

3. Two Dharmas That Subsume the Path to Buddhahood

There are also two dharmas that are able to subsume the path to buddhahood, namely:

> First, non-neglectfulness;
> And second, wisdom.

These are as described below:

> Non-neglectfulness and wisdom—
> The Buddha spoke of these as gateways to benefit.
> One does not see instances wherein one avoids neglectfulness,
> and yet those endeavors still fail to succeed.

4. Three Dharmas That Subsume the Path to Buddhahood

There are also three dharmas that are able to subsume the path to buddhahood, namely:

> First, training in the supreme moral virtue;
> Second, training in the supreme mind;
> And third, training in the supreme wisdom.

These are as described below:

> Moral virtue produces superior samādhi,
> samādhi produces wisdom,
> and wisdom scatters the afflictions
> just as wind blows away floating clouds.

5. Four Dharmas That Subsume the Path to Buddhahood

There are also four dharmas that are able to subsume the path to buddhahood, namely [the four bases of meritorious qualities]:

First, the truth basis;
Second, the relinquishment basis;
Third, the quiescence basis;
And fourth, the wisdom basis.

These are as described below:

By perfecting truth, relinquishment, and meditative concentration,
one acquires the pure benefits of wisdom.
One who vigorously pursues the path to buddhahood
should gather together these four dharmas.

6. Five Dharmas That Subsume the Path to Buddhahood

There are also five dharmas that are able to subsume the path to buddhahood, namely:

First, the faculty of faith;
Second, the faculty of vigor;
Third, the faculty of mindfulness;
Fourth, the faculty of meditative concentration;
And fifth, the faculty of wisdom.

These are as described below:

Through the faculty of faith and the faculty of vigor,
mindfulness, concentration, and wisdom are solid and durable.
Once these dharmas are joined with the great compassion,
one will never retreat from the path to buddhahood.

Just as a person who acquires the five sense faculties
is then able to completely comprehend the five sense objects,
similarly, if one acquires faith and the rest of the [five] faculties,
he is then able to know the [true] character of all dharmas.

7. Six Dharmas That Subsume the Path to Buddhahood

There are also six dharmas that are able to subsume the path to buddhahood, namely the *pāramitās*:

Giving;
Moral virtue;
Patience;
Vigor;
Dhyāna concentration;
And wisdom.

These are as described below:

If [one practices] the six perfections as explained,
one will overcome the afflictions,
will always bring about the growth of the roots of goodness,
and, before long, will succeed in attaining buddhahood.

8. Seven Dharmas That Subsume the Path to Buddhahood

There are also seven dharmas that are able to subsume the path to buddhahood, namely the so-called "seven right dharmas":

Faith;
A sense of shame;
A dread of blame;
Extensive learning;
Vigor;
Mindfulness;
And wisdom.

These are as described below:

One who aspires to acquire the seven right dharmas
should delight in meditative concentration pursued with vigor.
If one rids himself of the seven wrong dharmas,
he will be able to know all the meritorious qualities.

Such a person will be able to rapidly acquire
the unsurpassable bodhi of the Buddha,
extricate those sunken in *saṃsāra*,
and cause them then to reside in the safe and secure abode.

9. Eight Dharmas That Subsume the Path to Buddhahood

There are also eight dharmas that are able to subsume the path to buddhahood, namely the so-called "eight types of thought of great men," namely:

Having but few desires;
Being easily satisfied;
Renunciation;
Vigor;
Mindfulness;
Meditative concentration;
Wisdom;
And delighting in the avoidance of mere conceptual elaboration.

These are as described below:

If someone forms the definite resolve
to abide in the eight types of thought of great men, and then,
in order to pursue the path to buddhahood,
rids himself of the bad forms of ideation and reflection,

by proceeding in this manner, before long,
he will swiftly gain the unsurpassable path.
This is just as when someone practices goodness:
He is certainly bound to gain the sublime fruits [of the path].

10. Nine Dharmas That Subsume the Path to Buddhahood

There are also nine dharmas that are able to subsume the path to buddhahood, namely:

Great patience;
Great kindness;
Great compassion;
Wisdom;
Mindfulness;
Solid resolve;
Non-greed;
Non-hatred;
And non-delusion.

These are as described below:

If one is well equipped with great patience,
great kindness, and great compassion,
and is also able to abide in wisdom,
mindfulness, and solid resolve—

If with resolute intentions one enters the good roots
of non-greed, non-hatred, and non-delusion—
If one is able to act in this manner,
the path to buddhahood will then be in the palm of one's hand.

11. Ten Dharmas That Subsume the Path to Buddhahood

There are also ten dharmas that are able to subsume the path to buddhahood, namely the ten courses of good karmic action. [In the case of the first of them, these include]: not killing any being oneself, not instructing others to kill, not praising any killing that one observes, and not delighting in any killing [carried out by others]. And so the list continues similarly until we come to [the tenth], not holding wrong views. One then dedicates the merit [of adhering to these ten courses of good karmic action] to the attainment of *anuttarasamyaksaṃbodhi*. These are as described below:

One does not harass or harm any living being,
nor does one engage in any robbery or theft,
nor does one indulge in sexual transgressions with another's wife.
These are the three concerned with the karmic actions of the body.

One does not engage in false speech, divisive speech,
harsh speech, or frivolous speech,
nor does one indulge covetousness, ill will, or wrong views.
These are the seven actions of the mouth and the mind.

If one acts in this manner, then one is able to open
the gate to the unsurpassable path to buddhahood.
If one wishes to attain buddhahood,
one should practice in accordance with this initial gateway.

The bodhisattva should bring forth dharmas such as these, and then, having brought them forth, he should guard them. Having guarded them, he should then increase them so that every single good endeavor subsequently brings about an ever-increasing devotion to that form of goodness.

12. Faults to Be Urgently Abandoned on the Path to Buddhahood

a. One Fault That Must Be Urgently Abandoned on the Buddha Path

One should also realize that there is one bad dharma that one who pursues the path to buddhahood should urgently abandon. We refer here to the need to abandon neglectfulness.[452] This is as described here:

If one is unable to cross beyond
saṃsāra's dangerous wretched destinies,[453]
this is something worthy of rebuke
and is the worst of all offenses.

Although one delights in wealth's pleasures,
one may still be reborn into a poor and lowly family
in which one is unable to plant any roots of goodness
and in which one becomes a slave or a servant of others.

This is all brought about by the causes and conditions
associated with neglectfulness.
Therefore one who is wise
urgently leaves it behind as if it were a lethal poison.

If one has not yet developed the great compassion
and gained the unproduced-dharmas patience and irreversibility
and yet still indulges in neglectfulness,
this is synonymous with bring on one's own death.[454]

b. Two Faults That Must Be Urgently Abandoned on the Buddha Path

There are also two faults that one should urgently abandon, namely:

First, longing for the grounds of *śrāvaka* disciples.
And second, longing for the ground of *pratyekabuddhas*.

As the Buddha said:

If one falls down onto the grounds of the *śrāvaka* disciples
or onto the ground of the *pratyekabuddhas*,
for the bodhisattva, this is synonymous with dying
and is also synonymous with complete failure.

Even though one might fall into the hells,
one should still not feel any terror.
However, if he were to fall into the Two Vehicles,
the bodhisattva should then feel immensely fearful.

Although one might fall into the hells,
this would not forever block one's path to buddhahood.
However, if one were to fall into the Two Vehicles,
this would forever block one's path to buddhahood.

The Buddha has stated that one who loves his life,
would feel immensely fearful if faced with decapitation.
In this very same way, one who wishes to become a buddha
should feel immensely fearful of entering the Two Vehicles.[455]

c. Three Faults to Be Urgently Abandoned on the Buddha Path

There are also three faults that one should urgently abandon, namely:

First, hating bodhisattvas;
Second, hating the bodhisattva practices;
Third, hating any extremely profound Great Vehicle scripture.

These are as described below:

Those of lesser wisdom may, over but minor conditions,
come to hate Bodhisattvas,
hate the bodhisattva path,
or hate the sutras of the Great Vehicle.

Because they do not understand them, they have no faith in them
and then fall down into the great hells.
There, struck with fear, they scream in terror.
This is a situation that one should abandon.

d. Four Faults to Be Urgently Abandoned on the Buddha Path

There are also four faults that one should urgently abandon, namely:

First, flattery;
Second, deviousness;
Third, being quick-tempered;
And fourth, being bereft of kindness or pity.

These are as described below:

One who describes himself as a bodhisattva
who has a mind much given over to flattery and deviousness,

who is quick-tempered and intolerant,
and who does not act with a mind of kindness and pity—
This is to draw near to the Avīci Hells
and depart far from the path to buddhahood.

e. Five Faults to Be Urgently Abandoned on the Buddha Path

There are also five faults that one should urgently abandon, namely:

First, desire;
Second, ill will;
Third, lethargy-and-sleepiness;
Fourth, excitedness-and-regretfulness;[456]
And fifth, doubtfulness.

These are the five hindrances that may cover over a person's mind which are as described below:

If a person falls into neglectfulness,
the hindrances will cover his mind,
making even birth in the heavens difficult to achieve,
how much the less might one then attain the fruits of the path?

If one is diligent in the practice of vigor,
one can then tear through the hindrances.
If one is able to tear through the hindrances,
then, whatever one wishes for, it will all be obtained.

f. Six Faults to Be Urgently Abandoned on the Buddha Path

There are also six faults that are opposite to the six *pāramitās* and that one should urgently abandon:

First, miserliness;
Second, breaking the moral precepts;
Third, anger;
Fourth, indolence;
Fifth, excited agitation;
And sixth, delusion.

These are as described below:

Having the stain of miserliness defiling one's mind,
breaking the moral precepts, indulging in indolence,
being as ignorant as a cow or sheep,
being as fond of hatred as a venomous serpent,

or having a mind as scattered as that of a monkey—
If one fails to abandon the hindrances,
then, even gaining a celestial rebirth would be extremely difficult,
how much the less could one succeed in attaining buddhahood?

g. Seven Faults to Be Urgently Abandoned on the Buddha Path

There are also seven faults that one should urgently abandon:

First, delighting in pursuing many different endeavors;
Second, delighting in excessive study and recitation;
Third, delighting in sleep;
Fourth, delighting in talking;
Fifth, coveting offerings;
Sixth, always wanting to make people laugh;
And seventh, being so confused and befuddled in cultivating the path that one's mind follows the influence of craving.

These are as described below:

Inferior persons may delight in activities
or delight in much recitation of non-Buddhist scriptures.
Ignorant people may delight in sleeping
or delight in much talking amidst groups of people.

Although they aspire to become a buddha,
they are deeply attached to receiving offerings.
These slaves to craving have become confused
with regard to the path to buddhahood.

All such people as these who engage in what is bad
nonetheless claim to be bodhisattvas.

h. Eight Dharmas to Be Urgently Abandoned on the Buddha Path

There are also eight dharmas that one should urgently abandon, namely:

First, wrong views;
Second, wrong intentional thought;
Third, wrong speech;
Fourth wrong [physical] actions;
Fifth, wrong livelihood;
Sixth, wrong effort;
Seventh, wrong mindfulness;
And eighth, wrong meditative concentration.

These are as described below:

Wherever there are people who are so foolish
that they practice the eightfold wrong path,
pursue the study of deviant scriptures,
become fond of chasing after deviant spiritual guides,

and abandon the profound and sublime qualities
of the Āryas' eightfold path,
[these are people who] are solidly and deeply attached to afflictions,
and yet still may wish to succeed in realizing bodhi—

People who are so deluded as this
are like those who would wish to cross over a great ocean
by abandoning a fine, solid, and durable ship,
seeking instead to make the crossing by carrying stones.

i. Nine Dharmas to Be Urgently Abandoned on the Buddha Path

There are also nine dharmas that one should urgently abandon, namely:

First, failing to hear [the teachings on the attainment of] *anuttarasamyaksaṃbodhi;*

Second, having heard them, failing to have faith in them;

Third, having acquired faith in them, failing to take them on;

Fourth, having taken them on, nonetheless still failing to retain them through recitation;

Fifth, though one has also begun to retain them through recitation, one nonetheless still does not understand their meaning;

Sixth, having understood their meaning and significance, one nonetheless fails to explain them [for others];

Seventh, having explained them [for others], one nonetheless fails to accord with their explanation in one's own practice;

Eighth, having begun to practice in accordance with their explanation, one is still unable to always put them into practice;

And ninth, having become able to always put them into practice, one is unable to thoroughly practice them.

These are as described below:

Foolish people do not wish to even hear
[teachings on] the unsurpassable, right, and true path,
or, having heard them, they are unable to have faith in them,
or they are unable to retain them through recitation,

or they do not understand their meaning or explain them for others,
or they do not cultivate in accordance with how they were taught,
or they are unable to always or thoroughly put them into practice.
Moreover, they have no mindfulness or stable wisdom.

Such foolish people as these
cannot obtain the fruits of the path.
In this, they are like people who, having committed karmic offenses,
cannot succeed in gaining rebirth in the heavens.

j. Ten Dharmas to Be Urgently Abandoned on the Buddha Path

There are also ten dharmas that one should urgently abandon, namely those comprising the ten courses of bad karmic actions. These are as described below:

Foolish people, when still young,
begin to crave descending into the five desires,
abandoning the ten courses of good karmic action,
and engaging in the ten courses of bad karmic action.

Although the bliss of the heavens is in their own hands,
they still cast it aside and reject it,
just as, due to greedily pursuing the benefit of but little money,
one might somehow abandon a great treasury of jewels.

13. The 32 Dharmas of Genuine Bodhisattvas

Question: When you were explaining the characteristic aspects of the unsurpassable path, for many different reasons, you criticized and scolded empty-vow bodhisattvas, self-proclaimed bodhisattvas, and those who are bodhisattvas in name only. If those three types of individuals do not qualify as bodhisattvas, then, through the perfection of which dharmas does one qualify as a genuine bodhisattva?

Response:

It is not merely by making empty vows
by proclaiming oneself to be a bodhisattva,
or by being a bodhisattva only in name.
To state it briefly, it is those who are able to perfect
thirty-two dharmas
who then truly qualify as bodhisattvas.

If one brings forth the resolve by which he seeks to pursue the path to buddhahood and then claims himself to be a bodhisattva, merely emptily assuming the name but not cultivating the meritorious qualities, the mind of kindness and compassion, the *pāramitās,* and the other practices, this sort of person does not actually qualify as a bodhisattva, for he is comparable to some model city made of mud being referred to as "the jeweled city." In this, he only deceives himself, cheats all buddhas, and cheats all of the world's beings as well.

If a person comes to possess thirty-two sublime dharmas while also being able to bring forth the [bodhisattva's] vow, this is someone who qualifies as a genuine bodhisattva. What then are these thirty-two dharmas? They are:

1) He strives with resolute intentions to bring about every form of peace and happiness for all beings;
2) He is able to enter into the wisdom of all buddhas;
3) He knows through his own self-examination whether or not he is capable of becoming a buddha;
4) He does not hate or loathe anyone;
5) His resolve to succeed in the path is solid;

6) He does not form friendships or trusting relationships on false pretenses;
7) He always serves as a close friend to beings even up to the point of his entry into nirvāṇa;
8) Whether others are personally close or distant from him, his mind remains the same [in the way he treats them];
9) He does not retreat from good endeavors to which he has assented;
10) He never cuts off his great kindness for all beings;
11) He never cuts off his great compassion for all beings;
12) He always pursues right Dharma and his mind never becomes weary or prone to laziness;
13) He is diligent in bringing forth vigor and he has insatiable resolve;
14) He is possessed of extensive learning and comprehension of its meanings;
15) He always reflects upon his own faults;
16) He does not deride others for their shortcomings;
17) In all matters he observes or hears, he always cultivates the resolve to attain bodhi;
18) In giving, he seeks no reward;
19) His observance of the moral precepts is not motivated by the desire to take rebirth in any particular place;[457]
20) He exercises patience in his interactions with all beings and thus remains free of any hatred or obstructiveness toward them;
21) He is able to diligently and vigorously cultivate all roots of goodness;
22) He does not take on rebirths corresponding to the formless realm meditative absorptions;[458]
23) His wisdom is inclusive of appropriate expedient teaching methods;
24) His skillful means are those that lie within the four means of attraction;[459]
25) His kindness and pity for others do not differ with respect to those who observe the moral precepts versus those who break the moral precepts;
26) He is single-mindedly attentive when listening to the Dharma;
27) He remains single-mindedly focused when dwelling in a forest hermitage;
28) He does not delight in any of the many different sorts of endeavors that are admixed with worldly priorities;
29) He does not covet or retain any attachment for the Small Vehicle;

30) He perceives that the benefit brought about by the Great Vehicle is immense;
31) He stays away from bad spiritual guides;
32) He draws close to good spiritual guides.

14. Seven Additional Dharmas of Genuine Bodhisattvas

As the bodhisattva abides in these thirty-two dharmas, he is able to perfect seven additional dharmas. Specifically, they are:

The four immeasurable minds;[460]
The ability to roam about, delighting in the use of the five spiritual superknowledges;
Constant reliance on wisdom;
Never forsaking either good or evil beings;
Decisiveness in all pronouncements;
Definite truthfulness in all statements;
Insatiability in the accumulation of all good dharmas.

These constitute the thirty-two dharmas with their seven additional dharmas. Any bodhisattva who perfects these dharmas qualifies as a genuine bodhisattva.

The End of Chapter Twenty-Seven

Chapter 28

Distinctions in the 2nd Ground's Courses of Karmic Action

XXVIII. Ch. 28: Distinctions in the 2nd Ground's Karmic Actions

A. The Ten Resolute Intentions Necessary for Entering the 2nd Ground

> The bodhisattva who has already succeeded
> in the complete fulfillment of the first ground
> and then wishes to reach the second ground
> should bring forth ten types of resolute intentions.[461]

Those bodhisattvas who have already reached the first ground, the Ground of Joyfulness, next bring forth ten types of resolute intentions for the sake of reaching the second ground. It is because of these ten kinds of resolute intentions that one is able to reach the second ground. This is comparable to when someone wishes to go up to an upper-story balcony and must rely on the stairs to do so.

Question: What then are these ten kinds of resolute intentions that serve as means for reaching the second ground?

Response:

> The straight mind, the capable mind,
> the pliant, the restrained, and the quiescent minds,
> the truly sublime, the unmixed, and the non-covetous minds,
> the happy mind, and magnanimous mind make ten in all.

The bodhisattva who has already completely fulfilled the practices of the first ground and now wishes to reach the second ground proceeds to develop these ten kinds of resolute intentions as the appropriate means, namely:[462]

1) The straight mind;
2) The capable mind;
3) The pliant mind;
4) The restrained mind;
5) The quiescent mind;
6) The truly sublime mind;
7) The unmixed mind;
8) The unattached mind;
9) The expansively happy mind;
10) The magnanimous mind.

1. The Straight Mind and the Pliant Mind

Now, as for the straight mind, this is one that has abandoned flattery and deviousness. Because the mind has abandoned flattery and deviousness, it becomes characterized by pliancy. Pliancy refers to not being unyielding or gruff and ill-mannered. The bodhisattva who acquires this pliant mind develops many different *dhyāna* absorptions and also cultivates all good dharmas.

2. The Capable Mind

Once one has contemplated the true character of all dharmas, his mind then becomes capable. Because the mind has become capable, one develops the restrained mind.

3. The Restrained Mind

The restrained mind is one that is well able to restrain the eye and the other sense faculties. This is as stated in the sutras: "What is it that comprises the path of goodness? It is one wherein the bhikshu restrains his eye sense faculty and so forth until we come to his restraining of the mind faculty." It is due to restraint of the six sense faculties that we refer to "the restrained mind."

4. The Quiescent Mind

Once the mind has become restrained, it is then easy to bring forth the quiescent mind. Now, as for the quiescent mind, this refers to being able to extinguish greed, hatred, delusion, and the other afflictions. Having first restrained the mind, one is able to block [the arising of those afflictions] and bring about a state of quiescence.

There are others who claim that acquisition of the *dhyāna* absorptions that itself constitutes the quiescent mind. This is as described in the sutras where it says, "If a person thoroughly knows the characteristic features of the *dhyāna* absorptions, then he will not desire the delectability [of their pleasurable meditative states]. This then is what is meant by the quiescent mind."

5. The Truly Sublime Mind

Once one has acquired the quiescent mind, he will then definitely bring forth the truly sublime mind. "The truly sublime mind" is a state in which, whatever one wishes to accomplish in the *dhyāna* absorptions and spiritual powers, one will be able to put them to use in a manner that conforms to one's wishes. This is like having real gold that one is able to use however one wishes.

6. The Unmixed Mind

Once the practitioner has acquired these types of mind from the straight mind on through to the truly sublime mind, in order to preserve and protect these kinds of mind, he delights in bringing forth the unmixed mind. The unmixed mind is one in which one abstains from getting involved with either householders or monastics. This practitioner has this thought:

> Acquiring these types of mind depends entirely on the power of the *dhyāna* absorptions. It is by means of these types of mind that one acquires the measureless benefits of the second ground. If I allow [these types of mind] to become admixed with the affairs of these many other people, then I will lose these benefits.
>
> And why would this be so? If one allows his practice to become admixed with the affairs of other people, then, because of the eye faculty and the rest of the six sense faculties, one may sometimes then revert to the production of unwholesome dharmas. Why? Because, when one draws close to dharmas able to provoke lust, hatred, or delusion, [the sensations experienced through] the sense faculties may stir up the fires of the afflictions. It would be due to having ignited the fires of the afflictions that one would then lose these benefits.

It is because of having perceived these sorts of faults that one then develops the unmixed mind and realizes that he should not allow his practice to become admixed with the affairs of householders or other monastics.

7. The Unattached Mind

Having already developed this unmixed mind, this practitioner next develops the unattached mind. The unattached mind is that through which one does not become attached to any householders or monastics, including even one's father, one's mother, one's older or younger brother, one's preceptors, one's teachers, or one's elders. One reflects thus:

> If I become attached to householders or monastics, then this will surely involve the interactions involved with going thither and exchanging mutual greetings. In such circumstances, how could I possibly avoid the arising of mixed mind states? Therefore, if I wish to ensure that the benefits of the *dhyāna* absorptions continue to abide, doing so through preservation of the unmixed mind, then I should relinquish any thoughts of attachment for either householders or monastics.

a. Q: Doesn't an Unattached Mind Contradict the Bodhisattva Vow?

Question: The dharma of the bodhisattva prescribes that one should not forsake beings and should not entertain any thought of forsaking them. This is as stated in the *Bodhisaṃbhāra* [*Treatise*]:

From the very beginning, the bodhisattva exerts vigor
in the power of every form of skillful means
through which he should influence all beings
to abide in the Great Vehicle.

Even were one to teach beings as numerous as
the sands of the Ganges to abide in arhatship,
that would not equal [the merit of] instructing even one person
to abide in the Great Vehicle, for this would be the superior deed.

If one encounters someone possessed of only lesser strength
who is thus incapable of bringing forth Great Vehicle resolve,
one should, as a secondary priority, teach them to abide instead
in the *śrāvaka* disciple or *pratyekabuddha* vehicles.

If they find themselves incapable of abiding
in either *śrāvaka* disciple or *pratyekabuddha* vehicles,
then one should instruct such beings
in a way that causes them to cultivate the causal bases of merit.

If, however, they cannot take on any of the Three Vehicles
and cannot take on [causal bases] for human or celestial bliss, either,
then one should always resort to present-world endeavors
to benefit them in a manner corresponding to the situation.

If, even then, there happen to be those beings who
cannot accept benefit as offered by the bodhisattva,
one must still refrain from forsaking these beings,
but should bring forth great kindness and compassion for them.[463]

Also, why is it that you claim that the bodhisattva takes on the unmixed mind and brings forth the unattached mind? If the bodhisattva has no attachment to other beings, then that just amounts to abandoning them. How then could he liberate them?

b. A: No, One Must Accord with the Mind of Equanimity

Response: One should accord with the practice of the mind of equanimity as prescribed by the bodhisattva path. And why? It is because of the mind of equanimity that this person then develops the expansively happy mind. Thus, one reflects:

> If I relinquish these many sorts of disturbances, then I will be able to acquire the *dhyāna* absorptions and it is because of the *dhyāna* absorptions that I will bring forth that sublime dharma of expansive happiness. Once I have acquired this dharma, I will then be able to benefit beings in ways that are ten million times more beneficial than what I can do right now.

Consequently, in order to bring about far greater benefit for other beings, one temporarily uses the mind of equanimity to provisionally abandon the many disturbances so that one can then acquire the *dhyāna* absorptions, the five spiritual powers, and the associated qualities with which one can benefit beings.

So, why is it that the bodhisattva engages in these sorts of skillful means? In order to acquire the magnanimous mind, the bodhisattva reflects:

> Because the great man delights in providing great benefit, he does not settle for providing merely minor benefit. Therefore I should now seek to acquire the dharmas of great men and then cultivate the corresponding course of training. I should then pursue just such a diligent application of vigor for the sake of being able to provide such great benefit, namely by acquiring the *dhyāna* absorptions, the spiritual powers, the extinguishing of the sufferings, the liberations, and so forth.

Given the above, the challenge that you have presented here is wrongly conceived.

c. Q: Why Must the Bodhisattva Again Develop the Straight Mind, etc.?

Question: One already possesses the straight mind and other such dharmas on the first ground. Why then do you yet again state that the bodhisattva wishing to gain the second ground must develop these ten types of mind?

d. A: Now, on the 2nd Ground, These Minds Become Solidly Established

Response: Although one has already come into possession of these dharmas on the first ground, one still does not deeply delight in them and still has not yet solidly established them. One's mind is always joyous on this ground. One then becomes ever more solidly established [in these dharmas] and then develops the capacity to put them to use. Therefore, this challenge of yours is wrong.

e. Q: What Is the Result of Deep Delight and Solid Establishment?

Question: In the case of those who deeply delight in these dharmas and become ever more solidly established in them, what sorts of circumstances result from this?[464]

f. A: These Types of Mind Will Forever After Be Effortlessly Invoked

Response:

> If this person succeeds even one time in acquiring
> deep delight and solid establishment in these types of mind,
> then he will never again have to apply further effort in this,
> for they will then become like servants who always follow after him.

They will become like a servant that, from the time of his birth, then always follows along after his master. So too, once the bodhisattva has acquired deep delight in and solid establishment of these [ten types of] minds, they will immediately and always accompany him and never again require the application of special effort to cause them to arise. Thereafter, it requires only the most minor sort of causal circumstance for them to come forth yet again. Why is this so? It is because the roots [of goodness associated with these types of mind] have penetrated down so deeply that stems and branches continuously push forth [forever after].

g. Q: What Are the Fruits of Acquiring These Ten Types of Mind?

Question: If the bodhisattva succeeds in acquiring these ten types of mind, what sorts of fruits will he gain?

h. A: He Will Attain the Second Ground and a Threefold Stainlessness

Response:

If one acquires these types of mind,
then one will abide directly on the second ground
and will become completely equipped with a threefold stainlessness:
[Nominal]; in terms of bad karma; and in terms of the afflictions.

If the bodhisattva succeeds in acquiring these ten types of mind consisting of the straight mind as well as the others, he will then immediately qualify as abiding on the second bodhisattva ground.

The first type of stainlessness is the name of this ground, [i.e. the "stainlessness" ground]. The second type of stainlessness refers to the abandonment on this ground of the defilements associated with the karmic transgressions occurring in the ten courses of bad karmic action. The third type of stainlessness refers to abandonment of the defilements associated with greed, hatred, and the other sorts of afflictions.

It is for these reasons that this is called "the Ground of Stainlessness." Furthermore, regarding the meaning of "stainlessness":

B. The 2nd Ground Bodhisattva's Ten Courses of Good Karmic Action

The bodhisattva abiding on this ground
naturally abstains from engaging in bad actions.
Because he deeply delights in good dharmas,
he naturally practices the courses of good karmic action.

1. Q: How Many Are Physical, How Many Verbal & How Many Mental?

Question: Given that [this bodhisattva] naturally abstains from the ten courses of bad karmic action and naturally engages in the ten courses of good karmic action, how many of the actions comprising these two classes of courses of karmic action are physical, how many are verbal, and how many are mental?

2. A: Physical and Mental Are Threefold and Verbal Are Fourfold

Response:

The [bad] physical and mental actions are each of three types
and the [bad] verbal actions are fourfold. So too with good actions.
The brief explanation then is of this sort.
This is a subject that should be distinguished [further].

There are three types of bad physical karmic actions, namely killing, stealing, and sexual misconduct. There are four types of bad verbal karmic actions, namely false speech, divisive speech, harsh speech, and scattered or inappropriate speech. There are three types of bad mental karmic actions, namely covetousness, ill will, and wrong views.

There are also three types of good physical karmic actions, namely abandoning killing, stealing, and sexual misconduct. The good verbal karmic actions are also fourfold, namely abandoning false speech, divisive speech, harsh speech, and scattered or inappropriate speech. There are three types of good mental karmic actions, namely non-covetousness, refraining from ill will, and right views.

Whether the physical, verbal, or mental courses of karmic action are good or bad is a topic requiring further discussion so as to cause people to clearly understand such matters.

C. Definitions of Each of the Ten Courses of Good & Bad Karmic Action

1. Killing

First, "killing" as a course of bad karmic action involves the following factors:

The existence of another being;
The knowledge that there is this being;
The deliberate infliction of physical injury;
The loss of life due to this infliction of physical injury.

If one brings forth these physical karmic actions, this is what is known as "killing," the first of the courses of bad karmic action. It is the abandoning of these factors that defines the good karmic action of refraining from killing.

2. Stealing

As for "stealing," it involves the following factors:

There is something belonging to someone else;
One knows that this thing belongs to someone else;
One produces a thought intent on stealing it;
One's hand grasps this thing, picks it up, and then moves it away from its current location;
Whether one openly robs or surreptitiously steals the object, one then reckons, "This is my possession" and thinks, "This is mine."

These are the factors defining the act of stealing. It is the abandoning of these factors that defines the good karmic action of refraining from stealing.

3. Sexual Misconduct

As for "sexual misconduct," [it involves the following factors]:

There is some woman;[465]

She is under the protection of parents, under the protection of her clan, under the protection of her caste, under the protection of worldly convention or law, or under the protection of the moral precepts;

In the case of another man's wife, one may even know of the potential for such obstacles as being whipped, beaten with clubs, tormented, or afflicted with bodily injury;

Even in the midst of any of these circumstances, one nonetheless produces thoughts of lust and then actually commits one of the types of offending physical karmic actions.

In circumstances involving one's own wife, [the following factors constitute transgressions of this precept]:

She may have formally taken a [temporarily restricting] moral precept;

She may be pregnant;

She may still be nursing an infant;

The act may involve a restricted orifice.[466]

These are the factors defining the act of sexual misconduct. It is the abandonment of these factors that defines the good karmic action [of refraining from sexual misconduct].

4. False Speech

As for "false speech," [it involves the following factors]:

There is some deceptive sign;

There is the mental intent to deceive;

There is the perception that this action would constitute a deceptive falsehood;

There is the acquiescence in some circumstance constituting a deceptive falsehood;

There is the desire to deceive;

There is the knowledge that the circumstances are of this sort and yet one describes them as being otherwise.

These are the factors defining the action of false speech. It is the abandonment of these factors that defines the good karmic action of abstaining from false speech.

5. Divisive Speech

As for "divisive speech," [it involves the following factors]:

One wishes to cause others to separate;

One says something about this person to that person or says something about that person to this person in order to cause them to separate;

Those who previously were close are then caused to separate;

If they become separated, one is subsequently happy that they have separated, rejoices that they have separated, or is pleased that they have separated.

Factors such as these define an act of divisive speech. It is the abandonment of these factors that defines the good karmic action of abstaining from divisive speech.

6. Harsh Speech

As for "harsh speech," this is inclusive of all of the types of worldly speech that are inclined to cause anger or torment in others such as:

Harsh speech;

Injurious speech;

Bitter speech;

Coarse speech;

Abusive speech.

Factors such as these define an act of harsh speech. It is the abandonment of these factors that defines the good karmic action of abstaining from harsh speech.

7. Scattered or Inappropriate Speech

As for "scattered or inappropriate speech,"[467] [it may involve the following factors]:

Speaking [of particular topics] at an inappropriate time;

Non-beneficial speech;

Speech contrary to Dharma;

[Rambling] speech having neither beginning nor end;

Unreasonable speech.

Factors such as these define the action of scattered or inappropriate speech. It is the abandonment of these factors that defines the good karmic action of "abstaining from scattered or inappropriate speech."

8. Covetousness

As for "covetousness," [it involves the following factors]:

There are things belonging to someone else which that person wishes to keep such as his fields, lands, or wealth;

One's mind is influenced by covetousness;
One wishes to obtain that thing.

In whichever circumstance of this sort one refrains from coveting, refrains from envy, and refrains from wishing to obtain such an object, these factors constitute the good karmic action of "non-covetousness."

9. Ill Will

As for "ill will," [it may involve the following factors] directed toward some other being:

One produces thoughts of hatred;
Or one produces thoughts inclined toward obstructiveness;
Or one becomes angry;
Or one thinks, "Why not beat him up, tie him up, or murder him?"

Factors such as these define what is meant by "ill will." It is the abandoning of these factors that defines the good karmic action of "refraining from ill will."

10. Wrong Views

As for "wrong views," this refers to claims such as these:

There is no point in practicing giving;
There is no point in repaying others for kindnesses they have bestowed;
There are no corresponding karmic effects of good or bad karmic actions;
There is no [rebirth into] the present life and no [rebirth] into future lives;
There is no need to respect one's parents;
There are no *śramaṇas* or brahmans who are able to know of [rebirth into] this life or into future lives or who personally gain utterly clear and penetrating comprehension and realizations.

Factors such as these define what is meant by "wrong views."

11. Right View

As for right view, this is reflected in such views as:

There is giving [that should be done];
It is right to repay others for kindnesses they have bestowed;
There are corresponding karmic effects resulting from good and bad actions;
There is [rebirth into] the present life and into future lives;
The world does indeed have *śramaṇas* and brahmans who know [of rebirth into] this life and into future lives and who personally gain utterly clear and penetrating comprehension and realizations.

Factors such as these define the good karmic action of right view. It is in this manner that this bodhisattva enters the right view course [of good karmic action].

> The courses of good karmic actions and of bad karmic actions
> each involve twenty specific types of distinctions.
> Knowledge of factors such as point of origin and such
> each involve twelve different types of distinctions.

D. Abhidharma Categories Analyzing the 10 Courses of Karmic Action

With respect to the ten courses of bad karmic action and the ten courses of good karmic action, the bodhisattva knows twenty distinctions pertaining to their many different distinguishing aspects. He also thoroughly knows twelve kinds of distinctions pertaining to each of these twenty distinctions that include their point of origin and so forth.

1. Twenty Factors Used in Abhidharmic Analysis of Actions

For each of these component actions within the path of the ten bad karmic actions there are twenty distinguishing factors. For instance, in not abandoning the karmic offense of taking some other being's life, we have these factors:

First, it is an action that is not good.
Second, it is connected with the desire realm's planes of existence.
Third, it involves the contaminants.
Fourth, it is not a mental dharma.
Fifth, it is not associated with the mind.
Sixth, it does not follow the actions of the mind.
Seventh, it may or may not arise in conjunction with the mind.

What all is implied by "arising in conjunction with the mind"? [This involves the following]:

There is a truly existent being;
One knows it is a being;
One uses some physical action to take its life.

These factors define what is meant by "arising in conjunction with the mind."

What is meant by "not arising in conjunction with the mind"? In an instance where a person [merely] wished to kill a being, grab him, pull him forth, throw him down, and pin him to the ground, but only later was able to bring about his death, this would be a case of "[killing] not arising [directly] in conjunction with the mind."

Also, it might be that the body does not move and the mouth does not speak and one only brings forth the thought, "From this day on, I shall become someone who kills beings." This instance of the karmic offense of killing is one wherein [the actual act of taking a life] does not take place directly in conjunction with the mind.

Also, in an instance where this [ideational] non-abandonment of taking others' lives always accumulates habitual karmic propensities that continue to increase whether one is asleep or awake, this too qualifies as an instance where [the act of killing] does not arise in conjunction with the mind.

> Eighth, it may be [an offense] involving either form or non-form.

That initial case [directly above] in which the act of killing occurred in conjunction with the mind—that is one that involved form. That second [immediately subsequent] example of the karmic offense of killing as well as the third and the fourth—these are all instances not involving form.

> Ninth, it may involve performing an action or it may not involve performing an action.

That which involves form is one that does involve performing an action whereas any others do not involve the performing of an action.

> Tenth, it may or may not involve the presence of objective conditions.

That involving form does involve objective conditions whereas the rest are circumstances devoid of objective conditions.

Question: Are these states of mind that are possessed of objective conditions or devoid of objective conditions?

Response: They do not necessarily involve objective conditions.

Question: If these states of mind do not necessarily involve objective conditions, and we have a case of the body not moving and the mouth not speaking wherein there is only the production of the thought, "From this day forward, I shall be one who takes the lives of beings," how can it be that karmic offenses such as these do not involve an objective condition?

Response: If it is an instance wherein the karmic offense of killing takes place, then this mind should indeed have associated objective conditions. However, now, in truth, the karmic offense of killing is not [merely] mental. If the mind was what actually commits the karmic offense of killing, then that would itself involve a physical action. But, in truth the mind's actions are not physical actions. Therefore, this [merely mental] karmic offense of killing beings is not defined by the presence of objective conditions. Rather, [an actual] karmic offense of killing occurs in conjunction with the mind and arises within the physical body. It is because this [merely mental] instance does not involve any action that it is referred to as being one not involving objective conditions.

Eleventh, it may involve performing a karmic action.

Twelfth, it may not correspond to the commission of a karmic action.

Thirteenth, it may occur in a manner not in direct linkage with the commission of a karmic action.

Fourteenth, it may or may not be generated in conjunction with the commission of a given karmic action.

This is analogous to the case involving arising in conjunction with the mind and is no different than that. The only difference here is that it is not arising in conjunction with mind, but is instead arising in conjunction with volition.[468]

Fifteenth, it may not be a karmic result of actions carried out in previous existences.

Sixteenth, it is not to be cultivated.

Seventeenth, it is to be well understood.[469]

Eighteenth, it should be realized by wisdom and is not realized by the body.

Nineteenth, it can be severed.[470]

Twentieth, it can be known and seen.

[Now, as for the application of these factors to] the karmic offense of "not abandoning stealing," the karmic offense of "not abandoning sexual misconduct," and the karmic offense of "not abandoning false speech," these are just the same as when they were applied to the karmic offense of "killing" except that these involve:[471]

One instance that occurs in conjunction with the mind and two instances that do not occur in conjunction with the mind;

One instance that involves form and two instances that do not involve form;

One instance that involves the performance of an action and two instances that do not involve the performance of an action;

One instance that involves objective conditions and two instances that do not involve objective conditions.

As for "not abandoning divisive speech" and "not abandoning harsh speech," [the relevant distinctions] are just the same [as with the above-discussed actions].

In the case of "not abandoning scattered or inappropriate speech," [the relevant distinctions are as follows]:

It may be karmically bad;
It may be karmically neutral;
That which arises from bad intentionality is karmically bad;
That which arises from neutral intentionality is karmically neutral;
It may occur in connection with the desire realm;
It may occur in connection with the form realm.

As for that which occurs in connection with the desire realm, it is scattered or inappropriate speech arising in a desire-realm body and mind that occur in connection with the desire realm;

The basis for being categorized as "connected with the form realm" is similarly determined.

The remaining factors relevant to "scattered or inappropriate speech" are similar to those set forth earlier with regard to "false speech."

As for "covetousness," [the relevant distinctions are as follows]:[472]

It arises in connection with the desire realm;
It is a mental dharma influenced by the contaminants;
It is not associated with the mind;
It does not follow the actions of the mind;
It occurs in conjunction with the mind;
It is formless;
It does not involve an action;
It does involve an objective condition;
It does not correspond to a karmic action;
It does not follow and correspond to karmic action;
It does not arise in conjunction with karmic action;
It is not itself a karmic result from actions committed in a prior existence except when it is a karmic result of a [prior] cause;[473]
It cannot be cultivated;
It should be thoroughly understood;
It should be the object of wisdom-based realization;
It may involve realizations pertaining to the body;
It is subject to severance;
It is subject to being perceived and understood.

As for "ill will," [the relevant distinctions are as follows]:

It may be associated with the mind;
It may not be associated with the mind;
In instances where it is associated with the mind, it is included in the obsessions;

In instances where it is not associated with the mind, it is included among the latent afflictions;[474]

The cases are just the same with reference to its following or not following actions of the mind.

As for instances in which it occurs in conjunction with the mind or, alternatively, does not occur in conjunction with the mind, it is when it occurs in beings possessed of ideation that it occurs in conjunction with the mind and it is when it occurs in beings not possessed of ideation that it does not occur in conjunction with the mind.

Just as it is with occurrences associated with the mind, with occurrences following actions of the mind, with occurrences arising in conjunction with the mind, so too it is with occurrences associated with karmic actions, with occurrences following karmic action, and with occurrences in conjunction with the arising of karmic action.

And just as it is with occurrences unassociated with the mind, with occurrences not following actions of the mind, and with occurrences not arising in conjunction with the mind, so too it is with occurrences unassociated with karmic actions, with occurrences not following karmic action, and with occurrences not in conjunction with the arising of karmic action.

The remaining distinctions that could be made here [with regard to "ill will"] may be deduced from the earlier discussion of "covetousness."

[The distinctions that could be made regarding] "wrong views" are just the same as those already described above with regard to "ill will."

As for "abandonment of taking others' lives" among the ten courses of good karmic action, [the relevant distinctions are as follows]:

It is good in nature.

It may occur in connection with the desire-realm planes of existence.

It may be unconnected to the three realms of existence.[475]

In instances connected to the desire realm, one abides in a desire-realm body and abandons taking other beings' lives. This is what is meant by being "connected to the desire realm."

In instances "unconnected to the three realms of existence," this corresponds to actions included in the eightfold path of the Āryas engaged in by those at and beyond the stages of training who practice "right action" by abandoning the killing of beings.

It may involve the contaminants.

It may not involve the contaminants.

When it is "connected to the desire realm," it involves the contaminants. When it is "unconnected to the three realms," it is free of the contaminants.

> It is not a mental dharma.
> It is not a dharma associated with the mind.
> It is not [a dharma that] follows the mind.
> It may arise in conjunction with the mind.
> It may not arise in conjunction with the mind.

What all is implied by arising in conjunction with the mind? This is a circumstance like that of someone who is walking along, sees a bug, and thinks, "Through physical actions that abandon killing, I shall refrain from injuring it." This is what is meant by a good action of abandoning killing arising in conjunction with the mind.

How is it that the good action of abandoning killing other beings does not occur in conjunction with the mind? Take an instance where there is a person whose body does not move, whose mouth does not speak, and who only thinks, "From this very day forward, I shall no longer kill beings." This is a case in which [the action itself] does not occur in concert with the mind.

Then again, we may have a person who, from early on, has abandoned the killing of beings. Whether sleeping or awake, when his mind takes various other circumstances as objective conditions, in thought after thought, as he refrains from killing beings, his merit always increases and at the same time, this does not take place in conjunction with the mind.

This may or may not involve form. One instance involves form and two other instances do not involve form. One instance involves the performance of an action and two other instances do not involve the performance of an action. One instance involves objective conditions and two other instances do not involve objective conditions.

> It may constitute an action.
> It may not occur in conjunction with an action.
> It does not follow an action.

In instances where it may occur in conjunction with an action or may not occur in conjunction with an action, the determining factor is just the same [as in the case explained above] involving the issue of whether the action occurs in conjunction with the mind or does not occur in conjunction with the mind. The only difference is with regard to the presence of mind versus the presence of volition.

It is not itself a karmic result from actions committed in a prior [existence] except when it is a karmic result of a prior cause.
It can be cultivated.
It can be thoroughly understood.
It can be the object of physical realization or wisdom-based realization.
It may be subject to severance or may not be subject to severance.

If it is associated with the contaminants, then it may be subject to severance. If it is unassociated with the contaminants, then it is not subject to severance. So too with respect to its amenability to being known and seen.

[The relevant distinctions applicable to] "abandonment of stealing," "abandonment of sexual misconduct," "abandonment of false speech," "abandonment of divisive speech," and "abandonment of harsh speech" are all similar.

As for [the good karmic action of] "abandonment of scattered or inappropriate speech," [the relevant distinctions are as follows]:

It may be connected to the desire realm.
It may be connected to the form realm.
It may not be connected to any of the three realms.

When connected with the form realm, it is with a desire-realm body and mind that one abandons scattered and inappropriate speech. So too, when connected with the form realm, [it is with a form-realm body and mind that one abandons scattered and inappropriate speech]. When not connected with any of the three realms, [the distinguishing factors] are as explained above in the discussion of the good karmic action of abstaining from killing.

It may be associated with the contaminants.
It may be unassociated with the contaminants.

When associated with the contaminants, it is connected [with the three realms]. When unassociated with the contaminants, it is not connected [with any of the three realms]. The other applicable distinctions are as explained in the above discussion of "abandoning false speech."

As for [the good karmic action of] "abandonment of covetousness," [the relevant distinctions are as follows]:

It is good in nature.
It may be connected with the desire realm.
It may not be connected to any of the three realms.

When connected to the desire realm, this may be a desire-realm common person refraining from covetousness or else this may be someone who is a worthy or an *ārya* practicing the good karmic action of abstaining from covetousness. This is what is meant by being "connected with the desire realm."

When not connected to any of the three realms, this is an instance of refraining from covetousness that is a good karmic action unassociated with the contaminants done by either a worthy or an *ārya*.

This may be associated with the contaminants.
It may be unassociated with the contaminants.

When it is connected with the desire realm, it is associated with the contaminants. When not connected [to any of the three realms], it is unassociated with the contaminants.

This is a mental dharma.
It is associated with the mind.
It may follow actions of the mind.
It may arise in conjunction with the mind.
It is formless.
It does not involve performance of an action.
It has objective conditions.
It is not a karmic action.
It is associated with karmic actions.
It may follow karmic actions.
It may arise in conjunction with karmic actions.
It is not itself a karmic result from actions committed in a prior [existence] except when it is a karmic result of a prior cause.
It can be cultivated.
It can be thoroughly known.
It is amenable to physical realization.
It is amenable to wisdom-based realization.
It may be subject to severance.
It may not be subject to severance.

When associated with the contaminants, it is subject to severance. When unassociated with the contaminants, it is not subject to severance. So too with the distinctions regarding amenability to being directly known and seen.

As for [the good karmic action of] "abandoning ill will," [the relevant distinctions are as follows]:

It is good in nature.
It may be connected with the desire realm.
It may be connected with the form realm.

It may be connected to the formless realm.
It may be that it is not connected with any of the three realms.

When connected with the desire realm, it is in a desire-realm existence with roots of goodness arising [from previous practice] of restraint from ill will. When connected with existence in either of the other two realms, the bases are just the same.

As for when it is "not connected to any of the three realms," all other instances [aside from the above] are "not connected [to any of the three realms]."

> This may be associated with the contaminants or it may be unassociated with the contaminants.

When connected to any of the three realms, it is associated with the contaminants. All other instances are unassociated with the contaminants.

It is a mental dharma.
It may be associated with the mind.
It may be unassociated with the mind.

When opposing obsession, roots of goodness arising from refraining from ill will are associated with the mind. When opposing latent tendencies, roots of goodness arising from refraining from ill will are unassociated with the mind. The distinctions are the same with respect to following actions of the mind and arising in conjunction with the mind.

It is formless.
It does not involve performance of an action.
It may have objective conditions.
It may not have objective conditions.

When it is associated with the mind it has objective conditions. When it is unassociated with the mind it does not have objective conditions.

It is not a karmic action.
It may be associated with a karmic action.
Or it may not be associated with a karmic action.
It may follow the enactment of a karmic action.
Or it may not follow the enactment of a karmic action.
It may arise in conjunction with a karmic action.
Or it may not arise in conjunction with a karmic action.

[The distinctions applicable to this arising or not arising in conjunction with a karmic action] are the same as those that applied above when discussing mind.

It is not a karmic result from actions [committed in a prior existence] except when it is a karmic result of a prior cause.

It can be the object of physical realization or wisdom-based realization.

It may be subject to severance or may not be subject to severance.

When associated with the contaminants it is subject to severance. When unassociated with the contaminants, it is not subject to severance. So too with regard to its amenability to being known and seen.

As for [the good karmic action of] "right view," [the relevant distinctions are as follows]:

It is good in nature.

It may be connected with the desire realm.

It may be connected with the form realm.

It may be connected with the formless realm.

It may not be connected with any of the three realms.

When connected to the desire realm, it involves thoughts corresponding to right views produced in the desire realm by common persons, worthies, or *āryas*. When connected to the form realm and when connected to the formless realm, the circumstances are just the same.

When not connected to any of the three realms, these are right views unassociated with the contaminants as held by worthies or *āryas*.

It may be associated with the contaminants.

It may be unassociated with the contaminants.

When connected to any of the three realms, it is associated with the contaminants. When not connected to any of the three realms, it is unassociated with the contaminants.

It is a mental dharma.

It is a dharma associated with the mind.

It follows actions of the mind.

It arises in conjunction with the mind.

It is formless.

It does not involve the performance of an action.

It may have objective conditions.

It is not a karmic action.

It may be associated with a karmic action.

It may follow the enactment of a karmic action.

It may arise in conjunction with a karmic action.

It is not a karmic result from actions [committed in a prior existence] except when it is a karmic result of a prior cause.

It can be the object of physical realization or wisdom-based realization.
It may be subject to severance or may not be subject to severance.

When associated with contaminants, it is subject to severance. When unassociated with the contaminants, it is not subject to severance.

The differentiations here are the same with respect to amenability to knowing and seeing.

This [above discussion illustrates] what is meant by the application of twenty distinguishing factors such as "goodness," and so forth [to the understanding of the ten courses of good karmic action and the ten courses of bad karmic action.]

2. The Twelvefold Discussion of Origins and Such

As for the twelvefold discussion of "origins" and so forth, it is as follows:[476]

1) From what did it originate?
2) What does it produce?
3) From what cause did it originate?
4) For whom is it a cause?
5) What are the associated conditions?
6) For what is it a condition?
7) What does it take as an objective condition?
8) What is the benefit?[477]
9) What factors are dominant?
10) For whom is this dominant?
11) What losses does this incur?
12) What karmic effects does this entail?

In the case of the karmic offense of "killing," [these discussions are as follows]:

As for "From what did it originate?," it arises from the three types of bad karmic roots and additionally arises from wrong thought. Further, it arises from whichever thought the act of taking a being's life next followed upon. It originated from this thought.

As for "What does it produce?," these are all of the dharmas proximate to the karmic offense of killing whether those dharmas have already arisen, are now arising, or eventually will arise. So too with these causes and conditions.

As for "What does it take as an objective condition?," it takes a living being as its objective condition. Additionally, whichever thought precipitated the taking of that being's life—it also takes this thought as a condition.

As for "For what is it a condition?," all of the peripheral dharmas caused by the karmic offense of killing, whether already arisen, now arising, or eventually arising—these are all conditions associated with the karmic offense of killing.

As for "What losses does this incur?," this includes having a bad reputation in the present lifetime, being the object of others' distrust, and so forth.

As for "What karmic effects does this entail?," these include falling into the hell realm, the animal realm, the hungry-ghost realm, the *asura* realm, and other wretched destinies wherein one undergoes suffering and anguish.

As for "What factors are dominant?" and "For whom is this dominant?," these are the same as with above statement on the bases of origination.

These distinctions are the same in their application to stealing, sexual misconduct, false speech, divisive speech, harsh speech, scattered or inappropriate speech, covetousness, ill will, and wrong views. There are only differences with regard to what in each case serves as an objective condition.

For instance, in the case of stealing, it is the object that one appropriates to one's own use that serves as the objective condition. Sexual misconduct takes a being as the objective condition.

False speech, divisive speech, harsh speech, and scattered or inappropriate speech all take words as their objective condition.

Covetousness takes as its objective condition the particular object that one would appropriate to one's own use.

Ill will takes a being as the objective condition.

Wrong views take words as their objective condition.

All of the remaining distinctions are deducible from the differentiations described above.

"Refraining from killing beings" arises from the three types of good karmic roots as well as from right mindfulness. It also arises from the thought arising just prior to the act of refraining from killing a being.

As for "What does it produce?," these are all of the dharmas arising from this dharma, whether they have already arisen, are now arising, or eventually will arise. So too with the associated causes and conditions.

As for "What does it take as an objective condition?," it takes a living being as its objective condition.

As for "For what is it a condition?," all of the peripheral dharmas caused by the act of not killing whether already arisen, now arising, or eventually arising—these are all conditions associated with the act of not killing.

As for "dominant factors," the roots of goodness are dominant and right mindfulness is also dominant. Also whichever thought was followed by the restraint from killing a particular being—that thought was also dominant.

As for "For whom is this dominant?," this is determined by all of the dharmas peripheral to the act of not taking a being's life, whether they have already arisen, are now arising, or will eventually arise.

As for "What is the benefit?," being opposed to the karmic offense of killing—this is the benefit.

As for "What karmic effects does this entail?," these are whichever karmic effects are opposite to those entailed by killing beings.

These distinctions are the same in their application to not stealing, to not committing sexual misconduct, to not committing false speech, to not engaging in divisive speech, to not engaging in harsh speech, to not engaging in scattered or inappropriate speech, to non-covetousness, to refraining from ill will, and to right views. There are only differences with regard to what in each case serves as an objective condition.

For instance, in the case of not stealing, it is the object that one might otherwise appropriate to one's own use that serves as the objective condition.

Refraining from sexual misconduct takes a being [otherwise susceptible to one's sexual misconduct] as the objective condition.

Refraining from false speech, divisive speech, harsh speech, and scattered or inappropriate speech all take words as their objective condition.

Non-covetousness takes as its objective condition the particular object that one might otherwise desire to have available to one's own use.

Refraining from ill will takes a being as the objective condition.

Right views may take words as the objective condition or may take meaning as the objective conditions. Those associated with the contaminants take words as objective conditions. Those unassociated with the contaminants take meanings as the objective condition.

It is in this manner that this bodhisattva should distinguish and know with respect to the practice of the ten courses of good karmic actions the [twenty] analytic discussions of "goodness" and so forth as well as the twelve analytic discussions of "origination" and so forth.

In addition, he should know:

3. The Seven Types of Bad Actions, Their Origins, and Four Distinctions

The bases for the seven types of bad karmic actions,
how they may arise from greed, hatred, or delusion,
and also the application of four types of distinctions
of which two each are linked to karmic actions and to beings.

This bodhisattva knows that seven courses of bad karmic action may arise from greed, hatred, or delusion, and thus applies these distinctions to circumstances in the world. He is also aware of four categorical distinctions applicable to these seven types of bad karmic deeds.

This karmic offense of killing may arise from greed, hatred, or from delusion. [Consider the case in which killing] arises from greed. Suppose for example that a person sees some being, produces a thought of greed, and then, due to these causes and conditions, because he wishes to enjoy the use of that being's visual forms, sounds, fragrances, tastes, or touchables, or because he wants its tusks, horns, fur, hide, sinews, flesh, bones, marrow, and such—this person then, due to having this covetous thought, takes this being's life. This is a case of the karmic offense of killing arising from greed.

In a case where someone kills a being due to hating and being displeased [with that being], this is an instance of killing arising from hatred.

In a case where someone beset by wrong views fails to realize the effects of good and bad karmic actions as they unfold in subsequent lives and then, because of that, kills some being, this is an instance of the karmic offense of killing arising from delusion. In some cases, the killer may kill due to regarding the act as productive of merit. Or he may kill out of a desire to liberate [the being he is killing] from suffering. These cases are reflective of customs in the country of Parthia in the west and other such places.

There are yet other instances of killing motivated by the idea that it may serve as a cause and condition for the acquisition of merit. Thus one may wish to achieve rebirth in the heavens through the karma of killing. This latter situation is exemplified by a practice in East India of sacrificing beings in the temple of their deva, wishing through such deeds to be reborn in the heavens. These are all cases of killing occurring because of delusion.

There are yet other individuals who, because of greed, take the possessions of others, thinking: "This is because I deserve to freely acquire whichever fine visual forms, sounds, fragrances, flavors, or touchables appeal to me." This is just a case of stealing arising from greed.

There are yet other people who, due to hatred and dislike of others steal the wealth and possessions of others, wishing thereby to cause them anguish. These are cases of stealing arising from hatred.

Then again, there are people who, holding wrong views and failing to realize the karmic retribution involved, steal the possessions of others. This is stealing arising from delusion. This is exemplified by brahmans who state, "All the wealth and treasures of the world are rightfully mine. It is only because of the relative weakness of my power that all of these inferior classes of people have been able, using methods contrary to our dharma, to take these things for their own use. If I now seize them, this is just a case of someone retrieving his own possessions. Hence there is no karmic transgression in doing this." When someone uses such rationalizations to steal the belongings of others, this too is just a matter of stealing arising from delusion.

When someone commits sexual misconduct because of desire and attachment to sexual gratification, this is an instance of sexual misconduct arising from greed.

If someone motivated by hatred and aversion toward someone else thinks, "Because this fellow violated my mother, wife, sister, or daughter, I shall get back at him by sexually defiling his mother, wife, sisters, and daughters," this is an instance of sexual misconduct arising from hatred.

In someone holding wrong views and not realizing the karmic retributions involved violates [some woman], this is an instance [of sexual misconduct] arising from delusion. This is exemplified by a man who claims, "There is really no such thing as sexual misconduct between humans. Why? All women were born for the enjoyment of men and thus are just like any other thing we exploit for our own use. Thus, if one has a need for it and therefore becomes involved in this kind of affair, then there is no karmic offense of sexual misconduct involved here." When someone relying on this sort of rationalization goes ahead and indulges his sexual desire in this way, that is a case of sexual misconduct arising from delusion.

Just as it is with the karmic offense of stealing, so too it is with false speech. When someone tells lies because of greed for wealth, then this is referred to as false speech arising from greed. When someone deceives someone else in order to cause them anguish, this is referred to as false speech arising from hatred. When someone with wrong views who does not understand the karmic retributions involved tells a lie, this is referred to as false speech arising from delusion.

Divisive speech, harsh speech, and scattered or inappropriate speech are the same [as the above discussion of "false speech"] in that these three courses of bad karmic action also have these same foundational bases. From this, one can distinguish the arising of the karmic effects resulting from all seven physical and verbal karmic deeds.

Question: Is it or is it not the case that all instances of not abandoning killing beings constitute the karmic offense of killing? Are all instances of the karmic offense of killing necessarily instances of not abandoning killing?

Response: There are instances of not abandoning killing that constitute instances of the karmic transgression of killing beings and there are also instances of not abandoning killing that do not qualify as instances of the karmic transgression of killing beings.

This being the case, which of these instances of not abandoning killing constitute instances of the karmic transgression of killing? Taking for example a case where there is a being, one knows it is a being, one deliberately kills it, and in taking its life, one produces the associated physical karmic action—this is an instance of not abandoning killing also constituting an instance of the karmic offense of killing.

What would be an example of failure to abandon killing not qualifying as an instance of the karmic offense of killing? Take for instance a case where this person did in fact previously engage in the causes and conditions of killing but the being somehow did not die. Further, take the case in which someone makes no bodily movement and utters no words but merely thinks, "From this day on, I shall kill beings." Both of these instances qualify as cases of failure to abandon killing that do not actually entail the karmic offense of killing. This involves two categorical distinctions through which one makes a total of four distinctions, two for each of these two subcategories of the so-called "good" and "bad."

4. More Subsidiary Distinctions Related to the Good and Bad Actions

This is not just a matter of "good" versus "bad,"
but also of two types of karma, "physical" versus "mental."
One should also know
that there are still other distinctions.

There are other subsidiary physical actions aside from the actual killing of beings, stealing, or sexual misconduct, actions that, in the case of killing, include such abuses as beating, tying up, imprisoning, whipping, striking with staves, dragging [through the streets], and so forth. Because they fall short of actually inflicting death, these sorts of bad physical karmic actions are not subsumed under [the karmic offense of] taking life, and so forth [with the subsidiary physical actions associated with stealing and sexual misconduct].

[So too], among the actions that are good, actions such as welcoming eminences on arrival, escorting them off when they leave, pressing the palms together, bowing down in reverence, greeting with half bows, assisting with bathing, massage, and proffering of gifts, none of these good physical karmic actions are subsumed under non-killing, and so forth [with the wholesome subsidiary physical actions associated with stealing and sexual misconduct].

[So too], among the karmic actions of the mind, [the same principle applies] to all of the rest of the unwholesome [mental] dharmas aside from covetousness, ill will, and wrong views, dharmas such as not guarding or focusing the mind, the fetters, and so forth.

[So too], among the karmic actions of the mind, [the same principle applies] to all of the rest of the good [mental] dharmas aside from non-covetousness, refraining from ill will, and right views, dharmas such as guarding and focusing the mind, faith, observance of moral precepts, learning, meditative concentration, equanimity, wisdom, and so forth.

5. Distinguishing "Karmic Deeds" versus "Courses of Karmic Action"

Seven of the karmic deeds are also courses of karmic action
and three of the courses of karmic action are not karmic deeds.

These seven "karmic deeds" that consist of killing, stealing, sexual misconduct, false speech, divisive speech, harsh speech, and scattered or inappropriate speech are themselves both "karmic deeds" and "courses of karmic action." Covetousness, ill will, and wrong views are "courses of karmic action," but are not "karmic deeds" as such, for these three phenomena correspond to [intentional] thought, this type of [merely mental] activity.

Question: How is it that the previous seven endeavors qualify both as "karmic deeds" and "courses of karmic action"?

Response: It is due to progressively increasing habitual practice of these endeavors that one therefore arrives in the hell realm, the animal realm, and the realm of the hungry ghosts. It is because of this that they are referred to as "courses of karmic action." Because these seven are also endeavors that one can perform, they are also referred to as "karmic deeds."

As for the three which are "courses of karmic action" but not "karmic deeds" as such, this is because they serve as the foundation for those which do constitute bad karmic deeds. Consequently these three are referred to only as "courses of karmic action" but not as "karmic deeds."

The same principle applies in the sphere of the "good" [courses of karmic action]. Abandonment of killing, of stealing, of sexual misconduct, of false speech, of divisive speech, of harsh speech, and of scattered or inappropriate speech are all both "karmic deeds" and "courses of karmic action." The other three consisting of non-covetousness, refraining from ill will, and right view are all "courses of karmic action," but are not "karmic deeds" as such, for these three phenomena correspond to [volitional] thought, this type of [merely mental] activity.[478]

Question: How is it that, [within the ten courses of good karmic action] the first seven are both "karmic deeds" and "courses of karmic action"?

Response: They are referred to as "courses" [of karmic action] because it is due to always practicing these endeavors that one becomes able to arrive in good circumstances within the realms of humans and devas. It is because these seven are karmic deeds amenable to being performed that they are also referred to as "karmic deeds."

Question: How is it that, [within the ten courses of good karmic action] the remaining three are only "courses of karmic action," but are not "karmic deeds"?

Response: These three serve as the foundation for those that do qualify as good karmic actions. It is because the practice of all good karmic deeds comes forth from within them that they are referred to as "courses of karmic action," while not being referred to as "karmic deeds" as such.

Furthermore:

6. Four Distinctions: "Karmic Deeds" and "Courses of Karmic Action"

[Observances of] moral precept dharmas are karmic deeds.
karmic deeds may or may not be [observances of] moral precepts.
Qualification as a "karmic deeds" or as a "course of karmic action"
is a matter involving the application of four types of distinctions.

Physical and verbal karmic deeds may be [observances of] moral precepts. Mental actions may be karma, but they are not themselves [observances of] moral precepts.

As for the four types of categorical distinctions made with respect to qualification as either "karmic actions" or "courses of karmic action," they are as follows:

There are "karmic deeds" that are not "courses of karmic action."
There are "courses of karmic action" that are not "karmic deeds."
There are "karmic deeds" that are also "courses of karmic action."

There are [actions] that are neither "karmic deeds" nor "courses of karmic action."

As for those "karmic deeds" that are not "courses of karmic action," these are three types of bad physical deeds not subsumable within the sphere of "courses of karmic action," namely the wielding of fists to strike, whips to lash, cudgels to beat, and so forth. So too in the case of the three corresponding types of good physical deeds not subsumable in one of the categories of "courses of karmic action," namely: welcoming eminences on arrival, bowing down in reverence, and so forth. These two subcategories of good and bad deeds are not subsumable within the "courses of karmic action."

There are those who state that [these two subcategories of good and bad deeds] *are* also "courses of karmic action." Why? [They claim that], because these two types of deeds may have times when they lead one to [rebirth in] good or bad stations of rebirth, they are therefore "courses of karmic action." However, because this is not a fixed matter, we do not claim here that they constitute "courses of karmic action."

As for those that are "courses of karmic action" but which are not "karmic deeds," because the final three bad karmic deeds [of the ten courses of bad karmic action] and the final three good karmic deeds [of the ten courses of good karmic action] are, by nature, associated with the presence [or absence of] afflictions, they are not "karmic deeds" as such. However, because they are able to instigate the production of karmic deeds, they do therefore constitute "courses of karmic action."

[Among these], the three that are good, because they are, by nature, roots of goodness, they are not "karmic deeds" as such. But, because they are able to instigate the production of good karmic deeds, they do therefore constitute "courses of karmic action."

As for those that are both "karmic deeds" and "courses of karmic action," they are the seven deeds consisting of killing or not killing and the others [as well as their opposites].

As for those that are neither "karmic deeds" nor "courses of karmic action," they are all of the dharmas [not otherwise subsumed in the first three of these four categories].

In addition:

7. Three Kinds of Purity Used to Move Beyond the First Ground

If a bodhisattva still at the border with the first ground
uses three kinds of purity
to abide securely in the ten courses of good karmic action,
he will then be able to bring forth decisive resolve.

Once this bodhisattva comes to dwell on the second ground, he then distinguishes with utter clarity these ten good and bad courses of karmic action. Having come to know these matters, he applies three kinds of purity to his abiding in the ten courses of good karmic action, namely:

He does not personally kill any being;
He does not instruct others to kill any being;
And he does not delight in the karmic offense of killing.

In this same way, he also [applies these three kinds of purity to the rest of the courses of good karmic action] up to and including "right view."

Question: A bodhisattva dwelling on the first ground already abides in the ten courses of good karmic action. Why is this matter being discussed yet again here [in the context of the second ground]?

Response: It is not that he does not abide in the ten courses of good karmic action when dwelling on the first ground. However, due to the application of these three kinds of purity, such practice becomes ever more superior and ever more greatly increased here [on the second ground]. Previously, when still abiding on the first ground, although he might indeed become a monarch reigning over all of Jambudvīpa, he was still unable at that point to implement these three kinds of purity. It is for this reason that we discuss the three kinds of purity here. The bodhisattva who abides here on the second ground knows these distinctions as they apply to all sorts of karmic actions and thus brings forth decisive resolve.

8. The 10 Courses of Good and Bad Karma As Arbiters of One's Destiny

All the world's wretched destinies
are produced from the ten bad deeds.
All the world's good destinies
are produced because of the ten good deeds.

"All the world's wretched destinies" refers to:

The three types of hell-realm destinies, namely the hot hells, cold hells, and hells of blackness;

The three types of animal-realm destinies, namely the animals that live in the water, the animals that live on land, and the animals that fly through the air;

And the different types of ghost-realm destinies, namely the hungry ghosts, the ghosts who eat impure things, and those with flaming mouths, *asuras*, *yakṣas*, and so forth.

All of these arise from engaging in the ten courses of bad karmic action.

It is because of the presence of relatively superior, middling, or inferior causes and conditions that all of the world's good destinies are produced. Whether it be the deva realm or the human realm, they all arise from the practice of the ten courses of good karmic action. They are all included within the three realms of existence wherein there are the twenty-eight deva realms and, in the case of the human realm, these are all those peoples that inhabit the four continents.

9. Resolving to Abide in the 10 Good Actions & Teach This to Others

Having come to definitely know such matters, [this bodhisattva] reflects, "I wish that I myself will be born within these good stations of rebirth and wish also that I may be able to influence other beings to be reborn in these good stations of rebirth."

Therefore I should abide
within the ten courses of good karmic action
while also influencing other beings
to immediately abide within these courses of good karmic action.

Whether one is reborn in the good stations of rebirth or is instead born into bad stations of rebirth, this is all due to the ten courses of good karmic action or ten courses of bad karmic action. [Hence one reflects]:

> I realize that this world exists on the basis of all of the karmic causes and conditions and that there is no fixed subjective agent [involved in its creation].[479] Therefore, I should first ensure that I myself have become established in the practice of the ten courses of good karmic action and then, afterward, I should influence other beings to also abide in the practice of the ten courses of good karmic action.

Question: Why is it that one must first see that he himself abides within the ten courses of good karmic action and only later influences others to abide therein as well?

Response:

It is not easy for one who engages in bad deeds
to influence others toward goodness,
for, if one does not practice goodness oneself,
others will not believe and accept [one's teaching].

If someone who is a bad person does not practice goodness himself even as he wishes to influence others to practice goodness, this will be a very difficult to accomplish. Why? If this person does not practice goodness himself, other people will not believe in or accept his instruction. This is as described in a verse:

If one is not good oneself,
one will be unable to influence others toward goodness.

If one has not reached quiescence oneself,
one will be unable to influence others to reach quiescence.

It is for this reason that you should
first practice goodness and quiescence yourself
and then afterward instruct other people
to influence them to practice goodness and reach quiescence.

It is in this way that this bodhisattva should practice good dharmas.

10. One Should Learn the Rebirth Results of the 10 Good & Bad Actions

From the Avīci Hells
on up to the summit of existence,
one distinguishes the effects of ten courses of karmic action
as well as the places in which one undergoes their retribution.

In just this manner, one should rightly realize that, from down below in the Avīci Hells all the way on up to the station of neither perception nor non-perception, all of these are but places wherein one undergoes the resulting retribution from all of the many different sorts of good and bad karmic deeds. Among these [stations of rebirth]:

It is by habitually practicing the worst of the ten courses of bad karmic action that one is reborn in the Avīci Hells;
When the extent of evil karma is somewhat less, one is reborn instead in the Great Broiling Hell;
When somewhat less than that, one is reborn in the Lesser Broiling Hell;
When somewhat less again, one is reborn in the Great Screaming Hell;
When even less, one is reborn in the Lesser Screaming Hell;
When yet less than that, one is reborn in the Saṃgata Hell;
When less again, rebirth is in the Great Road Hell;
A yet lesser level brings birth in the Black Line Hell;
When lesser yet, one is reborn in the Living Hell;
Yet another increment less brings rebirth in the Sword Forest Hell or other lesser subsidiary hells for which one should also make ever finer distinctions [in these subcategories of hell-realm retributions].

It is through practicing an intermediate level of the ten courses of bad karmic action that one is reborn into the animal realm. One should also make ever finer distinctions regarding [the levels of karmic retribution as manifested within] the animal realm.

It is through practicing a relatively lesser level of the ten courses of bad karmic action that one is reborn into the realm of the hungry ghosts.

This represents only a general discussion of these matters. We should present a more expansive range of differentiating distinctions among these. There are the *asuras* and *yakṣas* born into the ghost realms, *nāga* kings reborn into the animal-realm wherein the bliss they enjoy may be identical to that experienced by the devas. All of these beings take these rebirths because of bad karma and then, having taken such rebirths, they may also enjoy the karmic fruits of their past good karmic actions.

In the case of those who have practiced only the very lowest level of the ten courses of good karmic action, they take rebirth in Jambudvīpa within poverty-stricken low-caste clans, namely among the *caṇḍālas*, or in remote regions, or as artisans, or as people of low social stature.

With a somewhat more superior level [of practice of the ten courses of good karmic action], one may be reborn into merchant-class families. When somewhat more superior, one is reborn into brahman clans. When more superior yet, one is reborn into a *kṣatriyan* clan. When more superior than that, one is reborn into a family of high governmental officials. When more superior yet, rebirth occurs into royal families.

When one's practice of the ten courses of good karmic action has been at a yet more superior level, one is reborn on the continent of Avara-godānīya. When more superior yet, rebirth is on the continent of Pūrva-videha. and when superior to that, rebirth is on the continent of Uttara-kuru.

When more superior yet, rebirth is into the abodes of the Four Heavenly Kings. At increasing levels of superiority to that, rebirth is into the Trāyastriṃśa Heaven, the Yāma Heaven, the Tuṣita Heaven, and the Nirmāṇarati Heaven. At the most superior level of practice of the ten courses of good karmic action, one is reborn in the Paranirmita Vaśavartin Heaven.

Here we should make all kinds of distinctions with regard to the minor and major differences. For instance, among humans, there are minor kings, major kings, the kings ruling over all of Jambudvīpa, and wheel-turning kings. The abode of the Four Heavenly Kings has Four Heavenly Kings. In the Trāyastriṃśa Heaven, there is Śakra, ruler of the devas. In the Yāma Heaven, there is the Suyāma Deva King. In the Tuṣita Heaven, there is the Saṃtuṣita Heaven King. In the Nirmāṇarati Heaven, there is the Skillful Transformations Heaven King. In the Paranirmita Vaśavartin Heaven, there is the Paranirmita Vaśavartin Heaven King. Beyond this, one must utilize volition associated with cultivation of the *dhyāna* absorptions to gain rebirth into the higher [celestial] realms.

Question: If in fact it is essential to utilize volition associated with the *dhyāna* absorptions, why was it just stated that, in every case, it is because of the ten courses of good karmic action that one gains every place of rebirth all the way up to the station of neither perception nor non-perception?

Response: Although one must cultivate the *dhyāna* absorptions to gain rebirth in the stations of either the form or formless realm, one must still first become solidly established in the practice of the ten courses of good karmic action. Only after this can one succeed in the cultivation of the *dhyāna* absorptions. It is for this reason that [acquisition of] those stations relies upon the great benefit provided by the ten courses of good karmic action. It is for this reason as well that it was stated here that, in every case, it is because of the ten courses of good karmic action that one attains every station of rebirth all the way up to the station of neither perception nor non-perception.

How is this so? After having first cultivated purity in the ten courses of good karmic action, by separating from sensual desire and cultivating the first *dhyāna* with relatively inferior volition, one may succeed in taking rebirth in the Brahma-kāyika Heaven. By cultivating the first *dhyāna* with relatively middling volition, one may take rebirth in the Brahma-purohita Heaven. And by cultivating the first *dhyāna* with relatively superior volition, one may succeed in taking rebirth in the Mahābrahma Heaven.

By cultivating the second *dhyāna* with relatively inferior volition, one may take rebirth in the Lesser Light Heaven. By cultivating the second *dhyāna* with relatively middling volition, one may succeed in taking rebirth in the Limitless Light Heaven. And by cultivating the second *dhyāna* with relatively superior volition, one may succeed in taking rebirth in the Sublime Light Heaven.

By cultivating the third *dhyāna* with relatively inferior volition, one may succeed in taking rebirth in the Lesser Purity Heaven. By cultivating the third *dhyāna* with relatively middling volition, one may succeed in taking rebirth in the Limitless Light Heaven. And by cultivating the third *dhyāna* with relatively superior volition, one may succeed in taking rebirth in the Universal Purity Heaven.

By cultivating the fourth *dhyāna* with relatively inferior volition, one may take rebirth in the Anabhraka Heaven. By cultivating the fourth *dhyāna* with relatively middling volition, one may take rebirth in the Puṇya-prasava Heaven. And by cultivating the fourth *dhyāna* with relatively superior volition, one may take rebirth in the Bṛhatphala Heaven.

By cultivating the non-perception absorption with relatively middling volition, one may succeed in taking rebirth in the Non-perception Heaven.

By repeated cultivation of contaminant-free concentration in the fourth *dhyāna* with relatively inferior volition, one may take rebirth in the "Non-Extensive"[480] or Avṛha Heaven. By repeated cultivation of contaminant-free concentration in the fourth *dhyāna* with [more] superior volition, one may take rebirth in the "Non-Hot" or Atapās Heaven. By repeated cultivation of contaminant-free concentration in the fourth *dhyāna* with [yet more] superior volition, one may take rebirth in the "Delightful Vision" or Sudarśana Heaven. By repeated cultivation of contaminant-free concentration in the fourth *dhyāna* with [even more] superior volition, one may take rebirth in the "Sublime Vision" or Sudṛśa Heaven. By repeated cultivation of contaminant-free concentration in the fourth *dhyāna* with the most superior volition, one may take rebirth in the Akaniṣṭha Heaven.

By cultivating the concentration associated with the station of infinite space with the corresponding volition, one may take rebirth in the Infinite Space Heaven. By cultivating the concentration associated with the station of infinite consciousness with the corresponding volition, one may take rebirth in the Infinite Consciousness Heaven. By cultivating the concentration associated with the station of nothing whatsoever with the corresponding volition, one may take rebirth in the Station of Nothing Whatsoever Heaven. By cultivating the concentration associated with the station of neither perception nor non-perception with the corresponding volition, one may take rebirth in the Neither Perception Nor Non-Perception Heaven.

The above discussion shows the stations to which beings go and from which they come as they undergo birth and death in the world, [as determined by their differing levels of cultivation of either the ten courses of bad karmic action or the ten courses of good karmic action].

The End of Chapter Twenty-Eight

Chapter 29
Distinctions Pertaining to Śrāvakas & Pratyekabuddhas

XXIX. Chapter 29: Distinctions Pertaining to the Two Vehicles

A. The Effectiveness of All 3 Vehicles Depends on the 10 Good Courses

Question: Do these ten courses of good karmic action function solely as causes and conditions for rebirths among humans and devas or do they also confer other additional benefits?

Response: They do have [additional benefits, as below]:

All of those cultivating the Śrāvaka Disciple Vehicle,
the Pratyekabuddha Vehicle, or the Great Vehicle,
in every instance rely upon the ten courses of good karmic action
to provide immense benefit for them.

Generally speaking, there are only three vehicles that serve as means for escaping *saṃsāra*'s cycle of births and deaths: the Śrāvaka Disciple Vehicle, the Pratyekabuddha Vehicle, and the Great Vehicle. These three vehicles all rely upon the ten courses of good karmic action to provide immense benefit for them. And how is this the case? These ten courses of good karmic action enable the practitioner to reach the grounds of the *śrāvaka* disciples, also enable him to reach the ground of the *pratyekabuddhas*, and also enable him to reach the ground of the Buddhas.

1. Q: Which Beings Can Use the 10 Courses to Fulfill the Śrāvaka Path?

Question: Which kinds of beings do these ten courses of good karmic action enable to reach the grounds of *śrāvaka* disciples?

Response:

Those reliant on others' teachings, who have no great compassion,
who are frightened by existence within the three realms,
who delight in but a minor measure of meritorious qualities,
and whose resolve is too inferior and weak—

Those whose minds delight in renunciation,
who always contemplate the impermanence of the world,
and who also know that all dharmas
have no self—

Those who do not for even a single mind-moment
wish to take on any rebirths,
and who always disbelieve that the world
is possessed of a stable and secure nature—[481]

Those who contemplate the great elements as like venomous snakes,
the aggregates as like knife-wielding thieves,
and the six sense bases as like a mere empty village,
and who do not delight in worldly wealth or pleasure—

Those who esteem solid observance of the moral precepts
and, for the sake of gaining the *dhyāna* absorptions,
always delight in sitting in *dhyāna* meditation
and in cultivating good dharmas—

Those who look only to nirvāṇa
to serve as the foremost rescuer and protector,
who always seek the wisdom that puts an end to suffering,
and who delight in accumulating the practices leading to liberation—

And those who only esteem the accomplishment of self-benefit
as they come forth through one or another of the supreme bases.
The courses of good karmic action cause these people
to have the ability to reach the grounds of Śrāvaka Disciples.

a. Stanza #1 Commentary

As for these [*śrāvaka* disciples] who accord with what is taught them by others,[482] they listen to what is taught them by others and practice in accordance with that, but are not otherwise able to develop wisdom of their own.

Question: Are the ten courses of good karmic action able in every case to cause all who hear the teachings from others to become *śrāvaka* disciples?

Response: No, that is not the way it is. For those who do not have the great compassion, the ten courses of good karmic action are indeed able to cause them to reach the grounds of the *śrāvaka* disciples. However, in the case of the bodhisattvas who have heard the Dharma from the Buddhas, because they are possessed of the great compassion, the ten courses of good karmic action cannot influence them to enter onto the grounds of the *śrāvaka* disciples.

Question: Is it the case then that whosoever does not possess the great compassion can be caused by the ten courses of good karmic action to reach the grounds of the *śrāvaka* disciples?

Response: No. It is not that way. For those who are frightened at the prospect of continued existence within the three realms, the ten courses of good karmic action are indeed able to cause them to reach the grounds of the *śrāvaka* disciples. For all of those others who are not fearful of existence in the three realms, the ten courses of good karmic action are able to cause them to gain rebirth in good stations of existence among humans and devas. This is because they delight in [continued existences within] the three realms.

Question: The ten courses of good karmic action are able to cause all who are frightened at the prospect of continued existences within the three realms to reach the grounds of the *śrāvaka* disciples. That being the case, bodhisattvas too are fearful of continued existence in the three realms. It is just that, in their diligent and vigorous striving for nirvana, they do so for the sake of both themselves and other beings. Therefore it must be that the ten courses of good karmic action are also able to cause even the bodhisattvas to reach the grounds of the Śrāvaka Disciples.

Response: It is not necessarily the case that everyone who is fearful of continued existence in the three realms is bound to fall down onto the grounds of the Śrāvaka Disciples. Who then is bound to fall? Those who delight in cultivation of but a minor measure of [the requisite] meritorious qualities and who take on but a minor measure of the six *pāramitās* as it was taught them by the Buddhas—it is people of this sort who are bound to fall down onto the grounds of the *śrāvaka* disciples.

In the case of a person who is able to acquire the meritorious qualities of the Buddhas and who is able as well to thoroughly train in their wisdom, the ten courses of good karmic action will definitely propel them directly to the realization of buddhahood.

Among those who rely upon what they have been taught by others, who are fearful of continued existence in the three realms, and who acquire only a minor measure of the meritorious qualities—these people are of two different types. There are those for whom the ten courses of good karmic action are able to cause them to reach the grounds of the *śrāvaka* disciples and there are those who are thereby caused to reach the ground of the *pratyekabuddhas*.

Question: Among these [two types of persons] who rely upon what they have been taught by others, who are fearful of continued existence in the three realms, and who acquire only a minor measure of the meritorious qualities, how is it that the ten courses of good karmic action cause some of them to reach the grounds of the *śrāvaka* disciples whereas others are instead caused to reach the grounds of the *pratyekabuddhas*?

Response: Those of [relatively] inferior and weak resolve end up becoming arhats whereas those whose resolve is somewhat more solid become *pratyekabuddhas*.

b. Stanza #2 Commentary

Question: Is it the case then that the ten courses of good karmic action cause all such people whose resolve is inferior and weak to reach the grounds of the *śrāvaka* disciples?

Response: No, that is not the way it is. Why? This refers to those whose resolve is relatively weak, but who still do delight in renouncing *saṃsāra*. It is not the case that this refers to those whose resolve is weak but who do not delight in renunciation [of *saṃsāra*], either.

Question: Through contemplation of which matters can one know whether one's mind delights in renunciation?

Response: If one contemplates conditioned dharmas as impermanent and contemplates all dharmas as having no self, one should then realize that he definitely delights in renunciation.

c. Stanza #3 Commentary

Question: Now that we know the bases for delighting in renunciation, since the bodhisattva also contemplates in the same way conditioned dharmas as impermanent and all dharmas as having no self, why do the ten courses of good karmic action not cause this person to fall down onto the grounds of the *śrāvaka* disciples?

Response: Because these people [who are drawn to the Śrāvaka Disciple and Pratyekabuddha Vehicles] have brought forth deep renunciation and have distanced themselves from the great compassion, they do not wish for even a single mind-moment to take on any further rebirths and they do not believe that the world is characterized by stability or security. As the Buddha told the bhikshus in a sutra:

> Just as even a small amount of excrement is smelly, defiled, and unclean, how much the more so a lot of it, so too, even a single mind-moment of rebirth existence is suffering, how much the more so a lot of it. Bhikshus, you should train in the severance of rebirths. Do not allow yourselves to undergo any more of them.[483]

Because *śrāvaka* disciples believe and accept these instructions, they do not wish for even a single mind-moment to undergo any further rebirths. These individuals additionally think thus:

> The world is impermanent. Whether it be the endeavors one pursues or the life span one experiences, these are all characterized by instability and insecurity. Given that death is always pursuing people, who can know the time of their own death? At the time of one's death, one cannot know what kind of karmic retribution one will undergo or what sort of thoughts will arise.[484] Because all such matters are unstable and insecure and because they cannot be trusted, one should urgently strive to put an end to suffering.

The bodhisattva, on the other hand, does not act in this manner, but rather commits himself to undergoing rebirths as numerous as the sands of the Ganges across the course of countless *asaṃkhyeya* kalpas for the sake of attaining *anuttarasamyaksaṃbodhi* and liberating beings.

Thus the verse says [of *śrāvaka* disciples] that they "do not for even a single mind-moment delight in taking on any rebirths." The [ten] courses of good karmic action enable these individuals to reach the grounds of the *śrāvaka* disciples.

d. Stanza #4 Commentary

Question: What sorts of endeavors do these people delight in cultivating and accumulating that they therefore so dislike undergoing further rebirth?

Response: Because, in contemplating the four great elements of earth, water, fire, and air, these people are fond of regarding them with animosity, and because they regard them as forming what is unlovely, foul-smelling, defiled, and ungrateful for kindnesses,[485] they therefore see them as analogous to poisonous snakes.

Because the five aggregates of form, feeling, perception, formative factors, and consciousness are able to rob one of one's wisdom life, they contemplate them as analogous to hostile bandits.

Because the sense bases of eye, ear, nose, tongue, body, and mind are destitute of permanence, unshakability, immutability, and indestructibility, and because they are devoid of self and are devoid of anything belonging to a self, they perceive them as like an empty village.

[They realize that], even if one were to have the advantage of every sort of natural endowment and life-enhancing provision for enjoyment, because those things are impermanent, false, deceptive, and do not abide for even a moment, they are not moved to delight in this. Hence people of this sort think of all stations of rebirth as devoid of any stability or security and they look only to the single dharma of nirvāṇa as their rescuer and protector. This is as described in a sutra:

> Bhikshus, the world is entirely ablaze, that is to say: The eye is ablaze, visual forms are ablaze, eye consciousness is ablaze, eye contact is ablaze, and whatever feeling is produced with eye contact as the causal condition—that too is ablaze.
>
> And with what is it ablaze? It is ablaze with the fire of desire, the fire of hatred, the fire of delusion, the fire of birth, aging, sickness, death, grief, lamentation, anguish, and torment. So too is this the case with the ear, nose, tongue, body, and mind faculty.[486]

e. Stanza #5–6 Commentary

They contemplate all conditioned dharmas as ablaze and regard only nirvāṇa's dharma of quiescent cessation as able to provide a source of rescue. Because they so esteem this single dharma of nirvāṇa, they abandon all other endeavors in favor of diligent practice of sitting in *dhyāna* meditation.

Question: If one contemplates all conditioned dharmas as ablaze and the quiescent cessation of nirvāṇa as the only source of rescue and protection, is it the case then that the ten courses of good karmic action are able in every case to cause these people to reach the grounds of the *śrāvaka* disciples?

Response: No, that is not so. Consider the moral precepts formulated by the Buddha. It is for the sake of attaining the *dhyāna* absorptions that these moral precepts are esteemed as so important. [Hence we refer here instead to] those with resolute aspiration who refrain from transgressing against the precepts, who abandon all other endeavors, who delight solely in sitting in *dhyāna* meditation, who seek the wisdom that extinguishes suffering, and who always diligently cultivate the causes and conditions for liberation. It is people of this sort who have come forth from cultivating one or two of the supreme bases [of meritorious qualities] in previous lives that the ten courses of good karmic action thus enable to reach the grounds of the *śrāvaka* disciples.

And how does this come about? If one upholds the moral precepts purely, one's mind becomes free of any regrets. Because one's mind is free of regrets, one becomes suffused with joyfulness. Having gained this state of joyfulness, one's body experiences a state of pliancy. Because one's body experiences this state of pliancy, one's mind becomes blissful. Because one's mind becomes blissful, one focuses the mind and gains meditative absorption. Because one focuses the mind and gains meditative absorption, one develops wisdom that accords with reality. Because one develops wisdom that accords with reality, one immediately develops disenchantment. From disenchantment, one develops detachment, and from detachment, one attains liberation.[487]

f. Stanza #7 Commentary

As for "coming forth from one or perhaps two of the supreme bases [of meritorious qualities]," this is exemplified by the Venerable Rāhula who came forth from the supreme basis of truthfulness, by the Venerable Sivali[488] who came forth from the supreme basis of relinquishment, by the Venerable Revata who came forth from the supreme basis of quiescence, and as exemplified by the Venerable Śāriputra who came forth from the supreme basis of wisdom.

Then again, it may perhaps be that one comes forth from the two supreme bases consisting of truthfulness and relinquishment, that one comes forth from the two supreme bases consisting of truthfulness and quiescence, that one comes forth from the two supreme bases consisting of truthfulness and wisdom, that one comes forth from the two supreme bases consisting of relinquishment and quiescence, that one comes forth from the two supreme bases consisting of relinquishment and wisdom, or that one comes forth from the two supreme bases consisting of quiescence and wisdom.

It is in this way that the ten courses of good karmic action may enable one to reach the grounds of the *śrāvaka* disciples.

2. Q: Who Can Use the Ten Courses to Become a Pratyekabuddha?

Question: What sorts of people do the ten courses of good karmic action cause to enter the grounds of the *pratyekabuddhas*?

Response:

In the ten courses of good karmic action
practiced by *śrāvaka* disciples, they are even more superior.
They cultivate deep *dhyāna,* don't rely on others' teaching,
and are always fond of abiding in seclusion, far from others.

They always delight in the thorough cultivation
of the extremely deep dharma of causes and conditions.
They remain detached from the power of skillful means
as well as from the mind of great compassion.

They pursue lesser aspirations and lesser endeavors.
They abhor and disdain boisterous chatter,
always enjoy abiding in secluded places,
and are possessed of awe-inspiring virtue and deep solemnity.

They delight in serving as fields of merit
and always contemplate what by nature promotes transcendence.
They accomplish those endeavors that are principled
and accord reverence to the Lords [of the Dharma].

Having already perfected anchoring of the mind,
the knowing mind focuses on whatever is taken as the object.
They always delight in *dhyāna* concentration
and in this possess the power of men of intermediate capacities.

They delight in the dharmas of the monastic
and in them the mind of goodness does not shrink or sink away.
Those who gain the light of wisdom
may come forth from two of the supreme bases.

Or perhaps they come forth from three of the supreme bases.
The ten courses of good karmic action
enable persons of this sort
to reach the ground of the Pratyekabuddhas.

a. Stanza#1 Commentary

As for "In the ten courses of good karmic action practiced by *śrāvaka* disciples, they are even more superior," they surpass that level of accomplishment in the ten courses of good karmic action reached by the *śrāvaka* disciples, but still do not approach the level of accomplishment in such dharmas as practiced by the bodhisattvas.

They reflect in this manner:

> The *śrāvaka* disciple practitioners respond to and accord with what they are taught by others in their practice of the path, after which they attain personal realizations of wisdom. As for myself, I am not thus inclined, for I do not delight in following others. Therefore I should cause the practice of the ten courses of good karmic action to become even more superior. For this reason I shall delight in the ten courses of good karmic action without relying on others and this shall enable me to reach the ground of the *pratyekabuddhas*.

Having reflected in this manner, they always delight in seclusion, thinking thus:

> If I forever delight in the boisterousness [of the common crowd], then that is bound to lead to the accumulation of all manner of evil and unwholesome dharmas due to close proximity to circumstances that can cause defilement, can cause hatred, and can cause delusion. In this seclusion, I should cultivate the extremely deep dharma of causes and conditions.

b. Stanza#2 Commentary

They additionally reflect in this way:

> If I do not cultivate the extremely deep dharma of causes and conditions, then I will be unable to gain that wisdom that is not reliant on the teachings of others. Why should I not now always cultivate the extremely deep dharma of causes and conditions so that I can later gain the wisdom that is not reliant on the teachings of others?

"Extremely deep" refers in this context to that which is difficult to fathom and that with regard to which one cannot reach an utterly penetrating comprehension. One can completely fathom all of the scriptures, texts, skills, and arts possessed by all common people across the beginningless course of *saṃsāra*. It is only the extremely deep dharma of causes and conditions that one cannot completely fathom. [The difficulty of fathoming it] is comparable to a rabbit's or other small creature's inability to fathom the very bottom of a great ocean.

If one possesses skillful means and the mind of great compassion while also increasingly cultivating the extremely deep dharma of causes and conditions, then he can proceed directly toward the attainment of *anuttarasamyaksaṃbodhi*. However, if one abandons these two requisites while increasingly cultivating the extremely deep knowledge of causes and conditions, then he will instead become a *pratyekabuddha*.

"Skillful means" refers here to perfecting in a manner free of error all the different sorts of thought used in teaching beings while also not seizing on merely superficial aspects of extremely profound dharmas.

"Great compassion" refers here to abiding in a deep and kindly sympathy for beings, one that is superior even to that of *śrāvaka* disciples and *pratyekabuddha*s, how much the more so common people.

c. Stanza #3 Commentary

As for "pursuing lesser aspirations and lesser endeavors," and "abhorring and disdaining boisterous chatter," those possessed of these qualities can reach the ground of the *pratyekabuddha*s.

If one is inclined toward great aspirations and great endeavors, if one enjoys gatherings of many people, and if one is protected by skillful means and great compassion, then it will become easy to reach *anuttarasamyaksaṃbodhi*.

Why is this so? One who pursues *pratyekabuddhahood*, possessed as he is of lesser aspirations, thinks: "One need only see to one's own liberation."

As for his "pursuing lesser endeavors," this practitioner devotes himself solely to the perfection of his own roots of goodness and does not extend his concern to other people. Because this person abandons the endeavor of teaching beings, he does not draw near to any of the many sorts of commotion.

The bodhisattva, being inclined toward great aspirations and great endeavors, thinks: "I should liberate all beings." It is because of this great aspiration that he then takes on the great endeavor of teaching beings. This teaching of beings is no minor endeavor. If one abhors boisterousness and talkativeness, then he will not succeed in this work. Therefore the bodhisattva enters into the midst of such commotion and resorts to discourse appropriate to such commotion, but he still has nothing to which he is attached.

Moreover, it is because [the *pratyekabuddha* practitioners] reject the cultivation of genuine meritorious qualities that they are said to have "lesser aspirations." It is because they take on but few responsibilities that these are referred to as "lesser endeavors." It is because of their abhorrence and disdain for commotion that they are said to have "lesser aspirations." And it is because they delight in residing in solitude that they are said to engage in "lesser endeavors."

As for persons such as these who have lesser aspirations, engage in lesser endeavors, do not delight in the commotion and chatter of the multitudes, and who delight in proximity to far away, fearsome, and very remote places, their determination is extremely great. These individuals reflect thus:

> If I dwell in a faraway, fearsome, and very remote place, then nobody will come there, and thus, by virtue of that abiding at a great distance, the mind itself will also be able to abide at an especially great distance. If one does not dwell extremely far from those who delight in frivolousness, then outsiders will not find it difficult to come and go there.

d. Stanza #4 Commentary

People of this sort do not live together with other beings. Although they have abandoned beings, they still wish to influence beings to plant roots of goodness and do wish to be of great benefit to them. Hence they reflect in this manner: "How might I not live together with other beings and yet still benefit beings?" Having pondered in this manner, they realize: "I should benefit beings by serving as a field of merit for them, doing so by accepting offerings from them. Thus, even though I do not live together with other beings, I shall still be able to be of great benefit to them."

Continuing in this vein, this person reflects: "How then might I become a field of karmic merit for others?" He then immediately sees and realizes the following, thinking:

> If I deeply delight in serving as a field of merit and in always contemplating whatever naturally leads to transcendence, then, later on, the means for serving as a field of merit will spontaneously come forth and whatever dharmas naturally lead to transcendence will spontaneously come forth as well.

These [dharmas that naturally lead to transcendence] are what we refer to as the observance of moral precepts, cultivation of *dhyāna* absorptions, development of wisdom, and so forth.

He also has this thought:

> How might I be able to swiftly reach that ground in which I may become a field of merit and acquire the dharmas leading to

transcendence? I should become one who is grounded in right contemplation, should accomplish all endeavors that are manifestly principled and of meaningful significance, and should make offerings to and demonstrate reverence for the Lords [of the Dharma]. If I proceed in this manner, then before too long I shall swiftly acquire that ground on which I can serve as a field of merit and shall also acquire the dharmas that naturally lead to transcendence.

Why should I proceed in this manner? I should accomplish those endeavors that are principled and should rightly contemplate dharmas for this shall enable me to realize the wisdom that is not reliant on the teachings of others.

Furthermore, it is because of making offerings to and revering the Lords [of the Dharma] that one's roots of goodness are able to increase and grow ever more fully developed. Due to such growth in one's roots of goodness, wisdom too shall then become extremely deep and full in its development.

It is because of wisdom's becoming extremely deep and full in its development that one is then able to gain an utterly penetrating comprehension of the true character of all phenomena. When one is able to gain an utterly penetrating comprehension of the true character of all phenomena, one can then generate disenchantment. It is from this disenchantment that one is then able to generate detachment. It is through this detachment that one gains liberation. And it is because of gaining liberation that the roots of goodness one has accumulated in the past and later on finally enable one to serve as a field of merit. Afterward, one then attains the realization of the dharmas naturally leading to transcendence.

As for "the Lords," this is a specific reference to the Buddhas, the Bhagavats. During the time that one is planting roots of goodness, this matter [of reverence for the Buddhas] is the very greatest of all causes and conditions in that endeavor.

e. Stanza #5 Commentary

This practitioner continues pondering these matters, thinking, "Now, how exactly will I be able to swiftly succeed in those endeavors that are principled and of meaningful significance?"

This person then immediately understands and sees: "If I anchor the mind in a single place, directly know what it takes as its object, and always delight in the cultivation of the *dhyāna* absorptions, [my aims may be accomplished in this way]."

If this practitioner is able to anchor his mind in a single place, he is then able to gain samādhi. Due to acquiring samādhi, all principled endeavors can then be accomplished. This is as described in the sutras:

"By gaining *dhyāna* concentration, one becomes able to know in accordance with reality and see in accordance with reality."

If one has already practiced anchoring of the mind, then he will swiftly enter samādhi. It is through this ability to swiftly enter samādhi that one becomes an adept in the *dhyāna* absorptions, one who always abides in meditative absorption.

If one becomes able in this manner to cultivate these dharmas, then this itself constitutes offerings and reverence to the Buddhas. If someone were to make offerings of incense, flowers, and the four requisites to the Buddhas, this would not truly qualify as making offerings to the Buddhas. Rather, if one can single-mindedly draw near to and cultivate the path of the Āryas, doing so without falling into neglectfulness, this would truly constitute offerings and reverence to the Buddhas. As stated in the sutras, at the time of his *parinirvāṇa*, the Buddha told Ānanda:

> The raining down of *māndārava* flowers and powdered *candana* incense accompanied by the music of the devas—this does not truly qualify as offerings and reverence to the Tathāgata. Ānanda, if a bhikshu, bhikshuni, *upāsaka*, or *upāsikā* were to single-mindedly and without neglectfulness draw near to and cultivate the dharmas of the Āryas, it is this that would truly constitute the making of offerings to the Buddha. Therefore, Ānanda, you should cultivate and train in this true offering to the Buddha.

Many meritorious qualities such as these characterize the practitioner of intermediate strength who delights in leaving the household life and who does not allow his devotion to goodness to retreat or fall away.

Those of the most superior strength are able to succeed in attaining buddhahood whereas those possessed of a lesser degree of strength become *śrāvaka* disciples. Hence it is those of intermediate strength who become *pratyekabuddhas*.

f. Stanza #6–7 Commentary

Because they delight in leaving behind the household life they are able to perfect a multitude of meritorious qualities. And why is this so? If one continues to abide within the household, one is unable to have but few desires and take on but few endeavors. One is unable to remain physically and mentally detached nor can one acquire the *dhyāna* absorptions.

If one's resolve retreats and sinks into impurity, one will be unable to successfully accomplish many endeavors, one will be unable to understand the extremely deep dharma of causes and conditions, one will be unable to achieve the realization of the nature of transcendence, and one will be unable to truly make offerings to and revere the Buddhas in a manner that accords with the Dharma.

Beings such as these possess an intermediate level of strength. They think, "I am a person of intermediate strength. If I always delight in leaving the household life and maintain a resolve that does not retreat or fall away, all the meritorious circumstances that I wish for will naturally come forth for me."

He also reflects, "Being one of middling capacities, which of the fruits of the path should I delight in acquiring?" He immediately realizes that he should acquire the fruit of wisdom. And why? Because wisdom can bring about brilliant illumination. This is as stated in the sutras where it says: "Bhikshus, of all the different sorts of illumination, the light of wisdom is supreme."[489]

He then also thinks: "How should I go about acquiring this light of wisdom in which I delight?" He then realizes that it will come forth through perfection of either two or three of the supreme bases [of meritorious qualities]. As for the twofold acquisitions of the supreme bases, those combinations were already discussed above.

As for threefold acquisitions of the supreme bases, those may consist of truth, relinquishment, and quiescence, may consist of truth, relinquishment, and wisdom, or may consist of truth, quiescence, and wisdom. [He thinks,] "Therefore I should cultivate and accumulate these supreme bases. Once I have cultivated and accumulated these [supreme bases], I shall gain the light of wisdom and thus that wisdom that I have vowed to gain will naturally arrive here for me."

When someone possessed of such characteristics as these cultivates and accumulates these path-assisting dharmas in this way, the ten courses of good karmic action will enable him to reach the ground of the *pratyekabuddha.*

The End of Chapter Twenty-Nine

Chapter 30
[Distinctions Pertaining to] the Great Vehicle

XXX. Chapter 30: [Distinctions Pertaining to] the Great Vehicle

A. Q: Which Beings Can Use the Ten Courses to Become Buddhas?

Question: As you have already explained, the ten courses of good karmic action enable one to reach the grounds of the *śrāvaka* disciples and *pratyekabuddhas*. Which sorts of beings can the ten courses of good karmic action also cause to reach the ground of buddhahood?

B. A: The Ten Courses Enable Buddhahood for Beings of This Sort (Verse)

Response:

The way they practice the ten courses of good karmic action
is superior to that of the two other classes of practitioners,
for they engage in measureless extraordinary cultivation
superior to that of anyone else in the world.

They bring forth vows that are both solid and good,[490]
perfect the great compassion that cannot be impeded,
thoroughly take on the practice of skillful means,
and patiently endure every sort of pain and anguish.

They do not abandon any being,
deeply cherish the wisdom of the Buddhas,
and delight in those who completely and thoroughly practice
the Buddhas' powers and sovereign masteries.

They are able to refute all ideas involving wrong views
and accept and protect the Buddhas' right Dharma.
They are valiant, able to endure, and vigorous,
and are possessed of solid resolve in teaching beings.

They do not covet or become attached to their own happiness
or to living a measurelessly long life.
They are supreme in all their endeavors
and free of fault in all the works they do.

They possess every kind of purity
and come forth through the practice of all the supreme bases.
The courses of good karmic action enable these persons
to reach the ground of the Bhagavats who possess the ten powers.

C. An Extensive Line-by-Line Explanation of the Verse's Deep Meaning

1. "Superiority of the Bodhisattva's Cultivation of the Ten Courses"

As for "the way they practice the ten courses of good karmic action is superior to that of the two other classes of practitioners,"[491] this refers to the fact that the bodhisattvas have become superior to the *śrāvaka* disciple and *pratyekabuddha* aspirants in the quality of their cultivation of the ten courses of good karmic action. "Becoming superior," [in their cultivation of the ten courses of good karmic action] means that the bodhisattvas cultivate them with single-minded focus, that they always cultivate them, that they cultivate them to benefit themselves, that they cultivate them to benefit others, and that they cultivate them purely.

"Cultivating them with single-minded focus" means that they employ full mental intention in their cultivation.

"Always cultivate them" means that they never rest in their cultivation of them.

"Cultivating them to benefit themselves" means that they do this to establish the causes and conditions for birth among humans and devas and to establish the causes and conditions for the attainment of nirvāṇa.

"Cultivating them to benefit others" means that, as the bodhisattvas cultivate the ten courses of good karmic action, they dedicate the merit to the benefit and peace of all beings. It is for this reason that they can liberate an incalculable number of beings.

"Cultivating them purely" means theirs is undamaged practice, unmixed practice, unsullied practice, practice in which one has sovereign mastery, perfectly complete practice, practice free of covetousness and attachment, and practice that is praised by the wise.

"Damaged" practice refers here to that in which some aspects of the practice are cultivated whereas others are left aside and not practiced. Practice that is opposite to this is "undamaged" practice.

"Mixed" practice refers here to that wherein one encourages others to practice what one does not practice oneself. Practice that is opposite to this is "unmixed" practice.

"Sullied" practice is practice that occurs in conjunction with afflictions and karmic offenses. Practice that is opposite to this is "unsullied" practice.

As for "sovereign mastery," because they are tied down by agricultural work, wives, children, or material possessions, those who are prone to breaking the precepts are unable to achieve a state of sovereign mastery [in their practice]. Having no such [encumbering] circumstances, those who uphold the precepts may freely achieve a state of sovereign mastery in which they are not tied down by anything at all.

"Perfectly complete" practice refers to exhaustively complete observance of all the major and minor moral precepts that blocks off the afflictions, that involves constant mindfulness of the need to preserve them and guard against transgression, that serves as a cause and condition for the *dhyāna* absorptions, that is dedicated to realization of buddhahood, and that enables one to unite with ultimate reality and the nature of dharmas. This is what is meant by "perfectly complete" in this context.

Practice "free of covetousness and attachment" does not direct its focus toward worldly priorities, does not seize on merely superficial aspects of the moral precepts, and remains free of any tendency to elevate oneself and disparage others.

As for practice "praised by the wise," in the Dharma of *śrāvaka* disciples, it is because it does not follow the cycle of births and deaths and is implemented solely for the sake of nirvāṇa that it is referred to as "praised by the wise."

In this Dharma of the Great Vehicle, its practitioners do not even dedicate their practice to success in the Śrāvaka Disciple Vehicle or the Pratyekabuddha Vehicle, how much the less could their practice be dedicated to *saṃsāra*? Rather, it is dedicated solely to the realization of *anuttarasamyaksaṃbodhi*. This is what is meant by practice of the ten courses of good karmic action that is "praised by the wise."

Question: What are the marks of cultivation that qualify it as "good" cultivation?

Response: It is that which incorporates countless extraordinary qualities into cultivation of the ten courses of good karmic action in a manner superior to the cultivation practiced by anyone else in the world. This is what is meant by "good" cultivation.

a. Five Ways in Which the Bodhisattva's Practice is Superior

Question: How do the bodhisattvas, employing this sort of cultivation, cultivate in a manner "superior to anyone else in the entire world"?

Response: It is on the basis of five aspects of their cultivation that the bodhisattvas' cultivation is "superior to that of anyone else in the world":[492]

First, their vows;
Second, their solid resolve;
Third, their resolute intentions;
Fourth, their thoroughgoing purity;[493]
And fifth, their use of skillful means.

1) Superiority of Vows

As for "their vows," the vows implemented by the bodhisattvas do not even exist among all common people, *śrāvaka* disciple practitioners, or *pratyekabuddha* practitioners. It is for this reason that the vows implemented by the bodhisattvas are superior to those of anyone else in the world. This is as described in the questions of the woman Vimaladattā in the *Mahāprajñāpāramitā Sūtra* in which the Buddha, because of Maudgalyāyana, said, "From the point of his initial generation of the vow all the way on forward to his arrival at the *bodhimaṇḍa,* the bodhisattva is able to serve the entire world's devas and humans as a field of merit, doing so in a manner that is superior to all *śrāvaka* disciples or *pratyekabuddhas.*"

This is also as set forth in the *Pure Vinaya Sutra* in which Mahākāśyapa said in the Buddha's presence, "The Bhagavat has here so well described this rarity, that is to say, the bodhisattva's initial generation of the vow which is superior to that of all *śrāvaka* disciples and *pratyekabuddhas.*"

This also accords with a verse in which it is proclaimed that:

As for the bodhisattva's initial generation of his resolve
conjoined to the great kindness and great compassion
for the sake of the unsurpassable path,
it is just this very resolve that is supreme.
It is therefore the case that, because of this vow,
he abides in a position superior to those in the world.

2) Superiority of Solid Resolve

As for his "solid resolve," the bodhisattva maintains it even in the midst of every sort of pain and torment, that is to say he maintains it even in the Living Hells, Black-line Hells, Unification Hells, Lesser Screaming Hells, Great Screaming Hells, Lesser Roasting Hells, Great Roasting Hells, Avīci Hells, Boiling Excrement Hells, Sword Forest Hells, River of Coals Hells, Abhuta Hells, Nirarbuda Hells, Aṭaṭa Hells, Apalāla Hells, Huhuva Hells, Utpala Hells, Kumuda Hells, Sumanā Hells, Puṇḍarīka Hells, and the Padma Hells. He maintains it even when tortured and whipped in these various cold and hot hells.

He maintains it even in the midst of the anguish and torment in the animal realms, the hungry ghost realms, the asura realms, and the realms of humans and devas in which beings devour each other, exist in a state of mutual fearfulness, and go hungry when food has become too expensive.

And he maintains it when he falls back from and loses celestial realm rebirth and when he then encounters jealousy, the torment of hatred, separation from those one loves, association with those one detests, birth, aging, sickness, death, sorrow, lamentation, misery, and the like.

Thus he maintains his resolve even in the midst of all these sufferings in the six destinies of rebirth. Whether observing them, whether hearing them occur, or whether actually undergoing them himself, the bodhisattva still continues to cultivate the ten courses of good karmic action for the sake of realizing *anuttarasamyaksaṃbodhi.* During that entire time, his resolve continues on and never deteriorates.

It is on these bases that this bodhisattva, by cultivating the ten courses of good karmic action with solid resolve, thereby surpasses everyone else in the entire world. This is as described here:

Even when in the hells, among the animals,
the hungry ghosts, the asuras,
the devas, or the humans, the sufferings of these six destinies,
are still incapable of shaking their resolve.

Therefore the bodhisattvas,
through such solid resolve as this,
are superior to the entire world
in their cultivation of the ten courses of good karmic action.

3) Superiority of Resolute Intentions

Regarding their "resolute intentions," they also possess great intentions, useful intentions, affectionate intentions, and mindful intentions. The bodhisattvas rely on such types of intentions as these in their cultivation of the ten courses of good karmic action and, in this, they are superior to everyone in the entire world with the exception of the Buddhas, the Bhagavats, and those bodhisattvas of long-enduring practice. This is as described here:

They possess resolute intentions, useful intentions,
and intentions that strive to benefit the world,
it is through their use of these types of intentions
that the bodhisattvas surpass the entire world.

4) Superiority of Thoroughgoing Purity

As for "their thoroughgoing purity,"[494] in cultivating the courses of good karmic action, the bodhisattvas maintain the three types of karmic purity to a degree not found in such cultivation as carried on by anyone else.[495] Consequently, they are superior in this to everyone else in the entire world. This is as described here:

The bodhisattvas are treasures of the human realm
completely possessed of resolute intentions and pure intentions.
It is because of the power of these good dharmas
that they are unequaled by anyone in the world.

5) Superiority in the Use of Skillful Means

As for "their use of skillful means," the bodhisattvas use the power of skillful means to cultivate good dharmas that others do not possess. Consequently, they are superior in this to everyone else in the entire world.

2. The Bodhisattva's "Measureless Cultivation"

Regarding their "measureless" cultivation,[496] it is on the basis of five types of causes and conditions that the cultivation of the bodhisattva qualifies as "measureless," namely:

First, immeasurability of time;
Second, immeasurability of roots of goodness;
Third, immeasurability of objective conditions;
Fourth, immeasurability of ultimate ends;
And fifth, immeasurability of dedication of merit.

a. Immeasurability of Time

As for "immeasurability of time," the cultivation of the courses of good karmic action as practiced by the bodhisattvas exceeds the very bounds of time. Because it exceeds the bounds of time, their cultivation of the courses of good karmic action is itself measureless. Therefore, in this, they are superior to everyone else in the entire world. This is as described here:

> As for the cultivation of the courses of good karmic action
> as practiced by the bodhisattvas, those lions among men,
> because its duration surpasses the bounds of calculable time,
> their cultivation of goodness is the most superior of all.

b. Immeasurability of Roots of Goodness

As for "immeasurability of roots of goodness," bodhisattvas cultivate measureless and boundless roots of goodness. Because the courses of good karmic action they cultivate in reliance upon these roots of goodness are also immeasurable, the bodhisattvas are in this respect superior to everyone else in the world.

As stated in the Great Vehicle Dharma's *Pure Vinaya Sutra*: "The Buddha told Kāśyapa, 'It is as if the four great seas were filled to the brim with buttermilk. Just so extensive are the bodhisattva's conditioned roots of goodness and provisions for the path.'" Because this merit is dedicated to the knowledge that cognizes the unconditioned, it is able to provide immense benefit to all beings. Therefore, even though the bodhisattva abides in the midst of conditioned existence, he is able to surpass everyone else in the world in this respect. This is as described here:

[Accumulated] for the sake of all beings
as well as for the sake of buddhahood,
their roots of goodness are immeasurable.
Because of this, they are superior to all others in the world.

c. Immeasurability of Objective Conditions

As for the "immeasurability of objective conditions," in his accumulation of roots of goodness, the bodhisattva does not take as his objective condition a merely measurable number of beings. He does not say that the roots of goodness he has cultivated are for benefiting some particular number of beings. Rather, the bodhisattva simply takes all beings as the objective condition for his accumulation of roots of goodness. Therefore, since the bodhisattva takes a measureless number of beings as the objective condition on which he focuses, the courses of good karmic action that he cultivates are also measureless. Consequently, he is superior in this respect to everyone else in the world. As stated in the *Pure Vinaya Sutra*:

> The Buddha told the *devaputras*, "This is just as in the case of the great bodhisattva possessed of the mind of kindness and compassion who strives to benefit others. This resolve of his is able to cause countless beings to receive benefit and happiness. So too it is with the bodhisattva who is deeply earnest in bringing forth his resolve. Being like this in his diligent application of vigor, he can thereby teach measurelessly many *asaṃkhyeyas* of beings, enabling them to gain the bliss of nirvāṇa."

This is as described here:

The bodhisattva adorns himself
with measurelessly many fine meritorious qualities,
all for the purpose of liberating beings
from their measureless great suffering.

d. Immeasurability of Ultimate Ends

As for "immeasurability of ultimate ends," "the ten ultimate ends" were already discussed during the explanation of the first ground when discussing the making of [the ten bodhisattva] vows.[497] It is because of this immeasurability of ultimate ends that the courses of good karmic action as cultivated by the bodhisattva are measureless. He is therefore superior in this respect to anyone in the world. This is as described here:

The bodhisattva's cultivation of the courses of good karmic action
comes forth from the ten ultimate ends.
Therefore it is superior to that of everyone else
and such that no one is able to ruin it.

e. Immeasurability of Dedication of Merit

"Immeasurability of dedication of merit" is as described earlier in the explanation of the first ground. The karmic fruits of the bodhisattva's dedication of merit are measureless. Because the karmic fruits of dedication of merit are measureless, the courses of good karmic action he cultivates are also measureless. He is therefore superior in this respect to anyone in the world. This is as described here:

On the basis of measureless causes and conditions,
they cultivate the courses of good karmic action.
Because they dedicate this to [the realization of] the Buddha Vehicle,
they are therefore the most superior of all.

3. The Bodhisattva's "Extraordinary Cultivation"

As for the "extraordinary" nature of their cultivation,[498] it is because of five causes and conditions that the bodhisattvas' cultivation of the courses of good karmic action is said to be "extraordinary":

First, because of their capacity to endure;
Second, because of their vigor;
Third, because of the solidity of their resolve;
Fourth, because of their wisdom;
Fifth, because of the karmic fruits.

a. His Extraordinary Capacity to Endure

As for [the extraordinary nature of] their capacity to endure, [they reflect], "I ought to become one who is the most revered among all devas and humans, one who is possessed of all-knowledge." If one is able to have a capacity such as this, this is extraordinary. Were someone to use his finger to lift a great trichiliocosm's worlds and hold them aloft in space for a hundred thousand myriads of kalpas, even this might be considered possible to do and not worthy of being deemed truly difficult. Yet if one makes the vow: "I shall become a buddha," it is this that is extraordinary and extremely difficult. This is as described here:

As for he who, for the sake of a buddha's measureless dharmas,
would make the vow: "I shall become a buddha,"
this person is one who is beyond compare,
how much the less could there be anyone who might surpass him?

b. His Extraordinary Vigor

Regarding [the extraordinary nature of] their vigor, there are many people who can bring forth the resolve to attain *anuttarasamyaksaṃbodhi* but who are then unable to vigorously practice the six *pāramitās*. If someone can bring forth the resolve to attain *anuttarasamyaksaṃbodhi* and then also be able to vigorously practice the six *pāramitās*, this is what is meant by truly having the capacity to take on the attainment of the measureless meritorious qualities. It is because of the extraordinary nature of their vigor that the courses of good karmic action they cultivate are also extraordinary in nature. This is as described here:

> Their practice of great vigor is so extraordinary that,
> having merely contemplated it, the common man is frightened.
> The bodhisattva actually practices it.
> How could this not be regarded as extraordinary?

c. His Solidity of Resolve

As for [the extraordinary nature of] their solidity of resolve, there are those who bring forth vigorous resolve to cultivate the path to buddhahood. However, if upon encountering obstacles, their resolve is not solid, they will be unable to succeed. Therefore, if they bring forth vigor and become securely established in extraordinarily solid resolve, they will succeed in their endeavors and demolish all obstacles. It is this that is the most extraordinary accomplishment in bodhisattvas' cultivation of the courses of good karmic action. This is as described here:

> If one has no solidity of resolve,
> he will be unable to succeed in even minor endeavors.
> How much the less could one attain buddhahood
> and become the one unsurpassed by anyone in the world?

d. His Extraordinary Wisdom

As for [the extraordinary nature of] their wisdom, this capacity to endure, this vigor, and this solidity of resolve all take wisdom as their foundation. Therefore it is the wisdom of the bodhisattva that is the most extraordinary. Because it is able to produce this capacity to endure, this vigor, and this solidity of resolve, wisdom is itself deemed to be extraordinary. It is because this wisdom is extraordinary that the courses of good karmic action that are cultivated are also extraordinary. This is as described here:

> If someone has the capacity to endure
> in pursuing his aspiration to realize the Buddha's Dharma,
> and if he possesses vigor and has achieved solidity of resolve,
> all of these capacities take wisdom as their foundation.

e. His Extraordinary Karmic Fruits

As for [the extraordinary nature of] the karmic fruits they achieve, due to their cultivation of the courses of good karmic actions, they gain all the measureless and boundless dharmas of the Buddhas. Therefore [the karmic fruits] are extraordinary in nature. This is as described here:

> By practicing this goodness, one realizes buddhahood,
> acquires the power of its measureless meritorious qualities,
> and then serves as the teacher of all beings.
> Who, on hearing this, could fail to practice them?

4. The Bodhisattva's Vows

a. The "Solidity" of His Vows

Regarding their "solid" vows,[499] it is for five reasons that the bodhisattva is deemed to have made solid vows, namely:

First, his resolve does not turn back toward the Śrāvaka Disciple Vehicle;

Second, his resolve does not turn back toward the Pratyekabuddha Vehicle;

Third, his resolve does not turn back in favor of the endeavors of the followers of non-Buddhist paths;

Fourth, his resolve does not turn back due to any of the works of Māra;

And fifth, his resolve does not turn back due to an absence of [conducive] causes and conditions.

This is as described here:

> One might hear of the liberations won through the Two Vehicles
> and think, "Why not take up these paths instead?"
> If one has not yet entered the station [of irreversibility],[500]
> then one might fall away from the bodhisattva path.
>
> Or one might covet the endeavors of followers of non-Buddhist paths,
> or one might be destroyed by the works of Māra,
> or else, due to an absence of conducive causes and conditions,
> one might voluntarily abandon the bodhisattva path.

b. The "Goodness" of His Vows

As for the "goodness" of their vows,[501] it is for five reasons that the bodhisattva's vows are said to be "good" vows, namely:

First, they reflect a prior assessment of gains or losses;

Second, they are based on a knowledge of the path;

Third, they reflect a knowledge of the fruits of the path;

Fourth, they reflect an absence of any selfish attachment to one's own pleasure;

Fifth, they reflect the wish to extinguish the immense sufferings endured by all beings.

Vows made in this manner are deemed to be good vows. This is as described here:

One first observes the faults and misery of the world
and the immense benefit bestowed by the path to buddhahood.
One knows and practices the unsurpassable path
as well as its measureless fruits.

One relinquishes the bliss of entering one's own quiescent cessation,
and wishes to rid beings of their sufferings.
One who brings forth such peerless vows as these
is someone who is praised by all buddhas.

5. The Bodhisattva's "Great Compassion"

Regarding "the great compassion" that cannot be impeded,[502] there are five grounds for knowing a bodhisattva is possessed of the great compassion, namely:

First, because he is devoted to benefiting and conferring happiness on countless beings, he does not covet or selfishly cherish any of the life-sustaining requisites;
Second, he does not selfishly cherish his own physical well-being;
Third, he does not selfishly cherish his own life-span;
Fourth, he is not concerned with the extensively long period of time involved;
Fifth, he maintains a mind of equal regard and motivation to benefit both adversaries and friends.

This is as described here:

He has no covetous attachment for any of those things
that people cherish, whether personal or external.
In order to be of benefit to beings,
he would even sacrifice his body and life.

The countless kalpas spent amidst *saṃsāra*
are for him like the mere blinking of an eye.
He acts with uniformly equal regard for both enemy and friend.
These are the factors defining a bodhisattva's great compassion.

6. The "Unimpeded" Nature of the Bodhisattva's Compassion

As for [their compassion's] being "unimpeded,"[503] there are five reasons why a bodhisattva's compassion might [otherwise] become impeded, namely:

First, by the sufferings of the hell realms;
Second, by the sufferings of the animal realms;
Third, by the sufferings of the hungry ghost realms;

Fourth, by evil people's ingratitude [for kindnesses bestowed on them];
Fifth, by the faults and evils encountered amidst *saṃsāra*.

If even these five circumstances fail to impede his resolve, then he qualifies as possessing the unimpeded great compassion. This is as described here:

If even the foremost sufferings encountered in the hell realms,
the sufferings met in the animal realms or hungry ghost realms,
[the ingratitude of] evil people, and *saṃsāra*
still fail to impede him, he is one possessed of the great compassion.
The bodhisattva who is able to be one who is like this
has been declared by the Buddha to possess unimpeded compassion.

7. The Bodhisattva's "Thorough Practice of Skillful Means"

Regarding "thoroughly taking on the practice of skillful means,"[504] there are five bases for a bodhisattva's qualification as "thoroughly taking on the practice of skillful means," namely:

First, he knows the correct place and time;
Second, he knows what delights the minds of others;
Third, he knows what will cause others to turn and enter the path;
Fourth, he knows what constitutes the correct sequence of events;
Fifth, he knows how to lead and guide beings.

a. His Knowledge of "the Correct Place and Time"

As for "knowing the correct place and time," he knows that, in this particular place, one should explain Dharma in this particular way and knows that, at this particular time, one should explain the Dharma in this other way. He knows that, in this particular place, one should employ these specific causes and conditions to bring about the liberation of these particular beings. And he knows that, at this particular time, one should employ just these particular causes and conditions to bring about the liberation of these other beings. Having assessed these specific factors in advance, the bodhisattva then proceeds to act accordingly. This is as described here:

If one takes up the intent of the Bhagavat
wishing then to explain it for others,
one should first know these two factors,
and then speak in accordance with the correct time and place.

Should one fail to know the correct time and place
and yet wish to proclaim the intent of the Buddhas,
he will [not only] fail to accomplish the intended benefit,
but moreover may thus commit a blameworthy error.

b. His Knowledge of "What Delights the Minds of Others"

As for "knowing what delights the minds of others," this involves knowing, due to their mental dispositions, which endeavors and which experiences will cause them to be pleased. Having known this in advance, the bodhisattva acquires a penetrating understanding of what beings know and delight in and then brings forth the appropriate skillful means to facilitate their liberation. If one acts in this way, then his efforts will not be in vain. This is as described here:

The bodhisattva knows with respect to beings
the difficult-to-assess intentions present in their mental dispositions,
and, having already first known the character of their intentions,
he gradually influences them to dwell in the Buddha's intent.

Through thoroughly knowing the affairs of the world,
he benefits himself while also benefiting others.
One who is able to proceed in this manner
is said to be adept in the practice of skillful means.

c. His Knowledge of "What Causes Others to Turn & Enter the Path"

As for their "knowing what will cause others to turn and enter the path," this refers to knowing whatever may induce the minds of common persons following non-Buddhist paths to turn away from them and instead enter the path of the Buddha. It also refers to knowing whatever will induce beings to turn away from evil deeds and instead engage in good deeds. And it also refers to knowing whatever will induce followers of the *śrāvaka* disciple and *pratyekabuddha* paths to turn away from them and instead enter into the Great Vehicle.

This refers as well to knowing with respect to those already abiding within the Buddha's Dharma, just what will prevent them from entering into non-Buddhist paths. Having first come to know these matters, one then implements the practice accordingly. This is as described here:

If one is able to induce beings
to abandon non-Buddhist paths
while also inducing those devoted to what is bad
to enter the Buddha's way to the supreme quiescent cessation,

and if one knows with respect to beings
the superior, middling, or inferior character of their minds,
and, having known this, one is then able to lead and guide them,
this is what is meant by being adept in the practice of skillful means.

d. His Knowledge of "What Constitutes the Correct Sequence"

As for "knowing what constitutes the correct sequence," take for instance the priorities in the Śrāvaka Disciple Vehicle wherein they first speak of giving, then of upholding the moral precepts, then of being reborn in the heavens, then of the faults and misery in pursuing the five kinds of sensual pleasures, then of the suffering and distress of the household life, and then of the benefits and bliss of abandoning the home life [in favor of the monastic path]. Following this, they explain the truth of suffering, then the truth of its origination, then the truth of its cessation, and then the truth of the path. After this, they speak of the stream enterer's fruit of the path, the fruit of the *sakṛdāgāmin*, the fruit of the *ānagamin*, and the fruit of arhatship. They next speak of the indestructible liberation and then speak of those that are unimpeded.

Beyond that, within the Pratyekabuddha Vehicle, they also speak of the faults and misery inherent in the self and everything deemed to be possessed by the self and speak as well of the immense benefit in the abandonment of such faults and misery. They then speak of the life of the householder as possessed of serious faults and of leaving behind the household life as beneficial.

They next explain that the many sorts of disputation and conceptual elaboration involve serious faults, that solitary practice bestows wholesome benefits, that village life involves serious faults, that abiding in a forest hermitage brings wholesome benefits, that one should renounce the many desires and the many sorts of [worldly] endeavors and instead delight in having but few wants and but few endeavors. [They teach that] one is to carefully guard the sense faculties, know moderation in drink and food, maintain vigilance at all times throughout the first watch and the last watch of the night,[505] contemplate an object, focus on its characteristics, and take delight in dwelling in an empty hut.

They esteem the upholding of the moral precepts, the cultivation of *dhyāna* absorptions, and the development of wisdom. They refrain from displaying idiosyncratic or strange personal appearances. Although they do inspire happiness in others [who observe them on the daily alms round], they are only concerned with benefiting themselves. They delight in profound dharmas and acquire wisdom that does not rely on [teachings provided by] others.

According to the Great Vehicle's priorities regarding the correct sequencing of events, one first speaks of the perfection of giving, then the perfection of moral virtue, then the perfection of patience, then the perfection of vigor, then the perfection of meditative concentration, and then the perfection of wisdom.[506]

[The Great Vehicle also] first speaks of the truthfulness supreme basis [for the generation of meritorious qualities], then the relinquishment basis, then the quiescence basis, and then the wisdom basis.

Then again, they also first praise the generation of the resolve to attain bodhi, then the ten vows, and then the ten ultimate ends. They then praise the renunciation of whatsoever dharma might conduce to retreat from the resolve to attain bodhi, then they praise cultivation of those dharmas that prevent retreat from the resolve to attain bodhi, followed by promoting vigor buttressed by solid resolve, solidly established capacity for endurance, and then solidity in sustaining one's vows.

Yet again, [the Great Vehicle]:

First speaks of the dharmas that enable acquisition of all the [bodhisattva] grounds;
Next speaks of the dharmas that enable dwelling on the grounds;
Next speaks of the dharmas that enable acquisition of the deepest aspects of the grounds;
Next speaks of the dharmas by which one abandons defilements on the grounds;
Next speaks of the dharmas enabling purification of the grounds;
Next speaks of the dharmas conducive to abiding for a long time on the grounds;
Next speaks of the dharmas enabling one to reach the most extreme limits of each of the grounds;
Next speaks of the dharmas enabling nonregression from the grounds;
Next speaks of the fruits associated with each of the grounds;
And then speaks of the powers associated with the fruits of each of the grounds.

Then again, it may be that [the Great Vehicle]:

First speaks of the Ground of Joyfulness;
Next speaks of the Ground of Stainlessness;
Next speaks of the Ground of Shining Light;
Next speaks of the Ground of Blazing Brilliance;
Next speaks of the Difficult-to-Conquer Ground;
Next speaks of the Ground of Direct Presence;
Next speaks of the Far-Reaching Ground;
Next speaks of the Ground of Immovability;
Next speaks of the Ground of Excellent Intelligence;
And then speaks of the Ground of the Dharma Cloud.

These [various Three-Vehicle sequences] are as described below:

[*Śrāvakas*] first speak of giving, next of upholding moral precepts, and then their karmic fruition in gaining rebirth in the heavens.

Next, impermanence, the faults of the household life,
and then the immense benefits achieved by leaving the home life.

Next, they speak of the unsurpassed dharma of the four truths,
the severance of the fetters, and attaining the four fruits [of the path].
This sequence of skillful means
induces people to abide in the first of the [Three] Vehicles.

[*Pratyekabuddhas*] first speak of the faults in *saṃsāra*
and then speak of the benefits associated with nirvāṇa,
guarding and restraining the sense faculties,
maintaining the moral precepts, the *dhyāna* absorptions,

the wisdom not reliant on [the teachings] of others,
the excellent qualities associated with delighting in dwelling alone,
relying upon oneself, not relying on others,
delighting in striving for one's own benefit and happiness

while still not abandoning others,
and deeply cultivating the dharmas of the *dhūta* austerities.
In the case of those who cultivate this mid-level vehicle,
such are the features of the dharmas they teach.

[The Great Vehicle] refers to the forty exclusive dharmas
in describing the measureless qualities of the Buddha,
speaks as well of all of the dharmas that he practiced
when he was a bodhisattva

in order to be of benefit to beings,
speaking of these dharmas according to their correct sequence,
describing self-benefit as well as the benefiting of others,
explaining all of his different sorts of meritorious qualities,

explaining also with regard to all the Buddha's sons
the ten grounds in which they delight.
Those who seek Dharma as set forth in the Great Vehicle
achieve liberation in accordance with just such a sequence as this.

e. His Knowledge of "How to Lead and Guide Beings"

"Leading and guiding beings" involves adapting to whatever subjects beings delight in, and then, having understood precisely what those subjects are, using those very subjects as the means by which one leads and guides them. By adapting to whatever they delight in, allowing for their individual strengths, one influences them toward the achievement of liberation. This is as described here:

There may be cases where there are beings
amenable [to being led and guided] through profound classics,
through recondite subjects, through trades or artisanal skills,
through techniques involving mantras, through pleasing words,

through skillful discourse, through resources or wealth,
or through giving, moral virtue, meditation, or wisdom.
After [the bodhisattva] has assessed such factors,
he leads them to enter into the Great Vehicle.

He might manifest in a woman's body
to lead and guide men,
or he might manifest in the body of a man
to lead and guide women,

first showing the many pleasures of the five types of sensual desire,
and, afterward, speaking of the faults inherent in those desires,
thereby leading every sort of person
to then abandon the five types of sensual desire.

It is just such a skillful implementation of [his awareness of] these five matters that constitutes the bodhisattva's "adeptly taking on the practice of skillful means."

8. The Bodhisattva's "Patient Endurance of Pain and Anguish"

Regarding "patiently enduring every sort of pain and anguish,"[507] this refers to the case of a person who, through an incalculable number of kalpas in the cycle of births and deaths, can endure all sorts of pain and anguish as he cultivates the ten courses of good karmic action that enable this person to eventually abide in *anuttarasamyaksaṃbodhi.*

Question: Every person delights in happiness and detests suffering. How then could such a person be able to endure [such an immense amount of] pain and anguish?

Response: There are five reasons for his ability to accomplish this:

First, delight in nonself;
Second, resolute belief in emptiness;
Third, assessment of the nature of worldly dharmas;
Fourth, contemplation of retributions resulting from karmic actions;
Fifth, mindfulness of an incalculable number of kalpas already spent fruitlessly undergoing pain and anguish.

These are as described here:

He delights in the dharmas of nonself and emptiness,
and also understands the retributions resulting from karmic actions
as well as gain, loss, and the rest of the eight worldly dharmas
that one must certainly endure while dwelling in the world.

He is also mindful of his past lives
in which he endured in vain a measureless amount of suffering,
[thinking], "How much the more so should I be willing to undergo it
when this would be for the sake of realizing buddhahood?"

9. The Bodhisattva's "Never Abandoning Any Being"

As for "They do not abandon any being,"[508] sometimes there are beings who engage in the most extreme sorts of pernicious evil, who are utterly devoid of meritorious qualities, and whom it is impossible to benefit. Nonetheless, the bodhisattva still never thinks to abandon such beings.

Question: If these sorts of evil people cannot be brought to liberation, why should one not simply abandon them?

Response: There are five reasons, namely:

First, because of disdain for the dharmas of petty people;
Second, because of esteem for the dharmas of the great men;
Third, because of fear of cheating the Buddhas;
Fourth, because of gratitude for the kindnesses one has received;
Fifth, it is because of these works within the world that one transcends the world.

These are as described here:

Because of one's aspiration to liberate beings,
one brings forth the resolve to carry a heavy burden.
Thus, even in the midst of evil adversaries,
one's mind should never be inclined to abandon them.

To disdain petty people and esteem those who are great[509]
is [to conceive of] some difference between the petty and the great.
When in the midst of beings, one should not allow
one's mind of kindly sympathy to withdraw or cease.

In the midst of [others'] urgent difficulties
wherein one has no personal interests, one still provides help.
When it is the time to bear a heavy burden,
one does not shrink from or diminish one's efforts in that work.

In a case where one has brought forth the unsurpassable resolve,
but may still have instances in which one abandons beings,
either due to mental weariness or anguish
or because of being harmed by evil men,
those are instances of cheating and deceiving
all buddhas of the ten directions and three periods of time.

The Buddhas, the honored ones within the world,
for the sake of bestowing benefit on beings,
engaged in all manner of austerities
in their cultivation of the path to buddhahood.
For kalpas in number as the sands of the Ganges, the Buddhas
sacrificed happiness as they performed meritorious karmic deeds.

Were one to abandon even a single evil person,
that would be to turn one's back on the kindness of the Buddhas.
Therefore one must not abandon in mid-course
even those beings who are evil.

In an instance where someone,
throughout countless *asaṃkhyeyas* of kalpas,
cultivates the path to buddhahood,
the great compassion is the very root of that endeavor.

If due to thoughts rooted in desire
or thoughts founded on hatred or fear,
one were to abandon even one being who could attain liberation,
this would be to sever the root of the Buddha path.

Therefore [one should realize that] the courses of good karmic action can enable one who does not abandon [any beings] to eventually reach *anuttarasamyaksaṃbodhi.*

10. The Bodhisattva's "Deep Delight in the Buddhas' Wisdom"

As for "deeply delighting in the wisdom of the Buddhas,"[510] if one deeply delights in the wisdom of the Buddhas, then he will thereby swiftly attain *anuttarasamyaksaṃbodhi.* There are five reasons why [the bodhisattva] feels deep delight in the wisdom of the Buddhas, namely:

First, the wisdom of the Buddhas is unequaled by any other;
Second, the wisdom of the Buddhas is able to cause someone to become one who is honored throughout the world;
Third, the Buddhas use the wisdom of the Buddhas to bring about their own liberation;
Fourth, the wisdom of the Buddhas also enables the liberation of others;
Fifth, the wisdom of the Buddhas is the abode of all meritorious qualities.

These are as described below:

As for this wisdom of all the Buddhas,
no matter whether it be up in the heavens or in the world,
there is no wisdom anywhere that can even equal it,
how much the less might there be any superior to it.

It is because of this very wisdom that all buddhas
receive deep respect and reverential obeisance
from the devas, from the *asuras,*
and from all the world's humans.

The Buddhas use this wisdom to liberate themselves
and also use it to liberate other people.

If one acquires this wisdom of the Buddhas,
this is someone who is a treasury of meritorious qualities.

11. "Delight in Those Who Practice the Buddhas' Powers & Masteries"

Regarding "delight in those who completely and thoroughly practice the Buddhas' powers and the sovereign masteries,"[511] "thorough practice" refers to long-enduring practice of all the practices. "The powers" refers to the ten wisdom powers. "Sovereign masteries" refers to the ability to do precisely as one wishes in whatever one does. If one feels profound delight in the complete and thorough practice of the dharmas of the Buddhas' ten powers and sovereign masteries, such a person will be able before long to swiftly attain *anuttarasamyaksaṃbodhi*.

There are five reasons for delighting in the complete and thorough practice [of the powers and sovereign masteries], namely:

First, due to reverential esteem for the teachings and directives of all buddhas;
Second, due to the fact that all buddhas have such great disciples;
Third, due to their personal realization of all dharmas;
Fourth, due to their ability to draw in those who have fallen away;
Fifth, due to their ability to then rescue those who have fallen away.

These are as described below:

[They delight] due to revering the Buddhas' incomparable teachings,
due to the existence of the fourfold and eightfold classes
of the Buddha's sons of six and threefold types,
due to their capacity to become the teachers even of the devas,
due to the Buddhas' wisdom eye
with which they see all dharmas manifest directly before them,

and due to their ability to draw in and rescue, bringing to liberation
even those people who have fallen away such as
those who, by heinous evil deeds, have severed roots of goodness,
those who have broken the moral precepts, and other such beings.

If there be a person who [delights] in those who thoroughly practice
the Buddhas' powers and sovereign masteries,
then nirvāṇa as well as the merit of the heavens
will always be as if resting in the palm of his hand.

12. The Buddhas' "Practice of the Powers"

[Regarding the "Buddhas' powers"],[512] in circumstances such as these, the Buddhas are able to use a buddha's powers to accomplish five types of endeavors, namely:

First, they may induce beings to train in the Śrāvaka Disciple Vehicle;

Second, they may induce beings to train in the Pratyekabuddha Vehicle;
Third, they may induce beings to train in the Dharma of the Great Vehicle;
Fourth, in the case of those whose powers have become perfectly complete, they may enable their attainment of liberation;
Fifth, in the case of those whose powers are as yet inferior, they may enable them to abide in worldly happiness.

These are as described below:

The Buddhas use their spiritual powers
to influence beings who have developed renunciation,
perhaps influencing them to train either in the Small Vehicle,
or in the Intermediate Vehicle, or in the Great Vehicle.

In the case of those whose powers are completely fulfilled,
they enable them to attain liberation.
For those whose powers are still incomplete,
they assist their celestial rebirth or their happiness within the world.

13. The Buddhas' "Practice of the Sovereign Masteries"

As for "their sovereign masteries,"[513] there are five matters in which the Buddhas possess sovereign mastery, namely:

First, sovereign mastery in the spiritual superknowledges;
Second, the attainment of sovereign mastery over their own minds;
Third, the attainment of sovereign mastery in complete cessation;
Fourth, the attainment of sovereign mastery in the psychic powers of the Āryas;[514]
Fifth, sovereign mastery in determining their own life spans.

These are as described below:

They have sovereign mastery in flying and other [superknowledges]
and they have sovereign mastery over their own minds
as well as in the *dhyāna* absorption of complete cessation
that for them is [as easy] as entering and exiting their own abodes.

They can transform all things, whether pure or impure,
in accordance with their own minds.[515]
Their life spans cannot be diminished by others,
for, so long as they sustain the conditions, their lives will be endless.

Just as it is for such sovereign masteries as these,
so too it is with respect to all dharmas.
It is for these reasons that [the Buddhas], the lions among men,
are known as those who possess the sovereign masteries.

14. The Bodhisattva's "Ability to Refute All Wrong Views"

Regarding being "able to refute all ideas involving wrong views,"[516] this is a reference to whatever strays far from the right path such as the ninety-six kinds of non-Buddhist paths favored by common people, and other such wrong views. A general characterization of such wrong ideas would include the claim that the five aggregates constitute a self, that there is a self that possesses the five aggregates, that there is a self contained within the five aggregates, that the five aggregates are contained within a self, or that there exists a self apart from the five aggregates. These ideas are as described below:

> If [one posits that] the five aggregates constitute a self,
> thereby falling into the annihilationist [fallacy],
> one thus dispenses with the efficacy of karmic causes and conditions
> and posits liberation in the absence of the requisite efforts.
>
> As for the rest [of the wrong views], they are of four types.
> As for those positing a signless self distinct from the aggregates,
> whatsoever is signless is necessarily a nonexistent dharma.
> All [of the other fallacies] should be refuted in this same way.

Then again, it is the five erroneous views that constitute wrong ideas, namely: wrong views, the view of [the five-aggregate] "person" as constituting a self, extreme views, seizing upon views, and views that seize on precept observance [alone as constituting the path]. These are as described below:

> One demolishes the wrong views about cause and effect,
> the twenty kinds of views referencing a "person,"
> views positing the ultimacy of existence or nonexistence,
> [views esteeming] inferior endeavors as supreme,
> and [the view that] it is solely by the power of precept observance
> that one succeeds in achieving liberation.
>
> As with the earlier refutation [of a self] identical to or distinct
> [from the five aggregates], these views are refuted in just such a way.
> Using right thought and the eightfold path to refute them,
> one explains that these are the bases for attaining liberation.

15. The Bodhisattva's "Preservation and Protection of Right Dharma"

Regarding "preserving and protecting the Buddhas' right Dharma,"[517] this refers to someone who is able to preserve and protect the Dharma as taught by all buddhas, namely the twelve categories of scriptural text. Because his mind is able to believe and accept them, the ten courses of good karmic action can cause this person to succeed in reaching *anuttarasamyaksaṃbodhi.*

There are five reasons why one should accept and protect right Dharma, namely:

First, because one realizes the obligation to repay the kindness of all buddhas;

Second, in order to cause the Dharma to abide for a long time;

Third, in order to perform the most supreme form of offering, thus making an offering to the Buddhas themselves;

Fourth, in order to be of benefit to an incalculable number of beings;

Fifth, because right Dharma is the rarest of all things.

These are as described below:

If a person wishes to devote himself
to those endeavors bequeathed by all buddhas
and also wishes to cause the Dharma to remain for a long time
by presenting the most supreme offering to the Buddhas,

then, because he wishes to heal
the serious diseases that afflict beings,
because he has realized that all the Bhagavats
obtained this Dharma through having to undergo suffering,

and because, understanding these conditions of its origination,
he realizes that the Dharma is a rarity difficult to come by—
[for all these reasons], he who is wise
should therefore cherish and protect the Dharma.

In this connection, there are five bases by which one's actions might qualify as "cherishing and protecting right Dharma," namely:

First, one cultivates [the path] according to the way it was taught;

Second, one influences others to practice in accordance with the Dharma;

Third, one extricates any thorns that might destroy the Buddha's Dharma;

Fourth, one abandons the four seals of darkness;

Fifth, one practices [in accordance with] the four seals of greatness.[518]

These are as described below:

In one's own relationship with the Dharma of the Buddhas,
one abides in accordance with how the Buddha taught it.
One retains a mind of compassion, is not miserly with Dharma,
and also influences others to abide within it.

Moreover, one crushes the armies of Māra
and also refutes the claims of the non-Buddhist treatise masters.
On encountering those who detest the Dharma of the Buddhas,
with a mind free of hatred, one refutes their claims.

One departs from the four seals of blackness
while taking on the practice of the four seals of greatness.
One who is able to act in such a way is deemed to be
someone who cherishes and protects right Dharma.

16. The Bodhisattva's "Valor"

As for their being "valiant,"[519] there are five bases because of which the bodhisattva is deemed to be valiant, namely:

First, because he crushes Māra's thieves;
Second, because he crushes the non-Buddhist partisan thieves;
Third, because he crushes the thieves of the afflictions;
Fourth, because he crushes the thieves of the sense faculties;
Fifth, because he crushes the thieves of the five aggregates.

These are as described below:

Māra the Evil One marshaled his armies
and, at the bodhi tree, sought to harm the Buddha.
Always seeking opportunities to take advantage of the Buddha
and disturb the minds of his audience.
Once the Buddha sun had arisen and shone upon the world,
Māra made the request intended to cause him to enter nirvāṇa.

He is forever confusing those who take on the training,
attempting to destroy their paths to liberation,
even to the point that, to this very day,
his determination to accomplish this still never ceases.

These who detest nirvāṇa
are the great thieves of good people.
One must use moral virtue, *dhyāna* concentration, and wisdom
to crush adversaries possessed of Māra's powers.

There are those who, of the opinion that they are wise,
always slight the Buddhas out of arrogance
and use all different sorts of tactics
to destroy the Buddha's Dharma, manifesting for that very reason.

They always detest the Buddha's disciples
and, having become failures themselves, they teach others to fail.
These various classes of non-Buddhists
are the great thieves in the world.

One ought to use a mind free of hatred
and one should use the wisdom based on extensive learning.
Then, availing oneself of the power of the great resolve,
one should utterly demolish these non-Buddhist adversaries.

The power of the afflictions brings forth karmic actions,
cyclic existence, and descent into the wretched destinies.
It is because of obstacles caused by the power of the afflictions
that one remains unable to practice the great path.

It is because of the power of the afflictions
that one falls into all sorts of wrong views.
It is because of the power of the afflictions
that one does not practice the path to the elixir of immortality.

It is because of all these reasons
that the afflictions are the worst of all the great thieves.
Through right mindfulness, concentration, and wisdom,
one becomes able to crush the thieves of the afflictions.

If one is dragged along by the thieves of the sense faculties,
they cause a person to descend into the wretched destinies
and also cause one to fall into celestial and human realms
wherein one does not succeed in reaching nirvāṇa.

Now, given [the plight caused by] these sense-faculty thieves,
how could one fail to use a sense of shame, dread of blame,
and right mindfulness as well as wisdom
to utterly crush the thieves of the sense faculties.

These are analogous to [the stratagems of] people of the world
who may resort to gently persuasive words, or to deception,
or to wealth and valuables, or even to swords and lances,
using these four means to drive away the thieves.

It is because of these five aggregates
that one undergoes birth, aging, sickness, and death,
also falls into the realms of immense terror,
and becomes subject to undergoing intense suffering and anguish.

It because of the five aggregates
that one is plunged into grief and then sobs and weeps.
It is also because of the five aggregates
that one undergoes all the different sorts of sufferings.

Therefore you should realize
the need to use the dharmas of knowledge and vision
to utterly crush [the ruinous power of] the five aggregates
just as one would defeat adversaries or thieves.

17. The Bodhisattva's "Ability to Endure"

As for [the bodhisattva's] being "able to endure,"[520] he is one whose resolve is strong, who is possessed of the marks of a great man, and who is possessed of a profound and distant vision. There are five grounds for his being deemed "able to endure," namely:

First, when he succeeds in the endeavors he has vowed to achieve, his mind does not become elated;

Second, when he does not succeed in the endeavors he has vowed to achieve, his mind does not become dejected;

Third, when pain and anguish cut close, his mind remains unmoved;

Fourth, when his body is beset by pleasurable experiences, his mind still remains unchanged;

Fifth, his state of mind runs deep and sees far. Thus whether he has been given cause for anger or cause for joy, his mind remains inscrutable.

These are as described below:

When his body or mind experience some new suffering,
his mind still remains unmoved.
No matter what sort of pleasurable experience comes,
his greatly wise mind does not change.

Even where he is given cause for anger, joy, or fear,
no one else can fathom [his state of mind].
Wherever one possesses marks of resolute intentions such as these,
this person is said to be one who is "able to endure."

18. The Bodhisattva's "Vigor"

Regarding [the bodhisattva's] diligent "vigor,"[521] there are five circumstances in which he is diligent in his practice of vigor, namely:

First, he is diligently vigorous in preventing the arising of bad dharmas that have not yet arisen;

Second, he is diligently vigorous in cutting off and destroying bad dharmas that may already have arisen;

Third, he is diligently vigorous in causing the arising of good dharmas that have not yet arisen;

Fourth, he is diligently vigorous in increasing any good dharmas that have already arisen;

Fifth, he is diligently vigorous in ensuring that nothing can obstruct whatever endeavors he has taken up in the world.

These are as described below:

He cuts off evil dharmas that have already arisen
just as one might get rid of a venomous snake.
He cuts off any evil dharmas that have not yet arisen
just as one might block off the waters of a flood.

He brings about the growth of [already arisen] good dharmas
just as one might water a sweet fruit's seedling.
He strives to bring forth goodness that has not yet arisen
just as one might use a wooden friction drill to light a fire.

In pursuing his good endeavors in the world,
he acts with such diligent vigor as permits no obstruction.
All buddhas say of a person such as this
that he is to be known as one who is diligently vigorous.

19. The Bodhisattva's "Solid Resolve in Teaching Beings"

As for "solid resolve in the teaching of beings,"[522] if, during all that time in which he teaches beings in the five vehicles, the bodhisattva's mind remains unturned even as he experiences at the hands of others the giving of offerings, slighting, arrogance, detestation, love, terror, suffering, bliss, extreme exhaustion, and other such situations, he thereby qualifies as one who "proceeds with solid resolve in the teaching of beings."

As for the five vehicles, they are:

First, the Buddha Vehicle;
Second, the Pratyekabuddha Vehicle;
Third, the Śrāvaka Disciple Vehicle;
Fourth, the Deva Vehicle;
Fifth, the Human Vehicle.

These are as described below:

You should use single-minded focus[523]
and all your powers,
while relying on many different sorts of skillful means
and abandoning any thoughts of hate or love

as you proceed to teach every sort of being,
doing so with a pure mind that has abandoned defilement,
thereby influencing them to gain what in countless lifetimes
is a rarity: the unsurpassable [Buddha] Vehicle.

If one enters among those who have no such strength
and thus have no capacity to abide in the Great Vehicle,
one may in sequence teach either the Pratyekabuddha Vehicle,
the Śrāvaka Disciple Vehicle, or the vehicles of devas or humans.

20. The Bodhisattva's "Not Coveting His Own Happiness"

As for "not coveting their own happiness,"[524] this refers to not being attached to any sort of bliss. There are five reasons why the bodhisattva does covet his own happiness, namely:

First, all pleasures are just as ephemeral as a bubble on the water;
Second, worldly pleasures transform into suffering;
Third, they are a product of the conjunction of many conditions;
Fourth, they are a product of cravings;
Fifth, they are but a minor bliss like that of a mere drop of honey.

These are as described below:

Pleasures abide for but a short time, like a bubble
and they transform into suffering like food laced with poison.
Relying on a three-part conjunction, they exist through contact
and arise because of the ulcerous boil of desire.

If one abandons desire and craving,
then there is no pleasure that exists apart from them.
[Pleasures] are like a dry well or a drop of honey,
for there is but little bliss and an abundance of suffering.

Whosoever aims to be of benefit to beings
should not have any sort of covetous attachment.

21. The Bodhisattva's "Not Coveting a Measurelessly Long Life"

Regarding [their refraining from covetous attachment] "to living a measurelessly long life,"[525] there are five reasons why the bodhisattva does not covet or selfishly cherish his own body, namely:

First, the body did not come forth from previous lives;
Second, it shall not go on to future lives;
Third, it is not a durable entity;
Fourth, it is devoid of any self;
Fifth, there is nothing in it qualifying as the property of a self.

These are as described below:

Your body is but a collection of many sorts of filth
entirely filled up with impurities.
It did not come forth to the present from previous lives,
and it will not be taken forth to one's future lives.

Even though one might provide for and serve it well for a long time,
it will still break its obligation to repay great kindness.
This body is not a durable entity,
for, like a foam bubble, it will be destroyed before long.

Whatsoever is the product of conditions has no fixed nature.
Having no fixed nature, it is therefore not a self-existent entity.
Therefore, one should realize that [the body]
is not a self and is not the possession of a self.

This body is possessed of countless faults.
Thus one should not selfishly cherish it.

There are five reasons why the bodhisattva does not selfishly cherish a long life span, namely:

First, because he delights in the life of wisdom;
Second, because he is frightened at the prospect of committing any karmic transgression [in order to preserve it];
Third, because he is mindful of the countless deaths one has undergone throughout the course of beginningless *saṃsāra;*
Fourth, because [death] is an experience jointly shared by all beings;
Fifth, because [death] is unavoidable.

These are as described below:

Because, through abundant learning and right discourse about it,
one comes to prize one's life of wisdom,
because one fears that, when [trying to avoid] losing one's life,
one might produce the evil of karmic transgressions,

and also, because one observes that no one
can escape [the clutches of] the king of death
and hence it cannot be avoided through the power
of expedients dependent on wealth or knowledge—

How then could anyone devoted to cultivating good dharmas
still continue to cherish this life?

22. The Bodhisattva's "Supremacy in All Endeavors"

As for "They are supreme in all their endeavors,"[526] if one absolutely must be able to complete whatever endeavor he begins, this is the mark of a superior person. There are five endeavors that, once the bodhisattva has begun them, he absolutely must bring to completion, namely:

First, [the accumulation of] wealth;
Second, giving;
Third, the observance of the moral precepts;
Fourth, the cultivation of meditative concentration;
Fifth, [the cultivation of] the virtues associated with the path.

These are as described below:

One strives diligently to accumulate wealth
and, with utmost sincerity, [uses it] to engage in giving.
In their sequence, he purifies his observance of the moral precepts
and then vigorously strives to acquire the *dhyāna* absorptions.

He implements many different skillful means
for bringing forth liberation through the eightfold path.
This is how, in all the endeavors that one takes up,
one comes to be known as a superior person.

23. The Bodhisattva's "Freedom from Fault in All the Works They Do"

Regarding being "free of fault in all the works they do,"[527] whatever endeavors this bodhisattva engages in is of the sort that is not criticized by the wise. There are five reasons that whatever he does is free of fault and is not criticized by the wise, namely:

First, he engages in works that he is capable of accomplishing;
Second, they produce a greatly beneficial result;
Third, they do no damage to the Dharma;
Fourth, they are free of any subsequently resulting faults;
Fifth, they result in an immensely fine reputation.

These are as described below:

He first makes all different sorts of assessments
regarding matters of his own ability and the ease of accomplishment,
ensuring that what is gained by this endeavor
will constitute an immeasurably great resulting benefit,

that it will not interfere with the good Dharma,
that, once it has been accomplished, nothing bad will follow from it,
that it will be of a sort that is praised by good people,
and that it will cause a fine reputation to spread widely.

Whichever works are initiated by the wise
are of a sort that they are free of any fault.
Issues of feasibility and ease of accomplishment
are matters for which one is individually responsible.
Those possessed of measureless great qualities,
will swiftly bring about a resulting benefit.

It is in this manner that the wise come to know
that there will be no subsequent fault arising from this,
and that they should devote diligent vigor to this task,
whereupon they then engage in endeavors such as these.

24. The Bodhisattva's "Complete Purity" & "Success in Supreme Bases"

Regarding "They abide in purity of every kind and come forth through the practice of all the supreme bases [of meritorious qualities],"[528] there are five causal bases for [the bodhisattva's coming forth through] all the supreme bases and for his possessing every kind of purity, namely:

First, he has resolute intentions that are pure;
Second, his dedications of merit are pure;
Third, his own practice of the supreme bases [of meritorious qualities] accords with the way he explains them to others;
Fourth, he influences others to practice them;

Fifth, he abandons all dharmas contrary to the supreme bases [of meritorious qualities], namely false speech, miserliness, covetousness, frivolous restlessness, and delusion.

These are as described below:

The bodhisattva possesses profound and pure intentions,
abandons flattery and deviousness,
always relies upon the four supreme bases,
and dedicates his merit to the realization of buddhahood.

He first cultivates good dharmas himself
and thereafter influences others to practice them.
The bodhisattva who proceeds in this manner
is one for whom the four supreme bases are pure.

25. How the Ten Courses Enable the Attainment of Buddhahood

As for "The ten courses of good karmic action enable these persons to reach the station of the Bhagavats who possess the ten powers,"[529] if one cultivates the ten courses of good karmic action in this manner, they enable a person to reach that state wherein he is possessed of the ten powers. "The ten powers" refers to the possession of right and universal knowledge. One who acquires right and universal knowledge is then himself a buddha. There are five causal bases for one's being referred to as a "*bhagavat*,"[530] namely:

First, [through his right and universal knowledge], he has severed all doubts with respect to the past;

Second, he has severed all doubts with respect to the future;

Third, he has severed all doubts with respect to the present;

Fourth, he has severed all doubts with respect to dharmas that transcend the three periods of time;

Fifth, he has severed all doubts regarding the ineffable dharmas.

These are as described below:

With regard to the beginningless past,
they have an utterly penetrating comprehension free of doubts.
With regard to the boundless future,
they know it with a penetrating comprehension free of doubts.

All of the boundless worlds
throughout the ten directions of the present
as well as what transcends the three periods of time,
including the sublime dharmas of the unconditioned

and also the fourteen ineffable dharmas—[531]
they know those too with a comprehension free of doubts.
They are therefore treasuries of meritorious qualities,
the Buddhas, those renowned as the World Honored Ones.

The ten courses of good karmic action are able to cause bodhisattvas who perfect such meritorious qualities as these to reach *anuttarasamyaksaṃbodhi.* Therefore whoever seeks to attain buddhahood should cultivate the ten courses of good karmic action in this manner.

The End of Chapter Thirty

Chapter 31
Guarding the Moral Precepts

XXXI. Chapter 31: Guarding the Moral Precepts

It is in this way that this bodhisattva practices the courses of good karmic action.

A. General and Specific Results of the Ten Courses of Karmic Action

In both good and bad courses of karmic action,
there are general characteristics as well as specific characteristics.
Each of these are to be clearly distinguished and known
as possessing two corresponding types of karmic results.

1. The Ten Courses of Good Karmic Action

a. General Karmic Results of the Ten Courses of Good Karmic Action

As for the general characteristics of the resulting retributions of the ten courses of good karmic action, these may consist of either rebirth in the heavens or rebirth among humans.

b. Specific Karmic Results of the Ten Courses of Good Karmic Action

As for the specific characteristics of the resulting retributions, they are as follows:

In the case of the good karmic action of abandoning the killing of beings, there are two resultant karmic retributions: First, long life span. Second, having but little illness.

From the good karmic action of abandoning stealing, there are two resultant karmic retributions: First, one obtains great wealth. Second, one becomes independently wealthy.

From the good karmic action of abandoning sexual misconduct, there are two resultant karmic retributions: First, one's wife will be chaste and good. Second, she cannot be "ruined" by others.[532]

From the good karmic action of abandoning false speech, there are two resultant karmic retributions: First, one will not be slandered by anyone. Second, one will not be cheated or deceived by others.

From the good karmic action of abandoning divisive speech, there are two resultant karmic retributions: First, one will gain a fine following. Second, one's [reputation] will not be ruined by others.

From the good karmic action of abandoning harsh speech, there are two resultant karmic retributions: First, one will hear whichever sounds one delights in hearing. Second, one will not become embroiled in disputes.

From the good karmic action of abandoning scattered or inappropriate speech, there are two resultant karmic retributions: First, people will trust and accept whatever one says. Second, whatever one says will be definitely decisive.

From the good karmic action of abandoning covetousness, there are two resultant karmic retributions: First, one will be easily contented. Second, one will have but few wants.

From the good karmic action of abandoning ill will, there are two resultant karmic retributions: First, wherever one is reborn, one will always seek to bring about fine circumstances for others. Second, one will not delight in tormenting or harming other beings.

From the good karmic action of maintaining right views, there are two resultant karmic retributions: First, one will abandon flattery and deviousness. Second, whatever one sees will be pure in character.

2. The Ten Courses of Bad Karmic Action

a. General Karmic Results of the Ten Courses of Bad Karmic Action

The same principles apply in the matter of the ten courses of bad karmic action. As for the general characteristics of their resulting karmic retributions, if one has engaged in them to a high degree, one falls into the hell realms. If one has engaged in them to a middling degree, one will fall into the animal realms. If one has engaged in them to a lesser[533] degree, then one will to fall into the realms of the hungry ghosts.

b. Specific Karmic Results of the Ten Courses of Bad Karmic Action

As for the specific karmic retributions [associated with the ten courses of bad karmic action], they are as follows:

From the bad karmic action of killing beings, there are two resultant retributions: First, a short life span. Second, much illness.

From the bad karmic action of stealing, there are two resultant karmic retributions: First, poverty. Second, loss of wealth.

From the bad karmic action of sexual misconduct, there are two resultant karmic retributions: First, one will have an ugly and evil wife who is also unchaste. Second, one will be ruined by her.

From the bad karmic action of false speech, there are two resultant karmic retributions: First, one will be slandered by others. Second, one will be cheated and deceived by others.

From the bad karmic action of divisive speech, there are two resultant karmic retributions: First, one will gain a bad following. Second, one will have a following vulnerable to destruction.

From the bad karmic action of harsh speech, there are two resultant karmic retributions: First, one will have to listen to sounds that one loathes. Second, one will be forever embroiled in disputes.

From the bad karmic action of scattered or inappropriate speech, there are two resultant karmic retributions: First, one's words will not be trusted and accepted. Second, one's speech will have neither beginning nor end.

From the bad karmic action of covetousness, there are two resultant karmic retributions: First, one's mind will never know contentment. Second, one will have an abundance of insatiable desires.

From the bad karmic action of ill will, there are two resultant karmic retributions: First, one will be bad-natured. Second, one will delight in tormenting other beings.

From the bad karmic action of maintaining wrong views, there are two resultant karmic retributions: First, one's mind will tend toward flattery and deviousness. Second, one will tend to fall into wrong views.

B. The Bodhisattva's Implementation of Moral Virtue on the Path

1. Cherishing the Dharma and Increasing Kindness and Compassion

Having known the Dharma, one cherishes and delights in it
and one's mind becomes unshakable in the Dharma.
When in the midst of beings,
one's mind of kindness and compassion becomes ever greater.

As for "cherishing the Dharma," one cherishes only the Dharma and sees nothing superior to the Dharma. In this context, "Dharma" refers to the ten courses of good karmic action discussed earlier.

As for "delighting in the Dharma," one delights only in the Dharma and in nothing else.

As for "one's mind remains unshakable in the Dharma," the bodhisattva never abandons the Dharma even when threatened with the loss of his life.

As the bodhisattva practices dharmas such as these, when he is in the midst of other beings, his kindness and compassion toward them become ever greater. Although kindness and compassion do exist on the first ground, their quality therein cannot match their quality as they exist on this ground. This is because he now has a penetrating comprehension of the causes and conditions for karmic offenses and karmic merit.

Beings are pitiable, for they are all under the influence of their own karma and are unable to gain independence from it. This being the case, one's mind then remains free of any thoughts affected by hatred or anger. For one who practices in this way, kindness and compassion do indeed become ever greater. He reflects in this manner:

2. The Motivation to Teach Beings and Cause Them to Enter the Path

Alas! These beings!
They have fallen so very deeply into wrong views.
I must explain right views for them
and thus cause them to gain entry into the path of what is right.

Having gained this penetrating comprehension of the causes and conditions for karmic offenses and karmic merit, the bodhisattva engages in the deep practice of kindness and compassion for all beings, thinking thus:

> Beings are so pitiable. Because they do not know the true character of dharmas, for the most part they engage in false thinking and thus develop all manner of wrong views. It is because of their wrong views that they produce all manner of afflictions, and it is because of their afflictions that then create all sorts of karma. And it is because they produce these karmic causes and conditions that they then turn about in *saṃsāra*'s cycle of births and deaths.
>
> I previously brought forth the resolve to seek *anuttara-samyak-saṃbodhi*. In order to bring about the liberation of beings, I should explain right views for them. I should liberate all of these beings and influence them to enter the true path so that are then caused to attain liberation.

Having reflected thus, one comes to realize that all beings are beset by all manner of afflictions, as described below:

3. The Genesis of a Bodhisattva's Wish to Rescue Beings from Suffering

One contemplates the afflictions they have brought forth
as well as the defilement associated with those afflictions,
all of the different sorts of black and evil karmic actions they do,
and all the diverse sorts of suffering and anguish they undergo.

One bears in mind all of these beings, feeling pity for their plight
and for the many ways in which they have become so deficient.
Having taken up all of these different contemplations,
one realizes, "They are all just as I myself have been."

One then immediately brings forth the mind of compassion
and uses the skillful means of bringing forth a great aspiration:
"Oh, how might I be able to influence these beings
to succeed in extinguishing all their many sufferings?"

Regarding "afflictions" and "defilement associated with those afflictions," "afflictions" refers to any of the dharmas subsumed by the fetters whereas "defilement" refers to [whatever arises from] being "obsessed"[534] [by the afflictions].

[More specifically], those afflictions subsumed by the fetters include greed, hatred, conceit, ignorance, the view of a real self in association with the body [or any of the other four aggregates],[535] extreme views, seizing on views, seizing on unprincipled precepts, wrong views, and doubt. These ten [consisting of three] root and [seven] subsidiary afflictions are distinguished according to their relationship to the three realms of existence and according to whether they are to be severed by directly seeing the [four] truths or whether they are to be severed by meditative cultivation.[536] As a consequence [of these distinctions], there are ninety-eight latent tendencies.[537]

Those not subsumed by the fetters include non-faith, absence of a sense of shame, absence of a dread of blame, flattery, deviousness, restlessness, regretfulness,[538] rigid attachment, indolence, neglectfulness, drowsiness, malice, miserliness, jealousy, arrogance, impatience, and gluttony. These too are distinguished according to their relationship to the three realms of existence and according to whether they are to be severed by directly seeing the [four] truths or whether they are to be severed by meditative cultivation. As a consequence [of these distinctions], there are one hundred and ninety-six obsessive defilements.

There are others who explain "afflictions" as phenomena residing in deep mental dispositions and explain "defilements" as phenomena abiding at a more superficial level of mind.

There are yet others who explain that it is all of the hindrances that constitute "obsessive defilements" whereas all else falls within the sphere of "afflictions."

Regarding "black and evil karmic actions," this refers to those seven courses of karmic action [among the ten courses of bad karmic action] that actually do constitute [physical or verbal] karmic actions together with thought that has come under the influence of covetousness, ill will, or wrong views. These are able to engender painful karmic retributions.

As for "all the different sorts of suffering and anguish," whatsoever bad experiences are undergone by the body correlate with "suffering" whereas whatsoever bad experiences are undergone by the mind correlate with "anguish." Alternatively, one may explain that present-life sufferings are what correlate with "suffering" whereas "anguish" corresponds to later experiences occurring through descent into the wretched destinies.

Regarding "the many ways in which they have become so deficient," "deficiencies" refers here to inadequacies in sense faculties, limbs, or physical bodies, in what is essential to sustain life, or in faith, observance of the moral precepts, or other such meritorious qualities.

Because the remaining lines are easy to interpret in accordance with the verse statements, no further explanation is necessary.

Once one has contemplated in this manner, one realizes:

4. The Vow to Cause 2 Vehicles Practitioners to Enter the Mahāyāna

Beings are ever so pitiable.
For those who have fallen into the Two Vehicles,
I shall make a vow for their sakes
to cause them to dwell in the Great Vehicle.[539]

This circumstance accords with this *Ten Grounds Sutra* wherein Vajragarbha Bodhisattva himself said:[540]

> This bodhisattva abandons the ten courses of bad karmic action while also influencing beings to abide in the ten courses of good karmic action. For the sake of these beings, he strives profoundly to gain the supreme mind, the fine mind, the delighting mind, the pitying mind, the kind and compassionate mind, the beneficial mind, the protective mind, the mind that sees other beings as one's own, the mind that acts as a great teacher, the mind that draws in others, and the mind that accepts others. He thinks:
>
> > All of these beings are so very pitiable. They have fallen into all different sorts of wrong thought and wrong views, and thus travel along in wrong and hazardous paths. I should now influence them to abide in the true path of right views.
> >
> > All these different groups of beings engage in mutual disputation and fighting. They always feel anger toward one another as mutual hatred and torment blaze up between them. This being the case, I should influence them to instead abide in the unsurpassably great kindness.
> >
> > These beings are insatiable, so much so that they covet any advantages enjoyed by others and pursue wrong livelihoods as their means of survival. I should influence them to instead abide in the pure actions of body, speech, and mind.
> >
> > Abiding among causes and conditions associated with greed, hatred, and delusion, these beings are forever generating all the different sorts of afflictions and fetters while never availing themselves of the means whereby they might seek to escape their plight. I should extinguish their sufferings and anguish and influence them to instead abide in the state that is free of sufferings and anguish.

These beings have had their vision obscured by ignorance and thus have wandered into a dense forest of darkness so deeply that they are unable to escape from it by themselves. Having abandoned the light of wisdom, they have strayed into the hazardous and evil path of the various [wrong] views. I should rescue them and cause them then to acquire the eye of unimpeded wisdom. Using this wisdom eye, they will not follow other people, but rather will know all dharmas in accordance with their true character.

These beings have fallen into the long river of births and deaths and are about to descend into the pit of the hell realms, animal realms, hungry ghost realms, and *asura* realms. They are on the verge of falling into the net trap of perversity and deviousness hidden from their view by the weeds of the many different afflictions.

Having no guide, they are not even motivated to escape from their predicament. They claim that the path is not the path and that what is not the path is indeed the path. The minions of Māra, their adversaries, always pursue them. Having no good guide, they obey the ideas of Māra and stray far from the Dharma of the Buddha.

I should cause beings such as these to pass beyond these hazardous and evil roads in the cycle of births and deaths so that they may be able to dwell in the city of all-knowledge that is free of fear and free of decay.

All these beings have become caught and carried along, drifting, in the current of the flood of desire, the flood of existence, the flood of [wrong] views, and the flood of ignorance in which they are pulled under by the great waves of the many different karmic offenses and are submerged in the river of craving. They are swept along by the waves of the cycle of births and deaths, caught in a swirling whirlpool that pulls them around and around in a current from which they cannot escape.

They are drowned and rotted by the salty waves of desirous ideation, hate-filled ideation, and tormenting ideation.[541] They are seized and held by that *rākṣasa* of the view of a real self in association with the body. They enter into the deep woods of the five desires, are seized by the defilements of sensual enjoyments, and are blown about on the high plateau of conceit.

[Beings] are so extremely pitiable. There is no island [of respite] for them, nor do they have any means of rescue. They are stuck in the empty village of the six sense bases from which they are unable to move. There is no one with the skill to take them on beyond. I should now transport all such beings in the sturdy and durable ship of the great compassion and wisdom, taking them to the continent of all-knowledge where they shall become safe, secure, and free of fear.

These beings produce such an abundance of suffering that they are indeed pitiable. They are confined within the prison of birth, death, sorrow, lamentation, suffering, and anguish wherein they are much inclined toward greed, anger, craving, and hatred. They fall into the four inverted views, are harmed by the venomous snakes of the four great elements, are tortured by their five-aggregate enemies, are ensnared by the deceptive thief of sensual enjoyments' defilements, and undergo measureless suffering and anguish in the empty village of the six sense bases.

I should demolish their prison of *saṃsāra* and cause them to attain unimpeded sovereign mastery in the security and bliss of nirvāṇa.

These beings are so extremely pitiable. With such narrow, inferior, and petty minds, they have come to delight in paltry sorts of benefit. They have shrunken back from, fallen away from, and become bereft of the resolve to attain all-knowledge. Even when they do seek a means of escape, they then only delight in the vehicles of *śrāvaka* disciples or *pratyekabuddhas*. I should cause them to gain the truly great resolve by influencing them to delight in the vast and magnificent dharmas of a buddha.

[Next, we have]:

5. The Power of the Precepts and Deep Entry into the Second Ground

If the bodhisattva carries forth his practice in this manner,
he will gain the power arising from upholding the moral precepts.
Having thoroughly known how to bring forth good karmic actions,
he strives to cause them to increase.
If one proceeds thus, he will thereby become a son of the Buddha
and will deeply enter the Ground of Stainlessness.

Regarding "the power arising from upholding the moral precepts," if one is single-minded in purely fulfilling the moral precepts associated with the ten courses of good karmic action, then he will acquire the power derived from cultivating and accumulating merit.

As for the ability "to bring forth good karmic actions," one knows well how to personally bring forth and increase the courses of good karmic action and also knows how to cause other beings to do so as well.

As for his "deeply entering" [the Ground of Stainlessness], his practices become ever more far-reaching to the point that they exhaust its very limits and depths.

As for the term "son of the Buddha," whosoever is able to carry on his practice in accordance with the Dharma is one who is known as "a son of the Buddha."

From the point of its initial arising on the first ground on through to the second ground in which it increases, this bodhisattva should diligently practice vigor in this manner.

6. Reaching the 2nd Ground, the Bodhisattva May See a 1000 Buddhas

When the bodhisattva succeeds in reaching
the boundaries of the Ground of Stainlessness,
he will then be able to see
a hundred or a thousand buddhas.

In discussing the first ground, we already explained the *pratyutpanna* samādhi and the dharmas assisting acquisition of the samādhi in which one sees the buddhas of the present era. Specifically, these included using the thirty-two major marks, eighty secondary characteristics, and forty dharmas exclusive to the Buddhas in practicing mindfulness of the Buddha without having any attachment to any dharma. We also discussed the means to enhance the samādhi and enable the complete development of the powers arising from its fruition.

Question: If, by virtue of having already reached the limits of the first ground, a bodhisattva is able to see the Buddhas, then, on entering the second ground, he should then be able to see the Buddhas. Why then do you now state that, only upon reaching the limits of the second ground, does one, then and only then, see the Buddhas? If that is truly the case, then it must be that one loses this samādhi on first entering the second ground and only then regains it later on.

Response: When first entering the second ground, one still sees the Buddhas and still does not fall back from this samādhi. It is only because you have not well understood the intended meaning of the verse that you have posed this challenge.

In the beginning and middle phases of the second ground, one still only sees a hundred buddhas. It is only when one reaches its very limits that one is then able to see from a hundred up to a thousand buddhas. Once one has seen the Buddhas, one's mind is filled with immense joy. It is because of one's zeal to achieve success in the Buddha's Dharma that one then becomes diligent in practicing vigor.

7. One Makes Offerings to the Buddhas & Receives the 10 Courses Again

One immediately becomes able to use the four requisites
to make offerings to the Buddhas.
He is then able to receive again the ten courses of karmic action
in the abodes of the Buddhas.

"The four requisites" refers to robes, food and drink, bedding, and medicines. One may deduce for himself the meaning of the rest of the verse.

8. Having Received Them Again, One Forever Upholds the Precepts

Having performed acts such as these,
one receives the courses of good karmic action from the Buddhas
and, even throughout a hundred thousand myriads of kalpas,
one never allows his practice to become damaged or lost.

"Never allowing this practice to become damaged" means that one does not allow one's practice of the moral precepts to become scant or weak. One may also say that it is purity in one's endeavors that defines non-damage. "Loss" refers to complete discontinuance of one's practice.

It is in this manner that this bodhisattva has passed through the first ground and entered the second ground. This matter is as described below:

9. One Abandons Miserliness, Practices Giving, & Delights in Precepts

One thoroughly abandons the defilement of miserliness
and delights in the practice of pure giving.
By thoroughly abandoning the defilement of miserliness,
one gains a deep love of purity in upholding the moral precepts.

"Purity" refers to practicing giving with a mind devoted exclusively to goodness, one that is not mixed with any of the afflictions. "Deep love" [of purity in the moral precepts] refers to abiding so solidly in it that one never relinquishes that practice.

On this ground, there are no further residual traces of the defilement associated with miserliness or the defilement associated with breaking precepts. It is because of this that this ground is referred to as "stainless."

The bodhisattva who in this manner remains free of thoughts inclined toward miserliness or the breaking of moral precepts is especially proficient in the practice within the four means of attraction known as "pleasing words" and is also especially proficient in the practice within the six *pāramitās* referred to as "the perfection of moral virtue."

"Proficient" refers here to having engaged in extensive practice whereby one's power in that practice has becomes ever more deeply developed.

C. Śīla Pāramitā's Aspects, Arising, Powers, Purification & Distinctions

Question: If on the second ground one has already acquired strength in one's practice of *śīla pāramitā,* the perfection of moral virtue, now, as one discusses this ground, one should explain the aspects, the arising, the powers, the purification, and the distinctions associated with *śīla pāramitā.*

Response:

In a general discussion of the perfection of *śīla,*
there are sixty-five aspects.
As for its arising, powers, purification, and distinctions,
these are discussed in place after place elsewhere in this treatise.

1. The Sixty-Five Aspects of the Perfection of Moral Virtue

Śīla pāramitā, as a topic of discussion, is measureless and boundless. To speak of it only in general terms, there are sixty-five aspects. As for the other subtopics, in particular the arising of moral virtue, the powers of moral virtue, the purification of moral virtue, and distinctions to be made with regard to moral virtue, these factors are discussed in detail both earlier and later on in this treatise.

[This interpretive approach] is in accordance with the "The Harmonious Dharma of the Buddha" chapter of *The Jeweled Summit Sutra* wherein, in the presence of the Buddha, Akṣayamati Bodhisattva spoke of the sixty-five aspects of *śīla pāramitā,* stating that *śīla* refers to the following: [542]

It is not [physically] tormenting any being;[543]
It is not having any thought of stealing the possessions of others;
It is not being attached to any outward visual forms;
It is not deceiving beings;
Through ensuring the complete unity of retinues, it is not engaging in divisive speech;
Through being well able to patiently endure harsh words [from others], it is being free of harsh speech;
Through always contemplating and evaluating whether one's speech is beneficial, it is being free of scattered or inappropriate speech;
Through delighting in the continued happiness of others, it is being free of covetousness;
Through patiently enduring every sort of suffering, it is being free of ill will;

Through not praising teachers of other paths, it is right view;
Through faith in purification of the mind, it is faith in the Buddha;[544]
Through knowing that the Dharma is genuine, it is faith in the Dharma;
Through delighting in venerating and revering the assemblies of worthies and *āryas*, it is faith in the Sangha;
Through full prostrations, the making of offerings, and other expressions of reverential respect, it is mindfulness of the Buddha;
Through having mental dispositions by which one is fearful of transgressing against even the most minor moral precept, it is moral virtue that does not become diminished or weak;
Through not relying on any of the other vehicles, it is moral virtue that is undamaged;
Through abandoning erroneous practice, it is moral virtue that does not become deficient;
Through the non-arising of evil afflictions, it is moral virtue that does not become admixed [with impure aspects];
Through the most ultimate and constant delight in increasing and strengthening good dharmas, it is moral virtue that remains unsullied;
Through practicing in accordance with one's wishes, it is moral virtue characterized by sovereign mastery;
Through not doing anything criticized by the wise, it is moral virtue that is praised by the Āryas;
Through always abiding in mindfulness guided by stable wisdom, it is easily practiced moral virtue;
Through the complete absence of karmic transgressions in all that one does, it is irreproachable moral virtue;
Through guarding the sense faculties, it is skillfully guarded moral virtue;
Through being one of whom all buddhas are mindful, it is illustrious moral virtue;
Through receiving in proper measure things obtained in accordance with the Dharma,[545] it is moral virtue characterized by but few wants;
Through the severance of covetousness, it is moral virtue that knows contentment;
Through renunciation in both body and mind, it is moral virtue characterized by renunciation;
Through abandoning the many sorts of boisterous speech, it is moral virtue appropriate to a forest hermitage;

Through having no need to look to anyone else in the hope of obtaining anything, it is moral virtue perfectly complete in the lineage bases of the Āryas;

Through being one who possesses roots of goodness, it is moral virtue characterized by refined practice of the *dhūta* austerities;

Through [its efficacy in bringing about] rebirth among humans and devas, it is moral virtue characterized by practice consistent with the manner in which it has been taught;

Through devotion to rescuing all beings, it is moral virtue characterized by kindness;[546]

Through enduring every sort of suffering, it is moral virtue characterized by compassion;

Through resolve that does not retreat and sink away, it is moral virtue characterized by joy;

Through abandoning both hatred and affection, it is moral virtue characterized by equanimity;

Through subduing the mind, it is moral virtue marked by seeing one's own faults;

Through protecting the minds of others, it is unerring moral virtue;

Through skillfully guarding the precepts, it is moral virtue that is well restrained.;[547]

Through devotion to the ripening of beings, it is moral virtue characterized by giving;

Through having nothing for which one wishes, it is moral virtue characterized by patience;

Through not desisting and withdrawing from endeavors, it is moral virtue characterized by vigor;

Through accumulating the dharmas assisting *dhyāna*, it is moral virtue characterized by *dhyāna*;

Through insatiable pursuit of abundant learning and roots of goodness, it is moral virtue characterized by wisdom;

Through gaining wisdom from abundant learning, it is moral virtue that seeks abundant learning;

Through accumulating the dharmas that assist the seven limbs of enlightenment, it is moral virtue that draws close to good spiritual guides;

Through relinquishing erroneous paths, it is moral virtue characterized by the abandonment of bad spiritual guides;

Through contemplating impermanence, it is moral virtue characterized by non-attachment to the body;

Through diligently accumulating roots of goodness, it is moral virtue characterized by not trusting [in the durability of] one's life;

Through purity in one's resolute intentions, it is moral virtue characterized by freedom from regrets;
Through purity in one's actions, it is moral virtue that is not false;
Through resolute intentions that are free of defilement, it is moral virtue that is free of heat;
Through skillfulness in initiating karmic actions, it is moral virtue that is free of sorrow;
Through not elevating oneself [above others], it is moral virtue that is free of conceit;
Through abandoning defiled desires, it is moral virtue that does not indulge frivolous restlessness;
Through maintaining a straightforward mind, it is moral virtue that does not elevate oneself [above others];
Through maintaining a well-regulated mind, it is moral virtue possessed of a sense of shame;
Through not bringing forth evil thoughts, it is moral virtue trained in goodness;
Through extinguishing all afflictions, it is moral virtue characterized by quiescence;
Through practicing in accordance with [the original] explanations, it is moral virtue that follows what has been taught;
Through practicing the dharmas constituting the four means of attraction, it is moral virtue characterized by the transformative teaching of beings;
Through not erring in [the practice of] one's own dharma, it is moral virtue that protects the Dharma;
Through [maintaining one's] fundamental purity, it is moral virtue in which all vows are fulfilled;
Through dedicating [one's merit] to realization of the unsurpassed path, it is moral virtue that leads to acquiring the dharmas of the Buddha;
Through maintaining a mind of uniformly equal regard for all beings, it is moral virtue that leads to acquiring the Buddha's samādhis.

Venerable Śāriputra, as for these sixty-five aspects [of the perfection of *śīla*], [were one to exhaustively list them], the aspects of all bodhisattva's pure moral virtue would be endlessly numerous.

2. The Arising of the Moral Precepts

Now, as for the arising of the moral precepts, this is a matter discussed in place after place [elsewhere in this treatise].

Briefly stated, there are eight categories involved in the arising of the moral precepts, four arising from association with the body and four arising from association with speech. Those arising from association with the body are the abandonment of taking life, the abandonment of inflicting torment and suffering on beings, the abandonment of stealing, and the abandonment of sexual misconduct. Those associated with the mouth are the abandonment of lying, divisive speech, harsh speech, and scattered or inappropriate speech. These are the eight.

These eight categories of moral precepts arise by taking them on [as ongoing obligations]. These dharmas associated with taking them on, when separately distinguished in terms of taking them on physically, taking them on verbally, and taking them on mentally result in a combined total of twenty-four subcategories. When further considered in terms of the twenty-four associated with [the injunction against] instructing others [to commit any of these transgressions], the twenty-four associated with [the injunction against] rejoicing in [transgressions directly committed by others], and the twenty-four associated with [the injunction against] carrying them out oneself, this results in a total of ninety-six, all of which occur in connection with the desire realm.

These [moral precepts] arise commencing with this very day and night. How is this the case? After the initial mental moment of taking on [the obligation imposed by the moral precept] has expired, throughout the entire day and night, during the second [and all subsequent] mental moments thereafter [the force of that moral precept] constantly arises.

One's use of the associated merit is also just the same. How is this the case? After the initial mind-moment associated with an act of giving expires, beginning with the second mind-moment, as one uses [this merit], it is constantly produced.[548] This is the nature of the process as it occurs in association with good physical karmic actions.

There are those [instances of the arising of the moral precepts] that are subsumed within the ten courses of good karmic action and those that are not subsumed therein. This is the situation as it occurs in connection with the desire realm.

As for those [instances of the arising of moral precepts] that occur in connection with the form realm, there are two kinds: first, those [moral precepts] arising from association with the body, and second, those [moral precepts] arising from association with speech. As for those arising from association with the body, this refers to the abandonment of karmic offenses not subsumed among the ten courses of bad karmic action.[549]

In the case of those [moral precepts] arising from association with speech, this refers to the abandonment of scattered or inappropriate speech.[550] Taking on this moral precept involves taking it on physically, taking it on verbally, and taking it on mentally. Taking all of these categories into account, this amounts to two times three, a subtotal of six.

Similarly, there are thus also another six associated with the injunction against instructing others [to carry out any given karmic transgression], another six associated with [the injunction against] rejoicing [in transgressions committed by others], and another six associated with [the injunction against] carrying out [any given transgression] oneself. This yields in total four times six, for a net total of twenty-four. When these are added to the previously cited ninety-six, this brings the grand total to one hundred and twenty.

In much the same fashion, moral precepts also arise in association with the character of one's actions. Thus there is also an arising of moral precepts at the time one attains the realization of the path and there is also an arising of moral precepts at the time one retreats from the path. So too, there may also be an arising of moral precepts in association with one's first taking on birth.

Because this subject [of the arising of moral precepts] is so very expansive in its scope, we now only present this condensed explanation.

3. The Powers of the Moral Precepts

As for the powers associated with the moral precepts, as growth occurs in the corresponding *pāramitā,* one's practice of moral virtue becomes ever stronger. Also, in direct correlation with whichever of the grounds one has entered, there will also be a corresponding enhancement in the solidity of one's practice of moral virtue and hence also in the powers associated with it.

4. The Purification of the Moral Precepts

As for the purification of the moral precepts, not damaging or destroying moral precepts, not allowing deficiencies or diminishment in their practice, and so forth—these are all just as previously explained.

Additionally, the characteristic features of purity or impurity in one's practice of moral virtue correspond to their treatment in the dharma of the seven types of brahmacarya.[551] As related in the sutras, it is by virtue of seven manifestations of sexual desire[552] that the moral virtue [of one who practices *brahmacarya*] is impure, namely:

First, although one may indeed have cut off sexual relations, with a defiled mind, one might nonetheless still accept either bathing or massage performed by a woman;

Second, with a defiled mind, one might smell the perfume of a woman, engage in conversation with her, or participate in mutual joking with her;

Third, with a defiled mind, one might engage in mutual gazing with her;

Fourth, even though there might be a physical barrier separating one from a woman, with a defiled mind, he might still listen to her voice;

Fifth, one might have earlier talked and joked with a woman and later, even though separate from her, he might still recall that experience, being unable to let it go;

Sixth, one has restricted oneself from sexual relations [only] for a particular period of time, after which one will indulge in it again later on;[553]

Seventh, someone might temporarily cut off all sexual relations, doing so hoping that he will thereby be reborn in the heavens and enjoy sexual pleasures there together with celestial maidens while also gaining wealth and pleasure in future lives.

Therefore, [in cases such as these, even though] one has cut off sexual relations, these are still instances of impurity [in moral virtue]. Apart from these seven types of situations, [the practice of *brahmacarya*] does constitute purity in the practice of moral virtue.

5. Distinctions in the Moral Precepts

Regarding distinctions in moral virtue, a twofold distinction consists of, first, that characterized by the presence of the contaminants, and second, that characterized by the absence of the contaminants.

A threefold distinction consists of that connected with the desire realm, that connected with the form realm, and that with no connections [anywhere in the three realms].

A fourfold distinction consists of two types of right speech and right karmic action subsumed within right livelihood together with a different two types of right speech and right karmic action not subsumed within right livelihood.

A fivefold distinction consists of the common person's moral virtue, a bodhisattva's moral virtue, a *śrāvaka* disciple's moral virtue, a *pratyekabuddha's* moral virtue, and the unsurpassable moral virtue of a buddha.

A sixfold distinction consists of:

First, desire realm [moral virtue] of body and speech subsumed within right livelihood;

Second, [desire realm moral virtue of body and speech] not subsumable within right livelihood;

Third, form realm [moral virtue] of body and speech subsumed within right livelihood;

Fourth, [form realm moral virtue of body and speech] not subsumable within right livelihood;

Fifth, [moral virtue] of body and speech that is free of the contaminants and which is subsumed within right livelihood;

Sixth, [moral virtue of body and speech that is free of the contaminants] but not subsumed within right livelihood.

A seven-fold distinction consists of the seven [physical and verbal] courses of good karmic action.

An eightfold distinction consists of the previously-mentioned eight [types of arising of moral virtue] consisting of those four associated with the body and those four associated with speech.

A ninefold distinction consists of the seven [physical and verbal] courses of good karmic action in addition to the twofold distinction [according to presence or absence of the contaminants] cited earlier.

A tenfold distinction consists of three types of moral virtue associated with the path, three types of antidotal moral virtue, and three types of simple moral virtue. These nine types are all free of the contaminants. With the addition of moral virtue involving the contaminants, the total number of types comes to ten.

So it is that we have all these many different categories of moral virtue.

D. The Essential Constituents of Śīla (Moral Virtue)

1. Q: Does Moral Virtue Consist Only of Good Actions of Body & Speech?

Question: The Śrāvaka Disciple Vehicle claims that karmic actions of body and speech are the bases of *śīla,* moral virtue. Where these two consist of good karmic actions, they are deemed to be good. Where these two consist of bad karmic actions, they are deemed to be bad. Thus they hold that good karmic actions of body and speech constitute [the practice of] *śīla*. Does this treatise take these to constitute *śīla* or does it instead take *śīla* to involve some other additional factor?

2. A: No, There Are Other Factors Integral to Moral Virtue

Response:

It is not merely karmic actions of body and speech
that constitute *śīla*.
Cultivation, close personal engagement, and delight in practice
also constitute what is meant by *śīla*.

These three factors each contribute to the meaning of this single concept: cultivation, close personal engagement, and delight in practice.

3. The Supreme Cultivation of Moral Virtue

a. Q: Please Explain the Bases of Supreme Cultivation of Moral Virtue

Question: If one takes cultivation, close personal engagement, and delight in practice as [also] determining what is meant by *śīla*, then all dharmas could be considered as associated with *śīla*. How so? Because they may all be associated with constant cultivation, close personal engagement, and delight in practice. Therefore, you should explain what constitutes the supreme cultivation of *śīla*.

b. A: No "I," No "Mine," No Elaboration, and Inapprehensibility

Response:

If it is based on the nonexistence of "I" and "mine,"
the renunciation of conceptual elaboration,
and realizes nothing at all is apprehensible as [inherently existent],
then this is what is meant by *śīla*.

If one does not know the true character of all inward and outward dharmas, then, because one may generate arrogance and clinging attachment due to one's attachment to *śīla*, one may thereby open the door to all sorts of karmic offenses.

Therefore, if one does not perceive any self among the inward dharmas, does not perceive anything belonging to a self among the outward dharmas, if one realizes that all these inward and outward dharmas are ultimately empty and devoid of anything that is apprehensible, and if one also refrains from conceptual elaboration seizing on any characteristics in what is ultimately empty, then this is what constitutes the supreme [practice of] *śīla*.

And why is this so? In *śīla* such as this, there is not even the slightest mental error, how much the less could there be any [error in the actions] of either body or speech? Therefore, the Buddhas and the Bodhisattvas are those who are foremost in their ability to practice *śīla*, for they do not apprehend any [inherent existence] in any dharma. This is what constitutes the supreme practice of *śīla*. As related in the *Kāśyapa Sutra*, the Buddha told Kāśyapa:[554]

c. Scriptural Descriptions of Supreme Cultivation of Moral Virtue

Śīla refers to the nonexistence of self, to the nonexistence of nonself, to the nonexistence of doing, to the nonexistence of anything that is done, to the nonexistence of a doer, to the nonexistence of practice, to the nonexistence of non-practice, to the nonexistence of name, to the nonexistence of form, to the nonexistence of characteristics, and to the nonexistence of the absence of characteristics. There is neither goodness nor non-goodness. There is neither quiescent cessation nor nonexistence of quiescent cessation. There is no grasping and no relinquishing. There are no beings and no causes and conditions for the existence of any being. There is no body, no speech, and no mind, no world, no worldly dharmas, no reliance on the world. There is no elevation of oneself by virtue of one's *śīla*, no belittling of others because of [their absence of] *śīla*, no development of overweening pride because of one's *śīla*, and no distinguishing between this one and that one because of *śīla*.

Kāśyapa, this is what constitutes the *śīla* of all worthies and *āryas*, the *śīla* that has gone beyond the three realms, that is free of all contaminants, and that retains no connections [anywhere within the three realms].

This also accords with Akṣayamati Bodhisattva's statement to Śāriputra in the chapter on *śīla*:[555]

Śīla refers to not making any discriminating assertion claiming the existence of any being. One does not claim that any self exists, does not claim that anyone possessed of a soul or anyone possessed of a life exists. One does not claim that there is any person, does not claim that there is anyone who has been raised up, does not claim that there is any form aggregate or any feeling, perception, formative-factor, or consciousness aggregate. One does not claim that there exists any earth element or any water, fire, or wind element;

Śīla refers to not discriminating the existence of any eye characteristic, to not discriminating the existence of any visual form characteristic, to not discriminating the existence of any ear characteristic, any sound characteristic, any nose characteristic, any smell characteristic, any tongue characteristic, any flavor characteristic, any body characteristic, any characteristic of tangible objects, any mind characteristic, or any characteristic of dharmas as objects of mind;

Śīla refers to not discriminating the existence of body, speech, or mind;

Because *śīla* involves maintaining a focused mind, it is therefore characterized by single-mindedness;

Because it involves skillful selection among dharmas, it is therefore characterized by wisdom;

Śīla refers to arriving at emptiness, to reaching the ultimate limit of signlessness that does not involve any admixture with the three realms of existence, and to wishlessness, non-arising, and the unproduced dharmas patience;

Śīla refers to not coming forth from the past, not going forth to the future, and not abiding between them, either;

Śīla refers to not dwelling in the conjunction of mind faculty, mind consciousness, and thoughts [as objects of mind];

Śīla refers to not relying on the desire realm, to not relying on the form realm, and to not relying on the formless realm;

Śīla refers to abandoning the dust of greed, to ridding oneself of the defilement of hatred, to extinguishing the darkness of ignorance, to not falling into either eternalism or annihilationism, and to not contradicting production as characterized by [the conjunction of] multiple conditions;

Śīla refers to abandoning the conception of a self, to relinquishing the conception of anything belonging to a self, and to not dwelling in the view of a real self in association with the body;

Śīla refers to not being attached to designations and characteristics being incompatible with name-and-form;[556]

Śīla refers to not being under the direction of any of the fetters;

[*Śīla* refers to] not being overpowered by any of the obsessions;

[*Śīla* refers to] not abiding in any of the hindering doubts or regrets;

Śīla refers to not abiding in roots of bad action associated with greed, to transcending roots of bad action associated with hatred, and to severing roots of bad action associated with delusion;

Śīla refers to the happiness of the delighted mind free of anxiety and free of mental fever;

Śīla refers to not destroying the Dharma body, this through not severing the lineage of the Buddhas, to not severing the lineage of the Dharma, this through not making discriminations regarding the nature of dharmas, and to not severing the lineage of the Sangha, this through being characterized by [cultivation of] the unconditioned.[557]

Śāriputra, this is what is meant by the supreme and unsurpassed *śīla* of bodhisattvas. *Śīla* of this sort is inexhaustible. With the sole additional exception of the Buddhas, *śīla* [as practiced by all others] is in every case exhaustible.

This is as stated herein:

d. The Inexhaustibility of the Bodhisattvas' Moral Virtue

Beginning with the *śīla* of the common person
and ending with that practiced by a *pratyekabuddha*,
all of these are characterized by exhaustibility.
It is only that of bodhisattvas that is inexhaustible.

Even though all of the *śīla* practice coming forth from the common person results in their long-enduring enjoyment of its karmic fruits, it is all finally completely exhausted. Even all *śīla* ever practiced by all arhats and *pratyekabuddhas* is finally exhausted as well.

However, because the bodhisattva's practice of *śīla* is based on the realization of the nonexistence of a self or anything belonging to a self, on the abandonment of the idea that any dharma can be apprehended at all, and on the extinguishing of all conceptual elaboration, it is therefore utterly inexhaustible. This is as described by Akṣayamati Bodhisattva in the chapter on *śīla:*[558]

> Because [the karmic fruits of] the *śīla* practiced by common people come to an end in accordance with the stations of rebirth into which they are reborn, [the karmic fruits of] their *śīla* become exhausted. Because the five spiritual powers acquired by non-Buddhist practitioners come to an end when they regress, [the karmic fruits of] their *śīla* become exhausted. Because [the karmic fruits of] the ten courses of good karmic action as practiced by humans are exhaustible, [the karmic fruits of] their *śīla* become exhausted
>
> Because the merit of the devas in the desire realm is exhaustible, [the karmic fruits of] their *śīla* become exhausted. Because the four *dhyāna*s and the four immeasurable minds as practiced by devas in the form realm are exhaustible, [the karmic fruits of] their *śīla* become exhausted. Because the stations into which the devas of the formless realm may be reborn in accordance with their meditative absorptions are exhaustible, [the karmic fruits of] their *śīla* become exhausted.
>
> Because learners and those beyond learning [in the Śrāvaka Disciple Vehicle] come to an end with their entry into nirvāṇa, [the karmic fruits of] their *śīla* are exhaustible. Because the *pratyekabuddhas* do not possess the great compassion, [the karmic fruits of] their *śīla* are exhaustible.
>
> Venerable Śāriputra, only the *śīla* of bodhisattvas is inexhaustible. Why? It is from the bodhisattva's practice of *śīla* that there emerge all the different manifestations of *śīla*. Because those karmic causes are inexhaustible, the associated karmic fruits are also inexhaustible. Because the *śīla* of bodhisattvas is inexhaustible, the *śīla* of the Tathāgatas is also inexhaustible. As a consequence, the *śīla* as practiced by all these great men is inexhaustible.

4. A Clarification Regarding Aspects versus Essence of Moral Virtue

Question: When you explained the more general aspects of *śīla*, you spoke of sixty-five different aspects of *śīla* [*pāramitā*] and stated that, among *śrāvaka* disciples, there are eight kinds of *śīla*, four arising in association with the body and four arising in association with speech. How is there no contradiction between these [two different ways of enumerating the types of *śila*]?

Response: They are not mutually contradictory. How is this so?

> Although [those aspects] are not the very essence of *śīla*,
> because they are beneficial, they are referred to as its aspects.

> As for those eight kinds of physical and verbal karmic actions,
> those do constitute the essence of *śīla*.

Although those sixty-five aspects do not constitute the very essence of *śīla*, because they are nonetheless beneficial to those eight relatively coarse categories of physical and verbal *śīla*, they are therefore referred to as aspects of *śīla*. In general, whatever is able to be of benefit [to this practice] is regarded as an aspect [of *śīla*]. This is analogous to the custom of referring to all the [monarch's] elephants, horses, feather fans, and canopies as aspects of kingship. Consequently, although the *dhyāna* absorptions, wisdom, and so forth are not themselves the very essence of *śīla*, because they are beneficial to the practice of *śīla*, they too are regarded as aspects of *śīla*.

The End of Chapter Thirty-One

Chapter 32
An Explanation of the Dhūta Austerities

XXXII. Chapter 32: An Explanation of the Dhūta Austerities

A. Having Seen 10 Benefits, Wear Correct Robes and Go on Alms Round

The bodhisattva practices the dharma of *śīla* in this way:[559]

> Having observed its ten benefits, one should wear
> the two and six types of robes in accordance with that dharma.
> Additionally, due to having observed its ten benefits,
> one should obtain food on the alms round for one's entire life.

Wishing to completely fulfill the practice of upholding the various categories of moral precepts and having observed that there are ten associated benefits from doing so, one should take up the practice of wearing the two types and the six types of robes. What are those ten benefits? They are:

1. The Ten Benefits of the Appropriate Robes

First, because this assists a sense of shame and a dread of blame;

Second, because this allows one to protect oneself from cold, heat, mosquitoes, horseflies, and poisonous insects;

Third, because this displays the proper deportment of a *śramaṇa;*

Fourth, because, whenever devas or humans lay eyes on the Dharma robes, they are moved to respect and veneration comparable to what they would feel when coming upon a stupa or temple;

Fifth, because one wears the dyed robes with the mind of renunciation and not out of some desire to wear what is considered fine;

Sixth, because one wears the robes to accord with the ideal of quiescence and not to be ablaze with the fire of afflictions.

Seventh, because when one wears the Dharma robes, if there is something bad in one's character, this is easy for others to observe.

Eighth, because when one wears the Dharma robes, one requires no additional adornments;

Ninth, because in wearing the Dharma robes, one acts in accordance with the eightfold path of the Āryas;

Tenth, because I should be vigorous in practice of the path, I should not wear the *kaṣāya* robes for even a moment during which I am beset with defiled thoughts.

Having observed these ten benefits, one should wear the two types of robes: First, robes contributed by a householder. Second, cast-off robes.

As for the six types of robes, they are: First, *kārpāsa* (cotton) cloth robes. Second, *kṣaumā* (linen) cloth robes. Third, *kauśeya* (silk) cloth robes. Fourth, animal hair robes. Fifth, red hemp robes. Sixth, white hemp robes.

2. The Ten Benefits of Obtaining One's Food from the Alms Round

As for, "having observed its ten benefits, one should obtain food on the alms round for one's entire life," [those ten benefits are]:

First, that what I obtain [on the alms round] is able to sustain my life is my own responsibility and no one else's;[560]

Second, [having reflected], "May those beings who provide me with food be caused to find refuge in the Three Jewels," one may then go ahead and eat;

Third, [one reflects], "Whenever someone provides me with food, I should bring forth a thought of compassion for them and resolve to be diligent in practicing vigor so they may abide well in their practice of giving." Having reflected thus, one may then eat;

Fourth, this is a practice that accords with the instructions of the Buddha;

Fifth, one is easily satisfied and easily nourished through this practice.

Sixth, one practices a dharma that crushes potential arrogance;

Seventh, this practice plants roots of goodness for gaining the invisible summit mark [of a buddha's body];

Eighth, by observing the practice of obtaining food on the alms round, others engaged in the cultivation of good dharmas will emulate my practice;

Ninth, through this practice one refrains from forming close ties with particular men or women, whether old or young;

Tenth, by practicing the strictly sequential method of obtaining food on the alms round, one develops a mind of uniformly equal regard for all beings that assists the acquisition of the knowledge of all modes.

B. Dwelling in a Forest Hermitage

1. To Derive the Benefits of Dhūta Practice, Do Not Accept Invitations

Although the Buddha did permit accepting invitations for meals,
if one wishes to provide for one's own benefit
while also benefiting other people,
one should not accept invitations for meals.

"One's own benefit" refers here to the ability to perfect [the cultivation of] all the *pāramitās*. "Benefiting others" refers here to teaching beings in such a way that one induces them to abide in [accordance with] the

Three Jewels. A practitioner who acts accordingly will benefit himself while also benefiting others.

2. Having Observed Ten Benefits, Remain in Solitude with 3 Exceptions

Because one has observed its ten benefits,
one never abandons residing in a solitary wilderness dwelling.
In order to visit and console the sick, to listen to Dharma,
or to provide teachings, one may then go to a temple.

For the bhikshu who has taken up the practice of dwelling in a forest hermitage, although it may increase many different sorts of meritorious qualities, generally speaking, it is due to seeing ten benefits from this that, for the rest of his life, he should never abandon this practice. What are the ten benefits? They are as follows:

3. The Ten Benefits of Dwelling in Solitude in Forest Hermitage

First, one retains complete freedom to come and go at will;
Second, one thus easily does away with conceptions of "I" and "mine";
Third, there is nothing to impede one's dwelling wherever one wishes;
Fourth, one's mind increasingly delights in forest hermitage practice;
Fifth, one's dwelling place conduces to but few wants and few responsibilities;
Sixth, for the sake of perfecting the meritorious qualities, one should give up any selfish cherishing for his own body or life;[561]
Seventh, one departs far from the boisterous chatter of the crowds;
Eighth, even though one's practice is [devoted to perfecting] the meritorious qualities, one seeks no kindness in return;
Ninth, it becomes easy to achieve single-mindedness in accordance with one's cultivation of *dhyāna* concentration;
Tenth, through abiding in a solitary wilderness location, one easily develops unimpeded reflections.[562]

4. When Leaving, One Should Maintain the Perception of Emptiness

As for coming to the temple to visit and console the sick or for the other above-mentioned reasons:

If there are situations where, for particular reasons,
one comes and abides at the stupa or temple,
Still, in every such situation,
one never abandons one's perception of emptiness and serenity.

Although a bhikshu may have taken on the dharma of lifetime forest hermitage dwelling, if situations emerge involving particular causes and conditions, he may then go and enter the stupa or temple, for the

Dharma of the Buddha has both exceptions and restrictions in such cases. In this respect, it is not like the non-Buddhist approaches to forest hermitage dwelling. [This practice] is defined by always delighting in abiding in an empty and serenely quiet place. Hence one never relinquishes the perception of all dharmas as empty. This is because the very essence of all dharmas is that they are all ultimately empty [of any inherent existence of their own].

5. Ten Reasons a Forest Dweller Might Come to a Temple or Stupa

Question: What are the reasons for which one might come to the stupa or temple?

Response:

First, to provide for the care of the sick;
Second, to seek medical supplies to treat one's own sickness;
Third, for one who is sick to search for a physician to treat his illness;
Fourth, to teach the Dharma to the sick;
Fifth, to teach the Dharma to the other bhikshus;
Sixth, to listen to teachings on Dharma;
Seventh, in order to pay respects and make offerings to greatly virtuous monastics;
Eighth, in order to provide for the needs of the Ārya Sangha;
Ninth, to study and recite profound scriptures;
Tenth, to instruct others in the study of profound scriptures.

There are reasons such as these that justify coming to the stupa or temple.

6. The Forest Dweller's Vigorous Cultivation of Right Dharma

One is vigorous in cultivating the various types of thought
as one accords with the dharma of the forest hermitage.
The bhikshu who has been residing
in a forest hermitage abode

should always be vigorous and diligent in bringing forth
the many different good dharmas,
in great courageousness in one's resolve to realize nonself,
and in extinguishing every sort of fear.

Regarding the application of vigor in a forest hermitage, this is exemplified by the bhikshu who, because he has cut off covetousness and does not cherish his body, life, or offerings, always strives with diligence and vigor both day and night as, for his entire life,[563] he accords with forest hermitage practice, doing so with the same urgency one would feel in putting out a fire in one's own turban.

As for "[cultivating the various types of] thought," this refers to the thought of renunciation, the thought of non-ill will, and the thought of nonharming as well as to the other types of wholesome thought.[564]

Then again, this also refers to:

Cultivating mindfulness of the Buddha as the possessor of right and universal knowledge and as the most revered among all beings;

Cultivating mindfulness of the Buddha's Dharma as well spoken;

Cultivating mindfulness of his Sangha of disciples as according with right practice [of the path].

Furthermore, cultivating thought appropriate to dwelling in a forest hermitage refers as well to cultivating all of the various contemplative ideation that accords with emptiness, that accords with signlessness, and that accords with wishlessness.

Additionally, this refers to contemplative thought accordant with the four supreme bases [for the development of meritorious qualities] and concordant with the six *pāramitās*.

These are the various sorts of thought that are accordant with the dharma for abiding in a forest hermitage.

Then again, this is similar to what the Buddha told Ugra, the Elder, when explaining the bodhisattva path practices of both laity and monastics:[565]

7. Scriptural Citation on the Correct Purposes of a Forest Dweller

If a monastic bodhisattva takes on the dharma of forest hermitage practice, he should reflect in this manner:

> "Why am I choosing to abide in a forest hermitage setting? It is not solely because I abide in a forest hermitage setting that I qualify as a *śramaṇa*, for there are many sorts of beings who abide in a forest hermitage setting. Mostly inclined toward evil and not toward goodness, they do not guard the sense faculties, do not cultivate with vigor, and do not cultivate the good dharmas. Take for example the musk deer, monkeys, the many sorts of birds, evil bandits, *caṇḍālas*, and other such people, none of whom are bhikshus. So, for what purpose am I choosing to abide in a forest hermitage setting?"
>
> One must indeed accomplish one's purpose. Elder, what sorts of things constitute one's purpose? [They include the following]:
>
> 1) So that one's thoughts will not be scattered;
> 2) To acquire [consummate practice of] the *dhāraṇis*;
> 3) To cultivate the mind of kindness;
> 4) To cultivate the mind of compassion;
> 5) To abide with sovereign mastery in the five types of spiritual superknowledges;

6) To completely fulfill the practice of the six *pāramitās*;
7) To avoid abandoning the resolve to realize all-knowledge;
8) To cultivate the knowledge of skillful means;
9) To attract beings [into the Dharma];
10) To facilitate beings' success [in cultivating the path];
11) To avoid abandoning the four means of attraction;
12) To become ever mindful of the six objects of mindfulness;[566]
13) To avoid abandoning vigor in the acquisition of extensive learning;
14) To engage in correct contemplative analysis of dharmas;
15) To practice in accordance with right liberation;
16) To achieve the realization of the fruits [of the path];
17) To abide in the right and definite position (*samyaktva-niyāma*);
18) To preserve and protect the Buddha's Dharma;
19) To abide in right views through faith in karmic retributions;
20) To abide in right intentional thought through abandoning all recollective and discriminating thought;
21) To abide in right speech through teaching Dharma for beings in accordance with their own resolute beliefs;
22) To abide in right action through acting in ways that extinguish [bad] karma;
23) To abide in right livelihood through extinguishing affliction driven habitual karmic propensities;
24) To abide in right effort through striving for the attainment of the unsurpassed path;
25) To abide in right mindfulness through contemplation of dharmas that are not false;
26) To abide in right meditative concentration through the attainment of comprehensive wisdom;
27) To not be frightened by emptiness;
28) To not be made fearful by signlessness;
29) To not be overwhelmed by wishlessness;
30) To be guided by wisdom in taking on one's bodies;
31) To rely on the meaning, not merely on the words;
32) To rely on wisdom, not merely on consciousness;
33) To rely on sutras of ultimate meaning, not on sutras whose meaning is non-ultimate;
34) To rely on Dharma, not on persons.

Elder, it is [purposes] such as these that constitute the beneficial endeavors that the renunciant bodhisattva bhikshu should bring forth.

8. The Appropriate Dharmas of a Forest Dweller

As for "according with the dharma of the forest hermitage," this refers to cultivation of the four *dhyānas*, the four immeasurable minds, the heavenly ear, the heavenly eye, cognition of others' thoughts, cognition of past lives, the spiritual superknowledges, and so forth.

9. The Means for Extinguishing Fear

As for "extinguishing every sort of fear," there are three reasons for this practitioner's ability to extinguish fear:

First, because he sees that dharmas are characterized by nonexistence of self and the nonexistence of anything belonging to a self, he is therefore able to dispel fear;

Second, because he has the power of skillful means;

Third, because he has the power of mental courage, he is able to dispel fear.

Regarding this matter of "seeing the nonexistence of self and the nonexistence of anything belonging to a self," this is just as presented earlier, in the [third chapter's] treatment of the first ground, where ridding oneself of five kinds of fear was discussed.[567]

As for "the power of skillful means," in this treatise, it is mindfulness that rightly reflects upon karma and its retributions that constitutes the power of skillful means. One should reflect in this way:

All of the great kings may be deep in their palaces where their security is ensured by the fourfold elephant, cavalry, chariot, and infantry battalions that surround and serve them. Even so, once the karmic causes and conditions sustaining their rule finally come to an end, even they are compelled to undergo all of the different events that eventually bring about their ruin and anguish.

Also, in the case of those who are protected by the causes and conditions of their karmic actions, even though they might travel a hazardous road, sail far out onto the waters of the great sea, or walk amidst the ranks of battling armies, they will still remain entirely safe and free of any personal calamities.

Given the karmic causes and conditions established in my previous lives, no matter whether I reside in the village or in a forest hermitage, I will still definitely be compelled to undergo its karmic retribution.

Having contemplated matters in this way, one thereby succeeds in extinguishing fear. Furthermore, one thinks:

If, to protect myself, I choose to go forth into the city or village, thus abandoning this living in a forest hermitage, there will be nothing

> there that is able to exceed the protection afforded me by good physical karmic actions, good verbal karmic actions, and good mental karmic actions.

This is just as told to King Prasenajit by the Buddha himself when he said:[568]

> If a person practices good physical karmic actions, practices good verbal karmic actions, and practices good mental karmic actions, this is what affords a person the best personal protection. Were this person to claim of himself, "I am hereby well protected," this would indeed be a proclamation of the truth.
>
> Great King, even though this man would not be surrounded and guarded by the fourfold battalions of the army, he can still be regarded as being well protected. And why is this so? It is because this form of protection is inward protection, not mere outward protection.

[Thus one may be moved to reflect]:

> Therefore I do in fact qualify as personally well protected by virtue of my practice of good physical karmic actions, good verbal karmic actions, and good mental karmic actions.

One may additionally reflect thus:

> All of these birds, beasts, snakes, and such that abide in the vicinity of this forest hermitage—even without practicing good physical karmic actions, good verbal karmic actions, or good mental karmic actions, they are free of fear due to dwelling far from the village. How could one as knowledgeable as I fail to even match [the fearlessness of] these birds, beasts, and other creatures?

Through reflecting in these various ways, one does away with all of one's fears.

Additionally, by resorting to mindfulness of the Buddha, one can dispel all fear-inducing circumstances that may arise in a forest hermitage. As is stated in a sutra:[569]

> When any of you bhikshus are dwelling in a forest hermitage setting, whether beneath a tree, or in some empty building, it could happen that you might be overcome with fear, even to the point that your heart sinks and your hair stands on end. At just that very point, you should become mindful of me [by my ten names]: the Thus Come One (*tathāgata*), Worthy of Offerings (*arhat*), of Right and Universal Enlightenment (*samyak-saṃbuddha*), Perfect in the Clear Knowledges and Conduct (*vidyā-caraṇa-saṃpanna*), the Well Gone One (*sugata*), the Knower of the Worlds (*lokavid*), the Unsurpassed Tamer of Those to

be Tamed (*anuttara-puruṣa-damya-sārathi*), the Teacher of Devas and Humans (*śāstā-deva-manuṣyāṇām*), the Enlightened One (*buddha*), the World Honored One (*bhagavat*). When you become mindful in this way, your fear will immediately disappear.

As for "great courageousness," this refers to possessing resolve that is not timid or weak and which is decisive in seeking the path. This is as described here:

The bhikshu who abides in the wilderness
should draw upon the power of courageous resolve
to extinguish all fears,
being mindful of the Buddha as the one who is fearless.

In a case where someone has created karma
and fears that he will be unable to escape [its retribution],
even if he is not fearful, he will still not escape it.
Hence, if one is fearful, then one loses his rightful benefit.

Thus, if one realizes that he cannot avoid it,
and yet allows this to destroy other benefits one might achieve,
then one thereby involves himself in the affairs of petty men
and engages in behavior a bhikshu should never adopt.

If one is to have something that one fears,
then one should instead fear *saṃsāra*.
All the various forms of fear
have this cycle of births and deaths as their cause.

Therefore, one who practices the path
wishing to gain liberation from *saṃsāra*
while also rescuing others
should not give rise to fear.

As stated by the Buddha in *The Sutra on Abandoning Fear* when discussing the dharma of fearfulness:[570]

In an instance where a *śramaṇa* or brahman is abiding in a forest hermitage, he should reflect as follows: "It is because of impure physical karma, because of impure verbal karma, because of impure mental karma, because of thoughts devoted to what is impure, because of elevating self and diminishing others, because of an indolent mind, because of false recollective thinking, because of an unconcentrated mind, and because of one's delusions that one is overcome by fear. And it is because of the very opposite qualities consisting of purity of physical karma and so forth that one then becomes free of fear."

Additionally, for the sake of Ugra, the Elder, the Buddha said:[571]

The monastic bodhisattva who resides in a forest hermitage should reflect thus: "For what purpose am I here?"

He should then immediately realize, "It is because of a desire to abandon fear that I have come here. Fear of what? It is fear of the many sorts of befuddling disturbances, fear of the chattering of crowds, fear of greed, hatred, and delusion, fear of arrogance, fear of anger and hostility, fear of jealousy over offerings received by others, fear of visual forms, sounds, smells, tastes, touchables, fear of the *māra* of the five aggregates, fear of all circumstances involving delusion-induced obstacles, fear of untimely speech, fear of claiming to have seen what one has not seen, fear of claiming to have heard what one has not heard, fear of claiming to have awakened when one has not yet awakened, fear of claiming to know what one does not know, fear of the *śramaṇa*'s defilements, fear of mutual detestation, fear of all the places of rebirth throughout the desire realm, the form realm, and the formless realm, and fear of falling into the hell realms, the animal realms, the hungry ghost realms, or any of the other difficulties.[572] To state it briefly, it is because of fear of all evil and unwholesome dharmas that I have come to abide here.

"If one lives as a householder, delights in its many sorts of commotion, does not cultivate the path, and abides in wrong thought, he will not be able to achieve emancipation from such points of fear as these.

"There were the bodhisattvas of the past, all of whom resided in a forest hermitage, abandoned all fears, reached the state of fearlessness, and gained all-knowledge. So too, all bodhisattvas of the future shall also dwell in a forest hermitage, abandon all fears, and gain all-knowledge. All of the bodhisattvas of the present also undertake the practice of residing in a forest hermitage and thereby abandon all fears, reach the station of fearlessness, and gain all-knowledge.

"Therefore, given that I fear all of these sorts of bad circumstances, in order to transcend all fears, I too should take up the practice of abiding in a forest hermitage dwelling.

"Furthermore, all fears arise due to attachment to a self, due to affection for and acceptance of a self, due to the conception of a self, due to the perception of a self, due to esteeming a self, due to discriminations conceiving of a self, and due to protection of a self.

"Were I to take up the practice of abiding in a forest hermitage dwelling but still fail to abandon this attachment to a self, then this would amount to abiding in a forest hermitage in vain."

Furthermore, Elder, whosoever perceives that there is anything at all that is apprehensible [as inherently existent] does not truly reside in a forest hermitage. Whosoever abides in the conception of a self or anything belonging to a self does not truly reside in a forest hermitage. Whosoever abides in thoughts affected by the inverted views does not truly abide in a forest hermitage.

> Elder, so it goes even up to the point that, not even one who conceives of nirvāṇa [as inherently existent] truly abides in a forest hermitage, how much the less could it be that someone who conceives of afflictions [as inherently existent] truly abides in a forest hermitage.
>
> Elder, just as the grass and trees in the vicinity of a forest hermitage are entirely free of fear, so too is the bodhisattva. When abiding in a forest hermitage, one should envision oneself as like the grass and trees, envision oneself as like stones or tiles, envision oneself as like a reflection in a pool of water, and envision oneself as like an image in a mirror. One should imagine speech to be echoes and should imagine one's thoughts to be like magical illusions. In any of this, who is it that could possibly be frightened? And who is it that could be struck with fear?

The bodhisattva then undertakes right contemplation of the body, observing the nonexistence of self and the nonexistence of anything belonging to a self. He observes that there is no being, no one possessed of a soul, no one possessed of a life, no one who has been raised up, no one identifiable as male, no one identifiable as female, no knower, and no perceiver.

Fear itself is but a product of false discriminations. Thus one reflects: "Then I should not simply follow along with false discriminations."

In just this way, the bodhisattva should be just like the grass or trees as he abides in a forest hermitage. He should also be aware that all dharmas are also just like this.

It is the cutting off of all forms of struggle and disputation that truly qualifies as abiding within a forest hermitage. It is the nonexistence of self, the nonexistence of anything belonging to a self, and the not belonging to anything at all that truly qualify as the bases of abiding in a forest hermitage.

One should not delight in the many sorts of noisy dwelling places of either householders or monastics. The Buddhas do not permit a bhikshu dwelling in a forest hermitage to abide together with either a householder or a monastic.

10. Four Cases in Which a Forest Dweller May Gather with Others

Question: Did the Buddha forbid one to gather together with anyone else in the community?

Response: No. He did not.

> The Buddha permitted meeting with others in four circumstances
> but did not permit it otherwise.
> Therefore one should draw near [to others] in those situations,
> while still abiding well apart in other circumstances.

Thus the bodhisattva who abides in a forest hermitage is permitted to join in four types of assemblies. Specifically, he may enter assemblies gathered to hear the teaching of Dharma, may enter assemblies to teach beings, may enter assemblies to make offerings to the buddha, and may enter assemblies gathered to prevent abandoning the resolve to gain all-knowledge.

Therefore one is only permitted to gather together with others in these four circumstances. [The bhikshu dwelling in a forest hermitage] should not draw near to others in other circumstances.

11. The Aspects Defining Hermitage Dwelling Approved by the Buddhas

Additionally, the bodhisattva should reflect in this manner: "How should I establishing a forest hermitage dwelling that is closely adherent to those permitted by all buddhas? Could it perhaps be that this is not actually a forest hermitage dwelling and that I merely suppose it to be a forest hermitage dwelling? Could I perhaps be mistaken about the meaning of this?"

Question: What then are the aspects of a forest hermitage dwelling that a bodhisattva should know?[573]

Response: In the sutras, thc Buddha himself declared:

> Abiding in a forest hermitage refers to not abiding in any dharma, to not taking refuge in any of the sense objects, to not seizing on any mark of any dharma, and to not coveting any visual forms, sounds, smells, tastes, or tangible objects;
>
> Abiding in a forest hermitage refers to dwelling in a manner wherein one has nothing upon which one relies, this because [one realizes that] all dharmas are uniformly equal;
>
> Dwelling in a forest hermitage refers to abiding in a manner free of contradictions because of the goodness of one's own mind;
>
> Dwelling in a forest hermitage refers to dwelling in a manner whereby one relinquishes all the burdens and abides in delighted happiness;
>
> Dwelling in a forest hermitage refers to abiding in a manner whereby one becomes liberated from all afflictions and one becomes free of all fears;
>
> Dwelling in a forest hermitage refers to dwelling in a manner whereby one crosses beyond the floods;[574]
>
> Dwelling in a forest hermitage refers to abiding in the lineage bases of the Āryas;[575]
>
> Dwelling in a forest hermitage refers to being satisfied with what one obtains in the course of things;
>
> Dwelling in a forest hermitage refers to dwelling in way that one is easily satisfied, easily supported, and inclined to but few wants;

Dwelling in a forest hermitage refers to abiding in a manner whereby one achieves the fulfillment of wisdom;

Dwelling in a forest hermitage refers to abiding in a manner whereby one rightly practices [what one has acquired through] extensive learning;

Dwelling in a forest hermitage refers to directly manifest realization of the emptiness, signlessness, and wishlessness gates to liberation;

Dwelling in a forest hermitage refers to abiding in a manner wherein one severs all the bonds and gains liberation;

Dwelling in a forest hermitage refers to abiding in a manner that accords with the twelvefold chain of causation;

Dwelling in a forest hermitage refers to abiding in a manner whereby one reaches the state of ultimate quiescence in which one has already done what is to be done;

Dwelling in a forest hermitage refers to abiding in a manner compliant with all classes of moral precepts, compliant with all types of practice assisting acquisition of the meditative absorptions, compliant with all types of practice beneficial to wisdom, compliant with all types of practice that facilitate easy achievement of liberation, compliant with all classes of practice facilitating easy acquisition of the knowledge and vision of liberation, compliant with whatever practices facilitate easy practice of the dharmas conducive to realization of bodhi, and compliant with whatever is able to conduce to accumulating all meritorious qualities associated with the *dhūta* austerities;

Dwelling in a forest hermitage refers to achieving a penetrating comprehension of the truths;

Dwelling in a forest hermitage refers to seeing and knowing the aggregates;

Dwelling in a forest hermitage refers to [realizing that] the nature of all things is identical to the nature of dharmas;[576]

Dwelling in a forest hermitage refers to abandoning the twelve sense bases;

Dwelling in a forest hermitage refers to never forgetting one's resolve to attain bodhi;

Dwelling in a forest hermitage refers to contemplating emptiness without being frightened by it;

Dwelling in a forest hermitage refers to being able to protect and preserve the Buddha's Dharma;

Dwelling in a forest hermitage refers to [practicing in a manner whereby] one who seeks liberation does not err with regard to the the meritorious qualities;

Dwelling in a forest hermitage refers to [practicing in a manner whereby], if one is a person capable of gaining all-knowledge, he will thus achieve increased benefit.

12. Hermitage Dwelling as a Means to Fulfill the Six Perfections

If a bodhisattva dwelling in a forest hermitage is able to practice in this way, he will swiftly achieve complete fulfillment of the six perfections. How might this be so?

If a bodhisattva abiding in a forest hermitage does not have a selfish cherishing even for his own body or life, this is the practice of *dāna pāramitā,* the perfection of patience;
If he maintains purity in the three kinds of good karmic actions and enters the refined practice of the *dhūta* austerities, this is the practice of *śīla pāramitā,* the perfection of moral virtue;
If he does not generate any hatred toward any other beings but rather extends a mind of universally inclusive kindness to all of them, and if he only accepts and delights in the vehicle of all-knowledge and no other vehicle, this is the practice of *kṣānti pāramitā,* the perfection of patience;
If he makes the solemn personal vow to abide in a forest hermitage and never leave this place so long as he has not yet rightly realized the [unproduced] dharmas patience, this is the practice of *vīrya pāramitā,* the perfection of vigor;
If, having gained the *dhyāna* absorptions, his cultivation of roots of goodness is not done with an eye toward taking rebirth in the stations of rebirth to which they correspond,[577] this is the practice of *dhyāna pāramitā,* the perfection of *dhyāna* meditation;
If one's person and the forest hermitage have become of the same suchness, if one's person and bodhi have become of the same suchness, and if these are all indistinguishable from ultimate reality, this is the practice of *prajñā-pāramitā,* the perfection of wisdom.

13. The Buddha's Four Prerequisite Dharmas for Hermitage Dwelling

The Buddha permitted those possessed of four dharmas
to abide in a forest hermitage.

What then are those four dharmas? As the Buddha told [Ugra], the Elder, they are:

First, extensive learning;
Second, thorough knowledge of the definitive meaning;
Third, delight in the cultivation of right mindfulness;
Fourth, practice accordant with the manner in which [the Dharma] was taught.

People of this sort should take up the practice of dwelling in a forest hermitage.

14. Other Bodhisattvas for Whom Hermitage Dwelling Is Beneficial

Additionally, there are bodhisattvas whose afflictions are deep and dense. If such a person abides in the midst of noisy crowds, he will bring forth yet more afflictions. Therefore he should dwell in a forest hermitage in order to subdue afflictions.

Then again, there are bodhisattvas who have acquired the five spiritual superknowledges. Because these practitioners may wish to teach devas, dragons, *yakṣas,* or *gandharvas* and assist their success [on the path], they should dwell in a forest hermitage.

Yet again, there are bodhisattvas who think thus: "Dwelling in a forest hermitage is the circumstance praised and permitted by all buddhas."

Moreover, dwelling in a forest hermitage assists the fulfillment of all good dharmas and increases roots of goodness. Afterward, one may then enter the village and teach Dharma for the welfare of beings. If one's intention is to develop such meritorious qualities, one may then dwell in a forest hermitage.

Also:

15. Four Fourfold Dharmas for the Forest Dweller

In the Sutra of the Resolute King,
The Buddha told Ānanda:
"The bhikshu who dwells in a forest hermitage
should dwell in four fourfold dharmas."

A bodhisattva who wishes to abide in a forest hermitage [may do so for these purposes]:

First, to depart far from both laypeople and monastics;
Second, out of a wish to study and recite profound scriptures;
Third, as a means of leading forth other beings, thereby influencing them to develop the meritorious qualities arising from dwelling in a forest hermitage;
Fourth, to engage in uninterrupted day and night practice of mindfulness of the Buddha.

There are another four dharmas:

First, one does not generate a thought of hatred toward other beings even for the duration of a finger snap;
Second, one should not allow drowsiness to blanket one's mind even for the briefest moment;

Third, one should not conceive of [an inherently existent] being even for the briefest moment;

Fourth, one should not forget one's resolve to attain bodhi even for the briefest moment.

There are yet four more dharmas:

First, one should always engage in quiet sitting [meditation] and refrain from joining together with groups;

Second, one should always delight in meditative walking;

Third, one always contemplates all dharmas without any conception of their being either new or old;

Fourth, one should never depart from the profound dharmas of emptiness, signlessness, and wishlessness.

Again, there are four additional dharmas:

First, one cultivates the four *dhyānas* but does not cultivate worldly *dhyāna* meditation. Thus, in one's cultivation of the four immeasurable minds, one brings forth thoughts of compassion focusing on beings as the objective condition, but without seizing on any mark [of the existence] of any being;

Second, although one cultivates the [immeasurable] mind of kindness, one does not perceive any [inherently existent] being as the object. Although one cultivates the [immeasurable] mind of sympathetic joy, one does not crave happiness [for oneself]. And, although one cultivates the [immeasurable] mind of equanimity, one never forsakes any being;

Third, although one may perceive oneself as compliant with the four lineage bases of the Āryas, one does not take that as a basis for elevating oneself and looking down on others;

Fourth, one personally engages in the accumulation of extensive learning while also practicing in accordance with what one has learned.

These are the [four sets of] four dharmas [as presented in that scripture]. There is an additional related topic, as below:

16. The Bad Results of Forest Dwelling without Wisdom and Vigor

One who has no wisdom and has no vigor
and yet dwells alone in an isolated place
then acquires four dharmas
and also acquires yet another four dharmas.
He also encounters three additional situations.
Circumstances such as these are as described by the Buddha.

Of all the meritorious qualities, the bhikshu who dwells in a forest hermitage should diligently cultivate these, [namely wisdom and vigor]. Why? Because, of all the meritorious qualities associated with a forest hermitage, it is these two factors that are able to generate all of the [other] meritorious qualities.

If a bhikshu were instead to give into delusion and indolence while abiding in a forest hermitage, he will acquire four wrong dharmas:

First, he will spend much of his time sleeping;
Second, he will become much inclined to want offerings;
Third, he will take advantage of these [special] circumstances[578] to pretend to be extraordinary;
Fourth, he will become unhappy with dwelling in a forest hermitage.

He will also acquire four additional dharmas:

First, he will develop overweening pride due to which he will think he has already attained what he has not yet attained;
Second, he will come to abhor profound scriptures;
Third, he will ruin [his ability to realize] the dharmas of emptiness, signlessness, and wishlessness;
Fourth, his mind will generate hatred for those who uphold the profound scriptures.

There are three additional circumstances that might occur. If he abides in a forest hermitage while failing in vigor and having no wisdom, he may meet some woman and fall into behavior contrary to the Dharma due to which he either becomes a ruined member of the Sangha, commits a grave offense, or transgresses against the moral precepts and returns to lay life.[579] These are the three.

C. Additional Discussions of the Dhūta Austerities

There are additional related topics, as below:

Extensive discussion of dharmas practiced in solitary wilderness life
as well as the dharmas associated with the alms round
and the virtues of practicing the other ten *dhūta* austerities—
all of these should also be extensively explained.

In the course of the preceding discussion, we have presented an extensive explanation of two of the twelve *dhūta* austerities.[580] The meritorious qualities of the other ten *dhūta* austerities should be similarly understood. How so? This is because these two practices have served to open the door into the other ten *dhūta* austerities. Thus the others may now be easily understood. As for those other ten *dhūta* austerities, they are:

1. A Listing and Brief Discussion of The Other Ten Dhūta Austerities

First, wearing robes made [only] of cast-off rags;
Second, [taking one's daily meal in but] a single sitting;
Third, always sitting, [even when sleeping];
Fourth, having taken the meal, not accepting food or drink at the wrong times;
Fifth, possessing only a single three-part set of robes;
Sixth, wearing an animal-hair robe;
Seventh, laying out one's sitting mat wherever one happens to be.
Eighth, dwelling at the foot of a tree;
Ninth, dwelling out in the open;
Tenth, dwelling in a charnel field.

"Cast-off rag robes" refers to those that have been thrown away by others. After having accepted them, one then wears them. "Accepting" refers here to either mental or verbal assent.

"In but a single sitting" refers to taking one's meal at the first place one accepted it and then refraining from taking any further food [for that entire day].

"Always sitting" means one never lies down, even at night.

"After the meal, refraining from any beverages" refers to not accepting any beverage at the wrong time,[581] not even those made merely with crystalized sugar or other nutritional substances.

"Possessing only the single set of three robes" means one only accepts that single set of three robes and does not collect any other clothing whatsoever.

"Wearing an animal-hair robe" refers to wearing an animal-hair robe made of cloth woven from coarse animal hairs such as felt cloth or *kambala* (wool) cloth.

"Laying out one's sitting mat wherever one happens to be" refers to simply going along with whatever sitting spot is available that does not involve causing someone else to get up and move.

"Dwelling at the foot of a tree" refers to delighting in dwelling out beneath the trees, never going into a sheltered location.

"Dwelling out in the open" simply refers to living out on the open ground.

"Dwelling in a charnel field" refers to always spending the night in the area where the dead bodies are cast off in order to accord with the mind of renunciation.

This is what is meant by the twelve *dhūta* austerities that facilitate purity in the observance of the moral precepts.

2. The Benefits of the Other Ten Dhūta Austerities

a. The Ten Benefits of Wearing Cast-Off Robes

There are ten benefits from wearing cast-off rag robes, namely:

First, one does not have to mix with the laity simply to acquire robes;
Second, one need not appear to solicit robes simply to acquire clothing;
Third, nor is one compelled to present the appearance of finding some expedient to discuss obtaining robes;
Fourth, one is not compelled to go off and search in the four directions in order to obtain robes;
Fifth, even if one does not obtain a robe, one is still free of distress;
Sixth, even if one does obtain a robe, one is not elated;
Seventh, worthless material is easily come by in a way that does not risk committing transgressions;
Eighth, this practice accords with the initially received explanation of the methods for obtaining the four requisites;[582]
Ninth, one thereby becomes just another one of those who wear coarse [and common] clothing;
Tenth, one thereby avoids becoming the object of others' covetousness.

b. The Ten Benefits of Taking One's Single Meal in a Single Sitting

[Taking one's meal in but] a single sitting also has ten benefits, as follows:

First, one does not experience the weariness and inconvenience of going off in search of a second meal;
Second, as a consequence, one accepts but little [food];
Third, there is none of the weariness and inconvenience entailed by what one would consume [by compelling others to provide additional meals];
Fourth, one is spared the weariness and inconvenience of readying oneself [for an additional meal];
Fifth, one adopts an approach to eating that is consistent with more refined practice;
Sixth, one eats only after one's previous meal has been entirely digested;
Seventh, one devotes less effort to fending off difficulties [associated with obtaining food];
Eighth, one has fewer illnesses;
Ninth, one's body feels lighter and more at ease;
Tenth, one's experience of the body is pleasant.

c. The Ten Benefits of Always Sitting and Never Lying Down

Always sitting [and never lying down to sleep] also has ten benefits, as follows:[583]

First, one does not seek physical pleasure;
Second, one does not seek pleasure from sleeping;
Third, one does seek pleasure from [good] bedding;
Fourth, one is spared the aches associated with lying down on a sleeping mat;
Fifth, one does not pursue physical desires;
Sixth, it becomes easy to achieve success in sitting in *dhyāna* meditation;
Seventh, it becomes easy to study and recite scriptures;
Eighth, one spends less time sleeping;
Ninth, one's body feels light and rises easily;
Tenth, one devotes but little mental effort to seeking sitting cushions, bedding, and clothing;

d. The Ten Benefits of Not Accepting Food at the Wrong Time

There are also ten benefits of refraining from accepting food or drink at the wrong time,[584] after one has already eaten, as follows:

First, one thereby avoids excessive eating;
Second, one does not become full when eating;
Third, one avoids desire for fine flavors;
Fourth, one has fewer things one otherwise desires;
Fifth, one has fewer interfering difficulties;
Sixth, one has fewer illnesses;
Seventh, one easily feels full;
Eighth, one is easily supported;
Ninth, one is easily satisfied;
Tenth, one's body remains free of weariness when sitting in *dhyāna* meditation or studying scriptures.

e. The Ten Benefits of Possessing Only One Three-Part Set of Robes

Possessing only the single three-part set of robes also has ten benefits, as follows:

First, one is spared the weariness and inconvenience associated with seeking robes beyond the single three-part set of robes;
Second, one is spared the weariness and inconvenience of storing and protecting [additional clothing];
Third, one collects fewer things;
Fourth, one is satisfied with whatever one is wearing;
Fifth, this refines one's practice of the moral precepts;

Sixth, one remains free of encumbrances when traveling;
Seventh, one's body feels lighter and more at ease;
Eighth, this practice accords with standards of practice for dwelling in a forest hermitage;
Ninth, no matter where one goes, one has nothing that one treasures;
Tenth, one's practice accords with the path.

f. The Ten Benefits of Accepting Robes Woven from Animal Hair

Accepting robes made of animal hair also has ten benefits, as follows:

First, one is a wearer of coarse clothes;
Second, one seeks but little;
Third, one can sit down anywhere;
Fourth, one can lie down anywhere;
Fifth, it is easy to wash;
Sixth, it is easy to dye;
Seventh, it is seldom ruined by insects;
Eighth, it is difficult to ruin;
Ninth, one has no need of any additional clothing;
Tenth, one does not neglect one's pursuit of the path.

g. The Ten Benefits of Laying out One's Sitting Mat Wherever One Is

Laying out one's sitting mat wherever one happens to be also has ten benefits, as follows:

First, one is spared the weariness and difficulty of seeking out a good monastic dwelling in which to live;
Second, one is spared the weariness and difficulty of seeking out a good seat and bed;
Third, one avoids aggravating those of senior monastic rank;
Fourth, one gives no cause for distress to those of junior monastic rank;
Fifth, one has few wants;
Sixth, one has few tasks;
Seventh, one uses whatever is available in the course of things;
Eighth, since one uses but little, one has but few responsibilities;
Ninth, one avoids the creation of causes or conditions for disputes;
Tenth, one avoids appropriating a spot used by someone else.

h. The Ten Benefits of Dwelling beneath a Tree

Dwelling beneath a tree also has ten benefits, as follows:

First, one is spared the weariness and inconvenience of seeking out a sheltered dwelling;

Second, one is spared the weariness and inconvenience of seeking lodging;[585]

Third, one is spared the weariness and inconvenience of indulging one's own preferences;

Fourth, one is spared the weariness and inconvenience of appropriating things for one's own use;

Fifth, one does not even have an address;

Sixth, one has no disputes;

Seventh, one complies with the dharma regulating the four necessities;

Eighth, one uses but little, uses only what is easily obtained, and avoids transgressions;

Ninth, one accords with correct cultivation of the path;

Tenth, one need not practice amidst the noisiness of groups.

i. The Ten Benefits of Dwelling in a Charnel Field

Dwelling in a charnel field also has ten benefits, as follows:

First, one is always acquiring the perception of impermanence; Second, one is always acquiring the perception of death;

Third, one is always acquiring the perception of the unloveliness [of the body];

Fourth, one is always acquiring the perception of the unenjoyability of all worldly existence;

Fifth, one is always developing renunciation of all who are dear to oneself;

Sixth, one is always attaining the mind of compassion;

Seventh, one abandons all frivolous restlessness;

Eighth, one's mind always abides in renunciation;

Ninth, one remains diligent in the cultivation of vigor;

Tenth, one is able to dispel all fears.

j. The Ten Benefits of Dwelling out in the Open

Dwelling out in the open also has ten benefits, as follows:

First, one does not have to find a tree to dwell beneath;

Second, one abandons everything one owns;

Third, one remains free of disputes;

Fourth, when going elsewhere, one has nothing one treasures;

Fifth, one seldom indulges frivolous restlessness;

Sixth, one is able to endure wind, rain, cold, heat, mosquitoes, horseflies, poisonous insects, and such;

Seventh, one remains unpierced by the thorn of noise;[586]

Eighth, one avoids arousing the hatred of other beings;

Ninth, one is himself also able to enjoy freedom from sorrow and hostility;

Tenth, one is able to avoid places frequented by noisy crowds;

3. Additional Discussion of Matters Related to Hermitage Dwelling

As explained for the five types of solitary wilderness dweller,
just so understand correctness in the other meritorious qualities.
In instances where one is to study, recite, or teach others,
one may leave one's solitary wilderness dwelling.

a. Five Types of Monks Who Dwell in a Forest Hermitage

There are five distinct categories of bhikshus who dwell in a forest hermitage, namely:

First, there are those who, with evil intentions, seek gain and offerings;

Second, there are those who practice in a forest hermitage because of their own stupidity and dull faculties;

Third, there are those who establish a forest hermitage because they are insane, deluded, or deranged;

Fourth, there are those who establish a forest hermitage in order to practice the *dhūta* austerities;

Fifth, there are those who establish a forest hermitage because it is a practice praised by all buddhas, bodhisattvas, worthies, and *āryas*.

Of these five categories of forest hermitage dwellers, those taking up the practice in order to cultivate the *dhūta* austerities and those taking up the practice because it has been praised by all buddhas, bodhisattvas, worthies, and *āryas* are both good, whereas the other three may be reprimanded.

Just as with this fivefold distinction among those dwelling in a forest hermitage, so too should one distinguish and know [the differences among] the practitioners of the other eleven *dhūta* austerities.

b. Additional Discussion of When One May Leave a Hermitage

Question: The Buddha said that whosoever has taken up the practice of dwelling in a forest hermitage should never abandon it. If there are extenuating circumstances, is it or is it not permissible to abandon it?

Response:

One may leave one's forest hermitage
in order to study or recite scriptures.

If a bhikshu wishes to receive others' teachings on the study or recitation of the Dharma of the scriptures, or, alternatively, if he wishes to instruct others in such study or recitation, he may leave his forest hermitage and come into the stupa or temple. It is permissible to leave for these purposes.

1) Proper Motivation When Leaving the Forest Hermitage

When teaching others in study and recitation,
one should not do so wishing to attract offerings or support.
Rather, one should immediately bring to mind the Buddha, [thinking],
"Even[587] the Buddha had endeavors he was intent on accomplishing."

When one emerges from his isolated forest hermitage to teach others in study and recitation, one should not do so seeking to attract respect or offerings of support. Rather, one should bring to mind the Buddha, thinking, "If even the Buddha[588] had endeavors he was intent on accomplishing, how much the more should this be so for someone like me?"

"Bringing to mind the Buddha" in this context refers to recalling that the Buddha is the Tathāgata, the One of Right and Universal Enlightenment, one to whom even the devas, dragons, spirits, *gandharvas, asuras, garudas, kinnaras, mahoragas,* Śakra, ruler of the devas, the Four Heavenly Kings, humans, and nonhumans all make offerings, one who serves as the unsurpassable field of merit for all beings. [One recalls that] not even he seeks offerings or support from anyone. He just continues on in devotion to the endeavors he has taken up. [Thus one reflects]: "Now I am one who still does not know anything, one who is just a beginner in the training. How then could I be worthy to receive anyone's offerings?"

Additionally, one should reflect as follows:

2) Generating the Motivation to Benefit Both Self and Others

I am the one who should be devoted
to making offerings to all beings,
for, rather than expecting them to make offerings,
I should be benefiting myself while also benefiting others.

What then is meant by "benefiting oneself"? If one esteems the receiving of offerings [from others], then he loses the merit that would otherwise arise through giving the gift of Dharma. If, on the other hand, one refrains from esteeming the receiving of offerings, then one may acquire the meritorious qualities arising from giving the Dharma to others.

What then is meant by "benefiting others"? If one esteems others' offerings and then teaches them to study and recite scriptures, they will then think, "The teacher instructs us only in order to gain worldly benefit for himself and not for the sake of the Dharma." If someone makes offerings to his spiritual teacher when under the influence of these sorts of thoughts, he will not reap a great amount of merit. If, on the other hand, he were to feel profound esteem for the teacher solely out of reverence for the Dharma, he would acquire an immense amount of merit. This is what constitutes "benefiting others."

> In one's striving to acquire wisdom from others,
> one should not cherish even one's own body or life.

If the practitioner wishes to seek wisdom from others, he should then be willing even to sacrifice his own body and life in this quest. "Sacrifice" means that, for the sake of acquiring wisdom, one is so diligent, vigorous, and reverently respectful of his spiritual teacher that he does not even cherish his own body and life.

c. On the Importance of Revering One's Spiritual Teacher

Question: Why should one, in striving for wisdom, revere the spiritual teacher even to the point that one does not even cherish one's own body and life?

1) On the Difficulty of Repaying the Kindness of One's Teacher

Response:

> If every one of his words and every one of his thoughts
> were to be accorded that very number of kalpas
> during which one might bow in reverence to the spiritual teacher
> able to teach this treatise,
>
> as one also took care to avoid any flattering or devious thought,
> and, suffused with deep affection, [bowed in] reverence to him
> day and night without cease, [one should indeed wish to do so],
> continuing on even to the end of just such a number of kalpas.

[If one allotted a number of kalpas of devotion] corresponding to however many words are in the treatises taught by one's spiritual teacher in addition to however many thoughts he used in providing that instruction, and if the mind of the beneficiary of the teachings remained entirely free of any flattery and deviousness in his demonstrations of reverence performed without cherishing his own body and life, and if he carried on with that reverence day and night with earnestness that remained undiminished from beginning to end—although one might indeed carry through with just such devotion, one still would be unable to adequately repay the kindness of the spiritual teacher's benefiting one with the wisdom of this treatise.

2) On Maintaining the Proper Attitude toward One's Teacher

The disciple should therefore abandon any thoughts of flattery or deviousness, should not selfishly cherish his own body and life, and should crush any arrogance. Even were the teacher to slight him, his thoughts of reverence and affectionate regard should remain undiminished. Rather, he should bring forth thoughts of deep affection for him, should bring forth the most profoundly sincere reverence for him, should think of the spiritual teacher as he would his own parents, should think of him as a great teaching master, should think of him as his good spiritual guide, should think of him as someone able to do what is most difficult, and should realize that [the teacher's kindness] is something difficult to ever adequately repay.

3) On Taking Direction from One's Teacher

If one's spiritual teacher has already permitted them, then one should take up the tasks one usually does, for one does not need the teacher's [additional] permission to do so. If there are other tasks that arise, then one is to consult the teacher for his opinion, whereupon one performs the tasks accordingly. Thus one should also cherish and esteem whatever one's teacher cherishes and esteems.

4) On Not Seeking Praise or Benefit in Relating to a Teacher

One must not seek to reap any worldly advantage from one's relationship with one's spiritual teacher. One must not seek the teacher's praise and must also not seek name and fame [on account of that relationship]. Rather, one should seek only to obtain the Dharma jewel of wisdom.

5) On Making the Teacher's Good Qualities Well Known

In the event the teacher makes some mistake, one should allow it to always remain a private matter. If the teacher has committed some infraction and it has come to light, one should use some expedient to conceal it.

One should proclaim and make widely known the meritorious qualities possessed by one's teacher while also sincerely delighting in listening to, accepting, upholding, comprehending, contemplating, and practicing in accord with the import of his teachings.

6) On the Need to Become a Good Lineage-Preserving Disciple

As for striving to "benefit oneself and also benefit others," one must not become a mere straw disciple, must not become a disastrous disciple,[589] must not become a defiled disciple, must not become a disciple who allows [the lineage to go to] ruin, and must not become a useless disciple. One must not allow oneself to fall into any such transgressions as these.

i) Scriptural Instructions on Right Behavior toward Teachers

One must abide solely within the dharma appropriate to a good disciple. One should make offerings to one's spiritual teacher. This is as described in *The Pratyutpanna [Samādhi] Sūtra* in which the Buddha told Bhadrapāla:

> If a bodhisattva wishes to acquire this samādhi, he should be diligent and vigorous in bringing forth thoughts of reverential esteem toward all his teachers, thoughts recognizing the rare good fortune to encounter them. In the case of those from whom one has received teachings personally spoken by them or those from whom one has obtained volumes of scriptural texts, one should express deeply sincere reverence for these teachers, regarding them as one would one's own parents, regarding them as one's good spiritual guides, and regarding them as great teaching masters. This is because they are able to teach Dharma such as this which is able to assist one's realization of bodhi.
>
> Bhadrapāla, whether one strives to follow in the bodhisattva path or one seeks the way of a *śrāvaka* disciple, if one were to fail to bring forth thoughts of deep reverence for the teacher as the source of one's becoming able to study and recite this Dharma, if one were to fail to think of one's teacher as one would one's own parents, regarding him as one's good spiritual guide, and regarding him as a great teaching master, it would then be impossible for one to correctly understand[590] this Dharma in such a way that it would not perish but rather would abide for a long time without disappearing.
>
> Why is this? Bhadrapāla, it is because of just such failure to accord reverence that the Buddha's Dharma disappears.
>
> Therefore, Bhadrapāla, whether one strives to follow in the bodhisattva path or one seeks the way of a *śrāvaka* disciple, were one to bring forth thoughts of reverential respect for whoever one heard this Dharma from and whoever was the source of one's being able to study, recite, or write out this Dharma, bringing forth thoughts regarding him as one would one's own parents, regarding him as one's good spiritual guide, and regarding him as a great master of the teachings—if one were able to do that, then it is indeed possible that whatsoever one has studied, recited, and written out, and whatsoever one had not obtained but has now obtained might now be able to remain [in this world] for a long time.
>
> And why is this? Because it is due to having a mind of reverential respect that the Buddha's Dharma does not disappear. Therefore,

Bhadrapāla, I am now telling you: One must bring forth thoughts of profound reverential respect toward teachers such as this, bringing forth thoughts regarding them as one would one's own parents, regarding them as good spiritual guides, and regarding them as great masters of the teachings. This being so, one is to comply with what I have herein instructed.

The End of Chapter Thirty-Two

Chapter 33
Aids to Gaining the Fruits of Śīla

XXXIII. Chapter 33: Aids to Gaining the Fruits of Śīla

A. On the Purification of Śīla, Moral Virtue

In order to pursue extensive learning and then practice in accord with the way it was taught after understanding the meaning of that extensive learning, a bodhisattva such as this becomes able to purify his practice of *śīla*. Thus one should cultivate the dharmas used to purify one's practice of *śīla* (moral virtue).

1. Four Dharmas Enabling Purification of Moral Virtue

Question: Which dharmas are able to purify one's practice of *śīla*?

Response:

Guard the actions of body, speech, and mind
while also not apprehending any dharma by which one guards it.
Never permit any admixture of the view of a self
or any of the other views.
Dedicate the merit from this to the attainment of all-knowledge.
These four methods purify one's practice of *śīla*.

If the practitioner cultivates these four dharmas, his observance of *śīla* will naturally become pure. "Guarding the actions of body, speech, and mind" refers to always using right mindfulness in one's physical, verbal, and mental actions even to the point that one does not allow oneself to err through committing even the most minor transgressions, acting in this like the tortoise who always takes such care in guarding his head and feet.

Because this practitioner deeply delights in emptiness, in his comprehension of the supreme meaning, he does not even apprehend [the existence of] any dharma by which one guards the three types of actions. There are others who, although they do indeed perceive the emptiness of dharmas, they are still of the opinion that the knower of emptiness remains [as an existent entity]. It is for this reason that [the verse] says, "Never permit any admixture of the view imputing a self," the view of a being, the view of a person, the view of a soul, the view of a life,[591] or the view of a knower.

"Dedicating [merit to the realization of] all-knowledge" means one does not dedicate the merit arising from upholding the moral precepts to any other sort of fortunate result, but rather only dedicates it to the liberation of all beings through one's quest to attain buddhahood. These are the four [dharmas that enable the purification of moral virtue].

2. Four More Dharmas Enabling Purification of Moral Virtue

There are yet another four dharmas by which one is able to bring about the purification of one's practice of *śīla*, namely:

> If one has no conceptions of a self or anything belonging to a self,
> if one also has no annihilationist or eternalist views,
> and if one penetrates the dharma explaining multiple conditions,
> one will then be able to purify one's practice of *śīla*.

"Freedom from conceptions of a self or anything belonging to a self" refers to not being attached to thoughts imputing the existence of a self or anything belonging to a self. One need only realize that these ideas are empty, false, and inverted and hence there is no dharma of [the existence of] a self.

One "has no annihilationist or eternalist views" because annihilationist and eternalist views are possessed of numerous faults.

As for "penetrating the dharma that explains multiple conditions," by knowing that all dharmas are products of many conditions and hence are devoid of any fixed nature of their own, one practices the Middle Way.

[By availing oneself of] four such dharmas such as these, one is able to purify one's practice of *śīla*.

3. Four More Dharmas Enabling Purification of Moral Virtue

There are four additional dharmas through which one is able to purify one's practice of *śīla*, namely:

> One practices the four lineage bases of the Āryas,
> adopts the twelve *dhūta* austerities,
> also does not delight in the noise of crowds,
> and bears in mind why one left home [to become a monastic].

"The four lineage bases of the Āryas" refers to being satisfied with whatever robes one has already obtained, to being satisfied with whatever food and drink one has already obtained, to being satisfied with whatever dwelling place[592] one has already obtained, and to delighting in severance and delighting in cultivation.

"The twelve *dhūta* austerities" are:

Adopting the dharma of dwelling in a forest hermitage;
Obtaining one's food through the alms round;
Wearing robes made of cast-off rags;
[Taking one's daily meal in but] a single sitting;

Always sitting [to sleep, never lying down];
Having taken the meal, not accepting food or drink at the wrong times;
Possessing only a single three-part set of robes;
Wearing only an animal-hair robe;
Laying out one's sitting mat wherever one happens to be;
Dwelling at the foot of a tree;
Dwelling out in the open (lit. "on empty ground");
Dwelling in a charnel field.

"Not delighting in the noise of crowds" refers to avoiding meeting together with either laypeople or monastics. There are those who, although they have taken up the dharma of dwelling in a forest hermitage, because they have many acquaintances and friends, often have many people coming and going. Therefore, it refers here to "not delighting in the noise of crowds," whether through not going off to other places or through being disinclined to gather together with others.

As for "bearing in mind why one left home [to become a monastic]," one who is focused on *śīla* practice reflects thus: "Why did I leave the home life to become a monastic?" Having pondered this, because one accords with the endeavors appropriate to the monastic's life and wishes to succeed in these, he practices in a manner that accords with the way [monastic cultivation] was taught. These are the four.

4. Four More Dharmas Enabling Purification of Moral Virtue

There are another four dharmas by which one can purify one's practice of *śīla*, namely:

[One sees that] the five aggregates have no arising or destruction,
[sees] the six elements[593] as like the nature of dharmas,
sees that the six sense faculties are empty [of inherent existence],
and does not become attached to worldly expressions.
[Practice] that accords with these four dharmas
also enables one to purify one's practice of *śīla*.

As for "[seeing that] the five aggregates have no arising or destruction," this means that, by contemplating the five aggregates from root to branch, one perceives their absence of arising and destruction.

As for "[seeing that] the six elements" consisting of earth and so forth "are like the nature of dharmas,"[594] this means that, just as the nature of dharmas cannot be apprehended, so too, the six elements cannot be apprehended, either.

One realizes that, although the six sense faculties involve pain, pleasure, and such, they do so through causes and conditions linked to the mind and mental dharmas. Thus, by resorting to investigative applications of right wisdom, one realizes that they are empty [of any inherent existence].

One then utterly comprehends the nature of all three of these associated categories, realizing that in every case they are entirely empty [of inherent existence].

There are practitioners who develop an attachment to emptiness that then also hinders cultivation of the path. Hence it states here that one must not develop an attachment to emptiness that simply conforms to worldly uses of the word "emptiness."

Dharmas such as these enable one to purify one's practice of *śīla*.

Question: If this is truly so, why do you speak here of the dharmas of the five aggregates?

Response: It is because they are empty. All dharmas of the five aggregates are empty. As for the very last part where it states that one must not become attached to emptiness, this means that even "emptiness" should be relinquished. If one accords with this, then there will be no dharma of erroneous doubtfulness impeding one's practice of *śīla*.

Question: Because the dharmas of the five aggregates are possessed of characteristic marks and that which can be marked, they do therefore definitely exist. Take for instance the [canonical] declarations that "the form aggregate is characterized by being assailed by what is painful"[595] and "awareness of pain and pleasure is the characteristic of the feeling aggregate." Given that they obviously possess such characteristics, how can one claim that [the aggregates] are neither empty nor non-empty?

Response:

Affliction and destruction are marks of the form aggregate.
What all goes into making this form?
If affliction is indeed a characteristic mark of form,
apart from its marks, there is nothing amenable to being marked.

And where then do these characteristic marks abide?
There is no mark nor anything that can be marked.
The entire world is finally nonexistent.
There is neither any mark nor anything that can be marked.

Characteristic marks and that which can be marked
are neither conjoined nor not conjoined.
In their coming forth, they have no place from which they come.
In going away, they also have no place to which they go.

If one posits either a conjoining or a nonconjoining
through which one establishes either marks or what is markable,

then to proceed in this way is mistaken
with regard to both marks and what is markable.

This would be to use marks to establish what is markable.
[However], marks themselves are not self established.
Since even marks themselves cannot be established,
how then could they [be used to] establish what is markable?

The beings of the world are so extremely pitiable,
for they distinguish marks and what is markable,
become deluded in pursuing all manner of deviant paths,
and are cheated and deceived by deviant teachers.

Marks and what is markable then are just
devoid of marks and devoid of anything that can be marked.
Given such a visibly apparent situation as this,
how could one fail to realize [what is so obvious]?

Pursuant to imputations of the existence of marks and the markable,
there exist such [merely] conceptual elaborations as these.
And whenever such conceptual elaborations as these arise,
one then falls into a position associated with afflictions.[596]

Moreover, the practitioner employs the gateway of [understanding that all phenomena] neither come into existence nor pass away to facilitate the contemplation of the aggregates, sense realms, and sense bases as empty [of inherent existence]. This is as described here:

The dharmas of birth, aging, sickness, and death,
when arising, have no place from which they come.
The dharmas of birth, aging, sickness, and death,
when extinguished, have no place to which they go.

It is the nature of the aggregates, sense realms, and sense bases that,
when arising, they have no place from which they come,
and, when extinguished, they have no place to which they go.
Just so is the meaning of the Buddha's Dharma.

So too with fire, which is not in the human effort used to make it,
is also not present in the friction drill or wood,
and is not in their coming together, either,
even as it still does exist due to their all having come together.

If the fuel is entirely consumed, the fire will then die out.
Yet, when it does die out, there is no place to which it goes.
It exists due to the coming together of conditions,
yet, if those conditions scatter, it becomes entirely nonexistent.

So too is this the case with the eye consciousness
that does not abide in the eye,

also does not abide in visual forms,
also does not abide between them,

also does not abide in their combination,
also is not found apart from them,
also does not come thither from elsewhere,
yet does exist due to such a combination,

and which, when the combining scatters, then becomes nonexistent.
So too it also is with all dharmas.
When arising, there is no place from which they come,
and when extinguished, there is no place to which they go.

This is analogous to a dragon's mental powers
through which the dark clouds appear.
They do not emerge from the body of the dragon,
nor do they arrive from some other place,

and yet the rain from these great dark clouds
pours down throughout the entire world,
after which it then evaporates,
yet has no place to which it goes.

Just as such clouds neither come nor go,
so too it is with all dharmas.
When they arise, there is no place from which they come,
and, when destroyed, there is no place to which they go.

They are also like a man who has been painted on a wall
that does not reside in any or all of the colors,
also does not reside in their combination,
and also does not abide in the wall.

It does not abide in the painter,
nor does it abide in the paintbrush.
It does not come forth from elsewhere,
yet it exists because of all of these coming together.

When that combination scatters, it then no longer exists.
So too it is with all dharmas.
When they exist, there is no place from which they come.
When they cease to exist, there is no place to which they go.

The lamp flame does not abide in its oil,
also does not emerge from its wick,
and also does not arrive from some other place,
and yet, because of the oil and the wick, it exists.

If its causes and conditions end, it is extinguished.
When it is extinguished, there is no place to which it goes.

All dharmas' characteristics of coming forth and departing
are in every case also just like this.

5. Four More Dharmas Enabling Purification of Moral Virtue

There are another four dharmas by which one can purify one's practice of *śīla*, namely:

One is able to contemplate the nature of one's own body
and refrains from elevating oneself or diminishing others.
Since these two cannot be apprehended,
one abides in mental pliancy, free of any conceit.
One contemplates all dharmas as uniformly equal.
These four serve to purify one's *śīla*.

As for being "able to contemplate the nature of one's own body," the practitioner has this thought: "This body of mine is characterized by impurity, impermanence, and mortality. What true worth[597] does it possess?"

Having reflected in this manner, one does not elevate oneself and look down on others.

Because one has a resolute belief that both self and others are devoid of "I" and "mine," one realizes that they cannot be apprehended at all.

As for "mental pliancy," having acquired these dharmas, one's mind then abides in lightness, suppleness, and the capacity to endure and acquiesce in dharmas. It is due to this mental pliancy and delight that one does not elevate himself above others.

As for "contemplating all dharmas as uniformly equal," this means that, because [one realizes] they are empty, one contemplates all conditioned and unconditioned dharmas as equal and devoid of any distinctions as to those which are superior, those which are middling, and those which are inferior. This is as described here:

If one would posit that, because of the inferior,
there thereby exist the middling and the superior,
since the inferior does not itself create the middling or the superior,
how then could they exist because of the inferior?
And for the inferior itself to have become "inferior,"
middling and superior would definitely have existed beforehand.

If one would posit that, because of the middling,
there thereby exist the inferior and the superior,
since the middling does not itself create the inferior or the superior,
how could they exist because of the middling?
And for the middling itself to have become "middling,"
inferior and the superior would definitely have existed beforehand.

If one would posit that, because of the superior,
there thereby exist the middling and the inferior,
since the superior does not itself create the middling or the inferior,
how could they exist because of the superior?
And for the superior itself to have become "superior,"
middling and inferior would definitely have existed beforehand.

It cannot be that, due to the inferior, [middling and superior exist].
Nor can it be that it is *not* because of it [that they exist].
If [the middling and superior] already existed previously,
they could not exist because of the inferior.
And if [the middling and superior] were previously nonexistent,
how could they succeed in becoming the middling and superior?

It cannot be that, due to the middling, [inferior and superior exist].
Nor can it be that it is *not* because of it [that they exist].
If [the inferior and the superior] already existed previously,
they could not exist because of the middling.
And if [the inferior and the superior] were previously nonexistent,
how could they succeed in becoming the inferior and the superior?

It cannot be that, due to the superior, [inferior and middling exist].
Nor can it be that it is *not* because of it [that they exist].
If [the middling and the inferior] definitely already existed,
they could not exist because of the superior.
And if [middling and inferior] were certainly previously nonexistent,
how could they succeed in becoming middling and inferior?

Additionally, because their emptiness is of a singular character, one contemplates all dharmas as uniformly equal. So too it is with beings. This is as described here:

In the midst of what is empty, the wise
do not speak of any distinguishable characteristic signs.
In the singularity of emptiness, there are no differentiations.
If one is able to perceive emptiness in this manner
this then is to see the Buddha,
for the Buddha is no different from emptiness.

It is said that all buddhas are one,
all beings are one,
all dharmas are but a single dharma,
and no distinctions exist between superior, middling, or inferior.

All of the Buddhas, the Bhagavats,
transcend both inherently existent and externally created nature.
So too do all beings
transcend both inherently existent and externally created nature.

All dharmas are also just so
in transcending inherently existent and externally created natures.
It is because of just such causes and conditions
that they are said to be of a singular character.

If one claims that buddhas exist, this is wrong.
If one claims no buddhas exist, this is also wrong.
If one claims that beings exist, this is wrong.
If one claims that no beings exist, this is also wrong.

If one claims dharmas exist, that is wrong.
If one claims that no dharmas exist, that is also wrong.
It is because they transcend both "existence" and "nonexistence"
that they are said to be uniformly equal.

All the Buddhas, the Bhagavats,
all beings, and also all dharmas
are in every case ungraspable.
This is what is meant by the uniform equality of all dharmas.

All buddhas, beings,
and dharmas have no differences.
Because one cannot make any distinctions among them,
they are said to be of a single uniform equality.

All buddhas, all beings,
and all dharmas,
even as they enter into arising, enduring, and destruction,
abide in quiescent cessation and do not exist at all.

Nor do they have any place from which they have come,
nor do they have any place to which they go.
It is because of their neither coming nor going
that they are said to be of a single uniform equality.

All buddhas, all beings,
and all dharmas
are, in every case, entirely nonexistent
and utterly beyond all of the paths of existence.

These three are not equal,
are not unequal,
are not both equal and unequal,
and are neither equal nor unequal.
It is in this way that one explains all dharmas
as being in every case equal and devoid of distinctions.

6. Four More Dharmas Enabling Purification of Moral Virtue

There are another four dharmas by which one can purify one's practice of *śīla*. They are as described below:

> Being well able to maintain a resolute belief in emptiness,
> not being frightened by the dharma of signlessness,
> maintaining the great compassion toward beings,
> and being able to acquiesce in the nonexistence of self—
> It is through four dharmas such as these
> that one is also able to purify one's practice of *śīla*.

It is because of a practitioner's complete comprehension of all dharmas as devoid of any self-existent nature or any externally created nature that he is referred to as having "a resolute belief in emptiness." This is as described here:

> All dharmas whatsoever
> never arise on the basis of any inherently existent nature.
> If they arise from multiple conditions,
> they should then exist through that which is other.
>
> Given they do not arise through any inherently existent nature,
> how then could they arise through that which is other?
> If an inherently existent nature is not established,
> then any nature existing through some "other" is also nonexistent.
>
> If they transcend any arising from an inherently existent nature,
> then they are devoid of any inherently existent nature.
> If they have transcended any inherently existent nature,
> then they are [also] devoid of any mark of inherent existence.
>
> An inherently existent nature and marks of inherent existence
> do not exist on the basis of conjoining
> and do not become nonexistent through separation.
> Hence they are both devoid of any fixed existence.
>
> Dharmas cannot be produced from that which is other,
> nor can they be produced from themselves,
> nor can they be produced by both self and other,
> and yet, apart from those two, they cannot be produced, either.
>
> If no inherent existence can be established for itself,
> how then could it possibly be produced from what is other?
> If one departs from dharmas that are mere worldly conventions,
> then "self" and "other" are entirely nonexistent.
>
> If that which is other were produced from that which is other,
> then that "other" would have no substance of its own.
> If it had no substance, then it could not even exist.
> From what thing then can there be the arising of what is other?

Because it has no substance of its own,
production from some other is also a nonexistent [possibility].
Since all four [tetralemma ideas] are empty [of inherent existence],
no dharma whatsoever has any fixed arising or destruction.

As for "not being frightened by signlessness," it is because of one's resolute belief [in signlessness] and one's utter transcendence of all signs that one is not frightened. This is as described here:[598]

If everything is signless,
then everything is identical with whatever possesses signs.
Quiescent cessation is signless
and is identical with whatever is an existent dharma.[599]

If one contemplates the dharma of signlessness,
whatever is signless is [seen as] the same as what possesses signs.
If one says that one is cultivating signlessness,
that is just a non-cultivation of signlessness.

Were one to relinquish all strategizing and attachments[600]
and designate that as constituting signlessness,
such seizing on this sign of having relinquished attachments
then becomes the very absence of liberation.

In general, it is because of the existence of grasping,
that then, because of that grasping, there then is relinquishing.
It is the abandonment of grasping and whatever thing is grasped[601]—
It is on this basis that one then refers to "relinquishing."

As for the one who grasps, the grasping to which he resorts,
as well as that dharma that is subject to being grasped,
whether as conjoined or separate, they are all entirely nonexistent,[602]
for these are all synonymous with quiescent cessation.

If any dharma's signs are established on the basis of causes,
this is just something devoid of any [inherently existent] nature.
Whatever is devoid of any [inherently existent] nature—
this is just something that is devoid of any [inherently existent] signs.

If a dharma has no [inherently existent] nature—
this is just something that is signless.
How can one assert that it has no [inherently existent] nature?
It is precisely because it is synonymous with signlessness.[603]

If one uses [such terms as] "existence" and "nonexistence,"
"both" and "neither" should be permissible as well,[604] for,
although one may speak thus, so long as one's mind is not attached,
one thereby remains free of any fault in doing so.

Where has there ever first existed some dharma
that, afterward, was not destroyed?
Wherever there was first some fire
that, afterward, was then extinguished,
the quiescent cessation of these existent signs
is identical to the quiescent cessation of whatsoever is signless.

Therefore, as for these words about quiescent cessation
as well as the one who speaks about quiescent cessation,
from the beginning onward, they have not been quiescent[605]
nor have they been nonquiescent,
nor have they been both quiescent and nonquiescent,
nor have they been neither quiescent nor nonquiescent.

Regarding "maintaining compassion toward beings," because beings are countless and boundless, one's mind of compassion is also expansive in that very same way. Also, the Dharma of all buddhas is measureless, boundless, and endless, like empty space. The mind of compassion is the very foundation of the Dharma of all buddhas. It is because it is able to bring about the realization of the great Dharma that it is referred to as the "great" compassion. Among all beings, the one who is the greatest is the Buddha. It is because it is practiced by the Buddha that it is referred to as the "great" compassion.

As for "acquiescence in the dharma of nonself," one accomplishes this because one has a resolute faith in the true Dharma. It is because it is the one path to nirvāṇa taken by all buddhas that it is known as "the Dharma of nonself."

If one enters into this dharma and one's mind is unable to endure it, this is like putting a small plant into a fire, whereupon it is entirely burned up. However, if one puts real gold into a fire, it is able to endure it and it remains entirely undiminished.

In the same way, if a common person, one who has not cultivated roots of goodness, attempts to enter [the dharma of] nonself, he will be unable to bear it and will immediately bring forth erroneous doubts about it. This bodhisattva, however, has cultivated roots of goodness for countless lifetimes. His wisdom has become fiercely sharp and he is sustained by the protective mindfulness of all buddhas. Although he may not yet have cut off the fetters, when he enters into the dharma of nonself, his mind is able to endure and accept it.

"The dharma of nonself" is a reference to all such dharmas as the aggregates, the sense realms, the sense bases, and the twelvefold chain of causation. The causes and conditions through which one demolishes [the view of] self are as discussed earlier.

Therefore, if one wishes to purify one's practice of *śīla,* one should practice these four dharmas.

Furthermore:

7. Four Kinds of Monks Who Break the Moral Precepts

There are four individuals who destroy *śīla*
even when seeming to uphold *śīla.*
The practitioner should be vigorous
in exerting self-control and taking care not to act [as they do].

In the "Kāśyapa" chapter of *The Jeweled Summit Sutra,* the Buddha told Kāśyapa:[606]

> There are four kinds of bhikshus who break the moral precepts while seeming as if they are bhikshus who uphold the moral precepts. What are those four? Kāśyapa, there are bhikshus who are completely able to perfectly practice the moral precepts of the scriptures and yet claim that a self exists. Kāśyapa, this is what is meant by breaking the moral precepts while seeming as if one is upholding the moral precepts.
>
> Then again, Kāśyapa, there are bhikshus who recite and retain the moral precept scriptures and guard their practice of the moral precepts, but who do not move from and never abandon their view of a real self in association with the body. This is what is meant by breaking the moral precepts while seeming as if one is upholding the moral precepts.
>
> Yet again, Kāśyapa, there are bhikshus who are perfect in their practice of the twelve *dhūta* austerities while nonetheless maintaining the view that dharmas have a fixed existence. This is what is meant by breaking the moral precepts while seeming as if one is upholding the moral precepts.
>
> Then again, Kāśyapa, there are bhikshus who focus on beings as the objective condition in their cultivation of the mind of kindness but who, on hearing that all conditioned things[607] are characterized by nonproduction, their minds are filled with terror. This is what is meant by breaking the moral precepts while seeming as if one is upholding the moral precepts.
>
> Kāśyapa, these are the four kinds of persons who break the moral precepts even while seeming as if they are upholding the moral precepts.

Furthermore:

8. Four Kinds of Monks of Which One Should Become the Fourth

According to what the Bhagavat has taught,
there are four types of *śramaṇas*

of which one should become the fourth
while distancing oneself from the first three kinds.[608]

As for these four kinds of bhikshus referred to here that are found in the "Kāśyapa" chapter, one should learn to become the fourth kind of *śramaṇa* while avoiding becoming any of the other three kinds. What then are those four? The Buddha told Kāśyapa:

There are four kinds of *śramaṇas*, namely:

First, those who, merely in form and appearance, seem to be *śramaṇas*;

Second, those *śramaṇas* who merely feign extraordinary deportment;

Third, those who are *śramaṇas* simply because they covet fame and self-benefit;

Fourth, *śramaṇas* who genuinely carry on right practice.

a. He Who Is a Monk Only in Form and Appearance

What is meant by one who is a *śramaṇa* merely in form and appearance? He adopts the form of the *śramaṇa* and adopts the appearance of a *śramaṇa*, doing so specifically through wearing a *saṃghāṭī* robe, shaving off his hair and beard, and carrying a blackened bowl, while nonetheless still engaging in impure physical actions, impure verbal actions, and impure mental actions. He does not seek to reach *nirvāṇa* and does not seek to become good. He is miserly and indolent and practices evil dharmas. He breaks the moral precepts and does not delight in cultivation of the path. This is what is meant by one who is a *śramaṇa* merely in form and appearance.

b. He Who Merely Feigns Extraordinary Deportment

What is meant by the *śramaṇa* who merely feigns extraordinary deportment? He is perfect in the four kinds of deportment. He investigates the truths, is comfortable and serene in getting by on whatever robes and food he has already acquired, is devoted to the practice of the [four] lineage bases of the Āryas, avoids gathering together with either laypeople or monastics, and speaks but little, but he does all these things in order to seize the attentions of others with a mind that is not pure.

Deportment of this sort is not done for the sake of goodness, is not done for the sake of reaching nirvāṇa, and is done with an implicit view that seizes on all dharmas as having a fixed and definite existence. [Such a practitioner] fears the dharmas of emptiness and nonexistence in just the same way as one might fear falling into a pit. Whenever he sees anyone who speaks of emptiness, he thinks of him as an enemy. This is what is meant by the *śramaṇa* who merely feigns extraordinary deportment.

c. He Who Is a Monk Only for Fame and Self-Benefit

What is meant by one who is a *śramaṇa* simply because he covets fame and self-benefit? There are those *śramaṇas* who, although they are able to force themselves to uphold the moral precepts, [as they do so, they think], "How can I cause other people to know me as one who upholds the moral precepts?"

Although they are able to force themselves to strive after extensive learning, [as they do so, they think], "How can I cause other people to know me as someone possessed of extensive learning?"

Although they are able to force themselves to take up the dharma of abiding in a forest hermitage, [as they do so, they think], "How can I cause other people to know that I am a forest hermitage dweller?"

Although they are able to force themselves to have but few wants, to be easily satisfied, and to practice the dharmas of one who dwells in solitude, as they do so, they think, "How can I cause other people to know that I have but few wants, am easily satisfied, and practice the dharmas of one who dwells in solitude?"

They do not do these things in order to develop a mind of renunciation, do not do them in order to destroy the afflictions, do not do them in order to strive in the eightfold right path of the Āryas, do not do them in order to reach nirvāṇa, and do not do them in order to bring about the liberation of all beings. This is what is meant by the *śramaṇa* who covets fame and self-benefit.

d. The Monk Who Genuinely Carries on Right Practice

What is meant by the *śramaṇa* who genuinely carries on right practice? There is a type of *śramaṇa* who does not retain any selfish cherishing even of his own body, how much the less might he cherish fame or self-benefit? On being taught that all dharmas are empty and that nothing whatsoever exists, his mind is filled with great joy and he proceeds to practice in accordance with that teaching.

He does not have any selfish cherishing even of nirvāṇa as he carries on his practice of *brahmacarya,* how much the less might he have any selfish cherishing of [any station of rebirth within] the three realms?

He is not even attached to the view that sees the emptiness [of all dharmas], how much the less might he become attached to the existence of a self, a person, a being, a soul, a life, a knower, or a seer?

He seeks liberation even in the midst of the afflictions and does not seek it anywhere outside. He contemplates all dharmas as fundamentally pure and undefiled. This person relies only on himself and does not rely on anyone else. Through [his direct knowing of] the true character of all dharmas, he does not even covet the Dharma body, how much the less the form body. He sees dharmas as transcending marks and as inexpressible in words. He does not even make any discriminating distinctions among those in the community of Āryas who course in the unconditioned, how much the less might he do so among those in the common multitude of people? He does not for the sake of severance or for the sake of cultivation abhor *saṃsāra* on the one hand and delight in nirvāṇa on the other. For him, there is neither bondage nor liberation. He realizes that the Dharma of the Buddhas has no fixed aspects and, having realized this, he neither comes and goes in *saṃsāra*, nor opts to enter nirvāṇa, either.

Kāśyapa, this is what is meant by the *śramaṇa* who accords with genuine practice. Kāśyapa, you should all be diligent in the practice of the genuine-practice *śramaṇa*. Do not allow yourselves to be harmed for the sake of a reputation.

9. Wrong Motivations for Upholding the Practice of Moral Virtue

Moreover:

Do not uphold the practice of *śīla*
merely for the sake of kingship or other such things.
Also, do not uphold the practice of *śīla*
to obtain a particular rebirth or other such aims.

The practitioner who wishes to purify his practice of *śīla* should not practice it for the sake of such things as kingship. With regard to such things as becoming a king, when speaking for the benefit of the stalwart, Pure Virtue, the Buddha said, "Son of Good Family, as for the bodhisattva who practices *śīla*:

He will never break a moral precept even at the cost of his own life;
He does not uphold the moral precepts hoping to become a king;
He does not uphold the moral precepts hoping to achieve celestial rebirth;
He does not uphold the moral precepts hoping to become Śakra, ruler of the devas, hoping to become the Brahma Heaven King, or hoping to gain wealth, happiness, or unconstrained and independent power;
He does not uphold the moral precepts for the sake of fame or praise, for the sake of offerings, for the sake of a long life span, or for the sake of drink, food, robes, bedding, medicines, or other life-sustaining things;
He does not uphold the moral precepts in reliance on dharmas concerned with rebirths and such. Hence he does not do so for the sake of being reborn among devas or humans;
He does not uphold the moral precepts because of concerns having to do with himself;

He does not uphold the moral precepts because of concerns having to do with others;

He does not uphold the moral precepts because of present-life concerns;

He does not uphold the moral precepts because of future-life concerns;

He does not uphold the moral precepts out of concerns associated with his physical form, out of concerns associated with feelings, perceptions, formative factors, or consciousnesses, out of concerns associated with the eyes, out of concerns associated with the sense bases, or out of concerns associated with the ears, nose, tongue, body, or mind faculty;

He does not uphold the moral precepts out of concerns associated with the desire realm, form realm, or formless realm;

He does not uphold the moral precepts to be liberated from the wretched destinies of the hell realm, the animal realm, the hungry ghost realm, or the *asura* realm;

He does not uphold the moral precepts out of fear of being poverty-stricken when reborn among the devas;

He does not uphold the moral precepts out of fear of being poverty-stricken when reborn among humans;

He does not uphold the moral precepts out of fear of being poverty-stricken when reborn among the *yakṣas*."

10. Right Motivations for Upholding the Practice of Moral Virtue

Question: If [this bodhisattva] does not [uphold the moral precepts] out of concern for these sorts of things, then for the sake of which sorts of things does he uphold the moral precepts?

Response:

It is because he wishes to cause the Three Jewels
to abide for a long time that he upholds the moral precepts.
It is because he wishes to obtain the many different sorts
of benefits that he upholds the moral precepts.

As for "causing the Three Jewels to abide for a long time":

It is in order to prevent the cutting off of the lineage of the Buddhas that he upholds the moral precepts;

It is in order to turn the wheel of Dharma that he upholds the moral precepts;

It is in order to attract a community of *āryas* that he upholds the moral precepts;

It is in order to gain liberation from birth, aging, sickness, death, lamentation, grief, pain, and melancholy that he upholds the moral precepts;

It is in order to facilitate the liberation of all beings that he upholds the moral precepts;

It is in order to cause all beings to gain peace and happiness that he upholds the moral precepts;

It is in order to cause beings to reach a peaceful and secure[609] place that he upholds the moral precepts;

It is in order to cultivate the *dhyāna* absorptions that he upholds the moral precepts;

It is in order to gain wisdom, liberation, and the knowledge and vision of liberation that he upholds the moral precepts.

These matters are just as extensively discussed in *The Pure Virtue Sutra.*

11. The Benefits of Perfecting the Practice of Moral Virtue

The bodhisattva who is able in this fashion
to perfect the practice of *śīla*
will not lose the ten benefits
or the many other different types of benefits.

Additionally, he will not fall down into
erroneous paths associated with the four difficulties.
He will not encounter the four dharmas associated with loss and
he will not encounter the four dharmas associated with destruction,

He will also gain the four dharmas
by which one does not deceive the Buddhas or others.
He is able to pass beyond susceptibility to falling into the hells
and the rest of the ten terror-inducing circumstances.

"Will not lose the ten benefits" refers to:

Not losing the ability to always become a wheel-turning king;

Not losing the non-neglectful mind when acting in that capacity;

Not losing the ability to always become Śakra, ruler of the devas;

Not losing the non-neglectful mind when acting in that capacity;

Never losing one's quest to seek the path of all buddhas;

Never losing those things that all bodhisattvas are taught;

Never losing the unimpeded knowledge of eloquence;

Never losing [the pursuit of] the planting of roots of goodness and merit and the fulfillment of whatsoever one has vowed to accomplish;

Never losing that due to which one is praised by all buddhas, bodhisattvas, worthies and *āryas*;

Never losing the ability to swiftly perfect the attainment of all-knowledge.

These are the ten [benefits of perfecting the practice of *śīla*.

"The many other different types of benefits" refers to never retreating from or losing one's many different sorts of meritorious qualities. This is as described in the sutras:

> The bodhisattva who skillfully guards his ability to uphold the moral precepts:
>
> Is always praised by the devas;
> Is well protected by the dragon kings;
> Is the beneficiary of people's offerings;
> Is always borne in mind by all buddhas;
> Always serves as a great teacher of those in the world;
> And is sympathetically mindful of beings.

As for "not falling down into erroneous paths associated with the four difficulties," the bodhisattva who is able to perfect the practice of *śīla* in this manner will not fall into places [of rebirth] beset with the four difficulties, namely:

> First, he will not be born into a place in which the Buddha is not present;
> Second, he will not be born into a household in which wrong views hold sway;
> Third, he will not take rebirth among the long-lived devas;
> Fourth, he will not be reborn into any of the wretched destinies.
> "The four dharmas associated with loss" are:
> First, he never loses the resolve to attain bodhi;
> Second, he never loses his mindfulness of the Buddha;
> Third, he never loses his constant quest for extensive learning;
> Fourth, he never loses his ability to call to mind the events experienced across the course of countless lifetimes.

Regarding "not encountering the four dharmas associated with destruction" this refers to:

> First, never encountering the destruction of the Dharma;
> Second, never encountering weapons or war;
> Third, never encountering noxious poisons;
> Fourth, never encountering hunger.

As for "gaining the four dharmas of non-deception," they are:

> First, one does not deceive the Buddhas of the ten directions;
> Second, one does not deceive devas, spirits, or other such beings;
> Third, one does not deceive beings;
> Fourth, one does not deceive oneself.

Also, regarding "passing beyond the ten terror-inducing circumstances," the bodhisattva who purifies the moral precepts in this way thereby becomes able to pass beyond any vulnerability to falling down into the hells or into any of the other situations contained in the ten terror-inducing circumstances. What then are those ten? They are:

First, one is able to pass beyond the fear of falling into the hell realms;

Second, one is able to pass beyond the fear of falling into the animal realms;

Third, one is able to pass beyond the fear of falling into the hungry ghost realms;

Fourth, one is able to pass beyond the fear of becoming poverty-stricken;

Fifth, one is able to pass beyond the fear of slander, rebuke, and bad reputation;

Sixth, one is able to pass beyond the fear of being overcome by the various sorts of afflictions;

Seventh, one is able to pass beyond the fear of reaching the [irreversible] "right and definite position" (*samyaktva niyāma*) [in the paths] of the *śrāvaka* disciples and the *pratyekabuddhas*;

Eighth, one is able to pass beyond the fear of [falling into the destinies of] devas, men, dragons, spirits, *yakṣas, gandharvas, asuras, garuḍas, kinnaras, mahoragas*, and others;

Ninth, one is able to pass beyond the fear of weapons or war, noxious poisons, water, fire, lions, tigers, wolves, and injury by other men;

Tenth, one is able to pass beyond the fear of adopting wrong views.

If the bodhisattva is able in this manner to purify his observance of the moral precepts, then he will be able to abide within the Dharma of all Buddhas, namely the forty exclusive dharmas, and he will also be able to become a Dharma vessel.

The End of Chapter Thirty-Three

Chapter 34
In Praise of the Moral Precepts

XXXIV. Chapter 34: In Praise of the Moral Precepts

The bodhisattva who purifies his observance of the moral precepts in this manner is able to gather together all sorts of meritorious qualities and derive all manner of benefits. This is as stated by Akṣayamati Bodhisattva when he said:

Then again, to offer but a brief praise of a few aspects of *śīla*:

Śīla is the basis for the monastic's experiencing the foremost joyous delight that is comparable to the most supreme delight enjoyed by a youth who has both wealth and noble birth;

[*Śīla*] brings about the proliferation and growth of good dharmas just as when a kind mother raises her child;

[*Śīla*] is able to protect one from ruinous calamity just as when a father protects his child;

Śīla is able to bring about for monastics complete accomplishment in all forms of great benefit just as great wealth is able to bring about great benefit for a householder;

Śīla is as able to rescue one from all forms of suffering torment just as when right action accords with what is principled;

Śīla is as revered by good people as the dharma of repaying others' kindnesses;

Śīla is just as cherished and esteemed by people as a long life span;

Śīla is as esteemed by the wise as wisdom itself;

Those who strive to gain liberation thoroughly guard their practice of *śīla* just as carefully as high officials guard the secrets of the king;

Those who delight in the benefits of the path cherish and value *śīla* just as deeply as those who delight in nirvāṇa cherish and value the Dharma of the Buddha;

The wise thoroughly guard their practice of *śīla* with the same urgency as those who cherish their own lives guard their physical safety and urgently seek rescue when death threatens;

The supreme [good fortune] of encountering *śila* is comparable to that of meeting a good guide in the midst of grave danger;

Śila adorns the worthy ones with purity and, in this, it is analogous to the daughter of nobility who, possessed of a sense of shame and dread of blame, remains undefiled;

Śila is the initial entryway into meritorious qualities just as not engaging in flattery and deviousness opens the way to acquiring fine benefits;

Śila is the most important foundation of *brahmacarya* just as the straight mind is the foundation of right views;

Śila is the origin of all dharmas of great people just as the straight mind is the origin of success in seeking an important position;

Śīla is a treasure trove of meritorious qualities comparable to non-negligence and right mindfulness in their ability to bring forth every sort of benefit;

[*Śīla*] is also comparable to a worthy friend who is good in the beginning, good in the middle, and good to the end;

[*Śīla*] is something beyond which one who trains in right Dharma must never go and, in this, he is like the ocean which always remains within its boundaries;[610]

Śīla is the dwelling place of meritorious qualities and, in this, it is also like the great earth upon which the myriad things depend;

Śīla serves to moisten all of the meritorious qualities of goodness and, in this, it is analogous to the rain falling down from the sky that moistens and benefits the seeds and enables the growth of the five kinds of roots;

[*Śīla*] is like fire in its ability to cook things and provide all sorts of benefits and, in this, it is like the [energetic] winds that sustain the body;

Śīla is able to accommodate all fruits of the path and, in this, it is also like empty space that contains and takes in the myriad things.

[*Śīla*] is also like the magically-auspicious vase that is able to bring forth anything that one might wish for, and it is also like fine cuisine in its ability to benefit all of one's faculties;

Śīla is well able to open all paths and it is able to cause all one's faculties to become purified and unimpeded;

One's wisdom life relies upon *śīla* as its foundation just as the life of the body depends upon the breath as its very foundation;

Śīla is the most superior of all points of reliance just as it is the king upon whom all his subjects rely;

Śīla serves as the lord of all the meritorious qualities just as the chief general commands the entire army;

Śīla is the source of the many varieties of happiness and, in this, it is like the compliant wife who is well able to satisfy all the wishes of her husband;

Whether it be in striving to reach nirvāṇa or in gaining rebirth in the heavens, *śīla* constitutes the provisions sustaining those training on the path and, in this, it is like the essential clothing and provisions that one traveling afar must take along on his travels;

Śīla leads people along in such a way that they are caused to reach a good place and, in this, it is like finding a good guide who escorts one along a hazardous road;

Śīla delivers people from the faults of *saṃsāra* and, in this, it is like a sturdy ship by which one is able to cross a great ocean;

Śīla is well able to put an end to all calamities wrought by the afflictions and, in this, it is like a good medicine that is able to eliminate the many sorts of diseases;

Śīla's weapons are able to defend one against Māra's thieves and, in this, they are like the weapons of a good army that are able to counter an enemy's troops;

Just as a beloved relative leads one through hardships and does not desert one, so too, *śīla* leads people through all manner of ruinous torment, continues to protect them, and never abandons them;

Śīla is able to illuminate even the darkness of delusion in one's future lives and, in this, it is like the light of a great lamp that is able to dispel the darkness;

Śīla is able even to deliver one out of the wretched destinies and, in this, it is like finding a good bridge when crossing deep waters;

Śīla is able to dispel the extreme fever of the afflictions and, in this, it is like a cool room that is able to get rid of scorching heat;

Even when on the verge of falling into the wretched destinies, *śīla* is able to come to the rescue and, in this, it is like a fierce sword-brandishing warrior rescuing someone in terror;

Every common person should feel a deeply cherishing fondness for *śīla* like that of the bodhisattvas training in the supreme basis of truthfulness;[611]

The practitioner's skillful practice of *śīla* is just like all bodhisattvas' practice of the supreme basis of relinquishment;

The skillful cultivation of *śīla* on the part of the practitioner who has gained the fruits [of the path] is just like all bodhisattvas' cultivation of the supreme basis of quiescence;

Guarding and upholding the practice of *śīla* causes one to attain the fruits [of the path] just like a bodhisattva who cultivates the wisdom supreme basis;

One who refrains from damaging the Dharma is able to purify his practice of *śīla* in a manner comparable to the purity and stainlessness of the bodhisattvas;

Bad people abandon *śīla* just as flattering and devious people abandon the straight mind;

Neglectful people do not practice *śīla* and, in this, they are like miserly people who do not practice kindly giving;

Neglectful people abandon *śīla* and, in this, they are like those prone to inappropriate and frivolous speech who abandon the dharma of quiescence;

Stupid people are bereft of *śīla* just as a blind man does not see the five colors;

An unreflective person is as far from *śīla* as one who has abandoned the eightfold right path is far from nirvāṇa;

Those who truly love themselves deeply delight in *śīla* just as an arhat deeply loves the Dharma;

Śīla is able to ensure that the good dharmas by which one remains free of afflictions continue on uninterruptedly just as the Buddha's emergence in the world ensures that goodness will continue without cease;

Śīla is able to cause the fruits of the path to abide [in the world] just as the Buddha's spiritual power causes the Dharma to remain for a long time;

Śīla is just like the Buddha in that it benefits both oneself and others;

Śīla thoroughly protects all good meritorious qualities just as a king who understands right timing, is able to defend the country's borders;

Śīla quiets the mind of the practitioner just as when a stream-enterer,[612] by revealing in timely fashion [moral code infractions] remains free of subsequent regrets;

Śīla ensures that one shall ultimately and definitely reach nirvāṇa just as the bodhisattva vow ensures that one will ultimately become a buddha;

Śīla is also like a good plot of farmland that is well irrigated which, when sown with seeds, produces a rapidly-growing crop;

Śīla is the cause of right conduct just as knowing the right time, knowing the right place, and so forth are the causes of success in all endeavors;

Just as a handsome man possessed of merit and wisdom is revered and esteemed by others, so too is *śīla* respected by both self and others;

Just as when one's merit has become ripe, one's mind is peaceful and secure, so too is *śīla* able to cause one's mind to become peaceful and secure and to enjoy all its beneficial rewards;

Śīla is able to cause the practitioner to be delighted just as a fine son is able to inspire delight in his father's mind;

Śīla is a dharma that causes fearlessness in one who is free of faults just as when a person becomes free of faults, his mind then becomes free of fear;

Śīla causes one to become free of all fear and free of the evil of moral transgressions in both the present life and future lives;

Others are inspired to make offerings and give praise to whoever upholds the practice of *śīla*, for others are moved by him to feel joy and realize that they too have some part in it;

Śīla causes one to feel affection for other beings, just as when one cultivates the meditation on [measureless] kindness;

Śīla motivates one to do away with the sufferings of others, just as when one cultivates the meditation on [measureless] compassion;

Śīla bestows joyfulness, just as when one cultivates the meditation on [measureless] sympathetic joy;

Śīla causes one to become free of both hatred and desire, just as when one cultivates the meditation on [measureless] equanimity;

Śīla inspires faith on the part of others, just as the four kinds of good speech are able to win the trust of others;

Śīla brings delight in its practice just as dharmas of the world always bring delight to the mind [of a worldly person];

Just as extensive learning is the cause of delight in speech, *śīla* is the cause of consistency between one's words and one's actions;

Śīla is the cause of fearlessness just as eloquence also brings about fearlessness;

Śīla is the cause of renown just as complete comprehension of all scriptures brings a fine reputation;

Śīla is a dharma capable of bringing about one's rescue just as being one who is easy to converse with ensures one will be rescued by them;

Śīla is a dharma that is able to bring about successful attainment of the clear knowledges and liberation and, in this, it is comparable to practicing in accordance with the teachings;

Śīla is the characteristic feature of all buddhas and, in this, it is comparable to *anuttarasamyaksaṃbodhi*;

Śīla is a dharma that aids cultivation of the path and, in this, it is like samādhi's role in assisting the attainment of wisdom;

Śīla causes a person to have no difficulties that he fears just as someone possessed of great courage has nothing that he fears;

Śīla is the gathering place of every form of meritorious quality, for just as the Himalayas are the repository of precious things, faith, the other meritorious qualities, and all marvelous phenomena[613] rely on *śīla* for their very existence;

Śīla is like the great sea in that it contains the many sorts of extraordinary things;

Also, just as, to obtain fine fruit, one relies on a tree, so too *śīla* is what provides people with whichever fruit they find pleasing. This is just as when one who pursues right wisdom then acquires [its fruits] in accordance with his practice;

Śīla is that by which one is cleansed even without the aid of water;

Śīla is the most superior of sublime incenses, one that does not come forth from some root, trunk, branch, leaf, blossom, or fruit;

Śīla is an adornment that surpasses that of any jewelry, for it always remains with one's person and cannot be stolen by anyone;

Śīla provides a great bliss not born of any of the five desires and it bestows the reward of sublime bliss in future lives as well;

Śīla is that which is praised by all worlds' devas, humans, *māras*, Brahmās, *śramaṇas*, and brahmans;

The happiness produced by *śīla* abides independently in one's own person for it is not obtained from anyone else and it is also the excellent means for gaining celestial rebirth or nirvāṇa;

Śīla is the right ford for crossing the river of faith, one that is free of quicksand, tiles, stones, thorns, or brambles, and one that may be entered at will so as to skillfully cross without being impeded by anything;

Śīla is a form of precious wealth free of ruin or anguish;

Śīla is the indestructible path of purity that is comparable to a level road that can be traveled without difficulty;

Śīla is a fine farm field that, even without having to plant it or harvest it, one naturally obtains its fruits;

Śīla is the fruit tasting of the elixir of immortality that, even though not obtained from a tree or produced from a plant, is incomparably delicious;

Śīla is a *mañjūṣaka* flower that does not grow forth from either water or land and never wilts;

Śīla dispels the fever of the afflictions and, in this, it is like bathing in cool waters;

Śīla provides complete protection superior to that of even swords or staves, hence the practitioner of *śīla* is respected, but not because others fear him;

Śīla is a station of sovereign mastery that is free of any disputation or struggle;

Śīla is a fine jewel not extracted from the mountains or drawn forth from the great sea, one whose value is incalculable;

Śīla is able to take one beyond the fear of not surviving, beyond the fear of entering the assembly, beyond the fear of interrogation and beating, and beyond the fear of falling into the hells;[614]
Śīla always follows along with a person in present and future lives just as a shadow follows its form.

The End of Chapter Thirty-Four

Chapter 35
The Karmic Rewards of the Moral Precepts

XXXV. Chapter 35: The Karmic Rewards of the Moral Precepts

A. The Second Ground Bodhisattva as a Wheel-Turnining King

The comprehensive explanation of purification related to the bodhisattva's Ground of Stainlessness is hereby concluded. The bodhisattva dwelling on this ground always becomes a wheel-turning king. This second of the ten grounds is referred to as the Ground of Stainlessness. It is because covetousness and the rest of the ten bad karmic actions are all cut off at the very root that it is referred to as "stainless." A bodhisattva on this ground engages in the deep practice of *śīla pāramitā*. In the event that this bodhisattva has not yet abandoned the desires, the causes and conditions associated with this ground's karmic rewards result in his becoming a wheel-turning king ruling over the four continents who obtains a thousand-spoked gold wheel.

B. The Wheel-Turning King's Treasures

1. His Gold Wheel Treasure

Its rim is adorned with many different sorts of precious jewels and its hub is made of real beryl. It has a circumference of fifteen *li*.[615] It is protected by a hundred kinds of *yakṣas*. It is able to fly through the air leading a fourfold army with agility, strength, and speed like that of the king of the golden-winged [*garuḍa*] birds, like that of the wind, or like that of a single thought, so that it is then able, wherever it goes, to put an end to all calamities and conquer any enemies.

All of the lesser kings come and declare their allegiance and submission. Of all of his relatives, clans, and subject peoples, there are none who do not both love and revere him. He is able to emanate radiance that illuminates everywhere. The sage king's clan members wear many different kinds of floral chaplets with interspersed adornments of pearls. The five kinds of music follow him wherever he goes. An extraordinarily marvelous jeweled canopy hangs down over and around him. As he walks along, many different sorts of flower blossoms, incenses, and powdered sandalwood rain down as offerings as there also burn genuine black aloewood incense and ox-head sandalwood incense. His body is scented with yellow sandalwood fragrance. On both sides of that wheel, heavenly maidens stand in attendance, holding white whisks. The canopy above him is composed of all sorts of precious jewels. The wheel itself has all sorts of different rare things adorning it. This is what is meant by his "gold wheel treasure."

2. His Elephant Treasure

[As for his elephant treasure] it possesses all the characteristics of an elephant and its body is huge and white like a king of mountains made of real silver. It comes from a herd of great elephants in the magic mountains. It is able to fly through the air, decisively defeat, and drive away in retreat all of the other great elephant kings, including Airāvaṇa, Añjana, Vāmana, and the rest. This is what is meant by his "white elephant treasure."

3. His Horse Treasure

[As for his horse treasure], it possesses all the characteristics of horses and is the color of a peacock's neck. Its body has agility and speed like that of the king of the golden-winged [*garuḍa*] birds and it can fly unimpeded through the air. This is what is meant by his "horse treasure."

4. His Prime Minister of Military Affairs Treasure

[As for his prime minister of military affairs treasure], he is one who has been born into a noble clan with a body that is free of illness, possessed of great strength, and a physical form of pristine appearance. His memory and thought are deep and far-reaching and he is possessed of a straight and resilient mind. He is solid in his observance of the precepts and he has deep reverence and affection for the king. He is able to penetrate the meaning of the many different classic scriptures as well as the technical skills and arts. This is what is meant by his "prime minister of military affairs treasure."

5. His Treasury Minister Treasure

As for his treasury minister treasure, like the heavenly king of great wealth, he is characterized by such repletion in wealth that a thousand myriads of *koṭis* of kinds of precious jewels form a treasury that always follows along with him wherever he goes, attended by retinue of a thousand myriads of *koṭis* of *yakṣas*. All of this is the karmic reward for his karmic actions in previous lives. [All of the precious jewels in the treasury] are well known and distinguished, including the gold, silver, *indranīla* sapphires, *mahānīla* sapphires, diamonds, malachite, *musāragalva*, carnelian, coral, *sphaṭika*, *maṇi* jewels, real pearls, beryl, and all of the other different kinds of precious things. Precisely how much goes out and how much comes in is also well known. In accordance with whatever is fitting, he is able to use these so that he is able to fulfill the wishes of the king. This is what is meant by his "treasury minister treasure."[616]

6. His Jewel Treasure

[As for his jewel treasure, it emanates] light like the sun or moon that produces illumination that extends for sixteen *yojanas*. It is shaped like a huge drum and it is able to extinguish many different kinds of insect venom, noxious energies, pestilences, and pain. Of all the humans and devas who see it, none fail to cherish it. It is adorned with fine flowers and necklaces, and, wherever it is placed, a banner is flown on high. It radiates an awe-inspiring and extraordinary radiance that is able to cause beings to bring forth thoughts of wonder and immense joy. This is what is meant by his "jewel treasure."

7. His Jade Maiden Treasure

[Regarding a wheel-turning king's "jade maiden" treasure], her fingernails are vermillion-colored and thin. Her physical form is straight, tall, and imposing. Her complexion is smooth, soft, and neither plump nor thin. Variations in the contours of her flesh are gradual in the transitions of her muscles and skin from dense and full to fine and delicate. Her tender skin would be ill-suited for coarse tasks. Her body is as stable and firm in its stance as the trunk of a *tāla* tree. In place after place on her body, auspicious characters are clearly visible. The silhouette outline of the auspicious tree adorns her body as well. The insignias of the king of elephants, king of bulls, and king of horses, as well as other such emblems as the imperial canopy emblem, the fish emblem, and the parks and forests emblems grace her body as adornments.

Her ankle bones appear flat and not prominent. Her feet have a profile like the shell of a tortoise. The sides of her feet are entirely red. Her heels are round and broad. Her calves are soft and smooth. Her knees are rounded and not prominent. Her thighs are shaped like golden pillars, like a plantain tree's trunk, or like an elephant's trunk while also being soft, smooth, radiantly lustrous, even, round, straight, and graced by three horizontal creases. Her belly is even and not prominent. Her umbilicus is round and deep. Her back is flat and straight. Her breasts are like *bimba* fruit or like [the breasts of] a pair of mandarin ducks. They are rounded and prominent, but not sagging, while also being soft, smooth, and fresh and pristine in appearance.

Also, her arms are slender, even, round, and long, with joints that are hidden and hence not apparent. The profile of her nose is straight and not jutting prominently outward. It is neither large nor small, and its nostrils are hidden and hence not visible.

Her two cheeks are not sunken, but rather are even and full. They are not high, but rather are full on both sides.

Her forehead is flat, broad, and graced with an auspicious emblem. Her ears are soft, hang downward, and wear priceless earrings.

Her teeth appear like a strand of real pearls or like a new crescent moon and are the color of snow or alabaster. Her lips, a rosy cinnabar-red, appear like *bimba* fruits, are well matched above and below, and are neither coarse nor fine. They resemble strands of red pearls.

Her eyes are white with dark blue[617] [irises] and the margin between the two colorations is clearly defined. [Her eyes] are graceful, long and wide. They glisten with brightness and clarity. The lashes are bluish, with close-grown hairs that are long, but not disarrayed.

Her eyebrows are neither too thick nor too thin, neither too high nor too low, and they form the shape of new crescent moons. They are prominent and long with their two sides symmetrical.

Her hair is soft while also being fine, smooth, glossy, and not disarrayed.

Her body always emanates an incense-like scent similar to the fragrance rising forth from newly opened containers of various fine perfumes. All of the pores of her body always emit a truly sublime *candana* sandalwood's famous scent that is well able to please anyone's mind.

Her mouth always has the fragrance of a blue lotus.

Her body is as soft as a *kalaviṇka* bird and she is perfectly adorned with the sublimely smooth raiment of the devas.

Her mind is free of any tendency toward flattery or deviousness. She is straightforward, trustworthy, and endowed with a sense of shame and dread of blame. She deeply loves and reveres the king. She knows the right time, knows the right place, and is well equipped with means for drawing the king's attentions. Whether sitting or standing, her words are well able to match the king's intentions and accord with the course of the king's thoughts. She always speaks pleasing words and, like a virtuous maiden among humans, she is replete in the many sorts of fine qualities. Her appearance is comparable to that of the heavenly maiden, *Tiluduoma*,[618] for it has a purity and clarity that shines like the moon on the fifteenth night of the month. Her appearance is also comparable to that of Indra's consort, Śācī. She wears heavenly raiment, a floral chaplet of the devas, celestial scents, and has many [strands of] radiant heavenly gold, *maṇi* jewels, and pearls adorning her body. She is well versed in singing, dancing, music, and all of the other arts of pleasurable entertainment and humor while also being well possessed of all the ways to be freely able to cause the king to be delighted. Among all women, this woman is the very best. Such is the description of the king's "jade-maiden treasure."

C. Four Qualities of the Wheel Turning King

The wheel-turning king also has four spontaneously manifesting qualities:

First, his physical appearance is handsome and dignified and, in this, he is foremost, unmatched by anyone living on any of the four continents;
Second, he remains free of sickness and pain;
Third, he is deeply loved by his people;
Fourth, he has a very long life span.

D. A Description of a Wheel-Turning King's Domain, Rule & Qualities

He teaches beings that, through abiding by the ten courses of good karmic action, they are able to keep the heavenly palaces full, are able to diminish the *asura* hordes, are able to diminish the number of beings in the wretched destinies, and are able to increase their numbers in the good stations of rebirth.

In whatever endeavors he undertakes, he primarily seeks what is most beneficial to beings. Thus, without using armies and weapons, he institutes order in accordance with the Dharma and ensures peace and happiness among all the feudal princes.

Outwardly, he has no fear of hostile countries on his borders. Inwardly, he has no fear of secret plots against his reign. Additionally, his country remains free of plague, famine, or any of the disasters, locusts, or other ruinous and anguishing circumstances.

All the kings in the border regions pledge their allegiance and submit to him. He is attended by a large retinue and is able to swiftly gather people [to become loyal followers]. Thus there are none able to attack and damage his domain. His fourfold army is possessed of abundant might. He is loved and respected by all brahmans, merchants, and common people.

Sweet, fragrant, and delectable food comes to him spontaneously. The boundaries of his domain increase by the day and never shrink. He is well able to reach a penetrating comprehension of all the classic scriptures, arts, mathematics, and spiritual incantations, all of which he can retain and invoke. He is skilled in his ability to debate, discuss, and clearly distinguish their meaning and import. Those in his assembly of officials are all well possessed of awe-inspiring virtue. He is always devoted to philanthropic giving that no one can match.

His thousand sons are all as handsome as the sons of the devas and they are possessed of awe-inspiring virtue, courage, strength, and the ability to crush even the strongest of enemies.

The palace in which he dwells is replete with halls, towers, and pavilions like those supreme palaces enjoyed by the Four Heavenly Kings and Indra.

Whatsoever the king instructs is unable to be subverted by anyone anywhere on the four continents. It is only this one king whose marks of awe-inspiring power are so complete that none are able to match him.

His voice is deep, carries far, is easily heard, easily understood, and is never scattered or disordered. And, like the sound of the *kalaviṇka* bird, it is beautiful, soft, harmonious, refined, and pleasing to the ear of the hearer.

His retinue is of like mind and incapable of obstructiveness. Wherever he abides, whether on the land, the water, or moving through the air, there is no one able to impede his travel. He has awesome power that is courageous and abundant with which he can undertake and succeed in great endeavors.

He thinks of and asks after the welfare of the aged. He never deceives anyone. His mind has no jealousy. He does not tolerate anything contrary to Dharma and he has no hatred.

His personal deportment is serene and dignified and it is neither restless nor impetuous. Whatever he says is sincere and true and he never utters divisive speech. In whatever he does, he upholds the moral precepts and cultivates a mind imbued with goodness. In initiating or halting endeavors, he knows the right time and never fails to employ appropriate methods.

His facial expression is amiable and, in speaking, he is always inclined to a subtle smile. He never scowls or glowers at anyone. For those who have encountered misfortune, he does whatever is beneficial for them. Those who have already been benefited thereby come to feel deep gratitude and to feel disposed toward a sense of shame and dread of blame.

He is possessed of great wisdom, awe-inspiring virtue, and a dignified manner while also being able to abide in patience. He has the marks of the great man and his nature is such that he may manifest fierce severity. He is able to swiftly complete every endeavor he takes up. He first assesses circumstances correctly and then acts accordingly. Because the King has the Dharma eye, whatever he does is exceptional.

Where he has those who are possessed of good judgment, he delegates tasks to them. If they are incapable of fulfilling their duties, he then seeks further for other surrogates who are worthy and wise.

He is skillful in accumulating karmic merit and wealth. By virtue of his own purity, he is able to guard his own actions and defend against breaking any of the moral precepts.

He bestows much wealth and treasure and, in this, he is comparable to King Vaiśravaṇa. He possesses great strength like Śakra, ruler of the devas.

He is as majestic and entrancing as the full moon and as radiant as the sun. He has the capacity to endure of the earth and his mind is as deep as the ocean. He is not shaken in the least by either pain or pleasure, and, like Sumeru, king of the mountains, none of the winds can make him quaver and he is the repository of all jewels and marvelous things.

He is one in whom all the excellent meritorious qualities reside. He acts as the close friend and relative of everyone in the entire world and he is a place of refuge for all who are beset by suffering or affliction. He is a refuge for those who have no refuge and a shelter for those who have no shelter. He can dispel the fear of those beset by fear.

Such are the characteristics of the wheel-turning sage king.

He is able to reverse the path of those who break moral precepts
and then influence them to abide in good dharmas.
All the other endeavors to which he is devoted
are as previously explained in the discussion of the first ground.

As for "reversing the path of those who break moral precepts," he is able to influence beings to relinquish evil actions and take up those endeavors that are conducive to peace and happiness.

As for "influencing them to abide in good dharmas," he is able to turn beings away from evil actions of body, speech, and mind and influence them to take up the good karmic actions of body, speech, and mind.

As for these endeavors being "as previously explained in the discussion of the first ground," this refers to being able to see the buddhas and acquire the samādhis. The only difference is that, on that ground, hundreds of buddhas are seen, whereas on this ground, thousands of buddhas are seen.

The End of Chapter Thirty-Five

The End of theTreatise on the Ten Grounds

Endnotes

1. This is a reference to the *wojiao shan* (沃焦山), "the boiling and burning mountain" also known as the *wojiao shi* (沃焦石), the "boiling and burning rock," a huge and intensely hot mountain of stone at the bottom of the ocean which, in traditional Indian geography, is responsible for keeping the oceans from overflowing by boiling away the excess water flowing into them from all the great rivers, large and small. This mountain is sometimes held to reside at the bottom of the *wojiao hai* (沃焦海), "the boiling and burning ocean."

2. The four inverted views (*viparyāsa-catuṣka*) consist of imputing permanence to the impermanent, pleasure to what cannot deliver it, self to what is devoid of any inherently existent self, and purity to what does not actually possess that quality.

   Standard objects of such upside-down perception are: thought, the six categories of "feeling" manifested in association with the six sense faculties, dharmas (as components of the falsely imputed "self"), and the body.

   VB, preferring "inversions" to render this term, rightly points out that, per *Aṅguttara nikāya* 4:49, these four *viparyāsa* involve not only views, but rather they infect perceptions and mind as well as view. That said, I still feel comfortable with the now rather common and standard rendering as "four inverted views," not least because, as a practical matter, perception (*saṃjñā*) and mind/thought (*citta*) are nearly always intimately intertwined with and inseparable from views (*dṛṣṭī*), all of which are "inverted" due to delusion.

3. VB recognized these statements about four types of people as similar to statements in the *Aṅguttāra nikāya* (see his *Numerical Discourses of the Buddha*, pp. 476–77).

4. I emend the reading of the text here to correct an apparent graphic-similarity scribal error, preferring on sensibility grounds the *zheng* (拯), "rescue," of the SYMG editions to the *Taisho* edition's *ji* (極), "extremely."

5. The bracketed verse is repeated here to facilitate immediate reference by the reader.

6. Although this could be a reference to the *Mahāprajñāpāramitā Sūtra* wherein such statements do exist, Nāgārjuna might well intend here to cite the *Avataṃsaka Sūtra* (the mother sutra in which this entire ten grounds text is incorporated as "The Ten Grounds Chapter"). We have a number of such statements in the *Avataṃsaka Sūtra* including the famous passage (quoted some 350 times in Sino-Buddhist canonical works): "It is with the very moment of bringing forth the initial

resolve that one thereby achieves the right enlightenment" (初發心時便成正覺), this from Buddhabhadra's circa 400 CE translation (T09; no. 278; 449c).

7. "Vajra path" is an indirect reference to the acquisition of the "vajra-like samādhi" (*vajropama-samādhi*). It is a feature of both Southern and Northern School Buddhist path schemas that refers to the point at which the practitioner destroys the last vestiges of the residual fetters and reaches, for a *śrāvaka*-disciple practitioner, "the stage beyond the need for further training" or, for the bodhisattva path practitioner, the next to last stage of the Mahāyāna path known as "equal enlightenment" (*samasaṃbodhi*). This latter is the stage immediately prior to "sublime enlightenment" wherein the bodhisattva's level of awakening has reached the point that it is virtually the same as that of a fully enlightened buddha.

   As a Mahāyāna technical term "vajra path" is in no way any sort of reference to the so-called "Vajrayāna," a very late Hindu-influenced transformation of Buddhism characterized by the tenets and practices of Hindu tantras (Vajrayana texts are all post 6th century in origin, i.e., more than 1000 years post-Śākyamuni).

8. For the most part, I rely here and hereafter on Étienne Lamotte's *Traité de la Grande Vertu De Sagesse de Nāgārjuna* for the parenthetically included Sanskrit equivalents for the Chinese names of the various hells.

9. For Nāgārjuna's very graphic and nearly encyclopedic discussion of each one of the hell realms and hungry ghost realms wherein he explains the causality at the root of each type of suffering therein, see my translation from his *Mahāprajñāpāramitā Upadeśa*: *Nagarjuna on the Six Perfections*, in particular, within his discussion of the perfection of vigor, Chapter 27: "Specific Aspects of the Perfection of Vigor," p. 513-37 in the original bilingual edition.

10. The inscrutably ambiguous nature of the *Taisho* version of the text's rendering of a number of the instruments of punishment here (鐵鏘[金疾]鏫鐵[矛贊]刀鐵臼) is such that I prefer the alternative reading employed in the Song, Yuan, and Ming editions (槍蒺[廾/梨]刀劍鐵網: "javelins, spikes, short swords, iron nets").

11. "*Bhūta* ghost" is here a conjectural Sanskrit reconstruction of 浮陀鬼. According to MW, one of the many meanings of *bhūta* is: "a spirit (good or evil), the ghost of a deceased person, a demon, imp, goblin."

12. Again, the bracketed verse from the beginning of the chapter is repeated here to facilitate immediate reference by the reader.

13. Nāgārjuna is not implying here that the practitioners of the Śrāvaka Disciple vehicle actually possess all of these eight dharmas of the

bodhisattva. (After all, although they are certainly well-accomplished in the other six, they are not particularly well known for either compassion or skillful means.) Rather, he is primarily pointing out that they are secondary beneficiaries of the bodhisattvas' implementation of these eight dharmas that result in the bodhisattvas' eventual buddhahood and the resulting eternal renewal of Dharma in the world again and again throughout the course of time.

14. This would seem to contradict Nāgārjuna's earlier statement that "all *śrāvaka* disciples and *pratyekabuddhas* come forth in direct reliance upon a buddha." Not so. Even though the *pratyekabuddha* may finally gain his realization when there is no buddha and no Dharma in the world, his ability to gain that realization is entirely rooted in his previous lives' exposure to a buddha's Dharma at such time as there *was* a buddha or his right Dharma still existing in the world. It is at least in part the fruition of the karmic seeds from such earlier learning and practice that finally allows the *pratyekabuddha* at a later time to gain realizations in the absence of a buddha or of any residual Dharma after the end of a buddha's Dharma-ending age.
15. A *vibhāṣā* is an extensively detailed explanatory treatise.
16. VB points out that there is a canonical source for the "four bases" in *Majjhima nikaya* 140, MN III 245-6 for which the Sanskrit correlates of the Pali *saccādhitthāna, cāgādhitthāna, upasamādhitthāna* (= base of peace), and *paññādhitthāna* would be *satyādhiṣṭhāna, tyāgādhiṣṭhāna, upaśamādhiṣṭhāna,* and *prajñādhiṣṭhāna.* He also notes that there is a Chinese canonical parallel at MĀ 162; T01n0026_p0692a11.
17. I emend the reading of the *Taisho* text here to correct an apparent scribal error, preferring the reading in the SYMG editions (說十地義) to that of *Taisho* (義說十地).
18. The logic of this statement may seem opaque to some. The point here is that, so long as one creates bad karma and does not purify it, one's mind can never be at peace even in conventional terms. As for entering deep states of meditative quiescence such as the *dhyānas,* this would be completely impossible. This is one of the reasons why moral purity is taught as one of the primary prerequisites for meditative accomplishment.
19. VB notes the existence of a slightly variant parallel source in the Pali Canon: AN 3:80 (NDB p. 314). That citation makes it clear that, if Ānanda had somehow died before achieving the arhatship the Buddha predicted of him, his merit would have been so abundant that he would have been reborn in those blissful heavens for such an immensely long time.

20. The first four and a half of these five verses correspond to the KB translation of *The Ten Grounds Sutra* (498b27-c04).
21. The first two of these five verses echo Vajragarbha's preliminary statements in *The Ten Grounds Sutra,* just before embarking on the explanation of the first ground.
22. In this sort of context, *biding* (必定),"stage of certainty," is usually a translation of the Sanskrit *niyata* or one of its synonyms that refer to the stage of irreversibility from which one can never again fall back in one's progress on the path.
23. I emend the reading of the *Taisho* text to agree with the SYM editions, this by adding the qualifier *shan* (善), "thorough," to *xing* (行), "practice."

    Also, regarding householder practice, N's implication here is that, even though it is extremely difficult to carry on the life of a householder while also accessing the *dhyānas*, householder-level practice should not be disqualified from being referred to as "thorough practice" just because householders are usually unable to develop those meditation states.
24. "Resolute intentions," *shenxin* (深心), here and in most occurrences throughout the text, corresponds to the Sanskrit *āśaya* which has a range of meanings not so easily captured in a single English translation. Hence, in its various occurrences in scriptures and commentaries related to the ten grounds, it may connote "resolute," "deep-seated," or "earnest" "intentions," "aspirations," "dispositions" or "inclinations." In KB and SA, *āśaya* is often translated into Chinese as just *xin* (心) where it would very easily be confused with *citta*. In those instances, depending on the context and especially depending on whether it is referring to bodhisattvas or simply to unenlightened worldly beings, it is probably best rendered into English as "intentions," "aspirations," "dispositions" or "inclinations."
25. I emend the reading of the text here in accordance with the SYMG editions by preferring on sensibility grounds *wei* (未), "not yet," to the *Taisho* edition's *wei* (味), "flavor," the presence of which seems to have been the result of a graphic-similarity scribal error.
26. VB points out that this passage resembles a passage in "The Akṣayamati Chapter" of "*The Great Compilation Sutra*" (*Mahāvaipulya-mahāsaṃnipāta-sūtra*) at T13, no. 0397, p. 187b01.
27. "Forest hermitage" here translates what KJ retained in transliteration as the antecedent term: *araṇya* which is hermitage usually intended for the cultivation of deep meditation and/or various austere (*dhūta*) practices. Since the Sanskrit term does not carry any untranslatable

nuances, from here on I shall for the most part just go ahead and translate it as "forest hermitage.

28. I emend the reading of the text here in accordance with the SYMG editions by preferring on sensibility grounds to eliminate the *gu* (故), "therefore," the inclusion of which seems to have been the result of scribal error.

29. I emend the reading of the text here to correct an apparent scribal error in recording this statement by preferring the zhu fo fa (諸佛法), "all buddhas' Dharma," of the SYMG editions to Taisho's zhu fa (諸法), "all dharmas."

30. Although the Chinese is slightly ambiguous (hence my translation's use of the euphemistic "quiescent cessation," citing an analogue passage VB points out that the final couplet is referring to nirvāṇa, noting the following:

"The verse is perhaps alluding to MN I 45: *So vata, cunda, attanā palipapalipanno paraṃ palipapalipannaṃ uddharissatīti netaṃ ṭhānaṃ vijjati. So vata, cunda, attanā apalipapalipanno paraṃ palipapalipannaṃ uddharissatīti ṭhānametaṃ vijjati. So vata, cunda, attanā adanto avinīto aparinibbuto paraṃ damessati vinessati parinibbāpessatīti netaṃ ṭhānaṃ vijjati. So vata, cunda, attanā danto vinīto parinibbuto paraṃ damessati vinessati parinibbāpessatīti ṭhānametaṃ vijjati.* See MLDB 8, part16."

VB's translation there of the most closely relevant part of that passage is: "That one who is himself untamed, undisciplined, [with defilements] unextinguished, should tame another, discipline him, and help extinguish [his defilements] is impossible; that one who is himself tamed, disciplined, [with defilements] extinguished, should tame another, discipline him, and help extinguish [his defilements] is possible."

31. VB points out that this is a reference to *Dhammapada* 158 for which the Acharya Buddharakkhita translation gives: "One should first establish oneself in what is proper; then only should one instruct others. Thus the wise man will not be reproached."

32. VB suggests comparing the version of the ten powers found in *Majjhima nikāya* no. 12 ("The Greater Discourse on the Lion's Roar"). See MLDB, pp. 165-6.

33. Although KJ here uses the *xing* (性) that is usually translated as "nature," the source texts indicate that he is once again translating the Sanskrit *dhātu* which here refers to "realms."

34. This aspect along with the next five emphasize the importance of the six perfections.

35. This aspect along with the next three emphasize the importance of the four immeasurable minds.
36. As suggested by VB, this very likely refers to the twelfth chapter of the *Mahāsaṃnipāta-sūtra,* the "Akṣayamati Chapter" (T13n0397_p0184a16–212c26). In particular, this resembles a passage that begins at 187a26.
37. N refers here to a line from the fourth of his five earlier stanzas on cultivating the first ground:

    For the sake of gaining the ten powers,
    one enters the congregation of those at the stage of certainty.
    Then one is born into the family of the Tathāgatas
    wherein one is free of any transgressions or faults.

38. VB notes that the Pali version of this passage is found at MLDB 140.26, MN III 245: "For this, bhikkhu, is the supreme noble truth, namely, *nibbāna,* which has an undeceptive nature."
39. The *pratyutpanna* samādhi is a samādhi wherein one becomes able to see the buddhas of the present and listen to them teach the Dharma. The sutra that describes this samādhi and teaches how to acquire it is preserved in the *Taisho* Canon as the *Banzhou Sanmei Jing* (般舟三昧經 / T13.no. 0418.902c23–919c05) of which Paul Harrison has produced a translation for the BDK English Tripitaka. Other Chinese editions and translations of the same text are preserved as *Taisho* text numbers 416, 417, and 419.
40. N alludes here to verse number thirty-four from his *Bodhisaṃbhāra śāstra* (菩提資糧論 / T32n1660_p0528c13–14). See my translation of this treatise, *Nāgārjuna's Guide to the Bodhisattva Path,* page 33:

    The solid samādhis
    on the ground of all buddhas' "direct presence"
    serve for the bodhisattva as his father,
    whereas the great compassion and patiences serve as his mother.

    (諸佛現前住
    牢固三摩提
    此為菩薩父
    大悲忍為母.)

    N's equating of the *pratyutpanna* samādhi (wherein one sees the buddhas of the present) with a samādhi experienced on the sixth bodhisattva ground associates rather well with the following passage from the discussion of the sixth ground in the KB translation of the Ten Grounds Sutra:

    "The bodhisattva dwelling on this Ground of Direct Presence succeeds in being able to see many hundreds of buddhas, many thousands of buddhas, and so forth on up to many hundreds of thousands of myriads of *koṭis* of buddhas, making offerings to them, paying reverence to them, venerating them, praising them, and presenting them with robes, food and drink, bedding, and medicines. He draws close to the Buddhas and listens to the teaching of the Dharma in the presence of the Buddhas. Having heard their teachings on Dharma, he employs the light of reality-concordant wisdom to implement those teachings in practice in a manner accordant with the way they were taught, doing so in a manner that delights all buddhas." (T10n0286_p515c17–21.)

41. N refers again to this earlier verse on cultivating the first ground:

    For the sake of gaining the ten powers,
    one enters the congregation of those at the stage of certainty.
    Then one is born into the family of the Tathāgatas
    wherein one is free of any transgressions or faults.

42. These four bases of meritorious qualities (四功德處: 諦, 捨, 滅, 慧 / truth, relinquishment, cessation, and wisdom) are brought up repeatedly in this treatise and are found as well in N's *Bodhisaṃbhāra Śāstra* and *Ratnāvalī*.

43. I emend the reading of the text here by adopting the variant reading found in the SYMG editions to correct the absence of a single character (出) obviously missing from the *Taisho* text.

44. Throughout this text, I go ahead and translate "*srota-āpanna*" as "stream enterer."

45. "Three wretched destinies" is a reference to rebirth in the realms of hungry ghosts (*pretas*), animals, and hells.

46. The point here is that, since a stream enterer is then bound to enter *nirvāṇa* within seven lifetimes, whereupon he will not be reborn into any of the twenty-eight realms of rebirth (and there are *only* twenty-eight realms of rebirth), he need have no fear that he might somehow stray into some supposed "twenty-ninth" realm of rebirth (because no such place even exists).

47. I emend the reading of the text here in accordance with the SYMG editions by preferring on sensibility grounds *duo* (多), "for the most part," to the *Taisho* edition's *mingwei* (名為), "is known as."

48. "Contaminants" here translates the slightly ambiguous pre-Buddhist Jain term *asrava*, translated into Chinese as "flows" (漏). The allusion is to the defiling influence (read "influents") of either three or four factors, as follows: 1) sensual desire (*kāma*); 2) [craving for] becoming (*bhāva*), i.e., the craving for continued existence; 3) ignorance (*avidyā*), i.e., delusion; 4) views (*dṛṣṭi*) This fourth type is not included in some listings. Often-encountered alternate translations of this term include "taints," "outflows," "influxes," and "fluxes."

49. These forty dharmas (discussed at great length in chapters 21–23) are as follows:
    1) Sovereign mastery of the ability to fly.
    2) [The ability to manifest] countless transformations.
    3) Boundless psychic powers of the sort possessed by *āryas.*
    4) Sovereign mastery of the ability to hear sounds.
    5) Immeasurable power of knowledge to know others' thoughts.
    6) Sovereign mastery in [training and subduing] the mind.
    7) Constant abiding in stable wisdom.
    8) Never forgetting.
    9) Possession of the powers of the vajra samādhi.
    10) Thorough knowing of matters that are unfixed
    11) Thorough knowing of matters pertaining to the formless realm's meditative absorptions.
    12) The completely penetrating knowledge of all matters associated with eternal cessation.
    13) Thorough knowing of the non-form dharmas unassociated with the mind.
    14) The great powers *pāramitā.*
    15) The [four] unimpeded [knowledges] *pāramitā.*
    16) The *pāramitā* of perfectly complete replies and predictions in response to questions.
    17) Invulnerability to harm by anyone.
    18) Their words are never spoken without a purpose.
    19) Their speech is free of errors and mistakes.
    20) Complete implementation of the three turnings [of the Dharma wheel] in speaking Dharma.
    21) They are the great generals among all *āryas.*
    22–25) They are able to remain unguarded in four ways.
    26–29) They possess the four types of fearlessness.
    30–39) They possess the ten powers.
    40) They have achieved unimpeded liberation.
50. I emend the reading of the *Taisho* text here by preferring on sensibility grounds the SYMG editions' *yi* (已), "already," to the *Taisho* edition's *yi* (以), "by means of," "due to," etc."
51. "Musth" refers to a state of increased testosterone in a bull elephant that is characterized by increased willfulness and aggressiveness in doing whatever he wants to do.
52. The first five of these types of fear are brought up at this point in the Ten Grounds Sutra itself. In previewing my translation of that sutra, Bhikkhu Bodhi pointed out that this same fivefold list appears in the Pali (albeit in slightly different order and with mild differences

in the interpretation of two of the five points). See his translation of *Numerical Discourses* 9:5, p. 1255.

53. In most cases, "mind-moment" (一念 or 一念頃) translates the Sanskrit *kṣaṇa* or *eka-kṣaṇika*. As for "*kṣaṇa*," according to PDB: "In Sanskrit, 'instant' or 'moment'; the shortest possible span of time, variously measured as either the ninth part of a thought moment or the 4,500th part of a minute."

54. An *asaṃkhyeya* is an incalculably large Sanskrit number.

55. This is a reference to the seven "treasures" (*sapta ratna*) of a *cakravartin* king. Different from the more common list of "the seven precious things," they are: the wheel treasure, elephant treasure, horse treasure, precious pearl treasure, female treasure, *kulapati* (wealth-accumulation) treasure, and the army-and-ministers lordship treasure.

56. This reconstruction of "*she-ti-luo*" (蛇提羅) as *kṣatriya* is conjectural. It is likely that N is referring to the lesser wheel-turning kings who, unlike the wheel-turning king who is a universal monarch, do not rule over all four continents, but rather over only one, two, or three continents.

57. *Jiaojumo* (憍瞿摩). I cannot find any Sanskrit equivalent for this.

58. The implication in the first foot of the *śloka* is that, if one refrains from erroneously imputing the existence of an inherently-existent self, then the concept of some event called "death" is discovered to be baseless. Similarly, the second foot of the *śloka* indicates that, if one simply refrains from erroneously imputing the existence of some independently-existing concept that one thinks of as "death," then the concept of "some entity that dies" is discovered to be baseless as well.

59. KJ retained the Sanskrit *sarvajña* which I have chosen here to translate.

60. The Taisho text inserts a ming (名) here to create the clearly accidentally erroneous duo mingwen (多名聞) which means "abundant fame" instead of the "abundant learning" (多聞) referenced in the verse upon which this sentence comments. For obvious reasons, I have aligned my translation here with the clearly intended meaning.

61. N uses the Sanskrit *dānapati*. I prefer to translate it as "benefactor" throughout the following discussion.

62. N uses the Sanskrit *niṣadana*. I prefer to translate it as "sitting mat."

63. VB gives the Pali Canon correlate to this as *Itivuttaka* section 100: "*Tassa me tumhe puttā orasā mukhato jātā dhammajā dhammanimmitā dhammadāyādā, no āmisadāyādā.*"

64. I have been unable to associate this work with any texts extant in the *Taisho* canon.

65. In my translation of the KB *Ten Grounds Sutra*, the complete text of this first vow is as follows:

    I vow that I shall make gifts of every sort of offering to all buddhas without exception, freely making such offerings with pure resolute faith." In making such a great vow as this, his implementation of it is as vast as the Dharma realm and as extensive as empty space as he continues on until the end of future time, exhaustively making offerings of every sort of great gift to all buddhas.

66. In my translation of the KB *Ten Grounds Sutra*, the complete text of this second vow is as follows:

    He also vows that he will uphold and preserve the scriptural Dharma proclaimed by all buddhas, that he will take on the realization of the *anuttarasamyaksaṃbodhi* of all buddhas, that he will always accord with the Dharma taught by all buddhas, and that he will always be able to protect and preserve the Dharma of all buddhas. In making such a great vow as this, his implementation of it is as vast as the Dharma realm and as extensive as empty space as he continues on incessantly until the end of future time, exhaustively protecting and preserving the Dharma of all buddhas in every kalpa.

67. In my translation of the KB *Ten Grounds Sutra*, the complete text of this third vow is as follows:

    He also vows that, in all worlds, with the arrival of all buddhas, when they come down from the Tuṣita Heaven, enter the womb, abide in the womb, are first born, leave behind the home life, and then gain buddhahood, in every case he will entreat them to turn the great wheel of the Dharma, vowing too that, when they manifest entry into the great nirvāṇa, "I will in every case go there, make offerings, and serve as a leader in the compilation of their Dharma," vowing to do these things in order to facilitate [the Dharma wheel's] turning throughout the three periods of time. In making such a great vow as this, his implementation of it is as vast as the Dharma realm and as extensive as empty space as he continues on until the end of future time and throughout all kalpas, incessantly raising up offerings to all buddhas.

68. In my translation of the KB *Ten Grounds Sutra*, the complete text of this fourth vow is as follows:

    He also vows that he will teach all of the practices coursed in by the bodhisattvas, so vast, lofty, and far-reaching, so immeasurable, indestructible, and free of discriminations, those practices that are subsumed within the *pāramitās*, that are purified on the grounds, that generate the dharmas assisting realization of the path, that constitute the path of signs and the path of signlessness, teaching how they may conduce to success and how they may lead to ruination, teaching the path of the grounds coursed in by all bodhisattvas, teaching too the *pāramitās'* foundational practices, teaching these things to others in a manner whereby they are caused to take up their practice and bring forth increased resolve. In making such a great vow as this, his implementation of it is as vast as the Dharma realm and as extensive as empty space as he continues on until the end of future time and throughout all kalpas, incessantly employing the practices coursed in by all bodhisattvas to provide teaching in accord with Dharma for the ripening of beings.

69. In my translation of the KB *Ten Grounds Sutra,* the complete text of this fifth vow is as follows:

    He also vows that he will teach all beings, whether possessed of form or formless, whether possessed of perception, free of perception, or abiding in a state of neither perception nor non-perception, whether egg-born, womb-born, moisture-born, or transformationally born, teaching them all, no matter to which of the stations in the triple world they have become connected, no matter in which of the six destinies of rebirth they have taken birth, no matter in which place they have taken rebirth, thus teaching all who are subsumed in the sphere of name-and-form, proceeding thus for the sake of teaching and ripening all beings, for the sake of influencing them to cut off their coursing through all the destinies of worldly existence, for the sake of influencing them to abide in the Dharma of the Buddha, for the sake of influencing them to accumulate all-knowledge, teaching all of them without exception. In making such a great vow as this, his implementation of it is as vast as the Dharma realm and as extensive as empty space as he continues on until the end of future time and throughout all kalpas, incessantly teaching all beings.

70. *Fawei* (法位), "Dharma position," usually corresponds to "the right and fixed Dharma position" (*samyaktva niyāma*) that in turn involves irreversibility in one's progress on the path to the fruits of the individual-liberation paths of either the *pratyekabuddha* or the arhat. This is usually understood (except in sutras such as the *Lotus Sutra*) to involve the subsequent impossibility of ever entering the universal-liberation path of the bodhisattvas and buddhas.

71. "Reveal, instruct, benefit, and delight" (示教利喜) is an often encountered them in Northern School texts that refers to standard teaching stratagems used to influence beings to enter the universal liberation path of bodhisattvas and buddhas.

72. In my translation of the KB *Ten Grounds Sutra,* the complete text of this sixth vow is as follows:

    He also vows to directly know all of the differentiating aspects of all worlds throughout the ten directions, including all aspects of those worlds that are wide, narrow, extremely towering, of so countlessly many varieties one could never distinguish them all, including those that are immovable, and those that are indescribably coarse, subtle, upright, inverted, formed with their crowns and bases opposing each other, flat, spherical, or cubical, thus being able in this knowing to freely enter the knowledge of all such worlds, knowing them as existing in a manner comparable to appearances in the net-like canopy of Indra wherein things manifest like the phenomena in a conjuration. In making such a great vow as this, his implementation of it is as vast as the Dharma realm and as extensive as empty space as he continues on until the end of future time and throughout all kalpas, incessantly carrying on the direct and complete knowing of all such worlds.

73. This refers to a list of six recommended reflections conducing to clarity of understanding: impermanence, suffering, nonself, impurity of food, unenjoyability of all stations of worldly existence, death (T28.1548.637b).

74. In my translation of the KB *Ten Grounds Sutra,* the complete text of this seventh vow is as follows:

    He also vows to bring about the purification of all buddha lands wherein all buddha lands enter a single buddha land, a single buddha land enters all buddha lands, and each and every buddha land is adorned with measurelessly many radiant phenomena, wherein they all become filled with measurelessly many wise beings who have abandoned all defilements and perfected the path of purification, and wherein he always possesses the power of all buddhas' great superknowledges, accords with the mental dispositions of beings, and thus appears for their sakes. In making such a great vow as this, his implementation of it is as vast as the Dharma realm and as extensive as empty space as he continues on until the end of future time and throughout all kalpas, incessantly purifying lands such as these.

75. The five categories of evil ending with this one are the same ones that were described and thoroughly explained by Nāgārjuna earlier in this text as "five types of wrong livelihood for monastics."

76. These last five categories of evils clearly refer directly to the five hindrances (*nīvaraṇa* or *āvaraṇa*) preventing entry into meditative absorption.

77. I have not been able to find the Sanskrit antecedents for these three Chinese transliterations or the two transliterations that appear a little farther down in this list.
78. VB points out that this is most likely a reference to the Digambara Jains.
79. VB points out that this is most likely a reference to the Śvetāmbara Jains.
80. VB points out that Maskarī Gośālīputra was the "founder of the Ājivikas, See DN 2.20. He held that everything was determined by fate."
81. VB suggests that this is Sañjaya Vairāṭīputra, a.k.a. Saṃjayin Vairāṭīputra (Pali: Sañjaya Belaṭṭhiputta), a skeptical ascetic teacher, a contemporary of the Buddha. See DN 2.32
82. Per VB: "Probably Pakudha Kaccāyana. See DN 2.26. He taught a kind of atomism."
83. Per VB: "Perhaps Ajita Kesakambali, who taught a moral nihilism. See DN 2.23."
84. Per VB: "On the above [various theorists on nirvāṇa], see the five types of "final nirvāṇa in this very life" mentioned in the *Brahmajāla Sutta,* DN 1.3.19."
85. One should understand that this does not refer to the *dhūta* austerities so extensively discussed and praised by N in the 32nd chapter of this treatise, but rather only to the non-beneficial ascetic practices (lying down on a bed of nails, etc.) adopted by non-Buddhist traditions.
86. This is probably a reference to the ten "entangling thickets" (*gahana*) of which the first is indeed "afflictions." They are routinely translated as "difficulties" in KJ and KB translations. They are listed in the translation of the *Ten Grounds Sutra* (T10.286.524c10–12) in the discussion of the ninth *bhūmi* as follows:

    The entangling difficulties associated with the afflictions;
    The entangling difficulties associated with karmic actions;
    The entangling difficulties associated with the faculties;
    The entangling difficulties associated with resolute dispositions;
    The entangling difficulties associated with sense realms;
    The entangling difficulties associated with the mind's deep-seated intentions;
    The entangling difficulties associated with latent tendencies;
    The entangling difficulties associated with births;
    The entangling difficulties associated with residual karmic propensities;

And the entangling difficulties associated with the differences in the three categories of beings.

87. Probably *adbhuta* (Pali: *abbhuta*), "wondrous, supernatural, etc." for which the standard Chinese rendering is: "rarely encountered" (希有).

88. Per VB: "We have here five terms that are characteristic of the Buddha's teaching which we encounter again and again in the *Nikāyas* (particularly the *Saṃyutta Nikāya,* where they are applied to all the doctrinal items: the five aggregates (in Ch. 22), the six or twelve sense bases (Ch. 35), feelings (Ch. 36), the elements (Ch. 14), etc. The five are: *samudaya, atthaṅgama, assāda, ādīnava, nissaraṇa,* 'arising, passing away, enjoyment, danger, and escape.'

   "See e.g. SN 22: 73–74, 107–109, 129–34, and many other suttas.

   "For example SN 22:74 says, 'The unlearned worldling does not correctly understand the arising (through 'escape') regarding form ... consciousness. The learned noble disciple correctly understands the arising (through 'escape') regarding form ... consciousness.'

   "On the five-term template, see SN 14:38; 17:26; 22:108; 23:6; 36:28. The threefold "enjoyment" template is also common—see 14:37; 17:25; 22:107; 23:5; 36:27; 48:6, 29, 34."

89. [With reference to the Pali tradition], VB notes: "Here we have *vimokṣa* as eight stages of samādhi."

90. The Pali meditation tradition refers to these as *kasiṇas.*

91. The earlier line (33a22) upon which this comments referred instead to *ligen* (利根) "sharp faculties."

92. I emend the *Taisho* reading here by accepting the variant "moths" (蛾) found in four other editions. Without this emendation, "ants" (蟻) would be duplicated in this list.

93. VB suggests that this most likely corresponds to *saṃhita.*

94. In my translation of the KB Ten Grounds Sutra, the complete text of this eighth vow is as follows:

    > He also vows that he will be of like mind with and pursue the same studies as all other bodhisattvas, joining together with them in the accumulation of every sort of goodness, remaining free of enmity or jealousy toward them, developing identical states of mental awareness as theirs, holding thoughts of equal regard toward them, maintaining harmonious relations with them, never becoming mutually estranged from them, being able as well to manifest buddha bodies according to what suits the needs of others, being able in one's own mind to completely understand and know the domains, spiritual powers, and powers of cognition of all buddhas, always being able to freely employ spiritual superknowledges to

roam at will to all lands, manifesting the appearance of one's body in the assemblies of all buddhas, being able as well to everywhere take up births into all stations of rebirth, being possessed of all such inconceivably great wisdom, and perfecting the practices of the bodhisattvas. In making such a great vow as this, his implementation of it is as vast as the Dharma realm and as extensive as empty space as he continues on until the end of future time and throughout all kalpas, incessantly carrying forth the practice of just such a great path of wisdom.

95. In my translation of the KB Ten Grounds Sutra, the complete text of this ninth vow is as follows:

> He also vows that he will take up the irreversible turning of the wheel of Dharma, that he will course in the bodhisattva path, that, of all of his physical, verbal, and mental actions, none will be such as are done in vain, that any being who merely sees him will thereby immediately become bound for definite success in the Buddha's Dharma, that, "Any being who so much as hears my voice will thereby immediately become bound for success in the path of genuine wisdom," that, "Any being who merely lays eyes on me will immediately be filled with joyous delight and abandon afflictions," that, in this, he will become like the great king of medicine trees, and that, in order to develop such resolve as this, he will course in the bodhisattva path. In making such a great vow as this, his implementation of it is as vast as the Dharma realm and as extensive as empty space as he continues on until the end of future time and throughout all kalpas, incessantly coursing along in the path of irreversibility, ensuring that none of his actions will have been done in vain.

96. In my translation of the KB Ten Grounds Sutra, the complete text of this tenth vow is as follows:

> He also vows that he will gain the realization of *anuttarasamyaksaṃbodhi* in all worlds, that even in those places manifesting within the tip of a single hair, he will manifest entry into the womb, leaving behind the home life, sitting in the *bodhimaṇḍa,* gaining buddhahood, turning the wheel of Dharma, bringing about the liberation of beings, and manifesting the appearance of entering the great nirvāṇa, that he will manifest the great spiritual and cognitive powers of the *tathāgatas,* that he will adapt to the circumstances of all individual beings and that, according to what is appropriate for their liberation, he will, even in every successive mind-moment, manifest realization of the buddha path, facilitate the liberation of beings, and bring about the extinguishing of their suffering and afflictions, that he will gain the cognition that realizes all dharmas are characterized by identity with nirvāṇa,

that, employing a single voice, he will be able to cause all beings to become established in joyfulness, that, even though he manifests entry into the great nirvāṇa, he will nonetheless never cut off his coursing in the bodhisattva practices, that he will reveal to beings the grounds of great knowledge, that he will cause them to realize all dharmas are in every case false and deceptive, accomplishing these endeavors by resort to great wisdom, great superknowledges, and freely manifested spiritual transformations. In making such a great vow as this, his implementation of it is as vast as the Dharma realm and as extensive as empty space as he continues on until the end of future time and throughout all kalpas, incessantly persisting in accomplishing the works associated with the path to buddhahood, in seeking great wisdom, and in acquiring the great spiritual powers and other such realizations.

97. We know from comparisons with Sanskrit editions that, in some of the translations attributed to Kumārajīva (such as the *Daśabhumika Sutra*), *xing* (性) (usually translated into English as "nature" from the Sanskrit antecedent *bhāva*) instead often translates the Sanskrit antecedent *dhātu* which most often corresponds to the English word "realm." This section of text appears to be one of those passages. Hence my repeated translation here of *xing* (性) as "realm" and not as "nature."

98. "Range of actions" here translates *xingchu* (行處), a standard translation for the Sanskrit *gocara* which, per MW, means "pasture ground for cattle, range, field for action, abode, dwelling place, district, etc."

99. To correct an obvious scribal error involving the dropping of a crucial character from this phrase already occurring twice in this section, I emend the reading of the *Taisho* text by accepting the SYMG editions' retention of *fo* (佛), "buddhas."

100. Since it only requires one of these seven reasons for generating the resolve to actually do so, one might wonder why N mentions: "it may find its origin in [one of] three reasons or else in [one of] four reasons." I suspect he is referring to two different lists of reasons prevalent in different teaching traditions.

101. VB notes: "I think this is alluding to the seven good dharmas. See *Majjhima Nikāya* 53 (also *Anguttara Nikāya* 7:67): *śraddhā, hrī, avatapta* [*apatrāpya*], *bāhuśrutya, vīrya, smṛti,* and *prajñā*." (Faith, sense of shame, dread of blame, abundant learning, vigor, mindfulness, wisdom.)

102. VB proposes that this may refer to "eleven benefits of loving-kindness" enumerated in the *Aṅguttara Nikāya*'s treatment of "The Elevens," this based on his observation that Chinese translators

sometimes use this *gongde* (功德), usually "meritorious qualities," to translate *ānusaṃsā*, "benefits."

103. "Seventeen physical dharmas" is a provisional translation for "*shen shi qi*" (身十七). The text is opaque and a digital search of the entire *Taisho* canon failed to turn up any plausible analogues for this list.

104. VB notes that there are five faculties here that are distributed among these four listed types.

105. Comparison with the Sanskrit of the occurrences of this *xinle* (信樂) compound in the KB translation of the Ten Grounds Sutra confirm that this is an alternate Kumārajiva translation for *adhimukti* which is more commonly rendered into Kumārajiva translations as *xinjie* (信解), lit. "faithful comprehension." This refers to a strong mental inclination toward a (usually) wholesome mental object, hence the need to translate it in some contexts as "resolute belief," "resolute comprehension," etc.

106. I emend the reading of the *Taisho* text here, preferring the *chang* (常), "always," of the SYMG editions to *Taisho*'s *dang* (當), "should," this to correct an apparent graphic-similarity scribal error.

107. As Nāgārjuna makes clear elsewhere (*Bodhisaṃbhāra Śāstra* [菩提資糧論 – T32, no. 1660]), for one who aspires to continue all the way along the bodhisattva path to ultimate realization of buddhahood, it is essential that they first genuinely and solidly generate the resolve to gain the utmost, right, and perfect enlightenment, doing so *prior* to entering this "stage of certainty" or "right and fixed position" (*samyaktva niyāma*), lest they otherwise fall irreversibly into the path to arhatship.

 Nāgārjuna's rationale for warning bodhisattva path practitioners about this possibility is that, absent prior genuine generation of highest-bodhi resolve, the diligent cultivator of good dharmas who gains such a realization will become irreversible on the path to arhatship, this effective with his realization of the unproduced-dharmas patience. As a consequence, he entirely eliminates the possibility of his own future buddhahood.

 In that treatise, Nāgārjuna even goes so far as to equate this prospect with a tragedy far worse than falling into the hells, this because the hells, unlike arhatship, do not eliminate the possibility of future buddhahood. For my complete English translation of Nāgārjuna's *Bodhisaṃbhāra Śāstra*, and its early Indian Commentary, see *Nāgārjuna's Guide to the Bodhisattva Path* and *The Bodhisaṃbhāra Treatise Commentary*, both published by Kalavinka Press.

108. The "stage of certainty" or "right and fixed position" referenced here is that of the bodhisattva who has by this point become invulnerable to being turned away from the path to buddhahood.

109. Bhikkhu notes: "Velāma is the subject of AN 9.20."

110. "*Weishouduoluo*" (韋首多羅), the Chinese transliteration of this bodhisattva's name, is found only in this once in the entire Taisho canon. VB suggests that the Pali reconstruction might be "Vessantara," the name of the marvelously generous bodhisattva celebrated in a *jātaka* tale of one of the Buddha's previous lives. He also suggests that a Sanskrit equivalent might be the "Viśvantara" that I have chosen to use here.

111. These five Sanskrit terms refer to increasingly serious levels of transgression against the monastic moral code ranging from relatively minor offenses (*duṣkṛta*) to offenses involving a meeting of the Sangha with a probationary period (*saṃghāvaśeṣa*) or permanent expulsion from the monastic community (*pārājika*).

112. Because the Chinese of this statement is terse and vague, my translation here is somewhat tentative.

113. This appears to be subcommentary on this earlier statement regarding the abandonment of dharmas conducing to loss of the bodhi resolve: "By 'abandonment,' it is meant that one entirely extinguishes those dharmas that are bad and thus prevents them from entering one's mind."

114. A *pārājika* offense entails expulsion from the monastic sangha. A *saṃgha-vaśeṣa* offense entails a meeting of the local monastic sangha to determine the penalty and how to achieve purification of the transgression.

115. An instance of "at the time of certification" would be, for instance, during the semimonthly recitation of monastic precepts, when one is asked with respect to precepts just recited, "Are you pure in this?"

116. "Two Vehicles" refers to the two non-Mahāyāna individual-liberation paths, those of the arhats and the *pratyekabuddhas*.

117. The *Taisho* annotations state that the SYMG editions all format these twenty characters as a quatrain. As it is obvious that the immediately following text comments on them as if they did indeed constitute a verse, I have emended the English formatting accordingly.

118. In accordance with the SYMG editions, I emend the *Taisho* text here by substituting *sui* (雖), "although," for *shui* (誰), "who," this to correct an obvious graphic-similarity scribal error.

119. Again, those four originally mentioned in the above verse are: unawareness of the work of *māras*; weakness of the resolve to attain bodhi; karmic obstacles; and Dharma obstacles.

120. I translate here as "monastic preceptor" and "monastic Dharma teacher" what the KJ text retains in transliteration as "*upādhyāya*" and "*ācārya*" respectively.

121. When KJ refers to "the true character of dharmas" (諸法實相), he is typically translating the Sanskrit term "*dharmatā*."

122. This is clearly a reference to the eight worldly dharmas. In this connection VB offers the following citation: "See AN 8:5–6; IV 156 foll."

123. This seems to be a situation where some monk or nun wants to divert to themselves the material support of families that currently support other monastics. VB suggests, "This is what is called in Pali *kulamacchariya*, 'miserliness regarding families.'" He offers the following citation: AN 5:254–255.

124. "Five objects of desire" refers not only to the five types of "sensual" desire (forms, sounds, smells, tastes, touchables), but also to wealth, sex, fame, food, and leisure.

125. VB notes that the following verses reflect ideas found in Nāgārjuna's *Mūlamadhyamaka-kārikā*, in particular chapters 18, 10, and 6.

126. These four lines comprise the Buddhist tetralemma used to point to the futility of capturing the nature of ultimate reality in logical formulations.

127. In other words, ash has been traditionally used in making bleaching agents. So too with words: They may be used to remove the stain of wrong views from the mind, but they cannot ever entirely embody the truth reached through right views. Thus they are always bound to be freighted to a degree with the "stains" of dual concepts that are then bound to sully the direct perception of the truth of the emptiness of all phenomena.

128. This same verse is repeated later in the treatise in Chapter 33, at 118b05–26. There are eight variant characters as noted below.

129. The Chapter 33 version of this verse has "and is identical with whatever is an existent dharma" instead of "and is identical with whatever is possessed of signs" (即為是有法 instead of 即為是有相).

130. The Chapter 33 version of this verse has "Were one to relinquish all strategizing and attachments" instead of "Were one to relinquish all covetousness" (若捨諸計著 instead of 若捨諸貪著).

131. The Chapter 33 version of this verse has "such seizing on this sign of having relinquished attachments" instead of "such seizing on this

sign of having relinquished covetousness" (取是捨著相 instead of 取是捨貪相).

132. The Chapter 33 version of this verse has "It is the abandonment of grasping and whatever thing is grasped—" instead of "There is someone who grasps and something that is grasped" (離取取何事 instead of 誰取取何事).

133. The Chapter 33 version of this verse has "whether as conjoined or separate, they are all entirely nonexistent" instead of "whether as conjoined or separate, they all do not exist" (共離俱無有 instead of 共離俱不有).

134. The Chapter 33 version of this verse has "It is precisely because it is synonymous with signlessness" instead of "It is precisely because it is signless" (即名為無相 instead of 即為是無相).

135. These first two verse lines are referring to the four alternative propositions of the tetralemma, as in: 1) It exists; 2) It does not exist; 3) It both exists and does not exist; and 4) It neither exists nor does not exist.

136. The Chapter 33 version of this verse has a fairly nonconsequential variant for one of the characters in this line (先來非寂滅 instead of 先亦非寂滅).

137. VB notes the following here: "This is the first alternative among the four ways of construing a self. See SN 22:47."

138. The usual Sanskrit antecedent for this "traceless vajra-wielding dharma protectors" is *guhyapāda vajra*.

139. These *ślokas* correspond to *ślokas* 24–28 of Nāgārjuna's *Bodhisambhāra Śāstra*. In my English translation of that entire text with its Indian commentary, they read as follows:

    So long as he has not generated great compassion or the patiences,
    even though he may have gained an irreversibility,
    the bodhisattva is still subject to a form of "dying"
    which occurs through allowing negligence to arise.

    The grounds of the *śrāvaka* disciples or the *pratyekabuddhas*,
    if entered, become for him the same as dying
    because he would thereby sever the bodhisattva's
    roots of understanding and awareness.

    Even at the prospect of falling into the hell-realms,
    the bodhisattva would not be struck with fright.
    The grounds of the *śrāvaka* disciples and the *pratyekabuddhas*,
    however,
    do provoke a great terror in him.

    It is not the case that falling into the hell realms

would bring about an ultimate obstacle to his bodhi.
The grounds of the *śrāvaka* disciples and the *pratyekabuddhas*, however,
do create just such an ultimate obstacle.

Just as is said of he who loves long life,
that he becomes fearful at the prospect of his own beheading,
so too, the grounds of the *śrāvaka* disciples and *pratyekabuddhas*
should bring about a fearfulness of just this sort.

140. The first two quatrains correspond to the *Bodhisambhāra Śāstra*'s *śloka* numbers 22 and 23 which read as follows:

In the bodhisattva's striving for bodhi,
so long as he has not yet gained irreversibility,
he acts as urgently as the person whose turban has caught fire.
Thus one should take up just such intensely diligent practice.

Thus it is that those bodhisattvas,
when striving for the realization of bodhi,
should not rest in their practice of vigor,
for they have shouldered such a heavy burden.

141. These last two quatrains correspond to the *Bodhisambhāra Śāstra*'s *śloka* numbers 91 and 92 which read as follows:

Even if one were to take up the vehicle of the *śrāvaka* disciples
or the vehicle of the *pratyekabuddhas*,
and hence practiced solely for one's own self benefit,
still, one would not relinquish the enduring practice of vigor.

How much the less could it be that a great man,
one committed to liberate himself and liberate others,
might somehow not generate
a measure of vigor a thousand *koṭis* times greater?

142. I emend here the verse-abbreviated "Three Practices Buddha" reading to "Three *Vehicles* Practices Buddha" to accord with the explanatory text which follows at 42a02–06.

143. See *The Sutra on the Youth Precious Moon's Questions on Dharma* (大乘寶月童子問法經 / T14n0437_p108c01–110a07). The names vary, but the ideas are the same, i.e., sincere mindfulness of ten buddhas in the ten directions can bring irreversibility with respect to one's future attainment of buddhahood.

144. "*Candana*" usually refers to sandalwood, but as noted in MW, it may also be used as a term to refer to anything that is the most excellent of its kind. MW: "mn. sandal (*Sirium myrtifolium*), either the tree, wood, or the unctuous preparation of the wood held in high estimation as perfumes; hence; a term for anything which is the most excellent of its kind."

145. The Chinese translation for this eightieth buddha's name, *guang-ming fo* (光明佛), "Light Buddha," is duplicated in the name of the ninety-sixth buddha (see next paragraph). Since we do not know the Sanskrit antecedents for these two buddhas' names, I have distinguished them here with slightly variant English translations ("Light Buddha," "Radiance Buddha").

146. The Chinese translation for this ninety-sixth buddha's name, *guang-ming fo* (光明佛), "Radiance Buddha," is duplicated in the name of the eightieth buddha (see previous paragraph). Since we do not know the Sanskrit antecedents for these two buddhas' names, I have distinguished them here with slightly variant English translations ("Light Buddha," "Radiance Buddha").

147. On sensibility grounds, I adopt here the SYMG editions' variant, *hua yuan fo* (華園佛), "Floral Garden Buddha," to correct what seems to be a graphic-similarity scribal error in the *Taisho* edition, *hua chi fo* (華齒佛), "Floral Teeth Buddha."

148. I reconstruct "*aśoka*," lit. "sorrowless" as the name of this bodhi tree as it is a tree that grows throughout India (*Saraca asoca*) and is in fact said to also be the same kind of tree under which the historical Buddha's mother gave birth to him.

149. VB provides the following citation: "See DN II 4: *Sikhī, bhikkhave, bhagavā arahaṃ sammāsambuddho puṇḍarīkassa mūle abhisambuddho.*"

150. The *śirīṣa* tree is identified by MW as *acacia sirissa*.

151. An "*aśvattha*" tree is an ancient name for what is more commonly known in Buddhist texts as the "bodhi" tree (*ficus religiosa*).

152. In the verses below (at 44b07), this Buddha's name is enhanced with an additional character to "Marks of the Sovereign's Canopy" (王幢相).

153. I suspect that there should only be ten buddhas in this list and that this buddha's name may appear here only as a result of an accidental scribal redundancy, this for two reasons:
    a) The Chinese name is identical to that of the previously listed buddha except that the characters are in reverse order (*wangx-iang* [王相] versus *xiangwang* [相王]); and
    b) Although the other ten buddhas' names are mentioned in the following praise verses, this buddha's name is not mentioned there at all.

154. This buddha's name is only slightly different in the verses that follow, occurring there (at 44b15) as "Peacefully Established" (安立).

155. I emend the reading of the reading here by preferring the *zi* (自), "personally," of the SYMG editions to the *mu* (目), "eyes" of the *Taisho* text, this to correct an apparent graphic-similarity scribal error.

156. "Three times three, nine kinds in all" appears to refer to the nine varieties of bad karma produced through physical, verbal, and mental actions under the influence of the three kinds of afflictions or poisons (greed, hatred, and delusion).

157. One of two types of "morally indeterminate" or "neutral dharmas," *yin mo wu ji* (隱沒無記) or *you fu wu ji* (有覆無記), "obscured morally indeterminate [dharmas]," (*nivṛta-avyākṛta-dharma*) are those that are karmically neutral, but which involve a mind that is accompanied by subtle hindrances that impede liberation. "Subtle hindrances" refers for example to having the view that assumes the existence of a "self," to having a the tendency to think, "I am," to engaging in self-cherishing thoughts, words, and deeds, and to being forever under the influence of ignorance.

158. I translate here as "monastic preceptor" and "monastic Dharma teacher" what the KJ text retains in transliteration as *"upādhyāya"* and *"ācārya"* respectively.

159. Rebirth as an *asura* is one of the six rebirth destinies within cyclic existence. *Asuras* are typically described as "titans" or "demigods" whose most emblematic characteristic aside from a deficiency of merit is a fondness for fighting, especially with the desire-realm devas, in particular with the devas of the Trāyastriṃśa Heaven ("The Heaven of the Thirty-three"). The term is also used more loosely to describe beings within other realms of cyclic existence whose dominant character traits are marked by an analogous fondness for hatred, disputation, and combat.

160. The "three objects of reverence" are variously interpreted. In descending order of intended likelihood here, they are: the Three Jewels (Buddha, Dharma, Sangha); those who have attained the three fruitions of valid Buddhist paths (the buddhas, the *pratyekabuddhas*, and the arhats); in Pure Land contexts, Amitābha Buddha, Avalokiteśvara Bodhisattva, and Mahāsthāmaprāpta Bodhisattva; and, especially in *Avataṃsaka Sutra* contexts, Śākyamuni Buddha, Mañjuśrī Bodhisattva, and Samantabhadra Bodhisattva.

161. By "the difficulties" (諸難), N most likely means to refer specifically to "the eight difficulties.". They refer to rebirth: in the hell realm; in the hungry ghost realm; in the animal realm; in the long life heavens (where there is no motivation to cultivate the path); on the Northern Continent of *Uttarakuru* (where, again, there is no context there for cultivating the path); in a body with impaired faculties (as when

deaf, dumb, or blind); in a circumstance where one's mentality is exclusively focused on worldly knowledge and eloquence in debating secular issues irrelevant to the path of liberation; or in a place where the Buddha Dharma is no longer extant in that world.

Referring to the above, VB offers further perspectives here:

> "The eight in the Pali Canon are at AN 8:29: (1–4) are the same; (5) rebirth in the outlying provinces among the uncouth foreigners (maybe Uttarakuru is one example, but there must be many other 'outlying provinces,' including most of Eurasia, Africa and the Americas); (6) one holds wrong view and has a distorted perspective: 'There is nothing given, nothing sacrificed, nothing offered ...' in other words, a view that denies karma and results; (7) 'one is unwise, stupid, obtuse, unable to understand the meaning of what has been well stated and badly stated' (probably = 'rebirth with impaired faculties'); (8) 'a Tathāgata has not arisen in the world ... and the Dhamma leading to peace, *nibbāna,* and enlightenment is not taught.'"

162. The Sanskrit for these: *cakṣu, jñāna, vidyā,* and *āloka.*

163. N is referring here specifically to the life span of a buddha who, certainly more readily than an unenlightened person, he is able to either extend or shorten his life span at will. Another example of this phenomenon is described in Vasubandhu's *Abhidharmakoṣa-bhāṣya* in which it is noted that an arhat may either extend or shorten his life span through a corresponding diminishment or enhancement of his stock of karmic merit.

164. In most traditional Dharma community contexts, this would refer to welcoming and seeing off eminent Dharma teachers, preceptors, visiting monks or nuns, etc.

165. Although "*dhyāna* concentration states" usually refers primarily to the four *dhyānas* associated with the form realm, it also refers to the four *dhyāna* concentration states associated with the formless realm, namely: infinite space, infinite consciousness, nothing whatsoever, and neither perception nor non-perception.

166. By "kindness, compassion, and so forth," N is very likely referring to the four immeasurable minds (*apramāṇa-citta*) consisting of kindness, compassion, sympathetic joy, and equanimity.

167. "Unobscured morally indeterminate (*anivṛta-avyākṛta*)" actions are those that are karmically neutral and involve a mind that is free of subtle hindrances that impede liberation. As mentioned in an earlier note, "subtle hindrances" refers for example to having the view that assumes the existence of a "self," to having a the tendency to think, "I am," to engaging in self-cherishing thoughts, words, and deeds, and

to being forever under the influence of ignorance. In this case, there are none of these hindrances that might impede liberation.

168. "Those in training and those beyond training" (*śaikṣa-aśaikṣa*) is a reference to the eight stages of realization culminating in arhatship, the eighth and final stage in the Śrāvaka Vehicle's individual-liberation path.

169. For similar passages in the KJ translation of the *Great Perfection of Wisdom Sutra*, see the "Rejoicing" chapter (chapter 39 in fascicle 11) of 摩訶般若波羅蜜經that begins at T08n0223_p0297b18.

170. I could not locate this title in the *Taisho* edition of the Buddhist canon.

171. A very long and very similar corresponding passage, beginning with precisely this statement of praise can be found in Kumārajīva's translation of this chapter of the *Mahāprajñāpāramitā Sūtra in 25,000 lines*, beginning at T08, no. 223, p. 300b26.

172. The three clear knowledges (*tri-vidya*) are the heavenly eye, the cognition of past lives of oneself and others, and the extinguishing of the contaminants.

173. For a complete explanation of these three types of retribution, see Harivarman's *Satyasiddhi Śāstra*, Chapter 104, "The Three Types of Karmic Retribution" (T32; no. 1646; p. 297b–c.).

174. This sutra is extant in the Taisho canon and the cited passage is easily identifiable (T15; no. 633; p. 472c06–14).

175. VB recognized this passage as a quote from *A Lump of Salt* in the *Anguttara Nikāya*, 3:100 (NDB pp.331 foll.) for which the *Taisho* canon parallel is found in the *Madhyama Āgama* at T01n0026, beginning at page 433a12.

176. To correct an apparent graphic-similarity scribal error, I emend the reading of the *Taisho* text here by preferring the SYMG editions' *er* (二), "two," to the *Taisho* edition's *san* (三), "three."

177. The Sanskrit name for this "Comprehensive Giving Bodhisattva" (一切施菩薩) is Sarvadāna. Its Chinese transliteration (薩和檀) is used directly below in the paragraph related to Sadāprarudita.

178. This is a reference to Jātaka tale number 316 as recorded in the Pali tradition. It describes a previous life of the Buddha when he was a rabbit who sacrificed his life as a meal for a hungry rishi.

179. VB traced this passage to the "Akṣayamati" Chapter in the *Taisho* canon's 413 CE Chinese translation by Dharmakṣema of the *Mahāsaṃnipāta Sūtra* (大方等大集經卷第二十七 –無盡意菩薩品第十二之一 T13n0397_p0189a18 foll.), noting that this text's version of the

passage seems somewhat more elaborate than the passage as found in the T397 Chinese translation.

180. I emend the reading of the text by following two alternate editions (YM) in including *huijian* (慧堅) "solidity in wisdom" which completes this traditional fivefold list of five categories of mastery.

181. As will become clear in due course, "emptiness and such" refers primarily to emptiness, signlessness, and wishlessness (the three gates to liberation) and secondarily to a whole host of other qualities associated with the bodhisattva path.

182. Per VB, see *Mahāsaṃnipāta Sūtra* (大方等大集經,卷第二十七, 無盡意菩薩品第十二之一 [T13n0397_p0189b20 foll.]).

183. I emend the reading of the text here to correct a fairly obvious scribal error by preferring on sensibility grounds the SYMG editions' *xinjie* (信解), "resolute conviction, firm belief, etc.," to *Taisho*'s *xinjietuo* (信解脫), "liberation of faith."

184. "Field of merit" is a characterization typically but not exclusively reserved for more advanced or spiritually pure practitioners of the path such as senior monastics. In fact, anyone truly in need is often also regarded as "a field of merit." The idea behind the metaphoric designation is that, if one gives such people a gift, the karmic reward to the benefactor in terms of merit thereby accrued will be abundant in a way that is analogous to the results one might expect from the planting of good seeds in especially fertile soil.

185. Per VB, this is probably a reference to non-Buddhist teachings such as those promoted by Maskarī-gośālī-putra and Ajita-keśakambala who denied the existence of karmic cause-and-effect in human affairs.

186. Lit., "no giving where the recipient is not a field of merit." This is a reference to instances of discriminating against some potential recipients because they are considered to be insufficiently virtuous or to be of only inferior monastic rank ("mere novices," etc.).

187. "Fallacious conceptual proliferation" translates *xilun* (戲論), lit. "frivolous discourse," a Chinese translation of the Sanskrit *prapañca*, a term with numerous connotations that usually refers primarily to conceptual proliferation that imputes a self where none exists and spins out all sorts of other egotistical ideation with no basis in ultimate reality.

188. For the corresponding Chinese translation, VB notes that the passage begins at T13n0397_p0189c12.

189. VB notes: "On the following, see *Majjhima Nikāya* 142 (at the end). The *Madhyama Āgama* parallel is found at T01n0026_p0722b28. See also: T01n0084_p0904a23."

190. Lest this statement seem somewhat confusing, these four types each contain two entities, namely a giver and a receiver. Three of them have at least one entity that serves as a basis for purity and three of them have at least one entity that serves as a basis for impurity.

191. As VB points out, in these contexts, this *she* (捨) which otherwise most directly connotes "relinquishing" usually translates the Sanskrit *tyāga* which is also often used in Indian Buddhist texts to connote "generosity," hence my use of that translation here. In support of this translation, VB points to a Pali texts classical definition at AN 4:61: *"Katamā ca, gahapati, cāgasampadā? Idha, gahapati, ariyasāvako vigatamala-maccherena cetasā agāraetasā agārasāvako vigatamalaion."*

192. I emend the reading of the text here to correct an apparent scribal error by preferring on sensibility grounds the SYMG editions' *puti* (菩提), "bodhi," to the *Taisho* edition's *pusa* (菩薩), "bodhisattva."

193. KJ retains the transliteration (*sarvajña*). I prefer to go ahead and translate it (as "all-knowledge").

194. The brahman caste corresponds to the priestly class.

195. The *kṣatriya* caste corresponds to the military class.

196. The *vaiśya* caste corresponds to the agricultural and merchant classes.

197. The *śūdra* caste, in traditional Indian culture, is considered a low class. Of course, the Buddha emphatically repudiated the caste system, stating that all castes flow with equality into the Dharma of the Buddha just as all waters, when they flow into the ocean, immediately become of but a single flavor.

198. "Self-benefit" here is one of the two types of benefit to which the bodhisattva is dedicated, namely the self-benefit that brings about one's own complete awakening and the other-benefit that facilitates the complete awakening of all other beings.

199. The "erroneous" of "erroneous interpretations" here translates the Chinese *yi* (異), literally "aberrant," "divergent," or "deviating."

200. VB offers this note: "The following is in the *Dīgha Nikāya* 16.4.7 foll. (Long Discourses of the Buddha, pp. 255–56). Also in *Aṅguttara Nikāya* 4:180. A Chinese parallel is at T01n0001_p0017c01."

201. Here and hereafter, I translate *zhu fa xiang yi* (諸法相義) as "the true character of dharmas. Although it might more literally translate as "the meaning of the character of dharmas," or as "the character and meaning of dharmas," it would seem to more probably correspond to the Sanskrit *dharmatā* which, in other KJ texts is rendered into Chinese as *zhu fa shi xiang* (諸法實相). This seems especially likely when one notes that Hirakawa (p. 190) gives *dharmatā* as the Sanskrit antecedent for "諸法實相義."

202. *Mātṛkās* were systematic "matrices" (same etymological root) and/or lists of the technical terms, topics, and other doctrinal details contained in the sutras. They served as memorization aids in the preservation of the sutras and the teachings contained within them, this during the time after the Buddha's nirvāṇa and before the sutras and the abhidharma literature based upon them were first systematically committed to writing on palm leaves or other transcription media.

203. Although the title of such a scripture is indeed referenced in numerous places in the Chinese Buddhist canon, I could not find this textual passage anywhere in the canon as an extant scriptural translation. Of course this does not rule out the possible presence of a slightly variant Chinese translation of these ideas in either in this so-named scripture or somewhere else in the canon.

204. *Dhāraṇīs* usually take the form of mantras serving to retain Dharma as dominant in one's karmic continuum from lifetime to lifetime and to also retain very precise memory of all teachings one has learned from lifetime to lifetime. They are also commonly used to protect the practitioner of the path from negative influences arising both from without and from within his own mind. They are also regularly used to bestow benefit on other beings and to enhance one's capabilities on the bodhisattva path in numerous additional ways. Nāgārjuna writes at great length on this topic in his exegesis on the 25,000-line *Great Perfection of Wisdom Sutra.*

205. Although the *dhūtas are* austerities, here they refer not to austerities in general, but rather specifically to the twelve *dhūtaguṇa* austerities.

206. *Baiyi* (白衣), "white-robed ones," is a Sino-Buddhist translation of the Sanskrit *avadāta-vasana,* a term specifically referring to members of the Buddhist laity.

207. The apparent implication here is not only that a monastic will find his mind distracted by conversation with villagers, but also that his unconventional activities will become the subject of disapproving rumors that degrade the laity's respect for all members of the monastic sangha.

208. "Three poisons" is an alternate designation for the three primary psycho-spiritual afflictions of greed, hatred, and delusion.

209. N refers here to the rest of the six perfections aside from the practice of giving.

210. VB notes: "Nāgārjuna probably has in mind a passage that occurs in Pāli Saṃyutta Nikāya 20:10, and elsewhere: 'Here some bhikkhu dresses in the morning and, taking bowl and robe, enters a village or town for alms with body, speech, and mind unguarded, without

setting up mindfulness, unrestrained in his sense faculties. He sees women there lightly clad or lightly attired and lust invades his mind. With his mind invaded by lust, he meets death or deadly suffering. For this, bhikkhus, is death in the Noble One's Discipline: that one gives up the training and returns to the lower life. This is deadly suffering: that one commits a certain defiled offence of a kind that allows for rehabilitation.' ...Giving up the training is "death in the Noble One's discipline, the equivalent of dying." Breaking a grave precept approaches death but does not cross the line."

211. The four bases of meritorious qualities (truth, relinquishment, quiescence, and wisdom) were introduced by N in Chapter One (at 22b28–9). Their importance as defining qualities of both buddhas and bodhisattvas was emphasized repeatedly in Chapter Two.

212. N's use of "Dharma position" or "right Dharma position" (*samyaktva niyāma*) refers in this context to a stage on the *śrāvaka* disciple's path that is synonymous with attainment of the path of seeing, a stage from which one cannot readily switch over to cultivation of the bodhisattva path to buddhahood. See Leo Pruden's translation of *Abhidharma Kośa Bhāṣyam* (321, 944, 1055–6n, 1243).

 In the Mahāyāna context, this "right Dharma position" connotes a stage of progress on the bodhisattva path wherein one directly perceives the emptiness of dharmas, yet nonetheless continues on with kindness and compassion in the universal-liberation path to buddhahood and remains invulnerable to retreating to the *śrāvaka* disciple's path to the attainment of individual liberation.

213. "Four fruitions" here is a reference to the four fruits of the *śrāvaka* disciples' path beginning with stream entry and ending with arhatship.

214. "Three matters" refers to mindfulness of the Buddha, mindfulness of the Dharma, and mindfulness of the Sangha in a manner accordant with the ensuing chapter-concluding discussion.

215. This statement is found in N's *Exegesis on the Mahāprajñāpāramitā Sūtra* (T25n1509.442c05–07) as well as in the *Mahāprajñāpāramitā Sūtra* itself (T08n0223.p273b29–c02).

216. VB Notes: "This must be *māraviṣaya* or *māradheyya*, the realm/domain of Māra, a metaphor for *saṃsāra*."

217. This is a reference to the "eight winds" or "eight worldly dharmas" (*aṣṭalokadharma*) that consist of four pairs of affective mind states strongly influencing the life priorities of beings trapped in cyclic existence: gain (*lābha*) and loss (*alābha*), fame (*yaśas*) and disgrace (*ayaśas*), praise (*praśaṃsā*) and blame (*nindā*), and pleasure (*sukha*) and pain (*duḥkha*).

218. Per the *Mahā-saṃgīti-sūtra* (佛說大集法門經) translated into Chinese by Dānapāla in 1005, these "six kinds of equanimity" (六捨) refer to equanimity or indifference at each of the six sense gates of eye, ear, nose, tongue, body, and mind with regard to the objects of those six sense faculties: visual forms, sounds, smells, tastes, touchables, and dharmas as objects of mind (T01n0012_p0231c15–18).

219. "Two kinds of afflictions" commonly refers to latent afflictions and manifest afflictions.

220. "The five hindrances" is a reference to desire, ill will, lethargy-and-sleepiness, excitedness-and-regretfulness, and afflicted doubtfulness. These five hindrances must be overcome in order to successfully enter deep states of meditation.

221. These are explained by the Buddha in the Ekottara Āgama Sūtra (T02.125.738b18–c17). In summary, these refer to avoidance of being taken advantage of by māras, i.e., "demons" (this is reiterated in all seven) by not retreating from these seven practices:
    1) Dwelling together in a single place with mutual respect involving mutual assistance between juniors and seniors while persisting in the cultivation of good dharmas;
    2) Accordance with the teachings within a harmonious and united Sangha;
    3) Non-attachment to worldly responsibilities or reputation;
    4) Avoidance of the recitation of miscellaneous (non-Buddhist) texts while forever goading on one's resolve;
    5) Non-indulgence of drowsiness and persistence in wakefulness;
    6) Avoidance of the study or propagation of "calculations" (probably referring to astronomically-based predictions and various sorts of divination, etc.);
    7) Bringing forth the reflection that there is nothing in the entire world that is worthy of delight, practicing *dhyāna* meditation, and persevering in accordance with the teachings.

222. Assuming that KJ is using the same Sanskrit-to-Chinese correspondences that we find in the KB translation of the *Daśabhūmika Sūtra*, what I translate here as "deep-seated aspirations and resolute belief" (*shenxin xinle* [深心信樂]) would correspond to *āśaya* and *adhimukti*.

223. "True character of dharmas" (usually *zhu fa shi xiang* - 諸法實相) is KJ's usual rendering for what Hirakawa notes (p. 1090) may be *tattvasya-lakṣaṇam, dharmatā, dharma-svabhāva,* etc. As such it is a reference to the true nature of dharmas as they really are. Hence it is a synonym for true suchness (*tathatā*).

224. I emend the reading of the *Taisho* text here by preferring on sensibility grounds the SYMG editions' *ming* (名), "is what is meant by," to the *Taisho* edition's *gu* (故), "therefore."

225. This extended sutra passage has direct correspondences to a section of a four-fascicle scripture that is included in the *Mahāvaipulya-mahāsamnipata-sūtra* (大方等大集經) otherwise known as the *Akṣayamati-nirdeśa* (無盡意菩薩品). That passage is in the *Taisho* canon at T13.397.186b–c.

226. On sensibility grounds, I emend the reading of the *Taisho* text's *xing* (性), "nature," here by preferring the SYMG editions' graphically similar *xing* (姓), "caste."

227. This *"jian wen jue zhi"* (見聞覺知) that I translate here as "seeing, hearing, sensing, or cognizing" corresponds to the Sanskrit *"dṛṣṭaṃ, śrutaṃ, mataṃ, vijñānam"* which collectively refer to the knowing of their respective objects by the six sense faculties of eye, ear, nose, tongue, body, and mind. In this tetrad, the cognitive functions of three of the senses (the olfactory, gustatory, and tactile sensing that are accomplished by the nose, tongue, and body) are collapsed under the single term "sensing" whereas the other three senses' functions are individually specified as "seeing" (the eye sense faculty), "hearing" (the ear sense faculty), and "cognizing" (the mind faculty).

228. The *Taisho* analogue text has *"jing jie gong de"* (境界功德), "qualities of the state of mind" (T13.397.0186b20).

229. "Joy" and "bliss" are two factors on a continuum of subtlety (joy being more coarse, bliss being more sublime) that arise and fall away in progressing through the four *dhyānas*. "Declining to indulge the delectable" refers to remaining unattached to delectably pleasurable meditation states (*āsvādana-samādhi*) encountered in one's meditation practice that would otherwise pose a danger to progress in meditation.

230. Lest the reader find this passage somewhat opaque, this paragraph is primarily referring to transcendence of the five aggregates.

231. N. may be referring here either to the immediately preceding "mindfulness of the true Buddha" discussion or else to his later six-chapter (20–25) discussion of "mindfulness of the buddha" and its associated *pratyutpanna* samādhi.

232. As inferred by the following discussion, this may be a reference to the layperson's option of starting out in the cultivation of moral purity by only formally obligating himself to observe whichever moral precepts he can confidently uphold. Hence it is not uncommon for a layperson to start by taking just the three precepts proscribing

killing, stealing, and lying and then only later on formally taking the other two of the five precepts which prohibit sexual misconduct and the consumption of intoxicants.

233. This is probably a reference to the seven (or eight) kinds of arrogance variously listed in the canon.

234. "The body that does endure" is probably intended to refer to the Dharma body shared by all buddhas.

235. This refers to the recognition that, wisely used, the wealth of this life may bring about a circumstance of being wealthy in the Dharma. This is accomplished through using such wealth to do good deeds, support the Dharma, and otherwise generate merit that brings forth success in encountering right Dharma, the good spiritual guide, and conditions for cultivating the path to buddhahood in life after life.

236. The Chinese is more literally "impurity of the body," however, the Indian Buddhist tradition refers to it more specifically as "contemplation of the unloveliness of the body (*aśubha-bhāvanā* or *aśubhā-saṃjñā*)." This practice involves such contemplations as the contemplation of the 32 (or 36) parts of the body, the contemplation of the nine stages of decomposition of a corpse, and the contemplation of the white-boned skeleton.

237. This statement is probably intended to apply to socially obligatory serving of alcoholic beverages in circumstances such as the hosting of a large wedding reception where many of the people in attendance will surely be drinking anyway. In this connection, however, it is perhaps useful to recall the major bodhisattva precept forbidding any purveyance of intoxicants. It is stated therein that something so apparently minor as passing a glass of wine to someone may result in being born for five hundred lifetimes with no hands. Also, if it is not already obvious, Nāgārjuna would not condone a precepted layperson's personal consumption of alcohol, even when attending the sorts of events alluded to here.

238. Many of the statements contained in this scriptural passage correlate quite closely with those recorded in the very short fourth chapter of the single-fascicle *Sutra on the Questions of Ugradatta* (郁迦羅越問菩薩行經 / T12.n0323.p23a–30b). This edition of the *Ugraparipṛcchā Sūtra*, one of three translations made into Chinese, was translated by Dharmarakṣa sometime in the late 3rd or early 4th century.

239. "Ideation and discursion" translates the standard Chinese rendering of *vitarka* and *vicāra* (覺觀).

240. "Foolish common person," translates the standard Chinese rendering of *pṛthagjana* (凡夫). Although obviously not very flattering, this

English translation by Edward Conze is unfortunately very accurate. It basically refers to anyone who has not yet attained one of the fruits of the path by which one would become an *ārya*. The rest of us are always running mental and spiritual software deeply encoded with ignorance which produces delusion which in turn generates every permutation of greed, hatred, and stupidity. Hence the "foolishness" to which the term alludes.

241. The text reflects conditions in ancient India dominated by tribal customs. Occurrences such as those listed here might have easily followed from offending tribal authorities, the rich, the powerful, organized crime, ad hoc groups of bandits, local Taliban-like zealots, or invading armies.
242. VB points out that these four causal influences of desire, hatred, delusion, and fear (*chanda, doṣa, moha,* and *bhaya*) are called "the four wrong courses" (*agati*) and cites AN 4:17–19 as a specific Pali canon reference.
243. Unlike today, during ancient times actors and entertainers did not necessarily possess a particularly high social status.
244. The almsman provides the opportunity to practice giving and by his presence influences one to engage in giving, a necessary practice for advancement on the path because it generates merit while also diminishing miserliness.
245. Giving to an almsman generates karmic merit which in turn brings about material abundance in the future lives of the benefactor.
246. This act of giving assists realization of bodhi for both the benefactor and the recipient. For the former, it contributes to an essential stock of merit without which one cannot make meaningful progress on the path. For the latter, it provides the physical sustenance without which the almsman could not continue cultivating the path.
247. All-knowledge is a quality exclusive to the Buddhas. When giving to an almsman cultivating the path that culminates in attaining this utmost, right, and perfect enlightenment, one's contemplation of this goal could then serve as an inspiration to one's own pursuit of this very same state of ultimately supreme liberation.
248. Although giving to an almsman is certainly productive of a rewarding karmic result, to give for the sake of a rewarding karmic result is just another form of covetousness. It does not accord with the path and it also massively diminishes the quality of the positive karmic result that this act of giving might otherwise bring about.
249. Māra, the Sixth Desire Heaven *devaputras,* demonic ghosts, and, figuratively speaking, the demon of one's own miserliness—all of these

types of "demons" may manipulate the mind state of the bodhisattva cultivator, thereby discouraging him from generating merit through the practice of giving. By resisting these, one overcomes the forces of Māra.

250. It is said to be karmically quite usual for the beneficiaries of such generosity to eventually become disciples or members of one's own familial or spiritual clan in this and/or future lives. Additionally, the almsman may indeed have been a previous-life clan member or Dharma-family relation.

251. The bodhisattva employs the four means of attraction (giving, pleasing words, beneficial actions, and joint endeavors) as essential skillful means to be used in drawing beings forth into pursuing the path to liberation.

252. "Dispassion" translates a standard Chinese rendering of *virāga* (離欲).

253. "Dispassion" (*virāga*) is most likely intended here in the sense of "indifference" or "detachment" with regard to one's own possessions.

254. Dedicating the merit arising from giving to the eventual attainment *anuttarasamyaksaṃbodhi* greatly elevates one's dedication to moral purity because focusing one's resolve exclusively on attaining buddhahood necessarily entails strict adherence ever-after to the highest level of moral virtue. If one fails to dedicate one's merit to the attainment of buddhahood, that merit will otherwise naturally just go merely to greater personal abundance in subsequent rebirths.

255. This manner of giving is consistent with the perfection of vigor because the benefactor has moved right along with the act, maintaining zeal, resolve, and a degree of determination that remains invulnerable to any tendency to retreat from this virtuous act.

256. "Worthy" (*bhadra*) and *ārya* are technical terms with specific meanings in Mahāyāna doctrine. Basically, a "worthy" has advanced well beyond the spiritually untutored mind of the foolish common person, but he is still vulnerable to being impeded in his progress to spiritual liberation. An *ārya,* on the other hand, has already reached one of the stages of realization through which progression to spiritual liberation is guaranteed.

257. "It endures" reflects the realization that the gift, once given, will continue to generate merit for the benefactor even after it is no longer in his possession.

258. "It will not endure" reflects the realization that this possession, like all other phenomena, is impermanent.

259. The text actually specifies "wife" here, but I deliberately instead translate with the rather more neutral term, "spouse." Nāgārjuna certainly would have used such a word if he had thought a woman might ever read this text which was, after all, written for a readership consisting entirely of men. This work was written at a time when only men were able to read. Thus it was never envisioned that women or prospective nuns might actually read the text (as opposed to having it orally taught in a lecture format more precisely tailored to the contemplations best suited to a woman reflecting on the suboptimal aspects and potential spiritual liabilities inherent in marriage). Obviously, in order to derive the intended salutary effect of reading this (and other similar) commentaries, a woman reading this text should simply "flip" any references specifying "women" or "wives" as objects of critical contemplation to "men" or "husbands."

260. There is a total of ninety-nine negative spousal contemplations here consisting of thirty-three sets of three, all of them intended to provoke the lay practitioner already weary of the tedium of married life to consider abandoning the householder's life in favor of monastic life, a path that is described step-by-step in the ensuing chapters of this treatise.

261. VB points out that the triple contemplations that follow are taken from the *Ugraparipṛcchā Sūtra*. See Jan Nattier's translation of this scripture, *A Few Good Men*, pp. 247–55.

262. "Contemplation of the body as unlovely" generally translates the Sanskrit *aśubha-bhāvanā* or *aśubhā-saṃjñā*.

263. Starting here and continuing for the rest of these spousal contemplations, the *Taisho* text has *xiang* (相) as a more-or-less standard short-form abbreviation for *xiang* (想) whilst the other four editions (SYMG) all have *xiang* (想) throughout.

264. The black-eared kite (*Milvus lineatus*) is a medium sized Asian raptor.

265. *Acipenser mikadoi*.

266. Responsible spiritual teachers will generally forbid married disciples from precipitously abandoning a marriage when the family is financially dependent on one's ongoing presence. They will usually instead counsel joint lay bodhisattva practice that includes the cultivation of patience, the planting of merit, the development of wisdom, and continued kindness and compassion in the context of the ongoing marriage until, by mutual agreement, the husband and wife together decide that more efficient progression along the bodhisattva path is best pursued in a monastic context.

Serious married lay practitioners may explore the option of celibacy by mutual agreement, beginning by formally taking on the eight precepts that include celibacy, observing those precepts for a day and a night on six days of each lunar month, usually, the eighth, fourteenth, fifteenth, twenty-third, twenty-ninth, and thirtieth of the lunar month.

267. Again, as in many other places in this text, rather than retain the Sanskrit term, I go ahead and translate KJ's *"sarvajña"* as "all-knowledge."

268. VB notes the parallels from *Āgama* and *Nikāya* sources: SA 861–863, EA 24.6, T 88, T 89, T 87, MA 202, AN 3.37–38, AN 3:70, AN 8.43 and points out that the full text of the eight precepts is found in AN 3:70 and 8:43.

269. "Consumption of intoxicants" here is literally "alcoholic beverages," but it also refers to any substance that, once consumed, skews normal clear consciousness. Hence the various forms and methods of ingesting mind-altering *cannabis* products (marijuana, hashish, etc.), opiates, amphetamines, psychedelics, and other such mind-altering substances would be included as well. Coffee and tea, although they can interfere with meditation, are not proscribed.

270. This scripture has apparently been lost as a search of the canon does not turn up any remotely similar texts with such a name.

271. Krakucchanda Buddha was the fourth of the seven buddhas of antiquity mentioned in the Nikāyas and Āgamas.

272. VB notes that this statement's corresponding Pali canon passage is found at AN 6:44. Hence, on page 913 of NDB, we find: "Therefore, Ānanda, do not be judgmental regarding people. Do not pass judgment on people. Those who pass judgment on people harm themselves. I alone, or one like me, may pass judgment on people."

273. VB notes that the following passage's corresponding Pali canon passage is found at AN 4:103 and NDB pp. 484–5.

274. 諸法無行經 / *Sarva-dharma-apravṛtti-nirdeśa-sūtra* (T15; no. 650; 750–761). See also other translations (T15; nos. 651, 652).

275. Perhaps *The Inquiry of Ugra, (Ugraparipṛcchā)*.

276. To correct an obvious graphic-similarity scribal error, I emend the reading of the *Taisho* text here by preferring the SYMG editions' *xiang* (相), "sign," to the *Taisho* edition's *xiang* (想), "thought." These three successive phrases are clearly intended to refer specifically to practitioners of the three gates to liberation (emptiness, signlessness, and wishlessness) of which this phrase refers to the second of those three gates.

277. "Kindness, compassion, sympathetic joy, and equanimity" is a direct reference to the four immeasurable minds (*apramāṇa-citta*).
278. VB notes corresponding Pali text passages: SN 15:3, 4, and 13.
279. This statement is slightly ambiguous, but most likely refers to the Indian layperson's caste origins and associated social stature which are entirely transcended and dispensed with once one becomes a monastic in the Buddha's Sangha.
280. "Elixir of immortality," lit. "sweet dew" (*ganlu* [甘露]) corresponds to the Sanskrit "*amṛta*," which, as with the western analogue term, "ambrosia," means "the undying" and refers to the nectar or food of the gods which confers immortality. "Poisons" likely refers to the three poisons: greed, hatred, and delusion along with their numerous subsidiary afflictions.
281. Although this statement is somewhat ambiguous, it likely refers to the layperson's relatively greater vulnerability to having his interests encroached upon and harmed by the power of the king, the power of thieves, the power of *māras*, or the power of the afflictions.
282. This is probably intended to refer to the "heat" of anger and lust.
283. VB notes the corresponding Pali text passage: SN 35:247; CDB pp. 1255–57.
284. The "three-part robe" consists of a sarong, an upper robe, and a *sanghāti* robe.
285. "*Avadāna* stories" are stories of the previous lives of a buddha.
286. The Chinese text preserves a transliteration of the Sanskrit word for "sitting cloth" (*niṣīdana*). I have preferred to go ahead and translate it.
287. To correct an apparent graphic-similarity scribal error, I emend the reading of the *Taisho* text here by preferring the SYMG editions' *yi* (遺), "omitted, left out, held back, or neglected," to the *Taisho* edition's *gui* (匱).
288. "The station of the *avaivartika*" corresponds to irreversibility on the bodhisattva path to buddhahood.
289. "Patience" here is to be construed in the sense of "acquiescence."
290. The Chinese term that I translate here as "resolute faith" (信解) is perhaps the most standard Sino-Buddhist translation of the Sanskrit *adhimukti*.
291. I insert the Sanskrit term "*dhāraṇī*" here in place of its sometimes slightly opaque Chinese translation as "comprehensive retention [formulae]." This Chinese translation (總持) as well as the Sanskrit term itself both refer to one of the most important types of *dhāraṇīs*, those which aid the remembrance of particular Dharma teachings

even for many lifetimes. There are other types of *dhāraṇīs* such as those that consist of untranslated Sanskrit syllables which serve as powerful mantra-like "mystic formulae." N discusses this topic at length in his Mppu.

292. These "universal bases" (*kṛtsnāyatana*) are ten visualization devices traditionally used as one of a number of basic techniques in early Buddhist meditation practice that were aimed at developing and strengthening deep meditative concentration. These are synonymous with the ten types of *kasiṇa* familiar to students of Southern Tradition Buddhism's meditation practice aimed at acquisition of the four *dhyāna* (*jhāna*) concentration states associated with the form realm.

 These *kasiṇas* may be discs representing earth, water, fire, air, blue, yellow, red, white, space, consciousness (or as an alternative to "consciousness": "bright light"), or empty space. Through correctly developed meditation on any one of these discs, one is able to produce a precise image of the given *kasiṇa* that then abides in the mind's eye or may be called forth to the mind's eye at will and independently of the original meditation object. Then one becomes able in response to one's own volition to freely develop any representational image that one wishes that incorporates the original elements, colors, etc. upon which the meditation was originally focused.

 These representational images are then no longer limited to an exact replica of that original meditation object. For example, one is then able to transform one element into another and produce certain supernormal effects as a result. Hence the analogy here to developing the practice through "resolve" "in accordance with one's wishes."

293. "Karmic propensities" (here: *qi* [氣] and *qixing* [氣性], more usually *xiqi* [習氣], lit. "habit energies") would usually correspond to the Sanskrit "*vāsanā*" which refers to the habitual tendencies created in the mind through repetition of similar volitions and actions that produce the likelihood one will quite readily stumble into repeating the same affliction-associated karmic errors.

294. Emendation: To correct an apparent scribal error, I'm reversing the order of the second and third lines of this four-line *śloka* to accord with the obviously correct order revealed in N's subsequent discussion and in the Ming edition of the text.

295. I emend the reading of the *Taisho* text here by preferring on sensibility grounds the SYMG editions' *dafahui* (大法會), "great Dharma assemblies," to the *Taisho* edition's *dahui* (大會), "great assemblies."

296. It is not clear to which *abhidharma* text Nāgārjuna is referring here.

297. The "tala palm" (*Borassus flabellifer*) is native to the Indian subcontinent and Southeast Asia.

298. "White hair tuft" = *ūrṇākeśa*.

299. "The *nyagrodha* tree" (*Ficus benghalensis*) is the Indian banyan tree.

300. According to MW, *"aiṇeya"* refers to the Indian black antelope. I suspect the intended species may be the Indian blackbuck (*Antilope cervicapra*).

301. I translate here as "monastic preceptor" and "monastic Dharma teacher" what the KJ text retains in transliteration as *"upādhyāya"* and *"ācārya"* respectively.

302. Although in later period literature *xiongdi* (兄弟) refers exclusively to elder and younger brothers, ancient texts used it to refer to elder and younger sisters as well.

303. In India, "merit halls" (*puṇya-śālā*) were a type of "hostel" for the lodging, sustenance, and medical care of travelers and the poor. These were usually donated by the kings and the wealthy.

304. The four lineage bases of the Āryas (*catur-āryavaṃśa*) are: delighting in mere sufficiency in clothing, delighting in mere sufficiency of food and drink, delighting in mere sufficiency of bedding, and delighting in the severance [of evil] and the cultivation [of goodness].

305. I translate here as "monastic preceptor" and "monastic Dharma teacher" what the KJ text retains in transliteration as *"upādhyāya"* and *"ācārya"* respectively.

306. In this translation, "good spiritual friend" and "good spiritual guide" are alternative renderings for the same Chinese terms (善知識) and Sanskrit (*kalyāṇa-mitra*). "Good spiritual friend" is used to refer to those who are companions on the spiritual path who support one's adherence to the teachings. "Good spiritual guide" is used to refer to spiritual friends who also serve as mentors upon whom one relies for spiritual guidance as one cultivates the path.

307. The Lokāyata school of ancient Indian philosophy is a materialist doctrine the founding of which is often attributed to Bṛhaspati who is thought to have lived around 1000 BCE.

308. Given the readings in the immediately preceding passage and in the verse which follows below, for consistency's sake, I emend the *Taisho* reading of *da zang* (大藏), "great treasuries," here in favor of the SYMG reading of *guangda zang* (廣大藏), "vast treasuries."

309. I emend the reading of the *Taisho* text here by preferring on sensibility grounds the SYM editions' *guang shuo* (廣說), "extensive explanation," to the *Taisho* edition's *guang* (廣), "extensive."

310. I translate here as "benefactors" what the KJ text retains in transliteration as *"dānapati."*

311. To correct an apparent graphic-similarity scribal error, I emend the reading of the *Taisho* text here by preferring the SYMG editions' *zengshang man* (增上慢), "overweening pride," to the *Taisho* edition's untranslatable *zengshang man* (憎上慢).

312. Although the arrangement of the *Taisho* text does not make this clear, it is obvious that these first four five-character phrases form a quatrain upon which the following paragraph comments. Hence I have formatted the text accordingly.

313. This most likely refers to "The Pratyutpanna Samādhi Sūtra" preserved in the *Taisho* Canon as the *Banzhou Sanmei Jing* (般舟三昧經 / T13.no. 0418.902c23–919c05). Paul Harrison has produced a translation of this text for the BDK English Tripitaka.

314. I emend the reading of the text here (but still keep the emendation in brackets since there are no supporting variants in any of the other editions), this to correct an obvious scribal error wherein the name of the third of these "four bases of meritorious qualities" is missing from this sentence. The missing "basis" here is *mie* (滅), "quiescence" (*upaśamādhiṣṭhāna*).

315. These four bases of meritorious qualities (四功德處: 諦, 捨, 滅, 慧; *satyādhiṣṭhāna, tyāgādhiṣṭhāna, upaśamādhiṣṭhāna, prajñādhiṣṭhāna*; truth, relinquishment [generosity], quiescence, and wisdom) are brought up repeatedly in this and other Nāgārjunian treatises, sometimes in slightly varying order and sometimes, as in the present case, with the Chinese translation using slightly variant terminological choices for one of the four list components.

316. "Arms appearing like golden gate bars" is a rather obscure simile that I have never encountered. The SYMG editions have *chan* (鋋) which would be the equally obscure "like golden spears."

317. To correct an apparent graphic-similarity scribal error, I emend the reading of the *Taisho* text here by preferring the SYMG editions' *sheng* (生), "growth," to the *Taisho* edition's *zhu* (主), "ruler."

318. The "reply that sets aside the question" is one of polite refusal to provide an answer, not because the answer is not known, but because the question involves a false premise making the query absurd on the face of it, because providing the answer would only promote endless frivolous and fruitless speculation on the part of the questioner (as with the fourteen imponderables), or because providing an answer would in no way serve the goal of spiritual liberation.

319. More specifically, the component lists comprising the thirty-seven wings of enlightenment are: the five faculties, the five powers, the seven limbs of bodhi, the eightfold path, the four stations of mindfulness, the four right efforts, and the four foundations of psychic power.

320. "Foes" refers here to the three poisons, i.e., the afflictions. An arhat has completely destroyed them. VB points out that this pronouncement references the word play in the word *"arahant"* where it is explained that they are those who are enemy (*ari*) destroyers (*hanta*).

321. Perhaps due to corruption of the manuscript at some point in its long history, the following list contains only 74 of the 80 secondary characteristics.

322. The *saṃkakṣikā* is the monastic's robe that is worn over the left shoulder and under the right arm.

323. The *nivāsana* is the monastic's skirt-like inner robe.

324. The *saṃghāṭī* is the monastic's outer robe.

325. "Eight kinds of *āryas*" usually refers to those eminences who reside at the four candidate stages and the four realization stages on the Śrāvaka Vehicle path. The first is candidate for stream entry and the eighth is the fully realized arhat.

326. *Garuḍa* birds prey on young dragons, hence the mention that, at least when attending Dharma teachings by buddhas, they manage to remain uncharacteristically free of any mutual hostility.

327. Although the *Taisho* text has *xiang* (相), "appearance," here it is as an often-encountered and more-or-less standard short-form abbreviation for *xiang* (想), "thought."

328. VB notes that this is a stock description of the Buddha's teaching of the Dharma as found in the *suttas* of the Nikāyas, as for example: *"ādikalyāṇaṃ majjhe kalyāṇaṃ pariyosāne kalyāṇaṃ sātthaṃ sabyañjanaṃ,* etc.," and *"sandiṭṭhiko akālika ehipassiko opanayako paccattaṃ veditabbo viññūhi."*

329. KJ transliterated rather than translated these fruits of the path (*srota-āpanna, sakṛdāgāmin, anāgamin*) that, with the exception of *"arhat,"* I have elected to translate.

330. The emendation proposed by the 2009 edition of CBETA ([和>知]) involving a supposed graphic-similarity scribal error is itself erroneous and irrelevant. This verse simply restates an idea clearly articulated late in Chapter 18: "Through not allowing estrangement to occur among other beings or among one's relatives, and through being able to cause those who have become estranged to be reunited, one acquires the mark of male genital ensheathment. Due to having

[planted the karmic causes that result in] this mark, one acquires many disciples." See 65b18-20: 能善調人不令眾生親里遠離。若有乖離還令和合故得陰藏相。有是相故多得弟子。

331. "Genital ensheathment" of course also associates with transcendence of sensual desire and, as an incidental implication, that there may therefore be no biological sons via which the patrilineal lineage might continue on.

Here, the metaphoric interpretation points out that it is the pure wisdom eye (pure by virtue of an absence of attachments) that leads to the continuance of the lineage of the Buddhas, this because it is a buddha's wise teachings flowing from his possession of the wisdom eye that beget "the sons of the Buddha," i.e., the bodhisattvas who will themselves become the buddhas of the future who carry on his Dharma lineage.

332. These are eight voice qualities possessed only by the Buddhas: 1) Extremely fine; 2) Gentle; 3) Appropriate; 4) Possessed of venerable wisdom; 5) Non-feminine; 6) Unmistaken; 7) Deep and far-reaching; and 8) Inexhaustible. These are discussed at length in Section 59 of "A Sequential Explanation of the Initial Gateway into the Dharma Realm" (法界次第初門 / T46n1925_p0697a15–b20) composed by the famous meditation master and immensely prolific Tiantai hermeneutic school exegete Zhiyi (沙門釋智顗, a.k.a. 陳隋國師智者大師).

333. Because the received text's listing of these 40 exclusive dharmas presents them in a somewhat different order than occurs as they are actually presented and discussed in the text, I reorder and renumber them here to follow the actual order of their presentation. I do so based on the usually factual assumption that the section titles and preliminary lists in translations of Sanskrit texts are for the most part *not* part of the original text, but rather are added by the Sanskrit-to-Chinese translator to assist the reader, or, in this case, perhaps by the editors and scribes in Kumārajīva's translation bureau. For those interested in the erroneously ordered and numbered list found here in the received text, it is as follows:

1) Sovereign mastery of the ability to fly;
2) [The ability to manifest] countless transformations;
3) Boundless psychic powers of the sort possessed by *āryas;*
4) Sovereign mastery of the ability to hear sounds;
5) Immeasurable power of knowledge to know others' thoughts;
6) Sovereign mastery in [training and subduing] the mind;
7) Constant abiding in stable wisdom;
8) Never forgetting;
9) Possession of the powers of the *vajra* samādhi;

10) Thorough knowing of matters that are unfixed;
11) Thorough knowing of matters pertaining to the formless realm's meditative absorptions;
12) The completely penetrating knowledge of all matters associated with eternal cessation;
13) Thorough knowing of the non-form dharmas unassociated with the mind;
14) The great powers *pāramitā;*
15) The [four] unimpeded [knowledges] *pāramitā;*
16) The *pāramitā* of perfectly complete replies and predictions in response to questions;
17) Perfectly complete implementation of the three turnings in speaking Dharma;
18) Their words are never spoken without a purpose;
19) Their speech is free of error;
20) Invulnerability to harm by anyone;
21) They are the great generals among all *āryas;*
22–25) They are able to remain unguarded in four ways;
26–29) They possess the four fearlessnesses;
30–39) They possess the ten powers;
40) They possess the unimpeded liberations.

334. VB notes: "This is a category in Sarvāstivāda Abhidharma (not in the Theravāda Abhidharma), which indicates the author is familiar with the Sarvāstivāda system."

335. "Without a purpose" here is literally "empty" (in the sense of "in vain" or "fruitlessly").

336. VB notes: "See Anguttara Nikaya 7:58. The four are: conduct of body, speech, and mind, and livelihood."

337. To correct an apparent graphic-similarity scribal error, I emend the reading of the *Taisho* text here by preferring the SYMG editions' *neng* (能), "able to," to the *Taisho* edition's *suo* (所), "that which."

338. VB notes: "See *Anguttara Nikaya,* Sevens, no. 40 (see, too, Sixes, no. 24):

'Bhikkhus, possessing seven qualities, a bhikkhu exercises mastery over his mind and is not a servant of his mind. What seven? Here, (1) a bhikkhu is skilled in concentration; (2) skilled in the attainment of concentration; (3) skilled in the duration of concentration; (4) skilled in emergence from concentration; (5) skilled in fitness for concentration; (6) skilled in the range of concentration; and (7) skilled in resolution regarding concentration. Possessing these seven qualities, a bhikkhu exercises mastery over his mind, and is not a servant of his mind.'"

339. This appears to be yet another instance of KJ's use of *xing* (性), usually translated as "nature," as a translation for *dhātu* which is more ordinarily translated into Sino-Buddhist Classical Chinese as *jie* (界), "realm."

340. VB notes: "In the above [passage: '諸相諸觸諸覺諸念亦知起知住知生知滅'], 相 is clearly another instance of the confusion between 相 and 想 so common in Chinese texts. The Pali part parallel has *saññā*. See the end of Majjhima Nikāya 123, where the Buddha says he knows the arising, persistence, and passing away of *vedanā*, *saññā*, and *vitakka*."

341. In response to my earlier draft translation of *emo* (惡魔) here as "an evil demon," VB notes: Here there is no doubt that 惡魔 is none other than the infamous Māra, a particular individual, not just any "evil demon." See *Samyutta Nikāya* 4:24 "Seven Years of Pursuit":

"On one occasion the Blessed One was dwelling at Uruvelā on the bank of the river Nerañjarā at the foot of the Goatherd's Banyan Tree. Now on that occasion Māra the Evil One had been following the Blessed One for seven years, seeking to gain access to him but without success….

"Then Māra the Evil One, in the presence of the Blessed One, recited these verses of disappointment:

"There was a crow that walked around
A stone that looked like a lump of fat.
'Let's find something tender here,' [he thought,]
'Perhaps there's something nice and tasty.'

But because he found nothing tasty there,
The crow departed from that spot.
Just like the crow that attacked the stone,
We leave Gotama disappointed."

342. These five are: past dharmas, present dharmas, future dharmas, unconditioned dharmas (referred to below as "those that transcend the three periods of time"), and ineffable dharmas.

343. I emend the text here to correct an apparent graphic-similarity scribal error, preferring SYMG's *san* (三), "three," to the *Taisho* text's *er* (二), "two." The rationale for the emendation is evident in the paragraph's discussion of "three" dharmas that are "strung together," not merely "two."

344. I have made the same emendation here as in the immediately previous note.

345. VB notes that this incident involving the elephant named Nālagiri is described in the Vinaya, Cūlavagga, II 194 foll. of PTS Pali edition.

346. As described later in the text, "The twelve *dhūta* austerities" are:

Adopting the dharma of dwelling in a forest hermitage;
Obtaining one's food through the alms round;
Wearing robes made of cast-off rags;
[Taking one's daily meal in but] a single sitting;
Always sitting to sleep, [never lying down];
Having taken the meal, not accepting food or drink at the wrong times;
Possessing only a single set of three robes;
Wearing only an animal-hair robe;
Laying out one's sitting mat wherever one happens to be;
Dwelling at the foot of a tree;
Dwelling out in the open (lit. "on empty ground");
Dwelling in a charnel field.

347. VB notes: "In the Pali these are laid out as parallel descriptive terms. The Pali actually has nine synonymous terms. See AN 1:174."

348. Based on VB's very sensible suggestion that "quiescent cessation" (寂滅) is probably here as elsewhere simply a somewhat opaque sounding sino-Buddhist translation of *"nirvāṇa,"* I have gone ahead and rendered it as such throughout this entire passage as well as in other places throughout the text where the context demands it.

349. I have been unable to find a Sanskrit antecedent for this Chinese transliteration of a type of rishi, a *"pisuo"* (脾娑) rishi. VB suggests that this may be a transliteration of *viśvarśi* (*viś ṛṣi*).

350. VB notes that one can find approximate Pali Canon parallels at MN 110.4, MLDB p. 892, and AN 3:3.

351. VB notes: "The story of Ciñcā the brahman girl occurs in the Dhammapada Commentary, commenting on verse 176. See Burlingame, *Buddhist Legends* III 19 foll."

352. VB notes: "In the Pali Canon, this incident is referred to in Udāna Section 38."

353. VB notes: "The incident is at SN 4:18 (PTS ed. I 113–14)."

354. VB notes: "The story is in the Pāli Vinaya in Cullavagga, chapter 7; PTS ed II 194–96."

355. VB notes: "This [story] is at the beginning of the Pārājika chapter of the Vinaya."

356. VB notes: "His departure from the Sangha and denunciation of the Buddha are mentioned at the beginning of MN 12. MN 105 is spoken to him, and his arguments with the Buddha about arahants are at DN 23."

357. VB notes: "See AN 7:58: Four things that the Tathāgata does not have to guard: conduct of body, speech, and mind, and livelihood."

358. "The *upoṣadha* dharma" is a reference to spiritual purification, in particular the two days of the month when monastics recite the precepts and the days of the month in which pious lay people voluntarily take on a semi-monastic level of moral precept observance.

359. This is verse 183 of the *Dhammapada*.

360. The first four lines here correspond to *Dhammapada* 361.

361. This corresponds to verse 362 of the *Dhammapada*.

362. VB notes: "See AN 5:181 foll.: 'Bhikkhus, there are these five kinds of forest dwellers. What five? (1) One who becomes a forest dweller because of his dullness and stupidity; (2) one who becomes a forest dweller because he has evil desires, because he is driven by desire; (3) one who becomes a forest dweller because he is mad and mentally deranged; (4) one who becomes a forest dweller, [thinking]: "It is praised by the Buddhas and the Buddhas' disciples"; (5) and one who becomes a forest dweller for the sake of fewness of desires, for the sake of contentment, for the sake of eliminating [defilements], for the sake of solitude, for the sake of simplicity. The fifth is pronounced the best.'"

363. VB notes: "I think the author here is referring to the Buddha's hesitation, immediately after his enlightenment, about going out and teaching the Dharma. See MN 26.19, SN 6:1, etc."

364. VB notes: "This is at MN 26.22–23. Interestingly the author here takes a similar perspective on *sarvajñatā* as the Theravāda commentaries, that knowledge arises when the Buddha directs his attention to some issue (*āvajjanapaṭibaddhaṃ buddhassa bhagavato ñāṇaṃ*), in contrast to the later Mahāyāna view that the Buddha perpetually knows everything simultaneously."

365. The second part of the Chinese text's title, "Forty Dharmas Exclusive to Buddhas: The Exclusive Dharma of Thoroughly Knowing What is Unfixed," is misleading because "the exclusive dharma of thoroughly knowing what is unfixed" only describes the first few pages of this long chapter that in fact discusses all of the remaining exclusive dharmas (nos. 10–40). I have therefore dropped this misleading phrase from the chapter title. One should be aware that these chapter titles almost certainly do not originate with Nāgārjuna but rather with Kumārajīva's translation team.

366. VB notes: "The above corresponds to Majjhima Nikaya no. 136."

367. Commenting on the corresponding passages as preserved in the Pali canon, VB notes: "The Pāli sutta with the simile of the raft mentions

all four fruits (MN 22; see the end). But the proposition about one of two fruits occurs in a number of other suttas, such as the Satipaṭṭhāna Sutta (see end of MN 10)."

368. Regarding this "*Ekottara Āgama*'s *Shejiali Sutra*" (舍迦梨經), I have so far been unable to locate the Sanskrit for its title.

369. VB comments: "The above corresponds to Anguttara Nikāya 10:217 (also 10:218). Note that there are three modes in which the karmic results may be received, both in Pāli and Chinese versions: in the present life (現受報), upon rebirth (that is, the next life; 生受), or in a subsequent life (after the next one; 後受). Here is the Pāli followed by my rendering:

    217. "*Nāhaṃ, bhikkhave, sañcetanikānaṃ kammānaṃ katānaṃ upacitānaṃ appaṭisaṃviditvā byantībhāvaṃ vadāmi. Tañca kho diṭṭheva dhamme upapajje vā apare vā pariyāye. Na tvevāhaṃ, bhikkhave, sañcetanikānaṃ kammānaṃ katānaṃ upacitānaṃ appaṭisaṃveditvā dukkhass'antakiriyaṃ vadāmi.*"

    "Bhikkhus, I do not say that there is a termination of volitional kamma that has been done and accumulated so long as one has not experienced [its results], and that may be in this very life, or in the [next] rebirth, or on some subsequent occasion. But I do not say that there is making an end of suffering so long as one has not experienced [the results of] volitional kamma that has been done and accumulated."

370. Again, I have so far been unable to find the Sanskrit name for this transliterated title.

371. VB notes: "The Pāli parallel is *Majjhima* 58: *Abhayarājakumāra Sutta*."

372. These "three groups" refers to the *tri-skandha* (三聚) as that term is used to categorize the karmic destinies of beings. Those who are "definitely deviant" or "erroneous" are definitely bound to be unsuccessful in reaching enlightenment whereas those who are "definitely righteous" or "correct" are definitely bound to succeed in becoming enlightened. In his Mppu, in commenting on a passage in the Great Perfection of Wisdom Sutra that brings up the topic of these three groups, N points out that it is the ability or inability to destroy the inverted views that is pivotal in determining one's position in this threefold categorization. It is those who may or may not encounter the karmic conditions enabling the destruction of these inverted views who are categorized as "indefinite." (See T25.n1509.647c27–648a01.)

373. These four "repositories of Dharma" (*dharma-piṭaka*) are identified by Nāgārjuna in his Mppu as: 1) the Sutra Piṭaka; 2) the Vinaya Piṭaka;

3) the Abhidharma Piṭaka; and 4) the Kṣudraka-piṭaka (T12; No. 1509; 143c23–25).

374. These are "delectable absorptions" (*āsvādana-samādhi*) which are characterized by the arising of extremely pleasurable meditation states to which the unskilled or unwise meditator is vulnerable to becoming attached.

375. VB notes: "The Pāli parallel is the opening passage of Dīgha Nikāya no. 14, almost verbatim the same."

376. I emend the reading of the *Taisho* text here by preferring on sensibility grounds the SYMG editions' *ci jing* (此經), "this sutra," to the *Taisho* edition's *jing ci* (經此), "sutra this."

The sutra to which this text refers is obviously the Ten Grounds Sutra upon which Nāgārjuna's SZPPS comments. This topic of the expansiveness of the Buddha's knowledge and vision is treated at great length in the sutra itself.

377. VB notes: "The names of *pratyekabuddhas* are mentioned in MN 116. I would posit the following equivalents [for a few of the *pratyekabuddhas* mentioned here]:

無垢 = Ariṭṭha
華相 = Tagarasikhī
喜見 = Piyadassī

378. VB notes: "Parallel to the above is AN 6:62 Section 6: (6) 'Then, Ānanda, having encompassed his mind with my own mind, I understand some person thus: "Wholesome qualities and unwholesome qualities are found in this person." On a later occasion, having encompassed his mind with my own mind, I understand him thus: "This person does not have even a mere fraction of a hair's tip of an unwholesome quality. This person possesses exclusively bright, blameless qualities. He will attain *nibbāna* in this very life."'"

379. VB notes: "[This passage is found] in MN 12."

380. VB notes: "The following passage comes toward the end of MN 12."

381. This long paragraph (beginning with "Supposing…") has the appearance of language quoted from a sutra. However, having failed to locate it, I frame it here as simply Nāgārjuna's amplification of the meaning of the immediately preceding passage that VB recognized as having a Pali analogue in MN 12.

382. This is the name as recorded in the Pali canon. I'm not sure about the Sanskrit for this name.

383. Ibid.

384. VB notes that the following passage is found in the beginning of MN 136.

385. Rāhula was the Buddha's son whereas Devadatta was someone intent on killing the Buddha.

386. VB suggest that this passage may be alluding to AN 4:111, "Kesi the Horse Trainer."

387. This refers to *satkāyadṛṣṭi.*

388. Again, although in these last two cases, the Chinese is literally "gain the path" (得道), per Hirakawa (p. 451, column 2) this corresponds to: "*bodhi, abhisaṃbuddha, saṃbodhi-prāpta.*" Edgerton in turn suggests "becoming perfectly enlightened" for *abhisambuddhana* (Page 58, column 2).

389. Although "*brahmacarya*" (梵行) generally refers to celibate spiritual practice, it may just as well be thought of as "the holy life" or "the spiritual life. VB notes that this scriptural quote "is found in many places in the Nikāyas: e.g., beginning of MN 148: "*Bhagavā etadavoca – 'dhammaṃ vo, bhikkhave, desessāmi ādikalyāṇaṃ majjhe kalyāṇaṃ pariyosānakalyāṇaṃ sātthaṃ sabyañjanaṃ, kevalaparipuṇṇaṃ parisuddhaṃ brahmacariyaṃ pakāsessāmi.'*"

390. VB notes: "In the Pali suttas, the second wonder is being able to declare another person's thoughts. For the three wonders, see AN 3:60: "There are, brahman, these three kinds of wonders. What three? The wonder of psychic potency, the wonder of mind-reading, and the wonder of instruction (*iddhipāṭihāriyaṃ ādesanāpāṭihāriyaṃ anusāsanīpāṭihāriyaṃ*; also at DN 11.3–8, I 212–14). The second is explained thus: There is one who ... declares: 'Your thought is thus, such is what you are thinking, your mind is in such and such a state.' And even if he makes many declarations, they are exactly so and not otherwise."

391. I have been unable to locate either the Sanskrit or Pali antecedents for the titles of these scriptures. VB also notes: "I'm not sure of the references here. Perhaps the former is the Potaliya Sutta, MN 54, but I'm not sure."

392. VB notes: "[The Pali canon analogue for] the following is at MN 12 and AN 4:8."

393. I emend the reading of the *Taisho* text here by preferring on sensibility grounds the SYMG editions' *wei wei* (微畏, "slightest fear," to the *Taisho* edition's *shi* (是), "this."

394. VB notes that the analogue passage in the Pali canon is found at DN no. 20.

395. VB notes: "See MN 115 and AN 1:277."

396. VB notes: "The above, too, is in MN 115 and AN 1:284 foll."
397. VB notes: "On this, see MN 45, 46."
398. VB notes: "This may be an allusion to AN 5:28."
399. VB notes: "This may be an allusion to AN 5:27."
400. This is a concept with numerous similar alternative explanations, most of which refer to the immense amount of merit and time required to acquire the thirty-two marks and eighty minor characteristics of a buddha's body and finally achieve buddhahood. This is discussed in greater detail in Nāgārjuna's commentary on the Great Perfection of Wisdom Sutra. See T25.1509.57b05–27.
401. Nārāyaṇa is a powerful celestial eminence regarded as a Dharma protector in Buddhism.
402. As is quite common with the syntax of multi-line Classical Chinese verses, this quatrain has require the rearrangement of its lines to produce a sensible and naturally flowing statement in English.
403. "Eight classes in four pairs" (四雙八輩) refers to the four preliminary phases and four fruition stages on the individual-liberation path of the *śrāvaka* disciples.
404. VB notes: "見聞覺知 = Pāḷi *diṭṭhaṃ, sutaṃ, mutaṃ, viññātaṃ,* where mutaṃ is explained as things sensed through the other three sense faculties: smell, taste, and touch."

    Hence, in "seen, heard, sensed, and known," (per Hirakawa's BCSD: *dṛṣṭa-śruta-mata-jñāta* or *dṛṣṭa-śruta-mata-vijñāta*) "sensed" (*mata*) refers to the sensory function of the olfactory, gustatory, and tactile sense faculties. Therefore this series is intended to refer to the functions of all six sense faculties and their corresponding consciousnesses.
405. To correct an apparent scribal error very likely originating in homophony, I emend the reading of the text here, preferring on sensibility grounds the homophonous *de* (得), "achieved" of the SYMG editions to the *Taisho* text's *de* (德), "qualities."
406. "Five characteristics" here is slightly ambiguous. It could refer particularly to the five types of desire which together constitute the first of the five hindrances (visible forms, sounds, smells, tastes, and touchables, or wealth, sex, fame, food, and leisure). Alternatively, it may be intended to refer to all five of the "five hindrances" that must be eliminated to access deep states of meditation (desire, ill will, lethargy-and-sleepiness, excitedness-and-regretfulness, and afflicted doubtfulness).

407. To correct an apparent graphic-similarity scribal error, I emend the reading of the *Taisho* text here by preferring the SYMG editions' *li* (力), "power," to the *Taisho* edition's *fen* (分), "portion."

408. I am not sure precisely what Nāgārjuna intended by "the six categories of meanings associated with the forty exclusive Dharmas," set forth in his preceding praise verses.

409. The Sanskrit antecedent of *shixiang* (實相) in KJ translations is usually *dharmatā*, i.e. the true nature of all dharmas, i.e. *śūnyatā*, i.e. the utter absence of inherent existence in any and all phenomena.

410. To correct an apparent graphic-similarity scribal error, I emend the reading of the *Taisho* text here by preferring the SYMG editions' *shen* (深), "deep" or "profound," to the *Taisho* edition's *ran* (染), "defiled." Nāgārjuna's discussion of this line corroborates the correctness of the emendation.

411. When translated into Chinese, "Tathāgata" means "Thus Come One."

412. Again, this most likely refers to "The Pratyutpanna Samādhi Sūtra" preserved in the *Taisho* Canon as the *Banzhou Sanmei Jing* (般舟三昧經 / T13.no. 0418.902c23–919c05).

413. "Overweening pride," *zeng shang man* (增上慢), corresponds to the Sanskrit *adhimāna*.

414. To correct an obvious graphic-similarity scribal error, I emend the reading of the *Taisho* text here by preferring the SYMG editions' *zeng* (增), "increase," to the *Taisho* edition's *zeng* (憎), "detest."

415. "Characteristic sign" refers here to any of the signs associated with three sequential levels of practice described at the very beginning of this chapter:

    1) The thirty-two marks and eighty secondary characteristics of a buddha's form body;
    2) The Dharma body of the Buddhas;
    3) The true character [of all dharmas], i.e. "emptiness of inherent existence" (*śūnyatā*). This "emptiness of inherent existence" is evidenced by: a) their being merely composite constructs of subsidiary conditions; b) their being merely evanescently transient states in a chain of serial causality; and c) their being mere names attached to a) and b) to which one falsely imputes individual reality.

416. To correct an obvious graphic-similarity scribal error, I emend the reading of the *Taisho* text here by preferring the SYMG editions' *zhai* (齋), "ritual purification," to the *Taisho* edition's *qi* (齊), "uniform."

Also, "Precepts of abstinence" refers here to the *aṣṭāṅgasamanvāgataṃ upavāsaṃ*, the laity's formal acceptance and observance of the practice of upholding the eight precepts that include celibacy and not eating after midday. One observes this enhanced level of lay precept practice either continuously or on the eighth, fourteenth, fifteenth, twenty-third, twenty-ninth, and thirtieth days of each lunar month.

417. This reference to laypeople staying in a monastery probably refers most usually to the not uncommon practice of allowing laypeople to live in separate quarters on monastery grounds when they are continuously training in these eight lay precepts for a predetermined period of time.

418. I translate here as "monastic preceptor" and "monastic Dharma teacher" what the KJ text retains in transliteration as "*upādhyāya*" and "*ācārya*" respectively.

419. KJ retained the Sanskrit term for "benefactor" (*dānapati*) which I have opted to translate here.

420. VB notes: "This is the practice of seeking alms at every door, without skipping over houses where the people do not give or give poor quality food." The rationale for observing this "proper sequence" is that, since providing alms to monks and nuns produces karmic merit, one would not want to deny that opportunity to anyone.

421. Lest "unwholesome remorsefulness" seem somewhat opaque, this would refer first and foremost to regretting having done something good or regretting not having done something bad.

422. "Demolishing through separation" most likely refers to the "deconstructive analysis" involved in such contemplations as the contemplation of the thirty-two (or 36) parts of the body, the nine stages of the decomposition of a rotting corpse, the white-boned skeleton contemplation, etc. All of these contemplations serve as powerful antidotes to sensual desire.

423. This attainment of the sign of unloveliness refers to directly perceiving the unloveliness of sensually attractive physical forms so completely that the image of their unloveliness is retained even in the absence of the initially contemplated meditation object. This is often accomplished by deeply practicing the contemplations of the parts of the body, the stages of decomposition of a rotting corpse, or the white-boned skeleton.

424. Hirakawa gives the Sanskrit as: "*saṃrañjanīyaṃ dharmam.*" These six dharmas refer to mutual harmoniousness, respect, equality, and fairness in matters pertaining to: body, speech, mind, precepts, views, and benefits received (food, robes, shelter, etc.).

425. These five bases of liberation (Skt. *vimukty-āyatanāni*) are five different circumstances under which, with or without the advantage of correct teaching from a qualified Dharma teacher or fellow practitioner, a practitioner may come to engage with and find success in cultivation, establish his mind in concentration, and then finally achieve liberation. VB refers us to AN 5:26 for the precise canonical explanation.

426. VB refers us to AN 9:29.

427. VB refers us to AN 8:80.

428. VB refers us to AN 8:80, noting that this is found in the second part of that sutta.

429. These are the *navasaṃjñā* for which VB refers us to AN 9:16.

430. VB refers us to AN 8:30.

431. "No apprehensible reality" (無所得) refers to emptiness of inherent existence, i.e. there is nothing in or about these *dhyāna* absorptions that can be gotten at as ultimately real.

432. VB notes: "Items 43-45 are at SN 35:238, 'The Simile of the Vipers.'"

433. VB notes: "This may also be in SN 35:238: 'The further shore, which is safe and free from danger': this is a designation for Nibbāna."

434. This appears to be a quotation from the "Pratyutpanna Samādhi Sūtra."

435. "Compulsory karmic retributions" most likely refers here to heinous karmic offenses that entail immediate retribution during or at the end of this very life such as: patricide, matricide, killing an arhat, drawing the blood of a buddha, or causing a schism in the monastic sangha.

436. This statement seems contradictory. As such, I am not particularly confident that this sentence is not corrupted or that I have interpreted its intent correctly.

437. The immediately preceding abhidharmic analytic categories are in some cases phrased so tersely in the Chinese as to be mildly obscure. Hence I may not have rendered all of them with definitively precise accuracy.

438. These eight verse lines are a verbatim quote from the very beginning of Chapter Three on the characteristic features of the first bodhisattva ground (26a19–22).

439. Again, the first two of these five verses roughly correspond to the KB translation of the *Ten Grounds Sutra* (500b08-11).

440. As noted in chapter two, again, *biding* (必定),"stage of certainty," is a translation of the Sanskrit *avaivartika*, the stage of irreversibility from which one can never again fall back in one's progress on the path.

441. These twenty verse lines are a verbatim quote from the very beginning of Chapter Two on entry into the first of the ten bodhisattva grounds (23a23-b03).

442. KJ retained the Sanskrit *sarvajña* which I have chosen here to translate as "all-knowledge."

443. With the exception of a minor phrase variation in the second of these twenty-eight lines, this is a verbatim quote from the opening lines of Chapter Four, "On the Purification of the Ground" (28c24–29a08).

444. Each of these seven are clearly explained at the very beginning of Chapter Three.

445. Again, these were: "disbelief, breaking of precepts, having but little learning, covetousness, indolence, chaotic thoughts, and absence of wisdom."

446. The Chinese text here simply transliterates a Sanskrit term for "passport" as *weipotuo* (韋婆陀), which I prefer to translate.

447. At this point in N's text, there is an interpolated note, most likely inserted by the KJ translation team: "The Chinese translation of the Sanskrit "*weituo*" (韋陀) is "unopposed" and it means 'passport.'"

448. Again, "the five hindrances" is a reference to desire, ill will, lethargy-and-sleepiness, excitedness-and-regretfulness, and afflicted doubtfulness, hindrances that must be overcome in order to successfully enter deep states of meditation.

449. "...the other [forms of wisdom]" most likely refers to "wisdom that arises from contemplation" and "great wisdom," both of which were mentioned just above in discussing the metaphoric significance of "firewood" in this extended analogy that forms the basis of two thirds of this chapter.

450. *Zhengwei* (正位), "right and fixed position," seems to usually correspond to the Sanskrit *samyaktva-niyāma* for which Conze's MDPL gives "certainty to have got safely out of this world," or, in the case of "*samyaktva-niyata*," "destined for salvation."

451. "Faculties" here is a reference to "the five root faculties" that, once developed, become "the five powers": faith, vigor, mindfulness, concentration, and wisdom.

452. I emend the reading per the SYMG editions to correct the *Taisho* edition's mistaken inclusion here of *bu* (不), "not." Absent this correction,

the statement would result in the exact opposite of the obviously intended meaning.

453. This line could also be plausibly rendered as: "the hazardous and bad road of *saṃsāra*."

454. In other words: "This is tantamount to committing suicide [on the path to spiritual liberation]."

455. In this particular passage, especially following on the heels of his warning about "neglectfulness," N. is presenting a very close paraphrase of five verses from his own Bodhisaṃbhāra Śāstra, verses 24–28. I quote them here from my own complete translation of that treatise along with its early Indian commentary:

    Until one develops the great compassion and the patiences,
    Even though he may have gained irreversibility,
    The bodhisattva is still subject to a form of "dying"
    Occurring through the arising of negligence.

    The grounds of the Śrāvakas or the Pratyekabuddhas,
    If entered, constitute "death" for him
    Because he would thereby sever the roots
    Of the bodhisattva's understanding and awareness.

    At the prospect of falling into the hell-realms,
    The bodhisattva would not be struck with fright.
    The grounds of the Śrāvakas and the Pratyekabuddhas
    Do provoke great terror in him.

    It is not the case that falling into the hell realms
    Would create an ultimate obstacle to bodhi.
    If one fell onto the grounds of the Śrāvakas or Pratyekabuddhas,
    That would create an ultimate obstacle.

    Just as is said of one who loves long life
    That he is frightened at the prospect of being beheaded,
    So too the grounds of the Śrāvakas and Pratyekabuddhas
    Should provoke in one this very sort of fear.

456. The Chinese translation preserved a short-hand rendering of the third hindrance (as "drowsiness") and fourth hindrance (as "excitedness") for which I have supplied the standard complete rendering of these classic Indian Buddhist technical terms, the third and fourth of which are dual-component hindrances.

457. This is most likely referring to the fact that his adherence to moral virtue is not pursued in order to achieve rebirth in the heavens.

458. This most likely refers to preventing oneself from taking rebirth in the form realm heavens because they constitute an obstacle to cultivation of the bodhisattva path.

459. "Four means of attraction" refers to giving, pleasing words, beneficial actions, and joint endeavors.

460. The four immeasurable minds are kindness, compassion, sympathetic joy, and equanimity.

461. As revealed by the DSBC Sanskrit of the Ten Grounds Sutra's discussion of the second bodhisattva ground, *shi zhong xin* (十種心) "ten types of *resolute intentions*" here and in the ensuing SZPPS discussion correspond to the Sanskrit *cittāśaya*.

462. The DSBC Sanskrit of the Ten Grounds Sutra accords fairly closely with the SZPPS order of this list of ten "resolute intentions" (*cittāśaya*) as it is presented in the following explanation. It records the Sanskrit antecedents as: *ṛjvāśaya* (= *ārjava*?), *mṛdvāśaya, karmaṇyāśaya, damāśaya, śamāśaya, kalyāṇāśaya, asaṃsṛṣṭāśaya, anapekṣāśaya, udārāśaya, māhātmyāśaya.*

463. These six verses correspond to verses 12 through 17 of N's *Bodhisaṃbhāra Śāstra*. I quote them here from my own complete translation of that treatise along with its early Indian commentary:

From the very beginning, the bodhisattva
Should accord with the power of his abilities
And use skillful means to instruct beings,
Causing them to enter the Great Vehicle.

Even if one taught beings as numerous as the Ganges' sands
So that they were caused to gain the fruit of arhatship,
Still, by instructing but a single person to enter the Great Vehicle,
One would generate merit superior to that.

Instructing through resort to the Śrāvaka Vehicle
Or through resort to the Pratyekabuddha Vehicle
Is undertaken where, on account of lesser abilities,
Beings are unable to accept instruction in the Great Vehicle.

Where even when relying on Śrāvaka or Pratyekabuddha Vehicles
In addition to the Great Vehicle teachings,
There are those who still cannot accept any such instruction,
One should strive to establish them in merit-creating situations.

If there be persons unable to accept
Instruction conducing either to the heavens or to liberation,
Favor them through bestowing present-life benefits.
Then, as befits one's powers, one should draw them in.

Where, with regard to particular beings, a bodhisattva
Has no conditions through which to instruct them,
He should draw forth the great kindness and compassion
And should refrain from abandoning them.

464. To correct an apparent graphic-similarity scribal error, I emend the reading of the *Taisho* text here by preferring the SYMG editions' *guo* (果), "resultant," to the *Taisho* edition's *yi* (異), "different." (The immediately following question in the ensuing text echoes this word choice and corroborates the validity of the emendation.)

465. Although this teaching seems to be addressed exclusively to men regarding their behaviors vis-à-vis women, that is only because most women were illiterate at the time and never would have encountered this treatise outside of a lecture format where its universal applicability would have been made clear.

466. In Buddhist texts, "restricted orifice" refers to oral sex, anal sex, etc.

467. This "scattered or inappropriate speech" usually translates *saṃbhinnapralāpa* which, in addition to the definitions mentioned here, is usually also interpreted to include "lewd, dirty, or off-color speech." This traditional subdefinition is implicitly and euphemistically referenced here a few lines below as one of the traditional meanings of "speech contrary to Dharma."

468. "Volition" (思) could be referring here to premeditation, i.e. deliberate intentionality.

469. VB notes: "Items sixteen and seventeen here correspond to functions relating to the four noble truths: the truth of the path is *bhāvetabba*, 'to be cultivated.' The truth of suffering is *pariññeyya*, 'to be well understood.'"

470. VB notes: "[This refers to] *pahātabba*: the function pertaining to the second noble truth."

471. I am not entirely sure about the accuracy of my translation of the following fourfold list. I may have misunderstood it or it may be slightly corrupted.

472. Because some of these listed distinctions seem contradictory, I am not confident that I have correctly rendered the intended meaning of the abhidharmic technical terms here. It may also be the case that the text has become somewhat corrupted.

473. Because this would seem to be a contradiction, I am not sure I have translated this correctly. There are five instances of this same statement (with minor variations) in this chapter.

474. VB notes: "The above [two cases] refer to two stages or degrees of an affliction: the stage of *anuśaya*, where it remains as a latent tendency; and the stage of obsession, where it arises and dominates the mind."

475. VB notes: "This latter alternative presumably refers to abandoning the taking of life in world-transcendent (*lokottara*) states of mind."

476. This twelvefold list has become slightly corrupted at some point, but not irretrievably so. (As noted below, I correct the corruption by emendation.) As received, it duplicates the sixth member of the list ("For what is it a condition?" ["與誰作緣?"]) and leaves out another member of the list which we encounter in the ensuing discussion ("What is the benefit?" ["何利益?"]).

477. The received editions of this text mistakenly duplicate list item number six here as "8) For what is it a condition?". I have emended the text to correct this obvious scribal error by inserting the missing list item ("What is the benefit?" ["何利益?"]) which is found in the ensuing discussion at 97a27–8.)

478. VB notes: "This may be alluding to a passage in the early sutras, see AN 6.63: 'It is volition, O monks, that I call karma. For having willed, one acts by body, speech, or mind.' Thus covetousness, etc., are here considered not to be karma (in the sense of actual action) because they are mental states associated with or corresponding to volition rather than actions in their own right. The Theravada Abhidhamma differs, considering covetousness, etc., both karma and paths of karma. They are mental karma (*manokamma*)."

479. The phrase "there is no fixed subjective agent [involved in its creation]" (無有定主) can refer to one or both of two ideas: a) The absence of any sort of creator god involved in the creation of the world; or b) The absence of any inherently existent "self" in oneself or in any of the other beings who collectively create all the causes and conditions for the creation, abiding, and destruction of the world, this through the causal power of their good and bad karmic deeds.

480. In referring to it as the "Non-extensive Heaven (不廣天), N uses an extremely rare name for this Avṛha Heaven. (There is only one other use of this name in the entire *Taisho* canon.) The more common Chinese name is the "No Affliction Heaven" (無煩天).

481. In commenting on this line that I might otherwise translate as "and who always disbelieve that the world / is possessed of *the dharma of* stability and security—," VB notes: "In Sanskrit and Pali, *-dharma* / *-dhamma* is often used as a suffix to indicate 'having the nature of' or 'subject to.' Thus (P) *sabbe sattā maraṇadhammā*, 'all beings are subject to death / have the nature of dying.' I suspect that the Sanskrit original of this line used *'dharma'* [法] in that function, thus [the sense of this may be] 'The world does not have a stable and secure nature.'"

482. "*Śrāvaka*" means, in essence, "auditor," i.e. "those who learn by listening."

483. VB notes: The Pali version, AN 1:328 NDB p.121: "Bhikkhus, just as even a trifling amount of feces is foul smelling, so too I do not praise even a trifling amount of existence, even for a mere finger snap."

484. N seems to be referring here to the pivotal importance of one's last thoughts at the moment of death that may so strongly influence whether or not one then enters good or bad rebirth circumstances.

485. Lest it not be so obvious, "what is unlovely, stinking, defiled, and ungrateful for kindnesses" is intended to refer to the human body.

486. VB notes: "See SN 35:28, Connected Discourses p. 1143."

487. VB notes: "This sequence is found in several places in the *Nikāyas*, especially in the *Anguttara*. See AN 10:1–4 and 11:1–4. Here, 厭 = *nibbidā*, which I render 'disenchantment,' while 離 is *virāga*, 'dispassion' or 'detachment.'"

488. VB notes: "尊者施曰羅. This is probably Ven. Sivali. Since 捨 can mean either 'generosity' or 'relinquishment,' the two connect Sivali's past-life merits with his special facility as a monk.

From Dictionary of Pali Proper Names: 'In Padumuttara Buddha's time he made the resolve to be pre-eminent among recipients of gifts, like Sudassana, disciple of Padumuttara. To this end he gave alms for seven days to the Buddha and his monks. In the time of Vipassī Buddha he was a householder near Bandhumatī. The people gave alms to the Buddha and the Order in competition with the king, and when they were in need of honey, curds and sugar, Sīvalī gave enough of these for sixty-eight thousand monks.... Sīvalī was declared by the Buddha (A.i.24) pre-eminent among recipients of gifts.... Sīvalī went to the Himālaya with five hundred others, to test his good luck. The gods provided them with everything. On Gandhamādana a deva, named Nāgadatta, entertained them for seven days on milk rice."

For more, see:

http://www.palikanon.com/english/pali_names/s/siivalii.htm."

489. VB notes: "*Anguttara* 4: 143 : 'Bhikkhus, there are these four lights. What four? The light of the moon, the light of the sun, the light of fire, and the light of wisdom. These are the four lights. Of these four lights, the light of wisdom is foremost.'"

490. Although slightly ambiguous, their "twofold vows" most likely refers to their vows to accomplish both self-benefit and other-benefit, i.e. to become buddhas themselves while also facilitating the awakening of all other beings.

491. See the chapter-commencing verse, line 1–2.

492. See the chapter-commencing verse, line 4.

493. As noted by VB, here this *shan* (善) does not have its somewhat more usual meaning of "goodness" (*kuśala*). Rather, as in many places in KJ translations, it serves here as an intensifying modifier. When modifying "purity," as in the "*su*" of *suviśuddha*, it would instead mean "thorough," "thoroughgoing," or "complete" purity.

494. See the preceding note for an explanation of this somewhat less usual use of the *shan* (善) in *shan qingjing* (善清淨).

495. Although not explicitly stated here, the "three types of purity" may refer to either (or both) of two explanations offered earlier in the sutra. Here are the two previous explanations:

1) In Chapter Five, we had: "As for 'purity,' this means that one has completely developed the three types of purity, namely purity in physical actions, purity in verbal actions, and purity in mental actions."

2) In Chapter Twenty-eight, specifically referring to the bodhisattva's practice of these ten courses of good karmic action on this second bodhisattva ground, we had a verse and the prose explanation immediately following it, as follows:

"If a bodhisattva still at the border with the first ground
employs three kinds of purity
to abide securely in the ten courses of good karmic action,
he will then be able to bring forth decisive resolve.

Once this bodhisattva comes to dwell on the second ground, he then distinguishes with utter clarity these ten good and bad courses of karmic action. Having come to know these matters, he applies three kinds of purity to his abiding in the ten courses of good karmic action, namely:

He does not personally kill any being;
He does not instruct others to kill any being;
And he does not delight in the karmic offense of killing."

496. See the chapter-commencing verse, line 3.

497. See Chapter Five, "The Explanation of the Vows," in which these ten "ultimate ends" that define the infinity of the bodhisattva vows are listed as follows:

"[Hence these vows are made]:

First, until the end of the realms of beings;
Second, until the end of the realms of worlds;
Third, until the end of the realms of empty space;
Fourth, until the end of the Dharma realm;
Fifth, until the end of the realm of nirvāṇa;
Sixth, until the end of the realms in which buddhas are born;

Seventh, until the end of the realms of all buddhas' knowledge;
Eighth, until the end of everything that can be taken as an object of mind;
Ninth, until the end of the knowledge associated with the range of all buddhas' actions;
And tenth, until the end of the permutations of the knowledge of worldly dharmas.

These are the ten [ways in which vows are] ultimately enduring."

498. See chapter-commencing verse, line 3.

499. See chapter-commencing verse, line 5.

500. This is clearly a reference to "the right and fixed position" (*samyaktva-niyāma*) wherein the bodhisattva becomes immune to the temptations of opting for the nirvāṇa prized by adherents of the Śrāvaka Disciple Vehicle and Pratyekabuddha Vehicles.

501. See chapter-commencing verse, line 5.

502. See chapter-commencing verse, line 6.

503. See chapter-commencing verse, line 6.

504. See chapter-commencing verse, line 7.

505. VB points out that this "... *maintaining vigilance* at all times throughout the first watch and the last watch of the night" is stock material in the early suttas that should not be misunderstood as referencing "achieving awakening" (覺悟) as such. See NDB pp. 212, 427, etc.

506. I prefer here to translate what the KJ text preserves as the transliterations of the Sanskrit for the perfections: "One first speaks of *dāna pāramitā*, then *śīla pāramitā*, then *kṣānti pāramitā*, then *vīrya pāramitā*, then *dhyāna pāramitā*, and then *prajñā pāramitā*."

507. See chapter-commencing verse, line 8.

508. See chapter-commencing verse, line 9.

509. Having already made it clear in the above fivefold list that it is a good thing to disdain the *dharmas* of petty people and esteem the *dharmas* of great men, here one is reminded to still retain completely equal compassionate regard for the people themselves.

510. See chapter-commencing verse, line 10. ("[They] deeply cherish the wisdom of the Buddhas ....")

511. See chapter-commencing verse, line 11–12.

512. See chapter-commencing verse, line 12.

513. See chapter-commencing verse, line 12.

514. VB notes: "For these, see AN 5:144 (NDB pp. 761–62 along with note 1144. Paṭisambhidāmagga calls them "powers of the noble ones" (*ariy'iddhi*)."
515. This is a reference to number four, "the psychic powers of the Āryas."
516. See chapter-commencing verse, line 13.
517. See chapter-commencing verse, line 14.
518. A search of the *Taisho* Canon indicates that, in both cases (whether "dark" or "great"), these "four seals" refer to four levels of trustworthiness in determining whether or not any given teaching that one has received is to be trusted as truly originating with the Buddha.
519. See chapter-commencing verse, line 15.
520. See chapter-commencing verse, line 15.
521. See chapter-commencing verse, line 15.
522. See chapter-commencing verse, line 16.
523. I emend the text here to accord with four other editions by substituting 汝 for 如 to correct an apparent homophonic scribal error, this because the resulting reading is much more plausible than the extremely forced reading that retaining 如 would yield.
524. See chapter-commencing verse, line 17.
525. See chapter-commencing verse, line 18.
526. See chapter-commencing verse, line 19.
527. See chapter-commencing verse, line 20.
528. See chapter-commencing verse, lines 21–22.
529. See chapter-commencing verse, lines 23–24.
530. Although, per MW, the meaning of the Sanskrit word *bhagavat* is "possessing fortune, fortunate, prosperous, happy" or "glorious, illustrious, divine, adorable, venerable," in Buddhism, it is one of the ten primary names of any and all buddhas that is intended to call to mind all of the Buddha's qualities including his perfect wisdom and virtue. The Chinese translation is "World Honored One" (世尊). Other common English translations (per PDB) are "Blessed One," "Exalted One," or "Lord." It is because of the wide range of connotations of the name that, rather than translate the Chinese honorific, I usually prefer to simply use the now fairly common Sanskrit name "Bhagavat." (I *do* translate it in the following verse, however.) "Bhagavan" is essentially the same word that one encounters in other translations and other traditions as (again per PDB) *bhagavān*, *bhagavad*, *bhagawan*, and *bhagwan*.

531. "The fourteen ineffable dharmas" is a reference to the fourteen "unanswered" or "undeclared" (*avyākṛta*) dharmas.

532. Although the language itself is not specific, the implicit reference is to extramarital relationships, perhaps voluntary, perhaps not.

533. I emend the text here (at 108a17, second character) by replacing the clearly erroneous *bu* (不), "not," with the doubtlessly intended *xia* (下), "lesser," to correct an obvious graphic-similarity scribal error not noticed in either *Taisho* or in any of its recorded alternate editions).

534. "Obsessed" (纏) corresponds to the Sanskrit *paryavasthāna* and refers to the active phase of entanglement by the afflictions.

535. "…the view of a real self in association with the body [or any of the other four aggregates]" (身見) corresponds to the Sanskrit *satkāya-dṛṣṭi*.

536. VB notes that, on the Śrāvaka Vehicle path, this severance via seeing the four truths occurs upon realizing stream-entry, whereas severance through meditative cultivation occurs on the three higher stages of the path to arhatship.

537. What is referred to here as "the ninety-eight fetters" (九十八使) is elsewhere rendered somewhat more precisely as "the ninety-eight latent tendencies" (九十八隨眠 [*anuśaya*]), hence I translate accordingly.

538. I emend the reading here to correct a fairly obvious graphic-similarity scribal error by preferring on doctrinal sensibility grounds SYMG's *hui* (悔), "regret," to the *Taisho* edition's *wu* (侮), "to insult."

539. I have followed four other editions (SYMG) in placing these four lines into verse format. The correctness of this couldn't be clearer, especially given the combination of even line length, context, and unavoidably obvious Chinese rhyming of the quatrain's third line with the first line and fourth line with the second line.

540. This very long quotation (2.5 pages, ending at the next set of stanza lines) corresponds fairly closely to a second-ground passage in the KB Ten Grounds Sutra translation (T10n0286_0505b05–c20) and also to the corresponding second-ground passage in the Śikṣānanda translation of the Avataṃsaka Sutra's "Ten Grounds" chapter (T10n0279_0186a10–b22).

541. VB notes: "This is a reference to the three wrong thoughts (*vitarka*): sensual thought, thought of ill will, and thought of harming."

542. The following passage corresponds quite closely with a long passage in the "Akṣayamati" Chapter of the *Mahāsaṃnipāta Sūtra* (in the *Taisho* canon's Chinese translation by Dharmakṣema in 413 CE: 大方等大集經卷第二十七 –無盡意菩薩品第十二之一 T13n0397_p0189c27–190b10).

However, that translation lists "sixty-seven" rather than the "sixty-five" to which Nāgārjuna refers in this treatise probably authored two centuries before Dharmakṣema's translation.

543. This aspect of moral virtue together with the next nine correspond to the ten courses of good karmic action.

544. This aspect of moral virtue together with the next two correspond to the Three Refuges.

545. VB points out that "things that accord with Dharma" (如法物) is probably best construed as "things *obtained* in accordance with the Dharma," this because it directly corresponds to "*yathādhammaṃ lābha*" in the Pali scriptures.

546. This aspect of moral virtue and the next three correspond to the four immeasurable minds.

547. This aspect of moral virtue together with the next five correspond to the six perfections. Here the first two perfections are listed in reverse order.

548. I emend the reading here to correct a fairly obvious graphic-similarity scribal error by preferring (due to issues of doctrinal sensibility and explicitly stated parallelism) the SYMG editions' *chang* (常), "constantly," to the *Taisho* edition's *dang* (當), "should."

549. VB notes: "This is referring to the abandoning of physical bad karma not included in the ten karmic paths, for, in the form realm, there is no killing, stealing, and sexual misconduct—indeed, there is no sexuality there, no private property, and the beings have fixed life spans. Since the three transgressions are impossible there, there is no abandoning them; but minor types of unwholesome physical conduct might exist there, and one must abstain from these."

550. VB offers a clarifying note here with respect to bad karmic actions associated with speech in the form realm: "This [mention of scattered or inappropriate speech] is not just an example; apparently there is no lying, divisive speech, or harsh speech in the form realm, but there is scattered speech."

551. "*Brahmacarya*," literally "brahman conduct" refers to the celibate spiritual life.

552. VB notes: "See *Anguttara Nikāya* 7:50, NDB pp. 1038–39. The sixth is different from the Pali version."

553. As mentioned in the above note, the Pali version of number six is different, as follows: "(6) '...he does not recollect laughing, talking, and playing with women in the past...but he looks at a householder or a householder's son enjoying himself furnished and endowed with the five objects of sensual pleasure....'"

554. VB located what appears to be very nearly this same passage in the Mahāratnakuta collection (大寶積經) at T11n0310_p0636c28.

555. VB located this passage in the *Mahāvaipulya-mahāsaṃnipāta Sūtra* (大方等大集經) at T13n0397_p0190b11.

556. "Name and form" (名色 = *nāmarūpa*) is a reference to the five aggregates.

557. The *Mahāvaipulya-mahāsaṃnipāta Sūtra* translation's version of this passage clarifies this Sangha-related clause with "by *cultivation* of the unconditioned" (T13n0397_p0190b28: 不斷僧種，[17]修無為故。[Note 17 in that edition tells us that the SYMG reading has 以修 instead of just 修]).

558. The *Mahāvaipulya-mahāsaṃnipāta Sūtra* translation's version of this passage is found at T13n0397_p0190c01.

559. VB offers the following supplementary note on the austerities:

> "Ten ascetic practices are mentioned in the *Anguttara Nikāya* at 5:181–90, each distinguished as fivefold in accordance with the reasons they are undertaken. In the Theravada tradition, the standard list of ascetic practices is expanded to thirteen, described and analyzed in *Visuddhimagga*, Chapter 2. Ten agree with those in this chapter. They differ in that the *Daśabhūmika-vibhāṣā-śāstra* includes two not in the *Visuddhimagga* system: wearing robes made of animal hairs, and not accepting drinks other than water after mid-day. The *Visuddhimagga* list includes three not in this *Daśabhūmika-vibhāṣā-śāstra*: walking on alms round by going to every house, without skipping any (a narrowing of the ascetic practice of eating only food collected on alms round); eating only from the alms bowl (refusing the use of other plates and saucers); and refusing food brought after one has started one's meal (but still within the time limits). The latter seems to be a different interpretation of the ascetic practice the *Daśabhūmika-vibhāṣā-śāstra* system interprets as refusing drinks after mid-day."

560. The Chinese text for this first reflection is ambiguous. It seems to allude to the idea that whatever one receives [or doesn't receive] on the alms round is a direct reflection of whether or not one has created enough merit, hence being able to continue in this is one's own responsibility and no one else's.

561. The implication here is that one should be willing to abandon any concerns for personal comfort as one vigorously pursues very rigorous bodhisattva path practices.

562. "Unimpeded reflections" here likely refers to such reflections as those devoted to deep understanding and realization of the three

gates to liberation, the four immeasurables, the four bases of meritorious qualities, and the six perfections (as implied just below at 112a27–29).

563. Due to the requirements of sensibility, I emend the reading of the text here in accordance with the SYMG editions by adding a missing *ji* (及) before *Taisho*'s *shen* (身) to produce *jishen* (及身) which I take here to mean "for one's entire life."

564. VB notes: "What is mentioned here are the three kinds of wholesome thought, namely, thought of renunciation, thought of non-ill will, and thought of nonharming. Note that *chujue* (出覺) is *nekkhamma-vitakka*, 'thought of renunciation.' See for example MN 19, on the three kinds of wholesome thought: '*Tassa mayhaṃ, bhikkhave, evaṃ appamattassa ātāpino pahitattassa viharato uppajjati nekkhammavitakko … abyāpādavitakko … pe … avihiṃsāvitakko.*'"

565. VB notes that this is Ugra, the subject of the *Ugraparipṛcchā Sūtra* and that this passage can be found in the *Mahāratnakūṭa Sūtra* (大寶積經卷第八十二，郁伽長者會第十九), beginning at T11n0310_p0477c24.

566. This likely refers to the "six recollections" (*anusmṛti*) of the Buddha, the Dharma, the Sangha, moral virtue, generosity, and the devas.

567. The relevant verse from chapter three (T26, no. 1521, 27a15–18) is:

He is free of the fear of not surviving,
the fear of death, the fear of the wretched destinies,
the fear of the Great Assembly's awesome virtue,
the fear of ill repute, and the fear of being disparaged.

As for fear of imprisonment, shackles, and manacles,
and the fear of beatings or capital punishment,
given that he is free of a self or any possessions of self,
how then could he have any such fears as these?

568. VB notes that the Pali parallel is *Samyutta Nikāya* 3:5.

569. VB notes: "The Pali parallel is *Saṃyutta Nikāya* 11: 3. The author of this work is evidently very familiar with the *Nikāyas/Āgama* collections."

570. VB notes: "The Pali parallel for this passage is the first part of *Majjhima Nikāya Sutta* 4; see MLDB pp.102–3."

571. As noted earlier by VB, again, this is Ugra, the subject of the *Ugraparipṛcchā Sūtra*. This particular passage can be found in the *Mahāratnakūṭa Sūtra* (大寶積經卷第八十二，郁伽長者會第十九), beginning at T11n0310_p0478a20.

572. "Difficulties" here is probably a reference to the eight difficulties of which the hells, animals, and hungry ghosts are the first three list members.

573. I emend the reading of the *Taisho* text here by preferring on sensibility grounds the SYMG editions' *zhi* (知), "to know," to the *Taisho* edition's *hehe* (和合), "to harmonize."

574. This is probably meant to refer to the four floods (Skt. *catvāra oghāḥ, catur-ogha*): sensual desire (*kāmarāga*), [craving for] continuing existence (*bhāva*), ignorance (*avidyā*), and views (*dṛṣṭi*). (These are identical to the "contaminants" [*āsrava*]).

575. Again, the four lineage bases of the Āryas (*catur-āryavaṃśa*) are: delighting in mere sufficiency in clothing, delighting in mere sufficiency of food and drink, delighting in mere sufficiency of bedding, and delighting in the severance [of evil] and the cultivation [of goodness].

576. "Nature of dharmas" usually corresponds to the Sanskrit *dharmatā*. Still, although somewhat less likely, given that KJ very regularly uses *xing* (性) to translate *dhātu*, this might also be construed to mean: "Dwelling in a forest hermitage refers to [realizing that] all realms together constitute the Dharma realm."

577. "The stations of rebirth to which they correspond" refers to rebirth in the heavens of the form realm.

578. I emend the reading of the *Taisho* text here by preferring on sensibility grounds the SYMG editions' *ci yinyuan* (此因緣), "these [special] circumstances," to the *Taisho* edition's *yinyuan* (因緣), "[special] circumstances."

579. A saṃghāvaśeṣa offense is a serious offense (such as touching a woman motivated by a thought of desire) that requires a meeting of the bhikshu sangha to determine the disciplinary penalty. "Grave offense" here is a euphemism for sexual intercourse, a pārājika offense entailing expulsion from the monastic community. The third case, "transgressing against the precept and returning to lay life," refers to committing either of the above sorts of offenses and then voluntarily setting aside the robes (rather than waiting for the bhikshu sangha's formal judgment on the matter).

580. These first two *dhūta* austerities just discussed at length were always gaining one's sustenance from the alms round and dwelling in a forest hermitage.

581. "Not accepting any beverage at the wrong time" means that that one does not accept any beverage but water outside of that very mealtime. "Wrong time" has the additional meaning of "not after midday."

582. VB notes: "When one first receives full ordination, the teacher explains the ideal form of the four requisites: using cast off robes,

food obtained on alms round, dwelling at the foot of a tree, and using cow's urine for medicine. Then he explains the more lenient alternatives. Thus *chushou* (初受), ["the initially received explanation"], refers to what was first explained at one's ordination."

583. Lest it not be obvious, this in no way restricts standing or walking. It is entirely a matter of never lying down, not even when one sleeps.

584. Again, although it is not mentioned here, in addition to its otherwise referenced meanings, "at the wrong time" also means "not after midday."

585. VB notes that this *zuo wo ju* (坐臥具), *senāsana*, literally "seats and beds" is a term of convenience for "a dwelling place."

586. VB notes: "This is an allusion to a sutra in which the Buddha says that "noise is a thorn for one attaining the first dhyāna." See *Anguttara Nikaya* 10:72 "Thorns": ... (5) Noise is a thorn to the first *jhāna.* (6) Thought and examination are a thorn to the second *jhāna.* (7) Rapture is a thorn to the third *jhāna.* (8) In-and-out breathing is a thorn to the fourth *jhāna.*"

587. To correct an apparent graphic-similarity and/or homophonic scribal error, I emend the reading of the *Taisho* text here by preferring the SYMG editions' *shang* (尚), "even," to the *Taisho* edition's *chang* (常), "always." The correctness of the emendation is corroborated by the commentary in the next paragraph.

588. To correct an apparent omission, I emend the reading of the *Taisho* text here by preferring on sensibility grounds the SYMG editions' insertion of an additional *fo* (佛), "Buddha," to begin this sentence. The emended reading then exactly echoes the text of the verse upon which this sentence comments.

589. I emend the reading of the *Taisho* text here by preferring on sensibility grounds the SYMG editions' *yang* (殃), "disastrous," to the *Taisho* edition's *da* (大), "great."

590. I emend the reading of the text here in accordance with the SYM (but not G) editions by preferring on sensibility grounds *tong* (通) "understand" to the *Taisho* edition's *song* (誦) "recite."

591. I emend the reading of the text here in accordance with the SYMG editions by preferring on sensibility grounds the inclusion of an apparently lost member of the often-encountered rather standard list that is found later on in this same chapter that includes *mingzhe jian* (命者見), "the view of a life."

592. Again, even though this *zuo wo ju* (坐臥具) would seem to refer to "seats and beds," it is a hyperliteral translation of the Sanskrit

senāsana which is just a term of convenience for "a lodging" or "a dwelling place."

593. Yet again, both here and directly below, KJ is translating *xing* (性) (more usually "nature") as *dhātu* (usually "realms" or "elements." We know this both from context and from comparisons of his Ten Grounds Sutra translation with a much later Sanskrit edition of that sutra. This rendering of *xing* is somewhat inconsistently applied by the KJ translation team, hence we must rely on context sensibility to determine which Sanskrit antecedent is being referenced in any given passage. This line presents a perfect example of that inconsistency of usage, for it is used in *both* senses here, first as "elements," then as "nature."

594. "The six elements" (*ṣaḍ-dhātu*) are: earth, water, fire, wind / air, space, and consciousness.

595. Regarding this statement that "the form aggregate is characterized by being assailed by what is painful," VB notes:

 "'如說色是苦惱相': There is a word play in the Pali (and, presumably its Sanskrit counterpart) that [although successfully captured in this passage translated by KJ], wasn't reflected in the Chinese translation [of the *Saṃyukta Āgama*]. A Pali sutta (SN 22:79) playfully tried to derive *rūpa* = material form from the verb *ruppati*, meaning something like "to be molested, to be assailed."—"assailed by cold, by heat, by hunger and thirst, etc." There is no real etymological connection between *rūpa* and *ruppati*, but the pun works. Here is the Pali: *"Kiñca, bhikkhave, rūpaṃ vadetha? Ruppatī ti kho, bhikkhave, tasmā 'rūpna' ti vuccati. Kena ruppati? Sītenapi ruppati, uṇhenapi ruppati, jighacchāyapi ruppati, pipāsāyapi ruppati, ḍaṃsamakasavātātapasiriṃsapasamphassenapi ruppati."*

 The Chinese parallel is *Saṃyukta Āgama* 46 (雜阿含經-T02n0099_p0011b26–29): "若可閡可分，是名色受陰。指所閡，若手、若石、若杖、若刀、若冷、若暖、若渴、若飢、若蚊、虻、諸毒虫、風、雨觸，是名觸閡，是故閡是色受陰。"

596. To correct an apparent graphic-similarity scribal error, I emend the reading of the *Taisho* text here by preferring the SYMG editions' *duo* (墮), "to fall," to the *Taisho* edition's *sui* (隨), "to follow."

597. In Classical Chinese literature, *zhi* (直), "straight, direct, etc.," is interchangeable with *zhi* (值), "worth, value, etc.," and I have translated it accordingly here as this is clearly the meaning intended by the KJ translation team.

598. This very long verse is a nearly verbatim repetition of the verse found earlier in the treatise in Chapter Eight, at 39c21–40a13. There are eight variant characters as endnoted directly below.

599. The Chapter Eight version of this verse has "and is identical with whatever is possessed of signs" instead of "and is identical with whatever is an existent dharma" (即為是有相 instead of 即為是有法).

600. The Chapter Eight version of this verse has "Were one to relinquish all covetousness" instead of "Were one to relinquish all strategizing and attachments" (若捨諸貪著 instead of 若捨諸計著).

601. The Chapter Eight version of this verse has "There is someone who grasps and something that is grasped" instead of "It is the abandonment of grasping and whatever thing is grasped" (誰取取何事 instead of 離取取何事).

602. The Chapter Eight version of this verse has "whether as conjoined or separate, they are all entirely nonexistent" instead of "whether as conjoined or separate, they are all devoid of existence" (共離俱不有 instead of 共離俱無有).

603. The Chapter Eight version of this verse has "It is precisely because it is signless" instead of "It is precisely because it is synonymous with signlessness" (即為是無相 instead of 即名為無相).

604. These first two verse lines are referring to the four alternative propositions of the tetralemma, as in: 1) It exists; 2) It does not exist; 3) It both exists and does not exist; and 4) It neither exists nor does not exist.

605. The Chapter Eight version of this verse has a fairly nonconsequential variant for one of the characters in this line (先亦非寂滅 instead of 先來非寂滅).

606. The following passage corresponds to a section of the *Great Jeweled Summit Sutra* (大寶積經: T11n0310_p0636c17–29).

607. *Xing* (行), more usually "action(s)," refers here instead to *saṃskāras*, hence here the translation as "all conditioned things."

608. This verse and the very long passage that follow are also found in the *Great Jeweled Summit Sutra* (大寶積經: T11n0310_p0636a29–b29).

609. I emend the reading of the text here in accordance with the SYMG editions by preferring on sensibility grounds *anwen* (安隱), "peaceful and secure" to the *Taisho* edition's *anle* (安樂), "peaceful and happy" which appears to be a result of scribal absent-mindedness reflexively repeating the immediately preceding concept which would produce an unlikely redundancy.

610. VB notes: "See AN 8:19, [where this is listed as] one of the qualities of the ocean."

611. Here and in the following three paragraphs, the text is referring to the four supreme bases for the generation of meritorious qualities, namely truth, relinquishment, quiescence, and wisdom.

612. "Stream enterer" here is literally "one who has acquired the fruit of the path of a *srota-āpanna*."

613. "Marvelous phenomena" (希有事) is generally intended to refer to miraculous occurrences brought about by spiritual powers. (希有= *adbhuta*, "supernatural.")

614. VB notes: "AN 9:5 mentions these four fears. See NDB p. 1255." This topic of the fears to which a bodhisattva is invulnerable is also extensively treated in Chapter Three of this treatise in the discussion of the characteristics of the bodhisattva who has reached the second bodhisattva ground.

615. As of the Tang Dynasty, a couple hundred years after Kumārajīva made this translation, a Chinese mile (*li* = 里) was roughly 1060 feet, i.e. a fifth of a U.S. mile or a third of kilometer. As of the end of the Han Dynasty, a couple hundred years before this translation was made, it was roughly 1365 feet, i.e. a quarter of a U.S. mile or four tenths of a kilometer. Using these measures as a basis, the circumference of this wheel would be between 3.0 and 3.9 U.S. miles, or between 5 and 6 kilometers.

616. Although this is literally the "householder treasure," (居士寶 / *gṛhapati ratna*), the literature makes it clear that this is a minister of the treasury.

617. To correct an apparent graphic-similarity scribal error, I emend the reading of the *Taisho* text here by preferring the SYMG editions' *qing* (青), "blue," to the *Taisho* edition's *jing* (睛), "eye."

618. A search of Cbeta suggests that this is the only place in the entire Chinese Buddhist canon that this transliteration appears, hence any Sanskrit reconstructions I might suggest for this celestial maiden's name would be mere conjecture.

Bibliography

Bodhi. (2000). *The Connected Discourses of the Buddha: A New Translation of the Saṃyutta Nikāya* ; translated from the Pāli ; original translation by Bhikkhu Bodhi. (Teachings of the Buddha). Somerville, MA: Wisdom Publications.

Bodhi. (2012). The Numerical Discourses of the Buddha: A Translation of the Aṅguttara Nikāya (Teachings of the Buddha). Boston: Wisdom Publications.

Burlingame, E., Buddhaghosa, & Lanman, Charles Rockwell. (1921). Buddhist legends (Harvard oriental series ; v. 28-30). Cambridge, Mass.: Harvard Univ. Press.

Conze, E., & Suzuki Gakujutsu Zaidan. (1967). Materials for a Dictionary of the Prajñāpāramitā Literature. Tokyo: Suzuki Research Foundation.

Dharmamitra. (2009) Nāgārjuna on the Six Perfections: An Ārya Bodhisattva Explains the Heart of the Bodhisattva Path. A translation of chapters 17-30 of Ārya Nāgārjuna's Exegesis on the Great Perfection of Wisdom Sutra. Seattle: Kalavinka Press.

Dharmamitra. (2009) Nāgārjuna's Guide to the Bodhisattva Path: Treatise on the Provisions for Enlightenment. A translation of the Bodhisaṃbhāra Śāstra by Ārya Nāgārjuna. Seattle: Kalavinka Press.

Edgerton, F. (1953). Buddhist Hybrid Sanskrit grammar and dictionary. (William Dwight Whitney linguistic series). New Haven: Yale University Press.

Hirakawa, A. (1997). Buddhist Chinese-Sanskrit Dictionary / Bukkyō Kan-Bon daijiten. Tokyo]; [Tokyo] :: Reiyūkai : Hatsubaimoto Innātorippusha; 霊友会 : 発売元いんなあとりっぷ社.

Malalasekera, G. (1937). Dictionary of Pāli proper names (Indian texts series). London: J. Murray.

Ñāṇamoli, & Bodhi. (1995). The Middle Length Discourses of the Buddha: A New Translation of the Majjhima Nikāya (Teachings of the Buddha). Boston: Wisdom Publications in association with the Barre Center for Buddhist Studies.

Nattier, J. (2003). A Few Good Men: The Bodhisattva Path According to the Inquiry of Ugra (Ugraparipṛcchā) (Studies in the Buddhist traditions). Honolulu: University of Hawai'i Press.

Powers, J. (2016). The Buddhist World (Routledge worlds). London ; New York: Routledge, Taylor & Francis Group.

Rahder, J. (1928). Glossary of the Sanskrit, Tibetan, Mongolian, and Chinese Versions of the Daśabhūmika-Sūtra. Compiled by J. Rahder. (Buddhica, Documents et Travaux pour l'Étude du

Bouddhisme publiés sous la direction de J. Przyluski; Deuxième Série; Documents—Tome I). Paris: Librarie Orientaliste Paul Geuthner, 1928.

Rahder, J., & Vasubandhu. (1926). Daśabhumikasutra. Leuven: J.B. Istas.

Ruegg, D. (1981). The Literature of the Madhyamaka school of Philosophy in India (History of Indian literature ; v. 7, fasc. 1). Wiesbaden: Harrassowitz.

Stefania Travagnin (2013) Yinshun's Recovery of ShizhuPiposha Lun 十住毗婆沙論: a Madhyamaka-based Pure Land Practice In Twentieth-Century Taiwan, Contemporary Buddhism, 14:2, 320-343, DOI: 10.1080/14639947.2013.832497 To link to this article: https://doi.org/10.1080/14639947.2013.832497

Takakusu, J., & Watanabe, Kaigyoku. (1924). Taishō shinshū Daizōkyō. Tōkyō; 東京 :: Taishō Issaikyō Kankōkai; 大正一切經刊行會.

Vaidya, P. L., ed. Daśabhūmikasūtram. Darbhanga: The Mithila Institute of Post-Graduate Studies and Research in Sanskrit Learning, 1969.

Williams, M. Monier, Sir. (n.d.). A Sanskrit-English Dictionary. Delhi: Sri Satguru.

Zhonghua dian zi fo dian xie hui. (2004). CBETA dian zi fo dian ji cheng = CBETA Chinese electronic Tripitaka collection (Version 2004. ed.). Taibei; 台北 :: Zhonghua dian zi fo dian xie hui; 中華電子佛典協會.

Glossary

A

Abhidharma: A category of Buddhist texts devoted to detailed scholastic analyses of the teachings contained in the sutras.

afflictions: Otherwise known as "the three poisons" (*triviṣa*) these are: 1) greed (including lust and desire in general); 2) hatred (including all of the permutations of aversion such as irritation, anger, and rage); and 3) delusion or ignorance. There are many subcategories of afflictions (*kleśa*) listed in the various dharma schemas. For example, in the Sarvāstivāda school, there are six root afflictions and ten subsidiary afflictions.

aggregates: See "five aggregates."

anāgamin: The *anāgamin* or "nonreturner" is one who has gained the third of the four fruits of the individual-liberation path of the śrāvaka disciple.

anuttarasamyaksaṃbodhi: "Anuttarasamyaksaṃbodhi" refers to "the utmost, right, and perfect enlightenment" of a buddha.

arhat: An arhat is one who, having put an end to all of the afflictions, fetters, and contaminants and having put an end to rebirth, has gained the fourth and final fruit on the individual-liberation path of the śrāvaka disciple.

ārya: One who has realized one of the fruits of the path from which they can never fall away. This includes any one of the eight fruits of the arhat path, or any of the irreversible stations on the bodhisattva path to Buddhahood.

asaṃkhya, asaṃkhyeya: In Sanskrit, this is an incalculably and infinitely large number.

asura: As one of the paths of rebirth, this refers to a demi-god or titan. More loosely, this refers to beings much characterized by anger, hatred, jealousy, and contentiousness who may also appear as humans, animals, hungry ghosts (*pretas*), or hell-dwellers.

avadāna stories: Stories of the previous lives of a buddha.

avaivartika: one who has become irreversible on either the individual liberation path of the arhats or on the universal-liberation path of the bodhisattvas and buddhas. Throughout this text, "stage of certainty" (必定, 必定地) is most likely a translation of *avaivartika*.

B

bases of psychic powers: The four bases of psychic power (*catvāra ṛddhi-pāda*) are: zeal (*chanda*); vigor (*vīrya*); [concentration of] mind/

thought (*citta*); and reflective or investigative consideration, examination, or imagination (*mīmāṃsā*).

Bhagavat: "Bhagavat" is one of the titles of a Buddha. It may be translated as "Blessed One," "Lord," or, as rendered in Chinese Buddhist texts, "World Honored One," *shizun* (世尊).

bhikshu: A fully ordained celibate Buddhist monk within one of the traditional schools of Buddhism.

bhikshuni: A fully ordained celibate Buddhist nun within one of the traditional schools of Buddhism.

bhūta ghost: According to MW, one of the many meanings of *bhūta* is: "a spirit (good or evil), the ghost of a deceased person, a demon, imp, goblin." PDB: "A class of harm-inflicting and formless obstructing spirits (i.e. 'elemental spirits')..."; "...sometimes equivalent to *preta* (hungry ghosts)...."; "Because they obstruct rainfall, the *bhūta* are propitiated by rituals to cause precipitation."

bodhi: "Enlightenment" or "awakening." In its most exalted form this refers exclusively to the utmost, right, and perfect enlightenment (*anuttarasamyaksaṃbodhi*) of a buddha.

bodhimaṇḍa: A *bodhimaṇḍa* is the "site of enlightenment" wherein enlightenment is cultivated and fully realized. It may be used as a general reference to Buddhist temples, though it often refers specifically to the site beneath the bodhi tree where a buddha gains complete realization of the utmost, right, and perfect enlightenment.

bodhisattva: A bodhisattva is a being who, in his pursuit of the utmost, right, and perfect enlightenment of buddhahood, is equally dedicated to achieving buddhahood for himself while also facilitating all other beings' achievement of buddhahood. His primary practice is classically described as focusing on the six (or ten) "perfections" (*pāramitā*): giving, moral virtue, patience, vigor, meditative skill (*dhyāna*), and world-transcending wisdom (*prajñā*).

bodhi tree: The tree in Bodhgaya in the Indian state of Bihar under which the Buddha reached enlightenment approximately 2600 years ago.

Brahmā: Per PDB: "An Indian divinity who was adopted into the Buddhist pantheon as a protector of the teachings and king of the Brahmaloka ["Brahma world"] (in the narrow sense of that term)." "Brahmaloka" here refers to the first three heavens of the form realm.

brahmacārin: Per MW, "A young Brahman who is a student of the veda (under a preceptor) or who practises chastity, a young Brahman before marriage (in the first period of his life)."

brahmacarya: Celibacy.

brahman: Someone who belongs to the highest caste in Hinduism; a member of the Hindu priestly caste.

buddha: Anyone who has achieved the utmost, right, and perfect enlightenment (*anuttarasamyaksaṃbodhi*), whether we speak of the Buddha of the present era in this world, Shakyamuni Buddha, any of the seven buddhas of antiquity, or, in Mahāyāna cosmology, any of the countless buddhas of the ten directions and three periods of time.

C

clear knowledges: "Clear knowledges" refers to the "three knowledges" (*trividyā*): 1) The remembrance of previous lives (*pūrvavanivāsānusmṛti*); 2) Knowledge of beings' rebirth destinies (*cyutyupapattijñāna*); and 3) Knowledge of the destruction of the defiling contaminants or "taints" (*āsravakṣaya*).

contaminants: "Contaminants" (āsrava) are usually defined as either threefold or fourfold: 1) sensual desire (*kāma*); 2) [craving for] becoming (*bhāva*), i.e. the craving for continued existence; 3) ignorance (*avidyā*), i.e. delusion; 4) views (*dṛṣṭi*) This fourth types is not included in some listings. Often-encountered alternate translations include "taints" and "outflows" and, less commonly "influxes" and "fluxes."

D

dāna pāramitā: The perfection of giving

deva: Devas are divinities residing in the heavens that collectively constitute the highest of the six rebirth destinies within the realm of *saṃsāra*. There are 27 categories of devas and their heavens in the desire realm, form realm, and formless realm. Although the life spans of the devas in these various heavens may be immensely long, when their karmic merit runs out, they are all still destined to eventually fall back into the other five paths of rebirth wherein they are reborn in accordance with their residual karma from previous lifetimes.

dhāraṇī: *Dhāraṇīs* are of many types, but the two main types are mantra-like spells that serve the purpose of protection from negative spiritual forces such as ghosts and demons and formulae that aid the retention even for countless lifetimes of the Dharma teachings one has acquired in this and previous lives.

Dharma: The teachings of the Buddha

dharmas: 1) Fundamental constituent aspects, elements, or factors of mental and physical existence, as for instance, "the 100 dharmas" with which Vasubandhu analytically catalogued all that exists. In this sense, dharmas are somewhat analogous to the elements of the periodic table in chemistry; 2) Any individual teaching, as for instance in "the dharma of conditioned origination."

Dharma realm: As a Buddhist technical term, "Dharma realm" or "dharma realm," *dharma-dhātu,* has at least several levels of meaning:

1) At the most granular level, "dharma realm" refers to one of the eighteen sense realms, dharmas as "objects of mind" (*dharma*-āyatana);

2) In the most cosmically and metaphysically vast sense, "Dharma realm" refers in aggregate to all conventionally-existent phenomena and the universally pervasive noumenal "true suchness" (*tathatā*) that underlies and characterizes all of those phenomena. In this sense, it is identical with the "Dharma body" (*dharma-kāya*);

3) As a classifying term, "dharma realm" is used to distinguish realms of existence (as in the ten dharma realms consisting of the realms of buddhas, bodhisattvas, śrāvaka disciples, *pratyekabuddhas,* devas, *asuras,* humans, animals, hungry ghosts, hell-dwellers) or metaphysical modes of existence (as in the "four dharma realms" of the Huayan hermeneutic tradition that speaks of: a] the dharma realm of the "noumenal" [synonymous with emptiness or śūnyatā]; b] the dharma realm of the "phenomenal"; c] the dharma realm of the unimpeded interpenetration of the phenomenal and the noumenal; and d] the dharma realm of the unimpeded interpenetration of all phenomena with all other phenomena in a manner that resonates somewhat with quantum entanglement and non-locality).

Dharma wheel: The "wheel of Dharma" or "Dharma wheel" (*dharma-cakra*) refers to the eight-spoked wheel emblematic of the Buddha's teaching of the eightfold path of the Āryas or "Noble Ones" consisting of right views, right volition or intentional thought, right speech, right physical action, right livelihood, right effort, right mindfulness, and right meditative concentration. This term is also synonymous with the three turnings of the four truths as initially taught by the Buddha to his original five disciples.

dhūta, dhūtaṅga, or *dhūtaguṇa* austerities: In contrast to the non-beneficial ascetic practices of non-Buddhists (lying on a bed of nails, etc.), these are austerities beneficial to progress on the path such as wearing only patchwork robes sewn from discarded cloth, eating only food obtained on the alms round, eating only a single meal each day, always sitting and never lying down, dwelling at the base of a tree, or residing in a charnel field where one observes the stages of the body's decomposition.

dhyāna: "*Dhyāna*" is a general term broadly corresponding to all forms of Buddhist meditative skill. The Chinese "*ch'an*" or "*chan*" (禪) and the Japanese term "*zen*" are transliterations of the same Sanskrit word "*dhyāna*." All forms of Buddhist "calming" and "insight" meditation are subcategories of "*dhyāna*."

dhyāna pāramitā: The perfection of meditative skill.

E

eight difficulties: Birth in the hells, birth as a hungry ghost, birth as an animal, birth as a long-lived deva, birth in a border region (where there is no Buddha Dharma), birth as someone who is blind, deaf, mute, or otherwise possessed of impaired physical or mental faculties, birth as someone who is possessed of merely worldly knowledge and intelligence (and hence who uses his cleverness to deny the truth of the Dharma); and birth at a time before or long after a buddha appears in the world.

eight precepts: Eight vows involving abstaining from: 1) killing; 2) taking what is not given; 3) sexual misconduct; 4) false speech; 5) intoxicants; 6) use of perfumes, jewelry, other personal adornments, dancing, singing, or watching such performances; 7) sleeping on high or wide beds; and 8) eating after midday.

eighteen sense realms: These consist of the six sense faculties (eye, ear, nose, tongue, body, and mind), the six sense objects (visual forms, sounds, smells, tastes, touchables, and ideas, etc. as objects of mind), and the six sense consciousnesses (visual, auditory, olfactory, gustatory, tactile, and mental).

F

fetters: The fetters (*saṃyojana*) are ten mental characteristics of unenlightened existence that bind beings to uncontrolled rebirths in the six destinies of rebirth. They are: 1) "Truly existent self view," the wrong view that believes in the existence of an eternally existent self in association with the five aggregates; 2) "Skeptical doubt" about the truth of the Dharma and the path to enlightenment; 3) "Clinging to [the observance of] rules and rituals" in and of themselves as constituting the path to spiritual liberation; 4) Sensual desire; 5) Ill will; 6) Desire for rebirth in the form realm [heavens]; 7) Desire for rebirth in the formless realm [heavens]; 8) "Conceit," i.e. the belief that "I" exist; 9) "Agitation" or "restlessness" that prevents deep concentration; and 10) "Ignorance."

five aggregates: 1) form; 2) feelings (i.e. sensations as received through eye, ear, nose, tongue, body, or mind); 3) perceptions; 4) karmic formative factors (such as volitions); and 5) consciousness (visual, auditory, olfactory, gustatory, tactile, and mental).

five desires: Wealth, sex, fame, flavors, and leisure or, alternatively, the objects of the five basic sense faculties (visual forms, sounds, smells, tastes, and touchables).

five faculties: faith; vigor; mindfulness; concentration; wisdom.

five powers: faith; vigor; mindfulness; concentration; wisdom.

five precepts: Five vows involving abstaining from killing, stealing, sexual misconduct, false speech, and intoxicants.

four bases of meritorious qualities: truth, relinquishment, quiescence, and wisdom. (Per VB, the Sanskrit correlates of the Pali *saccādhitthāna, cāgādhitthāna, upasamādhitthāna* (= base of peace), and *paññādhitthāna* would be *satyādhiṣṭhāna, tyāgādhiṣṭhāna, upaśamādhiṣṭhāna,* and *prajñādhiṣṭhāna*.)

four bases of supernatural power: Zeal; vigor; mind; investigation.

four great elements: earth, water, fire, wind.

four right efforts: Causing already arisen evil to cease; causing not yet arisen evil to not arise; causing already arisen goodness to increase; causing not yet arisen goodness to arise.

four requisites: Food obtained on the alms round; robes; residences; medicines.

four stations of mindfulness: Mindfulness of the body; mindfulness of feelings or sensations (experienced via the eye, ear, nose, tongue, body, and mind consciousnesses); mindfulness of thoughts or mind states; mindfulness of dharmas.

four truths / four truths of the Āryas: Suffering; its origination; its cessation; the path to its cessation.

G

gandharva: *Gandharvas* are a type of celestial music spirit that is said to rely on fragrances as their means of survival.

garuḍa: *Garuḍas* are a type of spirit that manifests as an immense golden-winged bird that feeds on young dragons.

ground, grounds: These are levels or planes of spiritual development through which a practitioner proceeds on the way to complete enlightenment.

H

hindrances: "Hindrances" usually refers to "the five hindrances" which are desire, ill will, lethargy-and-sleepiness, excitedness-and-regretfulness, and afflicted doubtfulness. These five hindrances must be overcome in order to successfully enter deep states of meditation.

I

inverted views: The four inverted views (*viparyāsa-catuṣka*) consist of imputing permanence to the impermanent, pleasure to what cannot deliver it, self to what is devoid of any inherently existent self, and purity to what does not actually possess that quality. Standard objects of such upside-down perception are: thought, or mind states, the six categories of "feeling" manifesting in association with the six sense faculties, dharmas (as components of the falsely imputed "self"), and the body.

K

kalaviṅka bird: The Himalayan cuckoo bird that sings with an incomparably beautiful sound even before it breaks out of its shell.

kalpa: The Sanskrit "*kalpa*" roughly corresponds to the English term "eon" with the primary distinction being that, in Buddhist and Hindu cosmology, kalpas occur in various relatively precisely designated immensely long durations.

kāṣāya robe: The robes of an fully ordained bhikshu or bhikshuni.

kinnara: *Kinnaras* (skt. *kiṃnara*) are a type of celestial music spirit with the body of a human and the head of a horse.

kumbhāṇḍa: According to MW: "Having testicles shaped like a *kumbha* [a winter melon]," a class of demons (at whose head stands Rudra). PDB: "In Sanskrit, a type of evil spirit, and typically listed along with especially *rākṣasa*, but also *piśāca*, *yakṣa*, and *bhūta* spirits. Virūḍhaka, one of the four world-guardians, who protects the southern cardinal direction, is usually said to be their overlord, although some texts give Rudra this role instead. The *kumbhāṇḍa* are also sometimes listed among the minions of Māra, evil personified.

koṭī: A *koṭī* is a number that is defined in the Flower Adornment Sutra Chapter Thirty as the product of multiplying a *lakṣa* (100,000) by a *lakṣa*. Hence it equals 10,000,000, i.e. ten million.

kṣaṇa: A *kṣaṇa,* corresponds to a micro-moment. This is variously defined, one traditional definition being "a ninetieth of a finger-snap." Elsewhere in the text, this may be referred to as "a single thought," "a mind-moment," or "a thought-moment" as approximate translations of the term.

kṣānti pāramitā: The perfection of patience.

kṣatriya: The second of the four castes of traditional Indian culture consisting primarily of the warrior and royalty class.

kṣetra: The Sanskrit word *kṣetra* refers to a land or realm or field and in Buddhist texts it may refer specifically to a "buddha land."

M

mahāsattva: A *mahāsattva* is a great bodhisattva, one who has cultivated the bodhisattva path for countless kalpas.

mātṛkā: *Mātṛkās* are "matrices" consisting of lists of dharmas, technical terms, and concepts discussed in the sutras. They served as the basis for the Abhidharma.

Māra, *māras*: In Buddhism, Māra is generally regarded as the personification of evil and death who is also a particular deity dwelling in one of the desire realm heavens who delights in interfering with spiritual liberation from perpetual rebirths in *saṃsāra*. More specifically, there are said to be four kinds of *māras*: 1) the *māra* of the five mental and physical aggregates in association with which all beings wander endlessly in *saṃsāra*; 2) the *māra* of the afflictions consisting of the three poisons of greed, hatred, and delusion and all of their subcategories; 3) the *māra* of death; and, as mentioned above, 3) the deity known as Māra as well as all of his *devaputra* minions. Additionally, there are also "ghost and spirit" *māras* who may manifest in countless ways to interfere with a practitioner's cultivation of the path.

mind-moment: See *kṣaṇa*.

mahorāga: *Mahorāgas* are a type of serpent spirit often portrayed as having the upper body of a human and the lower body of a snake.

N

nayuta: A very large number, usually defined as a one hundred billion.

nirvāṇa: Nirvāṇa is the ultimate goal of the path of Buddhist spiritual cultivation that corresponds to the elimination of the three poisons (covetousness, aversion, delusion) and the ending of compulsory and random rebirth in *saṃsāra*, the cycle of existences in the deva realm, the demigod realm, the human realm, the animal realm, the hungry ghost realm, and the hell realms.

In the case of the individual liberation path practitioner exemplified by arhats and *pratyekabuddhas*, all future existence ends for them with the acquisition of nirvāṇa.

In the case of the universal liberation practitioners exemplified by bodhisattvas and buddhas, they achieve the direct cognition of the emptiness of all beings and phenomena and realize an ongoing realization of a nirvana-like state even as, by force of vow, they continue to take on intentional rebirths within *saṃsāra* in order to facilitate the spiritual liberation of all beings.

nirvāṇa without residue: The final nirvāṇa realized at death by fully awakened beings whether they be arhats, *pratyekabuddhas*, or buddhas.

nivāsana robe: The *nivāsana* is the monastic's skirt-like inner robe.

O

once-returner: See *sākṛdāgāmin*.

P

pāramitā: One of the six (or ten) "perfections" cultivated and perfected by the bodhisattva on the path to buddhahood.

Paranirmita Vaśavartin Heaven: The Paranirmita Vaśavartin Heaven is the sixth of the six desire realm heavens. PDB: "The heaven of the gods who have power over the creations of others, or the gods who partake of the pleasures created in other heavens."

piśāca: PDB: "In Sanskrit, "flesh-eater," a class of ogres or goblins, similar to rākṣasa and yakṣa, who eat human flesh." The female is called *piśācī*.

prajñā: *Prajnā* is the world-transcending wisdom that cognizes and understands all phenomena associated with "self," others, and the world as they truly are and in accordance with ultimate reality.

prajñā pāramitā: The perfection of wisdom.

pratyekabuddha: One who, in the absence of a buddha or his Dharma, achieves a level of enlightenment comparable to that of an arhat, doing so on his own through the contemplation of the cycle of dependent origination (*pratītyasamutpāda*). Mahāyāna literature attributes this ability to awaken in the absence of a buddha or his Dharma to direct exposure to the Dharma in previous lives, the seeds of which enable enlightenment in the present life.

pratyutpanna samādhi: The *pratyutpanna* samādhi is a samādhi wherein one becomes able to see the buddhas of the present and listen to them teach the Dharma.

provisions (for enlightenment): The provisions for enlightenment (*bodhisaṃbhāra*) are the spiritual prerequisites for enlightenment that must be accumulated in order to fully realize the path to buddhahood. These are usually considered to be merit (*puṇya*) and knowledge (*jñāna*).

pūtana: Per PDB: "Stinking hungry demons."

R

rākṣasa: A swift flying malignant flesh-eating demon which changes its form to seduce humans and eat them.

S

sakṛdāgāmin: The *sakṛdāgāmin* or "once-returner" is one who has gained the third of the four fruits of the individual-liberation path of the śrāvaka disciple.

samādhi: Samādhi refers both to any single instance of one-pointed concentration and also, more usually, to enduring states of persistently maintained one-pointed concentration.

saṃghāṭī robe: The *saṃghāṭī* is the monastic's outer robe.

saṃkakṣikā robe: The *saṃkakṣikā* is the monastic's robe that is worn over the left shoulder and under the right arm.

saṃsāra: *Saṃsāra,* for which the usual Sino-Buddhist rendering is "births-and-deaths," *shengsi* (生死), refers to the endless cycle of rebirths in the six realms of rebirth: devas (gods), *asuras* ("demi-gods" or "titans"), humans, animals, hungry ghosts (*preta*), and hell-dwellers.

Sangha: A community of at least ten fully ordained bhikshus in Buddhist countries or at least five fully ordained bhikshus in countries where Buddhism is only just being established for the first time. As the third object of refuge in "the Three Refuges" or "the Three Jewels," this refers exclusively to those persons who have already acquired one of the fruits of the path from which they can never fall away, whether on the individual-liberation paths of the arhats or *pratyekabuddhas,* or on the bodhisattva path.

śarīra: *Śarīra* are the remains or "relics" of eminent monks, bodhisattvas, or buddhas that are contained in their cremation ashes.

seven enlightenment factors: assessment or skillful selection of dharmas; vigor; joy; mental pliancy; concentration; equanimity with respect to the saṃskāra (karmic formative factors) aggregate.

śīla pāramitā: The perfection of moral virtue.

six rebirth destinies: gods (*deva*), demi-gods or titans (*asura*), humans, hungry ghosts (*pretas*), animals, and hell-dwellers.

skandha: See "aggregates."

skillful means: "Skillful means" (*upāya*) are individually tailored skillful techniques adopted by the bodhisattva in teaching the various kinds of beings. These various techniques are adopted precisely because all beings are possessed of different capacities, karmic obstacles and predilections due to which they respond best to individually tailored teachings.

spiritual superknowledges: The usual Sanskrit antecedent for "spiritual superknowledges" is *abhijñā* ("superknowledges") or *ṛddhi* ("supernatural powers"). This includes such abilities as "the six superknowledges" (the spiritual powers, the heavenly eye, the heavenly ear, the cognition of others' thoughts, past life recall for both self and others, and complete elimination of all "defiling contaminants" or "taints" [*āsrava*]).

śramaṇa: More generally, a *śramaṇa* is a mendicant, one who has left the home life and relies on alms for sustenance. In the Buddhist context, this refers specifically to a bhikshu, i.e. a Buddhist monk.

śrāvaka, śrāvaka disciple: A follower of the individual-liberation path to arhatship.

stream enterer: The stream enterer (*srota-āpanna*) is one who has gained the first of the four fruits of the path to arhatship.

śūdra: A member of the fourth and lowest caste of traditional Indian culture consisting primarily of servants and such.

sutra: A scripture attributed to the Buddha.

T

tathatā: "Suchness," i.e. the true nature of the ultimate reality of any and all things as it really is.

Tathāgata: "*Tathāgata*" ("Thus Come One") is one of the ten primary titles by which all buddhas are known.

Ten directions: North, south, east, west, the four midpoints, the zenith, and the nadir.

Thirty-seven wings of enlightenment / thirty-seven enlightenment factors: These consist of: the four stations of mindfulness; the four right efforts; the four bases of supernatural powers; the five faculties; the five powers; the seven enlightenment factors; and the eightfold path of the Āryas.

Three Jewels: The Buddha, the Dharma, and the Ārya Sangha.

Three periods of time: Past, present, and future.

Three Refuges: The Buddha, the Dharma, and the Ārya Sangha, the Three Jewels in which one "takes the refuges" to become a Buddhist disciple and upon which one must rely to advance on the Buddhist path.

Three Vehicles: The Śrāvaka-disciple Vehicle, the Pratyekabuddha Vehicle, and the Great Vehicle (Mahāyāna) the endpoints of which are arhatship, pratyekabuddhahood, and Buddhahood.

three wretched destinies: The three wretched destinies are rebirth as either an animal, a hungry ghost (*preta*), or a hell dweller.

trichiliocosm: A world system consisting of countless worlds.

tripiṭaka: The three divisions of the three-fold Buddhist canon, otherwise known as "the Tripiṭaka": the sutras (scriptures attributed to the Buddha or disciples authorized by the Buddha), the commentarial treatises (śāstra), and the moral codes (*vinaya*).

tripiṭaka master: A "*tripiṭaka* master" is someone who has completely mastered the three divisions of the three-fold Buddhist canon.

twelve sense bases: the six sense faculties (eye, ear, nose, tongue, body, and mind) and their respective sense objects (visual forms, sounds, smells, tastes, touchables, and ideas, etc. as objects of mind).

Two Vehicles: The two individual liberation vehicles taught by the Buddha, the Śrāvaka-disciple Vehicle leading to arhatship and the Pratyekabuddha Vehicle leading to pratyekabuddhahood.

V

vaiśya: A member of the third caste in traditional Indian culture comprised primarily of the merchant and agricultural classes.

vajra: An indestructible substance equated with the diamond. A symbol of indestructibility. Also, a pestle shaped sceptre or "thunderbolt" weapon held by Dharma protectors and deities.

vibhāṣā: A *vibhāṣā* is an extensively detailed explanatory treatise.

vinaya: The Buddhist moral codes.

vīrya pāramitā: The perfection of vigor.

W

wheel-turning king: In Buddhism, a "wheel-turning king" (*cakravartin*) is a universal monarch.

worthy: In Mahāyāna literature, a "worthy" (*bhadra*) is a bodhisattva practitioner who has brought forth the bodhisattva vow but who is still cultivating the preparatory stages and thus has not yet reached the ten bodhisattva grounds and has not yet become an ārya.

Y

yakṣa: *Yakṣas* are a kind of either good or evil spirit possessed of supernatural powers that may either serve as a guardian or a demon.

yojana: A measure of distance in ancient India usually defined as being the distance that an ox cart would travel in a day without unharnessing (somewhat less than ten miles).

About the Translator

Bhikshu Dharmamitra (ordination name "Heng Shou" – 釋恆授) is a Chinese-tradition translator-monk and one of the earliest American disciples (since 1968) of the late Guiyang Ch'an patriarch, Dharma teacher, and pioneer of Buddhism in the West, the Venerable Master Hsuan Hua (宣化上人). He has a total of 34 years in robes during two periods as a monastic (1969–1975 & 1991 to the present).

Dharmamitra's principal educational foundations as a translator of Sino-Buddhist Classical Chinese lie in four years of intensive monastic training and Chinese-language study of classic Mahāyāna texts in a small-group setting under Master Hsuan Hua (1968–1972), undergraduate Chinese language study at Portland State University, a year of intensive one-on-one Classical Chinese study at the Fu Jen University Language Center near Taipei, two years of course work at the University of Washington's Department of Asian Languages and Literature (1988–90), and an additional three years of auditing graduate courses and seminars in Classical Chinese readings, again at UW's Department of Asian Languages and Literature.

Since taking robes again under Master Hua in 1991, Dharmamitra has devoted his energies primarily to study and translation of classic Mahāyāna texts with a special interest in works by Ārya Nāgārjuna and related authors. To date, he has translated more than fifteen important texts comprising approximately 150 fascicles, including most recently the 80-fascicle *Avataṃsaka Sūtra* (the "Flower Adornment Sutra"), Nāgārjuna's 17-fascicle *Daśabhūmika Vibhāśa* ("Treatise on the Ten Grounds"), and the *Daśabhūmika Sūtra* (the "Ten Grounds Sutra"), all of which are current or upcoming Kalavinka Press publications.

Kalavinka Buddhist Classics

(http: www.kalavinka.org)

Fall, 2019 Title List

<u>**Meditation Instruction Texts**</u>

The Essentials of Buddhist Meditation

A marvelously complete classic *śamathā-vipaśyanā* (calming-and-insight) meditation manual. By Tiantai Śramaṇa Zhiyi (538–597).

Six Gates to the Sublime

The early Indian Buddhist meditation method involving six practices used in calming-and-insight meditation. By Śramaṇa Zhiyi

<u>**Bodhisattva Path Texts**</u>

On Generating the Resolve to Become a Buddha

On the Resolve to Become a Buddha by Ārya Nāgārjuna
Exhortation to Resolve on Buddhahood by Patriarch Sheng'an Shixian
Exhortation to Resolve on Buddhahood by the Tang Literatus, Peixiu

Letter from a Friend - The Three Earliest Editions

The earliest extant editions of Ārya Nāgārjuna's *Suhṛlekkha*:
Translated by Tripiṭaka Master Guṇavarman (*ca* 425 CE)
Translated by Tripiṭaka Master Saṇghavarman (*ca* 450 CE)
Translated by Tripiṭaka Master Yijing (*ca* 675 CE).

Marvelous Stories from the Perfection of Wisdom

130 Stories from Ārya Nāgārjuna's *Mahāprājñāpāramitā Upadeśa.*

Nāgārjuna's Guide to the Bodhisattva Path

The *Bodhisaṃbhāra Treatise* with abridged Vaśitva commentary.

The Bodhisaṃbhāra Treatise Commentary

The complete exegesis by the Indian Bhikshu Vaśitva (*ca* 300–500).

Nāgārjuna on Mindfulness of the Buddha

Ch. 9 and Chs. 20–25 of Nāgārjuna's *Daśabhūmika Vibhāṣā*
Ch. 1, Subchapter 36a of Nāgārjuna's *Mahāprājñāpāramitā Upadeśa.*

Nāgārjuna on the Six Perfections

Chapters 17–30 of Ārya Nāgārjuna's *Mahāprājñāpāramitā Upadeśa.*

A Strand of Dharma Jewels (Ārya Nāgārjuna's *Ratnāvalī*)

The earliest extant edition, translated by Paramārtha: *ca* 550 CE

The Ten Bodhisattva Grounds

Śikṣānanda's translation of The Flower Adornment Sutra, Ch. 26

The Ten Grounds Treatise

Nāgārjuna's 35-chapter *Daśabhūmika Vibhāṣā*

The Ten Grounds Sutra

Kumārajīva's translation of the *Daśabhūmika Sūtra*

Vasubandhu's Treatise on the Bodhisattva Vow

By Vasubandhu Bodhisattva (*ca* 300 CE)